KB084871

CEDU 쎄듀는 A **C**omprehensive **E**nglish e**DU**cation(종합적 영어교육)의 약자입니다.

저자

김기훈   現 ㈜쎄듀 대표이사
現 메가스터디 영어영역 대표강사
前 서울특별시 교육청 외국어 교육정책자문위원회 위원

저서   천일문 / 천일문 Training Book / 천일문 GRAMMAR / 천일문 STARTER
어법끝 / 어휘끝 / 첫단추 / 쎈쓰업 / 파워업 / 빈칸백서 / 오답백서
쎄듀 본영어 / 문법의 골든룰 101 / ALL씀 서술형 / 수능실감
거침없이 Writing / Grammar Q / Reading Q / Listening Q 등

쎄듀 영어교육연구센터
쎄듀 영어교육센터는 영어 콘텐츠에 대한 전문지식과 경험을 바탕으로
최고의 교육 콘텐츠를 만들고자 최선의 노력을 다하는 전문가 집단입니다.

마케팅	콘텐츠 마케팅 사업본부
영업	문병구
제작	정승호
디자인	DOTS · 윤혜영
전산 편집	김명렬
삽화	플러스툰
영문교열	Michael A. Putlack

빠르게

쎄듀
중학영어듣기
모의고사 20회

2

Structure & Features
구성 및 특징

실전모의고사 20회

가장 최신의 출제 경향을 반영한 실전모의고사 20회를 수록했습니다. 1~5회는 〈시도교육청 주관 영어듣기능력평가〉에 비해 지문의 길이가 10~20% 정도 길고, 6회~20회는 20~30% 정도 긴 지문의 문제로 구성하여, 학생들이 점진적으로 문제 풀이 능력을 기를 수 있도록 구성했습니다.

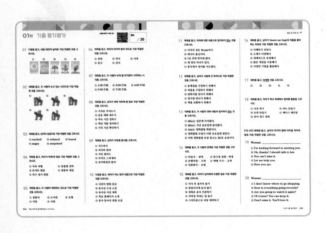

기출 듣기평가 5회

2013년부터 2015년까지 실시된 〈시도교육청 주관 영어듣기능력평가〉의 기출 문제를 총 5회분 수록했습니다. 시험 직전에 최종 점검을 하는 목적으로 문제를 풀어보시기 바랍니다.

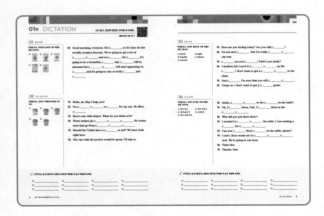

DICTATION

문제 풀이에 중요한 단서가 되는 명사, 동사, 형용사 등의 핵심 어휘와, 어휘 실력 향상에 도움이 되는 동사구, 전명구 등을 위주로 딕테이션 연습을 할 수 있도록 구성했습니다. 잘 안 들리거나 모르는 단어는 박스에 체크한 뒤 페이지 하단의 어휘복습 코너를 통해 확인하세요. 아울러, 문장과 문장 사이에 일정한 간격을 두어, 학생들이 단어를 직접 써볼 수 있도록 마련했습니다.

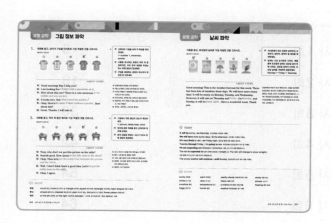

문제 유형 공략 및 필수 표현 익히기

〈시도교육청 주관 영어듣기능력평가〉 기출 문제를 면밀히 분석하여 총 17개의 유형으로 분류하고 문제 공략법을 소개했습니다. 또한 유형별 주요표현과 필수어휘 등도 함께 수록했으므로 시험을 보기 전에 꼭 확인해 보세요.

다양한 교사용 부가자료 및 학습 지원

쎄듀 홈페이지에 들어오시면 다양한 교사용 부가자료가 준비되어 있습니다.

- Q&A 게시판
- 본문 수록 어휘
- 딕테이션 음원
- 본문 스크립트
- 모의고사 음원
- 문항 단위 음원

Contents
목차

실전모의고사 20회

기출 듣기평가 5회

문제 유형 공략 및 필수 표현 익히기

01 다음을 듣고, 금요일의 날씨로 가장 적절한 것을 고르시오.

① ② ③ ④ ⑤

02 대화를 듣고, 남자가 구매할 티셔츠를 고르시오.

① ② ③

④ ⑤

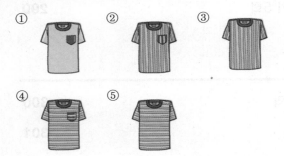

03 대화를 듣고, 남자의 심정으로 가장 적절한 것을 고르시오.

① bored   ② angry   ③ hopeful
④ relaxed   ⑤ worried

04 대화를 듣고, 여자가 한 일로 가장 적절한 것을 고르시오.

① 잡지 읽기   ② 식탁 차리기
③ 책상 옮기기   ④ 요리하기
⑤ 학교 과제 하기

05 대화를 듣고, 두 사람이 대화하는 장소로 가장 적절한 곳을 고르시오.

① 소아과   ② 치과   ③ 약국
④ 문구점   ⑤ 여행사

06 대화를 듣고, 남자의 마지막 말의 의도로 가장 적절한 것을 고르시오.

① 감사   ② 사과   ③ 비난
④ 충고   ⑤ 기원

07 대화를 듣고, 여자가 가장 좋아한 책을 고르시오.

① 전기   ② 동화책   ③ 역사책
④ 시집   ⑤ 소설

08 대화를 듣고, 남자가 대화 직후에 할 일로 가장 적절한 것을 고르시오.

① 숙제하기   ② 방 청소하기
③ 피아노 레슨 가기   ④ 축구 연습하기
⑤ 친구 집에 가기

09 다음을 듣고, 무엇에 관한 내용인지 가장 적절한 것을 고르시오.

① 신체 검사   ② 학교 일정
③ 점심 메뉴   ④ 도서관의 위치
⑤ 쓰레기 재활용

10 대화를 듣고, 여자의 장래 희망으로 가장 적절한 것을 고르시오.

① 농부   ② 요리사   ③ 과학자
④ 사업가   ⑤ 선생님

11 다음을 듣고, Galaxy War에 관한 내용과 일치하는 것을 고르시오.

① 연극이다.
② 지난 금요일에 개봉했다.
③ Eric Hampton이 감독이다.
④ 장르는 코미디이다.
⑤ 성공을 거둘 것이다.

12 대화를 듣고, 여자가 전화한 목적으로 가장 적절한 것을 고르시오.

① 책을 주문하려고
② 주문을 취소하려고
③ 주문한 책 값을 지불하려고
④ 책이 도착하는 시간을 문의하려고
⑤ 책을 가지고 있는지 확인하려고

13 다음을 듣고, 축구 경기에 관한 정보로 일치하지 <u>않는</u> 것을 고르시오.

① 시즌 첫 번째 경기이다.
② 오후 2시에 시작한다.
③ Bell Park에서 열린다.
④ 2시간 동안 진행될 것이다.
⑤ 오후 1시까지 공원에 도착해야 한다.

14 대화를 듣고, 두 사람의 관계로 가장 적절한 것을 고르시오.

① 학생 – 교사
② 감독 – 선수
③ 상사 – 부하
④ 교장 – 학생
⑤ 교사 – 학부모

15 대화를 듣고, 여자가 남자에게 요청한 일로 가장 적절한 것을 고르시오.

① 빌린 돈 갚기
② 농구 연습하러 가기
③ 남동생의 부탁 들어주기
④ 식료품점에서 장보기
⑤ 냉장고에 남은 우유 마시기

16 대화를 듣고, 남자가 공원에 가는 이유로 가장 적절한 것을 고르시오.

① 소풍을 가려고
② 자전거를 타려고
③ 친구를 만나려고
④ 스케이트보드를 타려고
⑤ 롤러블레이드를 타려고

17 다음을 듣고, 두 사람의 대화가 <u>어색한</u> 것을 고르시오.

①　　②　　③　　④　　⑤

18 다음을 듣고, 여자가 언급하지 <u>않은</u> 것을 고르시오.

① 전시 내용
② 실내 전시관 수
③ 점심식사 장소
④ 관람 비용
⑤ 관람 종료 시간

[19~20] 대화를 듣고, 남자의 마지막 말에 이어질 여자의 응답으로 가장 적절한 것을 고르시오.

19 Woman: _____

① Yes, I have it with me.
② It's almost dinnertime now.
③ Let's get some sandwiches.
④ Sure, we can study a bit longer.
⑤ I don't have my books with me.

20 Woman: _____

① I'm sure you'll have fun.
② Not really. I didn't like it.
③ Thanks for the invitation.
④ I saw lots of fish in the water.
⑤ Yes, we were there for one week.

01 날씨 파악

다음을 듣고, 금요일의 날씨로 가장 적절한 것을 고르시오.

① ② ③

④ ⑤

M: Good morning, everyone. It's □ _____, so it's time for the weekly weather forecast. We're going to get a lot of □ _____ □ _____ and on □ _____. On □ _____, it's going to be a beautiful, □ _____ day. □ _____ will be pleasant but □ _____. □ _____ will start appearing on □ _____, and it's going to rain on both □ _____ and □ _____.

02 그림 정보 파악

대화를 듣고, 남자가 구매할 티셔츠를 고르시오.

① ② ③

④ ⑤

W: Hello, sir. May I help you?

M: I'm □ _____ □ _____ a □ _____ for my son. He likes □ _____.

W: Here's one with stripes. What do you think of it?

M: Those stripes go □ _____ □ _____ □ _____. He wants ones that go from □ _____ □ _____ □ _____.

W: Should the T-shirt have a □ _____ or not? We have both right here.

M: The one with the pocket would be great. I'll take it.

✏️ **어휘복습** 잘 안 들리거나 몰라서 체크한 어휘를 써 놓고 복습해 보세요.

□ _____ □ _____ □ _____ □ _____

□ _____ □ _____ □ _____ □ _____

□ _____

03 심정 추론

대화를 듣고, 남자의 심정으로 가장 적절한 것을 고르시오.

① bored   ② angry
③ hopeful   ④ relaxed
⑤ worried

W: How are you feeling today? Are you still □ _____?

M: I'm not sick □ _____. But I'm really □ _____ □ _____ our test.

W: □ _____ are you □ _____? Didn't you study?

M: I studied, but I need to □ _____ □ _____ on the □ _____. I don't want to get a □ _____ □ _____ in the class.

W: Just □ _____. I'm sure that you will □ _____ □ _____.

M: I hope so. I don't want to get a □ _____ grade.

04 한 일 파악

대화를 듣고, 여자가 한 일로 가장 적절한 것을 고르시오.

① 잡지 읽기   ② 식탁 차리기
③ 책상 옮기기   ④ 요리하기
⑤ 학교 과제 하기

M: Linda, □ _____ □ _____ to the □ _____ on the table?

W: Oh, I □ _____ them, Dad. I □ _____ them in the □ _____ □ _____.

M: Why did you put them there?

W: I needed to □ _____ □ _____ the table. I was making a □ _____ for □ _____ □ _____.

M: Can you □ _____ them □ _____ on the table, please?

W: I can't. Mom wants me to □ _____ □ _____ □ _____ now. We're going to eat soon.

M: That's fine.

W: Thanks, Dad.

✏️ **어휘복습** 잘 안 들리거나 몰라서 체크한 어휘를 써 놓고 복습해 보세요.

□ _____   □ _____   □ _____   □ _____

□ _____   □ _____   □ _____   □ _____

□ _____   □ _____   □ _____   □ _____

05 장소 추론

대화를 듣고, 두 사람이 대화하는 장소로 가장 적절한 곳을 고르시오.

① 소아과　② 치과　③ 약국
④ 문구점　⑤ 여행사

W: Is there something I can help you with?

M: I hope so. I've been □ _____ a lot □ _____.

W: Do you have any other □ _____? Do you have a □ _____ □ _____?

M: No, I feel fine. The only problem is that I □ _____ □ _____ coughing.

W: □ _____ □ _____ you buy a bottle of this? □ _____ it □ _____ □ _____ a □ _____.

M: How long should I take it for?

W: Three days. If you don't □ _____ □ _____, then you'd better □ _____ □ _____ □ _____.

06 의도 파악

대화를 듣고, 남자의 마지막 말의 의도로 가장 적절한 것을 고르시오.

① 감사　② 사과　③ 비난
④ 충고　⑤ 기원

W: Jack, happy birthday.

M: You actually □ _____. I think everyone else □ _____.

W: □ _____ □ _____ I forget your birthday? You're my □ _____ □ _____.

M: Thanks for saying that. It really □ _____ □ _____ □ _____ to me.

W: So what are you going to do □ _____?

M: My mom is making my □ _____ □ _____. And we're going to have cake and ice cream, too.

W: That sounds great. By the way, here's □ _____ □ _____ □ _____. I hope you like it.

M: You □ _____ □ _____, Tina. I really □ _____ it.

✎ **어휘복습** 잘 안 들리거나 몰라서 체크한 어휘를 써 놓고 복습해 보세요.

□ _____　□ _____　□ _____　□ _____

□ _____　□ _____　□ _____　□ _____

□ _____　□ _____　□ _____　□ _____

07 특정 정보 파악

대화를 듣고, 여자가 가장 좋아한 책을 고르시오.

① 전기
② 동화책
③ 역사책
④ 시집
⑤ 소설

W: I finished □ _____ another □ _____ today.

M: You seem to be reading lots of books these days.

W: That's true. This was a □ _____. I have also read □ _____ books, □ _____, □ _____ books, and □ _____ _____.

M: Which one did you □ _____ □ _____ □ _____?

W: I read an □ _____ novel. It was written by my □ _____ □ _____.

M: Can you □ _____ it to me sometime?

W: I got it from the □ _____. You'll have to go there to □ _____ it.

08 할 일 파악

대화를 듣고, 남자가 대화 직후에 할 일로 가장 적절한 것을 고르시오.

① 숙제하기
② 방 청소하기
③ 피아노 레슨 가기
④ 축구 연습하기
⑤ 친구 집에 가기

W: Are you going to □ _____ your □ _____ soon? It's □ _____ □ _____ □ _____.

M: I can't, Mom. I've got to □ _____ the □ _____ in a few minutes.

W: But you don't have □ _____ □ _____ today. That's tomorrow.

M: Right. I've got my □ _____ □ _____ instead.

W: Oh, I □ _____ □ _____ about that. Do I need to □ _____ you □ _____ after it's finished?

M: You don't need to do that. I'm going to John's house to □ _____ some □ _____ afterward.

✏️ **어휘복습** 잘 안 들리거나 몰라서 체크한 어휘를 써 놓고 복습해 보세요.

□ _____   □ _____   □ _____   □ _____

□ _____   □ _____   □ _____   □ _____

□ _____   □ _____   □ _____   □ _____

09 화제 추론

다음을 듣고, 무엇에 관한 내용인지 가장 적절한 것을 고르시오.

① 신체 검사　　② 학교 일정
③ 점심 메뉴　　④ 도서관의 위치
⑤ 쓰레기 재활용

W: Everyone, listen closely, please. The school has finally added some □ _____ □ _____. So don't throw □ _____, □ _____, □ _____, or □ _____ □ _____ in the trashcans anymore. You need to put them in the recycling bins. You can find them □ _____ the front door, □ _____ □ _____ the library, and □ _____ □ _____ □ _____ room one oh seven. Let's all take good care of the environment.

10 특정 정보 파악

대화를 듣고, 여자의 장래 희망으로 가장 적절한 것을 고르시오.

① 농부　　② 요리사　　③ 과학자
④ 사업가　　⑤ 선생님

W: Here, □ _____ some of this and tell me □ _____ you think it □ _____.
M: Wow, this cookie □ _____ □ _____. Did you make it □ _____?
W: Yes, I did. I □ _____ □ _____ □ _____ a □ _____ when I grow up, so I practice making all kinds of foods.
M: □ _____ food can you cook □ _____ □ _____?
W: I make a really good dish with □ _____ and □ _____. You should try it □ _____.
M: I'd love to. Tell me the □ _____ □ _____ you're planning to make it.

✏️ **어휘복습** 잘 안 들리거나 몰라서 체크한 어휘를 써 놓고 복습해 보세요.

□ _____　　□ _____　　□ _____　　□ _____
□ _____　　□ _____　　□ _____　　□ _____
□ _____　　□ _____　　□ _____　　□ _____

11 내용 일치 파악

다음을 듣고, Galaxy War에 관한 내용과 일치하는 것을 고르시오.

① 연극이다.
② 지난 금요일에 개봉했다.
③ Eric Hampton이 감독이다.
④ 장르는 코미디이다.
⑤ 성공을 거둘 것이다.

M: In just a moment, we're going to □ _____ □ _____ Eric Hampton. He's one of the top □ _____ □ _____ in the world. He has a □ _____ □ _____ □ _____ □ _____ this Friday. The □ _____ is *Galaxy War*. He has the □ _____ □ _____ in the □ _____ movie, and it's sure to be a □ _____ . □ _____ are calling it one of the best movies of the year.

12 전화 목적 파악

대화를 듣고, 여자가 전화한 목적으로 가장 적절한 것을 고르시오.

① 책을 주문하려고
② 주문을 취소하려고
③ 주문한 책 값을 지불하려고
④ 책이 도착하는 시간을 문의하려고
⑤ 책을 가지고 있는지 확인하려고

M: Hello. This is David's □ _____ .
W: Hello. My name is Soyun Park. I □ _____ □ _____ □ _____ □ _____ books at your store yesterday.
M: Yes, I remember you. Is everything okay?
W: Actually, I want to □ _____ □ _____ . I need to □ _____ one more book □ _____ □ _____ □ _____ . It's *Daytime Troubles* by Linda Matters.
M: I know that book. I'll add it to your order. They will all be here tomorrow.
W: Great. I'll □ _____ them □ _____ in the evening.

✎ **어휘복습** 잘 안 들리거나 몰라서 체크한 어휘를 써 놓고 복습해 보세요.

□ _____ □ _____ □ _____ □ _____
□ _____ □ _____ □ _____ □ _____
□ _____ □ _____ □ _____ □ _____

13 내용 일치 파악

다음을 듣고, 축구 경기에 관한 정보로 일치하지 <u>않는</u> 것을 고르시오.

① 시즌 첫 번째 경기이다.
② 오후 2시에 시작한다.
③ Bell Park에서 열린다.
④ 2시간 동안 진행될 것이다.
⑤ 오후 1시까지 공원에 도착해야 한다.

M: We're going to have our first □ _____ □ _____ of the □ _____ this weekend. The game will □ _____ □ _____ two in the afternoon on □ _____. We're going to □ _____ □ _____ Bell Park. We're going to play □ _____ a team from Morristown. Please □ _____ at the park □ _____ one P.M. We need to □ _____ □ _____ and □ _____ □ _____ for the game.

14 관계 추론

대화를 듣고, 두 사람의 관계로 가장 적절한 것을 고르시오.

① 학생 – 교사   ② 감독 – 선수
③ 상사 – 부하   ④ 교장 – 학생
⑤ 교사 – 학부모

W: Thank you for coming to this □ _____ today.
M: It's no problem. My boss let me □ _____ □ _____ □ _____. So what do you want to □ _____ □ _____?
W: We need to talk about Minho. His □ _____ isn't very good these days.
M: It's not? What's the □ _____?
W: He □ _____ a lot of □ _____ on it.
M: I'll start □ _____ his homework at home after he finishes it.
W: That would be great. I want his work to □ _____.

✎ **어휘복습** 잘 안 들리거나 몰라서 체크한 어휘를 써 놓고 복습해 보세요.

□ _____   □ _____   □ _____   □ _____
□ _____   □ _____   □ _____   □ _____
□ _____   □ _____   □ _____   □ _____

대화를 듣고, 여자가 남자에게 요청한 일로 가장 적절한 것을 고르시오.

① 빌린 돈 갚기
② 농구 연습하러 가기
③ 남동생의 부탁 들어주기
④ 식료품점에서 장보기
⑤ 냉장고에 남은 우유 마시기

W: Are you □ _____ □ _____ now, Jaehwan?
M: Yes, I am. I'm going out to □ _____ □ _____ with my friends.
W: I see. But I need you to □ _____ a □ _____ □ _____ me, please.
M: Okay. What do you want me to do?
W: On your way home, □ _____ □ _____ the □ _____ □ _____ and □ _____ some milk, will you?
M: All right. Should I buy anything else?
W: No. □ _____ some □ _____ for you.

대화를 듣고, 남자가 공원에 가는 이유로 가장 적절한 것을 고르시오.

① 소풍을 가려고
② 자전거를 타려고
③ 친구를 만나려고
④ 스케이트보드를 타려고
⑤ 롤러블레이드를 타려고

W: Do you □ _____ any □ _____ right now, Tom?
M: Yes, I do. I'm on my way to the □ _____.
W: That's great. I'm □ _____ my □ _____ there, too. Shall we go together?
M: Sure. □ _____ □ _____?
W: I'm going there to take a walk. How about you?
M: I'm going to □ _____ □ _____ with some of my friends. Do you know how to skateboard?
W: No, but I can □ _____. That's a lot of fun.
M: You're right. I enjoy doing it, too.

✎ **어휘복습** 잘 안 들리거나 몰라서 체크한 어휘를 써 놓고 복습해 보세요.

□ _____   □ _____   □ _____   □ _____
□ _____   □ _____   □ _____   □ _____
□ _____   □ _____   □ _____   □ _____

17 어색한 대화 찾기

다음을 듣고, 두 사람의 대화가 <u>어색한</u> 것을 고르시오.

①   ②   ③   ④   ⑤

① W: What time do you □ _____ □ _____ □ _____?
    M: At ten P.M. every night.

② W: □ _____ did you □ _____ your classmate?
    M: To □ _____ □ _____ our □ _____.

③ W: How about □ _____ a □ _____?
    M: Good idea.

④ W: What are you planning to do □ _____ □ _____?
    M: On Saturday or Sunday.

⑤ W: Do you know □ _____ □ _____ □ _____ Mark's house?
    M: Yes, I have been there before.

18 미언급 파악

다음을 듣고, 여자가 언급하지 <u>않은</u> 것을 고르시오.

① 전시 내용
② 실내 전시관 수
③ 점심식사 장소
④ 관람 비용
⑤ 관람 종료 시간

W: Good morning, everyone. Thank you for coming to the □ _____. You can see many items □ _____ ancient □ _____, □ _____, and □ _____ at the museum. We have □ _____ □ _____ □ _____ here. We □ _____ visit the first two exhibit halls □ _____ □ _____. Then, we'll □ _____ in the □ _____ for an hour. Next, we'll go to the □ _____ exhibit hall. After that, we'll go to the museum's □ _____ exhibits. The tour will end □ _____ □ _____. Let's □ _____ □ _____ right now.

✏️ **어휘복습** 잘 안 들리거나 몰라서 체크한 어휘를 써 놓고 복습해 보세요.

□ _____   □ _____   □ _____   □ _____

□ _____   □ _____   □ _____   □ _____

□ _____   □ _____   □ _____   □ _____

19 알맞은 응답 찾기

대화를 듣고, 남자의 마지막 말에 이어질 여자의 응답으로 가장 적절한 것을 고르시오.

Woman: _____
① Yes, I have it with me.
② It's almost dinnertime now.
③ Let's get some sandwiches.
④ Sure, we can study a bit longer.
⑤ I don't have my books with me.

W: We should □ _____ □ _____ on this □ _____ for a while.
M: □ _____ do you want to do that?
W: I'm □ _____. I need some food.
M: Didn't you □ _____ □ _____ this morning?
W: I didn't have any time to eat. I □ _____ □ _____ □ _____, so I ran to the library to meet you.
M: Oh, I didn't □ _____ that. You should have told me.
W: I didn't want to □ _____ you.
M: So □ _____ would you like to □ _____?
W: _____

20 알맞은 응답 찾기

대화를 듣고, 남자의 마지막 말에 이어질 여자의 응답으로 가장 적절한 것을 고르시오.

Woman: _____
① I'm sure you'll have fun.
② Not really. I didn't like it.
③ Thanks for the invitation.
④ I saw lots of fish in the water.
⑤ Yes, we were there for one week.

M: Jean, it's good to see you. Did you have a good weekend?
W: Yes, I did. I went to the □ _____ with my family.
M: That □ _____ □ _____. What did you do there?
W: I □ _____ □ _____ in the □ _____. I also went □ _____.
M: I didn't know you enjoyed the ocean so much.
W: It was my □ _____ □ _____ to go there. I want to □ _____ □ _____ soon.
M: My family is going there next week. You can go with us.
W: _____

✎ **어휘복습** 잘 안 들리거나 몰라서 체크한 어휘를 써 놓고 복습해 보세요.

□ _____   □ _____   □ _____   □ _____
□ _____   □ _____   □ _____   □ _____
□ _____   □ _____   □ _____   □ _____

01 대화를 듣고, 탁자 위 물건 배치로 가장 적절한 것을 고르시오.

02 대화를 듣고, 여자의 심정으로 가장 적절한 것을 고르시오.

① excited   ② upset   ③ nervous
④ scared   ⑤ proud

03 대화를 듣고, 남자가 한 일로 가장 적절한 것을 고르시오.

① 친구 만나기
② 이메일 쓰기
③ 회의 참석하기
④ 골프 약속 확인 전화하기
⑤ 식당에서 점심 식사하기

04 대화를 듣고, 두 사람이 대화하는 장소로 가장 적절한 곳을 고르시오.

① 학교   ② 서점   ③ 도서관
④ 문구점   ⑤ 편의점

05 대화를 듣고, 여자의 마지막 말의 의도로 가장 적절한 것을 고르시오.

① 후회   ② 충고   ③ 사과
④ 축하   ⑤ 위로

06 대화를 듣고, 여자가 지불해야 할 금액을 고르시오.

① $4.00   ② $4.50   ③ $5.00
④ $5.50   ⑤ $6.00

07 대화를 듣고, 여자가 대화 직후에 할 일로 가장 적절한 것을 고르시오.

① 식당 가기
② 식당 예약하기
③ 인터넷 검색하기
④ 공항에서 친구 만나기
⑤ 한국 문화에 대해 배우기

08 대화를 듣고, 두 사람이 가려고 하는 장소를 고르시오.

① 공원   ② 해변   ③ 영화관
④ 백화점   ⑤ 여자의 집

09 다음을 듣고, 무엇에 관한 내용인지 가장 적절한 것을 고르시오.

① 정원용품 소개
② 토마토 주스 효능
③ 인기 있는 식물 소개
④ 식물 심는 방법 안내
⑤ 원예 동아리 가입 안내

10 대화를 듣고, Lisa에 관한 내용과 일치하는 것을 고르시오.

① 남자에게 편지를 보냈다.
② 남동생과 함께 이탈리아에 있다.
③ 이모와 여행 중이다.
④ 어제 공원에 갔다.
⑤ 8월에 이탈리아로 떠났다.

11 대화를 듣고, 여자가 전화한 목적으로 가장 적절한 것을 고르시오.

① 문제점을 알리려고
② 복사기를 주문하려고
③ 책에 대해 물어보려고
④ 수리 기사와 통화하려고
⑤ 도서 대출을 갱신하려고

12 대화를 듣고, 내용과 일치하지 <u>않는</u> 것을 고르시오.

① 여자는 잡지사에서 일한다.
② 남자의 직업은 배우이다.
③ 남자의 최근 작품은 성공적이다.
④ 여자는 배우가 되기를 원한다.
⑤ 남자는 작품의 줄거리를 좋아한다.

13 대화를 듣고, 두 사람의 관계로 가장 적절한 것을 고르시오.

① 교사 – 학생   ② 아빠 – 딸
③ 약사 – 고객   ④ 의사 – 환자
⑤ 간호사 – 환자

14 대화를 듣고, 남자가 여자에게 요청한 일로 가장 적절한 것을 고르시오.

① 서점 방문하기
② 주문 취소하기
③ 배송 상태 확인하기
④ 우편으로 책 보내기
⑤ 인터넷으로 책 조회하기

15 대화를 듣고, 여자가 쇼핑몰에 가려는 이유로 가장 적절한 것을 고르시오.

① 옷을 사려고
② 지갑을 사려고
③ 엄마와 쇼핑하려고
④ 엄마에게 뭔가를 갖다 주려고
⑤ 상점에 옷을 반품하려고

16 다음을 듣고, 두 사람의 대화가 <u>어색한</u> 것을 고르시오.

①   ②   ③   ④   ⑤

17 대화를 듣고, 상황을 가장 잘 표현한 속담을 고르시오.

① All's well that ends well.
② Better safe than sorry.
③ Bad news travels quickly.
④ A rolling stone gathers no moss.
⑤ A bird in the hand is worth two in the bush.

18 다음을 듣고, 목요일의 날씨로 가장 적절한 것을 고르시오.

[19-20] 대화를 듣고, 남자의 마지막 말에 이어질 여자의 응답으로 가장 적절한 것을 고르시오.

19 Woman: _____

① Who helped you make it?
② No, I haven't tasted it yet.
③ Okay. I think I'd like that.
④ Where did you buy this cake?
⑤ I want one more piece, please.

20 Woman: _____

① Sure. We can get together and do some work on the weekend.
② No, I'm going to be at my grandmother's house instead.
③ We need to hurry up and finish the assignment.
④ Why don't we work on our reports together?
⑤ No, I'm not going to my house right now.

다시 듣고, 빈칸에 알맞은 단어를 써 보세요.

◀█》 MP3 실전 02-1

01 그림 정보 파악

대화를 듣고, 탁자 위 물건 배치로 가장 적절한 것을 고르시오.

① ② ③
④ ⑤

W: I'm thinking about putting this □ _____ □ _____ □ _____ the □ _____.

M: That's a good idea. We can put it □ _____ □ _____ □ _____. It should go □ _____ the □ _____.

W: I think that looks nice. Do you think we should □ _____ the □ _____ □ _____ the flower vase and the clock?

M: No, I don't like that. □ _____ □ _____ put the telephone on the table.

W: Sure. That's fine with me.

02 심정 추론

대화를 듣고, 여자의 심정으로 가장 적절한 것을 고르시오.

① excited ② upset ③ nervous
④ scared ⑤ proud

M: Sarah, □ _____ are you still □ _____? It's □ _____ □ _____.

W: I want to □ _____ □ _____ I'm □ _____ □ _____ the school field trip tomorrow.

M: You need to □ _____ some □ _____. You're going to be really busy on your □ _____ □ _____ the □ _____.

W: I know. □ _____ □ _____ I am □ _____ my □ _____. I don't want to forget anything.

M: I know you're □ _____ □ _____ □ _____ going there, but you really have to □ _____ □ _____ □ _____.

W: But I can't sleep. All I'm doing is □ _____ □ _____ the trip.

✏ **어휘복습** 잘 안 들리거나 몰라서 체크한 어휘를 써 놓고 복습해 보세요.

□ _____ □ _____ □ _____ □ _____
□ _____ □ _____ □ _____ □ _____
□ _____ □ _____ □ _____ □ _____

03 한 일 파악

대화를 듣고, 남자가 한 일로 가장 적절한
것을 고르시오.

① 친구 만나기
② 이메일 쓰기
③ 회의에 참석하기
④ 골프 약속 확인 전화하기
⑤ 식당에서 점심 식사하기

W: Hello. □ _____ □ _____ Mr. Bradbury's office. How may I help you?

M: Hi. This is Jim Phillips. I'm Mr. Bradbury's friend. Can I □ _____ □ _____ him, please?

W: I'm sorry, but he's □ _____ □ _____ □ _____ right now.

M: Okay. Can I □ _____ a □ _____ then?

W: Yes. Go ahead.

M: Please tell him that we're going to □ _____ □ _____ □ _____ at □ _____ in the morning. He should be at the golf course □ _____ □ _____ □ _____.

W: Okay. I'll give him the message.

04 장소 추론

대화를 듣고, 두 사람이 대화하는 장소로 가
장 적절한 곳을 고르시오.

① 학교   ② 서점   ③ 도서관
④ 문구점   ⑤ 편의점

M: Good afternoon. I'd like to □ _____ □ _____ these □ _____.

W: Okay. I need to see your □ _____ □ _____.

M: I don't have one. Can I use my □ _____ □ _____ card instead?

W: □ _____, □ _____ you must have a library card.

M: Oh, I didn't know that. I □ _____ □ _____ here.

W: You can make one right now if you want.

M: Okay. What should I do?

W: Please □ _____ □ _____ this □ _____.

✎ **어휘복습** 잘 안 들리거나 몰라서 체크한 어휘를 써 놓고 복습해 보세요.

□ _____   □ _____   □ _____   □ _____

□ _____   □ _____   □ _____   □ _____

□ _____   □ _____   □ _____   □ _____

05 의도 파악

대화를 듣고, 여자의 마지막 말의 의도로 가장 적절한 것을 고르시오.

① 후회   ② 충고   ③ 사과
④ 축하   ⑤ 위로

W: □ _____ □ _____ with you, Eric? You look like you're □ _____.

M: I □ _____ my □ _____ while I was □ _____ □ _____ during gym class.

W: Did you visit the school □ _____?

M: No, I didn't. I don't think it's very □ _____.

W: But you □ _____ to be □ _____ □ _____.

M: I'm okay. Don't worry about me.

W: I hope you □ _____ □ _____ soon.

06 숫자 정보 파악

대화를 듣고, 여자가 지불해야 할 금액을 고르시오.

① $4.00   ② $4.50   ③ $5.00
④ $5.50   ⑤ $6.00

M: Good evening. Can I help you?

W: Yes, please. □ _____ □ _____ are these □ _____?

M: Each cupcake □ _____ □ _____ dollars.

W: And how much does a glass of □ _____ □ _____ cost?

M: It costs □ _____ dollar and □ _____ cents.

W: Okay. I'd like □ _____ cupcakes and □ _____ glass of apple juice, please.

M: All right. Hold on one moment, please.

✎ **어휘복습** 잘 안 들리거나 몰라서 체크한 어휘를 써 놓고 복습해 보세요.

□ _____   □ _____   □ _____   □ _____

□ _____   □ _____   □ _____   □ _____

□ _____   □ _____   □ _____   □ _____

07 할 일 파악

대화를 듣고, 여자가 대화 직후에 할 일로 가장 적절한 것을 고르시오.

① 식당 가기
② 식당 예약하기
③ 인터넷 검색하기
④ 공항에서 친구 만나기
⑤ 한국 문화에 대해 배우기

W: I'm so □ _____. My friend from the United States is □ _____ □ _____ □ _____ Korea next week.

M: That's wonderful news. □ _____ are you □ _____ □ _____ □ _____ when your friend is here?

W: I'm not sure where I should take her.

M: You should definitely □ _____ her □ _____ a □ _____ Korean □ _____.

W: That's a good idea. Do you know any □ _____ □ _____?

M: No, I don't. But I'm sure you can □ _____ some □ _____ □ _____ □ _____.

W: I think you're right. I'm going to do that □ _____ □ _____.

08 특정 정보 파악

대화를 듣고, 두 사람이 가려고 하는 장소를 고르시오.

① 공원   ② 해변   ③ 영화관
④ 백화점   ⑤ 여자의 집

W: There is a □ _____ □ _____ □ _____. Do you want to come to my house then?

M: What do you want to do there?

W: How about □ _____ some □ _____? We could also □ _____ a □ _____.

M: Sorry, but □ _____ □ _____ do something □ _____. Why don't we □ _____ □ _____ the □ _____ and play there?

W: Well, I □ _____ it's □ _____. We can do that.

✎ **어휘복습** 잘 안 들리거나 몰라서 체크한 어휘를 써 놓고 복습해 보세요.

□ _____   □ _____   □ _____   □ _____

□ _____   □ _____   □ _____   □ _____

□ _____   □ _____   □ _____   □ _____

09 화제 추론

다음을 듣고, 무엇에 관한 내용인지 가장 적절한 것을 고르시오.

① 정원용품 소개
② 토마토 주스 효능
③ 인기 있는 식물 소개
④ 식물 심는 방법 안내
⑤ 원예 동아리 가입 안내

M: Listen carefully, everyone. We're going to do some work □ _____ □ _____ □ _____ now. All of you should have a □ _____ □ _____ a tomato □ _____ in it. □ _____ your pot and go to a □ _____ in the garden. Then, □ _____ the tomato plant and the □ _____ in the pot and □ _____ it □ _____ the □ _____. Put dirt around the entire plant and then □ _____ it □ _____. When you're finished, □ _____ □ _____ here. I have some more work for you to do.

10 내용 일치 파악

대화를 듣고, Lisa에 관한 내용과 일치하는 것을 고르시오.

① 남자에게 편지를 보냈다.
② 남동생과 함께 이탈리아에 있다.
③ 이모와 여행 중이다.
④ 어제 공원에 갔다.
⑤ 8월에 이탈리아로 떠났다.

M: What are you looking at?
W: It's a □ _____ □ _____ Lisa. She sent it to me from Italy.
M: Is she in Italy now?
W: Yes, she's □ _____ the □ _____ there. She is there □ _____ her □ _____ and □ _____.
M: I didn't know that. Now I □ _____ □ _____ I haven't seen her at the park this month. □ _____ is she going to □ _____ □ _____?
W: She'll be back at the □ _____ □ _____ □ _____.

✎ **어휘복습** 잘 안 들리거나 몰라서 체크한 어휘를 써 놓고 복습해 보세요.

□ _____   □ _____   □ _____   □ _____
□ _____   □ _____   □ _____   □ _____
□ _____   □ _____   □ _____   □ _____

11 전화 목적 파악

대화를 듣고, 여자가 전화한 목적으로 가장 적절한 것을 고르시오.

① 문제점을 알리려고
② 복사기를 주문하려고
③ 책에 대해 물어보려고
④ 수리 기사와 통화하려고
⑤ 도서 대출을 갱신하려고

M: Hello. □ _____ □ _____. How may I help you?

W: Hi. There's a □ _____ □ _____ the □ _____ □ _____ at Vernon Library.

M: What's the problem?

W: It won't □ _____ any □ _____. I think there's some □ _____ □ _____ in it.

M: I see. I'll send a □ _____ over □ _____ □ _____. He should be there □ _____ □ _____ □ _____.

W: Thank you very much.

12 내용 일치 파악

대화를 듣고, 내용과 일치하지 <u>않는</u> 것을 고르시오.

① 여자는 잡지사에서 일한다.
② 남자의 직업은 배우이다.
③ 남자의 최근 작품은 성공적이다.
④ 여자는 배우가 되기를 원한다.
⑤ 남자는 작품의 줄거리를 좋아한다.

W: Good evening, Mr. Jefferson. My name is Cathy Powers. □ _____ □ _____ *World News Magazine*. It's a pleasure to meet such a □ _____ □ _____.

M: It's a pleasure to meet you, too.

W: Your □ _____ □ _____ is a □ _____ □ _____. Why do you think so many people like it?

M: All of the □ _____ □ _____ a □ _____ □ _____, and the story is amazing, too.

W: That's interesting. □ _____ did you □ _____ □ _____ in the movie?

M: It was difficult □ _____ □ _____, but I really enjoyed it □ _____.

W: That's good to hear. How about telling us □ _____ □ _____ that □ _____ when you were □ _____?

✎ **어휘복습** 잘 안 들리거나 몰라서 체크한 어휘를 써 놓고 복습해 보세요.

□ _____   □ _____   □ _____   □ _____

□ _____   □ _____   □ _____   □ _____

□ _____   □ _____   □ _____   □ _____

13 관계 추론

대화를 듣고, 두 사람의 관계로 가장 적절한 것을 고르시오.

① 교사 – 학생   ② 아빠 – 딸
③ 약사 – 고객   ④ 의사 – 환자
⑤ 간호사 – 환자

M: Hello. Are you □ _____ □ _____ something?
W: Yes, I am. My □ _____ really □ _____. I hurt it □ _____ □ _____ yesterday.
M: You should use this knee □ _____. It will □ _____ you □ _____ □ _____.
W: Can you □ _____ any □ _____ for me?
M: This aspirin will make the □ _____ □ _____ □ _____. Take two of these a day.
W: What should I do if it still hurts in □ _____ □ _____ □ _____ days?
M: You should go to □ _____ a □ _____ □ _____ □ _____ then.

14 부탁 파악

대화를 듣고, 남자가 여자에게 요청한 일로 가장 적절한 것을 고르시오.

① 서점 방문하기
② 주문 취소하기
③ 배송 상태 확인하기
④ 우편으로 책 보내기
⑤ 인터넷으로 책 조회하기

M: Hello.
W: Hello. I'm □ _____ □ _____ Orion Books. May I □ _____ □ _____ Mark Sullivan?
M: □ _____ □ _____ Mark.
W: Hi, I'd like to □ _____ □ _____ □ _____ that the □ _____ you requested has just □ _____.
M: Oh, that's good news. □ _____ □ _____ □ _____ for you to call me for over a week.
W: Really? Why don't you □ _____ □ _____ to □ _____ it □ _____?
M: Can you □ _____ the book to me □ _____ □ _____? I □ _____ □ _____ □ _____ to visit the store this week.

✎ **어휘복습** 잘 안 들리거나 몰라서 체크한 어휘를 써 놓고 복습해 보세요.

□ _____   □ _____   □ _____   □ _____
□ _____   □ _____   □ _____   □ _____
□ _____   □ _____   □ _____   □ _____

15 이유 파악

대화를 듣고, 여자가 쇼핑몰에 가려는 이유로 가장 적절한 것을 고르시오.

① 옷을 사려고
② 지갑을 사려고
③ 엄마와 쇼핑하려고
④ 엄마에게 뭔가를 갖다 주려고
⑤ 상점에 옷을 반품하려고

M: Alice, □ _____ are you □ _____ now?

W: I have to go to the □ _____ □ _____.

M: Why are you doing that?

W: I'm going there to □ _____ my □ _____. She just called me.

M: Is she all right?

W: She went to □ _____ some □ _____, but she □ _____ her □ _____. She asked me to □ _____ it there to her.

M: I see.

16 어색한 대화 찾기

다음을 듣고, 두 사람의 대화가 <u>어색한</u> 것을 고르시오.

①   ②   ③   ④   ⑤

① W: How have you been □ _____?
   M: Yes, I've □ _____ □ _____ □ _____.
② W: I think you should □ _____ more □ _____.
   M: Okay. □ _____ □ _____ to do that.
③ W: Will you □ _____ me □ _____ □ _____?
   M: Okay. What do you need?
④ W: Are you □ _____ □ _____ cooking?
   M: □ _____ □ _____.
⑤ W: □ _____ □ _____ does the game □ _____?
   M: It should begin at seven.

✎ **어휘복습** 잘 안 들리거나 몰라서 체크한 어휘를 써 놓고 복습해 보세요.

□ _____   □ _____   □ _____   □ _____
□ _____   □ _____   □ _____   □ _____
□ _____   □ _____   □ _____   □ _____

17 속담 추론

대화를 듣고, 상황을 가장 잘 표현한 속담을
고르시오.

① All's well that ends well.
② Better safe than sorry.
③ Bad news travels quickly.
④ A rolling stone gathers no moss.
⑤ A bird in the hand is worth two
   in the bush.

M: Who were you talking to □ _____ □ _____ □ _____?

W: Eric. I was asking him about our □ _____ □ _____.

M: Why did you call him? You asked me about it □ _____ □ _____ □ _____.

W: Yeah, but I wanted to □ _____.

M: How come?

W: One time, I asked a friend, and she gave me the □ _____ □ _____. So now I always □ _____ two people the □ _____ □ _____. I don't want to □ _____ □ _____ □ _____ like I did that time.

18 날씨 파악

다음을 듣고, 목요일의 날씨로 가장 적절한
것을 고르시오.

① ② ③
④ ⑤

W: It's time for the weather report for this week. We're going to have □ _____ and □ _____ weather on □ _____. On □ _____, it will □ _____ □ _____ a bit, but it will rain as well. It will be □ _____ on □ _____ morning, but it's going to become very □ _____ in the evening. It will start □ _____ again on □ _____, and the weather will be cold and □ _____ on □ _____. I'll be back in one hour with another □ _____.

✎ 어휘복습 잘 안 들리거나 몰라서 체크한 어휘를 써 놓고 복습해 보세요.

□ _____ □ _____ □ _____ □ _____
□ _____ □ _____ □ _____ □ _____
□ _____ □ _____ □ _____ □ _____

19 알맞은 응답 찾기

대화를 듣고, 남자의 마지막 말에 이어질 여자의 응답으로 가장 적절한 것을 고르시오.

Woman: _____

① Who helped you make it?
② No, I haven't tasted it yet.
③ Okay. I think I'd like that.
④ Where did you buy this cake?
⑤ I want one more piece, please.

M: Would you like to □ _____ some of this □ _____?

W: Sure. It looks good. □ _____ □ _____ it?

M: I did.

W: You made this all □ _____ □ _____? Why?

M: I'd like to become a □ _____ one day. So □ _____ does it □ _____?

W: It's amazing. I'd love to be able to □ _____ like this.

M: I can □ _____ you □ _____ to do it if you want.

W: _____

20 알맞은 응답 찾기

대화를 듣고, 남자의 마지막 말에 이어질 여자의 응답으로 가장 적절한 것을 고르시오.

Woman: _____

① Sure. We can get together and do some work on the weekend.
② No, I'm going to be at my grandmother's house instead.
③ We need to hurry up and finish the assignment.
④ Why don't we work on our reports together?
⑤ No, I'm not going to my house right now.

M: Are you □ _____ □ _____ with your family this □ _____?

W: No, I'm not going to do that.

M: Did your family □ _____ the □ _____?

W: No, my □ _____ and little □ _____ are □ _____ going.

M: But you're not? □ _____ □ _____?

W: I've got to □ _____ a □ _____ for class □ _____ □ _____ morning.

M: Are you going to □ _____ □ _____ your □ _____ all alone?

W: _____

✏️ **어휘복습** 잘 안 들리거나 몰라서 체크한 어휘를 써 놓고 복습해 보세요.

□ _____ □ _____ □ _____ □ _____

□ _____ □ _____ □ _____ □ _____

□ _____ □ _____ □ _____ □ _____

01 대화를 듣고, 남자가 구매할 엽서를 고르시오.

① ② ③

④ ⑤

02 대화를 듣고, 남자의 심정으로 가장 적절한 것을 고르시오.

① nervous ② upset
③ surprised ④ excited
⑤ thankful

03 대화를 듣고, 남자가 주말에 한 일로 가장 적절한 것을 고르시오.

① 쇼핑 가기 ② 캠핑 가기
③ 나무 심기 ④ 하이킹 가기
⑤ 친구 만나기

04 대화를 듣고, 두 사람이 대화하는 장소로 가장 적절한 곳을 고르시오.

① 은행 ② 공항 ③ 서점
④ 경찰서 ⑤ 학교

05 대화를 듣고, 여자의 마지막 말의 의도로 가장 적절한 것을 고르시오.

① 거절 ② 사과 ③ 허가
④ 요청 ⑤ 감사

06 대화를 듣고, 파티에 올 사람들의 수를 고르시오.

① 8 ② 9 ③ 10
④ 11 ⑤ 12

07 대화를 듣고, 여자가 대화 직후에 할 일로 가장 적절한 것을 고르시오.

① 수영복 사기
② 수영장에 가기
③ 수영 수업에 등록하기
④ 수영 코치와 이야기하기
⑤ 남자에게 수영을 가르치기

08 대화를 듣고, 여자가 등록할 수업으로 가장 적절한 것을 고르시오.

① 미술 수업 ② 음악 수업
③ 수학 수업 ④ 과학 수업
⑤ 자전거 수업

09 다음을 듣고, 무엇에 관한 내용인지 가장 적절한 것을 고르시오.

① 강연 공지
② 시험 공지
③ 지역 병원 홍보
④ 새로 온 학생 소개
⑤ 수업 시작 시간 공지

10 대화를 듣고, 여자가 구매하지 않은 물건을 고르시오.

① 스웨터 ② 바지 ③ 티셔츠
④ 귀걸이 ⑤ 블라우스

11 대화를 듣고, 남자가 음식점에 전화한 목적으로 가장 적절한 것을 고르시오.

① 음식을 주문하려고
② 자리를 예약하려고
③ 지배인과 이야기하려고
④ 폐점 시간을 문의하려고
⑤ 일자리에 대해 문의하려고

12 다음을 듣고, 투어에 관한 정보로 일치하지 <u>않는</u> 것을 고르시오.

① Jake가 여행가이드를 맡을 것이다.
② 박물관을 먼저 방문할 것이다.
③ 점심식사 전에 수족관을 방문할 것이다.
④ 함께 점심을 먹을 것이다.
⑤ 점심식사 후에 버스를 타고 시내를 구경할 것이다.

13 대화를 듣고, 두 사람의 관계로 가장 적절한 것을 고르시오.

① 엄마 – 아들
② 고객 – 웨이터
③ 승객 – 승무원
④ 고객 – 요리사
⑤ 고객 – 점원

14 대화를 듣고, 남자가 여자에게 요청한 일로 가장 적절한 것을 고르시오.

① 도서 재고 확인하기
② 역사책 추천하기
③ 폐점 시간 알려주기
④ 에스컬레이터를 타는 곳 알려주기
⑤ 역사 코너가 어디 있는지 알려주기

15 대화를 듣고, 남자가 소풍을 갈 수 <u>없는</u> 이유로 가장 적절한 것을 고르시오.

① 숙제를 끝내야 하기 때문에
② 아빠가 아프시기 때문에
③ 남동생을 돌봐야 하기 때문에
④ 집을 페인트칠해야 하기 때문에
⑤ 가족과 함께 여행을 가기 때문에

16 다음을 듣고, 두 사람의 대화가 <u>어색한</u> 것을 고르시오.

① ② ③ ④ ⑤

17 대화를 듣고, 상황을 가장 잘 표현한 속담을 고르시오.

① No pain, no gain.
② Look before you leap.
③ A stitch in time saves nine.
④ All that glitters is not gold.
⑤ There is no royal road to learning.

18 다음을 듣고, 내일 날씨로 가장 적절한 것을 고르시오.

① ② ③ ④ ⑤

[19-20] 대화를 듣고, 남자의 마지막 말에 이어질 여자의 응답으로 가장 적절한 것을 고르시오.

19 Woman: _____

① What kind of homework is it?
② Yes, you're doing your homework.
③ You need to prepare for your test next.
④ Why didn't you clean your room today?
⑤ Okay, but clean your room once you're finished.

20 Woman: _____

① Sure, we can go now.
② No, I didn't like the meal.
③ Yes, I've been here before.
④ A piece of cake would be nice.
⑤ That's right. This place has dessert.

03회 DICTATION

다시 듣고, 빈칸에 알맞은 단어를 써 보세요.

◀)» **MP3 실전 03-1**

01 그림 정보 파악

대화를 듣고, 남자가 구매할 엽서를 고르시오.

① ② ③
④ ⑤

W: You should □ _____ a □ _____ to your friend in Korea.

M: That's a good idea. □ _____ □ _____ this postcard of the □ _____?

W: I don't like that one. This one □ _____ the □ _____ on it □ _____ □ _____.

M: It's nice, but I think the postcard with the □ _____ on it is □ _____ □ _____ one.

W: I □ _____. You should get it.

M: Okay. I will.

02 심정 추론

대화를 듣고, 남자의 심정으로 가장 적절한 것을 고르시오.

① nervous
② upset
③ surprised
④ excited
⑤ thankful

W: It's late. Why haven't you □ _____ □ _____ □ _____ yet?

M: I can't sleep. I □ _____ □ _____ thinking about tomorrow.

W: Why? Do you have a □ _____ □ _____?

M: No. It's my □ _____ □ _____ □ _____. I'm really □ _____ □ _____ □ _____ playing.

W: Right. You must be □ _____.

M: I am. I hope we □ _____.

✏️ **어휘복습** 잘 안 들리거나 몰라서 체크한 어휘를 써 놓고 복습해 보세요.

□ _____　　□ _____　　□ _____　　□ _____

□ _____　　□ _____　　□ _____　　□ _____

□ _____　　□ _____　　□ _____

03 한 일 파악

대화를 듣고, 남자가 주말에 한 일로 가장 적절한 것을 고르시오.

① 쇼핑 가기　　② 캠핑 가기
③ 나무 심기　　④ 하이킹 가기
⑤ 친구 만나기

M: How was your □ _____, Mina?
W: I □ _____ a □ _____ and □ _____ □ _____ with her. What about you?
M: I □ _____ on a □ _____ to the □ _____.
W: The forest? What did you do there?
M: My father and I went □ _____ for □ _____ □ _____. We had lots of fun.
W: That sounds □ _____.

04 장소 추론

대화를 듣고, 두 사람이 대화하는 장소로 가장 적절한 곳을 고르시오.

① 은행　　② 공항
③ 서점　　④ 경찰서
⑤ 학교

W: I'd like to □ _____ an □ _____, please.
M: No problem. Do you have your □ _____ □ _____?
W: Yes, I do. Here you are.
M: Thank you. Do you want to open a □ _____ account?
W: Yes, and I will □ _____ one hundred dollars in it.
M: Okay. □ _____ □ _____ this □ _____, please.

✎ **어휘복습** 잘 안 들리거나 몰라서 체크한 어휘를 써 놓고 복습해 보세요.

□ _____　　□ _____　　□ _____　　□ _____
□ _____　　□ _____　　□ _____　　□ _____
□ _____　　□ _____　　□ _____　　□ _____

05 의도 파악

대화를 듣고, 여자의 마지막 말의 의도로 가장 적절한 것을 고르시오.

① 거절　　② 사과　　③ 허가
④ 요청　　⑤ 감사

M: Mom, some of my □ _____ are □ _____ □ _____ on Saturday night.

W: Where are they going to go?

M: They're going to □ _____ the □ _____ □ _____ at the stadium.

W: Do you want to go with them?

M: Yes, I'd like to.

W: Have you □ _____ all your □ _____?

M: Yes, I have. I finished it after school today.

W: Then I will □ _____ you to go with them.

06 숫자 정보 파악

대화를 듣고, 파티에 올 사람들의 수를 고르시오.

① 8　　② 9　　③ 10
④ 11　　⑤ 12

M: Did you □ _____ □ _____ the □ _____ to your birthday party?

W: Yes. I gave them out at school today.

M: □ _____ □ _____ of your friends can □ _____?

W: □ _____ said they will be there.

M: So □ _____ people are coming, □ _____?

W: Oh, wait. Elizabeth can't come. She has a □ _____ □ _____ that day.

M: Okay. I'll □ _____ □ _____ there is □ _____ □ _____ for everyone.

✎ **어휘복습** 잘 안 들리거나 몰라서 체크한 어휘를 써 놓고 복습해 보세요.

□ _____　　□ _____　　□ _____　　□ _____

□ _____　　□ _____　　□ _____　　□ _____

□ _____　　□ _____　　□ _____　　□ _____

07 할 일 파악

대화를 듣고, 여자가 대화 직후에 할 일로 가장 적절한 것을 고르시오.

① 수영복 사기
② 수영장에 가기
③ 수영 수업에 등록하기
④ 수영 코치와 이야기하기
⑤ 남자에게 수영을 가르치기

W: Joe, are you □ _____ right now?
M: No, I'm going to □ _____ to the □ _____ □ _____.
W: The pool? I didn't know you could □ _____.
M: I can't, but I'm □ _____ swimming □ _____ now. You should learn with me.
W: I'd like to. It sounds fun.
M: Let's □ _____ □ _____ today. You can watch people swim and □ _____ □ _____ □ _____.
W: Okay. I'll do that.

08 특정 정보 파악

대화를 듣고, 여자가 등록할 수업으로 가장 적절한 것을 고르시오.

① 미술 수업
② 음악 수업
③ 수학 수업
④ 과학 수업
⑤ 자전거 수업

W: Are you going to sign up for an □ _____ □ _____?
M: Yes. But there are so many good classes. I can't □ _____ one.
W: I'd like to □ _____ the □ _____ class.
M: That one looks okay. But the □ _____ class and □ _____ class look □ _____ for me.
W: I didn't know there's an art class. □ _____ □ _____ □ _____ study art. Shall we take it together?
M: Okay. Let's sign up for it now.

✎ **어휘복습** 잘 안 들리거나 몰라서 체크한 어휘를 써 놓고 복습해 보세요.

□ _____ □ _____ □ _____ □ _____

□ _____ □ _____ □ _____ □ _____

□ _____ □ _____ □ _____ □ _____

09 화제 추론

다음을 듣고, 무엇에 관한 내용인지 가장 적절한 것을 고르시오.

① 강연 공지
② 시험 공지
③ 지역 병원 홍보
④ 새로 온 학생 소개
⑤ 수업 시작 시간 공지

W: Listen carefully, everybody. We're □ _____ going to □ _____ □ _____ in the afternoon. □ _____, we're going to have a □ _____ □ _____. Dr. Douglas from the local hospital is going to come here. He's going to □ _____ □ _____ his □ _____. Then, you can □ _____ him □ _____ about his □ _____ as a □ _____. I think this will be a lot of fun. Please go to the □ _____ □ _____ □ _____. Thank you.

10 미언급 파악

대화를 듣고, 여자가 구매하지 <u>않은</u> 물건을 고르시오.

① 스웨터   ② 바지   ③ 티셔츠
④ 귀걸이   ⑤ 블라우스

M: □ _____ was □ _____ at the new store?

W: It was great. The store was □ _____ a big □ _____.

M: □ _____ did you □ _____?

W: I got a □ _____, □ _____, and □ _____ for myself.

M: Did you buy □ _____ □ _____ your □ _____?

W: Yes, I did. I bought her a □ _____ and some □ _____.

M: Wow. That was nice of you.

✎ **어휘복습** 잘 안 들리거나 몰라서 체크한 어휘를 써 놓고 복습해 보세요.

□ _____   □ _____   □ _____   □ _____

□ _____   □ _____   □ _____   □ _____

□ _____   □ _____   □ _____   □ _____

11 전화 목적 파악

대화를 듣고, 남자가 음식점에 전화한 목적으로 가장 적절한 것을 고르시오.

① 음식을 주문하려고
② 자리를 예약하려고
③ 지배인과 이야기하려고
④ 폐점 시간을 문의하려고
⑤ 일자리에 대해 문의하려고

W: Hello. This is Johnny's Steakhouse. How can I help you?
M: Hi. I read your □ _____ □ _____ online.
W: Are you □ _____ □ _____ the job for □ _____
    □ _____?
M: Yes, that's the one. Is it still □ _____?
W: Yes, it is. Would you like to □ _____ □ _____ an
    □ _____?
M: I'd love to. □ _____ a □ _____ □ _____ to go there?
W: Why don't you come here today at □ _____ □ _____?
M: All right. I'll □ _____ □ _____ then.

12 내용 일치 파악

다음을 듣고, 투어에 관한 정보로 일치하지 <u>않는</u> 것을 고르시오.

① Jake가 여행가이드를 맡을 것이다.
② 박물관을 먼저 방문할 것이다.
③ 점심식사 전에 수족관을 방문할 것이다.
④ 함께 점심을 먹을 것이다.
⑤ 점심식사 후에 버스를 타고 시내를 구경할 것이다.

M: Hello. □ _____ □ _____ is Jake Sullivan, and I'll be your
    □ _____ □ _____ today. We're going to □ _____
    □ _____ □ _____ for the next few hours. □ _____,
    we'll visit the □ _____, □ _____ □ _____ we'll go to
    the □ _____. At noon, we'll □ _____ □ _____ together.
    After lunch, we'll □ _____ □ _____ parts of the
    □ _____. Please □ _____ me □ _____ anytime. I hope
    you have fun. Let's get started.

✏ **어휘복습** 잘 안 들리거나 몰라서 체크한 어휘를 써 놓고 복습해 보세요.

□ _____   □ _____   □ _____   □ _____
□ _____   □ _____   □ _____   □ _____
□ _____   □ _____   □ _____   □ _____

13 관계 추론

대화를 듣고, 두 사람의 관계로 가장 적절한 것을 고르시오.

① 엄마 – 아들   ② 고객 – 웨이터
③ 승객 – 승무원   ④ 고객 – 요리사
⑤ 고객 – 점원

W: □ _____ so much □ _____ the □ _____.
M: Did you □ _____ it? Were there any problems with it?
W: No, not at all. This was □ _____ □ _____ meal I've had in a long time.
M: Thank you for saying that. I'll □ _____ the □ _____ □ _____ you said that.
W: I'll definitely □ _____ □ _____ to this □ _____ in the future.
M: I'm glad to hear that.

14 부탁 파악

대화를 듣고, 남자가 여자에게 요청한 일로 가장 적절한 것을 고르시오.

① 도서 재고 확인하기
② 역사책 추천하기
③ 폐점 시간 알려주기
④ 에스컬레이터를 타는 곳 알려주기
⑤ 역사 코너가 어디 있는지 알려주기

W: Hello. Are you □ _____ □ _____ a □ _____?
M: Yes, I'm trying to find the □ _____ □ _____.
W: It's on another floor. You need to go to the □ _____ □ _____.
M: Can you tell me □ _____ I can □ _____ □ _____?
W: Sure. Just □ _____ the □ _____ to the fourth floor. You'll find it there.
M: Thanks for your help.

✎ **어휘복습** 잘 안 들리거나 몰라서 체크한 어휘를 써 놓고 복습해 보세요.

□ _____   □ _____   □ _____   □ _____
□ _____   □ _____   □ _____   □ _____
□ _____   □ _____   □ _____   □ _____

15 이유 파악

대화를 듣고, 남자가 소풍을 갈 수 없는 이유로 가장 적절한 것을 고르시오.

① 숙제를 끝내야 하기 때문에
② 아빠가 아프시기 때문에
③ 남동생을 돌봐야 하기 때문에
④ 집을 페인트칠해야 하기 때문에
⑤ 가족과 함께 여행을 가기 때문에

M: Hello.

W: Hi, Rick. Would you like to □ _____ □ _____ a □ _____ tomorrow?

M: That sounds great, □ _____ I can't go.

W: □ _____ □ _____? Are you □ _____?

M: Yes. I'm going to help my dad □ _____ the □ _____.

W: Will that □ _____ a □ _____ □ _____?

M: It will take almost □ _____ □ _____ □ _____.

W: Okay. We can do that next weekend then.

16 어색한 대화 찾기

다음을 듣고, 두 사람의 대화가 어색한 것을 고르시오.

① ② ③ ④ ⑤

① W: □ _____ □ _____ do you □ _____ your grandmother?
   M: At least □ _____ □ _____ □ _____.

② W: □ _____ do you want to eat for □ _____?
   M: I want □ _____ and □ _____.

③ W: Can you □ _____ □ _____ for the concert?
   M: Sorry. They are all □ _____ □ _____.

④ W: □ _____ □ _____ does it □ _____ to get to your home?
   M: About two meters.

⑤ W: □ _____ □ _____ for giving me some □ _____.
   M: It's my □ _____.

✎ **어휘복습** 잘 안 들리거나 몰라서 체크한 어휘를 써 놓고 복습해 보세요.

□ _____   □ _____   □ _____   □ _____
□ _____   □ _____   □ _____   □ _____
□ _____   □ _____   □ _____   □ _____

17 속담 추론

대화를 듣고, 상황을 가장 잘 표현한 속담을 고르시오.

① No pain, no gain.
② Look before you leap.
③ A stitch in time saves nine.
④ All that glitters is not gold.
⑤ There is no royal road to learning.

W: You □ _____ □ _____, Phil. What's the matter?

M: I bought a new □ _____ yesterday, but it already □ _____.

W: What's wrong?

M: I don't know. I tried to □ _____ □ _____ the phone, but it doesn't □ _____.

W: Did you buy a □ _____ one?

M: Yes, it was cheap. But I □ _____ it because it □ _____ □ _____ and □ _____.

W: Don't buy things because they look nice and shiny.

18 날씨 파악

다음을 듣고, 내일 날씨로 가장 적절한 것을 고르시오.

① ② ③
④ ⑤

M: Good afternoon. I'm Bud Samuels, and I'm here with this week's weather report. You need to □ _____ your □ _____ □ _____ since it's cold and cloudy. But the □ _____ will □ _____ □ _____, so we'll enjoy □ _____ skies □ _____ □ _____ □ _____. We'll □ _____ □ _____ sunny weather on Wednesday and Thursday, and the □ _____ will □ _____, too. But the weather will be □ _____ on □ _____ and □ _____. Expect both □ _____ □ _____ and □ _____ on those two days.

✎ **어휘복습** 잘 안 들리거나 몰라서 체크한 어휘를 써 놓고 복습해 보세요.

□ _____ □ _____ □ _____ □ _____
□ _____ □ _____ □ _____ □ _____
□ _____ □ _____ □ _____ □ _____

대화를 듣고, 남자의 마지막 말에 이어질 여자의 응답으로 가장 적절한 것을 고르시오.

Woman: _____

① What kind of homework is it?
② Yes, you're doing your homework.
③ You need to prepare for your test next.
④ Why didn't you clean your room today?
⑤ Okay, but clean your room once you're finished.

W: Steve, did you remember to □ _____ your □ _____?
M: I didn't forget, but I □ _____ □ _____ □ _____ to do that now.
W: Why not? What are you doing now?
M: I need to □ _____ my □ _____ □ _____.
W: □ _____ are you □ _____ to clean your room?
M: After I finish my homework, I'm going out to □ _____ □ _____. So I'll clean my room □ _____. Is that okay?
W: _____

대화를 듣고, 남자의 마지막 말에 이어질 여자의 응답으로 가장 적절한 것을 고르시오.

Woman: _____

① Sure, we can go now.
② No, I didn't like the meal.
③ Yes, I've been here before.
④ A piece of cake would be nice.
⑤ That's right. This place has dessert.

M: How are you □ _____ your □ _____?
W: It's □ _____. Thanks for taking me here.
M: I'm □ _____ you like it.
W: Are you going to □ _____ some □ _____?
M: I think I will. □ _____ would you □ _____?
W: _____

✎ **어휘복습** 잘 안 들리거나 몰라서 체크한 어휘를 써 놓고 복습해 보세요.

□ _____   □ _____   □ _____   □ _____
□ _____   □ _____   □ _____   □ _____
□ _____   □ _____   □ _____   □ _____

01 대화를 듣고, 여자가 여행에 가져갈 물건을 고르시오.

① 　② 　③

④ 　⑤

02 대화를 듣고, 베트남의 날씨로 가장 적절한 것을 고르시오.

① 　② 　③ 　④ 　⑤

03 대화를 듣고, 여자의 심정으로 가장 적절한 것을 고르시오.

① unpleasant　　② proud
③ relaxed　　④ regretful
⑤ disappointed

04 대화를 듣고, 두 사람이 대화하는 장소로 가장 적절한 곳을 고르시오.

① 카페　　② 음식점　　③ 제과점
④ 구내식당　　⑤ 아이스크림 가게

05 대화를 듣고, 여자가 묘사하는 사람을 고르시오.

① 　② 　③

④ 　⑤

06 대화를 듣고, 여자가 지불해야 할 금액을 고르시오.

① $2　　② $4　　③ $6
④ $8　　⑤ $10

07 대화를 듣고, 남자가 전화한 목적으로 가장 적절한 것을 고르시오.

① 주문하려고
② 주문을 취소하려고
③ 배송 날짜를 변경하려고
④ 소파 가격을 문의하려고
⑤ 상품 색상을 변경하려고

08 대화를 듣고, 남자가 대화 직후에 할 일로 가장 적절한 것을 고르시오.

① 야구 연습하기　　② 병원에 가기
③ 약 복용하기　　④ 달리기하기
⑤ 휴식 취하기

09 대화를 듣고, 두 사람의 관계로 가장 적절한 것을 고르시오.

① 엄마 – 아들
② 교사 – 학생
③ 종업원 – 고객
④ 운전 기사 – 승객
⑤ 승무원 – 승객

10 다음을 듣고, 학생들에게 가장 인기 있는 스포츠를 고르시오.

① soccer　　② softball
③ basketball　　④ volleyball
⑤ baseball

11 대화를 듣고, 여자가 남자를 위해 할 일로 가장 적절한 것을 고르시오.

① 샌드위치 가져다 주기
② 보고서 제출해주기
③ 보고서 작성 도와주기
④ 선생님과 이야기하기
⑤ 구내식당이 어디 있는지 알려주기

12 다음을 듣고, 3시에 열리게 될 행사로 가장 적절한 것을 고르시오.

① 축구   ② 줄다리기   ③ 야구
④ 달리기   ⑤ 시상식

13 대화를 듣고, 남자가 대화 직후에 할 일로 가장 적절한 것을 고르시오.

① 축제 기획하기
② 학교 연극에 참여하기
③ 음악 숙제 제출하기
④ 선생님과 이야기하기
⑤ 학교 연극에서 자원봉사하기

14 다음을 듣고, 도표의 내용과 일치하지 않는 것을 고르시오.

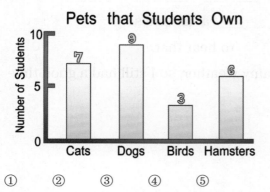

Pets that Students Own

①   ②   ③   ④   ⑤

15 대화를 듣고, 인도 음식점에 관한 정보로 일치하지 않는 것을 고르시오.

① 쇼핑몰 안에 있다.
② 여자는 그곳에서 점심을 먹었다.
③ 음식이 너무 매워서 먹을 수 없었다.
④ 식당의 가격은 저렴했다.
⑤ 최근에 개점했다.

16 다음을 듣고, 두 사람의 대화가 어색한 것을 고르시오.

①   ②   ③   ④   ⑤

17 다음을 듣고, 오늘 일정에 관해 언급되지 않은 것을 고르시오.

① 학생들은 운동장으로 모일 것이다.
② 학생들은 공원에서 점심을 먹을 것이다.
③ 12시에 교실 밖으로 모여야 한다.
④ 음식과 음료는 무료로 제공된다.
⑤ 점심식사 후에 게임을 할 것이다.

[18-19] 대화를 듣고, 여자의 마지막 말에 이어질 남자의 응답으로 가장 적절한 것을 고르시오.

18 Man: _____

① Yes, I'm all ready for school.
② I went to the park last week.
③ I'll do that on Thursday or Friday.
④ I'm going shopping with my family.
⑤ No, I don't need any school supplies.

19 Man: _____

① Let's buy one at the bakery.
② No, you don't have to do that.
③ I want a cake with vanilla icing.
④ How about buying me a present?
⑤ You should make a card for Mom.

20 다음을 듣고, Tom이 Amy에게 할 말로 가장 적절한 것을 고르시오.

Tom: _____

① We can go another time.
② I'm so glad you feel that way.
③ I helped you clean your room.
④ I had a great time at the movie.
⑤ Of course, your father must be proud.

01 그림 정보 파악

대화를 듣고, 여자가 여행에 가져갈 물건을 고르시오.

① ② ③
④ ⑤

M: Nancy, have you □ _____ your □ _____?

W: Not yet. Can you help me pack my □ _____, Dad?

M: Okay. □ _____ do you need to □ _____? Do you need a □ _____ and some □ _____?

W: No, I don't. Brazil will be □ _____ and □ _____.

M: Okay. Then you don't need any □ _____ □ _____ either.

W: I think I should take my □ _____ with me.

M: Okay. Let me get it for you.

02 날씨 파악

대화를 듣고, 베트남의 날씨로 가장 적절한 것을 고르시오.

① ② ③
④ ⑤

M: □ _____ was your □ _____ to Vietnam?

W: I □ _____ a □ _____ □ _____ there. It was my first □ _____ trip.

M: Was it really □ _____ there?

W: No, it wasn't. It □ _____ □ _____ □ _____. I had to □ _____ my □ _____ at all times.

M: □ _____ □ _____ to hear that.

W: It's okay. I like rainy weather, so I still had a good time there.

✎ 어휘복습 잘 안 들리거나 몰라서 체크한 어휘를 써 놓고 복습해 보세요.

□ _____   □ _____   □ _____   □ _____
□ _____   □ _____   □ _____   □ _____
□ _____   □ _____   □ _____   □ _____

03 심정 추론

대화를 듣고, 여자의 심정으로 가장 적절한
것을 고르시오.

① unpleasant   ② proud
③ relaxed   ④ regretful
⑤ disappointed

W: Did you have a good time at the □ _____ □ _____ today?

M: Yes. It was □ _____. There were so many good □ _____ □ _____.

W: □ _____ did your □ _____ □ _____?

M: Everyone there liked it a lot.

W: I'm glad to hear that.

M: The □ _____ gave me a □ _____ □ _____.

W: Wow. You did an amazing job.

04 장소 추론

대화를 듣고, 두 사람이 대화하는 장소로 가
장 적절한 곳을 고르시오.

① 카페   ② 음식점   ③ 제과점
④ 구내식당   ⑤ 아이스크림 가게

M: Excuse me. Can I □ _____ some □ _____?

W: Sure. □ _____ do you □ _____?

M: Today is my wife's □ _____, so I need a □ _____.

W: Does she □ _____ chocolate or vanilla?

M: She □ _____ □ _____.

W: We have many chocolate cakes here. Do you like any of them?

M: That □ _____ one looks nice. I'll take it.

W: That's a □ _____ □ _____. It's the □ _____ □ _____ in our store.

✎ **어휘복습** 잘 안 들리거나 몰라서 체크한 어휘를 써 놓고 복습해 보세요.

□ _____   □ _____   □ _____   □ _____

□ _____   □ _____   □ _____   □ _____

□ _____   □ _____   □ _____   □ _____

05 그림 정보 파악

대화를 듣고, 여자가 묘사하는 사람을 고르
시오.

① ② ③

④ ⑤

M: □ _____ one is the new □ _____ □ _____?

W: He's standing □ _____ □ _____ with the other men.

M: Many of those guys over there are □ _____ □ _____. Is he wearing glasses, too?

W: Yes, he is. But he isn't wearing a □ _____. Can you find him?

M: I'm not quite sure. Is he □ _____ or □ _____?

W: He's □ _____ □ _____ the other men.

06 숫자 정보 파악

대화를 듣고, 여자가 지불해야 할 금액을 고
르시오.

① $2   ② $4   ③ $6
④ $8   ⑤ $10

M: Hello. How can I help you?

W: Hi. I'd like to have one □ _____ for the □ _____ □ _____. □ _____ □ _____ does it cost?

M: Each ticket □ _____ □ _____ dollars. Do you have a □ _____ □ _____?

W: No, I don't. But I have a □ _____ □ _____. Can I □ _____ □ _____ □ _____ with it?

M: Yes, you can get a two-dollar discount.

W: Great. Here you are.

✎ **어휘복습** 잘 안 들리거나 몰라서 체크한 어휘를 써 놓고 복습해 보세요.

□ _____   □ _____   □ _____   □ _____

□ _____   □ _____   □ _____   □ _____

□ _____   □ _____   □ _____   □ _____

07 전화 목적 파악

대화를 듣고, 남자가 전화한 목적으로 가장 적절한 것을 고르시오.

① 주문하려고
② 주문을 취소하려고
③ 배송 날짜를 변경하려고
④ 소파 가격을 문의하려고
⑤ 상품 색상을 변경하려고

W: Hello. This is Fine □ _____. May I help you?

M: Hello. My name is Dave Thomas. I □ _____ a □ _____ there yesterday.

W: Yes, Mr. Thomas. What can I do for you?

M: Can I □ _____ the □ _____? I don't want □ _____.

W: What color do you want?

M: I'd like a □ _____ sofa. The black one would □ _____ □ _____ □ _____ the other furniture in my house.

W: No problem. We will □ _____ a black sofa to you □ _____ □ _____.

08 할 일 파악

대화를 듣고, 남자가 대화 직후에 할 일로 가장 적절한 것을 고르시오.

① 야구 연습하기
② 병원에 가기
③ 약 복용하기
④ 달리기하기
⑤ 휴식 취하기

W: Hi, John. What's □ _____ □ _____ your leg?

M: I □ _____ it □ _____ I was □ _____ early this morning.

W: You should □ _____ some □ _____ then.

M: I can't. I have □ _____ □ _____ today. I really can't □ _____ it.

W: Don't go to it. Go to □ _____ □ _____ □ _____ instead. I'm □ _____ □ _____ your health.

M: Okay. I'll do that. Thanks for your □ _____.

✎ **어휘복습** 잘 안 들리거나 몰라서 체크한 어휘를 써 놓고 복습해 보세요.

□ _____   □ _____   □ _____   □ _____

□ _____   □ _____   □ _____   □ _____

□ _____   □ _____   □ _____   □ _____

09 관계 추론

대화를 듣고, 두 사람의 관계로 가장 적절한 것을 고르시오.

① 엄마 – 아들
② 교사 – 학생
③ 종업원 – 고객
④ 운전 기사 – 승객
⑤ 승무원 – 승객

M: Ms. Kim, can I □ _____ a □ _____?

W: Sure, Minsu. What is it?

M: Can you □ _____ □ _____ □ _____ I got a C on my paper? I don't □ _____.

W: You □ _____ a lot of □ _____ on it.

M: Can I write it again and then □ _____ it □ _____ to you?

W: □ _____, □ _____ you can't. Just □ _____ □ _____ on the next class □ _____.

M: Okay. I understand.

10 특정 정보 파악

다음을 듣고, 학생들에게 가장 인기 있는 스포츠를 고르시오.

① soccer   ② softball
③ basketball   ④ volleyball
⑤ baseball

W: Students at our school □ _____ □ _____ many different □ _____. The boys love some sports □ _____ the girls enjoy playing other ones. For example, □ _____ and □ _____ are □ _____ girls' sports. □ _____ and □ _____ are two of the □ _____ sports for boys. However, □ _____ □ _____ popular sport at the school is □ _____. Both boys and girls like it very much.

✎ **어휘복습** 잘 안 들리거나 몰라서 체크한 어휘를 써 놓고 복습해 보세요.

□ _____   □ _____   □ _____   □ _____

□ _____   □ _____   □ _____   □ _____

□ _____   □ _____   □ _____   □ _____

11 할 일 파악

대화를 듣고, 여자가 남자를 위해 할 일로
가장 적절한 것을 고르시오.

① 샌드위치 가져다 주기
② 보고서 제출해주기
③ 보고서 작성 도와주기
④ 선생님과 이야기하기
⑤ 구내식당이 어디 있는지 알려주기

M: Julie, □ _____ are you □ _____ now?

W: I'm going to the □ _____. I'm hungry.

M: Can you □ _____ me □ _____ □ _____ then?

W: Sure. What do you need?

M: Can you □ _____ me a □ _____ when you □ _____
□ _____?

W: Okay. But why can't you go there?

M: I am □ _____ □ _____ on this □ _____. I need to give
it to Mr. Smith by one.

12 특정 정보 파악

다음을 듣고, 3시에 열리게 될 행사로 가장
적절한 것을 고르시오.

① 축구   ② 줄다리기   ③ 야구
④ 달리기   ⑤ 시상식

M: Good morning, everyone. Today is our school's □ _____
□ _____. We're going to have lots of fun today. From
□ _____ □ _____ □ _____, we'll play □ _____. After
that, we're going to have □ _____. At one, we're going
to play □ _____ □ _____ □ _____. And at □ _____,
we will have a □ _____ game. When the game ends, we'll
have an □ _____ □ _____ as the □ _____ □ _____.
I hope everyone has fun.

✏ **어휘복습** 잘 안 들리거나 몰라서 체크한 어휘를 써 놓고 복습해 보세요.

□ _____   □ _____   □ _____   □ _____
□ _____   □ _____   □ _____   □ _____
□ _____   □ _____   □ _____   □ _____

13 할 일 파악

대화를 듣고, 남자가 대화 직후에 할 일로 가장 적절한 것을 고르시오.

① 축제 기획하기
② 학교 연극에 참여하기
③ 음악 숙제 제출하기
④ 선생님과 이야기하기
⑤ 학교 연극에서 자원봉사하기

W: I □_____ □_____ Ms. Lee today. The school needs □_____ for the □_____.

M: Are you going to help?

W: Yes. I'm going to volunteer at the □_____ □_____.

M: That's good. □_____ □_____ □_____ help the school have a good festival?

W: You should □_____ □_____ Ms. Lee. She can tell you what to do.

M: Okay. I'll □_____ her □_____ after music class ends.

14 도표 · 실용문 파악

다음을 듣고, 도표의 내용과 일치하지 <u>않는</u> 것을 고르시오.

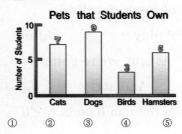

Pets that Students Own

①   ②   ③   ④   ⑤

① □_____ are □_____ by □_____ students.
② Dogs are owned by □_____ students.
③ □_____ are owned by □_____ students.
④ Birds are owned by □_____ □_____ students.
⑤ Hamsters are owned by □_____ students □_____ cats are.

✎ **어휘복습** 잘 안 들리거나 몰라서 체크한 어휘를 써 놓고 복습해 보세요.

□_____   □_____   □_____   □_____

□_____   □_____   □_____   □_____

□_____   □_____   □_____   □_____

15 내용 일치 파악

대화를 듣고, 인도 음식점에 관한 정보로 일치하지 <u>않는</u> 것을 고르시오.

① 쇼핑몰 안에 있다.
② 여자는 그곳에서 점심을 먹었다.
③ 음식이 너무 매워서 먹을 수 없었다.
④ 식당의 가격은 저렴했다.
⑤ 최근에 개점했다.

W: You'll never □ _____ what I did today.

M: I □ _____ □ _____. Go ahead and tell me.

W: Jenny and I went to the Sandstone Mall and □ _____ □ _____ at the new Indian □ _____.

M: Are you □ _____? I've heard so much about it. □ _____ was the □ _____?

W: It was □ _____. Some of it was □ _____, but it wasn't so hot that you couldn't eat it.

M: Were the □ _____ □ _____?

W: Yes, they were. And the restaurant was having a □ _____ □ _____ to □ _____ its □ _____. So we only paid □ _____ □ _____.

M: Wow. I really □ _____ you. I'd love to go there.

16 어색한 대화 찾기

다음을 듣고, 두 사람의 대화가 <u>어색한</u> 것을 고르시오.

①   ②   ③   ④   ⑤

① M: □ _____ you □ _____ eaten Mexican food?
  W: Yes, but I did not like it.

② M: □ _____ □ _____ is your □ _____ to Jeju Island?
  W: I will be there for one week.

③ M: Did you □ _____ to □ _____ your brother?
  W: No, I □ _____ to do that.

④ M: What's the □ _____ □ _____ now?
  W: It's cold and □ _____.

⑤ M: What do you usually do □ _____ □ _____ □ _____?
  W: I □ _____ my □ _____ and stay at their home.

✎ **어휘복습** 잘 안 들리거나 몰라서 체크한 어휘를 써 놓고 복습해 보세요.

□ _____   □ _____   □ _____   □ _____

□ _____   □ _____   □ _____   □ _____

□ _____   □ _____   □ _____   □ _____

17 미언급 파악

다음을 듣고, 오늘 일정에 관해 언급되지 <u>않</u>은 것을 고르시오.

① 학생들은 운동장으로 모일 것이다.
② 학생들은 공원에서 점심을 먹을 것이다.
③ 12시에 교실 밖으로 모여야 한다.
④ 음식과 음료는 무료로 제공된다.
⑤ 점심식사 후에 게임을 할 것이다.

M: Good morning, students. Today, we will not □ _____ □ _____ in the □ _____. □ _____, we will □ _____ a □ _____ □ _____ on the school grounds. At twelve, everyone should □ _____ □ _____. We will □ _____ □ _____ and □ _____ for all of you. After lunch, we will □ _____ some □ _____, too.

18 알맞은 응답 찾기

대화를 듣고, 여자의 마지막 말에 이어질 남자의 응답으로 가장 적절한 것을 고르시오.

Man: _____
① Yes, I'm all ready for school.
② I went to the park last week.
③ I'll do that on Thursday or Friday.
④ I'm going shopping with my family.
⑤ No, I don't need any school supplies.

M: □ _____ is almost □ _____. We start school next week.
W: What are you going to do □ _____ □ _____ □ _____?
M: I'm going to □ _____ □ _____.
W: What for?
M: I need some □ _____ □ _____.
W: When are you going to visit the □ _____ □ _____ then?
M: _____

✎ **어휘복습** 잘 안 들리거나 몰라서 체크한 어휘를 써 놓고 복습해 보세요.

□ _____   □ _____   □ _____   □ _____
□ _____   □ _____   □ _____   □ _____
□ _____   □ _____   □ _____   □ _____

19 알맞은 응답 찾기

대화를 듣고, 여자의 마지막 말에 이어질 남자의 응답으로 가장 적절한 것을 고르시오.

Man: _____
① Let's buy one at the bakery.
② No, you don't have to do that.
③ I want a cake with vanilla icing.
④ How about buying me a present?
⑤ You should make a card for Mom.

M: Mom's □ _____ is □ _____.

W: Oh, I □ _____ □ _____. What should we do?

M: We should □ _____ a □ _____ for her.

W: Okay. That's a good idea. □ _____ are you □ _____ to do for it?

M: We need a □ _____ and a □ _____. I can □ _____ a cake.

W: What do you want me to do?

M: _____

20 상황에 적절한 말 찾기

다음을 듣고, Tom이 Amy에게 할 말로 가장 적절한 것을 고르시오.

Tom: _____
① We can go another time.
② I'm so glad you feel that way.
③ I helped you clean your room.
④ I had a great time at the movie.
⑤ Of course, your father must be proud.

W: Tom and Amy are planning to □ _____ a □ _____ together □ _____ □ _____. However, on Saturday, Amy's father tells her she can't □ _____ □ _____. She has to □ _____ her □ _____ and □ _____ some other □ _____. Amy is very □ _____, but she calls Tom and tells him the news. In this situation, what could Tom say to make Amy feel better?

Tom: _____

✎ **어휘복습** 잘 안 들리거나 몰라서 체크한 어휘를 써 놓고 복습해 보세요.

□ _____　　□ _____　　□ _____　　□ _____
□ _____　　□ _____　　□ _____　　□ _____
□ _____　　□ _____　　□ _____　　□ _____

01 다음을 듣고, 토요일의 날씨로 가장 적절한 것을 고르시오.

① ② ③ ④ ⑤

02 대화를 듣고, 여자가 구매할 스웨터를 고르시오.

① ② ③

④ ⑤

03 대화를 듣고, 여자의 심정으로 가장 적절한 것을 고르시오.

① angry   ② proud   ③ regretful
④ bored   ⑤ pleased

04 대화를 듣고, 여자가 어제 한 일로 가장 적절한 것을 고르시오.

① 쇼핑 가기
② 선물 사기
③ 친구 만나기
④ 생일 파티 하기
⑤ 엄마의 심부름하기

05 대화를 듣고, 두 사람이 대화하는 장소로 가장 적절한 곳을 고르시오.

① bank   ② restaurant
③ supermarket   ④ bus station
⑤ repair center

06 대화를 듣고, 여자의 마지막 말의 의도로 가장 적절한 것을 고르시오.

① 동의   ② 제안   ③ 충고
④ 거절   ⑤ 허가

07 대화를 듣고, 핼러윈 파티에 오는 사람들의 수를 고르시오.

① 18   ② 19   ③ 20
④ 21   ⑤ 22

08 대화를 듣고, 여자가 대화 직후에 할 일로 가장 적절한 것을 고르시오.

① 숙제하기
② 전화하기
③ 선생님과 대화하기
④ 새 휴대폰 사기
⑤ 전자제품 매장 방문하기

09 대화를 듣고, 남자가 가장 좋았다고 생각한 운동으로 가장 적절한 것을 고르시오.

① 농구   ② 배드민턴   ③ 탁구
④ 테니스   ⑤ 야구

10 다음을 듣고, 무엇에 관한 내용인지 가장 적절한 것을 고르시오.

① 채소 보관법
② 농산물 가격 폭락
③ 특별 할인 안내
④ 연휴 기간 영업 안내
⑤ 신선한 과일 고르는 방법

11 대화를 듣고, 남자의 주문에서 언급되지 <u>않은</u> 것을 고르시오.

① 치킨　　　② 샐러드　　　③ 수프
④ 감자　　　⑤ 아이스티

12 대화를 듣고, 여자가 전화한 목적으로 가장 적절한 것을 고르시오.

① 책을 빌리려고
② 집에 초대하려고
③ 책을 돌려달라고 요청하려고
④ 과학 숙제에 대해서 물어보려고
⑤ 과학 시험에 대해서 물어보려고

13 대화를 듣고, 요리에 필요하지 <u>않은</u> 재료를 고르시오.

① 밀가루　　　② 버터　　　③ 달걀
④ 설탕　　　⑤ 초콜릿칩

14 대화를 듣고, 두 사람의 관계로 가장 적절한 것을 고르시오.

① 학부모 – 교사
② 학부모 – 감독
③ 의사 – 환자
④ 감독 – 선수
⑤ 약사 – 환자

15 대화를 듣고, 여자가 남자에게 요청한 일로 가장 적절한 것을 고르시오.

① 텔레비전 켜기　　　② 옷 다리기
③ 빨래 널기　　　④ 빨래 개기
⑤ 세탁기 돌리기

16 대화를 듣고, 남자가 버스 터미널에 가는 이유로 가장 적절한 것을 고르시오.

① 표를 사려고
② 버스를 타려고
③ 친구를 만나려고
④ 아빠를 데리러 가려고
⑤ 잃어버린 물건을 찾으려고

17 다음을 듣고, 두 사람의 대화가 <u>어색한</u> 것을 고르시오.

①　　　②　　　③　　　④　　　⑤

18 대화를 듣고, 상황을 가장 잘 표현한 속담을 고르시오.

① Better late than never.
② Look before you leap.
③ Rome wasn't built in a day.
④ After a storm comes a calm.
⑤ All work and no play makes Jack a
　 dull boy.

[19-20] 대화를 듣고, 남자의 마지막 말에 이어질 여자의 응답으로 가장 적절한 것을 고르시오.

19 Woman: _____

① Yes, his class is fun.
② Thanks for your help.
③ I love his math class.
④ No, I don't have any homework.
⑤ No, I haven't seen him all day.

20 Woman: _____

① Have you been to the park?
② I jog around 10 kilometers.
③ I'm trying to get in good shape.
④ I go jogging at 6 in the morning.
⑤ Not at all. You can meet me at 6 in
　 the morning.

05회 DICTATION

다시 듣고, 빈칸에 알맞은 단어를 써 보세요.

◀◎» MP3 실전 05-1

01 날씨 파악

다음을 듣고, 토요일의 날씨로 가장 적절한 것을 고르시오.

① ② ③ ④ ⑤

M: Good evening. It's time for the □ _____ □ _____ □ _____. It finally □ _____ □ _____ this morning. So we had a □ _____, □ _____ day today. The □ _____ is □ _____ □ _____ tomorrow. We will have □ _____ skies all day on □ _____. But it will be □ _____ again on □ _____. You'll need your □ _____ on □ _____. It's going to start raining again.

02 그림 정보 파악

대화를 듣고, 여자가 구매할 스웨터를 고르시오.

① ② ③ ④ ⑤

M: Hello. How may I help you?
W: Hi. I'd like to buy a □ _____ □ _____ my □ _____.
M: How about this one □ _____ □ _____?
W: No, I don't think she'll like that. She likes □ _____. □ _____ □ _____ on them.
M: □ _____ □ _____ this one with a □ _____ on it?
W: She loves dolphins. I'll take it.

03 심정 추론

대화를 듣고, 여자의 심정으로 가장 적절한 것을 고르시오.

① angry　② proud
③ regretful　④ bored
⑤ pleased

M: What's the matter, Karen?
W: Jason just □ _____ my MP3 player.
M: □ _____ □ _____ □ _____. He's only six years old.
W: But it □ _____ a lot of money. I can't buy a new one.
M: I understand. I'll □ _____ a □ _____ □ _____ for you.

✎ 어휘복습 잘 안 들리거나 몰라서 체크한 어휘를 써 놓고 복습해 보세요.

□ _____　□ _____　□ _____　□ _____
□ _____　□ _____　□ _____　□ _____
□ _____　□ _____　□ _____　□ _____

56　쎄듀 빠르게 중학영어듣기 모의고사

04 한 일 파악

대화를 듣고, 여자가 어제 한 일로 가장 적절한 것을 고르시오.

① 쇼핑 가기　　② 선물 사기
③ 친구 만나기　④ 생일 파티 하기
⑤ 엄마의 심부름하기

M: Sarah, you're □ _____ a nice □ _____ today.

W: Thanks. I just got it □ _____.

M: Was it a □ _____ □ _____ from someone?

W: No, my birthday is □ _____ □ _____. I □ _____ □ _____ with my mom yesterday.

M: I see. Tell me □ _____ your birthday □ _____. Then, I'll get you a present on your birthday.

05 장소 추론

대화를 듣고, 두 사람이 대화하는 장소로 가장 적절한 곳을 고르시오.

① bank　　　　② restaurant
③ supermarket　④ bus station
⑤ repair center

W: Hello. Can I help you, sir?

M: Yes, please. There's a □ _____ □ _____ my □ _____.

W: □ _____ □ _____ with it?

M: I □ _____ □ _____ anything when people call me.

W: There must be a problem with it. Let me □ _____ □ _____ □ _____.

M: Here it is. Can you □ _____ it?

W: Yes, we can. It will □ _____ about □ _____ □ _____.

06 의도 파악

대화를 듣고, 여자의 마지막 말의 의도로 가장 적절한 것을 고르시오.

① 동의　　② 제안　　③ 충고
④ 거절　　⑤ 허가

W: You look □ _____ today. What's going on?

M: I think I got an A on my □ _____ □ _____.

W: Really? □ _____ □ _____ □ _____. Did you think it was easy?

M: Yes, I did. The teacher didn't ask many difficult questions.

W: I □ _____ just about □ _____ □ _____ as you do. I think I □ _____ pretty □ _____, too.

✏ **어휘복습** 잘 안 들리거나 몰라서 체크한 어휘를 써 놓고 복습해 보세요.

□ _____　□ _____　□ _____　□ _____

□ _____　□ _____　□ _____　□ _____

□ _____　□ _____　□ _____　□ _____

07 숫자 정보 파악

대화를 듣고, 핼러윈 파티에 오는 사람들의 수를 고르시오.

① 18   ② 19   ③ 20
④ 21   ⑤ 22

W: Are you □ _____ □ _____ tonight's Halloween party?
M: Yes. It's going to be a lot of □ _____.
W: □ _____ from your □ _____ is □ _____, right?
That's □ _____ people.
M: No. Sarah and Jay can't □ _____ □ _____. They're
□ _____ □ _____.
W: So □ _____ of your friends are going to come?
M: That's right.

08 할 일 파악

대화를 듣고, 여자가 대화 직후에 할 일로 가장 적절한 것을 고르시오.

① 숙제하기
② 전화하기
③ 선생님과 대화하기
④ 새 휴대폰 사기
⑤ 전자제품 매장 방문하기

M: Did you □ _____ a new □ _____ yet?
W: No. I don't know □ _____ □ _____ I should buy.
M: Why don't you □ _____ □ _____ Jeff?
W: Jeff? Why should I □ _____ □ _____ him?
M: His father □ _____ an □ _____ □ _____. He knows all the good smartphones.
W: Thanks for the □ _____. I'll □ _____ him □ _____
□ _____ right now.

09 특정 정보 파악

대화를 듣고, 남자가 가장 좋았다고 생각한 운동으로 가장 적절한 것을 고르시오.

① 농구   ② 배드민턴   ③ 탁구
④ 테니스   ⑤ 야구

W: Did you □ _____ □ _____ at the community center today?
M: Yes, I did. My friends and I □ _____ lots of □ _____ there.
W: What games did you play?
M: We played □ _____, □ _____, □ _____, and □ _____.
W: That sounds fun. Which game did you □ _____ □ _____
□ _____?
M: □ _____ was the □ _____. My team □ _____ the
□ _____.

✎ **어휘복습** 잘 안 들리거나 몰라서 체크한 어휘를 써 놓고 복습해 보세요.

□ _____   □ _____   □ _____   □ _____
□ _____   □ _____   □ _____   □ _____
□ _____   □ _____   □ _____   □ _____

10 화제 추론

다음을 듣고, 무엇에 관한 내용인지 가장 적절한 것을 고르시오.

① 채소 보관법
② 농산물 가격 폭락
③ 특별 할인 안내
④ 연휴 기간 영업 안내
⑤ 신선한 과일 고르는 방법

W: Hello, shoppers. Let me tell you about a □ _____ □ _____ we are having. All □ _____ and □ _____ in the store are now □ _____ □ _____. Please go to the back of the store. Our workers will help you find the □ _____ fruits and vegetables. This sale will □ _____ when the □ _____ □ _____ tonight. Enjoy your □ _____.

11 미언급 파악

대화를 듣고, 남자의 주문에서 언급되지 않은 것을 고르시오.

① 치킨   ② 샐러드   ③ 수프
④ 감자   ⑤ 아이스티

W: Good evening. May I □ _____ your □ _____, please?
M: Yes, I'd like to have the □ _____ □ _____ and a □ _____.
W: Would you like □ _____ □ _____?
M: I'd love to have a □ _____ □ _____, please.
W: Okay, and do you want □ _____ □ _____ □ _____?
M: Yes. I'd like a glass of □ _____ □ _____.
W: Very good. Just a moment, please.

12 전화 목적 파악

대화를 듣고, 여자가 전화한 목적으로 가장 적절한 것을 고르시오.

① 책을 빌리려고
② 집에 초대하려고
③ 책을 돌려달라고 요청하려고
④ 과학 숙제에 대해서 물어보려고
⑤ 과학 시험에 대해서 물어보려고

M: Hi, Julie. How are you?
W: Hi, Steve. I'm good. □ _____ □ _____ □ _____, do you have my □ _____ □ _____?
M: □ _____ □ _____ □ _____ the science book you lent me?
W: Yes, that one. I need it to □ _____ my □ _____.
M: Do you need it □ _____ □ _____?
W: Yes. Can you please □ _____ it to my house?
M: Oh, okay. I'll be at your house □ _____ □ _____ □ _____ □ _____.

✎ **어휘복습** 잘 안 들리거나 몰라서 체크한 어휘를 써 놓고 복습해 보세요.

□ _____   □ _____   □ _____   □ _____
□ _____   □ _____   □ _____   □ _____
□ _____   □ _____   □ _____   □ _____

13 특정 정보 파악

대화를 듣고, 요리에 필요하지 <u>않은</u> 재료를 고르시오.

① 밀가루 ② 버터 ③ 달걀
④ 설탕 ⑤ 초콜릿칩

M: □ _____ are you □ _____, Mom?

W: I'm □ _____ □ _____. Do you want to help?

M: Sure. Do we □ _____ □ _____?

W: Yes, we do. We also need □ _____, □ _____, and □ _____.

M: □ _____ □ _____ chocolate chips?

W: No. I'm not making chocolate chip cookies. I'm making sugar cookies.

14 관계 추론

대화를 듣고, 두 사람의 관계로 가장 적절한 것을 고르시오.

① 학부모 – 교사
② 학부모 – 감독
③ 의사 – 환자
④ 감독 – 선수
⑤ 약사 – 환자

M: Hello. □ _____ □ _____ Coach Young □ _____.

W: Hello, Coach Young. This is Tim's mother. Do you □ _____ □ _____ □ _____ to talk?

M: Sure. What can I do for you?

W: I'm sorry to say this, but Tim □ _____ □ _____ to □ _____ □ _____ today.

M: Is he □ _____? What's the □ _____?

W: No, he's not sick, so please don't worry. I have to □ _____ □ _____ □ _____ see his □ _____.

M: I understand. □ _____ □ _____ □ _____ he'll be at practice □ _____?

W: Yes, he will.

✎ **어휘복습** 잘 안 들리거나 몰라서 체크한 어휘를 써 놓고 복습해 보세요.

□ _____   □ _____   □ _____   □ _____

□ _____   □ _____   □ _____   □ _____

□ _____   □ _____   □ _____   □ _____

15 부탁 파악

대화를 듣고, 여자가 남자에게 요청한 일로 가장 적절한 것을 고르시오.

① 텔레비전 켜기　② 옷 다리기
③ 빨래 널기　④ 빨래 개기
⑤ 세탁기 돌리기

M: Hi, Mom.

W: Hi, Joe. Where are you?

M: I'm □ _____ □ _____. I'm watching TV.

W: Can you □ _____ □ _____ for me, please?

M: Sure. What is it?

W: Can you □ _____ the □ _____ □ _____ □ _____?
I forgot. The □ _____ are already □ _____ it.

M: □ _____ □ _____. I'll do that.

16 이유 파악

대화를 듣고, 남자가 버스 터미널에 가는 이유로 가장 적절한 것을 고르시오.

① 표를 사려고
② 버스를 타려고
③ 친구를 만나려고
④ 아빠를 데리러 가려고
⑤ 잃어버린 물건을 찾으려고

W: Where are you going now, Jeff?

M: I'm going to the □ _____ □ _____.

W: Yeah? Are you □ _____ a □ _____?

M: No, I'm not. My □ _____ □ _____ is □ _____ to
□ _____ me. So I'm going there to □ _____ him
□ _____.

W: □ _____ □ _____ will his bus □ _____?

M: In about thirty minutes. So I need to □ _____.

✎ **어휘복습** 잘 안 들리거나 몰라서 체크한 어휘를 써 놓고 복습해 보세요.

□ _____　□ _____　□ _____　□ _____
□ _____　□ _____　□ _____　□ _____
□ _____　□ _____　□ _____　□ _____

17 어색한 대화 찾기

다음을 듣고, 두 사람의 대화가 <u>어색한</u> 것을 고르시오.

①   ②   ③   ④   ⑤

① M: □ _____ □ _____ met the new teacher?

    W: □ _____, □ _____ □ _____. He's a very humorous
       person.

② M: □ _____ was the □ _____ you saw?

    W: I liked it a lot.

③ M: This was a □ _____ □ _____, wasn't it?

    W: I haven't □ _____ □ _____ yet.

④ M: Do you usually □ _____ □ _____ on weekends?

    W: Yes, I □ _____ □ _____ that

⑤ M: □ _____ □ _____ you □ _____ me last night?

    W: Sorry. I forgot.

18 속담 추론

대화를 듣고, 상황을 가장 잘 표현한 속담을 고르시오.

① Better late than never.
② Look before you leap.
③ Rome wasn't built in a day.
④ After a storm comes a calm.
⑤ All work and no play makes Jack a dull boy.

W: □ _____ is your Chinese class □ _____, Tom?

M: Terrible. I □ _____ speak Chinese □ _____ □ _____.

W: Didn't you just □ _____ □ _____ it □ _____ □ _____?

M: Yes, and I still don't know much.

W: Relax. You're just a □ _____. You need to □ _____ a lot more □ _____ learning it.

M: What do you mean?

W: It □ _____ □ _____ to learn a new language. You need to be □ _____.

✎ **어휘복습** 잘 안 들리거나 몰라서 체크한 어휘를 써 놓고 복습해 보세요.

□ _____   □ _____   □ _____   □ _____

□ _____   □ _____   □ _____   □ _____

□ _____   □ _____   □ _____   □ _____

19 알맞은 응답 찾기

대화를 듣고, 남자의 마지막 말에 이어질 여자의 응답으로 가장 적절한 것을 고르시오.

Woman: _____
① Yes, his class is fun.
② Thanks for your help.
③ I love his math class.
④ No, I don't have any homework.
⑤ No, I haven't seen him all day.

W: Hi, Jay. Are you □ _____ □ _____ someone?

M: Yes. I need to find Mr. Stephens.

W: Do you mean the □ _____ □ _____? Why do you want to see him?

M: I have some □ _____ □ _____ the math □ _____ he assigned. Do you know where he is?

W: _____

20 알맞은 응답 찾기

대화를 듣고, 남자의 마지막 말에 이어질 여자의 응답으로 가장 적절한 것을 고르시오.

Woman: _____
① Have you been to the park?
② I jog around 10 kilometers.
③ I'm trying to get in good shape.
④ I go jogging at 6 in the morning.
⑤ Not at all. You can meet me at 6 in the morning

M: Do you still □ _____ a lot, Amy?

W: Yes. I □ _____ □ _____ every day.

M: □ _____ □ _____ do you jog for?

W: I jog □ _____ □ _____ one hour every day.

M: Wow, that's amazing. □ _____ do you go jogging?

W: I usually □ _____ □ _____ the □ _____.

M: □ _____ □ _____ □ _____ □ _____ I do that with you sometime?

W: _____

✎ **어휘복습** 잘 안 들리거나 몰라서 체크한 어휘를 써 놓고 복습해 보세요.

□ _____ □ _____ □ _____ □ _____
□ _____ □ _____ □ _____ □ _____
□ _____ □ _____ □ _____ □ _____

01 대화를 듣고, 두 사람이 만들 카드를 고르시오.

① 　② 　③

④ 　⑤

02 다음을 듣고, 로스앤젤레스의 날씨로 가장 적절한 것을 고르시오.

①　②　③　④　⑤

03 대화를 듣고, 두 사람이 대화하는 장소로 가장 적절한 곳을 고르시오.

① 음식점　　② 엘리베이터　③ 헬스클럽
④ 슈퍼마켓　⑤ 교실

04 대화를 듣고, 무엇에 관한 내용인지 가장 적절한 것을 고르시오.

① 테니스 경기　② 분리수거　③ 집안 청소
④ 공원 청소　⑤ 체육 대회

05 대화를 듣고, 여자가 전화한 목적으로 가장 적절한 것을 고르시오.

① 친구 주소를 물어보려고
② 조별 과제에 대해 물어보려고
③ 친구 전화번호를 물어보려고
④ 숙제를 함께 하자고 말하려고
⑤ 개학 날짜를 물어보려고

06 대화를 듣고, 여자의 심정 변화로 가장 적절한 것을 고르시오.

① nervous - happy
② concerned - proud
③ proud - relieved
④ angry - sorry
⑤ happy - upset

07 대화를 듣고, 남자가 좋아하는 TV 프로그램이 시작하는 시각을 고르시오.

① 7:00　　② 7:30　　③ 8:00
④ 8:15　　⑤ 8:30

08 대화를 듣고, 두 사람의 관계로 가장 적절한 것을 고르시오.

① 영화배우 - 팬　　② 교사 - 학생
③ 미용사 - 고객　　④ 판매원 - 고객
⑤ 엄마 - 아들

09 대화를 듣고, 남자가 도서관에 가는 방법으로 언급하지 않은 것을 고르시오.

① 길 건너기　　　② 택시 타기
③ 7번 버스 타기　④ 지하철 타기
⑤ 도서관까지 걷기

10 대화를 듣고, 남자가 대화 직후에 할 일로 가장 적절한 것을 고르시오.

① 전화하기　　　② 요리하기
③ 친구 만나기　　④ 티켓 구매하기
⑤ 놀이공원에 가기

11 대화를 듣고, 여자가 운동을 싫어하는 이유로 가장 적절한 것을 고르시오.

① 운동이 지루하기 때문에
② 무릎이 좋지 않기 때문에
③ 운동할 시간이 없기 때문에
④ 운동을 잘하지 못하기 때문에
⑤ 운동을 하면 몸이 아프기 때문에

12 대화를 듣고, 대화의 내용과 일치하지 않는 것을 고르시오.

① Tina는 다른 나라로 이사 간다.
② Tina는 이번 주에 이사 간다.
③ Tina와 남자는 공원에서 자주 연날리기를 했다.
④ Tina의 취미는 연날리기다.
⑤ 송별회는 금요일에 열릴 것이다.

13 대화를 듣고, 남자가 지불해야 할 금액을 고르시오.

① $15   ② $25   ③ $40
④ $50   ⑤ $60

14 대화를 듣고, 남자의 마지막 말의 의도로 가장 적절한 것을 고르시오.

① 후회   ② 동의   ③ 충고
④ 요청   ⑤ 칭찬

15 대화를 듣고, 남자가 대화 직후에 할 일로 가장 적절한 것을 고르시오.

① 독후감 쓰기
② 도서관에 가기
③ 숙제 제출하기
④ 책 빌리기
⑤ 선생님과 이야기하기

16 다음 표를 보면서 대화를 듣고, 공지 내용과 일치하지 않는 것을 고르시오.

Basketball Practice
① Date: October 20
② Place: Gym on Pine Street
③ Starting Time: 10 A.M.
④ Finishing Time: 1 P.M.
⑤ Snacks to Bring: Oranges & Sports Drink

17 다음을 듣고, 두 사람의 대화가 어색한 것을 고르시오.

①   ②   ③   ④   ⑤

18 대화를 듣고, 남자가 원하는 몸무게로 가장 적절한 것을 고르시오.

① 65kg   ② 66kg   ③ 67kg
④ 72kg   ⑤ 75kg

19 대화를 듣고, 남자의 마지막 말에 이어질 여자의 응답으로 가장 적절한 것을 고르시오.

Woman: _____

① No, I've never been there before.
② Every store there is having a sale.
③ Yes, it opens at 10 in the morning.
④ It's about an hour away from here.
⑤ There are more than 200 stores in it.

20 다음을 듣고, Sarah가 경찰관에게 할 말로 가장 적절한 것을 고르시오.

Sarah: _____

① Could you repeat that one more time, please?
② Yes, I'm going there to meet my friend.
③ Thanks for your help. I appreciate it.
④ Okay, so I'll take a left at the light.
⑤ How far away is it by bus?

01 그림 정보 파악

대화를 듣고, 두 사람이 만들 카드를 고르시오.

① ② ③ ④ ⑤

M: We need to □_____ a □_____ for Mom □_____ it's her □_____.

W: Okay. □_____ □_____ □_____ card should we make?

M: Let's make a □_____ card that has some □_____ on it.

W: How about a □_____ □_____ □_____ flowers? Won't that be □_____?

M: Good thinking. We can □_____ that and put "Happy Birthday, Mom" on the card.

W: All right. Let's start making it.

02 날씨 파악

다음을 듣고, 로스앤젤레스의 날씨로 가장 적절한 것을 고르시오.

① ② ③ ④ ⑤

M: It's □_____ □_____ the weather forecast for California. There will be □_____, □_____ weather in San Francisco today. It's going to be □_____ in Los Angeles. There will be □_____ in San Diego. In Sacramento, it will be hot and sunny. □_____ □_____ the state is going to get really nice weather today.

✎ 어휘복습 잘 안 들리거나 몰라서 체크한 어휘를 써 놓고 복습해 보세요.

□_____   □_____   □_____   □_____
□_____   □_____   □_____   □_____
□_____   □_____   □_____   □_____

03 장소 추론

대화를 듣고, 두 사람이 대화하는 장소로 가장 적절한 곳을 고르시오.

① 음식점　　　② 엘리베이터
③ 헬스클럽　　④ 슈퍼마켓
⑤ 교실

W: Pardon me. Can you □ _____ the □ _____ □ _____, please?

M: □ _____ □ _____. Where are you going?

W: I'm going up to the □ _____ □ _____.

M: I believe that's the □ _____ □ _____. Let me □ _____ the □ _____.

W: Thanks a lot. Where are you going?

M: I'm going to □ _____ □ _____ at a restaurant.

W: Is it on the □ _____ floor?

M: That's right. It's an Italian restaurant. You should □ _____ there □ _____.

W: Thanks. I will.

04 화제 추론

대화를 듣고, 무엇에 관한 내용인지 가장 적절한 것을 고르시오.

① 테니스 경기　　② 분리수거
③ 집안 청소　　　④ 공원 청소
⑤ 체육 대회

M: How about □ _____ □ _____ the □ _____ this weekend?

W: Sure. We can □ _____ □ _____ there.

M: Why don't we □ _____ □ _____ □ _____ there?

W: What do you mean?

M: The park is really □ _____ these days. So I want to help □ _____ it □ _____.

W: □ _____ □ _____ of you! Do you do that □ _____?

M: No. It's my □ _____ □ _____. You can go with me if you want.

W: Sure, □ _____ □ _____ □ _____.

✎ **어휘복습** 잘 안 들리거나 몰라서 체크한 어휘를 써 놓고 복습해 보세요.

□ _____　　□ _____　　□ _____　　□ _____
□ _____　　□ _____　　□ _____　　□ _____
□ _____　　□ _____　　□ _____　　□ _____

05 전화 목적 파악

대화를 듣고, 여자가 전화한 목적으로 가장 적절한 것을 고르시오.

① 친구 주소를 물어보려고
② 조별 과제에 대해 물어보려고
③ 친구 전화번호를 물어보려고
④ 숙제를 함께 하자고 말하려고
⑤ 개학 날짜를 물어보려고

M: Hi, Tina.

W: Hey, Chris. Do you know Eric?

M: □ _____ □ _____ I know him. He's one of my friends.

W: That's great. Do you know his □ _____ □ _____?

M: Yes, □ _____ do you need it □ _____?

W: I have to □ _____ him about our □ _____ □ _____.

M: Oh, okay. It's four zero nine, five four zero five.

W: Thanks a lot. See you at school tomorrow.

06 심정 추론

대화를 듣고, 여자의 심정 변화로 가장 적절한 것을 고르시오.

① nervous - happy
② concerned - proud
③ proud - relieved
④ angry - sorry
⑤ happy - upset

M: Kate, what's the matter?

W: I can't find my new □ _____ □ _____.

M: That's too bad. □ _____ do you think you □ _____ it?

W: I'm sure it's □ _____ here in the □ _____. I have been looking but can't find it.

M: Let me help you. Where did you look?

W: I □ _____ □ _____ my desk.

M: Oh, is it a □ _____ ring?

W: That's right.

M: Here it is. It's under this desk □ _____ □ _____.

W: Seriously? Thank you very much.

✎ **어휘복습** 잘 안 들리거나 몰라서 체크한 어휘를 써 놓고 복습해 보세요.

□ _____ □ _____ □ _____ □ _____

□ _____ □ _____ □ _____ □ _____

□ _____ □ _____ □ _____ □ _____

07 숫자 정보 파악

대화를 듣고, 남자가 좋아하는 TV 프로그램이 시작하는 시각을 고르시오.

① 7:00   ② 7:30   ③ 8:00
④ 8:15   ⑤ 8:30

W: Would you like to ☐ _____ ☐ _____ ☐ _____ ☐ _____ tonight?

M: ☐ _____ ☐ _____ do you want to do that?

W: ☐ _____ ☐ _____ at seven?

M: I'd rather not. My ☐ _____ TV ☐ _____ is coming on at that time.

W: ☐ _____ ☐ _____ we go out after the show ends?

M: Okay. It will ☐ _____ at ☐ _____ since it's an ☐ _____ ☐ _____.

W: All right. We can leave around ☐ _____ ☐ _____ then.

08 관계 추론

대화를 듣고, 두 사람의 관계로 가장 적절한 것을 고르시오.

① 영화배우 – 팬   ② 교사 – 학생
③ 미용사 – 고객   ④ 판매원 – 고객
⑤ 엄마 – 아들

W: Good afternoon, Tom.

M: Good afternoon. How are you?

W: I'm great. ☐ _____ should I ☐ _____ your ☐ _____ today?

M: ☐ _____ ☐ _____ ☐ _____ ☐ _____ this picture.

W: I know him. He's a famous ☐ _____ ☐ _____.

M: Yeah. I love his ☐ _____. Can you cut my hair ☐ _____ ☐ _____ ☐ _____?

W: Sure. That won't be a problem. ☐ _____ ☐ _____ ☐ _____ in the chair.

M: Thanks.

✎ **어휘복습** 잘 안 들리거나 몰라서 체크한 어휘를 써 놓고 복습해 보세요.

☐ _____   ☐ _____   ☐ _____   ☐ _____

☐ _____   ☐ _____   ☐ _____   ☐ _____

☐ _____   ☐ _____   ☐ _____   ☐ _____

09 미언급 파악

대화를 듣고, 남자가 도서관에 가는 방법으로 언급하지 <u>않은</u> 것을 고르시오.

① 길 건너기
② 택시 타기
③ 7번 버스 타기
④ 지하철 타기
⑤ 도서관까지 걷기

W: Pardon me. I'm trying to □ _____ □ _____ the public □ _____ . Where is it?

M: You need to □ _____ the □ _____ first. You have to □ _____ a □ _____ at the bus □ _____ over there.

W: All right. □ _____ bus goes to the library?

M: You should take the number seven bus. □ _____ □ _____ the bus at Western Station. Then, take the □ _____ .

W: Which subway □ _____ should I get off at?

M: Go three stops to Main Street Station. After that, just □ _____ to the library.

W: Thanks a lot for your help.

M: It's my pleasure.

10 할 일 파악

대화를 듣고, 남자가 대화 직후에 할 일로 가장 적절한 것을 고르시오.

① 전화하기
② 요리하기
③ 친구 만나기
④ 티켓 구매하기
⑤ 놀이공원에 가기

W: Hello. □ _____ □ _____ □ _____ □ _____ Jim?

M: □ _____ □ _____ he.

W: Hi, Jim. It's Wendy. Do you want to go to the □ _____ □ _____ with me today?

M: Yeah, that sounds like fun. □ _____ □ _____ shall we □ _____ ?

W: □ _____ □ _____ going there □ _____ ?

M: I'm eating lunch. Can we go there □ _____ □ _____ □ _____ ?

W: Okay. That's fine.

M: Should we □ _____ Eric, too? I can □ _____ him now and □ _____ him.

W: □ _____ . I know he □ _____ amusement parks.

✎ **어휘복습** 잘 안 들리거나 몰라서 체크한 어휘를 써 놓고 복습해 보세요.

□ _____   □ _____   □ _____   □ _____
□ _____   □ _____   □ _____   □ _____
□ _____   □ _____   □ _____   □ _____

11 이유 파악

대화를 듣고, 여자가 운동을 싫어하는 이유로 가장 적절한 것을 고르시오.

① 운동이 지루하기 때문에
② 무릎이 좋지 않기 때문에
③ 운동할 시간이 없기 때문에
④ 운동을 잘하지 못하기 때문에
⑤ 운동을 하면 몸이 아프기 때문에

M: Jane, I'm going to □ _____ □ _____ with Chris. Do you want to □ _____ □ _____ with us?

W: No, thanks.

M: Would you □ _____ to go □ _____ instead?

W: No. I don't really like □ _____ □ _____ □ _____.

M: Why not? Do you think it's □ _____?

W: My □ _____ always □ _____ after I finish exercising.

M: I see. Let's do something else together next time then.

12 내용 일치 파악

대화를 듣고, 대화의 내용과 일치하지 <u>않는</u> 것을 고르시오.

① Tina는 다른 나라로 이사 간다.
② Tina는 이번 주에 이사 간다.
③ Tina와 남자는 공원에서 자주 연날리기를 했다.
④ Tina의 취미는 연날리기다.
⑤ 송별회는 금요일에 열릴 것이다.

W: Did you hear that Tina is □ _____ □ _____ another country?

M: Yes, I know. She's moving to Tokyo □ _____ □ _____.

W: I'm really going to □ _____ her. She's one of my best friends.

M: Yeah, I'm going to miss her, too. We often flew kites together at the park.

W: I know. □ _____ □ _____ is one of her □ _____.

M: We should have a □ _____ □ _____ for her.

W: You're right. Let's talk to some of our friends about that.

M: Okay. We should □ _____ □ _____ it □ _____ □ _____.

✎ **어휘복습** 잘 안 들리거나 몰라서 체크한 어휘를 써 놓고 복습해 보세요.

□ _____   □ _____   □ _____   □ _____
□ _____   □ _____   □ _____   □ _____
□ _____   □ _____   □ _____   □ _____

13 숫자 정보 파악

대화를 듣고, 남자가 지불해야 할 금액을 고르시오.

① $15 ② $25 ③ $40
④ $50 ⑤ $60

W: Can I help you, sir?
M: Yes, please. Tomorrow is my mother's □ _____. Can you □ _____ something for a woman □ _____ □ _____ □ _____?
W: She might like this □ _____.
M: It □ _____ □ _____. □ _____ □ _____ does it □ _____?
W: It's □ _____ dollars for one □ _____.
M: Oh, that's too expensive for me. How about these □ _____?
W: The gloves cost □ _____ dollars.
M: Okay, and what about the □ _____ □ _____?
W: It costs □ _____ dollars. Which would you like?
M: □ _____ □ _____ the gloves. I think she'll like them.
W: I think so as well. Let me □ _____ them for you.

14 의도 파악

대화를 듣고, 남자의 마지막 말의 의도로 가장 적절한 것을 고르시오.

① 후회 ② 동의 ③ 충고
④ 요청 ⑤ 칭찬

W: Look outside. It's □ _____ □ _____.
M: That's too bad. I'm □ _____ □ _____ the □ _____ to meet Steve.
W: □ _____ are you going to get there?
M: I'm planning to □ _____ the □ _____.
W: You need to take the □ _____ □ _____.
M: Why? The bus □ _____ is □ _____ to here □ _____ the subway □ _____ is.
W: That's true. But □ _____ always moves □ _____ in the rain.
M: You're right about that. I'll take the subway then.

✎ **어휘복습** 잘 안 들리거나 몰라서 체크한 어휘를 써 놓고 복습해 보세요.

□ _____ □ _____ □ _____ □ _____
□ _____ □ _____ □ _____ □ _____
□ _____ □ _____ □ _____ □ _____

15 할 일 파악

대화를 듣고, 남자가 대화 직후에 할 일로 가장 적절한 것을 고르시오.

① 독후감 쓰기
② 도서관에 가기
③ 숙제 제출하기
④ 책 빌리기
⑤ 선생님과 이야기하기

M: What are you doing now, Jean?

W: I'm □ _____ this □ _____ for English class.

M: Oh, right. I □ _____ □ _____ reading it □ _____.

W: Why not? We have to read the book □ _____ □ _____.

M: □ _____ □ _____ □ _____ about that?

W: Yes, I am. Mr. Bennett told us that in class today.

M: □ _____ □ _____ go to the library. I need a □ _____ of it.

W: Don't worry. You can □ _____ mine. I'm □ _____ □ _____ reading it.

M: Great. Thanks a lot.

16 도표 · 실용문 파악

다음 표를 보면서 대화를 듣고, 공지 내용과 일치하지 <u>않는</u> 것을 고르시오.

Basketball Practice
① Date: October 20
② Place: Gym on Pine Street
③ Starting Time: 10 A.M.
④ Finishing Time: 1 P.M.
⑤ Snacks to Bring: Oranges & Sports Drink

W: Did you read the □ _____ about □ _____ □ _____, son?

M: Yes, I did. The first practice is on □ _____ □ _____. Can you □ _____ me to the □ _____ at □ _____ A.M. then?

W: Yes, I can do that. You're going to the gym on Pine Street, right?

M: That's right. Practice is going to □ _____ at □ _____. Can you □ _____ me □ _____ then?

W: Sure. Do you need any □ _____ for practice?

M: Yes. I should □ _____ some □ _____ and a sports drink. Thanks.

✎ **어휘복습** 잘 안 들리거나 몰라서 체크한 어휘를 써 놓고 복습해 보세요.

□ _____   □ _____   □ _____   □ _____

□ _____   □ _____   □ _____   □ _____

□ _____   □ _____   □ _____   □ _____

17 어색한 대화 찾기

다음을 듣고, 두 사람의 대화가 <u>어색한</u> 것을 고르시오.

①   ②   ③   ④   ⑤

① W: I □ _____ □ _____ we had a test today.

    M: Me □ _____.

② W: □ _____ do you □ _____ to your uncle's house?

    M: I always □ _____ the □ _____.

③ W: Can you show me □ _____ □ _____ □ _____ this □ _____?

    M: No, I can't answer the □ _____ now.

④ W: □ _____ □ _____ does your father come home?

    M: □ _____ □ _____ in the evening.

⑤ W: What did you get for your □ _____?

    M: Some □ _____ and money.

18 숫자 정보 파악

대화를 듣고, 남자가 원하는 몸무게로 가장 적절한 것을 고르시오.

① 65kg   ② 66kg   ③ 67kg
④ 72kg   ⑤ 75kg

W: Aren't you □ _____? Why aren't you eating much □ _____ □ _____?

M: I'm trying to □ _____ □ _____.

W: You're not □ _____. Why do you want to get slimmer?

M: My baseball coach thinks I □ _____ □ _____ □ _____. He wants me to lose weight to run faster.

W: □ _____ □ _____ weight do you want to lose?

M: I was seventy-five kilograms, but now I'm down to □ _____ kilograms. I'd like to lose □ _____ □ _____ kilograms though.

W: □ _____ □ _____ every day. That will help you lose weight.

✎ **어휘복습** 잘 안 들리거나 몰라서 체크한 어휘를 써 놓고 복습해 보세요.

□ _____   □ _____   □ _____   □ _____

□ _____   □ _____   □ _____   □ _____

□ _____   □ _____   □ _____   □ _____

19 알맞은 응답 찾기

대화를 듣고, 남자의 마지막 말에 이어질 여자의 응답으로 가장 적절한 것을 고르시오.

Woman: _____

① No, I've never been there before.
② Every store there is having a sale.
③ Yes, it opens at 10 in the morning.
④ It's about an hour away from here.
⑤ There are more than 200 stores in it.

W: Do you □ _____ any special □ _____ for the □ _____?
M: No, I don't. What about you?
W: My parents and I are going to the new □ _____ □ _____.
M: Ah, □ _____ □ _____ about that place. What are you going to buy there?
W: I need some clothes, and my parents want a new □ _____.
M: Is it □ _____ □ _____? □ _____ □ _____ will it take to get there?
W: _____

20 상황에 적절한 말 찾기

다음을 듣고, Sarah가 경찰관에게 할 말로 가장 적절한 것을 고르시오.

Sarah: _____

① Could you repeat that one more time, please?
② Yes, I'm going there to meet my friend.
③ Thanks for your help. I appreciate it.
④ Okay, so I'll take a left at the light.
⑤ How far away is it by bus?

W: Sarah is □ _____ to a □ _____ to meet her friend. She □ _____ the □ _____ and □ _____ □ _____ after seven stops. She □ _____ for a while, but she □ _____ she is □ _____. She sees a □ _____, so she □ _____ him □ _____ □ _____. The policeman tells her to □ _____ □ _____ □ _____ at the light and to walk □ _____ for five minutes. Sarah doesn't know the □ _____ well, so she is not sure about the directions. In this case, what would Sarah most likely say to the policeman?

Sarah: _____

✏️ **어휘복습** 잘 안 들리거나 몰라서 체크한 어휘를 써 놓고 복습해 보세요.

□ _____ □ _____ □ _____ □ _____
□ _____ □ _____ □ _____ □ _____
□ _____ □ _____ □ _____ □ _____

◀◀≫ MP3 실전 07

점수 / 20

01 다음을 듣고, 설명에 가장 알맞은 그림을 고르시오.

①   ②   ③

④ ⑤

02 다음을 듣고, 새해 첫날의 날씨로 가장 적절한 것을 고르시오.

① ② ③   ④ ⑤

03 대화를 듣고, 두 사람의 관계로 가장 적절한 것을 고르시오.

① 상점 주인 – 고객　② 시민 – 경찰관
③ 택시 기사 – 승객　④ 학생 – 교사
⑤ 승무원 – 승객

04 대화를 듣고, 두 사람이 대화하는 장소로 가장 적절한 곳을 고르시오.

① 공원　② 수영장　③ 해변
④ 산　⑤ 휴게소

05 대화를 듣고, 남자의 마지막 말의 의도로 가장 적절한 것을 고르시오.

① 동의　② 칭찬　③ 꾸중
④ 조언　⑤ 후회

06 다음을 듣고, 여자의 현재 심정으로 가장 적절한 것을 고르시오.

① bored　② satisfied
③ disappointed　④ worried
⑤ upset

07 대화를 듣고, 여자가 전화한 목적으로 가장 적절한 것을 고르시오.

① 소포를 배달하려고
② 배송 일정을 정하려고
③ 소포에 대해 문의하려고
④ 부재중 전화에 회신하려고
⑤ 집으로 오는 길을 알려주려고

08 대화를 듣고, 남자가 역사 시험을 망친 이유로 가장 적절한 것을 고르시오.

① 시험에 늦어서
② 시험 기간에 아파서
③ 정답을 잘못 표기해서
④ 시험 날짜를 착각해서
⑤ 잘못된 범위를 공부해서

09 대화를 듣고, 각자 지불해야 할 금액을 고르시오.

① $20　② $25　③ $30
④ $35　⑤ $40

10 대화를 듣고, 남자가 조깅하러 갈 장소로 가장 적절한 곳을 고르시오.

① 강가　② 호숫가　③ 산책로
④ 운동장　⑤ 숲

11 대화를 듣고, 두 사람이 대화 직후에 할 일로 가장 적절한 것을 고르시오.

① 소풍 가기   ② 음식 사기
③ 쿠키 가져오기   ④ 샌드위치 만들기
⑤ Tina에게 전화하기

12 대화를 듣고, Eric Lee에 대해 언급되지 <u>않은</u> 것을 고르시오.

① 신문 기사에 실렸다.
② 20대 사업가이다.
③ 일본어를 전공했다.
④ 세 개의 회사를 가지고 있다.
⑤ 세 개의 언어를 말할 수 있다.

13 대화를 듣고, 무엇에 관한 내용인지 가장 적절한 것을 고르시오.

① 복사기 사용 방법
② 종이 재활용 방법
③ 프린터 고치는 방법
④ 컴퓨터 파일 정리 방법
⑤ 삭제 파일 복원 방법

14 대화를 듣고, 남자가 한 일로 가장 적절한 것을 고르시오.

① 병문안 가기   ② 외식하기
③ 자전거 타기   ④ 바닷가에 가기
⑤ 이모의 생일파티에 가기

15 다음을 듣고, 도표의 내용과 일치하지 <u>않는</u> 것을 고르시오.

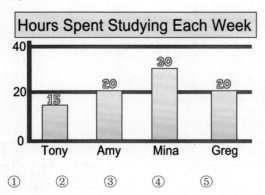

Hours Spent Studying Each Week

①   ②   ③   ④   ⑤

16 다음을 듣고, 두 사람의 대화가 <u>어색한</u> 것을 고르시오.

①   ②   ③   ④   ⑤

17 대화를 듣고, 반에서 가장 키가 큰 사람이 누구인지 고르시오.

① Joe   ② Paul   ③ Mary
④ Tim   ⑤ Sue

18 대화를 듣고, 여자가 오늘 할 일이 <u>아닌</u> 것을 고르시오.

① 고양이 밥 주기
② 미용실 가기
③ 병원 가기
④ 우체국 가기
⑤ 도서관 가기

19 대화를 듣고, 여자의 마지막 말에 이어질 남자의 응답으로 가장 적절한 것을 고르시오.

Man: _____

① It's a ten-page report.
② I'm looking forward to dinner.
③ It's still only 6:00 in the evening.
④ I thought I could finish it soon.
⑤ Yes, the teacher needs it tomorrow.

20 다음을 듣고, Julie가 여동생에게 할 말로 가장 적절한 것을 고르시오.

Julie: _____

① Don't cross the street yet.
② Please stop bothering me so much.
③ We're going to have fun at the park.
④ I think the park is closed for the day.
⑤ How about playing a game at the park?

01 그림 정보 파악

다음을 듣고, 설명에 가장 알맞은 그림을 고르시오.

① ② ③ ④ ⑤

W: I'd like everyone to □ _____ a □ _____ right now. First, draw a large □ _____. □ _____ the triangle, draw a □ _____. Be sure that the circle □ _____ all three □ _____ of the triangle. After that, I want you to draw □ _____ □ _____ inside the circle. One square should be □ _____ □ _____ □ _____ the other.

02 날씨 파악

다음을 듣고, 새해 첫날의 날씨로 가장 적절한 것을 고르시오.

① ② ③ ④ ⑤

W: Happy new year, everybody. It's □ _____ □ _____ □ _____ today, and it's time for the updated weather forecast. It's afternoon now, and the □ _____ is starting to □ _____ □ _____. It's still sunny, but it will be □ _____ and □ _____ this □ _____. On New Year's Day, we're going to get □ _____ □ _____ □ _____. □ _____ □ _____ □ _____, it will clear up and be □ _____ □ _____. But there will be cold temperatures all week long.

✎ **어휘복습** 잘 안 들리거나 몰라서 체크한 어휘를 써 놓고 복습해 보세요.

□ _____   □ _____   □ _____   □ _____
□ _____   □ _____   □ _____   □ _____
□ _____   □ _____   □ _____   □ _____

대화를 듣고, 두 사람의 관계로 가장 적절한
것을 고르시오.

① 상점 주인 – 고객
② 시민 – 경찰관
③ 택시 기사 – 승객
④ 학생 – 교사
⑤ 승무원 – 승객

W: Can I help you with something?

M: Yes. I □ _____ this □ _____ at the □ _____.

W: Where in the park did you find it?

M: It was □ _____ a □ _____.

W: Did you see anyone □ _____ it there?

M: No, I didn't. I saw it when I □ _____ □ _____ the park.
   Half an hour later, it was still there.

W: Okay. Thanks for bringing it here. We'll try to □ _____ it
   □ _____ its □ _____.

M: All right. Have a great day, □ _____.

대화를 듣고, 두 사람이 대화하는 장소로 가
장 적절한 곳을 고르시오.

① 공원   ② 수영장   ③ 해변
④ 산   ⑤ 휴게소

M: This place is really □ _____.

W: Yeah, everyone wants to □ _____ the beautiful □ _____.

M: It is a great day. And the □ _____ is so □ _____, too.

W: Do you want to □ _____ □ _____?

M: Not now. I want to □ _____ here □ _____ the □ _____.

W: Okay. I'm going to □ _____ □ _____ the water.

M: Sounds good. I'll □ _____ you in a few minutes.

✎ **어휘복습** 잘 안 들리거나 몰라서 체크한 어휘를 써 놓고 복습해 보세요.

□ _____   □ _____   □ _____   □ _____

□ _____   □ _____   □ _____   □ _____

□ _____   □ _____   □ _____   □ _____

05 의도 파악

대화를 듣고, 남자의 마지막 말의 의도로 가장 적절한 것을 고르시오.

① 동의   ② 칭찬   ③ 꾸중
④ 조언   ⑤ 후회

M: I □ _____ □ _____ it. I got the □ _____ □ _____ in □ _____ class.

W: Don't be □ _____. These things happen □ _____.

M: But I always get bad grades in math. I don't think I'll ever □ _____ □ _____.

W: You shouldn't □ _____ □ _____ □ _____. Think □ _____.

M: Why do you say that?

W: You can □ _____ □ _____ your □ _____. Keep studying hard, and you will □ _____ get better.

M: Yeah, I □ _____ you're right. I'll do what you suggest.

06 심정 추론

다음을 듣고, 여자의 현재 심정으로 가장 적절한 것을 고르시오.

① bored   ② satisfied
③ disappointed   ④ worried
⑤ upset

W: In spring, I □ _____ some □ _____ outside my house. I □ _____ very good □ _____ □ _____ them. I was so □ _____ to see them come up above the ground. But they grew so □ _____. It was really □ _____ to me. However, I was □ _____, so I waited. I kept taking good care of the flowers. Suddenly, they began to □ _____ □ _____. Now, they are taller than me, and the flowers are huge. I'm so □ _____ □ _____ how well they have grown.

✎ **어휘복습** 잘 안 들리거나 몰라서 체크한 어휘를 써 놓고 복습해 보세요.

□ _____   □ _____   □ _____   □ _____
□ _____   □ _____   □ _____   □ _____
□ _____   □ _____   □ _____   □ _____

대화를 듣고, 여자가 전화한 목적으로 가장 적절한 것을 고르시오.

① 소포를 배달하려고
② 배송 일정을 정하려고
③ 소포에 대해 문의하려고
④ 부재중 전화에 회신하려고
⑤ 집으로 오는 길을 알려주려고

M: Hello.
W: Hello. □ _____ am I □ _____ □ _____?
M: I'm sorry. Who are you?
W: You called me an hour ago, but I □ _____ the □ _____.
M: Oh, do you live at forty-nine Watson Street?
W: That's correct.
M: I'm a □ _____. I have a □ _____ for you.
W: That's great. I □ _____ □ _____ now, so you can come here □ _____.
M: Thank you.

대화를 듣고, 남자가 역사 시험을 망친 이유로 가장 적절한 것을 고르시오.

① 시험에 늦어서
② 시험 기간에 아파서
③ 정답을 잘못 표기해서
④ 시험 날짜를 착각해서
⑤ 잘못된 범위를 공부해서

W: What's wrong, Dave?
M: I think I □ _____ my history □ _____ today.
W: I'm sorry. Was the test □ _____?
M: Yes, it was really hard □ _____ □ _____.
W: I can help you the □ _____ □ _____. History is my □ _____ □ _____.
M: I like history, too. But I studied the □ _____ □ _____.
W: What do you □ _____ □ _____ □ _____?
M: The test was on chapter two, but I studied chapter three.
W: Oh, you need to be □ _____ the next time.

✏️ **어휘복습** 잘 안 들리거나 몰라서 체크한 어휘를 써 놓고 복습해 보세요.

□ _____   □ _____   □ _____   □ _____
□ _____   □ _____   □ _____   □ _____
□ _____   □ _____   □ _____   □ _____

09 숫자 정보 파악

대화를 듣고, 각자 지불해야 할 금액을 고르시오.

① $20   ② $25   ③ $30
④ $35   ⑤ $40

M: Tomorrow is Jane's □ _____. We should buy her
a □ _____.

W: That's a good idea. Why don't we □ _____ her a □ _____?
I saw a good one at the □ _____ □ _____.

M: □ _____ □ _____ did it □ _____?

W: The tag said it was □ _____ dollars. But it's □ _____
□ _____, so it's only □ _____ dollars now.

M: That's a lot of money. But we could buy it for her □ _____.

W: Yeah. Let's each □ _____ □ _____.

10 특정 정보 파악

대화를 듣고, 남자가 조깅하러 갈 장소로 가장 적절한 곳을 고르시오.

① 강가   ② 호숫가   ③ 산책로
④ 운동장   ⑤ 숲

W: Good morning. Is this your □ _____ □ _____ at
Hamilton Park?

M: Yes, it is. I'm here to □ _____ □ _____.

W: There are many great places for jogging.

M: Really? □ _____ do most people do that?

W: A lot of them □ _____ on the □ _____ in the park.

M: How about you?

W: I prefer to run □ _____ □ _____ □ _____. It's very nice
there.

M: Thanks. I think I'll do that.

✎ **어휘복습** 잘 안 들리거나 몰라서 체크한 어휘를 써 놓고 복습해 보세요.

□ _____   □ _____   □ _____   □ _____

□ _____   □ _____   □ _____   □ _____

□ _____   □ _____   □ _____   □ _____

11 할 일 파악

대화를 듣고, 두 사람이 대화 직후에 할 일로 가장 적절한 것을 고르시오.

① 소풍 가기
② 음식 사기
③ 쿠키 가져오기
④ 샌드위치 만들기
⑤ Tina에게 전화하기

W: □ _____ □ _____ the weather forecast, it will be □ _____ today.

M: That's good news. We can □ _____ □ _____ a □ _____ like we planned.

W: That's right. Did we □ _____ □ _____ we need?

M: I think so. We have sandwiches, potato chips, and sodas.

W: I have some paper plates and napkins. And Tina is going to bring some cookies for dessert.

M: It □ _____ □ _____ we have everything already then. □ _____ □ _____.

12 미언급 파악

대화를 듣고, Eric Lee에 대해 언급되지 않은 것을 고르시오.

① 신문 기사에 실렸다.
② 20대 사업가이다.
③ 일본어를 전공했다.
④ 세 개의 회사를 가지고 있다.
⑤ 세 개의 언어를 말할 수 있다.

W: Did you read this □ _____ in the □ _____? It's about Eric Lee. He's a famous □ _____ from Korea.

M: No, I didn't read it. What □ _____ does it have about him?

W: He is only twenty-five, but he □ _____ three companies.

M: That's □ _____.

W: He can □ _____ three □ _____, too. He knows Korean, English, and Japanese.

M: Wow. I guess he □ _____ □ _____ at school.

✎ **어휘복습** 잘 안 들리거나 몰라서 체크한 어휘를 써 놓고 복습해 보세요.

□ _____   □ _____   □ _____   □ _____
□ _____   □ _____   □ _____   □ _____
□ _____   □ _____   □ _____   □ _____

13 화제 추론

대화를 듣고, 무엇에 관한 내용인지 가장 적절한 것을 고르시오.

① 복사기 사용 방법
② 종이 재활용 방법
③ 프린터 고치는 방법
④ 컴퓨터 파일 정리 방법
⑤ 삭제 파일 복원 방법

W: Hi, Kevin. It's Wendy.

M: Hi, Wendy. How are you doing?

W: I'm okay, but I have a □ _____ □ _____ my □ _____.

M: What's going on?

W: It has a □ _____ □ _____. I don't know □ _____ □ _____ □ _____ it.

M: It's really easy. □ _____, you need to □ _____ □ _____ the □ _____ of the printer. □ _____, you should be able to see some paper in it.

W: What should I □ _____ □ _____ the paper?

M: □ _____ it □ _____. Then, the printer should □ _____ well □ _____.

W: Thanks a lot for your help.

14 한 일 파악

대화를 듣고, 남자가 한 일로 가장 적절한 것을 고르시오.

① 병문안 가기
② 외식하기
③ 자전거 타기
④ 바닷가에 가기
⑤ 이모의 생일파티에 가기

M: Janet, did you □ _____ a □ _____ □ _____ at your aunt's birthday party?

W: I did. We went to a restaurant and □ _____ her □ _____ there.

M: Wow. □ _____ □ _____ she was really happy.

W: Yeah. How about you? Did you go to the □ _____?

M: We planned to go there, but we had to □ _____ our plans. My brother □ _____ a bike □ _____.

W: Oh, no. Is he □ _____ □ _____?

M: My parents took him to the □ _____, and I visited him in the hospital. He's □ _____ □ _____ now.

✎ **어휘복습** 잘 안 들리거나 몰라서 체크한 어휘를 써 놓고 복습해 보세요.

□ _____   □ _____   □ _____   □ _____

□ _____   □ _____   □ _____   □ _____

□ _____   □ _____   □ _____   □ _____

15 도표 · 실용문 파악

다음을 듣고, 도표의 내용과 일치하지 <u>않는</u> 것을 고르시오.

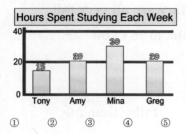

Hours Spent Studying Each Week

① ② ③ ④ ⑤

① Tony studies □ _____ □ _____ Greg.
② Amy studies □ _____ □ _____ amount □ _____ Greg.
③ Mina studies □ _____ □ _____.
④ Greg studies □ _____ □ _____ Tony.
⑤ Amy studies more than Tony and Mina.

16 어색한 대화 찾기

다음을 듣고, 두 사람의 대화가 <u>어색한</u> 것을 고르시오.

① ② ③ ④ ⑤

① M: May I □ _____ in this □ _____?
   W: Sorry, but that seat is □ _____ □ _____.
② M: □ _____ □ _____ pencils are in your pencil case?
   W: □ _____, but I have a few pens.
③ M: I'm so □ _____ right now.
   W: I'm glad I just ate dinner.
④ M: Can I □ _____ your □ _____?
   W: Sure. It's six oh four, three oh four three.
⑤ M: Have you ever □ _____ the □ _____ to get there?
   W: Sure. It □ _____ about fifteen minutes.

✎ **어휘복습** 잘 안 들리거나 몰라서 체크한 어휘를 써 놓고 복습해 보세요.

□ _____   □ _____   □ _____   □ _____
□ _____   □ _____   □ _____   □ _____
□ _____   □ _____   □ _____   □ _____

17 특정 정보 파악

대화를 듣고, 반에서 가장 키가 큰 사람이 누구인지 고르시오.

① Joe   ② Paul   ③ Mary
④ Tim   ⑤ Sue

W: Tim, which student is the □ _____ □ _____ our □ _____?

M: Let me think, Sue. Joe, Paul, and Mary are all very tall.

W: But you're □ _____ □ _____ Paul, aren't you?

M: Yes. That's right.

W: Are you taller than Joe?

M: No, I'm not. He's □ _____ □ _____ taller than me.

W: And Joe is also taller than Mary, isn't he?

M: Yes, that's □ _____.

18 특정 정보 파악

대화를 듣고, 여자가 오늘 할 일이 <u>아닌</u> 것을 고르시오.

① 고양이 밥 주기
② 미용실 가기
③ 병원 가기
④ 우체국 가기
⑤ 도서관 가기

M: Do you □ _____ a lot of □ _____ □ _____ □ _____ today?

W: Yes, I do. I need to □ _____ my □ _____ in the morning and then go to the □ _____ □ _____.

M: Don't you have a □ _____ □ _____, too?

W: That's right. I'm going there after I □ _____ □ _____ with Sue. Then, I'll go to the □ _____ □ _____ to mail a package.

M: Do you have time to □ _____ □ _____ the □ _____?

W: □ _____ □ _____. I can go there tomorrow.

✎ **어휘복습** 잘 안 들리거나 몰라서 체크한 어휘를 써 놓고 복습해 보세요.

□ _____   □ _____   □ _____   □ _____

□ _____   □ _____   □ _____   □ _____

□ _____   □ _____   □ _____   □ _____

19 알맞은 응답 찾기

대화를 듣고, 여자의 마지막 말에 이어질 남자의 응답으로 가장 적절한 것을 고르시오.

Man: _____

① It's a ten-page report.
② I'm looking forward to dinner.
③ It's still only 6:00 in the evening.
④ I thought I could finish it soon.
⑤ Yes, the teacher needs it
   tomorrow.

W: It's almost □ _____. Are you ready to eat?

M: I'll eat □ _____. I'm a bit busy now.

W: What are you doing?

M: I'm writing a □ _____ □ _____ for English class.

W: □ _____ do you have to give it to the teacher?

M: It's □ _____ □ _____.

W: Tomorrow? Are you □ _____ □ _____?

M: No, I □ _____ □ _____ a while ago.

W: Why didn't you start working on it □ _____?

M: _____

20 상황에 적절한 말 찾기

다음을 듣고, Julie가 여동생에게 할 말로 가장 적절한 것을 고르시오.

Julie: _____

① Don't cross the street yet.
② Please stop bothering me so
   much.
③ We're going to have fun at the
   park.
④ I think the park is closed for the
   day.
⑤ How about playing a game at
   the park?

M: Julie and her little sister are □ _____ □ _____ the □ _____. They □ _____ from their house to the park. Before they get to the park, they have to □ _____ the □ _____. It's a big street, and there are many cars on it. Julie's little sister is □ _____ to go to the park, so she starts running □ _____ it. However, the □ _____ in the □ _____ has not □ _____ □ _____ yet. In this situation, what would Julie most likely say to her little sister?

Julie: _____

✎ **어휘복습** 잘 안 들리거나 몰라서 체크한 어휘를 써 놓고 복습해 보세요.

□ _____   □ _____   □ _____   □ _____

□ _____   □ _____   □ _____   □ _____

□ _____   □ _____   □ _____   □ _____

01 대화를 듣고, 남자가 구매할 재킷을 고르시오.

①   ②   ③

④   ⑤

02 다음을 듣고, 내일 낮의 날씨로 가장 적절한 것을 고르시오.

①   ②   ③   ④   ⑤

03 대화를 듣고, 남자의 장래 희망으로 가장 적절한 것을 고르시오.

① 작곡가 ② 가수 ③ 댄서
④ 농구선수 ⑤ 피아니스트

04 대화를 듣고, 두 사람이 출발하기로 한 시각을 고르시오.

① 5:00 ② 5:30 ③ 6:00
④ 6:30 ⑤ 7:00

05 대화를 듣고, 여자의 마지막 말에 드러난 심정으로 가장 적절한 것을 고르시오.

① excited ② regretful ③ proud
④ bored ⑤ worried

06 다음을 듣고, 무엇에 관한 내용인지 가장 적절한 것을 고르시오.

① 인터넷 쇼핑몰
② 신상품 소개
③ 가방 할인 판매
④ 분실물 공지
⑤ 회원 가입 혜택

07 대화를 듣고, 여자가 배우려고 하는 것으로 가장 적절한 것을 고르시오.

① 스쿠버 다이빙 ② 수상 스키
③ 스노클링 ④ 수영
⑤ 낚시

08 대화를 듣고, 남자가 할 일로 가장 적절한 것을 고르시오.

① 쇼핑 가기 ② 수업 가기
③ 영화 보기 ④ 점심 먹기
⑤ 여름 캠프 가기

09 대화를 듣고, 남자가 지불해야 할 금액을 고르시오.

① $2 ② $3 ③ $4
④ $5 ⑤ $6

10 다음을 듣고, 여자가 언급하지 <u>않은</u> 것을 고르시오.

① 신발 종류 ② 신발 사이즈
③ 신발 가격 ④ 신발 색상
⑤ 신발이 필요한 이유

11 대화를 듣고, 두 사람이 대화하는 장소로 가장 적절한
곳을 고르시오.

① 교실 　　② 도서관 　　③ 영화관

④ 경기장 　　⑤ 스포츠 용품점

12 대화를 듣고, 여자가 할 일로 가장 적절한 것을 고르시
오.

① 산책하기 　　　② 침대에 눕기

③ 병원에 가기 　　④ 공원에서 놀기

⑤ 친구 만나기

13 대화를 듣고, 두 사람의 관계로 가장 적절한 것을 고르
시오.

① 택시 기사 – 승객

② 매표소 직원 – 고객

③ 버스 기사 – 승객

④ 감독 – 운동선수

⑤ 여행 가이드 – 여행객

14 대화를 듣고, 여자의 개에 관한 정보로 일치하지 <u>않는</u>
것을 고르시오.

> **Please help me find my dog.**
> ① I lost her at the park.
> ② She has black and white fur.
> ③ Her name is Sally.
> ④ She loves people.
> ⑤ If you find her, please call 631-
> 　 9054.

15 대화를 듣고, 남자가 전화한 목적으로 가장 적절한 것을
고르시오.

① 저녁식사에 초대하려고

② 저녁 약속을 취소하려고

③ 숙제에 대해서 물어보려고

④ 영화 보러 가자고 말하려고

⑤ 숙제가 있다는 것을 상기시키려고

16 대화를 듣고, 여자의 마지막 말의 의도로 가장 적절한
것을 고르시오.

① 조언 　　② 사과 　　③ 감사

④ 거절 　　⑤ 후회

17 다음을 듣고, 두 사람의 대화가 <u>어색한</u> 것을 고르시오.

① 　　② 　　③ 　　④ 　　⑤

18 대화를 듣고, 여자가 늦은 이유로 가장 적절한 것을 고
르시오.

① 늦게 일어나서

② 약속 시간을 잊어서

③ 버스를 놓쳐서

④ 교통 체증이 심해서

⑤ 지갑을 가지러 집에 돌아가야 해서

19 대화를 듣고, 여자의 마지막 말에 이어질 남자의 응답으
로 가장 적절한 것을 고르시오.

Man: _____

① What's my flight number?

② Great. Then I'll take the subway.

③ So I should cancel my reservation.

④ No, I've never been there before.

⑤ Okay. Thanks for the information.

20 다음을 듣고, Tina가 배달원에게 할 말로 가장 적절한
것을 고르시오.

Tina: _____

① The pizza looks delicious.

② How much do I owe you?

③ I can't wait to see the movie.

④ How about having some pizza?

⑤ You delivered the wrong food.

01 그림 정보 파악

대화를 듣고, 남자가 구매할 재킷을 고르시오.

① ② ③

④ ⑤

W: Good evening. Can I help you find something?

M: Yes, please. I'd like to □ _____ a □ _____.

W: How about this jacket □ _____ a □ _____?
   It's a □ _____ □ _____ these days.

M: No, thanks. That's □ _____ □ _____ □ _____.

W: Would you like this jacket with □ _____ □ _____ on it?

M: No. I want a jacket □ _____ any pockets. Oh, this jacket
   with □ _____ □ _____ the □ _____ looks great.

W: □ _____ □ _____. It's perfect for cold weather.

M: I love it. I'll take it.

02 날씨 파악

다음을 듣고, 내일 낮의 날씨로 가장 적절한 것을 고르시오.

① ② ③

④ ⑤

W: If you have plans to go outside tomorrow, you'd better do
   that in the morning. The □ _____ will be □ _____ and
   □ _____. However, around one in the □ _____, it's going
   to □ _____ □ _____. The rain will □ _____ in the
   □ _____, but it's going to be quite □ _____ the rest of
   the □ _____. Expect □ _____ □ _____ the next
   □ _____. In addition, the weather will □ _____
   □ _____ throughout the day.

✎ 어휘복습 잘 안 들리거나 몰라서 체크한 어휘를 써 놓고 복습해 보세요.

□ _____   □ _____   □ _____   □ _____

□ _____   □ _____   □ _____   □ _____

□ _____   □ _____   □ _____   □ _____

03 장래 희망 파악

대화를 듣고, 남자의 장래 희망으로 가장 적절한 것을 고르시오.

① 작곡가　② 가수　③ 댄서
④ 농구선수　⑤ 피아니스트

W: Steve, I haven't seen you in a while.

M: I've been busy. I've been □_____ □_____ □_____.

W: What have you been doing?

M: □_____ the □_____. I'd love to □_____ a □_____ in the future.

W: Are you □_____? I thought you wanted to be a □_____ □_____.

M: That would be fun, but I don't think I'm □_____ □_____.

W: Be sure to practice □_____, too. That might be □_____.

M: Thanks for the □_____.

04 숫자 정보 파악

대화를 듣고, 두 사람이 출발하기로 한 시각을 고르시오.

① 5:00　② 5:30　③ 6:00
④ 6:30　⑤ 7:00

M: Do we have □_____ for □_____ tomorrow?

W: Yes, and we're going to □_____ an □_____ after that.

M: □_____ □_____ does everything □_____?

W: We'll □_____ □_____ at □_____ P.M. And the □_____ □_____ at □_____ □_____ P.M.

M: □_____ □_____ will it □_____ to get to the restaurant?

W: It will take around □_____ minutes.

M: We'd better □_____ an □_____ □_____ just in case.

W: All right. I can be ready to go □_____ □_____.

M: Great. I can't wait.

✎ **어휘복습** 잘 안 들리거나 몰라서 체크한 어휘를 써 놓고 복습해 보세요.

□ _____　□ _____　□ _____　□ _____

□ _____　□ _____　□ _____　□ _____

□ _____　□ _____　□ _____　□ _____

05 심정 추론

대화를 듣고, 여자의 마지막 말에 드러난 심정으로 가장 적절한 것을 고르시오.

① excited   ② regretful
③ proud   ④ bored
⑤ worried

W: Did you enjoy the □ _____ □ _____?
M: Yes, it was great. Why didn't you go with us?
W: I wanted to □ _____ □ _____ to □ _____ some □ _____.
M: I see. Well, □ _____ □ _____ happened while we were there?
W: I don't know. What?
M: They were □ _____ a □ _____ at the amusement park.
W: A movie? □ _____?
M: Yeah, and we got to be in a scene.
W: No way. I □ _____ I □ _____ □ _____ there with you.

06 화제 추론

다음을 듣고, 무엇에 관한 내용인지 가장 적절한 것을 고르시오.

① 인터넷 쇼핑몰
② 신상품 소개
③ 가방 할인 판매
④ 분실물 공지
⑤ 회원 가입 혜택

M: Hello, everyone. Thank you for shopping at Sullivan's Department Store. A customer just □ _____ □ _____ a □ _____. It's a black leather □ _____ with a □ _____ and some □ _____ in it. If you lost your bag, please □ _____ □ _____ a □ _____ right now. The salesperson will □ _____ □ _____ come down here and □ _____ your bag □ _____.

✏ **어휘복습** 잘 안 들리거나 몰라서 체크한 어휘를 써 놓고 복습해 보세요.

□ _____   □ _____   □ _____   □ _____
□ _____   □ _____   □ _____   □ _____
□ _____   □ _____   □ _____   □ _____

대화를 듣고, 여자가 배우려고 하는 것으로
가장 적절한 것을 고르시오.

① 스쿠버 다이빙
② 수상 스키
③ 스노클링
④ 수영
⑤ 낚시

W: What do you like doing □ _____ your □ _____ □ _____, Fred?

M: I love □ _____ □ _____ in the water. □ _____ and □ _____ are lots of fun.

W: I enjoy swimming, too. I go to the □ _____ a lot, but I have □ _____ □ _____ snorkeling before.

M: Do you want me to □ _____ you?

W: Can you do that? That would be great.

M: Sure. We can □ _____ □ _____ the □ _____ on Saturday.

대화를 듣고, 남자가 할 일로 가장 적절한
것을 고르시오.

① 쇼핑 가기
② 수업 가기
③ 영화 보기
④ 점심 먹기
⑤ 여름 캠프 가기

W: Joe, it's nice to see you. What have you been doing □ _____?

M: I was at □ _____ □ _____ all last week. I had a great time there.

W: That's good.

M: What are you doing here?

W: I'm going to □ _____ some □ _____. Would you like to □ _____ □ _____ some □ _____ with me?

M: I'd □ _____ □ _____, □ _____ I can't. My friend Jina is coming soon. We're going to □ _____ a □ _____.

W: That sounds like fun. Let's □ _____ □ _____ together later.

✎ **어휘복습** 잘 안 들리거나 몰라서 체크한 어휘를 써 놓고 복습해 보세요.

□ _____   □ _____   □ _____   □ _____
□ _____   □ _____   □ _____   □ _____
□ _____   □ _____   □ _____   □ _____

09 숫자 정보 파악

대화를 듣고, 남자가 지불해야 할 금액을 고르시오.

① $2　　② $3　　③ $4
④ $5　　⑤ $6

W: Good evening, sir.

M: Hello. I'd like to □ _____ this DVD I □ _____.

W: No problem. □ _____ did you □ _____ the □ _____?

M: It was nice. My entire family liked it.

W: That's good to hear. Hmm... It looks like you're □ _____ this DVD □ _____. You needed to return it three days ago

M: Three days ago? Really?

W: Yes. So you need to □ _____ a □ _____ □ _____.

M: □ _____ □ _____ does that □ _____?

W: It's □ _____ dollars per day. And you have to pay a fine for □ _____ □ _____.

M: Okay. Here's the money.

10 미언급 파악

다음을 듣고, 여자가 언급하지 <u>않은</u> 것을 고르시오.

① 신발 종류
② 신발 사이즈
③ 신발 가격
④ 신발 색상
⑤ 신발이 필요한 이유

W: I'd like to buy □ _____ new □ _____ □ _____ □ _____. They need to be □ _____ shoes □ _____ I □ _____ a lot. I wear a □ _____ □ _____ shoe, and I don't want to spend □ _____ □ _____ □ _____ dollars on them. They □ _____ □ _____ □ _____ at the store □ _____ since I have to □ _____ them tomorrow morning when I □ _____ □ _____.

✎ **어휘복습** 잘 안 들리거나 몰라서 체크한 어휘를 써 놓고 복습해 보세요.

□ _____　　□ _____　　□ _____　　□ _____

□ _____　　□ _____　　□ _____　　□ _____

□ _____　　□ _____　　□ _____　　□ _____

11 장소 추론

대화를 듣고, 두 사람이 대화하는 장소로 가장 적절한 곳을 고르시오.

① 교실　　　　② 도서관
③ 영화관　　　④ 경기장
⑤ 스포츠 용품점

M: I'm sorry I'm late. How is the game going?

W: □_____ a □_____. You've □_____ an exciting □_____.

M: Oh, yeah? That's □_____ □_____. What's the □_____?

W: It's four to three.

M: Who's winning?

W: Our school's team is. Jeff Baker □_____ a □_____ a few minutes ago.

M: Yeah? □_____ □_____ □_____ I missed it.

W: You should have seen it. It went really far.

12 할 일 파악

대화를 듣고, 여자가 할 일로 가장 적절한 것을 고르시오.

① 산책하기　　② 침대에 눕기
③ 병원에 가기　④ 공원에서 놀기
⑤ 친구 만나기

M: How do you feel today, Cindy?

W: I'm doing □_____ □_____ □_____ I was. I think I'm □_____ □_____ my □_____.

M: That's good to hear.

W: I had to □_____ □_____ □_____ for almost a week.

M: I bet that was hard.

W: It was. I □_____ □_____ □_____ out and playing at the park.

M: Don't do that. You're still not □_____. You can □_____ □_____ □_____ if you really want to be outside. Just □_____ □_____ you put on a □_____ □_____.

W: Okay. I think I'll do that.

✎ **어휘복습** 잘 안 들리거나 몰라서 체크한 어휘를 써 놓고 복습해 보세요.

□ _____　　□ _____　　□ _____　　□ _____

□ _____　　□ _____　　□ _____　　□ _____

□ _____　　□ _____　　□ _____　　□ _____

13 관계 추론

대화를 듣고, 두 사람의 관계로 가장 적절한 것을 고르시오.

① 택시 기사 – 승객
② 매표소 직원 – 고객
③ 버스 기사 – 승객
④ 감독 – 운동선수
⑤ 여행 가이드 – 여행객

M: □ _____ are you □ _____?

W: I'd like to □ _____ the □ _____.

M: No problem.

W: □ _____ □ _____ will it take to □ _____ □ _____?

M: It's about □ _____ □ _____ □ _____ from here if traffic is okay.

W: That's great. I'm glad I □ _____ a □ _____. There was no bus stop on Pine Street.

M: □ _____ you □ _____ □ _____ in this city □ _____?

W: No, I haven't. I just □ _____ □ _____ to see the big game.

M: I hope you □ _____ a □ _____ □ _____.

14 내용 일치 파악

대화를 듣고, 여자의 개에 관한 정보로 일치하지 <u>않는</u> 것을 고르시오.

Please help me find my dog.
① I lost her at the park.
② She has black and white fur.
③ Her name is Sally.
④ She loves people.
⑤ If you find her, please call 631-9054.

M: Are you all right?

W: No, I'm not. I □ _____ my □ _____ □ _____ the □ _____ two days ago.

M: That's too bad. Can I □ _____ you □ _____ □ _____ her?

W: Yes, please. She has □ _____ □ _____.

M: □ _____ her □ _____?

W: Sally. She will come to you if you call her. She □ _____ □ _____.

M: If I find her, □ _____ can I □ _____ you?

W: □ _____ me □ _____ six three one, nine oh five four, please.

✎ **어휘복습** 잘 안 들리거나 몰라서 체크한 어휘를 써 놓고 복습해 보세요.

□ _____ □ _____ □ _____ □ _____

□ _____ □ _____ □ _____ □ _____

□ _____ □ _____ □ _____ □ _____

15 전화 목적 파악

대화를 듣고, 남자가 전화한 목적으로 가장 적절한 것을 고르시오.

① 저녁식사에 초대하려고
② 저녁 약속을 취소하려고
③ 숙제에 대해서 물어보려고
④ 영화 보러 가자고 말하려고
⑤ 숙제가 있다는 것을 상기시키려고

W: Hello.

M: Hi, □ _____ □ _____ Joe. Is Sam there?

W: I'm sorry, Joe, but Sam isn't here now. □ _____ □ _____ with his father.

M: When are they going to □ _____ □ _____?

W: They'll be back very □ _____ □ _____.

M: Oh... I guess he □ _____ □ _____ to my house □ _____ □ _____ this evening.

W: No, he can't. Why don't you □ _____ □ _____ in the morning?

16 의도 파악

대화를 듣고, 여자의 마지막 말의 의도로 가장 적절한 것을 고르시오.

① 조언   ② 사과   ③ 감사
④ 거절   ⑤ 후회

W: Are you □ _____ □ _____, Sean?

M: No, I'm not. I □ _____ □ _____ a □ _____ □ _____ my friend John today.

W: Why did you have a fight with him?

M: I told him that we shouldn't be friends □ _____.

W: Why did you tell him that?

M: He wouldn't □ _____ his □ _____ □ _____ to me. I □ _____ □ _____ about that now □ _____.

W: You should □ _____ him □ _____ □ _____ and □ _____ □ _____ him right now.

✎ **어휘복습** 잘 안 들리거나 몰라서 체크한 어휘를 써 놓고 복습해 보세요.

□ _____   □ _____   □ _____   □ _____

□ _____   □ _____   □ _____   □ _____

□ _____   □ _____   □ _____   □ _____

17 어색한 대화 찾기

다음을 듣고, 두 사람의 대화가 <u>어색한</u> 것을 고르시오.

① ② ③ ④ ⑤

① W: My brother was □ _____ □ _____ □ _____.
   M: I saw you □ _____ a new □ _____.
② W: □ _____ would you □ _____ to □ _____?
   M: □ _____ □ _____ we play computer games?
③ W: You need to □ _____ a □ _____ □ _____ the □ _____.
   M: Thanks for the □ _____.
④ W: The coach told me □ _____ □ _____ the □ _____ □ _____.
   M: □ _____. I'm so proud of you.
⑤ W: What's our □ _____ for today?
   M: We □ _____ □ _____ read the rest of the chapter.

18 이유 파악

대화를 듣고, 여자가 늦은 이유로 가장 적절한 것을 고르시오.

① 늦게 일어나서
② 약속 시간을 잊어서
③ 버스를 놓쳐서
④ 교통 체증이 심해서
⑤ 지갑을 가지러 집에 돌아가야 해서

M: You're finally here. □ _____ are you □ _____?
W: Sorry. The bus got □ _____ □ _____ bad □ _____.
M: You were late □ _____ □ _____ □ _____, too.
W: I know. I □ _____ my □ _____ that time and had to □ _____ □ _____ □ _____ to get it.
M: Well, let's go to the □ _____. I'm □ _____.
W: Okay. I'll □ _____ □ _____ the pizza since I was late.

✎ **어휘복습** 잘 안 들리거나 몰라서 체크한 어휘를 써 놓고 복습해 보세요.

□ _____ □ _____ □ _____ □ _____
□ _____ □ _____ □ _____ □ _____
□ _____ □ _____ □ _____ □ _____

대화를 듣고, 여자의 마지막 말에 이어질 남자의 응답으로 가장 적절한 것을 고르시오.

Man: _____
① What's my flight number?
② Great. Then I'll take the subway.
③ So I should cancel my reservation.
④ No, I've never been there before.
⑤ Okay. Thanks for the information.

W: Hello. Daydream Travel. This is Linda speaking.
M: Hi. This is Mr. Jacobs. I □ _____ a □ _____ to New York with you.
W: Yes, Mr. Jacobs. I remember. How can I help you?
M: I reserved a □ _____ at the Westside Hotel. Do you know it?
W: Yes, I do.
M: I don't know □ _____ □ _____ □ _____ □ _____. Should I □ _____ a □ _____ or a □ _____ to the hotel?
W: A taxi would be □ _____. The bus □ _____ □ _____ there.
M: _____

다음을 듣고, Tina가 배달원에게 할 말로 가장 적절한 것을 고르시오.

Tina: _____
① The pizza looks delicious.
② How much do I owe you?
③ I can't wait to see the movie.
④ How about having some pizza?
⑤ You delivered the wrong food.

W: Tina and two of her friends are at her house. They are going to □ _____ a □ _____, but they want to □ _____ some □ _____ first. Tina □ _____ a pizza □ _____ and orders a pepperoni pizza and spaghetti. When the □ _____ arrives, Tina looks at the order. She sees a pepperoni pizza and breadsticks. In this situation, what would Tina most likely say to the deliveryman?
Tina: _____

✏️ **어휘복습** 잘 안 들리거나 몰라서 체크한 어휘를 써 놓고 복습해 보세요.

□ _____ □ _____ □ _____ □ _____
□ _____ □ _____ □ _____ □ _____
□ _____ □ _____ □ _____ □ _____

■)) MP3 실전 09

점수 / 20

01 대화를 듣고, 남자가 구매할 케이크를 고르시오.

①   ②   ③

④   ⑤

02 대화를 듣고, 남자의 마지막 말에 드러난 심정으로 가장 적절한 것을 고르시오.

① angry   ② disappointed
③ tired   ④ relieved
⑤ amused

03 대화를 듣고, 두 사람이 만날 시각을 고르시오.

① 8:00   ② 9:00   ③ 10:00
④ 11:00   ⑤ 12:00

04 대화를 듣고, 오늘의 날씨로 가장 적절한 것을 고르시오.

①   ②   ③   ④   ⑤

05 다음을 듣고, 방송이 이루어지고 있는 장소로 가장 적절한 곳을 고르시오.

① 공항   ② 박물관   ③ 도서관
④ 백화점   ⑤ 놀이공원

06 대화를 듣고, 여자가 남자에게 빌릴 금액을 고르시오.

① $5   ② $6   ③ $7
④ $8   ⑤ $9

07 대화를 듣고, 남자가 할 일로 가장 적절한 것을 고르시오.

① 축제에 가기   ② 친구들 만나기
③ 숙제 끝내기   ④ 시험 공부하기
⑤ 포스터 만들기

08 대화를 듣고, 두 사람의 관계로 가장 적절한 것을 고르시오.

① 엄마 – 아들
② 식당 종업원 – 고객
③ 승무원 – 승객
④ 버스 기사 – 승객
⑤ 호텔 직원 – 투숙객

09 대화를 듣고, 여자가 남자에게 요청한 일로 가장 적절한 것을 고르시오.

① 책 정리하기
② 상자 구매하기
③ 짐 싸는 일 돕기
④ 내일 도와주러 오기
⑤ 이삿짐회사에 연락하기

10 대화를 듣고, 대화의 내용과 일치하지 않는 것을 고르시오.

① Mary는 오늘 병원에 갔다.
② Mary는 고열이 났다.
③ 두 사람은 병문안을 갈 것이다.
④ 병원은 경찰서 맞은편에 있다.
⑤ 두 사람은 꽃을 살 것이다.

11 대화를 듣고, 남자가 이메일을 쓰는 이유로 가장 적절한 것을 고르시오.

① 일자리에 지원하려고
② 웨이터를 칭찬하려고
③ 식당을 예약하려고
④ 식당 예약을 취소하려고
⑤ 서비스에 대해 불평하려고

12 대화를 듣고, 남자가 받은 선물로 가장 적절한 것을 고르시오.

13 다음을 듣고, 여자가 기분이 안 좋은 이유로 가장 적절한 것을 고르시오.

① 친구와 다퉈서
② 호텔 시설이 나빠서
③ 호텔 예약을 실패해서
④ 블로그에 오류가 생겨서
⑤ 블로그에 안 좋은 댓글이 달려서

14 다음을 듣고, 무엇에 관한 내용인지 가장 적절한 것을 고르시오.

① hockey
② ping-pong
③ volleyball
④ basketball
⑤ baseball

15 대화를 듣고, 상황을 가장 잘 표현한 속담을 고르시오.

① 끼리끼리 모인다.
② 뿌린 대로 거둔다.
③ 펜은 칼보다 강하다.
④ 빛나는 것이 모두 금은 아니다.
⑤ 겉을 보고 속을 판단하지 마라.

16 대화를 듣고, 두 사람이 가져가지 않을 것을 고르시오.

① 배낭
② 물병
③ 수건
④ 티셔츠
⑤ 우산

17 다음을 듣고, 도표의 내용과 일치하지 않는 것을 고르시오.

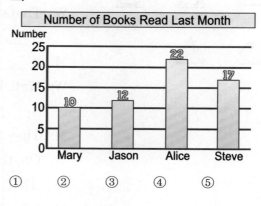

① ② ③ ④ ⑤

18 다음을 듣고, 두 사람의 대화가 어색한 것을 고르시오.

① ② ③ ④ ⑤

19 대화를 듣고, 남자의 마지막 말에 이어질 여자의 응답으로 가장 적절한 것을 고르시오.

Woman: _____

① Yes, it's a good picture.
② No, that's not my email.
③ Can you send it to my email?
④ Do you know my email address?
⑤ Let me tell you my home address.

20 다음을 듣고, Chris가 Dave에게 할 말로 가장 적절한 것을 고르시오.

Chris: _____

① I can't believe I won the game.
② Let's play a few more minutes.
③ Why didn't you help me up?
④ I'm really sorry about that.
⑤ That was a great shot.

다시 듣고, 빈칸에 알맞은 단어를 써 보세요.

◀◀◉》 MP3 실전 09-1

01 그림 정보 파악

대화를 듣고, 남자가 구매할 케이크를 고르시오.

① ② ③

④ ⑤

W: Hello. Are you □ _____ □ _____ something?

M: Yes, today is my friend's □ _____. So I want to buy him a birthday □ _____.

W: That's great. How do you like this one with a □ _____ □ _____ on it?

M: □ _____, □ _____ I don't think he would want that.

W: Well, here's a nice □ _____ cake. And this one has □ _____ on top of it.

M: They look nice, but they're not big enough.

W: Oh, then □ _____ □ _____ this one? It has □ _____ □ _____ on it.

M: It looks nice. □ _____ □ _____ is it?

W: It's thirty-five dollars.

M: Okay, I'll take it.

02 심정 추론

대화를 듣고, 남자의 마지막 말에 드러난 심정으로 가장 적절한 것을 고르시오.

① angry   ② disappointed
③ tired   ④ relieved
⑤ amused

W: I haven't seen you in a while, Jeff.

M: I was □ _____ □ _____ an □ _____ for school.

W: □ _____ □ _____ were you doing that for?

M: It was for Ms. Parker. She's my □ _____ teacher.

W: She was my teacher last year. She always gave □ _____ □ _____ □ _____. What did you have to do?

M: I had to write a story, read a book, and write a □ _____ □ _____. I was really □ _____ □ _____ that.

W: I understand. She gave you a lot of work. Did you finish?

M: Yes, so now I □ _____ so □ _____ □ _____. I'm □ _____ I'm done.

✎ **어휘복습** 잘 안 들리거나 몰라서 체크한 어휘를 써 놓고 복습해 보세요.

□ _____   □ _____   □ _____   □ _____
□ _____   □ _____   □ _____   □ _____
□ _____   □ _____   □ _____   □ _____

03 숫자 정보 파악

대화를 듣고, 두 사람이 만날 시각을 고르시오.

① 8:00   ② 9:00   ③ 10:00
④ 11:00   ⑤ 12:00

M: Do you want to □ _____ □ _____ with me tomorrow?

W: Okay. Where do you want to go?

M: I'd like to go □ _____ the □ _____.

W: The lake? Isn't it □ _____ □ _____?

M: It's about □ _____ kilometers □ _____ □ _____, but it's really nice.

W: Okay. □ _____ □ _____ should we meet?

M: How about at □ _____ in the □ _____? Is that all right?

W: I'd rather leave □ _____ □ _____ □ _____. I need to be home □ _____ □ _____.

M: Okay. That's fine with me.

04 날씨 파악

대화를 듣고, 오늘의 날씨로 가장 적절한 것을 고르시오.

①   ②   ③
④   ⑤

M: What's the □ _____ □ _____ for tomorrow?

W: It's going to □ _____ all day long.

M: Are you serious? I'm getting □ _____ □ _____ all this rain.

W: So am I, but we're in the □ _____ □ _____ the □ _____ □ _____ now.

M: Is it supposed to rain □ _____?

W: No, it's going to stay □ _____, but it won't rain.

M: When are we going to see the sun again?

W: I heard it will be □ _____ on the □ _____. So we can enjoy some nice weather then.

✎ **어휘복습** 잘 안 들리거나 몰라서 체크한 어휘를 써 놓고 복습해 보세요.

□ _____   □ _____   □ _____   □ _____
□ _____   □ _____   □ _____   □ _____
□ _____   □ _____   □ _____   □ _____

05 장소 추론

다음을 듣고, 방송이 이루어지고 있는 장소로 가장 적절한 곳을 고르시오.

① 공항　② 박물관　③ 도서관
④ 백화점　⑤ 놀이공원

W: □ _____, everyone. We are going to open in five minutes. You can □ _____ □ _____ by the □ _____. Tickets cost □ _____ dollars □ _____ □ _____ and □ _____ dollars for □ _____. Please do not □ _____ any □ _____ or □ _____ inside. You may not □ _____ □ _____ of the □ _____, and do not □ _____ them either. Some of them are very old and they can □ _____ □ _____. You can buy □ _____ and □ _____ of them at the □ _____ □ _____. We hope you enjoy the exhibits.

06 숫자 정보 파악

대화를 듣고, 여자가 남자에게 빌릴 금액을 고르시오.

① $5　② $6　③ $7
④ $8　⑤ $9

M: □ _____ do you need to □ _____ here?

W: I've got to get a □ _____ for my history class. The notebooks here cost □ _____ dollars □ _____.

M: □ _____ □ _____ any □ _____? I think they each □ _____ a dollar here.

W: Yes, I should buy □ _____ □ _____ □ _____. Oh, no.

M: What's wrong?

W: I don't have any money with me. Can I □ _____ some □ _____?

M: Sure. So, you need to buy a notebook and two pens?

W: That's right. Thanks a lot. I'll □ _____ you □ _____ tomorrow.

✎ **어휘복습** 잘 안 들리거나 몰라서 체크한 어휘를 써 놓고 복습해 보세요.

□ _____　　□ _____　　□ _____　　□ _____

□ _____　　□ _____　　□ _____　　□ _____

□ _____　　□ _____　　□ _____　　□ _____

07 할 일 파악

대화를 듣고, 남자가 할 일로 가장 적절한
것을 고르시오.

① 축제에 가기
② 친구들 만나기
③ 숙제 끝내기
④ 시험 공부하기
⑤ 포스터 만들기

W: Why are you □ _____ □ _____? You don't have class today.

M: Actually, I need to go to □ _____.

W: Why? It's Sunday. Do you have to □ _____ □ _____ a □ _____?

M: No. The school □ _____ is this week.

W: Oh, are you going to □ _____ □ _____ □ _____ the festival?

M: No, I'm not. But I'm going to help □ _____ for it.

W: That sounds interesting. How will you do that?

M: I'm going to □ _____ some □ _____ for it. Then, I'll □ _____ them □ _____ around the school.

08 관계 추론

대화를 듣고, 두 사람의 관계로 가장 적절한
것을 고르시오.

① 엄마 – 아들
② 식당 종업원 – 고객
③ 승무원 – 승객
④ 버스 기사 – 승객
⑤ 호텔 직원 – 투숙객

M: Hi. You look □ _____. Can I help you?

W: Yes, please. I'm trying to □ _____ my □ _____.

M: What's your room □ _____?

W: It's room four two three.

M: □ _____ □ _____ past the elevators. Then, □ _____ □ _____ and walk to the □ _____ □ _____ the □ _____.

W: That's easy. Thanks. Oh, I have one more question.

M: Sure. What is it?

W: Where is the □ _____ □ _____?

M: It's on the tenth floor.

✎ **어휘복습** 잘 안 들리거나 몰라서 체크한 어휘를 써 놓고 복습해 보세요.

□ _____   □ _____   □ _____   □ _____

□ _____   □ _____   □ _____   □ _____

□ _____   □ _____   □ _____   □ _____

09 부탁 파악

대화를 듣고, 여자가 남자에게 요청한 일로
가장 적절한 것을 고르시오.

① 책 정리하기
② 상자 구매하기
③ 짐 싸는 일 돕기
④ 내일 도와주러 오기
⑤ 이삿짐회사에 연락하기

W: Tim, can you give me that □ _____ □ _____ □ _____?
M: Sure. □ _____ do you need it □ _____?
W: I'm □ _____ tomorrow. So I have to □ _____ all of my □ _____ today.
M: Tomorrow? Do you have enough time to □ _____ □ _____? You must be really □ _____.
W: I am. Do you mind □ _____ me □ _____ now?
M: Not at all. What do you want me to do?

10 내용 일치 파악

대화를 듣고, 대화의 내용과 일치하지 <u>않는</u>
것을 고르시오.

① Mary는 오늘 병원에 갔다.
② Mary는 고열이 났다.
③ 두 사람은 병문안을 갈 것이다.
④ 병원은 경찰서 맞은편에 있다.
⑤ 두 사람은 꽃을 살 것이다.

W: Mary's sister just called me. Mary had to □ _____ □ _____ the □ _____ last night.
M: Seriously? What was □ _____ with her?
W: She had a □ _____ □ _____. She's still not well.
M: We should □ _____ her there now.
W: Good idea. She's at the hospital □ _____ □ _____ the □ _____ □ _____.
M: Okay. What should we get for her?
W: How about a □ _____ and some □ _____?
M: All right. Let's do it.

✎ **어휘복습** 잘 안 들리거나 몰라서 체크한 어휘를 써 놓고 복습해 보세요.

□ _____ □ _____ □ _____ □ _____
□ _____ □ _____ □ _____ □ _____
□ _____ □ _____ □ _____ □ _____

11 이유 파악

대화를 듣고, 남자가 이메일을 쓰는 이유로 가장 적절한 것을 고르시오.

① 일자리에 지원하려고
② 웨이터를 칭찬하려고
③ 식당을 예약하려고
④ 식당 예약을 취소하려고
⑤ 서비스에 대해 불평하려고

W: What are you doing □ _____ □ _____ □ _____?
M: I'm □ _____ an □ _____ to a restaurant manager. I had a □ _____ □ _____ there.
W: What happened?
M: The □ _____ was very □ _____. My □ _____ was so □ _____ □ _____ me.
W: Did you not like the □ _____ either?
M: No, the food was □ _____ □ _____, but I couldn't □ _____ my □ _____ because of the waiter.

12 특정 정보 파악

대화를 듣고, 남자가 받은 선물로 가장 적절한 것을 고르시오.

① ② ③
④ ⑤

M: Guess what. My parents □ _____ me a □ _____ today.
W: Cool. What did you get?
M: I got a □ _____. It's a □ _____ □ _____.
W: Is it a large animal?
M: No, it's actually very □ _____. It has □ _____ □ _____.
W: □ _____ do you □ _____ your pet?
M: I have a □ _____ for it. There's a big □ _____ in the cage for it to run on.
W: I want to see it soon. It must be really □ _____.

✎ **어휘복습** 잘 안 들리거나 몰라서 체크한 어휘를 써 놓고 복습해 보세요.

□ _____   □ _____   □ _____   □ _____
□ _____   □ _____   □ _____   □ _____
□ _____   □ _____   □ _____   □ _____

13 이유 파악

다음을 듣고, 여자가 기분이 안 좋은 이유로 가장 적절한 것을 고르시오.

① 친구와 다퉈서
② 호텔 시설이 나빠서
③ 호텔 예약을 실패해서
④ 블로그에 오류가 생겨서
⑤ 블로그에 안 좋은 댓글이 달려서

W: I □ _____ □ _____ my last □ _____ □ _____ my □ _____ today. I wrote that I didn't like the □ _____ I □ _____ □ _____. Someone who works at the hotel wrote a □ _____ on my blog. He told me that the hotel was great. Then, he said I was a □ _____ □ _____. I □ _____ him □ _____ he thought that. He just called me □ _____. I □ _____ □ _____ it. It was the □ _____ □ _____ of my life.

14 화제 추론

다음을 듣고, 무엇에 관한 내용인지 가장 적절한 것을 고르시오.

① hockey   ② ping-pong
③ volleyball   ④ basketball
⑤ baseball

M: This is a □ _____ that people □ _____ □ _____. It's a □ _____ sport, so there are □ _____ □ _____ on each team. To play the sport, the players □ _____ a □ _____ and a □ _____. They have to □ _____ the ball □ _____ their □ _____, make it □ _____ □ _____ the net, and try to make it hit the □ _____ □ _____ □ _____ □ _____ team's □ _____. A team can hit the ball □ _____ □ _____ before they have to hit it over the net. The first team to score □ _____ □ _____ wins the game.

✎ **어휘복습** 잘 안 들리거나 몰라서 체크한 어휘를 써 놓고 복습해 보세요.

□ _____   □ _____   □ _____   □ _____
□ _____   □ _____   □ _____   □ _____
□ _____   □ _____   □ _____   □ _____

15 속담 추론

대화를 듣고, 상황을 가장 잘 표현한 속담을
고르시오.

① 끼리끼리 모인다.
② 뿌린 대로 거둔다.
③ 펜은 칼보다 강하다.
④ 빛나는 것이 모두 금은 아니다.
⑤ 겉을 보고 속을 판단하지 마라.

M: Hey, why are you still □ _____ □ _____? I thought you were □ _____ □ _____.

W: I was □ _____ □ _____, but I didn't want to □ _____ that □ _____.

M: □ _____ movie are you □ _____ □ _____?

W: Do you know the new action movie?

M: Are you talking about *The Last Hero*?

M: Yeah. That movie looks really □ _____, so I just decided to □ _____ home.

W: No way. I saw it yesterday, and it was a lot of □ _____. Everyone □ _____ it.

M: Really? Maybe I □ _____ a □ _____.

16 특정 정보 파악

대화를 듣고, 두 사람이 가져가지 않을 것을
고르시오.

① 배낭   ② 물병   ③ 수건
④ 티셔츠   ⑤ 우산

W: We're going to have fun □ _____ □ _____ the □ _____ today.

M: I agree. Don't forget to □ _____ a □ _____ with you.

W: Right. I'm going to bring a □ _____ □ _____, too.

M: Good. And you should also bring a □ _____.

M: Why is that?

W: You'll □ _____ a lot. You can use it to □ _____ yourself □ _____.

M: Good point. I'll bring an □ _____ T-shirt and an □ _____, too.

W: The □ _____ □ _____ doesn't say it will rain.

M: Okay. Then my umbrella is □ _____ the □ _____.

✎ **어휘복습** 잘 안 들리거나 몰라서 체크한 어휘를 써 놓고 복습해 보세요.

□ _____   □ _____   □ _____   □ _____

□ _____   □ _____   □ _____   □ _____

□ _____   □ _____   □ _____   □ _____

17 도표 · 실용문 파악

다음을 듣고, 도표의 내용과 일치하지 않는 것을 고르시오.

Number of Books Read Last Month

① ② ③ ④ ⑤

① Mary read □ _____ □ _____ books.

② Jason read □ _____ books □ _____ Alice.

③ Alice read more books than Steve.

④ Steve read □ _____ books □ _____ Jason.

⑤ Steve read □ _____ □ _____ books.

18 어색한 대화 찾기

다음을 듣고, 두 사람의 대화가 어색한 것을 고르시오.

① ② ③ ④ ⑤

① W: Can you buy some □ _____ at the store?

M: Sure. What do you need me to get?

② W: May I □ _____ this □ _____ for a while?

M: Sorry, but I'm □ _____ it now.

③ W: Hello. How may I □ _____ you?

M: Yes, he's □ _____ me.

④ W: Have you □ _____ □ _____ Jane lately?

M: No, she hasn't □ _____ me □ _____ last week.

⑤ W: □ _____ □ _____ is the game going to □ _____?

M: I think it will □ _____ at seven.

✏️ **어휘복습** 잘 안 들리거나 몰라서 체크한 어휘를 써 놓고 복습해 보세요.

□ _____   □ _____   □ _____   □ _____

□ _____   □ _____   □ _____   □ _____

□ _____   □ _____   □ _____   □ _____

19 알맞은 응답 찾기

대화를 듣고, 남자의 마지막 말에 이어질 여자의 응답으로 가장 적절한 것을 고르시오.

Woman: _____
① Yes, it's a good picture.
② No, that's not my email.
③ Can you send it to my email?
④ Do you know my email address?
⑤ Let me tell you my home address.

M: I love coming to this □ _____. It's so □ _____.
W: I agree. I love all of the □ _____ □ _____.
M: Do you want me to □ _____ a □ _____ □ _____ you in front of them?
W: Sure. That would be great.
M: Okay. □ _____ □ _____ □ _____.
W: □ _____ □ _____?
M: Yes. One, two, three... There you go. You □ _____ □ _____ in the picture. I'll □ _____ a □ _____ to your email.
W: _____

20 상황에 적절한 말 찾기

다음을 듣고, Chris가 Dave에게 할 말로 가장 적절한 것을 고르시오.

Chris: _____
① I can't believe I won the game.
② Let's play a few more minutes.
③ Why didn't you help me up?
④ I'm really sorry about that.
⑤ That was a great shot.

W: Dave and Chris are □ _____ a □ _____ of □ _____ against each other. They are having a good time, but the game is very □ _____. □ _____ □ _____ them wants to □ _____ the game. Dave takes a □ _____, and Chris tries to □ _____ it. Chris □ _____ hits Dave and □ _____ him to the ground. Chris □ _____ □ _____ about that, so he helps Dave up. In this situation, what would Chris most likely say to Dave?
Chris: _____

✎ **어휘복습** 잘 안 들리거나 몰라서 체크한 어휘를 써 놓고 복습해 보세요.

□ _____ □ _____ □ _____ □ _____
□ _____ □ _____ □ _____ □ _____
□ _____ □ _____ □ _____ □ _____

01 대화를 듣고, 두 사람이 찾고 있는 아이를 고르시오.

①   ②   ③

④   ⑤

02 다음을 듣고, 도시별 오늘 날씨가 바르게 연결되지 <u>않은</u> 것을 고르시오.

① 런던 – 안개
② 로마 – 해
③ 모스크바 – 눈
④ 뭄바이 – 구름
⑤ 시드니 – 비

03 대화를 듣고, 두 사람이 대화하는 장소로 가장 적절한 곳을 고르시오.

① 시청   ② 버스   ③ 지하철
④ 기차역   ⑤ 버스 정류장

04 대화를 듣고, 두 사람의 심정으로 가장 적절한 것을 고르시오.

① angry   ② relaxed
③ pleased   ④ nervous
⑤ disappointed

05 대화를 듣고, 남자가 어제 한 일로 가장 적절한 것을 고르시오.

① 극장 가기   ② 선생님과 면담하기
③ 영화 보기   ④ 보고서 쓰기
⑤ 친구와 저녁 먹기

06 대화를 듣고, 남자가 비행기를 탈 시각을 고르시오.

① 6:00 A.M.   ② 10:30 A.M.
③ 11:00 A.M.   ④ 12:00 P.M.
⑤ 2:30 P.M.

07 대화를 듣고, 남자가 할 일이 <u>아닌</u> 것으로 가장 적절한 것을 고르시오.

① 빨래하기   ② 설거지하기
③ 쓰레기 버리기   ④ 거실 청소하기
⑤ 개에게 밥 주기

08 대화를 듣고, 여자가 지불할 금액을 고르시오.

① $10   ② $11   ③ $12
④ $13   ⑤ $14

09 대화를 듣고, 무엇에 관한 내용인지 가장 적절한 것을 고르시오.

① 분리수거 방법
② 도시 대기 오염
③ 도시 교통 문제
④ 봉사활동 지원 동기
⑤ 봉사활동 참가 안내

10 대화를 듣고, 두 사람의 관계로 가장 적절한 것을 고르시오.

① 교사 – 학생   ② 친구 – 친구
③ 엄마 – 아들   ④ 교사 – 학부모
⑤ 교장 – 교사

11 다음을 듣고, 십 대의 체중이 증가하는 원인으로 가장 적절한 것을 고르시오.

① 초콜릿을 많이 먹어서
② 스트레스를 많이 받아서
③ 패스트푸드를 많이 먹어서
④ 잠을 충분히 자지 않아서
⑤ 운동을 충분히 하지 않아서

12 대화를 듣고, 남자가 여자에게 제안한 것으로 가장 적절한 것을 고르시오.

① 비싼 노트북 사기
② 노트북으로 게임하기
③ 화면이 큰 노트북 사기
④ 용량이 큰 노트북 사기
⑤ 적당한 가격의 노트북 사기

13 다음을 듣고, 전화 메시지의 내용과 일치하지 <u>않는</u> 것을 고르시오.

① 아들을 위한 생일 케이크이다.
② 초콜릿 2단 케이크를 원한다.
③ 케이크 위에 축하 메시지를 넣는다.
④ 케이크는 7시까지 준비되어야 한다.
⑤ 케이크는 집으로 배달되어야 한다.

14 다음을 듣고, 여자가 언급하지 <u>않은</u> 것을 고르시오.

① 수영장 근처에서 뛰지 않기
② 수영하기 전에 샤워하기
③ 수영하기 전에 준비운동하기
④ 수영장에서 다이빙하지 않기
⑤ 안전요원의 말을 듣기

15 대화를 듣고, 두 사람이 대화 직후에 할 일로 가장 적절한 것을 고르시오.

① 은행 가기
② 집에 가기
③ 음식 주문하기
④ 휴대폰을 수리하기
⑤ 아이스크림 가게 가기

16 다음을 듣고, 두 사람의 대화가 <u>어색한</u> 것을 고르시오.

①　　②　　③　　④　　⑤

17 대화를 듣고, 여자가 선택할 수업의 일정으로 알맞은 것을 고르시오.

	Sewing Classes	
①	Tuesday	11:00 A.M.
②	Wednesday	7:00 P.M.
③	Friday	11:00 A.M.
④	Saturday	2:00 P.M.
⑤	Sunday	3:00 P.M.

18 대화를 듣고, 남자가 한 말을 가장 잘 표현한 속담을 고르시오.

① Easy come, easy go.
② Practice makes perfect.
③ Too many cooks spoil the broth.
④ The early bird catches the worm.
⑤ Look on the bright side of things.

[19-20] 대화를 듣고, 남자의 마지막 말에 이어질 여자의 응답으로 가장 적절한 것을 고르시오.

19 Woman: _____

① Not me. I love reading novels.
② Yes, I'm reading this book now.
③ I already finished that book.
④ I'm going to the library now.
⑤ No, I haven't read that story.

20 Woman: _____

① Please give me a chicken burger then.
② Okay. I'll have some vanilla ice cream.
③ I'll take a chocolate shake, please.
④ That's right. I ordered an apple pie.
⑤ Yes, I'll take one of those.

10회 DICTATION

다시 듣고, 빈칸에 알맞은 단어를 써 보세요.

■◀)》 MP3 실전 10-1

01 그림 정보 파악

대화를 듣고, 두 사람이 찾고 있는 아이를 고르시오.

① ② ③ ④ ⑤

W: Kevin, what are you doing here?

M: I'm □ _____ my □ _____ here in the park. How about you?

W: I'm here □ _____ my □ _____. It's his □ _____.

M: You have a □ _____ brother? I didn't know that. □ _____ is he?

W: Hmm... I don't see him right now.

M: Is that him □ _____ the □ _____ over there?

W: No, it isn't.

M: Is he the boy □ _____ the □ _____ □ _____?

W: No, that's □ _____ him □ _____.

M: What's he □ _____?

W: He's wearing □ _____ and a □ _____. He's also got a birthday □ _____ on his head.

02 날씨 파악

다음을 듣고, 도시별 오늘 날씨가 바르게 연결되지 <u>않은</u> 것을 고르시오.

① 런던 – 안개
② 로마 – 해
③ 모스크바 – 눈
④ 뭄바이 – 구름
⑤ 시드니 – 비

M: Hello, everybody. It's time for the □ _____ weather □ _____. Here's the weather for some □ _____ □ _____ around the world. In London, it's going to be □ _____ all day. It's □ _____ in Rome but □ _____ and □ _____ in Moscow. In Mumbai, it's going to be □ _____, and there will be □ _____ □ _____ in Sydney.

✎ **어휘복습** 잘 안 들리거나 몰라서 체크한 어휘를 써 놓고 복습해 보세요.

□ _____   □ _____   □ _____   □ _____
□ _____   □ _____   □ _____   □ _____
□ _____   □ _____   □ _____   □ _____

03 장소 추론

대화를 듣고, 두 사람이 대화하는 장소로 가장 적절한 곳을 고르시오.

① 시청　② 버스　③ 지하철
④ 기차역　⑤ 버스 정류장

W: Pardon me, but I □ _____ a □ _____.

M: Sure.

W: I'm going to City Hall. □ _____ □ _____ should I □ _____ □ _____ at?

M: I'm □ _____, □ _____ this □ _____ doesn't go to City Hall. You □ _____ □ _____ □ _____ the number forty-two bus to get there.

W: □ _____ □ _____ the number forty-two bus?

M: No, this is the number forty-four bus.

W: Oh, that's □ _____.

04 심정 추론

대화를 듣고, 두 사람의 심정으로 가장 적절한 것을 고르시오.

① angry　② relaxed
③ pleased　④ nervous
⑤ disappointed

W: This is □ _____.

M: I know, but we can't □ _____ □ _____. It's □ _____ too □ _____.

W: □ _____ □ _____ playing a game?

M: We □ _____ □ _____ some games.

W: Then □ _____ □ _____ watching TV?

M: There's □ _____ □ _____ on TV now.

W: Look. It's not raining □ _____.

M: Seriously? □ _____ □ _____ □ _____. You're right. Now we can go outside.

W: Wait a minute. You □ _____ □ _____ □ _____.

M: Why? What's the matter?

W: It just started raining □ _____.

✎ **어휘복습** 잘 안 들리거나 몰라서 체크한 어휘를 써 놓고 복습해 보세요.

□ _____　□ _____　□ _____　□ _____

□ _____　□ _____　□ _____　□ _____

□ _____　□ _____　□ _____　□ _____

05 한 일 파악

대화를 듣고, 남자가 어제 한 일로 가장 적절한 것을 고르시오.

① 극장 가기
② 선생님과 면담하기
③ 영화 보기
④ 보고서 쓰기
⑤ 친구와 저녁 먹기

W: You look □ _____.
M: I am. My □ _____ just □ _____ my □ _____.
W: Why did he do that?
M: He wants to □ _____ to her □ _____ my □ _____.
W: Are you getting □ _____ □ _____?
M: Not really, but I didn't write a report last night. It's the □ _____ □ _____ this month I □ _____ □ _____ my □ _____ for that class.
W: Was the report □ _____ □ _____?
M: Yeah, and I didn't □ _____ it □ _____.
W: □ _____ did you do □ _____ □ _____ then?
M: I went to my □ _____ □ _____ and □ _____ a couple of □ _____.

06 숫자 정보 파악

대화를 듣고, 남자가 비행기를 탈 시각을 고르시오.

① 6:00 A.M.   ② 10:30 A.M.
③ 11:00 A.M.   ④ 12:00 P.M.
⑤ 2:30 P.M.

W: You must be □ _____. □ _____ going to France tomorrow, □ _____ □ _____?
M: Yeah, it's going to be lots of fun.
W: Shouldn't you go to bed soon? Your □ _____ □ _____ □ _____ in the morning, □ _____ □ _____?
M: No, I'm not taking the six A.M. flight.
W: Did you □ _____ □ _____?
M: Yes, I did. Now, I'm going to be on the □ _____ □ _____ P.M. flight.
W: That's □ _____ □ _____.
M: You're right. So I'm going to get to the □ _____ □ _____ □ _____ P.M.
W: □ _____ □ _____ will you □ _____ home?
M: I'm going to leave the house □ _____ □ _____ □ _____ A.M.
W: That's good. You'll have □ _____ □ _____ □ _____.

✎ **어휘복습** 잘 안 들리거나 몰라서 체크한 어휘를 써 놓고 복습해 보세요.

□ _____   □ _____   □ _____   □ _____

□ _____   □ _____   □ _____   □ _____

□ _____   □ _____   □ _____   □ _____

07 미연급 파악

대화를 듣고, 남자가 할 일이 <u>아닌</u> 것으로 가장 적절한 것을 고르시오.

① 빨래하기
② 설거지하기
③ 쓰레기 버리기
④ 거실 청소하기
⑤ 개에게 밥 주기

M: Happy birthday, Mom.
W: Thanks for remembering, dear.
M: □ _____ today is your □ _____, I'm going to □ _____ all of the □ _____.
W: That's very nice of you.
M: First, I'll □ _____ the □ _____, and then I'll □ _____ □ _____ the □ _____.
W: You □ _____ □ _____ □ _____ take out the trash.
M: Why not?
W: □ _____ day is on Friday, not today.
M: Okay. Well, then I'll □ _____ the □ _____ □ _____ and □ _____ the □ _____, too.
W: □ _____ □ _____ □ _____ feeding the dog?
M: □ _____ □ _____ □ _____. I can give Rusty his dinner.

08 숫자 정보 파악

대화를 듣고, 여자가 지불할 금액을 고르시오.

① $10   ② $11   ③ $12
④ $13   ⑤ $14

M: Hi. Can I help you?
W: Good morning. What □ _____ do you □ _____?
M: The □ _____ are □ _____. Each orange □ _____ □ _____ dollars.
W: I don't really like oranges. □ _____ □ _____ the □ _____?
M: They're □ _____ □ _____ now, so they cost □ _____ dollar □ _____. But I'll give you □ _____ apples □ _____ □ _____ □ _____ of □ _____.
W: That sounds good.
M: Would you like to □ _____ □ _____?
W: Yes. I'd like □ _____ apples, please.

✎ **어휘복습** 잘 안 들리거나 몰라서 체크한 어휘를 써 놓고 복습해 보세요.

□ _____   □ _____   □ _____   □ _____
□ _____   □ _____   □ _____   □ _____
□ _____   □ _____   □ _____   □ _____

09 화제 추론

대화를 듣고, 무엇에 관한 내용인지 가장 적절한 것을 고르시오.

① 분리수거 방법
② 도시 대기 오염
③ 도시 교통 문제
④ 봉사활동 지원 동기
⑤ 봉사활동 참가 안내

M: Do you think the city has too much □ _____ □ _____ the □ _____? Then why don't you □ _____? You can help □ _____ □ _____ the streets. Make our city beautiful once again. □ _____ five oh nine, six four nine six and tell the person you want to □ _____ □ _____. You'll find out □ _____ □ _____ □ _____ to go. You'll □ _____ □ _____ a team of □ _____ for □ _____ □ _____ □ _____ hours every □ _____. By working together, we can clean up our city □ _____.

10 관계 추론

대화를 듣고, 두 사람의 관계로 가장 적절한 것을 고르시오.

① 교사 – 학생
② 친구 – 친구
③ 엄마 – 아들
④ 교사 – 학부모
⑤ 교장 – 교사

W: Stuart, have you □ _____ your □ _____ yet?
M: Almost, but I'm going to go to Bruce's house □ _____ □ _____ □ _____.
W: □ _____, you □ _____ do that.
M: □ _____ □ _____?
W: You haven't done your schoolwork or your □ _____.
M: But you and □ _____ give me too many chores.
W: That's not true. You only have to do □ _____ □ _____ □ _____ □ _____.
M: Okay. I'll □ _____ the □ _____ now.
W: Good. □ _____ □ _____.

✎ **어휘복습** 잘 안 들리거나 몰라서 체크한 어휘를 써 놓고 복습해 보세요.

□ _____   □ _____   □ _____   □ _____
□ _____   □ _____   □ _____   □ _____
□ _____   □ _____   □ _____   □ _____

다음을 듣고, 십 대의 체중이 증가하는 원인으로 가장 적절한 것을 고르시오.

① 초콜릿을 많이 먹어서
② 스트레스를 많이 받아서
③ 패스트푸드를 많이 먹어서
④ 잠을 충분히 자지 않아서
⑤ 운동을 충분히 하지 않아서

M: Nowadays, □ _____ in many countries are □ _____ too much □ _____ . Many of them are □ _____ . The main □ _____ □ _____ □ _____ they □ _____ a lot of □ _____ □ _____ . □ _____ □ _____ eating □ _____ food, they prefer □ _____ food, so they enjoy hamburgers, French fries, and fried chicken. Fast food has □ _____ □ _____ , but it has lots of □ _____ and □ _____ . This is causing teens to gain a lot of weight. □ _____ □ _____ they □ _____ a lot, they will □ _____ become obese.

대화를 듣고, 남자가 여자에게 제안한 것으로 가장 적절한 것을 고르시오.

① 비싼 노트북 사기
② 노트북으로 게임하기
③ 화면이 큰 노트북 사기
④ 용량이 큰 노트북 사기
⑤ 적당한 가격의 노트북 사기

W: I'm thinking about □ _____ a □ _____ □ _____ .
M: That's good. □ _____ are you going to □ _____ it □ _____ ?
W: I'll probably just □ _____ the □ _____ and □ _____ □ _____ .
M: □ _____ □ _____ going to play games, □ _____ □ _____ ?
W: No, I never play computer games. They aren't interesting to me.
M: □ _____ □ _____ □ _____ , you don't need an □ _____ laptop. Just get an □ _____ one.
W: Why is that?
M: The expensive ones are □ _____ □ _____ . But since you're going to do □ _____ □ _____ on yours, you □ _____ □ _____ to □ _____ a lot of money on it.

✎ **어휘복습** 잘 안 들리거나 몰라서 체크한 어휘를 써 놓고 복습해 보세요.

□ _____ □ _____ □ _____ □ _____
□ _____ □ _____ □ _____ □ _____
□ _____ □ _____ □ _____ □ _____

13 내용 일치 파악

다음을 듣고, 전화 메시지의 내용과 일치하지 <u>않는</u> 것을 고르시오.

① 아들을 위한 생일 케이크이다.
② 초콜릿 2단 케이크를 원한다.
③ 케이크 위에 축하 메시지를 넣는다.
④ 케이크는 7시까지 준비되어야 한다.
⑤ 케이크는 집으로 배달되어야 한다.

M: Hello. My name is Tom Roberts. I'd like to □ _____ a □ _____ □ _____. I want to get a □ _____ □ _____ cake. It should have vanilla □ _____ though. It's for my son's birthday, so please □ _____ "Happy Birthday, John" on it. You □ _____ □ _____ to □ _____ it. I'll □ _____ your place to □ _____ it □ _____ tonight at seven. Thanks a lot.

14 미언급 파악

다음을 듣고, 여자가 언급하지 <u>않은</u> 것을 고르시오.

① 수영장 근처에서 뛰지 않기
② 수영하기 전에 샤워하기
③ 수영하기 전에 준비운동하기
④ 수영장에서 다이빙하지 않기
⑤ 안전요원의 말을 듣기

W: Please □ _____ close □ _____ □ _____ the □ _____ of the □ _____ □ _____. Do not □ _____ anywhere near the pool. And you may not □ _____ any □ _____ or □ _____ by the pool. □ _____ a □ _____ before you go swimming. When you're in the pool, you may not □ _____ others. And you may not □ _____ □ _____ the pool either. Finally, always □ _____ □ _____ the □ _____. Do everything he says. Thank you.

✎ **어휘복습** 잘 안 들리거나 몰라서 체크한 어휘를 써 놓고 복습해 보세요.

□ _____   □ _____   □ _____   □ _____
□ _____   □ _____   □ _____   □ _____
□ _____   □ _____   □ _____   □ _____

15 할 일 파악

대화를 듣고, 두 사람이 대화 직후에 할 일로 가장 적절한 것을 고르시오.

① 은행 가기
② 집에 가기
③ 음식 주문하기
④ 휴대폰을 수리하기
⑤ 아이스크림 가게 가기

W: Let's □ _____ some □ _____ □ _____.

M: That's a good idea. Where should we go?

W: Let's go to the ice cream shop □ _____ the □ _____.

M: We □ _____ □ _____ there now.

W: Why not?

M: It's □ _____ □ _____ □ _____.

W: Oh... □ _____ is it going to □ _____ again?

M: I think it will □ _____ next week.

W: So □ _____ □ _____ we find □ _____ ice cream shop?

M: Good thinking. Do you know where one is?

W: Yes, I do. We have to □ _____ □ _____ □ _____ to get there.

16 어색한 대화 찾기

다음을 듣고, 두 사람의 대화가 <u>어색한</u> 것을 고르시오.

① ② ③ ④ ⑤

① M: Would you like to □ _____ □ _____ this □ _____?
   W: Yes, I want to see □ _____ □ _____ □ _____.

② M: □ _____ □ _____ should we □ _____ tomorrow?
   W: How about □ _____ □ _____ □ _____?

③ M: Hello. Are you □ _____ □ _____ something?
   W: Yes, I need to □ _____ a new □ _____.

④ M: There were two □ _____ □ _____ at □ _____ today.
   W: I □ _____ the □ _____ □ _____ of school, too.

⑤ M: Let's □ _____ a □ _____ this evening.
   W: That □ _____ □ _____ to me.

✏ **어휘복습** 잘 안 들리거나 몰라서 체크한 어휘를 써 놓고 복습해 보세요.

□ _____   □ _____   □ _____   □ _____

□ _____   □ _____   □ _____   □ _____

□ _____   □ _____   □ _____   □ _____

17 특정 정보 파악

대화를 듣고, 여자가 선택할 수업의 일정으로 알맞은 것을 고르시오.

	Sewing Classes	
①	Tuesday	11:00 A.M.
②	Wednesday	7:00 P.M.
③	Friday	11:00 A.M.
④	Saturday	2:00 P.M.
⑤	Sunday	3:00 P.M.

M: Good afternoon. What can I do for you?

W: Hi. I'd like to ☐ _____ ☐ _____ ☐ _____ the ☐ _____
☐ _____.

M: No problem. When do you ☐ _____ ☐ _____?

W: I'm ☐ _____ on ☐ _____ and ☐ _____ at eleven A.M. I
have ☐ _____ ☐ _____ then.

M: ☐ _____ ☐ _____ on ☐ _____?

W: Do you have a ☐ _____ class then?

M: No. We only have an ☐ _____ class on Saturday.

W: ☐ _____ ☐ _____ on ☐ _____ ☐ _____?

M: Yes, we have one of those.

W: Great. I'd like to sign up for it.

18 속담 추론

대화를 듣고, 남자가 한 말을 가장 잘 표현한 속담을 고르시오.

① Easy come, easy go.
② Practice makes perfect.
③ Too many cooks spoil the broth.
④ The early bird catches the worm.
⑤ Look on the bright side of things.

M: ☐ _____ ☐ _____ with you nowadays?

W: I'm ☐ _____ a ☐ _____ ☐ _____ at work. My boss
keeps giving me ☐ _____ ☐ _____ ☐ _____.

M: I ☐ _____ ☐ _____ you ☐ _____.

W: You do?

M: Sure. My ☐ _____ always gives me work to do, so I have
to ☐ _____ ☐ _____ at the office almost ☐ _____
☐ _____.

W: ☐ _____ do you ☐ _____ that?

M: I try to ☐ _____ ☐ _____, and ☐ _____ my ☐ _____.
In the future, I'm sure that I'll be ☐ _____.

W: That's a good ☐ _____.

✎ **어휘복습** 잘 안 들리거나 몰라서 체크한 어휘를 써 놓고 복습해 보세요.

☐ _____ ☐ _____ ☐ _____ ☐ _____
☐ _____ ☐ _____ ☐ _____ ☐ _____
☐ _____ ☐ _____ ☐ _____ ☐ _____

19 알맞은 응답 찾기

대화를 듣고, 남자의 마지막 말에 이어질 여자의 응답으로 가장 적절한 것을 고르시오.

Woman: _____
① Not me. I love reading novels.
② Yes, I'm reading this book now.
③ I already finished that book.
④ I'm going to the library now.
⑤ No, I haven't read that story.

W: Good afternoon, Jim. What are you doing?

M: I'm □ _____ in my □ _____.

W: I didn't know you □ _____ a diary.

M: I try to write in it every day. I enjoy writing □ _____
   □ _____ □ _____, and I also like to □ _____ □ _____.

W: □ _____ □ _____ □ _____ stories?

M: They are just stories that I □ _____ □ _____. How about
   you? What's your □ _____?

W: I enjoy □ _____ □ _____ in my free time.

M: □ _____ □ _____ □ _____. I like to read history books.

W: _____

20 알맞은 응답 찾기

대화를 듣고, 남자의 마지막 말에 이어질 여자의 응답으로 가장 적절한 것을 고르시오.

Woman: _____
① Please give me a chicken burger
   then.
② Okay. I'll have some vanilla ice
   cream.
③ I'll take a chocolate shake,
   please.
④ That's right. I ordered an apple
   pie.
⑤ Yes, I'll take one of those.

M: Thank you for coming to Fred's Fried Chicken. May I
   □ _____ your □ _____, please?

W: Yes. I'll □ _____ an order of □ _____ □ _____.

M: □ _____ □ _____ □ _____ would you like?

W: I'll take three pieces.

M: Do you want □ _____, □ _____, or □ _____?

W: Hmm... I think I'll take spicy. I need some □ _____
   □ _____, too.

M: Sure. Would you like a □ _____ order of fries?

W: Yes, and what kinds of □ _____ do you have?

M: We have apple pie, shakes, and cheesecake.

W: _____

✏️ **어휘복습** 잘 안 들리거나 몰라서 체크한 어휘를 써 놓고 복습해 보세요.

□ _____   □ _____   □ _____   □ _____

□ _____   □ _____   □ _____   □ _____

□ _____   □ _____   □ _____   □ _____

■◀》） MP3 실전 11

점수
/ 20

01 대화를 듣고, 남자가 구매할 셔츠로 가장 적절한 것을 고르시오.

①   ②   ③

④   ⑤

02 대화를 듣고, 남자의 장래 희망으로 가장 적절한 것을 고르시오.

① 과학자   ② 화가
③ 음악가   ④ 교사
⑤ 비행기 조종사

03 다음을 듣고, 금요일의 날씨로 가장 적절한 것을 고르시오.

① ② ③ ④ ⑤

04 대화를 듣고, 두 사람이 대화하고 있는 장소로 가장 적절한 곳을 고르시오.

① 해변   ② 미술관   ③ 수족관
④ 극장   ⑤ 수산시장

05 대화를 듣고, 여자가 남자의 제안을 거절한 이유로 가장 적절한 것을 고르시오.

① 돈이 충분하지 않아서
② 시간이 충분하지 않아서
③ 동대문에 가본 적이 없어서
④ 동대문을 좋아하지 않아서
⑤ 남자와 함께 가고 싶지 않아서

06 대화를 듣고, 콘서트가 시작하는 시각을 고르시오.

① 7:00   ② 7:15   ③ 7:30
④ 7:45   ⑤ 8:00

07 대화를 듣고, 여자가 남자에게 전화한 목적으로 가장 적절한 것을 고르시오.

① 책을 빌리려고
② 파티에 초대하려고
③ 병에 대해 물어보려고
④ 시험에 대해 말해주려고
⑤ 수학 숙제에 대해 물어보려고

08 다음을 듣고, 무엇에 관한 내용인지 가장 적절한 것을 고르시오.

① 화학 시험 범위
② 위기 대처 방법
③ 실험실 정리 방법
④ 화학약품의 종류
⑤ 실험실 행동 수칙

09 대화를 듣고, Mr. Jackson이 가르친 과목으로 가장 적절한 것을 고르시오.

① 미술   ② 과학   ③ 수학
④ 음악   ⑤ 역사

10 대화를 듣고, 남자가 대화 직후에 할 일로 가장 적절한 것을 고르시오.

① 치과 가기   ② 전화 걸기
③ 충치 뽑기   ④ 양치질하기
⑤ 초콜릿 먹기

11 대화를 듣고, 여자가 남자에게 부탁한 일로 가장 적절한 것을 고르시오.

① 설거지하기　　　　② 우유 따르기
③ 가게에 가기　　　　④ 식탁 차리기
⑤ 샐러드 만들기

12 대화를 듣고, 여자의 심정으로 가장 적절한 것을 고르시오.

① upset　　　　　　② happy
③ confident　　　　④ worried
⑤ relieved

13 대화를 듣고, 남자의 친구에 관해 언급되지 <u>않은</u> 것을 고르시오.

① 이름　　　　② 키　　　　③ 나이
④ 헤어스타일　　⑤ 옷

14 다음을 듣고, 도표의 내용과 일치하지 <u>않는</u> 것을 고르시오.

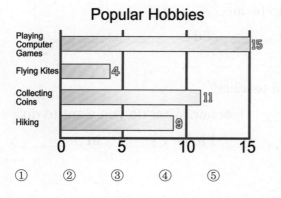

Popular Hobbies

Playing Computer Games — 15
Flying Kites — 4
Collecting Coins — 11
Hiking — 9

① 　② 　③ 　④ 　⑤

15 대화를 듣고, 두 사람의 관계로 가장 적절한 것을 고르시오.

① 경찰관 – 시민
② 재단사 – 고객
③ 세탁업자 – 고객
④ 식당 직원 – 고객
⑤ 인터넷 쇼핑몰 운영자 – 고객

16 다음을 듣고, 두 사람의 대화가 <u>어색한</u> 것을 고르시오.

①　　②　　③　　④　　⑤

17 다음을 듣고, 학교 축제에 관한 내용과 일치하는 것을 고르시오.

① 5월 20일에 시작된다.
② 3일 동안 진행된다.
③ 매일 오후 1시부터 열린다.
④ 다양한 게임이 펼쳐진다.
⑤ 밴드 공연이 6시 30분에 있다.

[18–19] 대화를 듣고, 여자의 마지막 말에 이어질 남자의 응답으로 가장 적절한 것을 고르시오.

18 Man: _____

① These gloves are made of leather.
② Yes, I think I should do that.
③ I'm wearing them right now.
④ No, I don't have my gloves.
⑤ Okay. I'll buy new gloves.

19 Man: _____

① Nobody wants to be punished.
② No, we can go out. Where do you want to go?
③ That's right. I'm studying for a test right now.
④ Don't worry. I'm almost finished with my assignment.
⑤ I came home late last night, so they're mad at me.

20 다음 상황 설명을 듣고, Joe가 Mina에게 할 말로 가장 적절한 것을 고르시오.

Joe: _____

① No, you didn't wait for me.
② Why was your phone turned off?
③ I'm glad we decided to meet today.
④ Did you finish all of the homework?
⑤ I thought you were coming upstairs.

01 그림 정보 파악

대화를 듣고, 남자가 구매할 셔츠로 가장 적절한 것을 고르시오.

① ② ③

④ ⑤

M: Hi. I need to □ _____ a new □ _____ for work.

W: Okay. How about a shirt □ _____ □ _____ □ _____?

M: No thanks. That's □ _____ □ _____ □ _____.

W: This shirt has □ _____ that □ _____ □ _____.

M: I don't like those. But stripes going □ _____ □ _____ □ _____ are fine.

W: We have a shirt like that. Here it is.

M: Wait a minute. I think this □ _____ style is □ _____.

W: That's a □ _____ shirt. Do you want it?

M: Yes, I'll take it. How much does it cost?

02 특정 정보 파악

대화를 듣고, 남자의 장래 희망으로 가장 적절한 것을 고르시오.

① 과학자 ② 화가
③ 음악가 ④ 교사
⑤ 비행기 조종사

W: What do you want to do □ _____ □ _____ □ _____?

M: Well, I really like □ _____. □ _____ □ _____ is fun.

W: So do you want to be an □ _____?

M: No, it's just my □ _____. I'd □ _____ □ _____ a □ _____.

W: Isn't your father a teacher?

M: Yes. He's a □ _____ teacher. What do you want to do?

W: I'd like to be a □ _____. I love □ _____ in □ _____.

✎ **어휘복습** 잘 안 들리거나 몰라서 체크한 어휘를 써 놓고 복습해 보세요.

□ _____   □ _____   □ _____   □ _____
□ _____   □ _____   □ _____   □ _____
□ _____   □ _____   □ _____   □ _____

다음을 듣고, 금요일의 날씨로 가장 적절한 것을 고르시오.

① ② ③
④ ⑤

M: Good evening. We had beautiful □ _____ weather □ _____. On □ _____, the sunny weather will □ _____ in the morning. Then, it's going to become □ _____ in the □ _____. On □ _____, it will be very □ _____ in the □ _____, but it won't rain. On □ _____, there will be □ _____ skies □ _____ □ _____ □ _____. And you can expect sunny skies □ _____ on □ _____.

대화를 듣고, 두 사람이 대화하고 있는 장소로 가장 적절한 곳을 고르시오.

① 해변 ② 미술관 ③ 수족관
④ 극장 ⑤ 수산시장

M: What do you think we should □ _____ □ _____?

W: We can see the □ _____ □ _____.

M: But that starts □ _____ □ _____ □ _____. What should we do now?

W: I'm not sure.

M: Why don't we go to see the □ _____ □ _____?

W: Don't you think sharks are □ _____ □ _____ □ _____?

M: Sure, but don't worry. They're in a big tank. It's □ _____ □ _____.

W: You're right. Do you know where it is?

M: Yeah. We just have to □ _____ □ _____ □ _____.

✏ 어휘복습 잘 안 들리거나 몰라서 체크한 어휘를 써 놓고 복습해 보세요.

□ _____   □ _____   □ _____   □ _____
□ _____   □ _____   □ _____   □ _____
□ _____   □ _____   □ _____   □ _____

05 이유 파악

대화를 듣고, 여자가 남자의 제안을 거절한 이유로 가장 적절한 것을 고르시오.

① 돈이 충분하지 않아서
② 시간이 충분하지 않아서
③ 동대문에 가본 적이 없어서
④ 동대문을 좋아하지 않아서
⑤ 남자와 함께 가고 싶지 않아서

M: □ _____ are you going to □ _____ this □ _____?
W: I'm going to □ _____ Seoul □ _____ my □ _____.
M: Oh, yeah? Where are you going to go?
W: We're going to visit Namdaemun. She wants to go to the □ _____ there.
M: □ _____ □ _____ you go to Dongdaemun, □ _____? That will be fun.
W: That's a good idea, but we □ _____ □ _____ □ _____ □ _____. We'll go there □ _____.
M: Okay. Well, □ _____ □ _____ with your friend.

06 숫자 정보 파악

대화를 듣고, 콘서트가 시작하는 시각을 고르시오.

① 7:00   ② 7:15   ③ 7:30
④ 7:45   ⑤ 8:00

W: Hi, Steve. Where are you?
M: I'm still □ _____ the □ _____.
W: What's the □ _____? Why are you still there?
M: □ _____ is □ _____. The cars are □ _____ very □ _____.
W: But it's □ _____ □ _____, and the concert □ _____ □ _____ □ _____ □ _____.
M: Don't worry. I think I can be there □ _____ □ _____ minutes.
W: □ _____ □ _____ □ _____ by seven fifteen? Okay. I'll be □ _____ □ _____ for you.
M: All right. I'll get there as fast as I can.

✎ **어휘복습** 잘 안 들리거나 몰라서 체크한 어휘를 써 놓고 복습해 보세요.

□ _____   □ _____   □ _____   □ _____
□ _____   □ _____   □ _____   □ _____
□ _____   □ _____   □ _____   □ _____

07 전화 목적 파악

대화를 듣고, 여자가 남자에게 전화한 목적으로 가장 적절한 것을 고르시오.

① 책을 빌리려고
② 파티에 초대하려고
③ 병에 대해 물어보려고
④ 시험에 대해 말해주려고
⑤ 수학 숙제에 대해 물어보려고

M: Hello.

W: Hello. Is Tim there?

M: □ _____ □ _____ Tim. □ _____ □ _____, please?

W: It's Wendy. Why were you □ _____ □ _____ □ _____ today?

M: I □ _____ □ _____ in the morning. So I □ _____ □ _____ □ _____ all day.

W: Do you □ _____ □ _____ now?

M: Yes, I do. Thanks for asking.

W: Anyway, I'm calling to □ _____ you about our □ _____ □ _____ tomorrow. □ _____ □ _____ to study for it.

M: Oh, that's right. Thanks for □ _____ □ _____ □ _____.

08 화제 추론

다음을 듣고, 무엇에 관한 내용인지 가장 적절한 것을 고르시오.

① 화학 시험 범위
② 위기 대처 방법
③ 실험실 정리 방법
④ 화학약품의 종류
⑤ 실험실 행동 수칙

W: Good morning, class. Before we begin, I need to □ _____ you some □ _____. □ _____, do not □ _____ □ _____ any of the □ _____ in the □ _____. Some of them are □ _____. □ _____, you need to □ _____ my instructions very □ _____. Only do what I tell you. □ _____, if you have any □ _____, please □ _____ me. Now, let's □ _____ □ _____.

✎ **어휘복습** 잘 안 들리거나 몰라서 체크한 어휘를 써 놓고 복습해 보세요.

□ _____   □ _____   □ _____   □ _____

□ _____   □ _____   □ _____   □ _____

□ _____   □ _____   □ _____   □ _____

09 특정 정보 파악

대화를 듣고, Mr. Jackson이 가르친 과목으로 가장 적절한 것을 고르시오.

① 미술　② 과학　③ 수학
④ 음악　⑤ 역사

M: □ _____ □ _____ □ _____ □ _____ this picture. Who is this?

W: That's Mr. Jackson. He □ _____ □ _____ be our □ _____.

M: Oh, right. I remember him.

W: Do you remember the □ _____ that he used to □ _____ us □ _____ in class?

M: Yeah, I do. And we got to □ _____ some □ _____ □ _____, too.

W: That was a fun class.

10 할 일 파악

대화를 듣고, 남자가 대화 직후에 할 일로 가장 적절한 것을 고르시오.

① 치과 가기　　② 전화 걸기
③ 충치 뽑기　　④ 양치질하기
⑤ 초콜릿 먹기

M: Ouch. My □ _____ really □ _____. I think I have a cavity.

W: You shouldn't eat so much chocolate. It's □ _____ □ _____ your □ _____.

M: I know. But it □ _____ so □ _____.

W: Anyway, you need to □ _____ a □ _____.

M: Do you know a good one?

W: Yes, but he's very busy. Here's the □ _____ □ _____. Why don't you □ _____ his clinic and □ _____ □ _____ □ _____?

M: Okay. I think I'll do that.

W: Good luck. I hope your tooth □ _____ □ _____.

✎ **어휘복습** 잘 안 들리거나 몰라서 체크한 어휘를 써 놓고 복습해 보세요.

□ _____　□ _____　□ _____　□ _____

□ _____　□ _____　□ _____　□ _____

□ _____　□ _____　□ _____　□ _____

11 부탁 파악

대화를 듣고, 여자가 남자에게 부탁한 일로 가장 적절한 것을 고르시오.

① 설거지하기　② 우유 따르기
③ 가게에 가기　④ 식탁 차리기
⑤ 샐러드 만들기

M: Mom, is □ _____ almost □ _____?

W: Not yet. I still have to make the □ _____.

M: Okay. Should I □ _____ the □ _____?

W: Your sister already did it. But there is something you can do for me.

M: What's that?

W: We □ _____ have □ _____ □ _____. Can you □ _____ to the □ _____ and get some?

M: Sure. I'll do that □ _____ □ _____.

W: Thanks a lot.

12 심정 추론

대화를 듣고, 여자의 심정으로 가장 적절한 것을 고르시오.

① upset　　② happy
③ confident　④ worried
⑤ relieved

M: What did you want to tell me earlier, Sue?

W: I □ _____ some possible □ _____ □ _____.

M: What is it?

W: My mom promised to □ _____ me □ _____ □ _____ the rock □ _____ this Saturday. I just have to get an A on my □ _____ □ _____.

M: Science? But that's your □ _____ □ _____.

W: I know. I'm □ _____ □ _____. □ _____ □ _____ I don't do well?

M: You just need to □ _____ □ _____.

W: I'll □ _____ □ _____ □ _____.

✎ **어휘복습** 잘 안 들리거나 몰라서 체크한 어휘를 써 놓고 복습해 보세요.

□ _____　□ _____　□ _____　□ _____
□ _____　□ _____　□ _____　□ _____
□ _____　□ _____　□ _____　□ _____

13 미언급 파악

대화를 듣고, 남자의 친구에 관해 언급되지 <u>않은</u> 것을 고르시오.

① 이름　　② 키　　③ 나이
④ 헤어스타일　⑤ 옷

M: Excuse me. Could you □ _____ □ _____ for me?

W: Sure. □ _____ do you □ _____?

M: My □ _____ is going to be □ _____ □ _____ with me. When he □ _____ □ _____, can you □ _____ him □ _____ my □ _____?

W: Of course. What's his □ _____?

M: His name is Allen Simmons. He's □ _____ one hundred eighty □ _____ □ _____, and he has □ _____ □ _____ □ _____.

W: Do you know □ _____ he is □ _____?

M: He's wearing a □ _____ □ _____ and a □ _____ □ _____.

14 도표 파악

다음을 듣고, 도표의 내용과 일치하지 <u>않는</u> 것을 고르시오.

Popular Hobbies

Playing Computer Games	15
Flying Kites	4
Collecting Coins	11
Hiking	9

0　5　10　15

①　②　③　④　⑤

① □ _____ □ _____ is □ _____ □ _____ □ _____ hobby.

② More students □ _____ □ _____ □ _____ □ _____ □ _____.

③ Playing computer games is □ _____ □ _____ popular hobby.

④ □ _____ □ _____ □ _____ students enjoy hiking the most.

⑤ □ _____ students like flying kites □ _____ playing computer games.

✎ **어휘복습** 잘 안 들리거나 몰라서 체크한 어휘를 써 놓고 복습해 보세요.

□ _____　□ _____　□ _____　□ _____

□ _____　□ _____　□ _____　□ _____

□ _____　□ _____　□ _____　□ _____

15 관계 추론

대화를 듣고, 두 사람의 관계로 가장 적절한 것을 고르시오.

① 경찰관 – 시민
② 재단사 – 고객
③ 세탁업자 – 고객
④ 식당 직원 – 고객
⑤ 인터넷 쇼핑몰 운영자 – 고객

M: Hello.

W: Hi. I'd like to □ _____ a □ _____ □ _____ my □ _____.

M: □ _____ □ _____ with the order you made?

W: I ordered some □ _____ □ _____ your □ _____, but you sent me the □ _____ □ _____.

M: I'm sorry. What's your order number?

W: It's four oh five nine five. My name is Soyun Park.

M: □ _____ □ _____ one moment, please.

16 어색한 대화 찾기

다음을 듣고, 두 사람의 대화가 <u>어색한</u> 것을 고르시오.

①   ②   ③   ④   ⑤

① M: I just □ _____ my □ _____, so there's a □ _____ on the □ _____.
   W: You need to □ _____ it □ _____.

② M: Do you know where the □ _____ □ _____ is?
   W: It should be □ _____ the □ _____.

③ M: Would you like a cup of □ _____?
   W: Yes, I'm going to □ _____ some □ _____.

④ M: □ _____ did you □ _____ your parents' home?
   W: I was just there two days ago.

⑤ M: □ _____ □ _____ DVDs are you going to □ _____?
   W: I'll just get □ _____ □ _____ □ _____.

✎ **어휘복습** 잘 안 들리거나 몰라서 체크한 어휘를 써 놓고 복습해 보세요.

□ _____   □ _____   □ _____   □ _____

□ _____   □ _____   □ _____   □ _____

□ _____   □ _____   □ _____   □ _____

17 내용 일치 파악

다음을 듣고, 학교 축제에 관한 내용과 일치하는 것을 고르시오.

① 5월 20일에 시작된다.
② 3일 동안 진행된다.
③ 매일 오후 1시부터 열린다.
④ 다양한 게임이 펼쳐진다.
⑤ 밴드 공연이 6시 30분에 있다.

W: Please □ _____ □ _____, everyone. The □ _____ □ _____ is going to begin on May tenth. It's going to □ _____ □ _____ □ _____ □ _____. On the □ _____ □ _____ of the festival, we will □ _____ □ _____ until one P.M. Then, there won't be □ _____ □ _____ for the □ _____ □ _____ □ _____ □ _____. On the □ _____ day, there will not be any classes. We hope all of you will come to the festival. There will be many □ _____ □ _____. The school □ _____ is also going to □ _____. The □ _____ will be on the second day of the festival □ _____ □ _____ P.M.

18 알맞은 응답 찾기

대화를 듣고, 여자의 마지막 말에 이어질 남자의 응답으로 가장 적절한 것을 고르시오.

Man: _____
① These gloves are made of leather.
② Yes, I think I should do that.
③ I'm wearing them right now.
④ No, I don't have my gloves.
⑤ Okay. I'll buy new gloves.

W: Are you □ _____ □ _____ now? Why don't you □ _____ your □ _____?
M: □ _____ do I need them □ _____?
W: It's going to □ _____ really □ _____ today.
M: Is it? I didn't hear the □ _____ □ _____.
W: □ _____ □ _____ the weatherman, it's going to be □ _____ □ _____ □ _____ later in the day.
M: Wow. It is going to be cold.
W: Why don't you □ _____ □ _____ inside and get your gloves then?
M: _____

✏ **어휘복습** 잘 안 들리거나 몰라서 체크한 어휘를 써 놓고 복습해 보세요.

□ _____ □ _____ □ _____ □ _____
□ _____ □ _____ □ _____ □ _____
□ _____ □ _____ □ _____ □ _____

대화를 듣고, 여자의 마지막 말에 이어질 남자의 응답으로 가장 적절한 것을 고르시오.

Man: _____

① Nobody wants to be punished.
② No, we can go out. Where do you want to go?
③ That's right. I'm studying for a test right now.
④ Don't worry. I'm almost finished with my assignment.
⑤ I came home late last night, so they're mad at me.

W: Hi, Tim. It's Wendy.

M: What's going on, Wendy?

W: I'm □ _____ right now. How about going out and □ _____ □ _____?

M: I'd really □ _____ □ _____, □ _____ I can't leave the house today.

W: Why not? Are you □ _____ a school □ _____?

M: No, I'm not. □ _____, my parents □ _____ □ _____ me □ _____ out this □ _____ □ _____.

W: They won't? Are they □ _____ you for something?

M: _____

다음 상황 설명을 듣고, Joe가 Mina에게 할 말로 가장 적절한 것을 고르시오.

Joe: _____

① No, you didn't wait for me.
② Why was your phone turned off?
③ I'm glad we decided to meet today.
④ Did you finish all of the homework?
⑤ I thought you were coming upstairs.

W: Joe and Mina are going to □ _____ at the □ _____ to □ _____ their □ _____. Joe goes to the □ _____ □ _____ of the library and □ _____ □ _____ Mina. However, Mina doesn't □ _____ □ _____. He □ _____ for □ _____ □ _____, and then he decides to go home. When he goes to the □ _____ floor, he sees Mina □ _____ by the □ _____ □ _____. In this situation, what would Joe say to Mina?

Joe: _____

✎ **어휘복습** 잘 안 들리거나 몰라서 체크한 어휘를 써 놓고 복습해 보세요.

□ _____ □ _____ □ _____ □ _____

□ _____ □ _____ □ _____ □ _____

□ _____ □ _____ □ _____ □ _____

01 대화를 듣고, 그림에서 Tom을 고르시오.

02 다음을 듣고, 내일 오후의 날씨로 가장 적절한 것을 고르시오.

① ② ③ ④ ⑤

03 대화를 듣고, 두 사람이 가져가지 <u>않을</u> 것을 고르시오.

04 대화를 듣고, 남자가 지불할 금액을 고르시오.

① 5,000원
② 5,500원
③ 6,000원
④ 6,500원
⑤ 7,000원

05 다음을 듣고, 무엇에 관한 내용인지 가장 적절한 것을 고르시오.

① 연주될 음악
② 음악가 소개
③ 티켓 예매 방법
④ 공연 관람 규칙
⑤ 공연 녹화 방법

06 대화를 듣고, 여자가 남자와 함께 여행을 가지 <u>못하는</u> 이유를 고르시오.

① 몸이 아파서
② 돈이 없어서
③ 일이 너무 바빠서
④ 환자를 돌봐야 해서
⑤ 다른 여행 계획이 있어서

07 대화를 듣고, 두 사람이 대화하는 장소로 가장 적절한 곳을 고르시오.

① 공항
② 식당
③ 은행
④ 우체국
⑤ 문구점

08 대화를 듣고, 여자의 장래 희망으로 가장 적절한 것을 고르시오.

① 건축가
② 의상 디자이너
③ 과학자
④ 수학 교사
⑤ 컴퓨터 프로그래머

09 대화를 듣고, 여자의 마지막 말의 의도로 가장 적절한 것을 고르시오.

① 동의
② 격려
③ 허가
④ 부탁
⑤ 추천

10 대화를 듣고, 두 사람의 관계로 가장 적절한 것을 고르시오.

① 정육점 직원 – 고객
② 과일 상인 – 고객
③ 광고 모델 – 감독
④ 택시 기사 – 승객
⑤ 식당 주인 – 종업원

11 대화를 듣고, 두 사람이 대화 직후에 할 일로 가장 적절한 것을 고르시오.

① 옷 구매하기
② 컴퓨터 게임하기
③ 온라인 쇼핑하기
④ 생일 파티에 가기
⑤ 전자제품 매장 방문하기

12 대화를 듣고, 남자의 심정으로 가장 적절한 것을 고르시오.

① angry ② regretful
③ pleased ④ satisfied
⑤ disappointed

13 대화를 듣고, 내용과 일치하지 <u>않는</u> 것을 고르시오.

① 두 사람은 보석 가게에 있다.
② 여자는 딸을 위한 선물을 찾는다.
③ 남자는 먼저 금목걸이를 추천한다.
④ 여자는 은팔찌를 마음에 들어 한다.
⑤ 팔찌는 포장해주지 않는다.

14 다음을 듣고, 표의 내용과 일치하는 것을 고르시오.

Great Lakes Amusement Park

	Weekdays	Weekends & Holidays
Open	8:00 A.M. – 10:00 P.M.	8:00 A.M. – 11:30 P.M.
Closed	Christmas Day, New Year's Day, Thanksgiving Day	

① ② ③ ④ ⑤

15 대화를 듣고, 남자가 대화 직후에 할 일로 가장 적절한 것을 고르시오.

① 숙제 끝마치기
② 친구의 집에 가기
③ 친구에게 전화하기
④ 방 청소하기
⑤ 쓰레기 내다버리기

16 다음을 듣고, 두 사람의 대화가 <u>어색한</u> 것을 고르시오.

① ② ③ ④ ⑤

17 대화를 듣고, 상황을 가장 잘 표현한 속담을 고르시오.

① Better late than never.
② Rome wasn't built in a day.
③ The early bird catches the worm.
④ Too many cooks spoil the broth.
⑤ A fool and his money are soon parted.

[18–19] 대화를 듣고, 남자의 마지막 말에 이어질 여자의 응답으로 가장 적절한 것을 고르시오.

18 Woman: _____

① Sure. I know the time.
② That sounds good to me.
③ I'm really sorry to hear that.
④ Okay. We can watch a movie.
⑤ What do you want me to watch?

19 Woman: _____

① That sounds fine to me.
② Yes, that's the correct answer.
③ Right. He is a good assistant.
④ Sure. The experiments are easy.
⑤ No, I've never made a poster before.

20 대화를 듣고, 여자의 마지막 말에 이어질 남자의 응답으로 가장 적절한 것을 고르시오.

Man: _____

① Okay. Make sure to wear warm clothes.
② Do you want to go with your brother?
③ Yes, the park is closed.
④ How many friends did you meet?
⑤ No, the car isn't parked outside now.

01 그림 정보 파악

대화를 듣고, 그림에서 Tom을 고르시오.

W: What are you □ _____ □ _____, Joe?

M: This is a □ _____ from my □ _____ □ _____.

W: Wow. All of these people are in your family?

M: That's right. Can you find my □ _____ Tom?

W: Is he the man □ _____ □ _____ and □ _____ a □ _____?

M: No, that's my uncle Jim. Tom is wearing □ _____.

W: Does he have □ _____ □ _____?

M: □ _____, he has □ _____ hair.

02 날씨 파악

다음을 듣고, 내일 오후의 날씨로 가장 적절한 것을 고르시오.

① ② ③
④ ⑤

M: □ _____ is □ _____, May twenty fifth. The □ _____ is finally □ _____ □ _____ several days of □ _____. Today, it will be □ _____ most of the day. At □ _____, the □ _____ will mostly □ _____. □ _____ some □ _____ early in the □ _____ on □ _____, but there will be □ _____ □ _____ starting □ _____ □ _____. On □ _____, however, it is probably going to □ _____ and be very □ _____.

✎ 어휘복습 잘 안 들리거나 몰라서 체크한 어휘를 써 놓고 복습해 보세요.

□ _____   □ _____   □ _____   □ _____

□ _____   □ _____   □ _____   □ _____

□ _____   □ _____   □ _____   □ _____

03 특정 정보 파악

대화를 듣고, 두 사람이 가져가지 <u>않을</u> 것을 고르시오.

① ② ③
④ ⑤

M: Did you remember to □ _____ our □ _____?

W: Yes, I did. They are already □ _____ the □ _____.

M: What about some □ _____ and □ _____?

W: Don't worry. Everything is □ _____ □ _____ our □ _____ _____.

M: That's great.

W: Do you think we should □ _____ some □ _____?

M: □ _____, the hotel will have those for us. But we should bring some □ _____ for the ship.

W: Good thinking.

04 숫자 정보 파악

대화를 듣고, 남자가 지불할 금액을 고르시오.

① 5,000원 ② 5,500원
③ 6,000원 ④ 6,500원
⑤ 7,000원

M: Pardon me. □ _____ □ _____ does it cost to □ _____ the □ _____?

W: □ _____ must pay □ _____ □ _____ won, and □ _____ must pay □ _____ □ _____ □ _____ □ _____ won.

M: My □ _____ is only □ _____. How much should he pay?

W: He only has to pay □ _____ □ _____ won.

M: Great. I need □ _____ adult tickets, □ _____ student ticket, and □ _____ child ticket.

W: □ _____ will you be □ _____ □ _____ this?

M: Cash. Here's ten thousand won.

✏ **어휘복습** 잘 안 들리거나 몰라서 체크한 어휘를 써 놓고 복습해 보세요.

□ _____   □ _____   □ _____   □ _____
□ _____   □ _____   □ _____   □ _____
□ _____   □ _____   □ _____   □ _____

05 화제 추론

다음을 듣고, 무엇에 관한 내용인지 가장 적절한 것을 고르시오.

① 연주될 음악
② 음악가 소개
③ 티켓 예매 방법
④ 공연 관람 규칙
⑤ 공연 녹화 방법

W: Please □＿＿＿＿ □＿＿＿＿. The □＿＿＿＿ is □＿＿＿＿ □＿＿＿＿ begin. Please □＿＿＿＿ □＿＿＿＿ your □＿＿＿＿ and other □＿＿＿＿ □＿＿＿＿ during the performance. You may □＿＿＿＿ □＿＿＿＿ □＿＿＿＿ at all. And you are not □＿＿＿＿ to □＿＿＿＿ the show either. Please do not □＿＿＿＿ □＿＿＿＿ to □＿＿＿＿ the theater □＿＿＿＿ the concert. There will be a short □＿＿＿＿ after about one hour. The concert will begin soon. I hope you enjoy the show.

06 이유 파악

대화를 듣고, 여자가 남자와 함께 여행을 가지 못하는 이유를 고르시오.

① 몸이 아파서
② 돈이 없어서
③ 일이 너무 바빠서
④ 환자를 돌봐야 해서
⑤ 다른 여행 계획이 있어서

W: Are you □＿＿＿＿ □＿＿＿＿ your trip to Spain?
M: Almost. I still □＿＿＿＿ □＿＿＿＿ pack a few things.
W: You're going to □＿＿＿＿ a □＿＿＿＿ □＿＿＿＿ there.
M: I hope so. It's □＿＿＿＿ □＿＿＿＿ you can't go with me.
W: Yeah, but the doctor told me not to travel.
M: When does he think you'll □＿＿＿＿ □＿＿＿＿?
W: He said I should be better □＿＿＿＿ my □＿＿＿＿ in two weeks.
M: That's good to hear.

✎ **어휘복습** 잘 안 들리거나 몰라서 체크한 어휘를 써 놓고 복습해 보세요.

□＿＿＿＿＿＿＿ □＿＿＿＿＿＿＿ □＿＿＿＿＿＿＿ □＿＿＿＿＿＿＿
□＿＿＿＿＿＿＿ □＿＿＿＿＿＿＿ □＿＿＿＿＿＿＿ □＿＿＿＿＿＿＿
□＿＿＿＿＿＿＿ □＿＿＿＿＿＿＿ □＿＿＿＿＿＿＿ □＿＿＿＿＿＿＿

07 장소 추론

대화를 듣고, 두 사람이 대화하는 장소로 가장 적절한 곳을 고르시오.

① 공항 ② 식당 ③ 은행
④ 우체국 ⑤ 문구점

W: Can you □ _____ the □ _____ □ _____ the □ _____ here, please?

M: Sure. I'd like to □ _____ it □ _____ □ _____.

W: No problem. Did you write the □ _____ □ _____ on it?

M: Yes, it's in the left-hand corner.

W: Thank you. That will be □ _____ dollars, please.

M: Here's my credit card.

08 특정 정보 파악

대화를 듣고, 여자의 장래 희망으로 가장 적절한 것을 고르시오.

① 건축가 ② 의상 디자이너
③ 과학자 ④ 수학 교사
⑤ 컴퓨터 프로그래머

W: Thanks for helping me with my □ _____ □ _____.

M: It's □ _____ □ _____. I □ _____ □ _____ math problems.

W: Do you want to teach math □ _____ □ _____ □ _____?

M: No. I would like to be a □ _____ □ _____.

W: That seems like a good job.

M: You still want to be an □ _____, right?

W: Yes. I □ _____ □ _____ homes and buildings.

M: Good luck. I know you can do it.

✎ **어휘복습** 잘 안 들리거나 몰라서 체크한 어휘를 써 놓고 복습해 보세요.

□ _____   □ _____   □ _____   □ _____

□ _____   □ _____   □ _____   □ _____

□ _____   □ _____   □ _____   □ _____

09 의도 파악

대화를 듣고, 여자의 마지막 말의 의도로 가장 적절한 것을 고르시오.

① 동의　② 격려　③ 허가
④ 부탁　⑤ 추천

W: It's noon. Why don't we □ _____ some □ _____?

M: All right. Should we go to a □ _____?

W: Okay. □ _____ would you like to □ _____?

M: I □ _____ □ _____ a new □ _____ restaurant. I think it's called Delhi Delights.

W: Oh, I ate there yesterday.

M: Really? □ _____ did you □ _____ it?

W: It was □ _____. I □ _____ □ _____ will □ _____ the food there.

10 관계 추론

대화를 듣고, 두 사람의 관계로 가장 적절한 것을 고르시오.

① 정육점 직원 – 고객
② 과일 상인 – 고객
③ 광고 모델 – 감독
④ 택시 기사 – 승객
⑤ 식당 주인 – 종업원

M: Can I □ _____ you □ _____ something?

W: What do you □ _____ today?

M: Well, the bananas are □ _____.

W: I □ _____ □ _____ like them.

M: How about some peaches? They're very □ _____.

W: □ _____ □ _____ are they?

M: They are two for a dollar.

W: That's a □ _____ □ _____. I'll take ten of them.

M: □ _____ □ _____ □ _____ five dollars, please.

✎ **어휘복습** 잘 안 들리거나 몰라서 체크한 어휘를 써 놓고 복습해 보세요.

□ _____　□ _____　□ _____　□ _____

□ _____　□ _____　□ _____　□ _____

□ _____　□ _____　□ _____　□ _____

11 할 일 파악

대화를 듣고, 두 사람이 대화 직후에 할 일로 가장 적절한 것을 고르시오.

① 옷 구매하기
② 컴퓨터 게임하기
③ 온라인 쇼핑하기
④ 생일 파티에 가기
⑤ 전자제품 매장 방문하기

M: What are you looking at □ _____ your □ _____?
W: I'm □ _____ □ _____ an □ _____ □ _____.
M: What are you going to buy?
W: I want to get my brother a □ _____ □ _____.
    I'm □ _____ □ _____ getting him some □ _____.
M: Clothes? He won't like those.
W: What should I do □ _____?
M: Let's go to the □ _____ store. I'll find a □ _____
    □ _____ he'll like.
W: Okay. Let me □ _____ my □ _____, and then we can
    □ _____.
M: Sure.

12 심정 추론

대화를 듣고, 남자의 심정으로 가장 적절한 것을 고르시오.

① angry   ② regretful
③ pleased   ④ satisfied
⑤ disappointed

M: I □ _____ □ _____ it.
W: What's up?
M: Do you remember that I was planning to □ _____
    a □ _____ this weekend?
W: Sure. You're □ _____ □ _____ Los Angeles, right?
M: That was my plan, but I had to □ _____ my trip because I
    need to □ _____ □ _____ □ _____ over the weekend.
W: That's disappointing.
M: □ _____ □ _____, the airline won't □ _____ my
    □ _____ because I bought a □ _____ □ _____. I'm so
    □ _____ about that.
W: I'm sorry to hear that. Your ticket was probably □ _____.

✎ **어휘복습** 잘 안 들리거나 몰라서 체크한 어휘를 써 놓고 복습해 보세요.

□ _____   □ _____   □ _____   □ _____

□ _____   □ _____   □ _____   □ _____

□ _____   □ _____   □ _____   □ _____

13 내용 일치 파악

대화를 듣고, 내용과 일치하지 <u>않는</u> 것을 고르시오.

① 두 사람은 보석 가게에 있다.
② 여자는 딸을 위한 선물을 찾는다.
③ 남자는 먼저 금목걸이를 추천한다.
④ 여자는 은팔찌를 마음에 들어 한다.
⑤ 팔찌는 포장해주지 않는다.

M: Hello. Are you looking for something?
W: Yes, I'd like to buy some □ _____ for my □ _____.
M: Here's a nice □ _____ □ _____.
W: I'm sorry, but gold is too expensive for me.
M: Would you □ _____ □ _____ then?
W: Yes. Do you have any silver □ _____?
M: Sure. □ _____ □ _____ □ _____ these.
W: This one looks very nice. I'll take it.
M: All right. Let me □ _____ it □ _____ for you.

14 도표 파악

다음을 듣고, 표의 내용과 일치하는 것을 고르시오.

Great Lakes Amusement Park

	Weekdays	Weekends & Holidays
Open	8:00 A.M. – 10:00 P.M.	8:00 A.M. – 11:30 P.M.
Closed		Christmas Day, New Year's Day, Thanksgiving Day

① ② ③ ④ ⑤

① The amusement park is □ _____ □ _____ □ _____ a □ _____.
② The amusement park □ _____ at □ _____ on □ _____.
③ The amusement park □ _____ at eight □ _____ □ _____ Day.
④ The amusement park closes □ _____ □ _____ □ _____ on weekdays and weekends.
⑤ The amusement park □ _____ at □ _____ on □ _____.

✎ **어휘복습** 잘 안 들리거나 몰라서 체크한 어휘를 써 놓고 복습해 보세요.

□ _____   □ _____   □ _____   □ _____
□ _____   □ _____   □ _____   □ _____
□ _____   □ _____   □ _____   □ _____

대화를 듣고, 남자가 대화 직후에 할 일로
가장 적절한 것을 고르시오.

① 숙제 끝마치기
② 친구의 집에 가기
③ 친구에게 전화하기
④ 방 청소하기
⑤ 쓰레기 내다버리기

M: Mom, Eric □ _____ me to his house □ _____ □ _____.
   May I go there?

W: □ _____ □ _____ does he want you to go?

M: It's □ _____ □ _____, and his family eats □ _____
   □ _____ every evening.

W: You can go if you □ _____ your □ _____ and your
   □ _____.

M: But that might □ _____ me a □ _____ □ _____.

W: Then you'd better □ _____ □ _____ now. Are you going
   to □ _____ your □ _____ first?

M: No, I think I'll □ _____ □ _____ the □ _____. Then, I'll
   do my math □ _____.

W: That's good.

다음을 듣고, 두 사람의 대화가 어색한 것을
고르시오.

①   ②   ③   ④   ⑤

① M: You □ _____ really □ _____ □ _____ the □ _____.
   W: You're welcome.

② M: □ _____ □ _____ does your dog eat?
   W: Pepper eats □ _____ □ _____ □ _____.

③ M: Would you like me to □ _____ the □ _____?
   W: Yes, that would be great.

④ M: □ _____ are you going to □ _____ the □ _____?
   W: I'll go there □ _____ □ _____.

⑤ M: How about □ _____ our □ _____ for a while?
   W: I'd love to, but I'm □ _____ □ _____.

✎ **어휘복습** 잘 안 들리거나 몰라서 체크한 어휘를 써 놓고 복습해 보세요.

□ _____   □ _____   □ _____   □ _____
□ _____   □ _____   □ _____   □ _____
□ _____   □ _____   □ _____   □ _____

17 속담 추론

대화를 듣고, 상황을 가장 잘 표현한 속담을 고르시오.

① Better late than never.
② Rome wasn't built in a day.
③ The early bird catches the worm.
④ Too many cooks spoil the broth.
⑤ A fool and his money are soon parted.

M: □ _____ is your history report □ _____?

W: What □ _____ □ _____?

M: Don't you remember? We have to □ _____ □ _____ a famous person in history.

W: Oh, right. I □ _____ □ _____. When is it □ _____?

M: We have to give it to Mr. Smith □ _____ □ _____.

W: I'd better get to □ _____ □ _____ it.

M: It's ten P.M. now. How can you □ _____ □ _____ □ _____?

W: I might not finish in the morning. But □ _____ □ _____ I can finish it □ _____ □ _____ tomorrow.

18 알맞은 응답 찾기

대화를 듣고, 남자의 마지막 말에 이어질 여자의 응답으로 가장 적절한 것을 고르시오.

Woman: _____
① Sure. I know the time.
② That sounds good to me.
③ I'm really sorry to hear that.
④ Okay. We can watch a movie.
⑤ What do you want me to watch?

M: Excuse me. Could you □ _____ □ _____ big □ _____ for me, please?

W: Sure. What do you need?

M: Would you please □ _____ my □ _____ for a moment? I have to □ _____ □ _____ the □ _____.

W: No problem. I'll □ _____ □ _____ □ _____ □ _____ it.

M: Thanks a lot. I don't want to □ _____ □ _____ else.

W: Why? Did you lose something □ _____?

M: Yes. I □ _____ my □ _____. Somebody □ _____ it a couple of days ago.

W: _____

✎ **어휘복습** 잘 안 들리거나 몰라서 체크한 어휘를 써 놓고 복습해 보세요.

□ _____   □ _____   □ _____   □ _____
□ _____   □ _____   □ _____   □ _____
□ _____   □ _____   □ _____   □ _____

19 알맞은 응답 찾기

대화를 듣고, 남자의 마지막 말에 이어질 여자의 응답으로 가장 적절한 것을 고르시오.

Woman: _____

① That sounds fine to me.
② Yes, that's the correct answer.
③ Right. He is a good assistant.
④ Sure. The experiments are easy.
⑤ No, I've never made a poster before.

M: I think we can □ _____ well □ _____ on this □ _____ □ _____.

W: I agree. It should be fun, too.

M: What kind of work do you want to do?

W: I'm □ _____ □ _____ □ _____, so I can □ _____ the □ _____.

M: That sounds good. And what should I do?

W: You can □ _____ the □ _____. I'm not that good at □ _____.

M: Okay, but I can't do it □ _____. You'll have to □ _____ me.

W: _____

20 알맞은 응답 찾기

대화를 듣고, 여자의 마지막 말에 이어질 남자의 응답으로 가장 적절한 것을 고르시오.

Man: _____

① Okay. Make sure to wear warm clothes.
② Do you want to go with your brother?
③ Yes, the park is closed.
④ How many friends did you meet?
⑤ No, the car isn't parked outside now.

M: Take a look outside. It □ _____ a lot last night.

W: That's great, Dad. Since it's Saturday, I can □ _____ in the snow □ _____ □ _____.

M: Why don't you □ _____ your □ _____ with you?

W: Okay. He can come □ _____ □ _____ me.

M: Thanks. □ _____ are you going to go?

W: I think we'll go to the □ _____ and play with my friends.

M: _____

✏ **어휘복습** 잘 안 들리거나 몰라서 체크한 어휘를 써 놓고 복습해 보세요.

□ _____ □ _____ □ _____ □ _____
□ _____ □ _____ □ _____ □ _____
□ _____ □ _____ □ _____ □ _____

01 대화를 듣고, 여자가 구매할 넥타이로 가장 적절한 것을 고르시오.

02 대화를 듣고, 여자의 심정으로 가장 적절한 것을 고르시오.

① afraid　　　　② nervous
③ pleased　　　　④ confused
⑤ satisfied

03 대화를 듣고, 홍콩의 날씨로 가장 적절한 것을 고르시오.

04 대화를 듣고, 여자가 커피를 마시지 않는 이유로 가장 적절한 것을 고르시오.

① 카페인이 싫어서
② 커피가 집중력을 높여줘서
③ 커피를 마시면 잠을 못 자서
④ 커피의 맛을 좋아하지 않아서
⑤ 뜨거운 커피에 혀를 덴 적이 있어서

05 대화를 듣고, 여자의 마지막 말의 의도로 가장 적절한 것을 고르시오.

① 꾸중　　　② 동의　　　③ 허락
④ 충고　　　⑤ 칭찬

06 다음을 듣고, 남자가 언급하지 않은 것을 고르시오.

① 고향
② 사는 곳
③ 한국에 온 시기
④ 아버지의 직업
⑤ 취미

07 대화를 듣고, 두 사람의 관계로 적절한 것을 고르시오.

① 엄마 – 아들
② 교사 – 학생
③ 승무원 – 승객
④ 사장 – 종업원
⑤ 코치 – 운동선수

08 대화를 듣고, 여자의 장래 희망으로 가장 적절한 것을 고르시오.

① 화가　　　② 기자　　　③ 조각가
④ 음악가　　⑤ 사진작가

09 대화를 듣고, 남자가 여자에게 전화한 목적으로 가장 적절한 것을 고르시오.

① 과제에 대해 물어보려고
② 피자를 만들자고 말하려고
③ 시험에 대해 상기시키려고
④ 친구의 전화번호를 물어보려고
⑤ 음식점에 같이 가자고 말하려고

10 다음을 듣고, 무엇에 관한 내용인지 가장 적절한 것을 고르시오.

① 콘센트　　② 건전지　　③ 충전기
④ 휴대폰　　⑤ 리모컨

11 다음을 듣고, 두 사람이 대화하는 장소로 가장 적절한 곳을 고르시오.

① 애견 카페   ② 치과   ③ 공원
④ 음식점   ⑤ 동물병원

12 대화를 듣고, 내용과 일치하지 <u>않는</u> 것을 고르시오.

① 여자가 쿠키를 만들었다.
② 남자는 쿠키가 맛있다고 생각한다.
③ 쿠키에 설탕과 달걀이 사용되었다.
④ 쿠키에는 초콜릿칩이 들어갔다.
⑤ 쿠키에는 체리가 들어갔다.

13 대화를 듣고, 남자가 지불할 금액을 고르시오.

① $5.00   ② $5.50   ③ $6.00
④ $6.50   ⑤ $7.00

14 대화를 듣고, TV 프로그램이 시작하는 시각을 고르시오.

① 8:15   ② 8:20   ③ 8:25
④ 8:30   ⑤ 8:35

15 다음을 듣고, 두 사람의 대화가 <u>어색한</u> 것을 고르시오.

①   ②   ③   ④   ⑤

16 대화를 듣고, 두 사람이 대화하고 있는 장소로 가장 적절한 곳을 고르시오.

① 병원   ② 약국   ③ 응급실
④ 보험사   ⑤ 은행

17 다음을 듣고, 도표의 내용과 일치하지 <u>않는</u> 것을 고르시오.

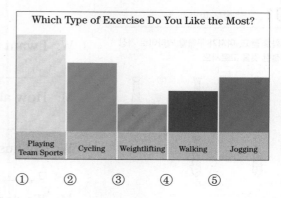

Which Type of Exercise Do You Like the Most?

Playing Team Sports | Cycling | Weightlifting | Walking | Jogging

①   ②   ③   ④   ⑤

18 대화를 듣고, 여자가 내일 할 일로 가장 적절한 것을 고르시오.

① 등산하기
② 영화 보기
③ 가족과 함께 걷기
④ 조부모님 방문하기
⑤ 과학 프로젝트 완성하기

[19-20] 대화를 듣고, 남자의 마지막 말에 이어질 여자의 응답으로 가장 적절한 것을 고르시오.

19 Woman: _____

① Here's the menu.
② No, I'm not a cook.
③ It's one of my hobbies.
④ May I take your order, please?
⑤ Yes, she works in a restaurant.

20 Woman: _____

① Do you expect to do well on the tests?
② What exam should I study for first?
③ No, I haven't handed it in yet.
④ I would appreciate that a lot.
⑤ I hope I do well on my exams.

01 그림 정보 파악

대화를 듣고, 여자가 구매할 넥타이로 가장 적절한 것을 고르시오.

① ② ③ ④ ⑤

W: I want to buy a □ _____ □ _____ my □ _____ for his □ _____. What do you □ _____?

M: How about this □ _____ □ _____? It's □ _____ □ _____ many men.

W: My husband doesn't like stripes. He □ _____ □ _____ □ _____ or ties □ _____ □ _____ on them.

M: We don't have any solid colors. But □ _____ □ _____ this one with □ _____ on it?

W: No, that doesn't look good. But that tie with □ _____ on it is nice.

M: □ _____ □ _____ □ _____ this one here?

W: Yes, I'll take it.

02 심정 추론

대화를 듣고, 여자의 심정으로 가장 적절한 것을 고르시오.

① afraid   ② nervous
③ pleased   ④ confused
⑤ satisfied

W: □ _____ □ _____ with Tony today?

M: Nothing. He seems □ _____ □ _____ to me.

W: I don't think so. I wanted to borrow his notebook, but he □ _____ really □ _____ □ _____ me. He's being □ _____.

M: That's strange. Tony is very □ _____ and □ _____ to everyone.

W: That's what I thought, too. But he was really □ _____ a few minutes ago.

M: Maybe he's □ _____ a □ _____ we don't know about.

W: That's possible. I □ _____ □ _____ □ _____ though.

✎ 어휘복습 잘 안 들리거나 몰라서 체크한 어휘를 써 놓고 복습해 보세요.

□ _____   □ _____   □ _____   □ _____
□ _____   □ _____   □ _____   □ _____
□ _____   □ _____   □ _____   □ _____

03 날씨 파악

대화를 듣고, 홍콩의 날씨로 가장 적절한 것을 고르시오.

① ② ③

④ ⑤

W: Did you hear about that big □ _____ in the □ _____ □ _____?

M: Yeah, it's dropping □ _____ □ _____ □ _____ □ _____ everywhere.

W: That's right. It's □ _____ □ _____ in Jakarta and Manilla, too.

M: □ _____ □ _____ in Shanghai? Is it □ _____ there?

W: No, it's only □ _____ there. The typhoon □ _____ □ _____ China yet.

M: So Hong Kong should be all right □ _____ □ _____.

W: That's correct. I just saw the weather report. It's very □ _____ there, but it hasn't started raining.

04 이유 파악

대화를 듣고, 여자가 커피를 마시지 <u>않는</u> 이유로 가장 적절한 것을 고르시오.

① 카페인이 싫어서
② 커피가 집중력을 높여줘서
③ 커피를 마시면 잠을 못 자서
④ 커피의 맛을 좋아하지 않아서
⑤ 뜨거운 커피에 혀를 덴 적이 있어서

W: You □ _____ a lot of □ _____, don't you?

M: That's right. I drink □ _____ □ _____ each day.

W: Wow, that's a lot of coffee. Why do you drink so much of it?

M: I love the □ _____ in it. It helps me □ _____ □ _____ and □ _____ □ _____ my work. Don't you drink coffee?

W: Actually, I've only had it once. I □ _____ □ _____ the □ _____, so I don't drink it.

M: That's interesting. So what do you drink □ _____?

W: I like □ _____ □ _____. I □ _____ cold drinks □ _____ hot ones.

✎ **어휘복습** 잘 안 들리거나 몰라서 체크한 어휘를 써 놓고 복습해 보세요.

□ _____ □ _____ □ _____ □ _____
□ _____ □ _____ □ _____ □ _____
□ _____ □ _____ □ _____ □ _____

05 의도 파악

대화를 듣고, 여자의 마지막 말의 의도로 가장 적절한 것을 고르시오.

① 꾸중　② 동의　③ 허락
④ 충고　⑤ 칭찬

W: You forgot to □ _____ the □ _____ □ _____ in the living room before you □ _____ to □ _____.

M: Sorry, Mom. I □ _____ forget the □ _____ □ _____.

W: I hope not. We shouldn't □ _____ □ _____.

M: How else can we □ _____ electricity?

W: We shouldn't □ _____ the computer or TV □ _____ when nobody is using them.

M: That's a good idea.

W: And we shouldn't leave the □ _____ door open □ _____ □ _____ □ _____. Open it, get some food, and then close it quickly.

M: Okay. I'll do that, too.

W: Great. Do those things, and you'll be able to □ _____ electricity.

06 미언급 파악

다음을 듣고, 남자가 언급하지 <u>않은</u> 것을 고르시오.

① 고향
② 사는 곳
③ 한국에 온 시기
④ 아버지의 직업
⑤ 취미

M: Hi, everyone. My □ _____ is Ralph, and □ _____ □ _____ □ _____ Canada. Now, my family and I □ _____ here □ _____ Daegu. We □ _____ □ _____ two years ago □ _____ □ _____ my father's job. I'm trying to □ _____ □ _____, but it's a difficult □ _____. On the weekend, I often □ _____ □ _____ in the local area, and I sometimes go □ _____ with my friends. I like □ _____ □ _____ as well.

✎ **어휘복습** 잘 안 들리거나 몰라서 체크한 어휘를 써 놓고 복습해 보세요.

□ _____　　□ _____　　□ _____　　□ _____
□ _____　　□ _____　　□ _____　　□ _____
□ _____　　□ _____　　□ _____　　□ _____

07 관계 추론

대화를 듣고, 두 사람의 관계로 적절한 것을 고르시오.

① 엄마 – 아들
② 교사 – 학생
③ 승무원 – 승객
④ 사장 – 종업원
⑤ 코치 – 운동선수

W: Steve, are you □ _____ □ _____ these days?
M: Yes, Ms. Martin. I'm □ _____. Why do you ask?
W: You haven't □ _____ □ _____ any □ _____ for two weeks.
M: I'm sorry about that.
W: So what's going on? Is there a □ _____?
M: The work is □ _____ □ _____ for me. I don't □ _____ it.
W: Then why don't you □ _____ □ _____ after school tomorrow? I can □ _____ you □ _____ to do it.
M: Okay. Thanks a lot.

08 특정 정보 파악

대화를 듣고, 여자의 장래 희망으로 가장 적절한 것을 고르시오.

① 화가 ② 기자 ③ 조각가
④ 음악가 ⑤ 사진작가

M: This is a really good □ _____. Did you make it?
W: No, one of my friends did. But I □ _____ the □ _____ she used for the painting.
M: Can I see it?
W: Sure. It's right here. I'd like to be a □ _____ □ _____ □ _____ □ _____.
M: The picture and the painting □ _____ almost □ _____ □ _____. I'm □ _____.
W: My friend is an □ _____ □ _____. Don't you agree?
M: Yes, I think so.

✎ **어휘복습** 잘 안 들리거나 몰라서 체크한 어휘를 써 놓고 복습해 보세요.

□ _____   □ _____   □ _____   □ _____
□ _____   □ _____   □ _____   □ _____
□ _____   □ _____   □ _____   □ _____

09 전화 목적 파악

대화를 듣고, 남자가 여자에게 전화한 목적으로 가장 적절한 것을 고르시오.

① 과제에 대해 물어보려고
② 피자를 만들자고 말하려고
③ 시험에 대해 상기시키려고
④ 친구의 전화번호를 물어보려고
⑤ 음식점에 같이 가자고 말하려고

W: Hi, Chris. How are you?

M: I'm good, Mina. What are you doing?

W: I'm □ _____ □ _____ my □ _____. I need to finish □ _____ a □ _____.

M: □ _____ □ _____ do you think you're going to □ _____?

W: I need about thirty more minutes. Why?

M: Wendy and I are going to get some □ _____ at the □ _____. Would you like to □ _____ □ _____ us?

W: Sure. That sounds great. □ _____ □ _____ □ _____ waiting a bit?

M: □ _____ □ _____ □ _____. □ _____ me □ _____ when you are ready to go.

W: Okay. I'll do that.

10 화제 추론

다음을 듣고, 무엇에 관한 내용인지 가장 적절한 것을 고르시오.

① 콘센트   ② 건전지   ③ 충전기
④ 휴대폰   ⑤ 리모컨

M: This is an □ _____ that many different □ _____ □ _____. This is usually □ _____, and this □ _____ □ _____. Without this, many items cannot □ _____. A person □ _____ this □ _____ an item such as a □ _____ □ _____, and then the person can use the remote control to change the channels. This often □ _____ □ _____ □ _____ □ _____ □ _____. But when this □ _____ □ _____ □ _____ power, people □ _____ this □ _____ a new one.

✏ **어휘복습** 잘 안 들리거나 몰라서 체크한 어휘를 써 놓고 복습해 보세요.

□ _____   □ _____   □ _____   □ _____
□ _____   □ _____   □ _____   □ _____
□ _____   □ _____   □ _____   □ _____

11 장소 추론

다음을 듣고, 두 사람이 대화하는 장소로 가장 적절한 곳을 고르시오.

① 애견 카페   ② 치과   ③ 공원
④ 음식점   ⑤ 동물병원

M: Good afternoon. □ _____ seems to be the □ _____?

W: It's Sandy. She keeps □ _____ her □ _____.

M: When did this start?

W: About two days ago. I looked at her right ear, and it's really red.

M: She might □ _____ an □ _____. Can you □ _____ her up □ _____ the □ _____?

W: Sure. Here she is. Don't worry. She won't □ _____ you. She's □ _____ her □ _____ now. She's very friendly.

M: Thanks. Hmm… Yes, her ear is very red.

W: Is it bad?

M: Let me □ _____ her □ _____ □ _____ and some □ _____. She'll be fine in a few days.

12 내용 일치 파악

대화를 듣고, 내용과 일치하지 <u>않는</u> 것을 고르시오.

① 여자가 쿠키를 만들었다.
② 남자는 쿠키가 맛있다고 생각한다.
③ 쿠키에 설탕과 달걀이 사용되었다.
④ 쿠키에는 초콜릿칩이 들어갔다.
⑤ 쿠키에는 체리가 들어갔다.

M: These cookies look great. □ _____ □ _____ □ _____ □ _____ I have one?

W: □ _____ □ _____ □ _____. Please □ _____ □ _____. I just made them.

M: Thanks. It's □ _____. What did you put in it?

W: Well, it has □ _____, □ _____, and □ _____ in it.

M: I can see the □ _____ □ _____, too.

W: Yes, I □ _____ some of those.

M: What are these red pieces? Are these □ _____?

W: No, they aren't. They're cranberries. They give the cookies their □ _____ □ _____.

✐ **어휘복습** 잘 안 들리거나 몰라서 체크한 어휘를 써 놓고 복습해 보세요.

□ _____   □ _____   □ _____   □ _____

□ _____   □ _____   □ _____   □ _____

□ _____   □ _____   □ _____   □ _____

13 숫자 정보 파악

대화를 듣고, 남자가 지불할 금액을 고르시오.

① $5.00   ② $5.50   ③ $6.00
④ $6.50   ⑤ $7.00

W: Hello. Welcome to Dave's □ _____ Shop.

M: Hi. Which donuts do you recommend?

W: The chocolate donuts are excellent. They □ _____ □ _____ □ _____ each.

M: □ _____ □ _____ the □ _____ donuts? I like them a lot.

W: We have cherry, blueberry, and raspberry jelly donuts.

M: What do they cost?

W: They are each □ _____ dollar and □ _____ cents. Would you like some?

M: I'll take □ _____ raspberry jelly donuts and □ _____ chocolate donuts.

W: □ _____ □ _____ just one moment, please.

14 숫자 정보 파악

대화를 듣고, TV 프로그램이 시작하는 시각을 고르시오.

① 8:15   ② 8:20   ③ 8:25
④ 8:30   ⑤ 8:35

W: Why are you watching TV?

M: My □ _____ □ _____ is □ _____ □ _____ in a while.

W: But it's □ _____ □ _____, and you have to □ _____ □ _____ for your piano lesson.

M: I know, Mom, but can't I watch this TV program first?

W: When does it start?

M: □ _____ □ _____ □ _____.

W: Well, □ _____ □ _____ □ _____ a bit before the piano teacher gets here? That will only take about five minutes.

M: Okay. I'll do that now.

W: Good. You need to □ _____ □ _____ you □ _____ the song you learned during your last lesson.

✎ **어휘복습** 잘 안 들리거나 몰라서 체크한 어휘를 써 놓고 복습해 보세요.

□ _____   □ _____   □ _____   □ _____
□ _____   □ _____   □ _____   □ _____
□ _____   □ _____   □ _____   □ _____

다음을 듣고, 두 사람의 대화가 <u>어색한</u> 것을 고르시오.

①　　②　　③　　④　　⑤

① M: □ _____ did you □ _____ that dress?

W: □ _____ a store downtown.

② M: What time is your □ _____ □ _____?

W: It's at two thirty.

③ M: Could you □ _____ □ _____ that □ _____ for me, please?

W: Sure. □ _____ should I □ _____ it?

④ M: Why don't we □ _____ □ _____ tonight?

W: Okay. I'll □ _____ a □ _____.

⑤ M: □ _____ do you □ _____ □ _____ the new student?

W: She □ _____ □ _____ a nice girl.

대화를 듣고, 두 사람이 대화하고 있는 장소로 가장 적절한 곳을 고르시오.

① 병원　　② 약국　　③ 응급실
④ 보험사　　⑤ 은행

M: Hi. How can I help you?

W: I have this □ _____ from Dr. Norby. I need to □ _____ it □ _____.

M: All right. That will □ _____ a few minutes.

W: Okay, I'll □ _____.

M: Do you have □ _____ □ _____?

W: Yes. Here's my insurance card.

M: Thanks. How will you □ _____ □ _____ this?

W: I'll pay with □ _____.

✎ **어휘복습** 잘 안 들리거나 몰라서 체크한 어휘를 써 놓고 복습해 보세요.

□ _____　□ _____　□ _____　□ _____

□ _____　□ _____　□ _____　□ _____

□ _____　□ _____　□ _____　□ _____

17 도표 · 실용문 파악

다음을 듣고, 도표의 내용과 일치하지 않는 것을 고르시오.

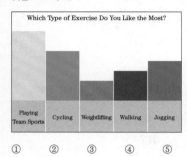

Which Type of Exercise Do You Like the Most?

| Playing Team Sports | Cycling | Weightlifting | Walking | Jogging |

①   ②   ③   ④   ⑤

① Playing □ _____ □ _____ is the □ _____ □ _____ type of □ _____.

② The □ _____ □ _____ of students like □ _____ and □ _____.

③ □ _____ is not □ _____ popular with students □ _____ □ _____.

④ Cycling is □ _____ popular □ _____ playing team sports.

⑤ Weightlifting is □ _____ □ _____ □ _____ □ _____ popular activities.

18 할 일 파악

대화를 듣고, 여자가 내일 할 일로 가장 적절한 것을 고르시오.

① 등산하기
② 영화 보기
③ 가족과 함께 걷기
④ 조부모님 방문하기
⑤ 과학 프로젝트 완성하기

M: Hi, Anna. What are you doing now?

W: I'm □ _____ □ _____ my science □ _____.

M: □ _____ □ _____ are you going to do that?

W: I'll □ _____ work on it for two more hours.

M: When you're finished, how about □ _____ a □ _____ with me?

W: I can't. I need to □ _____ □ _____ □ _____ early tonight. I'm □ _____ □ _____ with my family early in the morning.

M: Really? Where are you going to go?

W: We're □ _____ □ _____ □ _____ □ _____ in the countryside.

✎ **어휘복습** 잘 안 들리거나 몰라서 체크한 어휘를 써 놓고 복습해 보세요.

□ _____ □ _____ □ _____ □ _____

□ _____ □ _____ □ _____ □ _____

□ _____ □ _____ □ _____ □ _____

19 알맞은 응답 찾기

대화를 듣고, 남자의 마지막 말에 이어질 여자의 응답으로 가장 적절한 것을 고르시오.

Woman: _____
① Here's the menu.
② No, I'm not a cook.
③ It's one of my hobbies.
④ May I take your order, please?
⑤ Yes, she works in a restaurant.

W: How are you □ _____ the □ _____?
M: I'm having a great time here. □ _____ □ _____ the □ _____.
W: □ _____ □ _____. And thank you for coming here.
M: I didn't want to □ _____ this party. Everyone from school is here.
W: Yeah. □ _____ □ _____ □ _____ □ _____ the food?
M: It's great. Did your mother make everything?
W: □ _____, she and I □ _____ □ _____ to □ _____ all of the food.
M: You made this? I didn't know you could cook.
W: _____

20 알맞은 응답 찾기

대화를 듣고, 남자의 마지막 말에 이어질 여자의 응답으로 가장 적절한 것을 고르시오.

Woman: _____
① Do you expect to do well on the tests?
② What exam should I study for first?
③ No, I haven't handed it in yet.
④ I would appreciate that a lot.
⑤ I hope I do well on my exams.

M: Are you ready for our □ _____ □ _____?
W: Not yet. I □ _____ started studying □ _____.
M: But the tests start □ _____ □ _____ □ _____ □ _____. Why haven't you studied for them?
W: I've been working on my history project.
M: Oh, I □ _____ it □ _____ □ _____.
W: You did? I'm □ _____. Was it hard?
M: □ _____ □ _____. Would you like me to □ _____ you □ _____ □ _____ with yours?
W: _____

✎ **어휘복습** 잘 안 들리거나 몰라서 체크한 어휘를 써 놓고 복습해 보세요.

□ _____   □ _____   □ _____   □ _____
□ _____   □ _____   □ _____   □ _____
□ _____   □ _____   □ _____   □ _____

13회 DICTATION **159**

MP3 실전 14

점수 / 20

01 대화를 듣고, 여자가 구매할 시계로 가장 적절한 것을 고르시오.

①   ②   ③

④   ⑤

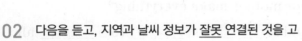

02 다음을 듣고, 지역과 날씨 정보가 잘못 연결된 것을 고르시오.

① 부산 – 안개 ② 대구 – 비
③ 광주 – 구름 ④ 인천 – 해
⑤ 원주 – 바람

03 대화를 듣고, 남자의 마지막 말에 드러난 심정으로 가장 적절한 것을 고르시오.

① excited ② nervous
③ worried ④ shocked
⑤ disappointed

04 대화를 듣고, 남자가 도서관에 가는 이유로 가장 적절한 것을 고르시오.

① 책을 대출하려고
② 책을 반납하려고
③ 친구를 만나려고
④ 과학 시험을 준비하려고
⑤ 연체료를 지불하려고

05 대화를 듣고, 남자가 여자에게 부탁한 일로 가장 적절한 것을 고르시오.

① 계단 이용하기
② 서류에 서명하기
③ 메시지 전달하기
④ 신분증 보여주기
⑤ 엘리베이터 수리하기

06 대화를 듣고, 두 사람의 관계로 가장 적절한 것을 고르시오.

① 아빠 – 딸
② 교사 – 학생
③ 화가 – 모델
④ 사진 작가 – 고객
⑤ 버스 기사 – 승객

07 대화를 듣고, 두 사람이 만날 시각을 고르시오.

① 9:00 A.M. ② 1:00 P.M.
③ 2:00 P.M. ④ 5:00 P.M.
⑤ 6:00 P.M.

08 대화를 듣고, 여자가 받을 거스름돈을 고르시오.

① $0.50 ② $1.00 ③ $1.50
④ $2.00 ⑤ $2.50

09 대화를 듣고, 남자에 대한 설명으로 일치하지 않는 것을 고르시오.

① 버스를 타고 등교한다.
② 등교하는 데 보통 30분이 걸린다.
③ 등굣길에 지루함을 느낀다.
④ 스마트폰을 갖고 다닌다.
⑤ 버스에서 게임을 한다.

10 대화를 듣고, 여자가 남자에게 전화한 목적으로 가장 적절한 것을 고르시오.

① 숙제 검토를 요청하려고
② 보고서 작성을 요청하려고
③ 보고서 마감일을 물어보려고
④ 역사 시험 범위를 물어보려고
⑤ 여동생 돌보는 일을 부탁하려고

11 대화를 듣고, 남자가 대화 직후에 할 일로 가장 적절한 것을 고르시오.

① 풍선 불기　　　② 집안 꾸미기
③ 제과점 가기　　④ 케이크 만들기
⑤ 선물 찾으러 가기

12 대화를 듣고, 두 사람이 대화하는 장소로 가장 적절한 곳을 고르시오.

① 유치원　　　　② 놀이공원
③ 전자제품 매장　④ 서점
⑤ 장난감 가게

13 다음을 듣고, 두 사람의 대화가 어색한 것을 고르시오.

①　　　②　　　③　　　④　　　⑤

14 다음을 듣고, 남자가 하는 말의 내용으로 가장 적절한 것을 고르시오.

① 수리기사 모집
② 비상계단 위치
③ 건물 청소 일정
④ 엘리베이터 고장
⑤ 3층과 4층의 공사 일정

15 대화를 듣고, 여자가 한 일이 아닌 것을 고르시오.

① 수영하기
② 해돋이 보기
③ 사촌 만나기
④ 자전거 타기
⑤ 스키 타기

16 다음을 듣고, 내용과 일치하지 않는 것을 고르시오.

① 정육 코너에서 할인을 한다.
② 닭고기와 돼지고기는 할인 비율이 같다.
③ 쇠고기는 20% 할인해서 판매된다.
④ 상점은 이틀 동안 할인 판매를 한다.
⑤ 판매원들이 고객들을 도울 것이다.

17 대화를 듣고, 상황을 가장 잘 표현한 속담을 고르시오.

① All that glitters is not gold.
② There's no place like home.
③ The early bird catches the worm.
④ Too many cooks spoil the broth.
⑤ If at first you don't succeed, try, try again.

18 대화를 듣고, 남자가 여자에게 제안한 것으로 가장 적절한 것을 고르시오.

① 새 공책 사기
② 문구점에 가기
③ 숙제 적어 두기
④ 선생님께 사과하기
⑤ 보고서 오류 수정하기

19 대화를 듣고, 남자의 마지막 말에 이어질 여자의 응답으로 가장 적절한 것을 고르시오.

Woman: _____

① This blouse was on sale.
② I just bought this new bag.
③ No, I haven't been there yet.
④ We're looking for some clothes.
⑤ Yes, that's what we're going to do.

20 대화를 듣고, 여자의 마지막 말에 이어질 남자의 응답으로 가장 적절한 것을 고르시오.

Man: _____

① It's open 24 hours a day.
② Okay. I'm getting hungry, too.
③ Yes, that's where the store is.
④ Mom said dinner's almost ready.
⑤ Why don't we just make lunch?

01 그림 정보 파악

대화를 듣고, 여자가 구매할 시계로 가장 적절한 것을 고르시오.

① ② ③

④ ⑤

W: Hi. I need to buy an □ _____ □ _____.

M: No problem. We have many of them. Do you like this □ _____ □ _____ □ _____ the □ _____ on top?

W: Not really. It's □ _____ □ _____ □ _____.

M: We also have a round one with no bell on it. How about that?

W: □ _____ □ _____ have a □ _____ one.

M: We have □ _____ □ _____ □ _____ them. This one has □ _____ on it.

W: Do you have any □ _____ clocks?

M: Yes, we have a rectangular one and a □ _____ one.

W: Give me the one □ _____ like a □ _____, please.

02 날씨 파악

다음을 듣고, 지역과 날씨 정보가 **잘못** 연결된 것을 고르시오.

① 부산 – 안개
② 대구 – 비
③ 광주 – 구름
④ 인천 – 해
⑤ 원주 – 바람

M: Here's the weather report for Korea today. In Busan, it's very □ _____ □ _____ □ _____. In Daegu, it's going to □ _____ all day long. There are □ _____ □ _____ in Gwangju and Daegu. In Incheon, it's □ _____ a bit now, but there are □ _____ skies in Seoul. And in Wonju, it's □ _____ and □ _____ right now.

✎ **어휘복습** 잘 안 들리거나 몰라서 체크한 어휘를 써 놓고 복습해 보세요.

□ _____   □ _____   □ _____   □ _____
□ _____   □ _____   □ _____   □ _____
□ _____   □ _____   □ _____   □ _____

03 심정 추론

대화를 듣고, 남자의 마지막 말에 드러난 심정으로 가장 적절한 것을 고르시오.

① excited
② nervous
③ worried
④ shocked
⑤ disappointed

M: □ _____ this □ _____. I have some great news.
W: What is it?
M: The Brazilian □ _____ □ _____ is going to be □ _____ the □ _____ team next week.
W: Really? That's □ _____. □ _____ □ _____ □ _____ see that game.
M: □ _____ □ _____ this □ _____, we can get □ _____ □ _____.
W: All right. Let's go to the □ _____ and □ _____ our tickets.
M: Oh, no. Look at this. This is □ _____.
W: What's the matter? Is there □ _____ □ _____?
M: There aren't any tickets left. They're all □ _____ □ _____.

04 이유 파악

대화를 듣고, 남자가 도서관에 가는 이유로 가장 적절한 것을 고르시오.

① 책을 대출하려고
② 책을 반납하려고
③ 친구를 만나려고
④ 과학 시험을 준비하려고
⑤ 연체료를 지불하려고

W: □ _____ are you □ _____ right now, Dave?
M: I've got to go to the □ _____.
W: Are you going to meet John? I know he's studying there now.
M: Oh, I didn't know that.
W: Yeah, he needs to □ _____ □ _____ the □ _____ □ _____ tomorrow.
M: I'm not going there to meet him. I need to □ _____ this □ _____.
W: Is it □ _____?
M: No, but it is □ _____ □ _____. So I need to return it □ _____ the library □ _____ tonight.
W: □ _____ □ _____ □ _____ then. It closes in half an hour.

✎ **어휘복습** 잘 안 들리거나 몰라서 체크한 어휘를 써 놓고 복습해 보세요.

□ _____   □ _____   □ _____   □ _____
□ _____   □ _____   □ _____   □ _____
□ _____   □ _____   □ _____   □ _____

05 부탁 파악

대화를 듣고, 남자가 여자에게 부탁한 일로 가장 적절한 것을 고르시오.

① 계단 이용하기
② 서류에 서명하기
③ 메시지 전달하기
④ 신분증 보여주기
⑤ 엘리베이터 수리하기

W: Excuse me. Where are you going?

M: I'm here to see Mr. Kent □ _____ the □ _____ □ _____.

W: I'm sorry, but you can't just □ _____ □ _____ the □ _____.

M: Why not?

W: All □ _____ to this building have to □ _____ □ _____.

M: Oh, I didn't know that.

W: Please sign your □ _____ here. And I need to see your □ _____ □ _____, too.

M: I think I left my wallet in my car. □ _____ □ _____ just □ _____ Mr. Kent □ _____ I'll be waiting in the lobby?

06 관계 추론

대화를 듣고, 두 사람의 관계로 가장 적절한 것을 고르시오.

① 아빠 – 딸
② 교사 – 학생
③ 화가 – 모델
④ 사진 작가 – 고객
⑤ 버스 기사 – 승객

M: Can I □ _____ you □ _____ something?

W: Yes, I need to □ _____ a □ _____.

M: What is the □ _____ for?

W: It's for my □ _____ □ _____ □ _____.

M: That's □ _____ □ _____. We can do that right now.

W: All right. Should I □ _____ □ _____ over there?

M: Yes. Let me □ _____ □ _____ the □ _____. This will just □ _____ □ _____ □ _____.

✎ **어휘복습** 잘 안 들리거나 몰라서 체크한 어휘를 써 놓고 복습해 보세요.

□ _____   □ _____   □ _____   □ _____
□ _____   □ _____   □ _____   □ _____
□ _____   □ _____   □ _____   □ _____

07 숫자 정보 파악

대화를 듣고, 두 사람이 만날 시각을 고르시오.

① 9:00 A.M.   ② 1:00 P.M.
③ 2:00 P.M.   ④ 5:00 P.M.
⑤ 6:00 P.M.

W: Are we still □ _____ □ _____ tomorrow morning □ _____ □ _____?

M: □ _____, □ _____ I can't go in the morning.

W: Why not?

M: My dad wants me to help around the house.

W: Should we go □ _____ □ _____ □ _____ □ _____ then?

M: It will probably be □ _____ □ _____ then. □ _____ □ _____ sometime □ _____ □ _____ □ _____? □ _____ is good for me.

W: □ _____ would be □ _____ though.

M: □ _____ □ _____. Let's go jogging then.

08 숫자 정보 파악

대화를 듣고, 여자가 받을 거스름돈을 고르시오.

① $0.50   ② $1.00   ③ $1.50
④ $2.00   ⑤ $2.50

M: Are you ready to □ _____?

W: Yes. I want a □ _____ □ _____, two orders of □ _____, and two □ _____, please.

M: Your □ _____ □ _____ □ _____ □ _____ dollars.

W: □ _____ □ _____ a moment. How much is a □ _____ of □ _____ □ _____?

M: It's □ _____ dollars.

W: □ _____ also □ _____ □ _____ of those, please.

M: □ _____ □ _____ □ _____?

W: Yes. Here's □ _____ dollars.

M: And □ _____ your □ _____.

✎ 어휘복습 잘 안 들리거나 몰라서 체크한 어휘를 써 놓고 복습해 보세요.

□ _____   □ _____   □ _____   □ _____
□ _____   □ _____   □ _____   □ _____
□ _____   □ _____   □ _____   □ _____

09 내용 일치 파악

대화를 듣고, 남자에 대한 설명으로 일치하지 <u>않는</u> 것을 고르시오.

① 버스를 타고 등교한다.
② 등교하는 데 보통 30분이 걸린다.
③ 등굣길에 지루함을 느낀다.
④ 스마트폰을 갖고 다닌다.
⑤ 버스에서 게임을 한다.

W: You □ _____ to □ _____ □ _____ □ _____, don't you?
M: That's right. I do that every morning.
W: □ _____ □ _____ does it □ _____?
M: It usually takes around □ _____ □ _____ □ _____ to get to school.
W: That's a long time. You □ _____ □ _____ □ _____ on the bus.
M: Not really.
W: Why not? What do you do?
M: I often □ _____ □ _____ on my □ _____. And I sometimes □ _____ the □ _____.
W: Ah, so you have something to do the □ _____ □ _____.

10 전화 목적 파악

대화를 듣고, 여자가 남자에게 전화한 목적으로 가장 적절한 것을 고르시오.

① 숙제 검토를 요청하려고
② 보고서 작성을 요청하려고
③ 보고서 마감일을 물어보려고
④ 역사 시험 범위를 물어보려고
⑤ 여동생 돌보는 일을 부탁하려고

M: Hi, Sue. How's it going?
W: I'm good, Eric. Are you busy now?
M: A little. I'm □ _____ my baby □ _____.
W: □ _____ □ _____ □ _____ □ _____ I come over for a while?
M: □ _____ □ _____?
W: I want you to look at the □ _____ I □ _____ □ _____ □ _____ class.
M: Why do you want me to look at it?
W: You're the □ _____ □ _____ in class. I know you'll □ _____ some □ _____ in my paper.
M: Okay. You can come over now.

✎ **어휘복습** 잘 안 들리거나 몰라서 체크한 어휘를 써 놓고 복습해 보세요.

□ _____   □ _____   □ _____   □ _____
□ _____   □ _____   □ _____   □ _____
□ _____   □ _____   □ _____   □ _____

11 할 일 파악

대화를 듣고, 남자가 대화 직후에 할 일로 가장 적절한 것을 고르시오.

① 풍선 불기　　② 집안 꾸미기
③ 제과점 가기　　④ 케이크 만들기
⑤ 선물 찾으러 가기

W: Wow. The house □ _____ □ _____.
M: Thanks. I've been □ _____ □ _____ □ _____ for the past two hours.
W: Is it your birthday?
M: No, it's my brother's birthday.
W: Are you □ _____ a □ _____ for him today?
M: That's right. It's a □ _____ party, so I need to □ _____ everything □ _____ □ _____. He's coming home then.
W: Where's the □ _____?
M: Oh, I □ _____ □ _____ about it. I need to □ _____ □ _____ the □ _____. Can you put up □ _____ □ _____ □ _____ these balloons for me?
W: Sure. I'll do that while you're gone.

12 장소 추론

대화를 듣고, 두 사람이 대화하는 장소로 가장 적절한 곳을 고르시오.

① 유치원　　② 놀이공원
③ 전자제품 매장　　④ 서점
⑤ 장난감 가게

W: Are you looking for something?
M: Yes. I need to buy □ _____ □ _____ my □ _____ for Christmas.
W: □ _____ □ _____ is he?
M: He's □ _____ □ _____ old.
W: Does he enjoy □ _____? Here are some games he could □ _____.
M: I think those aren't □ _____ □ _____ him. Do you have any □ _____?
W: Yes, we have □ _____ □ _____ robots. Please □ _____ me, and I'll □ _____ you.

✏ **어휘복습**　잘 안 들리거나 몰라서 체크한 어휘를 써 놓고 복습해 보세요.

□ _____　　□ _____　　□ _____　　□ _____

□ _____　　□ _____　　□ _____　　□ _____

□ _____　　□ _____　　□ _____　　□ _____

13 어색한 대화 찾기

다음을 듣고, 두 사람의 대화가 <u>어색한</u> 것을 고르시오.

①   ②   ③   ④   ⑤

① W: ☐ _____ you ☐ _____ Alice yet?

    M: Yes, we talked after class today.

② W: When are you ☐ _____ ☐ _____ ☐ _____?

    M: For three days and two nights.

③ W: Do you know ☐ _____ ☐ _____ ☐ _____ ☐ _____?

    M: Sorry, but I'm not wearing a ☐ _____.

④ W: ☐ _____ ☐ _____ does John play sports?

    M: ☐ _____ ☐ _____ after school.

⑤ W: Could I ☐ _____ a pen, please?

    M: Sure, but you need to ☐ _____ it ☐ _____.

14 화제 추론

다음을 듣고, 남자가 하는 말의 내용으로 가장 적절한 것을 고르시오.

① 수리기사 모집
② 비상계단 위치
③ 건물 청소 일정
④ 엘리베이터 고장
⑤ 3층과 4층의 공사 일정

M: Everyone, please ☐ _____ ☐ _____. I'm very sorry, but there's a ☐ _____ ☐ _____ the ☐ _____. It's ☐ _____ ☐ _____ the third and fourth floors. A ☐ _____ is coming to look at it now. But he won't be here for about twenty minutes. Until he ☐ _____ the ☐ _____, you need to ☐ _____ ☐ _____ ☐ _____ to get to another floor. Please ☐ _____ ☐ _____. I ☐ _____ ☐ _____ this problem.

✎ **어휘복습** 잘 안 들리거나 몰라서 체크한 어휘를 써 놓고 복습해 보세요.

☐ _____   ☐ _____   ☐ _____   ☐ _____

☐ _____   ☐ _____   ☐ _____   ☐ _____

☐ _____   ☐ _____   ☐ _____   ☐ _____

15 미언급 파악

대화를 듣고, 여자가 한 일이 <u>아닌</u> 것을 고르시오.

① 수영하기
② 해돋이 보기
③ 사촌 만나기
④ 자전거 타기
⑤ 스키 타기

M: Did you enjoy the □ _____ □ _____ □ _____, Sally?

W: I had a great time. I □ _____ to the □ _____.

M: Did you see the □ _____ □ _____ on the □ _____ □ _____ of the year?

W: That's right. It was so beautiful.

M: What did you do after that?

W: My cousin and I □ _____ □ _____ even though it was cold. Then, we went to a □ _____ □ _____ later in the day.

M: You can ski? I didn't know that.

W: It was my □ _____ □ _____. I □ _____ some □ _____.

M: It □ _____ □ _____ you had a really □ _____ holiday.

16 내용 일치 파악

다음을 듣고, 내용과 일치하지 <u>않는</u> 것을 고르시오.

① 정육 코너에서 할인을 한다.
② 닭고기와 돼지고기는 할인 비율이 같다.
③ 쇠고기는 20% 할인해서 판매된다.
④ 상점은 이틀 동안 할인 판매를 한다.
⑤ 판매원들이 고객들을 도울 것이다.

W: Good afternoon, everyone, and □ _____ □ _____ Super Saver Mart. Right now, we've got a □ _____ □ _____ in the □ _____ □ _____. Fresh □ _____ and □ _____ are □ _____ □ _____ for □ _____ □ _____ □ _____, and you can □ _____ □ _____ percent on fresh □ _____ and □ _____. This sale is going to □ _____ □ _____ the next □ _____ □ _____. So go to the back of the store right now and □ _____ □ _____ the □ _____ in the meat section. They will help you get the □ _____ □ _____.

✎ **어휘복습** 잘 안 들리거나 몰라서 체크한 어휘를 써 놓고 복습해 보세요.

□ _____ □ _____ □ _____ □ _____

□ _____ □ _____ □ _____ □ _____

□ _____ □ _____ □ _____ □ _____

17 속담 추론

대화를 듣고, 상황을 가장 잘 표현한 속담을 고르시오.

① All that glitters is not gold.
② There's no place like home.
③ The early bird catches the worm.
④ Too many cooks spoil the broth.
⑤ If at first you don't succeed, try, try again.

W: □ _____ are you □ _____ so much, Joe?
M: I just came back from □ _____ □ _____. Coach Patterson said that I □ _____ the □ _____.
W: That's great news. □ _____.
M: Thanks a lot.
W: Wait a minute. You □ _____ □ _____ □ _____ □ _____ but didn't make the team, right?
M: That's right. But I □ _____ really □ _____ all year long.
W: Did you □ _____ a lot?
M: Yeah, I did. I really wanted to make the team. I'm glad that I practiced so much.

18 제안 파악

대화를 듣고, 남자가 여자에게 제안한 것으로 가장 적절한 것을 고르시오.

① 새 공책 사기
② 문구점에 가기
③ 숙제 적어 두기
④ 선생님께 사과하기
⑤ 보고서 오류 수정하기

M: It's already four, Sally. Why are you □ _____ □ _____ our □ _____?
W: I had to □ _____ □ _____ after class.
M: Did a teacher □ _____ you □ _____ □ _____ □ _____?
W: Yes, Mr. Harding □ _____ □ _____ □ _____ me today.
M: What happened?
W: I forgot to □ _____ □ _____ my □ _____ assignment. It's the □ _____ □ _____ this month I have □ _____.
M: You should □ _____ □ _____ your homework assignments □ _____ a □ _____. Then, you □ _____ forget them □ _____.
W: You're right. I'm going to buy a notebook this evening.
M: That's smart.

✎ **어휘복습** 잘 안 들리거나 몰라서 체크한 어휘를 써 놓고 복습해 보세요.

□ _____   □ _____   □ _____   □ _____
□ _____   □ _____   □ _____   □ _____
□ _____   □ _____   □ _____   □ _____

19 알맞은 응답 찾기

대화를 듣고, 남자의 마지막 말에 이어질 여자의 응답으로 가장 적절한 것을 고르시오.

Woman: _____
① This blouse was on sale.
② I just bought this new bag.
③ No, I haven't been there yet.
④ We're looking for some clothes.
⑤ Yes, that's what we're going to do.

W: I'm □ _____ □ _____ the Hamilton □ _____ □ _____ with Mindy this weekend.
M: □ _____ □ _____ you'll have a great time there.
W: □ _____ you □ _____ to the mall □ _____?
M: Yes, I have. I went there □ _____ the □ _____ it □ _____. My family and I spent a few hours there.
W: Mindy and I are planning to □ _____ □ _____ there. Then, we'll □ _____ some □ _____.
M: □ _____ are you thinking of □ _____?
W: _____

20 알맞은 응답 찾기

대화를 듣고, 여자의 마지막 말에 이어질 남자의 응답으로 가장 적절한 것을 고르시오.

Man: _____
① It's open 24 hours a day.
② Okay. I'm getting hungry, too.
③ Yes, that's where the store is.
④ Mom said dinner's almost ready.
⑤ Why don't we just make lunch?

W: I'm □ _____. I want something to eat now.
M: Mom said we're going to have dinner □ _____ about □ _____ □ _____.
W: I can't □ _____ that □ _____. What's □ _____ the □ _____?
M: I think you're going to be □ _____.
W: Why? Don't we have any food?
M: No, the refrigerator is □ _____ □ _____.
W: □ _____ □ _____ going to the □ _____ □ _____ on the corner?
M: _____

✎ **어휘복습** 잘 안 들리거나 몰라서 체크한 어휘를 써 놓고 복습해 보세요.

□ _____   □ _____   □ _____   □ _____
□ _____   □ _____   □ _____   □ _____
□ _____   □ _____   □ _____   □ _____

01 다음을 듣고, 내일의 날씨로 가장 적절한 것을 고르시오.

① ② ③ ④ ⑤

02 대화를 듣고, 남자의 아기를 고르시오.

① ② ③ ④ ⑤

03 다음을 듣고, 무엇에 관한 내용인지 가장 적절한 것을 고르시오.

① 인터넷 ② 컴퓨터
③ 스마트폰 ④ 이메일
⑤ 소셜 네트워크 서비스

04 대화를 듣고, 남자가 호텔 예약을 취소하는 이유로 가장 적절한 것을 고르시오.

① 호텔이 너무 비싸서
② 출장 날짜가 변경돼서
③ 주말에 여행할 수 없게 돼서
④ 친구의 집에 머물 예정이어서
⑤ 시드니에 더 좋은 호텔을 찾아서

05 대화를 듣고, 두 사람이 대화하는 장소로 가장 적절한 곳을 고르시오.

① 영화관 ② 미술관 ③ 산
④ 동물원 ⑤ 동물병원

06 대화를 듣고, 남자의 마지막 말의 의도로 가장 적절한 것을 고르시오.

① 제안 ② 감사 ③ 사과
④ 동의 ⑤ 격려

07 대화를 듣고, 여자가 남자에게 전화한 목적으로 가장 적절한 것을 고르시오.

① 직원에 대해 항의하려고
② 특별 배송을 요청하려고
③ 환불이 가능한지 알아보려고
④ 제품 세탁 방법을 물어보려고
⑤ 제품 교환 방법을 물어보려고

08 대화를 듣고, 두 사람의 관계로 가장 적절한 것을 고르시오.

① 승무원 – 승객
② 버스 기사 – 승객
③ 호텔 직원 – 숙박객
④ 여행 가이드 – 여행자
⑤ 박물관 매표원 – 관람객

09 대화를 듣고, 여자의 심정으로 가장 적절한 것을 고르시오.

① proud ② shocked
③ satisfied ④ confused
⑤ disappointed

10 대화를 듣고, 남자가 지불한 금액을 고르시오.

① $90 ② $105 ③ $120
④ $150 ⑤ $165

11 대화를 듣고, 여자가 대화 직후에 할 일로 가장 적절한 것을 고르시오.

① TV 보기 ② 빨래하기 ③ 숙제 끝내기
④ 공원에 가기 ⑤ 방 청소하기

12 다음을 듣고, 학교 축제에 관한 내용과 일치하는 것을 고르시오.

① 4월 24일에 열린다.
② 교사들이 연극을 선보인다.
③ 축구, 배구, 야구 경기가 펼쳐진다.
④ 벼룩시장이 열린다.
⑤ 재학생들만 입장할 수 있다.

13 대화를 듣고, 남자가 여자에게 부탁한 일로 가장 적절한 것을 고르시오.

① 함께 등산 가기
② 사진 찍어주기
③ 카메라 빌려주기
④ 단풍잎 가져다주기
⑤ 북한산 가는 길 알려주기

14 다음을 듣고, 과학 동아리에 관한 내용과 일치하지 <u>않는</u> 것을 고르시오.

① 학기마다 현장학습을 간다.
② 과학실에서 실험을 할 수 있다.
③ 야외에서 지역의 동식물을 공부한다.
④ 과학 다큐멘터리를 제작한다.
⑤ 회장은 투표로 선출된다.

15 대화를 듣고, 남자가 개를 좋아하는 이유로 언급하지 <u>않은</u> 것을 고르시오.

① 재미있어서
② 다정해서
③ 집을 잘 지켜서
④ 활동적이어서
⑤ 부르면 곁으로 와서

16 다음을 듣고, 두 사람의 대화가 <u>어색한</u> 것을 고르시오.
①　　②　　③　　④　　⑤

17 다음을 듣고, 도표의 내용과 일치하지 <u>않는</u> 것을 고르시오.

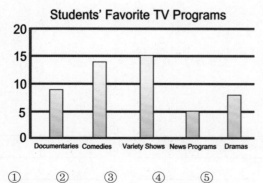

Students' Favorite TV Programs

①　　②　　③　　④　　⑤

[18-19] 대화를 듣고, 여자의 마지막 말에 이어질 남자의 응답으로 가장 적절한 것을 고르시오.

18 Man: _____

① Sure. We can try to erase the writing from the walls.
② That should work. Let's write the note now.
③ Okay. I'll stop doing that from now on.
④ What did you just write on the wall?
⑤ Yes, I'm going up to the fifth floor.

19 Man: _____

① I'm at the market right now.
② No, I didn't buy any of them.
③ Would you mind doing that?
④ Yes, I'm cooking green peppers.
⑤ Okay. What do you want from the market?

20 다음 상황 설명을 듣고, 엄마가 Kate에게 할 말로 가장 적절한 것을 고르시오.

Mom: _____

① Your teacher called and said you did a great job.
② Try rewriting your presentation to make it better.
③ I'm so proud of you. You didn't get nervous at all.
④ I think this is the best present you've ever given me.
⑤ Forget about everyone watching you and do your best.

01 날씨 파악

다음을 듣고, 내일의 날씨로 가장 적절한 것을 고르시오.

① ② ③
④ ⑤

W: Good evening. It's six thirty, so it's time to □ _____ you □ _____ □ _____ □ _____ the weather. The □ _____ is □ _____ now, so it's going to be □ _____ the rest of the □ _____. The skies are □ _____ □ _____, but they'll be □ _____ in a few hours. It looks like there's a winter □ _____ □ _____. It's going to □ _____ □ _____ □ _____ □ _____, but the rain will □ _____ □ _____ □ _____ the day after tomorrow. It looks like we're going to have bad weather for the next few days.

02 그림 정보 파악

대화를 듣고, 남자의 아기를 고르시오.

① ② ③ ④ ⑤

W: □ _____ □ _____ everyone in this □ _____.
M: We had a □ _____ □ _____ last month. There are many babies in that picture.
W: That □ _____ with the □ _____ in her hand is □ _____. Is she your □ _____?
M: No, she's my □ _____. She's my sister's daughter.
W: □ _____ one of them is □ _____ then? Is she the one who is □ _____?
M: No, that's my cousin's daughter. My daughter has a □ _____ □ _____ □ _____ □ _____ her □ _____.
W: Wow. She looks □ _____.
M: Thanks for saying that.

✎ **어휘복습** 잘 안 들리거나 몰라서 체크한 어휘를 써 놓고 복습해 보세요.

□ _____ □ _____ □ _____ □ _____
□ _____ □ _____ □ _____ □ _____
□ _____ □ _____ □ _____ □ _____

03 화제 추론

다음을 듣고, 무엇에 관한 내용인지 가장 적절한 것을 고르시오.

① 인터넷
② 컴퓨터
③ 스마트폰
④ 이메일
⑤ 소셜 네트워크 서비스

W: This is something that people □ _____ the □ _____ can □ _____. They use this to □ _____ □ _____ about all kinds of things. They also use this to □ _____ items and to □ _____ □ _____ their friends and family members. Many people use this □ _____ their □ _____, and lots of other people use this with their □ _____. This is very □ _____ nowadays, so people don't like being without this for a long period of time.

04 이유 파악

대화를 듣고, 남자가 호텔 예약을 취소하는 이유로 가장 적절한 것을 고르시오.

① 호텔이 너무 비싸서
② 출장 날짜가 변경돼서
③ 주말에 여행할 수 없게 돼서
④ 친구의 집에 머물 예정이어서
⑤ 시드니에 더 좋은 호텔을 찾아서

W: Good morning. This is the Prince □ _____. How may I help you?

M: Hello. My □ _____ is Tim Stuart. I □ _____ a □ _____ at your hotel.

W: Yes, Mr. Stuart. How can I help you?

M: I'm very □ _____, □ _____ I have to □ _____ my reservation.

W: Is there a problem?

M: I have to □ _____ this □ _____, so I □ _____ □ _____ □ _____ a □ _____.

W: I'm very sorry to hear that, Mr. Stuart. I □ _____ you can □ _____ □ _____ us the □ _____ □ _____ you come to Sydney.

M: I hope so, too. Thank you.

✎ **어휘복습** 잘 안 들리거나 몰라서 체크한 어휘를 써 놓고 복습해 보세요.

□ _____   □ _____   □ _____   □ _____

□ _____   □ _____   □ _____   □ _____

□ _____   □ _____   □ _____   □ _____

05 장소 추론

대화를 듣고, 두 사람이 대화하는 장소로 가장 적절한 곳을 고르시오.

① 영화관   ② 미술관   ③ 산
④ 동물원   ⑤ 동물병원

M: Wow, today is □ _____ □ _____ □ _____ day.

W: I agree. I'm glad we decided to come here □ _____ □ _____ going to the movies.

M: I □ _____ □ _____ □ _____ way. This is one of the nicest days in summer. It's good to be □ _____.

W: So where should we □ _____ □ _____?

M: I'd like to stay outdoors □ _____ □ _____ □ _____, so let's see the □ _____.

W: All right. They're near the □ _____, and I want to see them. They're my favorite animals.

M: Let's □ _____ the □ _____ house though. I'm scared of those animals.

W: Sure. I □ _____ want to see them □ _____.

06 의도 파악

대화를 듣고, 남자의 마지막 말의 의도로 가장 적절한 것을 고르시오.

① 제안   ② 감사   ③ 사과
④ 동의   ⑤ 격려

M: Mina, are you going to □ _____ your □ _____ to school tomorrow?

W: I can't. It's □ _____ □ _____ for me □ _____ □ _____.

M: But we need to do our □ _____ □ _____ tomorrow. And all of the □ _____ are on your laptop.

W: What should I do then?

M: Well, I can ask Gary to bring his.

W: And □ _____ □ _____ the files?

M: □ _____ them to a □ _____ □ _____ and bring that with you when you come to school.

✎ **어휘복습** 잘 안 들리거나 몰라서 체크한 어휘를 써 놓고 복습해 보세요.

□ _____   □ _____   □ _____   □ _____

□ _____   □ _____   □ _____   □ _____

□ _____   □ _____   □ _____   □ _____

대화를 듣고, 여자가 남자에게 전화한 목적
으로 가장 적절한 것을 고르시오.

① 직원에 대해 항의하려고
② 특별 배송을 요청하려고
③ 환불이 가능한지 알아보려고
④ 제품 세탁 방법을 물어보려고
⑤ 제품 교환 방법을 물어보려고

M: Hello. This is the Fairway Department Store.
W: Hi. I'm □ _____ □ _____ an □ _____ I bought there today.
M: Sure. □ _____ did you □ _____?
W: I bought a pair of □ _____ □ _____.
M: Is there a □ _____ □ _____ them?
W: Yes, there is. They're the □ _____ □ _____. Is it □ _____ to □ _____ them?
M: Of course. Simply □ _____ the jeans and the □ _____ to the store. A salesperson can □ _____ you □ _____.
W: Where should I take them?
M: Go to the returns desk □ _____ □ _____ □ _____ □ _____.

대화를 듣고, 두 사람의 관계로 가장 적절한
것을 고르시오.

① 승무원 – 승객
② 버스 기사 – 승객
③ 호텔 직원 – 숙박객
④ 여행 가이드 – 여행자
⑤ 박물관 매표원 – 관람객

W: □ _____ are you □ _____ your time in Shanghai?
M: It's a very □ _____ city. I really like it here.
W: Is your hotel □ _____?
M: Yes, it is. It's □ _____ right □ _____ the □ _____, so it has a □ _____ □ _____.
W: I'm glad to hear that.
M: So what are we going to □ _____ □ _____?
W: When everyone □ _____ □ _____ to the □ _____, we're going to □ _____ □ _____.
M: And after lunch?
W: We'll visit the best □ _____ in the □ _____ □ _____.

✎ 어휘복습 잘 안 들리거나 몰라서 체크한 어휘를 써 놓고 복습해 보세요.

□ _____   □ _____   □ _____   □ _____
□ _____   □ _____   □ _____   □ _____
□ _____   □ _____   □ _____   □ _____

09 심정 추론

대화를 듣고, 여자의 심정으로 가장 적절한 것을 고르시오.

① proud
② shocked
③ satisfied
④ confused
⑤ disappointed

M: How was your □ _____ at the new Italian □ _____?

W: It was an □ _____ □ _____.

M: Why do you say that?

W: Well, the restaurant itself was beautiful. It was □ _____ □ _____ many beautiful □ _____.

M: How was the food?

W: The lasagna I had □ _____ □ _____. But there was only a □ _____ □ _____.

M: What's that?

W: I □ _____ spaghetti. But the waiter brought me the □ _____ □ _____, and then he wouldn't □ _____. He □ _____ my □ _____.

10 숫자 정보 파악

대화를 듣고, 남자가 지불한 금액을 고르시오.

① $90　② $105　③ $120
④ $150　⑤ $165

W: Are those new □ _____ you are wearing, Mark?

M: Yes. They just □ _____ □ _____.

W: Did you □ _____ them □ _____?

M: That's right. I love online □ _____.

W: How was the □ _____?

M: The shoes □ _____ □ _____ □ _____ □ _____ dollars □ _____ a shoe □ _____, but they □ _____ cost me □ _____ dollars online.

W: That's a great □ _____. Did you have to □ _____ □ _____ □ _____, or was it □ _____?

M: I was □ _____ □ _____ dollars for delivery since I requested □ _____ □ _____.

✎ **어휘복습** 잘 안 들리거나 몰라서 체크한 어휘를 써 놓고 복습해 보세요.

□ _____　□ _____　□ _____　□ _____

□ _____　□ _____　□ _____　□ _____

□ _____　□ _____　□ _____　□ _____

11 할 일 파악

대화를 듣고, 여자가 대화 직후에 할 일로 가장 적절한 것을 고르시오.

① TV 보기
② 빨래하기
③ 숙제 끝내기
④ 공원에 가기
⑤ 방 청소하기

M: What are you planning to do □ _____ □ _____?

W: I was □ _____ □ _____ just watching TV and □ _____.

M: Don't you have any □ _____ to do?

W: Not today. I □ _____ my □ _____ and □ _____ the □ _____ in the morning.

M: In that case, □ _____ □ _____ going to the □ _____?

W: What do you want to do there?

M: We could go to the □ _____ and relax □ _____ the □ _____.

W: That sounds good. But I have to □ _____ my □ _____ □ _____. Can we do that in thirty minutes?

M: All right.

12 내용 일치 파악

다음을 듣고, 학교 축제에 관한 내용과 일치하는 것을 고르시오.

① 4월 24일에 열린다.
② 교사들이 연극을 선보인다.
③ 축구, 배구, 야구 경기가 펼쳐진다.
④ 벼룩시장이 열린다.
⑤ 재학생들만 입장할 수 있다.

M: May I □ _____ your □ _____, please? Remember that the □ _____ □ _____ will be on April twenty fifth. That's the day □ _____ □ _____ □ _____ finish. The festival is going to be lots of fun. There will be a □ _____ performed □ _____ some □ _____. We'll play □ _____ such as □ _____, □ _____, and □ _____. There will be a □ _____ and □ _____ □ _____. And we'll have a □ _____ □ _____ as well. Your □ _____ and □ _____ can come to the festival, so please □ _____ them.

✏ 어휘복습 잘 안 들리거나 몰라서 체크한 어휘를 써 놓고 복습해 보세요.

□ _____ □ _____ □ _____ □ _____
□ _____ □ _____ □ _____ □ _____
□ _____ □ _____ □ _____ □ _____

13 부탁 파악

대화를 듣고, 남자가 여자에게 부탁한 일로 가장 적절한 것을 고르시오.

① 함께 등산 가기
② 사진 찍어주기
③ 카메라 빌려주기
④ 단풍잎 가져다주기
⑤ 복한산 가는 길 알려주기

M: □ _____ you □ _____ □ _____ □ _____ Bukhan Mountain?

W: No, I □ _____. Is it nice?

M: It is, and it's near Seoul, so it's □ _____ to □ _____ □ _____.

W: Are you □ _____ to go there □ _____?

M: Yes, my friends and I are going □ _____ there this Saturday.

W: Really? That sounds fun.

M: By the way, would you □ _____ □ _____ me your □ _____?

W: □ _____ □ _____ □ _____. The leaves must be very colorful there □ _____ □ _____ □ _____ □ _____.

M: Exactly. We'd like to □ _____ some nice □ _____ □ _____ we are at the □ _____.

14 내용 일치 파악

다음을 듣고, 과학 동아리에 관한 내용과 일치하지 <u>않는</u> 것을 고르시오.

① 학기마다 현장학습을 간다.
② 과학실에서 실험을 할 수 있다.
③ 야외에서 지역의 동식물을 공부한다.
④ 과학 다큐멘터리를 제작한다.
⑤ 회장은 투표로 선출된다.

W: Thank you for □ _____ the first □ _____ of the school's science □ _____. We have many □ _____ □ _____ planned for this year. Each □ _____, we'll go on a □ _____ □ _____. We're going to do some science □ _____ in the □ _____ as well. We'll go on some nature hikes to □ _____ □ _____ the □ _____ and □ _____ in our region, and we're planning to □ _____ some great science □ _____. But first, we □ _____ □ _____ □ _____ the club □ _____.

✎ **어휘복습** 잘 안 들리거나 몰라서 체크한 어휘를 써 놓고 복습해 보세요.

□ _____ □ _____ □ _____ □ _____
□ _____ □ _____ □ _____ □ _____
□ _____ □ _____ □ _____ □ _____

대화를 듣고, 남자가 개를 좋아하는 이유로
언급하지 <u>않은</u> 것을 고르시오.

① 재미있어서
② 다정해서
③ 집을 잘 지켜서
④ 활동적이어서
⑤ 부르면 곁으로 와서

W: Do you □ _____ any □ _____?
M: Sure. I have □ _____ □ _____.
W: Three? You must really like dogs.
M: That's right. Dogs are lots of □ _____. They're very
□ _____, too.
W: Don't you like □ _____?
M: I □ _____ □ _____ cats. They often □ _____ and
□ _____ people.
W: Dogs do that □ _____.
M: Not my dogs. My dogs □ _____ □ _____, so we go to the
park and play a lot. That's fun. Cats can't do that.
W: You've □ _____ □ _____ good □ _____.
M: And my dogs □ _____ □ _____ to me when I □ _____
them.

16 어색한 대화 찾기

다음을 듣고, 두 사람의 대화가 <u>어색한</u> 것을
고르시오.

①   ②   ③   ④   ⑤

① M: □ _____ should we □ _____ to the museum?
W: We can □ _____ the □ _____ or the □ _____.
② M: □ _____ does your uncle □ _____ now?
W: He just □ _____ □ _____ a city in China.
③ M: Do you think you can □ _____ □ _____ to the
restaurant □ _____ □ _____?
W: I'm □ _____ a □ _____ now.
④ M: □ _____ our □ _____ going to be □ _____?
W: It's on chapters □ _____ and □ _____.
⑤ M: When is your □ _____?
W: It's on the □ _____ □ _____ of November.

✏ **어휘복습** 잘 안 들리거나 몰라서 체크한 어휘를 써 놓고 복습해 보세요.

□ _____   □ _____   □ _____   □ _____
□ _____   □ _____   □ _____   □ _____
□ _____   □ _____   □ _____   □ _____

17 도표 · 실용문 파악

다음을 듣고, 도표의 내용과 일치하지 <u>않는</u>
것을 고르시오.

Students' Favorite TV Programs

① ② ③ ④ ⑤

① □ _____ are □ _____ as popular as □ _____ □ _____.

② Students □ _____ variety shows □ _____ comedies.

③ □ _____ □ _____ popular programs are variety shows.

④ News programs are the □ _____ □ _____ shows with
students.

⑤ Dramas are □ _____ □ _____ popular □ _____
documentaries.

18 알맞은 응답 찾기

대화를 듣고, 여자의 마지막 말에 이어질 남
자의 응답으로 가장 적절한 것을 고르시오.

Man: _____

① Sure. We can try to erase the
   writing from the walls.
② That should work. Let's write
   the note now.
③ Okay. I'll stop doing that from
   now on.
④ What did you just write on the
   wall?
⑤ Yes, I'm going up to the fifth
   floor.

W: Look at this. I □ _____ □ _____ it.

M: What's the □ _____?

W: So many people □ _____ □ _____ the □ _____ in this
   □ _____ building. I hate that.

M: Why would people do that?

W: They think it's funny. But it really just □ _____ the
   □ _____ look □ _____.

M: Do you think we can □ _____ □ _____ □ _____ did it?

W: Probably not. But we can □ _____ a □ _____ by the
   elevator □ _____ people not to write on the walls any
   more.

M: _____

✎ **어휘복습** 잘 안 들리거나 몰라서 체크한 어휘를 써 놓고 복습해 보세요.

□ _____   □ _____   □ _____   □ _____

□ _____   □ _____   □ _____   □ _____

□ _____   □ _____   □ _____   □ _____

19 알맞은 응답 찾기

대화를 듣고, 여자의 마지막 말에 이어질 남자의 응답으로 가장 적절한 것을 고르시오.

Man: _____

① I'm at the market right now.
② No, I didn't buy any of them.
③ Would you mind doing that?
④ Yes, I'm cooking green peppers.
⑤ Okay. What do you want from the market?

W: Hi, Jim. What are you doing right now?
M: I'm □ _____ □ _____ for my parents.
W: That's really □ _____ □ _____ □ _____.
M: They are both □ _____ home □ _____ □ _____, so I decided to do the cooking since they will be □ _____.
W: What are you making?
M: I'm making spaghetti □ _____ □ _____ □ _____. But I just □ _____ I don't have any green peppers.
W: Do you want me to □ _____ □ _____ the □ _____ and buy some?
M: _____

20 상황에 적절한 말 찾기

다음 상황 설명을 듣고, 엄마가 Kate에게 할 말로 가장 적절한 것을 고르시오.

Mom: _____

① Your teacher called and said you did a great job.
② Try rewriting your presentation to make it better.
③ I'm so proud of you. You didn't get nervous at all.
④ I think this is the best present you've ever given me.
⑤ Forget about everyone watching you and do your best.

M: Kate has to □ _____ a □ _____ to her □ _____ tomorrow. She is □ _____ □ _____ writing, but she □ _____ very □ _____ speaking in front of people. Before she makes her presentations, she always starts to □ _____, and her □ _____ □ _____. She also has □ _____ □ _____ since she □ _____ what she's going to say. In this situation, what would Kate's mom most likely say to her to encourage her?
Mom: _____

✏ **어휘복습** 잘 안 들리거나 몰라서 체크한 어휘를 써 놓고 복습해 보세요.

□ _____   □ _____   □ _____   □ _____
□ _____   □ _____   □ _____   □ _____
□ _____   □ _____   □ _____   □ _____

01 대화를 듣고, 여자의 마지막 말의 의도로 가장 적절한 것을 고르시오.

① 꾸중   ② 설득   ③ 허락
④ 격려   ⑤ 축하

02 대화를 듣고, 주말의 날씨로 가장 적절한 것을 고르시오.

①   ②   ③   ④   ⑤

03 대화를 듣고, 여자의 마지막 말에 드러난 심정으로 가장 적절한 것을 고르시오.

① happy   ② excited
③ nervous   ④ shocked
⑤ concerned

04 대화를 듣고, 두 사람이 대화하는 장소로 가장 적절한 곳을 고르시오.

① 공항   ② 여행사
③ 중국 음식점   ④ 중국 대사관
⑤ 신용카드 회사

05 다음을 듣고, 무엇에 관한 내용인지 가장 적절한 것을 고르시오.

① 오페라   ② 인형극   ③ 오디션
④ 콘서트   ⑤ 뮤지컬

06 대화를 듣고, 남자가 대화 직후에 할 일로 가장 적절한 것을 고르시오.

① 학교 가기   ② 영어책 사기
③ 영어 숙제하기   ④ 여자의 집에 가기
⑤ 친구에게 전화하기

07 다음을 듣고, 여자가 메시지를 남긴 이유로 가장 적절한 것을 고르시오.

① 자신이 여행 중임을 알리려고
② 메시지를 남겨 달라고 말하려고
③ 전화번호를 남겨 달라고 말하려고
④ 자신의 휴대폰 번호를 알려주려고
⑤ 나중에 다시 전화해줄 것을 요청하려고

08 대화를 듣고, 남자가 지불할 금액을 고르시오.

① $12   ② $15   ③ $20
④ $27   ⑤ $35

09 대화를 듣고, 여자가 남자에게 전화한 목적으로 가장 적절한 것을 고르시오.

① 병원 진료를 예약하려고
② 송별회 장소를 물어보려고
③ 친구의 전화번호를 물어보려고
④ 파티에 불참한 이유를 설명하려고
⑤ 병원에 데려가 줄 것을 부탁하려고

10 다음을 듣고, 기차표를 구매할 때 세 번째로 해야 하는 것을 고르시오.

① 시간과 목적지 확인하기
② 기차 선택하기
③ 좌석 선택하기
④ 지불 방법 선택하기
⑤ 엔터 버튼 누르기

11 대화를 듣고, 두 사람이 하는 말의 내용으로 가장 적절한 것을 고르시오.

① 소송 사건   ② 고아원 설립
③ 자원봉사 신청   ④ 익명의 기부자
⑤ 저축 잘하는 법

12 대화를 듣고, 미술관에 관해 언급되지 <u>않은</u> 것을 고르시오.

① 전시회는 2층에서 열린다.
② 엘리베이터가 여러 대 있다.
③ 전시품에 대한 사진 촬영은 허용되지 않는다.
④ 기념품점에서 그림의 사진을 판매한다.
⑤ 평일 7시에 문을 닫는다.

13 대화를 듣고, 남자가 여자에게 부탁한 일로 가장 적절한 것을 고르시오.

① 택시 잡기
② 함께 가게에 가기
③ 옷 가격 할인해주기
④ 카페 위치 알려주기
⑤ 아내의 옷 함께 고르기

14 대화를 듣고, 남자가 주말에 한 일로 가장 적절한 것을 고르시오.

① 생일 파티에 갔다.
② 시험 공부를 했다.
③ 영어 에세이를 썼다.
④ 생일선물을 샀다.
⑤ 새 노트북을 샀다.

15 다음을 듣고, 광고문의 내용과 일치하지 <u>않는</u> 것을 고르시오.

> **For Rent**
> 2-bedroom house; the house has a
> living room, a kitchen, and a bathroom;
> the house is furnished with 2 beds, a
> sofa, a dining table, and four chairs
> Rent: $400 per month
> Telephone: 409-3423
> No pets are allowed.

①   ②   ③   ④   ⑤

16 대화를 듣고, 두 사람의 관계로 가장 적절한 것을 고르시오.

① 요리사 – 손님   ② 웨이터 – 손님
③ 승무원 – 승객   ④ 배달원 – 손님
⑤ 호텔 직원 – 손님

17 다음을 듣고, 두 사람의 대화가 <u>어색한</u> 것을 고르시오.

①   ②   ③   ④   ⑤

18 다음을 듣고, 시험에 관한 내용과 일치하지 <u>않는</u> 것을 고르시오.

① 내일은 중간고사가 있다.
② 제시간에 시작해야 완료할 가능성이 크다.
③ 검정색 펜을 준비해야 한다.
④ 연필을 사용할 수 없다.
⑤ 모든 문제가 쉽게 출제될 것이다.

[19-20] 대화를 듣고, 남자의 마지막 말에 이어질 여자의 응답으로 가장 적절한 것을 고르시오.

19 Woman: _____

① How about getting Chinese food for a change?
② Okay. That's exactly what I was thinking.
③ I'd love something from Pizza Express.
④ No, I haven't had anything for dinner.
⑤ Yes, I already ordered.

20 Woman: _____

① No, I didn't send a package to anyone.
② Sorry, but I haven't packed my bags yet.
③ You should leave it with the security guard.
④ Yes, I'm going to be home ten minutes from now.
⑤ I'm at home now. You can come here and drop it off.

다시 듣고, 빈칸에 알맞은 단어를 써 보세요.

◀◎)) **MP3 실전 16-1**

01 의도 파악

대화를 듣고, 여자의 마지막 말의 의도로 가장 적절한 것을 고르시오.

① 추궁 ② 설득 ③ 허락
④ 격려 ⑤ 축하

W: What are you □ _____ □ _____ in your bag?
M: I'm trying to find my □ _____ □ _____.
W: Did you □ _____ it □ _____?
M: Yes, I don't know □ _____ □ _____ □ _____. I guess I'll have to go to the □ _____ □ _____ □ _____ Office. Maybe someone □ _____ it □ _____.
W: You ought to □ _____ a □ _____. Let's go to the store and buy one right now.
M: A wallet? Do I really need that?
W: Listen. Aren't you □ _____ and □ _____ □ _____ losing your ID? □ _____ you □ _____ a wallet, you can □ _____ your ID and other cards □ _____ □ _____ □ _____ □ _____.

02 날씨 파악

대화를 듣고, 주말의 날씨로 가장 적절한 것을 고르시오.

① ② ③
④ ⑤

M: I'm so happy that □ _____ is finally □ _____.
W: So am I. I'm looking forward to □ _____ and □ _____ □ _____.
M: Mark and I are □ _____ □ _____ the □ _____ this □ _____. We're going to □ _____ □ _____.
W: That sounds like fun, but have you □ _____ the □ _____ □ _____?
M: No, why? Is it going to □ _____?
W: I just saw it. We're □ _____ to get □ _____ weather all weekend. Will that □ _____ you □ _____ surfing?
M: Actually, it will help □ _____ the □ _____ □ _____.
W: It looks like you're going to □ _____ a □ _____ □ _____ then.

✎ **어휘복습** 잘 안 들리거나 몰라서 체크한 어휘를 써 놓고 복습해 보세요.

□ _____ □ _____ □ _____ □ _____
□ _____ □ _____ □ _____ □ _____
□ _____ □ _____ □ _____ □ _____

03 심정 추론

대화를 듣고, 여자의 마지막 말에 드러난 심정으로 가장 적절한 것을 고르시오.

① happy　　　② excited
③ nervous　　④ shocked
⑤ concerned

M: □ _____ are you □ _____ so much, Dana?

W: I'm □ _____ □ _____ □ _____ this afternoon.

M: What are you going to do?

W: I'm going to □ _____ □ _____ for that □ _____ □ _____ on TV. I want to become a □ _____.

M: Are you □ _____ □ _____ the □ _____ *Who Wants to Be a Singer*?

W: Right. □ _____ □ _____ □ _____ I'm going to try out for.

M: The □ _____ for that program was yesterday. My friend Jeff □ _____ □ _____ to the □ _____ □ _____.

W: You aren't □ _____, are you? I □ _____ □ _____ I □ _____ it.

04 장소 추론

대화를 듣고, 두 사람이 대화하는 장소로 가장 적절한 곳을 고르시오.

① 공항　　　　② 여행사
③ 중국 음식점　④ 중국 대사관
⑤ 신용카드 회사

W: Good afternoon.

M: Hi. How can I help you?

W: I need to □ _____ a □ _____ for a □ _____ to □ _____.

M: All right. Are you □ _____ on □ _____ there?

W: Yes. I need to go there □ _____ □ _____ □ _____.

M: Do you already have a □ _____ □ _____ China?

W: No, I don't. Can you □ _____ me □ _____ that □ _____ □ _____?

M: Yes, we can get you a visa. But it will □ _____ □ _____ dollars to do that.

✎ **어휘복습** 잘 안 들리거나 몰라서 체크한 어휘를 써 놓고 복습해 보세요.

□ _____　　□ _____　　□ _____　　□ _____

□ _____　　□ _____　　□ _____　　□ _____

□ _____　　□ _____　　□ _____　　□ _____

05 화제 추론

다음을 듣고, 무엇에 관한 내용인지 가장 적절한 것을 고르시오.

① 오페라　② 인형극　③ 오디션
④ 콘서트　⑤ 뮤지컬

M: This is a □ _____ that people give □ _____ a □ _____.
This □ _____ a □ _____ that the □ _____ tell.
Sometimes this is a □ _____ story, and other times it's
a □ _____. But the actors don't speak their □ _____.
Instead, they □ _____ them. This also □ _____ an
□ _____. The orchestra □ _____ □ _____ while the
performers sing.

06 할 일 파악

대화를 듣고, 남자가 대화 직후에 할 일로 가장 적절한 것을 고르시오.

① 학교 가기
② 영어책 사기
③ 영어 숙제하기
④ 여자의 집에 가기
⑤ 친구에게 전화하기

W: Hello.
M: Hi, Karen. It's Joe. I didn't go to school today, so could you
□ _____ my English □ _____ home □ _____ □ _____?
I can □ _____ □ _____ your house and □ _____ it
□ _____ later.
W: Sorry, Joe, but I'm □ _____ □ _____ □ _____ now.
I □ _____ twenty minutes ago.
M: Oh, no. I □ _____ you □ _____ □ _____. □ _____
should I □ _____ □ _____ my English homework?
W: I can □ _____ you my book □ _____ this □ _____.
M: □ _____ □ _____ can you do that?
W: Around eight. I will be □ _____ with my homework
□ _____ □ _____.
M: That's □ _____ □ _____ for me. I'd better call someone
else to □ _____ □ _____ □ _____.
W: Talk to Jenny. She's still at school, and she lives □ _____
your □ _____. Maybe she can bring your book to you.
M: Thanks for □ _____ □ _____ □ _____. I'll do that right
now.
W: Good luck.

✎ **어휘복습** 잘 안 들리거나 몰라서 체크한 어휘를 써 놓고 복습해 보세요.

□ _____　□ _____　□ _____　□ _____

□ _____　□ _____　□ _____　□ _____

□ _____　□ _____　□ _____　□ _____

다음을 듣고, 여자가 메시지를 남긴 이유로 가장 적절한 것을 고르시오.

① 자신이 여행 중임을 알리려고
② 메시지를 남겨 달라고 말하려고
③ 전화번호를 남겨 달라고 말하려고
④ 자신의 휴대폰 번호를 알려주려고
⑤ 나중에 다시 전화해줄 것을 요청하려고

W: Hello. □ _____ □ _____ Mary Sanders. I'm really sorry, but I □ _____ □ _____ your □ _____ at this moment. I'm □ _____ in class □ _____ doing something else important. If you □ _____ a □ _____ □ _____ for me, I'll listen to it and □ _____ you □ _____ at once. Or you can just □ _____ a □ _____ message to my □ _____. Thanks for □ _____ me □ _____ □ _____. Goodbye.

대화를 듣고, 남자가 지불할 금액을 고르시오.

① $12   ② $15   ③ $20
④ $27   ⑤ $35

M: Look at all of these □ _____.
W: □ _____ are you going to □ _____?
M: Well, the □ _____ pie looks □ _____, and it only □ _____ □ _____ dollars.
W: How about the □ _____ pie for □ _____ dollars?
M: I love cherry, □ _____ my □ _____ □ _____, so I shouldn't buy it.
W: Oh, look □ _____ □ _____. There's a □ _____ pie, and it's only □ _____ dollars.
M: That's a □ _____ □ _____. I'm □ _____ going to □ _____ that.
W: Are you going to buy □ _____ □ _____ □ _____ pie?
M: Why not? The □ _____ here are □ _____. I'll get the strawberry pie, too.

✎ **어휘복습** 잘 안 들리거나 몰라서 체크한 어휘를 써 놓고 복습해 보세요.

□ _____   □ _____   □ _____   □ _____
□ _____   □ _____   □ _____   □ _____
□ _____   □ _____   □ _____   □ _____

09 전화 목적 파악

대화를 듣고, 여자가 남자에게 전화한 목적으로 가장 적절한 것을 고르시오.

① 병원 진료를 예약하려고
② 송별회 장소를 물어보려고
③ 친구의 전화번호를 물어보려고
④ 파티에 불참한 이유를 설명하려고
⑤ 병원에 데려가 줄 것을 부탁하려고

W: Hello, Jake.

M: Hey, Julie. Are you □ _____ □ _____? We missed you at Tom's □ _____ □ _____.

W: □ _____ □ _____ I'm calling. I'm really □ _____ that I □ _____ it. I want to □ _____ □ _____ Tom.

M: He was □ _____ you didn't □ _____ □ _____. What happened?

W: I suddenly □ _____ really □ _____ around lunchtime. I felt □ _____, so I □ _____ □ _____ on the sofa. Then, I □ _____ □ _____.

M: Did you just □ _____ □ _____ now?

W: Yes, but I still □ _____ □ _____ □ _____. I think I'm going to □ _____ the □ _____ soon.

M: Yeah, □ _____ □ _____ do that.

10 특정 정보 파악

다음을 듣고, 기차표를 구매할 때 세 번째로 해야 하는 것을 고르시오.

① 시간과 목적지 확인하기
② 기차 선택하기
③ 좌석 선택하기
④ 지불 방법 선택하기
⑤ 엔터 버튼 누르기

W: It's very □ _____ to use this machine to □ _____ a □ _____ □ _____. □ _____ □ _____ □ _____ you what to do. □ _____, you need to □ _____ the □ _____ and □ _____ of the train that you want. □ _____, □ _____ the train that you want to □ _____. □ _____ □ _____, choose the □ _____ you want to sit in. You can □ _____ an □ _____ or □ _____ seat. □ _____, □ _____ the □ _____ to □ _____ either cash or with a credit card and □ _____ the '□ _____' button. It's simple.

✎ **어휘복습** 잘 안 들리거나 몰라서 체크한 어휘를 써 놓고 복습해 보세요.

□ _____ □ _____ □ _____ □ _____

□ _____ □ _____ □ _____ □ _____

□ _____ □ _____ □ _____ □ _____

11 화제 추론

대화를 듣고, 두 사람이 하는 말의 내용으로 가장 적절한 것을 고르시오.

① 소송 사건
② 고아원 설립
③ 자원봉사 신청
④ 익명의 기부자
⑤ 저축 잘하는 법

M: Did you see the □ _____ today?
W: No, I missed it. Did □ _____ □ _____ happen?
M: □ _____, there was some □ _____ news.
W: Really? Tell me □ _____ □ _____.
M: Do you know the □ _____ downtown?
W: Sure. I □ _____ there □ _____ □ _____.
M: Well, somebody □ _____ one □ _____ dollars to the orphanage today.
W: That's □ _____. Who did that?
M: Nobody knows. A □ _____ went there □ _____ a □ _____ and said that his □ _____ didn't want anybody to □ _____ his □ _____.
W: □ _____ □ _____. I love it when people do things like that.

12 미언급 파악

대화를 듣고, 미술관에 관해 언급되지 않은 것을 고르시오.

① 전시회는 2층에서 열린다.
② 엘리베이터가 여러 대 있다.
③ 전시품에 대한 사진 촬영은 허용되지 않는다.
④ 기념품점에서 그림의 사진을 판매한다.
⑤ 평일 7시에 문을 닫는다.

W: Hello. Can you tell me □ _____ the □ _____ □ _____ is?
M: You need to □ _____ □ _____ the □ _____ □ _____ for that. Just □ _____ □ _____ ahead and go □ _____ the □ _____.
W: Thank you. Are visitors □ _____ to □ _____ □ _____?
M: I'm □ _____, □ _____ □ _____ is not allowed. You can □ _____ □ _____ or □ _____ of the paintings in the □ _____ □ _____ though.
W: That's □ _____ □ _____ □ _____.
M: Do you have any other questions?
W: Yes, one more. □ _____ □ _____ does the museum □ _____?
M: Since today is □ _____, we close □ _____ □ _____. We close at □ _____ on □ _____.

✎ **어휘복습** 잘 안 들리거나 몰라서 체크한 어휘를 써 놓고 복습해 보세요.

□ _____   □ _____   □ _____   □ _____
□ _____   □ _____   □ _____   □ _____
□ _____   □ _____   □ _____   □ _____

13 부탁 파악

대화를 듣고, 남자가 여자에게 부탁한 일로 가장 적절한 것을 고르시오.

① 택시 잡기
② 함께 가게에 가기
③ 옷 가격 할인해주기
④ 카페 위치 알려주기
⑤ 아내의 옷 함께 고르기

M: That's a very nice □ _____ you're □ _____.
W: Thank you for the □ _____.
M: □ _____ did you □ _____ it? My □ _____ would love that.
W: I bought it at the □ _____ □ _____ □ _____ □ _____ □ _____ from the cafe on Baker Street.
M: Oh, I know where that is.
W: It was only □ _____ dollars because I got it □ _____ □ _____.
M: That's a great □ _____.
W: I'm □ _____ □ _____ to the store in a few minutes. I need to □ _____ some more □ _____ there.
M: Do you □ _____ □ _____ I go there □ _____ □ _____?
W: Not at all. Shall we □ _____ a □ _____?

14 한 일 파악

대화를 듣고, 남자가 주말에 한 일로 가장 적절한 것을 고르시오.

① 생일 파티에 갔다.
② 시험 공부를 했다.
③ 영어 에세이를 썼다.
④ 생일선물을 샀다.
⑤ 새 노트북을 샀다.

M: Are you still □ _____ □ _____ your English □ _____?
W: Yes, I am. I □ _____ □ _____ □ _____ on the weekend, so I need to □ _____ it □ _____.
M: □ _____ □ _____ with that.
W: Have you finished □ _____?
M: Yes, I did it this morning.
W: What did you do □ _____ □ _____ □ _____ then?
M: I went to a □ _____ □ _____.
W: What were you doing there? Did you buy a new □ _____ □ _____ □ _____?
M: No, I didn't do that. I bought a computer □ _____ for Mark.
W: □ _____ did you do that?
M: Today is his □ _____. I'm going to his □ _____ after school.

✏️ **어휘복습** 잘 안 들리거나 몰라서 체크한 어휘를 써 놓고 복습해 보세요.

□ _____   □ _____   □ _____   □ _____
□ _____   □ _____   □ _____   □ _____
□ _____   □ _____   □ _____   □ _____

다음을 듣고, 광고문의 내용과 일치하지 않는 것을 고르시오.

> **For Rent**
> 2-bedroom house; the house has a living room, a kitchen, and a bathroom; the house is furnished with 2 beds, a sofa, a dining table, and four chairs
> Rent: $400 per month
> Telephone: 409-3423
> No pets are allowed.

①   ②   ③   ④   ⑤

① There are □ _____ □ _____ in the house.

② The house has □ _____ in it.

③ The house □ _____ □ _____ □ _____ dollars to □ _____ each month.

④ A person can □ _____ a □ _____ to ask about the house.

⑤ A person □ _____ a □ _____ can □ _____ in the house.

대화를 듣고, 두 사람의 관계로 가장 적절한 것을 고르시오.

① 요리사 – 손님
② 웨이터 – 손님
③ 승무원 – 승객
④ 배달원 – 손님
⑤ 호텔 직원 – 손님

W: Hello. □ _____ □ _____.

M: Hi. This is John Taylor in room four two three.

W: Yes, how can I help you?

M: I'd like to □ _____ some □ _____, please.

W: Sure. □ _____ do you want to □ _____?

M: I'd like the □ _____, a □ _____ □ _____, and a cola.

W: All right. Your food will □ _____ □ _____ in about twenty minutes. How would you like to □ _____ □ _____ it?

M: Please □ _____ it □ _____ my room.

✏️ **어휘복습** 잘 안 들리거나 몰라서 체크한 어휘를 써 놓고 복습해 보세요.

□ _____   □ _____   □ _____   □ _____

□ _____   □ _____   □ _____   □ _____

□ _____   □ _____   □ _____   □ _____

17 어색한 대화 찾기

다음을 듣고, 두 사람의 대화가 <u>어색한</u> 것을 고르시오.

①   ②   ③   ④   ⑤

① M: Do you know □ _____ I can □ _____ □ _____ the flower shop?

W: □ _____ right □ _____ this □ _____ and □ _____ □ _____ at the □ _____.

② M: □ _____ □ _____ times did you □ _____ Doug today?

W: I only called him □ _____.

③ M: How would you like to □ _____ □ _____ this?

W: I'm going to use my □ _____ □ _____.

④ M: Would you □ _____ pizza □ _____ sandwiches for lunch?

W: Yes, that would be great.

⑤ M: May I please □ _____ □ _____ Mr. Simmons?

W: He's □ _____ □ _____ □ _____. Hold, please.

18 내용 일치 파악

다음을 듣고, 시험에 관한 내용과 일치하지 <u>않는</u> 것을 고르시오.

① 내일은 중간고사가 있다.
② 제시간에 시작해야 완료할 가능성이 크다.
③ 검정색 펜을 준비해야 한다.
④ 연필을 사용할 수 없다.
⑤ 모든 문제가 쉽게 출제될 것이다.

M: Please □ _____ □ _____. You're going to □ _____ your midterm □ _____ tomorrow, so please □ _____ the □ _____. First, do not be □ _____ □ _____ □ _____ because the test will □ _____ the □ _____ □ _____ to complete. Next, you must use a □ _____ □ _____. You may not use a □ _____ or blue pen. When you take the test, you must □ _____ the □ _____ □ _____. Some of them are a bit □ _____. You must also □ _____ all of the □ _____. Even if you don't know an answer, try to □ _____ it anyway. □ _____ □ _____ and good luck tomorrow.

✎ **어휘복습** 잘 안 들리거나 몰라서 체크한 어휘를 써 놓고 복습해 보세요.

□ _____   □ _____   □ _____   □ _____

□ _____   □ _____   □ _____   □ _____

□ _____   □ _____   □ _____   □ _____

19 알맞은 응답 찾기

대화를 듣고, 남자의 마지막 말에 이어질 여자의 응답으로 가장 적절한 것을 고르시오.

Woman: _____

① How about getting Chinese food for a change?
② Okay. That's exactly what I was thinking.
③ I'd love something from Pizza Express.
④ No, I haven't had anything for dinner.
⑤ Yes, I already ordered.

M: Why don't we □ _____ a □ _____ tonight?

W: But we had pizza two nights ago.

M: I know. But Pizza Express is □ _____ □ _____ □ _____. If we buy one pizza, we can get □ _____ □ _____ □ _____.

W: I □ _____ □ _____ like the food there.

M: I thought you loved it. You always eat the pizza when we order it.

W: I □ _____ eat it □ _____ I know how much you love it.

M: I □ _____ □ _____ □ _____. In that case, what would you like to □ _____ □ _____ □ _____ tonight?

W: _____

20 알맞은 응답 찾기

대화를 듣고, 남자의 마지막 말에 이어질 여자의 응답으로 가장 적절한 것을 고르시오.

Woman: _____

① No, I didn't send a package to anyone.
② Sorry, but I haven't packed my bags yet.
③ You should leave it with the security guard.
④ Yes, I'm going to be home ten minutes from now.
⑤ I'm at home now. You can come here and drop it off.

M: Hello. May I □ _____ □ _____ Ms. Gordon, please?

W: □ _____ □ _____ Ms. Gordon. □ _____ □ _____?

M: I'm □ _____ □ _____ Speedy Delivery. I have a □ _____ I'd like to □ _____ to you in ten minutes.

W: I'm terribly sorry, but I'm □ _____ □ _____ □ _____ right now.

M: Would it be okay if I □ _____ the package in your □ _____?

W: I □ _____ □ _____ that's a □ _____ □ _____. It contains some □ _____ □ _____.

M: Then □ _____ do you want me to □ _____ □ _____ the package?

W: _____

✏️ **어휘복습** 잘 안 들리거나 몰라서 체크한 어휘를 써 놓고 복습해 보세요.

□ _____ □ _____ □ _____ □ _____
□ _____ □ _____ □ _____ □ _____
□ _____ □ _____ □ _____ □ _____

MP3 실전 17

점수 / 20

01 대화를 듣고, 두 사람이 구매할 물건을 고르시오.

 ① ② ③

 ④ ⑤

02 다음을 듣고, 무엇에 관한 내용인지 가장 적절한 것을 고르시오.

① 수표   ② 은행   ③ 통장
④ 체크카드   ⑤ 현금지급기

03 대화를 듣고, 오늘의 최저 기온을 고르시오.

① –4℃   ② –2℃   ③ 0℃
④ 2℃   ⑤ 11℃

04 대화를 듣고, 여자의 마지막 말의 의도로 가장 적절한 것을 고르시오.

① 거절   ② 제안   ③ 초대
④ 명령   ⑤ 꾸중

05 대화를 듣고, 남자가 책을 늦게 반납하는 이유로 가장 적절한 것을 고르시오.

① 책을 잃어버려서
② 반납일을 잊고 있어서
③ 책을 친구에게 빌려줘서
④ 책을 끝까지 읽으려고 해서
⑤ 도서관에 올 시간이 없어서

06 대화를 듣고, 여자가 남자에게 전화한 목적으로 가장 적절한 것을 고르시오.

① 장미를 주문하려고
② 장미 주문을 취소하려고
③ 백합의 가격을 물어보려고
④ 주문한 꽃의 수량을 변경하려고
⑤ 주문한 꽃의 종류를 변경하려고

07 대화를 듣고, 두 사람이 먹지 않을 음식을 고르시오.

① 라면   ② 김밥   ③ 순대
④ 탄산음료   ⑤ 오렌지 주스

08 대화를 듣고, 남자가 대화 직후에 할 일로 가장 적절한 것을 고르시오.

① 연필 빌리기   ② 공책 빌리기
③ 교과서 사기   ④ 컴퓨터 사기
⑤ 문구점에 가기

09 대화를 듣고, 여자의 심정으로 가장 적절한 것을 고르시오.

① afraid   ② upset   ③ satisfied
④ worried   ⑤ pleased

10 다음을 듣고, 내일 오후의 날씨로 가장 적절한 것을 고르시오.

① ② ③ ④ ⑤

11 다음 표를 보면서 대화를 듣고, 남자가 지불해야 할 금액을 고르시오.

Age	Residents	Nonresidents
Adult	$12.00	$15.00
Children (12 or Younger)	$7.00	$9.00
Elderly (60 or Older)	$5.00	$7.00

① $39   ② $45   ③ $47
④ $51   ⑤ $63

12 대화를 듣고, 남자가 여자에게 부탁한 일로 가장 적절한 것을 고르시오.

① 함께 친구를 기다리기
② 신청서 양식 가져오기
③ 선생님 전화번호 적어주기
④ 방과 후 수업 목록 가져오기
⑤ 방과 후 수업 대신 신청하기

13 다음을 듣고, 두 사람의 대화가 <u>어색한</u> 것을 고르시오.

①   ②   ③   ④   ⑤

14 다음을 듣고, 내용과 일치하지 <u>않는</u> 것을 고르시오.

① 중국은 세계에서 인구가 가장 많다.
② 인도에는 10억 명 이상이 산다.
③ 미국의 인구는 세계에서 네 번째로 많다.
④ 브라질의 인구는 인도네시아보다 많다.
⑤ 바티칸 시티는 인구가 가장 적은 나라 중 하나다.

15 대화를 듣고, 두 사람이 대화하는 장소로 가장 적절한 곳을 고르시오.

① 버스   ② 해변   ③ 음식점
④ 비행기   ⑤ 공항

16 대화를 듣고, 상황을 가장 잘 표현한 속담을 고르시오.

① The grass is always greener on the other side of the fence.
② A penny saved is a penny earned.
③ All that glitters is not gold.
④ A stitch in time saves nine.
⑤ Seeing is believing.

17 대화를 듣고, 여자가 남자에게 부탁한 일로 가장 적절한 것을 고르시오.

① 병원에 같이 가기
② 할머니 병문안 가기
③ 수업내용 정리해주기
④ 선생님 전화번호 알아보기
⑤ 선생님에게 메시지 전달하기

18 대화를 듣고, John's Health Club에 관해 언급되지 <u>않은</u> 것을 고르시오.

① 운동 프로그램   ② 회비
③ 할인제도   ④ 운영 시간
⑤ 위치

[19-20] 대화를 듣고, 여자의 마지막 말에 이어질 남자의 응답으로 가장 적절한 것을 고르시오.

19 Man: _____

① No, I haven't met Karen before.
② How has Cindy been doing lately?
③ So what are you and Cindy doing tonight?
④ Why don't you try meeting her more often?
⑤ It's good to hear that you're getting along well.

20 Man: _____

① The park looks like it's clean to me.
② What should we do here at the park?
③ Why didn't we ask them to meet us here?
④ You're right. I shouldn't have brought them.
⑤ Yeah. We could meet here every weekend.

01 특정 정보 파악

대화를 듣고, 두 사람이 구매할 물건을 고르시오.

① ② ③ ④ ⑤

W: Mom's □ _____ is this □ _____. You □ _____ forget, □ _____ □ _____?

M: Of course not. I've been □ _____ □ _____ to buy her a present.

W: That's great. I've saved some money □ _____ □ _____.

M: Why don't we □ _____ our money and buy her something from □ _____ □ _____ us?

W: That's a good idea. What should we buy for her?

M: □ _____ □ _____ some □ _____? She loves □ _____.

W: Yeah, but I want to get her something she can □ _____ □ _____ □ _____ □ _____ □ _____. We could get her a new □ _____.

M: She has □ _____ □ _____ those. How about some □ _____?

W: Yeah, she said she wants some □ _____ □ _____ □ _____. Let's buy □ _____ □ _____ for her.

02 화제 추론

다음을 듣고, 무엇에 관한 내용인지 가장 적절한 것을 고르시오.

① 수표 ② 은행 ③ 통장
④ 체크카드 ⑤ 현금지급기

M: People can □ _____ this all the time. This □ _____ □ _____ in all sorts of places. This is □ _____ □ _____, □ _____ people's homes, and even □ _____ □ _____ □ _____ sometimes. People can use this to □ _____ □ _____ at any time. They need to have a special □ _____ □ _____ the □ _____. But they don't have to go to the bank if they use this. This is very □ _____ on □ _____ and □ _____.

✎ 어휘복습 잘 안 들리거나 몰라서 체크한 어휘를 써 놓고 복습해 보세요.

□ _____   □ _____   □ _____   □ _____
□ _____   □ _____   □ _____   □ _____
□ _____   □ _____   □ _____   □ _____

03 특정 정보 파악

대화를 듣고, 오늘의 최저 기온을 고르시오.

① -4°C ② -2°C ③ 0°C
④ 2°C ⑤ 11°C

M: I'm really happy that □ _____ is finally □ _____.
W: I feel the same way. I'm □ _____ □ _____ □ _____ □ _____.
M: Yeah, I want □ _____ weather. I want to go outside □ _____ wearing a □ _____ □ _____.
W: So □ _____ you □ _____ the weather forecast for today?
M: Not yet. What's the □ _____ □ _____ going to be?
W: It's going to get □ _____ □ _____ □ _____ degrees, but it's going to go □ _____ □ _____ □ _____ degrees □ _____ □ _____ tonight.
M: That's □ _____ □ _____ yesterday's weather.
W: I know. It was □ _____ □ _____ degrees □ _____. It was □ _____.

04 의도 파악

대화를 듣고, 여자의 마지막 말의 의도로 가장 적절한 것을 고르시오.

① 거절 ② 제안 ③ 초대
④ 명령 ⑤ 구충

M: What are you □ _____ □ _____, Mom?
W: This month's □ _____ □ _____. It's a lot □ _____ □ _____ normal.
M: I guess we □ _____ □ _____ □ _____ electricity, didn't we?
W: That's right. We need to □ _____ □ _____ electricity. We should □ _____ □ _____ the □ _____ in rooms when we leave them.
M: Will that really □ _____?
W: Yes, it will. □ _____ □ _____ it seems small, it will □ _____ a □ _____ □ _____ over a month.
M: □ _____ □ _____ can we do then?
W: □ _____ □ _____ using the □ _____ rather than the □ _____ □ _____?

✏ **어휘복습** 잘 안 들리거나 몰라서 체크한 어휘를 써 놓고 복습해 보세요.

□ _____ □ _____ □ _____ □ _____
□ _____ □ _____ □ _____ □ _____
□ _____ □ _____ □ _____ □ _____

05 이유 파악

대화를 듣고, 남자가 책을 늦게 반납하는 이유로 가장 적절한 것을 고르시오.

① 책을 잃어버려서
② 반납일을 잊고 있어서
③ 책을 친구에게 빌려줘서
④ 책을 끝까지 읽으려고 해서
⑤ 도서관에 올 시간이 없어서

W: Hello. Do you need to □ _____ □ _____ a □ _____?
M: No, but I have a book I □ _____ □ _____ □ _____.
   Here you are.
W: Thank you very much.
M: □ _____, the book is □ _____, so I guess I need to
   □ _____ a □ _____.
W: □ _____ □ _____ □ _____. Yes, it's three days late.
M: I'm really □ _____ □ _____ that.
W: What happened? Did you □ _____ about it?
M: No. It's a great book, and I wanted to □ _____ □ _____
   it □ _____ □ _____ it.
W: I see. Well, your fine is three dollars.

06 전화 목적 파악

대화를 듣고, 여자가 남자에게 전화한 목적으로 가장 적절한 것을 고르시오.

① 장미를 주문하려고
② 장미 주문을 취소하려고
③ 백합의 가격을 물어보려고
④ 주문한 꽃의 수량을 변경하려고
⑤ 주문한 꽃의 종류를 변경하려고

M: Hello. This is the Green Thumb □ _____ □ _____. Can I
   help you?
W: Hi. □ _____ □ _____ Melissa Reynolds. I □ _____
   some □ _____ about thirty minutes ago.
M: Yes, Ms. Reynolds. Is there something I can do for you?
W: I need to □ _____ my order.
M: Sure. □ _____ do you want to change it?
W: Well, I ordered □ _____ □ _____ □ _____ and a dozen
   □ _____, right?
M: That's correct.
W: I □ _____ □ _____ the carnations □ _____. I'd like a
   dozen □ _____ □ _____.
M: No problem. I'll □ _____ □ _____ □ _____ that right
   away.

✎ **어휘복습** 잘 안 들리거나 몰라서 체크한 어휘를 써 놓고 복습해 보세요.

□ _____   □ _____   □ _____   □ _____
□ _____   □ _____   □ _____   □ _____
□ _____   □ _____   □ _____   □ _____

07 특정 정보 파악

대화를 듣고, 두 사람이 먹지 <u>않을</u> 음식을 고르시오.

① 라면 ② 김밥 ③ 순대
④ 탄산음료 ⑤ 오렌지 주스

W: Are you □ _____? I need some food.
M: Okay, let's □ _____ □ _____ □ _____ and get □ _____
□ _____ □ _____.
W: Thanks. What do you □ _____ □ _____ eating?
M: □ _____ □ _____ going to the □ _____ □ _____? We
can get some □ _____ □ _____ there.
W: That sounds fine. And some gimbap and sundae would be nice,
too.
M: All right. Do you want a □ _____?
W: □ _____ □ _____. Let's just get some □ _____
□ _____ instead.
M: Sure. My □ _____ is □ _____ now. Let's □ _____
□ _____ and go there.

08 할 일 파악

대화를 듣고, 남자가 대화 직후에 할 일로 가장 적절한 것을 고르시오.

① 연필 빌리기 ② 공책 빌리기
③ 교과서 사기 ④ 컴퓨터 사기
⑤ 문구점에 가기

M: Are you all □ _____ □ _____ the new □ _____ to begin?
W: I think so. I □ _____ all of my □ _____ already.
M: I □ _____ □ _____ □ _____ thing yesterday.
W: And I went to the □ _____ □ _____ to buy some
□ _____, □ _____, and □ _____.
M: I □ _____ done that □ _____. I probably have a few
pencils □ _____ □ _____ though.
W: But □ _____ □ _____ □ _____ any notebooks? You
really need some of them.
M: No, I □ _____. I □ _____ □ _____ buy them today.
W: □ _____ □ _____ going to the store and getting them now?
M: Okay. But □ _____ □ _____ □ _____ going along with
me?
W: □ _____ □ _____ □ _____. Let's do that right now.

✎ 어휘복습 잘 안 들리거나 몰라서 체크한 어휘를 써 놓고 복습해 보세요.

□ _____ □ _____ □ _____ □ _____
□ _____ □ _____ □ _____ □ _____
□ _____ □ _____ □ _____ □ _____

09 심정 추론

대화를 듣고, 여자의 심정으로 가장 적절한 것을 고르시오.

① afraid   ② upset
③ satisfied   ④ worried
⑤ pleased

M: What are you doing here? I thought you were ☐ _____ ☐ _____ ☐ _____.

W: I was ☐ _____ ☐ _____ ☐ _____ ☐ _____ Guam today.

M: Why didn't you go?

W: You ☐ _____ ☐ _____ what happened. I ☐ _____ ☐ _____ early and ☐ _____ ☐ _____ the ☐ _____.

M: Did you get on the ☐ _____ bus?

W: No. The bus was ☐ _____ ☐ _____ ☐ _____ on the highway, and I ☐ _____ ☐ _____ at the airport, so I ☐ _____ my ☐ _____.

M: That's ☐ _____. You must feel ☐ _____.

W: You can ☐ _____ ☐ _____ ☐ _____.

10 날씨 파악

다음을 듣고, 내일 오후의 날씨로 가장 적절한 것을 고르시오.

① ② ③
④ ⑤

W: Remember that we're going to ☐ _____ our class ☐ _____ ☐ _____. I ☐ _____ the ☐ _____ ☐ _____. Apparently, it's going to ☐ _____ in the ☐ _____. So all of you should ☐ _____ ☐ _____ or ☐ _____ ☐ _____. But don't worry too much. The rain will ☐ _____ ☐ _____ ☐ _____, and the ☐ _____ will begin to ☐ _____ ☐ _____. We should have ☐ _____ weather ☐ _____ around ☐ _____ P.M. I'm sure we're going to ☐ _____ a ☐ _____ ☐ _____ tomorrow.

✎ **어휘복습** 잘 안 들리거나 몰라서 체크한 어휘를 써 놓고 복습해 보세요.

☐ _____   ☐ _____   ☐ _____   ☐ _____
☐ _____   ☐ _____   ☐ _____   ☐ _____
☐ _____   ☐ _____   ☐ _____   ☐ _____

11 도표·실용문 파악

다음 표를 보면서 대화를 듣고, 남자가 지불해야 할 금액을 고르시오.

Age	Residents	Nonresidents
Adult	$12.00	$15.00
Children (12 or Younger)	$7.00	$9.00
Elderly (60 or Older)	$5.00	$7.00

① $39　　② $45　　③ $47
④ $51　　⑤ $63

W: Good morning. □ _____ □ _____ the arts center.
M: Hi. I need to buy □ _____ □ _____, please.
W: Are you a local □ _____, or do you □ _____ □ _____ □ _____?
M: We □ _____ □ _____ the □ _____. Here's my □ _____ □ _____.
W: Ah, yes, I can see your □ _____ on it. Thank you.
M: There are □ _____ □ _____ and □ _____ □ _____.
W: All right. Will you be □ _____ □ _____ your credit card?
M: Yes. Here you are.

12 부탁 파악

대화를 듣고, 남자가 여자에게 부탁한 일로 가장 적절한 것을 고르시오.

① 함께 친구를 기다리기
② 신청서 양식 가져오기
③ 선생님 전화번호 적어주기
④ 방과 후 수업 목록 가져오기
⑤ 방과 후 수업 대신 신청하기

M: Have you □ _____ a □ _____ for the □ _____ program yet?
W: No, I haven't.
M: □ _____ do we need to do that □ _____?
W: I think we need to □ _____ □ _____ by tomorrow morning.
M: Oh, I didn't know that.
W: I'm going to Mr. Park's office. He has the □ _____ □ _____ and _____. Would you like to □ _____ □ _____ □ _____?
M: I □ _____ □ _____, □ _____ I'm waiting for Minsu. Can you □ _____ □ _____ a form for me?
W: Sure. I'll □ _____ it to you □ _____ □ _____.
M: Thanks a lot.

✎ **어휘복습** 잘 안 들리거나 몰라서 체크한 어휘를 써 놓고 복습해 보세요.

□ _____　□ _____　□ _____　□ _____
□ _____　□ _____　□ _____　□ _____
□ _____　□ _____　□ _____　□ _____

13 어색한 대화 찾기

다음을 듣고, 두 사람의 대화가 <u>어색한</u> 것을 고르시오.

①　②　③　④　⑤

① M: □ _____ did you □ _____ the pie?
   W: It was a cherry pie.

② M: Let's □ _____ □ _____ □ _____ this afternoon.
   W: Sorry. I □ _____ □ _____ enough □ _____.

③ M: □ _____ does soccer practice □ _____?
   W: It □ _____ □ _____ three thirty.

④ M: You □ _____ really □ _____ in that dress.
   W: Thank you for saying that.

⑤ M: □ _____ didn't you □ _____ □ _____ □ _____ yesterday?
   W: I □ _____ a very bad □ _____.

14 내용 일치 파악

다음을 듣고, 내용과 일치하지 <u>않는</u> 것을 고르시오.

① 중국은 세계에서 인구가 가장 많다.
② 인도에는 10억 명 이상이 산다.
③ 미국의 인구는 세계에서 네 번째로 많다.
④ 브라질의 인구는 인도네시아보다 많다.
⑤ 바티칸 시티는 인구가 가장 적은 나라 중 하나다.

M: There are around □ _____ □ _____ □ _____ in the world. Each country has a different number of people in it. □ _____ has the □ _____ □ _____ □ _____ □ _____ □ _____ has the □ _____ largest. Each country has more than □ _____ □ _____ □ _____ living in them. □ _____ □ _____ □ _____ has the □ _____ most people. □ _____ and □ _____ are numbers □ _____ and □ _____. Vatican City is a country with □ _____ □ _____ □ _____ □ _____ populations. Only □ _____ □ _____ □ _____ people live there.

✎ **어휘복습** 잘 안 들리거나 몰라서 체크한 어휘를 써 놓고 복습해 보세요.

□ _____　　□ _____　　□ _____　　□ _____
□ _____　　□ _____　　□ _____　　□ _____
□ _____　　□ _____　　□ _____　　□ _____

15 장소 추론

대화를 듣고, 두 사람이 대화하는 장소로 가장 적절한 곳을 고르시오.

① 버스　② 해변　③ 음식점
④ 비행기　⑤ 공항

M: Would you like □ _____ □ _____ □ _____, ma'am?

W: What are my □ _____?

M: You can have □ _____ or □ _____.

W: Seafood □ _____ □ _____ to me.

M: How about something to □ _____?

W: □ _____ □ _____ a cola, please.

M: Is there □ _____ □ _____ you need?

W: Yes, I have a question. □ _____ are we going to □ _____ in Hawaii?

M: We should be □ _____ there □ _____ about □ _____ □ _____.

16 속담 추론

대화를 듣고, 상황을 가장 잘 표현한 속담을 고르시오.

① The grass is always greener on the other side of the fence.
② A penny saved is a penny earned.
③ All that glitters is not gold.
④ A stitch in time saves nine.
⑤ Seeing is believing.

M: Did you see the new □ _____ that Dave got □ _____ his □ _____?

W: Yeah, it's really nice.

M: □ _____ □ _____ I □ _____ a bike like that.

W: But you have a □ _____. Your parents gave you a new one □ _____ □ _____ □ _____.

M: I know, but Dave's bike looks □ _____ □ _____ □ _____.

W: □ _____ □ _____ about his bike? You've got a great one, and you □ _____ □ _____ □ _____ you have it.

M: I don't know. I □ _____ think he has a □ _____ bike □ _____ I do.

✎ **어휘복습** 잘 안 들리거나 몰라서 체크한 어휘를 써 놓고 복습해 보세요.

□ _____　　□ _____　　□ _____　　□ _____
□ _____　　□ _____　　□ _____　　□ _____
□ _____　　□ _____　　□ _____　　□ _____

17 부탁 파악

대화를 듣고, 여자가 남자에게 부탁한 일로 가장 적절한 것을 고르시오.

① 병원에 같이 가기
② 할머니 병문안 가기
③ 수업내용 정리해주기
④ 선생님 전화번호 알아보기
⑤ 선생님에게 메시지 전달하기

M: Clara, how are you doing?
W: □ _____ □ _____ □ _____. Do you happen to know Ms. Carpenter's □ _____ □ _____?
M: Sorry, but I □ _____ □ _____ □ _____. □ _____ do you need it?
W: I need to □ _____ □ _____ her □ _____ □ _____.
M: What's going on?
W: My □ _____ is □ _____ the □ _____, so my family is going to □ _____ her. Can you □ _____ her □ _____ I'm □ _____ □ _____ □ _____ tomorrow?
M: Of course, I'll tell her. And I hope your grandmother □ _____ □ _____.
W: Thanks a lot.

18 미언급 파악

대화를 듣고, John's Health Club에 관해 언급되지 <u>않은</u> 것을 고르시오.

① 운동 프로그램
② 회비
③ 할인제도
④ 운영 시간
⑤ 위치

W: I'm thinking of □ _____ a □ _____ □ _____. Do you know a □ _____ □ _____?
M: Sure. You should go to John's Health Club. I □ _____ □ _____ there.
W: What do you do?
M: I □ _____ □ _____ and □ _____ there. But there are also □ _____ □ _____.
W: That sounds interesting. □ _____ □ _____ is it?
M: It costs □ _____ dollars □ _____ □ _____. The hours are good, too. It's □ _____ □ _____ □ _____ in the morning □ _____ □ _____ at night every day of the year.
W: Wow. I should go there. □ _____ is it?
M: It's at sixty-eight Maple Street. It's really □ _____ □ _____ the school.

✎ **어휘복습** 잘 안 들리거나 몰라서 체크한 어휘를 써 놓고 복습해 보세요.

□ _____   □ _____   □ _____   □ _____
□ _____   □ _____   □ _____   □ _____
□ _____   □ _____   □ _____   □ _____

19 알맞은 응답 찾기

대화를 듣고, 여자의 마지막 말에 이어질 남자의 응답으로 가장 적절한 것을 고르시오.

Man: _____

① No, I haven't met Karen before.
② How has Cindy been doing lately?
③ So what are you and Cindy doing tonight?
④ Why don't you try meeting her more often?
⑤ It's good to hear that you're getting along well.

M: Are you □ _____ □ _____ this evening?

W: I am. Karen and I are planning to □ _____ a □ _____ together.

M: Why don't you □ _____ □ _____ □ _____ Cindy anymore?

W: Karen and I have a great time together. She's □ _____ □ _____ □ _____ Cindy.

M: But you've been □ _____ □ _____ with Cindy for five years.

W: That's true, but we □ _____ □ _____ □ _____ □ _____ nowadays.

M: _____

20 알맞은 응답 찾기

대화를 듣고, 여자의 마지막 말에 이어질 남자의 응답으로 가장 적절한 것을 고르시오.

Man: _____

① The park looks like it's clean to me.
② What should we do here at the park?
③ Why didn't we ask them to meet us here?
④ You're right. I shouldn't have brought them.
⑤ Yeah. We could meet here every weekend.

M: I □ _____ □ _____ □ _____ □ _____ the park is.

W: I know. People just □ _____ their □ _____ on the ground.

M: Why don't we □ _____ □ _____ some of this trash?

W: We could do that, but there's so much of it.

M: You're right. But we could still make the park □ _____ □ _____.

W: We should bring some friends to □ _____ us □ _____ □ _____ the park.

M: _____

✏️ **어휘복습** 잘 안 들리거나 몰라서 체크한 어휘를 써 놓고 복습해 보세요.

□ _____ □ _____ □ _____ □ _____
□ _____ □ _____ □ _____ □ _____
□ _____ □ _____ □ _____ □ _____

점수
/ 20

---

01 대화를 듣고, 남자가 원하는 신발로 가장 적절한 것을 고르시오.

① ② ③

④ ⑤

02 다음을 듣고, 오늘 파리의 날씨로 가장 적절한 것을 고르시오.

① ② ③ ④ ⑤

03 다음을 듣고, 남자가 하는 말의 내용으로 가장 적절한 것을 고르시오.

① 응급처치 방법
② 준비운동의 종류
③ 보호장비의 종류
④ 부상을 피하는 방법
⑤ 건강을 유지하는 방법

04 대화를 듣고, 여자의 마지막 말의 의도로 가장 적절한 것을 고르시오.

① 거절 ② 설득 ③ 사과
④ 요청 ⑤ 칭찬

05 대화를 듣고, 키가 가장 큰 사람을 고르시오.

① Kevin ② Steve ③ Peter
④ Joe ⑤ Mark

06 대화를 듣고, 두 사람이 만날 시각을 고르시오.

① 3:00 ② 3:30 ③ 4:00
④ 4:30 ⑤ 5:00

07 대화를 듣고, 여자가 남자에게 부탁한 일로 가장 적절한 것을 고르시오.

① 열쇠 찾기
② 차 태워주기
③ 차 빌려주기
④ 일기장 찾기
⑤ 고양이와 놀기

08 다음을 듣고, 남자의 심정으로 가장 적절한 것을 고르시오.

① pleased ② excited ③ sad
④ angry ⑤ lonely

09 대화를 듣고, 내용과 일치하지 않는 것을 고르시오.

① 남자는 어제 TV를 봤다.
② 남자는 어제 숲에 가지 않았다.
③ 여자는 어제 꽃을 수집했다.
④ 여자는 어제 호수에 갔다.
⑤ 여자는 어제 동물에게 먹이를 주었다.

10 대화를 듣고, 남자가 지불할 금액을 고르시오.

① $850 ② $900 ③ $1,000
④ $1,050 ⑤ $1,200

11 다음을 듣고, 두 사람의 대화가 어색한 것을 고르시오.

① ② ③ ④ ⑤

12 대화를 듣고, 여자가 숙제를 제출하지 <u>않은</u> 이유로 가장 적절한 것을 고르시오.

① 아파서
② 숙제를 깜빡해서
③ 숙제가 어려워서
④ 자원봉사를 해서
⑤ 다른 숙제가 많아서

13 대화를 듣고, 두 사람의 관계로 가장 적절한 것을 고르시오.

① 교사 – 학생
② 승무원 – 승객
③ 판매원 – 쇼핑객
④ 여행사 직원 – 고객
⑤ 여행 가이드 – 여행객

14 대화를 듣고, 여자가 남자에게 부탁한 일로 가장 적절한 것을 고르시오.

① 휴대폰 교체하기
② 휴대폰 배달하기
③ 사무실로 전화하기
④ 사무실 전화번호 적기
⑤ 휴대폰 수리비 할인해주기

15 대화를 듣고, 내용과 일치하는 것을 고르시오.

① 남자의 삼촌은 도시에 살고 있다.
② 남자는 동물을 돌보는 일이 무서웠다.
③ 남자는 자전거를 탈 줄 모른다.
④ 여자는 바다에서 낚시를 했다.
⑤ 여자는 햇볕에 몸이 탔다.

16 대화를 듣고, 남자가 친구를 데려갈 곳을 고르시오.

① 경주   ② 인사동   ③ 부산
④ 한국민속촌   ⑤ 경복궁

17 다음을 듣고, 소방 훈련의 내용으로 언급되지 <u>않은</u> 것을 고르시오.

① 신속하게 줄 서기
② 엘리베이터 타지 않기
③ 다른 학생들 밀지 않기
④ 물이 든 양동이 나르기
⑤ 선생님이 출석 부르는 것 듣기

18 대화를 듣고, 남자가 여자에게 전화한 목적으로 가장 적절한 것을 고르시오.

① 개를 돌봐 달라고 부탁하려고
② 여자를 인천 여행에 초대하려고
③ 남자의 집에 들를 것을 부탁하려고
④ 과학 다큐멘터리에 대해 얘기하려고
⑤ 여자의 이모가 어떻게 지내는지 물어보려고

[19-20] 대화를 듣고, 남자의 마지막 말에 이어질 여자의 응답으로 가장 적절한 것을 고르시오.

19 Woman: _____

① That's right. I made a robot.
② I like working with machines a lot.
③ I want to go to space in the future.
④ No, that wasn't an interesting topic.
⑤ The robot cleans the house really well.

20 Woman: _____

① No, I'm not hungry now.
② I'd like to have some Spanish food.
③ I want to try Russian food again.
④ No, I haven't tasted Brazilian food before.
⑤ I've been to that country a couple of times.

🔊 MP3 실전 18-1

01 그림 정보 파악

대화를 듣고, 남자가 원하는 신발로 가장 적절한 것을 고르시오.

① ② ③

④ ⑤

W: Hello. May I help you?

M: Yes, please. I need some □ _____ □ _____ my □ _____.

W: Does he need □ _____ shoes □ _____ □ _____?

M: No, he needs some □ _____.

W: Okay. How about these shoes □ _____ □ _____ □ _____ on them?

M: I'm not sure. Do you have □ _____ □ _____?

W: Here are a pair of □ _____ shoes with □ _____ □ _____ on them.

M: Oh, I like the □ _____ ones. Do you have them in a □ _____ □ _____?

W: Yes, I do. □ _____ □ _____ get it for you.

02 날씨 파악

다음을 듣고, 오늘 파리의 날씨로 가장 적절한 것을 고르시오.

① ② ③

④ ⑤

M: It's time for the weather report. Let's look at some □ _____ □ _____ in □ _____. London has warm and □ _____ weather today. Berlin has very □ _____ and □ _____ weather though. It's □ _____ in Spain and Italy, so both Rome and Madrid are □ _____ □ _____ □ _____. In □ _____, the □ _____ are □ _____. And it's very □ _____ in Oslo. That's it for the weather report. I'll □ _____ □ _____ in thirty minutes with another one.

✎ 어휘복습 잘 안 들리거나 몰라서 체크한 어휘를 써 놓고 복습해 보세요.

□ _____ □ _____ □ _____ □ _____

□ _____ □ _____ □ _____ □ _____

□ _____ □ _____ □ _____ □ _____

03 화제 추론

다음을 듣고, 남자가 하는 말의 내용으로 가장 적절한 것을 고르시오.

① 응급처치 방법
② 준비운동의 종류
③ 보호장비의 종류
④ 부상을 피하는 방법
⑤ 건강을 유지하는 방법

M: □ _____ □ _____ is one way to □ _____ □ _____ and to have fun. Many people □ _____ □ _____ while playing sports these days because they don't know □ _____ □ _____ □ _____ □ _____ □ _____ themselves. There are several ways to □ _____ □ _____. One of them is to have the □ _____ □ _____. People need the □ _____ □ _____ and □ _____ equipment for certain sports. They should also be sure to □ _____ □ _____ □ _____ before playing a sport. Warming up can help them □ _____ injuries. By doing these two activities, people can □ _____ their □ _____ of getting hurt.

04 의도 파악

대화를 듣고, 여자의 마지막 말의 의도로 가장 적절한 것을 고르시오.

① 거절   ② 설득   ③ 사과
④ 요청   ⑤ 칭찬

W: I'm thinking of cooking □ _____ □ _____ □ _____ tonight.

M: Why don't we have some □ _____ instead?

W: □ _____ do you want to eat leftovers?

M: Take a look at the □ _____. There's a lot of □ _____ in there □ _____.

W: You're right. I didn't □ _____ that.

M: If we have some leftovers, we can □ _____ □ _____ all of the food we have.

W: Wow. I □ _____ a lot □ _____ you.

✏️ **어휘복습** 잘 안 들리거나 몰라서 체크한 어휘를 써 놓고 복습해 보세요.

□ _____   □ _____   □ _____   □ _____
□ _____   □ _____   □ _____   □ _____
□ _____   □ _____   □ _____   □ _____

05 특정 정보 파악

대화를 듣고, 키가 가장 큰 사람을 고르시오.

① Kevin ② Steve ③ Peter
④ Joe ⑤ Mark

W: □ _____ □ _____ are you, Kevin?
M: I'm one hundred seventy centimeters tall. I'm about □ _____ □ _____.
W: Are you □ _____ □ _____ your friend Mark?
M: That's □ _____. □ _____ Mark and Steve are around one hundred sixty-six centimeters tall.
W: Are you □ _____ □ _____ boy in your class?
M: No, I'm not. Joe and Peter are both taller than me. Joe's one hundred seventy-five centimeters tall.
W: Wow. And what about Peter?
M: He's one hundred eighty-two centimeters tall. He's □ _____ the □ _____ □ _____.
W: I □ _____ he's really good.

06 숫자 정보 파악

대화를 듣고, 두 사람이 만날 시각을 고르시오.

① 3:00 ② 3:30 ③ 4:00
④ 4:30 ⑤ 5:00

M: Do you □ _____ a few □ _____ □ _____ help me?
W: What do you need me to do?
M: I have to □ _____ □ _____ this □ _____ for the school □ _____ by five P.M., but I'd like you to □ _____ it for □ _____.
W: I □ _____ □ _____ □ _____ right now. How about at three?
M: I've got to meet Sue □ _____. Is three thirty □ _____ □ _____ you?
W: No, I've got □ _____ □ _____. But I can meet you □ _____ practice is □ _____.
M: When's that?
W: □ _____ □ _____ □ _____.
M: Sounds great. I'll see you then.

✎ **어휘복습** 잘 안 들리거나 몰라서 체크한 어휘를 써 놓고 복습해 보세요.

□ _____ □ _____ □ _____ □ _____
□ _____ □ _____ □ _____ □ _____
□ _____ □ _____ □ _____ □ _____

대화를 듣고, 여자가 남자에게 부탁한 일로
가장 적절한 것을 고르시오.

① 열쇠 찾기
② 차 태워주기
③ 차 빌려주기
④ 일기장 찾기
⑤ 고양이와 놀기

W: What are you doing right now, Eric?

M: I'm just □ _____ in my □ _____.

W: Do you □ _____ some □ _____ □ _____ □ _____ me?

M: Sure. What do you □ _____?

W: Whiskers isn't □ _____ □ _____. I need to □ _____ her
to the □ _____.

M: Would you like me to □ _____ you and your □ _____
□ _____ the □ _____?

W: That would be great. It's □ _____ □ _____ □ _____
□ _____ □ _____ there.

M: All right. Let me get my □ _____ □ _____.

W: Thanks a lot. I really □ _____ your □ _____.

다음을 듣고, 남자의 심정으로 가장 적절한
것을 고르시오.

① pleased   ② excited
③ sad   ④ angry
⑤ lonely

M: Today, I □ _____ my older brother's □ _____. He is
twenty-six years old, and his wife is twenty-four. It was
really □ _____ □ _____ □ _____ him and his wife so
□ _____. However, □ _____ □ _____ he is □ _____,
he is □ _____ □ _____ of my parents' home. He's going
to move to another city, so I'm not going to see him very
much □ _____. I think I'm starting to □ _____ □ _____
without him around.

✏️ **어휘복습** 잘 안 들리거나 몰라서 체크한 어휘를 써 놓고 복습해 보세요.

□ _____   □ _____   □ _____   □ _____
□ _____   □ _____   □ _____   □ _____
□ _____   □ _____   □ _____   □ _____

09 내용 일치 파악

대화를 듣고, 내용과 일치하지 <u>않는</u> 것을 고르시오.

① 남자는 어제 TV를 봤다.
② 남자는 어제 숲에 가지 않았다.
③ 여자는 어제 꽃을 수집했다.
④ 여자는 어제 호수에 갔다.
⑤ 여자는 어제 동물에게 먹이를 주었다.

W: What did you do □ _____, Lewis?
M: I just □ _____ □ _____ □ _____ and watched TV most of the day.
W: You □ _____ □ _____ □ _____ to the □ _____ with us. We had a great time.
M: Yeah? What did you do there?
W: We □ _____ □ _____ and □ _____ lots of □ _____ and □ _____.
M: Collecting leaves and flowers? □ _____ did you do that?
W: We were trying to □ _____ □ _____ □ _____ of them □ _____ □ _____ □ _____. After that, we went to the □ _____ and □ _____ lots of □ _____. I even saw a □ _____.
M: Wow. I'll □ _____ □ _____ □ _____ you the next time.

10 숫자 정보 파악

대화를 듣고, 남자가 지불할 금액을 고르시오.

① $850   ② $900   ③ $1,000
④ $1,050   ⑤ $1,200

W: Hello. Star □ _____. How may I help you?
M: I'd like to □ _____ with my family □ _____ Seoul □ _____ Osaka □ _____.
W: You're □ _____ □ _____. We have lots of □ _____ □ _____, and we're □ _____ a □ _____ □ _____ all □ _____ to Japan.
M: That's wonderful. □ _____ □ _____ are □ _____?
W: Tickets are □ _____ three hundred fifty dollars □ _____ □ _____ and two hundred fifty dollars for □ _____.
M: But □ _____ □ _____ the discount?
W: Now, they're □ _____ □ _____ □ _____ dollars for adults and □ _____ □ _____ dollars for children.
M: Wonderful. I need two tickets for adults and two tickets for children, please.

✎ **어휘복습** 잘 안 들리거나 몰라서 체크한 어휘를 써 놓고 복습해 보세요.

□ _____   □ _____   □ _____   □ _____
□ _____   □ _____   □ _____   □ _____
□ _____   □ _____   □ _____   □ _____

다음을 듣고, 두 사람의 대화가 어색한 것을
고르시오.

①   ②   ③   ④   ⑤

① M: I'm planning to □ _____ □ _____ □ _____ Amy
     tonight.
   W: □ _____ □ _____ □ _____ □ _____ I go with you?

② M: □ _____ are you planning to □ _____ India?
   W: I'll be there in □ _____ □ _____ □ _____.

③ M: □ _____ did you manage to □ _____ so much
     □ _____?
   W: I □ _____ every day and ate □ _____ □ _____.

④ M: □ _____ is the □ _____ □ _____ located?
   W: You need to □ _____ the □ _____ to the □ _____
     □ _____.

⑤ M: □ _____ did you □ _____ the □ _____ was?
   W: I had to □ _____ ten □ _____ □ _____.

대화를 듣고, 여자가 숙제를 제출하지 않은
이유로 가장 적절한 것을 고르시오.

① 아파서
② 숙제를 깜빡해서
③ 숙제가 어려워서
④ 자원봉사를 해서
⑤ 다른 숙제가 많아서

M: Janet, everyone □ _____ □ _____ their □ _____ except
   you.
W: I'm sorry, Mr. Walker. I'll □ _____ it to you □ _____
   □ _____ morning.
M: Sorry, but I don't □ _____ □ _____ homework.
W: But I have a □ _____ □ _____ this time.
M: □ _____ □ _____ going to tell me that you were
   □ _____ again, □ _____ □ _____?
W: No, it wasn't that. I □ _____ some □ _____ □ _____
   □ _____ the □ _____ all weekend, so I was □ _____
   □ _____ to do that.
M: I see. Well, it's nice to see that you □ _____ □ _____
   others.
W: So can I please turn my homework in late?

✎ **어휘복습** 잘 안 들리거나 몰라서 체크한 어휘를 써 놓고 복습해 보세요.

□ _____   □ _____   □ _____   □ _____
□ _____   □ _____   □ _____   □ _____
□ _____   □ _____   □ _____   □ _____

13 관계 추론

대화를 듣고, 두 사람의 관계로 가장 적절한 것을 고르시오.

① 교사 – 학생
② 승무원 – 승객
③ 판매원 – 쇼핑객
④ 여행사 직원 – 고객
⑤ 여행 가이드 – 여행객

M: Hello. How can I help you today?

W: I'm thinking about □ _____ □ _____ an □ _____.

M: □ _____ □ _____ you □ _____ Saipan? It's beautiful there.

W: I □ _____ just □ _____ five months ago.

M: □ _____ you □ _____ □ _____ the Philippines? The □ _____ there are □ _____ this time of the year.

W: No, I haven't been there. □ _____ do you □ _____ that I go?

M: Lots of people □ _____ the □ _____ at Cebu.

W: That's interesting. □ _____ □ _____ are □ _____ there?

14 부탁 파악

대화를 듣고, 여자가 남자에게 부탁한 일로 가장 적절한 것을 고르시오.

① 휴대폰 교체하기
② 휴대폰 배달하기
③ 사무실로 전화하기
④ 사무실 전화번호 적기
⑤ 휴대폰 수리비 할인해주기

M: Good morning, ma'am. What can I do for you?

W: I □ _____ my □ _____ in the □ _____ and it got □ _____ all over it. Now, it □ _____ even □ _____ □ _____.

M: Oh, that's not good. Would you like us to □ _____ it?

W: Yes. □ _____ □ _____ will that □ _____?

M: This □ _____ going to be □ _____ to fix, so it's going to take □ _____ □ _____ □ _____.

W: I have to □ _____ □ _____ □ _____ □ _____. Can you □ _____ me at my □ _____ □ _____ to let me know when the phone is □ _____?

M: Sure. Just □ _____ it □ _____ for me, and I'll do that.

✎ **어휘복습** 잘 안 들리거나 몰라서 체크한 어휘를 써 놓고 복습해 보세요.

□ _____   □ _____   □ _____   □ _____

□ _____   □ _____   □ _____   □ _____

□ _____   □ _____   □ _____   □ _____

대화를 듣고, 내용과 일치하는 것을 고르시오.

① 남자의 삼촌은 도시에 살고 있다.
② 남자는 동물을 돌보는 일이 무서웠다.
③ 남자는 자전거를 탈 줄 모른다.
④ 여자는 바다에서 낚시를 했다.
⑤ 여자는 햇볕에 몸이 탔다.

W: John, did you have a good □ _____ □ _____?
M: Yes. I □ _____ a lot of □ _____ □ _____.
W: Like what?
M: I □ _____ some □ _____ at my uncle's □ _____,
so I □ _____ □ _____ □ _____ the animals and
□ _____ in the □ _____.
W: That doesn't sound fun.
M: Actually, I really □ _____ it. I got to □ _____ □ _____
and □ _____ in the country, too.
W: Wow. I just spent most of my time □ _____ □ _____
□ _____.
M: That's why you □ _____ □ _____ really good □ _____.

대화를 듣고, 남자가 친구를 데려갈 곳을 고르시오.

① 경주   ② 인사동
③ 부산   ④ 한국민속촌
⑤ 경복궁

M: My □ _____ from America is □ _____ here □ _____
□ _____. What should I do with him?
W: Why don't you □ _____ □ _____ □ _____ the Korean
□ _____ □ _____? He'll love it.
M: He □ _____ □ _____ □ _____ □ _____, so he went
there. □ _____ also □ _____ □ _____ Insadong and
Gyeongbokgung, too.
W: □ _____ □ _____ you take him to Busan or Gyeongju
then? That might be a fun trip.
M: Hmm... He □ _____ □ _____, so Gyeongju would be a
good place to go. Thanks for the □ _____, Sumi.
W: You're welcome.
M: Now, I need to □ _____ □ _____ everything for when he
gets here.

✏ **어휘복습** 잘 안 들리거나 몰라서 체크한 어휘를 써 놓고 복습해 보세요.

□ _____ □ _____ □ _____ □ _____
□ _____ □ _____ □ _____ □ _____
□ _____ □ _____ □ _____ □ _____

17 미언급 파악

다음을 듣고, 소방 훈련의 내용으로 언급되지 <u>않은</u> 것을 고르시오.

① 신속하게 줄 서기
② 엘리베이터 타지 않기
③ 다른 학생들 밀지 않기
④ 물이 든 양동이 나르기
⑤ 선생님이 출석 부르는 것 듣기

M: We will □ _____ a □ _____ □ _____ in a few minutes. First of all, if you hear the □ _____ □ _____, everyone needs to □ _____ □ _____ quickly and quietly □ _____ □ _____ □ _____. I'll check to □ _____ □ _____ the fire isn't right □ _____ the door. Then, we'll all □ _____ quickly □ _____ □ _____ the □ _____. We can't □ _____ the □ _____ in case of a fire, so we'll take the □ _____. Don't □ _____ or □ _____ other students. When we get out of the building, go to the □ _____ □ _____ □ _____ and listen as I □ _____ □ _____. I need to make sure everyone is there with me.

18 전화 목적 파악

대화를 듣고, 남자가 여자에게 전화한 목적으로 가장 적절한 것을 고르시오.

① 개를 돌봐 달라고 부탁하려고
② 여자를 인천 여행에 초대하려고
③ 남자의 집에 들를 것을 부탁하려고
④ 과학 다큐멘터리에 대해 얘기하려고
⑤ 여자의 이모가 어떻게 지내는지 물어보려고

W: Hi, Minsu. □ _____ □ _____?
M: Hi, Soyun. Do you □ _____ some □ _____ right now?
W: A bit. I'm just □ _____ a □ _____ for science class.
M: Do you mind □ _____ □ _____ □ _____ my □ _____ for a couple of days?
W: □ _____ □ _____ □ _____. But why can't you do it?
M: My □ _____ in Incheon is very □ _____, so we're going there to □ _____ □ _____ □ _____ her. I □ _____ □ _____ Snowy with me.
W: Okay. □ _____ I go to your house now to □ _____ her □ _____?
M: No. We'll □ _____ □ _____ there soon and □ _____ her □ _____ with you.

✎ **어휘복습** 잘 안 들리거나 몰라서 체크한 어휘를 써 놓고 복습해 보세요.

□ _____   □ _____   □ _____   □ _____

□ _____   □ _____   □ _____   □ _____

□ _____   □ _____   □ _____   □ _____

대화를 듣고, 남자의 마지막 말에 이어질 여자의 응답으로 가장 적절한 것을 고르시오.

Woman: _____

① That's right. I made a robot.

② I like working with machines a lot.

③ I want to go to space in the future.

④ No, that wasn't an interesting topic.

⑤ The robot cleans the house really well.

M: Jenny, I heard your □ _____ □ _____ □ _____ □ _____ □ _____ at the science □ _____. Congratulations.

W: Thanks, Jake. I □ _____ a lot of □ _____ doing it.

M: What was your project?

W: I □ _____ a □ _____ that can □ _____ the □ _____.

M: Wow. That's both □ _____ and □ _____.

W: My □ _____ □ _____ me the □ _____, but I □ _____ the entire robot □ _____.

M: □ _____ are you so □ _____ □ _____ robots?

W: _____

대화를 듣고, 남자의 마지막 말에 이어질 여자의 응답으로 가장 적절한 것을 고르시오.

Woman: _____

① No, I'm not hungry now.

② I'd like to have some Spanish food.

③ I want to try Russian food again.

④ No, I haven't tasted Brazilian food before.

⑤ I've been to that country a couple of times.

M: There's an international □ _____ □ _____ □ _____ the □ _____ today. Shall we go?

W: Why not? It □ _____ like □ _____.

M: I went to the festival last year. I got to □ _____ □ _____ □ _____ □ _____ good food.

W: What did you eat?

M: I had food from Brazil, Thailand, Russia, and Ethiopia.

W: Wow. I □ _____ □ _____ to go there.

M: Which country's food are you □ _____ □ _____ □ _____?

W: _____

✏ **어휘복습** 잘 안 들리거나 몰라서 체크한 어휘를 써 놓고 복습해 보세요.

□ _____   □ _____   □ _____   □ _____

□ _____   □ _____   □ _____   □ _____

□ _____   □ _____   □ _____   □ _____

◀◎》 MP3 실전 19

점수 / 20

01 대화를 듣고, 남자가 구매할 공책으로 가장 적절한 것을 고르시오.

① ② ③

④ ⑤

02 대화를 듣고, 남자의 심정으로 가장 적절한 것을 고르시오.

① nervous ② bored
③ afraid ④ confident
⑤ proud

03 대화를 듣고, 두 사람이 대화하는 장소로 가장 적절한 곳을 고르시오.

① 학교 ② 서점 ③ 도서관
④ 출판사 ⑤ 전자제품 매장

04 대화를 듣고, 여자가 남자에게 전화한 목적으로 가장 적절한 것을 고르시오.

① 할인권을 받으려고
② 햄버거를 주문하려고
③ 광고 제작을 요청하려고
④ 웹사이트 주소를 물어보려고
⑤ 일자리 지원 방법을 물어보려고

05 대화를 듣고, 남자가 환전 후 받게 될 금액을 고르시오.

① $100 ② $120 ③ $200
④ $240 ⑤ $1,000

06 대화를 듣고, 여자가 지난 주말에 한 일로 가장 적절한 것을 고르시오.

① 연극 보기
② 병문안 가기
③ 카페에 가기
④ 건강검진 받기
⑤ 여행 계획 세우기

07 대화를 듣고, 두 사람의 관계로 가장 적절한 것을 고르시오.

① 비행기 조종사 – 승무원
② 버스 기사 – 승객
③ 택시 기사 – 승객
④ 여행 가이드 – 관광객
⑤ 승무원 – 승객

08 다음을 듣고, 사람들이 기내에 가장 많이 두고 내리는 물건을 고르시오.

① baggage ② phones ③ clothes
④ newspapers ⑤ books

09 대화를 듣고, 여자가 남자에게 부탁한 일로 가장 적절한 것을 고르시오.

① 식탁 차리기 ② 저녁 요리하기
③ 거실 청소하기 ④ 아빠에게 전화하기
⑤ 식당에서 음식 가져오기

10 대화를 듣고, 여자가 음악 동아리에 가입한 이유로 가장 적절한 것을 고르시오.

① 노래를 잘 부르고 싶어서
② 악기 연주를 배우고 싶어서
③ 밴드의 멤버가 되고 싶어서
④ 춤 실력을 자랑하고 싶어서
⑤ 음악 점수를 잘 받고 싶어서

11 다음을 듣고, 두 사람의 대화가 어색한 것을 고르시오.

① ② ③ ④ ⑤

12 대화를 듣고, 여자의 마지막 말의 의도로 가장 적절한 것을 고르시오.

① 요청   ② 위로   ③ 제안
④ 거부   ⑤ 승인

13 대화를 듣고, 내용과 일치하지 <u>않는</u> 것을 고르시오.

① 여자는 자신의 시에 만족한다.
② 시의 길이는 20행 이상이다.
③ 시는 완성되는 데 이틀이 걸렸다.
④ 시에는 기사와 용이 등장한다.
⑤ 남자는 여자의 시를 읽고 싶어 한다.

14 다음을 듣고, 남자가 하는 말의 내용으로 가장 적절한 것을 고르시오.

① 캠프 규정   ② 하루 일정
③ 조별 과제   ④ 숙소 배정
⑤ 캠핑장 구성

15 다음을 듣고, 내용과 일치하지 <u>않는</u> 것을 고르시오.

①	Chinese	12
②	Latin	10
③	Spanish	9
④	French	10
⑤	Russian	4

16 다음을 듣고, 남자가 성적을 향상시키는 방법으로 언급하지 <u>않은</u> 것을 고르시오.

① 수업에 귀 기울이기
② 스터디 그룹에 참여하기
③ 공책에 필기하기
④ 필기 내용 복습하기
⑤ 숙제하기

17 대화를 듣고, 두 사람이 만날 시각을 고르시오.

① 1:15   ② 1:30   ③ 2:15
④ 2:45   ⑤ 4:00

18 대화를 듣고, 상황을 가장 잘 표현한 속담을 고르시오.

① Actions speak louder than words.
② A penny saved is a penny earned.
③ He who laughs last laughs best.
④ A watched pot never boils.
⑤ Early to bed, early to rise.

[19-20] 대화를 듣고, 남자의 마지막 말에 이어질 여자의 응답으로 가장 적절한 것을 고르시오.

19 Woman: _____

① No, I haven't seen that picture yet.
② Here's a picture I took with my camera.
③ I'll probably start with pictures of fruit.
④ I've painted several pictures in the past week.
⑤ Yes, my mother painted that picture on the wall.

20 Woman: _____

① I wrote my paper earlier this morning.
② You should have written two pages by now.
③ Yes, I worked there for the past three years.
④ Yes, Ms. Durham works very hard every day.
⑤ Write down anything you think of on your paper.

다시 듣고, 빈칸에 알맞은 단어를 써 보세요.

◀◖》 **MP3 실전 19-1**

01 그림 정보 파악

대화를 듣고, 남자가 구매할 공책으로 가장 적절한 것을 고르시오.

① ② ③
④ ⑤

W: Hi. Are you □ _____ □ _____ something?

M: Yes. I need to □ _____ a □ _____ for my sister.

W: Why don't you get this one □ _____ the □ _____ □ _____ the □ _____?

M: She □ _____ □ _____ □ _____ animals.

W: Okay. Here's a notebook with a □ _____ on the front.

M: That's nice. But I think she'll □ _____ the □ _____ □ _____ the □ _____.

W: Do you want the notebook with □ _____ hearts □ _____ □ _____?

M: The □ _____ □ _____ □ _____ hearts, please.

W: All right. Here you are.

02 심정 추론

대화를 듣고, 남자의 심정으로 가장 적절한 것을 고르시오.

① nervous ② bored
③ afraid ④ confident
⑤ proud

M: The □ _____ □ _____ is putting on a □ _____ tomorrow.

W: Oh, I didn't know that. Are you going to □ _____ it?

M: Actually, I'm going to be □ _____ □ _____. I □ _____ the □ _____.

W: Wow. You must be □ _____. Have you played □ _____ □ _____ □ _____ many □ _____ before?

M: I've been in many □ _____, so I'm □ _____ □ _____ □ _____ □ _____.

W: Do you know all of the □ _____?

M: Yes, I do. I have □ _____ □ _____ □ _____ a day for the past month. I'm sure I'll □ _____ □ _____.

W: Excellent. I'll □ _____ attend the concert □ _____.

✎ **어휘복습** 잘 안 들리거나 몰라서 체크한 어휘를 써 놓고 복습해 보세요.

□ _____ □ _____ □ _____ □ _____
□ _____ □ _____ □ _____ □ _____
□ _____ □ _____ □ _____ □ _____

03 장소 추론

대화를 듣고, 두 사람이 대화하는 장소로 가장 적절한 곳을 고르시오.

① 학교　　② 서점　　③ 도서관
④ 출판사　⑤ 전자제품 매장

M: Hi. Can I help you?

W: Yes, I'm looking for a □ _____ of the new □ _____ by Jeff Mercer.

M: Ah, yes. I □ _____ that we have it.

W: That's great. Can you tell me □ _____ □ _____ □ _____ ?

M: Let me □ _____ the □ _____ for a moment. It's in □ _____ number □ _____ in the □ _____ section.

W: Great. And do you know □ _____ □ _____ it □ _____ ?

M: It's □ _____ □ _____ □ _____ dollars.

W: Thanks.

04 전화 목적 파악

대화를 듣고, 여자가 남자에게 전화한 목적으로 가장 적절한 것을 고르시오.

① 할인권을 받으려고
② 햄버거를 주문하려고
③ 광고 제작을 요청하려고
④ 웹사이트 주소를 물어보려고
⑤ 일자리 지원 방법을 물어보려고

M: Hello. This is Burger World. How can I help you?

W: Hi. I □ _____ a □ _____ for you.

M: Yes, we're still having a □ _____ □ _____ □ _____ burgers.

W: Oh, it's not that. I □ _____ an □ _____ for your restaurant □ _____ .

M: Are you interested in □ _____ here □ _____ □ _____ ?

W: Yes, I am. What should I do?

M: □ _____ □ _____ you come here □ _____ at □ _____ ? You can □ _____ □ _____ the manager.

W: Great. Thanks for your □ _____ .

✎ **어휘복습**　잘 안 들리거나 몰라서 체크한 어휘를 써 놓고 복습해 보세요.

□ _____　□ _____　□ _____　□ _____

□ _____　□ _____　□ _____　□ _____

□ _____　□ _____　□ _____　□ _____

05 숫자 정보 파악

대화를 듣고, 남자가 환전 후 받게 될 금액을 고르시오.

① $100   ② $120   ③ $200
④ $240   ⑤ $1,000

W: Next □ _____ □ _____, please.
M: Good morning.
W: How can I □ _____ □ _____ □ _____ today?
M: What is the □ _____ □ _____ for Korean □ _____ □ _____ American □ _____?
W: You can get □ _____ □ _____ dollars for □ _____ □ _____ □ _____ □ _____ won.
M: That's great.
W: □ _____ □ _____ do you want to exchange?
M: I've got □ _____ hundred □ _____ thousand won.

06 한 일 파악

대화를 듣고, 여자가 지난 주말에 한 일로 가장 적절한 것을 고르시오.

① 연극 보기
② 병문안 가기
③ 카페에 가기
④ 건강검진 받기
⑤ 여행 계획 세우기

M: How was your □ _____, Tina?
W: It □ _____ very □ _____, Mark.
M: □ _____ □ _____? I thought you were going to □ _____ □ _____ □ _____.
W: I was □ _____ □ _____, □ _____ my friend Betty couldn't go.
M: That's too bad. □ _____ □ _____ to her?
W: She □ _____ □ _____ □ _____ while we were at a café before the play.
M: Oh, that's terrible. What did you do?
W: I □ _____ her □ _____ □ _____ her □ _____.
M: That was very □ _____ □ _____ □ _____.
W: I guess. Anyway, she's □ _____ □ _____ now, so I'm happy about that.

✎ **어휘복습** 잘 안 들리거나 몰라서 체크한 어휘를 써 놓고 복습해 보세요.

□ _____   □ _____   □ _____   □ _____
□ _____   □ _____   □ _____   □ _____
□ _____   □ _____   □ _____   □ _____

07 관계 추론

대화를 듣고, 두 사람의 관계로 가장 적절한 것을 고르시오.

① 비행기 조종사 – 승무원
② 버스 기사 – 승객
③ 택시 기사 – 승객
④ 여행 가이드 – 관광객
⑤ 승무원 – 승객

W: Excuse me. Are you going to Incheon □ _____ or Gimpo Airport?
M: We're going to Incheon.
W: That's great. I □ _____ I □ _____ the □ _____ bus.
M: Are you going to □ _____ your □ _____ while we go there?
W: Yes, this is just a □ _____ □ _____.
M: Okay. It □ _____ □ _____ □ _____ won for a ticket.
W: Here you are.
M: Thank you. Don't forget to □ _____ □ _____ □ _____.
W: I won't. Thanks.

08 특정 정보 파악

다음을 듣고, 사람들이 기내에 가장 많이 두고 내리는 물건을 고르시오.

① baggage
② phones
③ clothes
④ newspapers
⑤ books

M: Many □ _____ □ _____ are □ _____ □ _____ □ _____ when they □ _____ □ _____ their □ _____. So they frequently □ _____ things □ _____. Which □ _____ do they leave behind □ _____ □ _____? You might think it's their □ _____. But it's not. Only a few people forget that. The items people most □ _____ leave on airplanes are □ _____. Mobile phones, magazines, and clothes are some other items they □ _____ forget □ _____ □ _____.

✎ **어휘복습** 잘 안 들리거나 몰라서 체크한 어휘를 써 놓고 복습해 보세요.

□ _____   □ _____   □ _____   □ _____
□ _____   □ _____   □ _____   □ _____
□ _____   □ _____   □ _____   □ _____

09 부탁 파악

대화를 듣고, 여자가 남자에게 부탁한 일로 가장 적절한 것을 고르시오.

① 식탁 차리기
② 저녁 요리하기
③ 거실 청소하기
④ 아빠에게 전화하기
⑤ 식당에서 음식 가져오기

W: Joe, are you □_____ □_____ now?
M: Yes, Mom. Why?
W: I need you to □_____ □_____ □_____ for me, please.
M: Sure. Do you want me to □_____ the □_____ or □_____ □_____ some □_____ from the restaurant?
W: No, you □_____ □_____ □_____ do □_____ of those two things.
M: All right.
W: I need you to □_____ the □_____ □_____. Your father is bringing some □_____ home □_____ □_____.
M: Oh, so we need the house to look nice, right?
W: That's right.

10 이유 파악

대화를 듣고, 여자가 음악 동아리에 가입한 이유로 가장 적절한 것을 고르시오.

① 노래를 잘 부르고 싶어서
② 악기 연주를 배우고 싶어서
③ 밴드의 멤버가 되고 싶어서
④ 춤 실력을 자랑하고 싶어서
⑤ 음악 점수를 잘 받고 싶어서

M: Did you □_____ any □_____ this □_____?
W: Yes. I just □_____ □_____ □_____ the school's □_____ club.
M: Music? Can you □_____ an □_____?
W: Actually, I □_____ play any instruments □_____ □_____.
M: So □_____ □_____ did you join the club □_____?
W: I'd like to learn □_____ □_____ □_____.
M: □_____? I didn't know you were □_____ □_____ singing.
W: I'd like to □_____ □_____ □_____ one of those TV programs, so I need to □_____ a new □_____. You know, I can dance, but I can't sing.
M: I see. Well, good luck.

✏ **어휘복습** 잘 안 들리거나 몰라서 체크한 어휘를 써 놓고 복습해 보세요.

□_____ □_____ □_____ □_____
□_____ □_____ □_____ □_____
□_____ □_____ □_____ □_____

11 어색한 대화 찾기

다음을 듣고, 두 사람의 대화가 <u>어색한</u> 것을 고르시오.

①   ②   ③   ④   ⑤

① W: Do you □ _____ baseball □ _____ soccer?

    M: □ _____. I like basketball □ _____ □ _____ them.

② W: Is this sweater □ _____ □ _____ right now?

    M: Yes, we □ _____ □ _____ □ _____ one a while ago.

③ W: □ _____ do you □ _____ □ _____ my new idea?

    M: It's pretty □ _____, but you could □ _____ it a bit.

④ W: □ _____ are you □ _____ □ _____ in the lake?

    M: I'll probably do that □ _____ □ _____.

⑤ W: □ _____ □ _____ is this program going to □ _____?

    M: It's going to finish □ _____ □ _____.

12 의도 파악

대화를 듣고, 여자의 마지막 말의 의도로 가장 적절한 것을 고르시오.

① 요청   ② 위로   ③ 제안
④ 거부   ⑤ 승인

W: This is very □ _____.

M: What's the matter?

W: I have my own □ _____, but some people are □ _____ □ _____ □ _____ on it.

M: What kind of comments are they making?

W: They're □ _____ □ _____ □ _____ about my friends and me.

M: That's not nice at all.

W: What can I do about that?

M: You should □ _____ the comments and then □ _____ those people □ _____ □ _____ on your blog.

W: I don't know □ _____ □ _____ □ _____ that. Would you mind □ _____ me what to do?

✎ **어휘복습** 잘 안 들리거나 몰라서 체크한 어휘를 써 놓고 복습해 보세요.

□ _____   □ _____   □ _____   □ _____

□ _____   □ _____   □ _____   □ _____

□ _____   □ _____   □ _____   □ _____

13 내용 일치 파악

대화를 듣고, 내용과 일치하지 <u>않는</u> 것을 고르시오.

① 여자는 자신의 시에 만족한다.
② 시의 길이는 20행 이상이다.
③ 시는 완성되는 데 이틀이 걸렸다.
④ 시에는 기사와 용이 등장한다.
⑤ 남자는 여자의 시를 읽고 싶어 한다.

M: Did you □ _____ □ _____ your □ _____?
W: Yes, I did. I'm really □ _____ with it.
M: □ _____ □ _____ is it?
W: It's □ _____ □ _____ □ _____ lines. It's pretty long.
M: Wow. □ _____ □ _____ did it □ _____ for you to write it?
W: Actually, I was planning to finish it □ _____ □ _____ □ _____, but it took me more than □ _____ □ _____.
M: What's it about?
W: It's a □ _____ poem about a □ _____ and a □ _____. Would you like to read it?
M: Sure. It sounds interesting.

14 화제 추론

다음을 듣고, 남자가 하는 말의 내용으로 가장 적절한 것을 고르시오.

① 캠프 규정   ② 하루 일정
③ 조별 과제   ④ 숙소 배정
⑤ 캠핑장 구성

M: Attention, □ _____. Welcome to Lake Shady. We've got an □ _____ □ _____ planned for you. First, you need to □ _____ □ _____ your □ _____ and □ _____ your □ _____ there. After that, we'll □ _____ □ _____ □ _____ □ _____ of the camp. Then, we're going to □ _____ a □ _____ for lunch. When lunch is finished, we're going to □ _____ □ _____ □ _____ the □ _____, and then we'll □ _____ in the □ _____ for a while. We've got a busy day, so let's □ _____ □ _____. Please take your bags to your cabins and be back here □ _____ □ _____ □ _____.

✎ **어휘복습** 잘 안 들리거나 몰라서 체크한 어휘를 써 놓고 복습해 보세요.

□ _____   □ _____   □ _____   □ _____
□ _____   □ _____   □ _____   □ _____
□ _____   □ _____   □ _____   □ _____

15 내용 일치 파악

다음을 듣고, 내용과 일치하지 <u>않는</u> 것을 고르시오.

①	Chinese	12
②	Latin	10
③	Spanish	9
④	French	10
⑤	Russian	4

16 미언급 파악

다음을 듣고, 남자가 성적을 향상시키는 방법으로 언급하지 <u>않은</u> 것을 고르시오.

① 수업에 귀 기울이기
② 스터디 그룹에 참여하기
③ 공책에 필기하기
④ 필기 내용 복습하기
⑤ 숙제하기

W: The school is giving the students a ☐ _____ ☐ _____ ☐ _____ a new ☐ _____ ☐ _____ . The ☐ _____ decide to ☐ _____ to see which language they will study. ☐ _____ students request to study ☐ _____ while ☐ _____ of them want to learn ☐ _____ . ☐ _____ students ask to learn ☐ _____ . The ☐ _____ ☐ _____ of them want to learn ☐ _____ . ☐ _____ ☐ _____ students would like to learn ☐ _____ . It's the ☐ _____ ☐ _____ language.

M: If you want to ☐ _____ a ☐ _____ ☐ _____ , you need to ☐ _____ ☐ _____ ☐ _____ . First, always ☐ _____ ☐ _____ when the ☐ _____ is ☐ _____ in class. Don't ☐ _____ ☐ _____ your ☐ _____ or ☐ _____ ☐ _____ your ☐ _____ . Instead, ☐ _____ ☐ _____ what the teacher is saying. Next, be sure to ☐ _____ good ☐ _____ . ☐ _____ write ☐ _____ your ☐ _____ though. Get a ☐ _____ and take notes in it. ☐ _____ your notes ☐ _____ ☐ _____ every day, and you'll be able to ☐ _____ the lesson ☐ _____ . Be sure to ☐ _____ ☐ _____ of your ☐ _____ as well. Doing homework will help you learn the ☐ _____ you studied in class a lot ☐ _____ .

✏ **어휘복습** 잘 안 들리거나 몰라서 체크한 어휘를 써 놓고 복습해 보세요.

☐ _____ ☐ _____ ☐ _____ ☐ _____
☐ _____ ☐ _____ ☐ _____ ☐ _____
☐ _____ ☐ _____ ☐ _____ ☐ _____

17 숫자 정보 파악

대화를 듣고, 두 사람이 만날 시각을 고르시오.

① 1:15　② 1:30　③ 2:15
④ 2:45　⑤ 4:00

W: Hi, Jason. It's Amy.
M: □ _____ □ _____, Amy?
W: Did you □ _____ □ _____ our □ _____ to go to the □ _____ today?
M: Not at all. We're still □ _____ □ _____ □ _____, right?
W: Actually, we were □ _____ □ _____ □ _____ at □ _____ □ _____.
M: Oh, that's □ _____ minutes □ _____ □ _____. I don't think I can □ _____ □ _____ downtown by then.
W: Then when can you be there?
M: How about at a □ _____ □ _____ □ _____? I can be there then if I □ _____ the □ _____ now.
W: Okay. □ _____ me when you □ _____ □ _____.
M: I will. Bye.

18 속담 추론

대화를 듣고, 상황을 가장 잘 표현한 속담을 고르시오.

① Actions speak louder than words.
② A penny saved is a penny earned.
③ He who laughs last laughs best.
④ A watched pot never boils.
⑤ Early to bed, early to rise.

M: You won't □ _____ □ _____ □ _____ to me.
W: What? Tell me.
M: Wendy said she was going to □ _____ □ _____ to □ _____ □ _____ our group □ _____, but she didn't □ _____ □ _____.
W: Did you □ _____ □ _____ her?
M: I did, but her □ _____ is □ _____ □ _____.
W: □ _____ she just has a lot of □ _____ □ _____ □ _____.
M: I don't think so. This is the □ _____ □ _____ she has done that.
W: I'm sure she didn't □ _____ □ _____. She always tries to □ _____ her □ _____.
M: She □ _____ □ _____ to keep them, but she □ _____ does.

✎ **어휘복습** 잘 안 들리거나 몰라서 체크한 어휘를 써 놓고 복습해 보세요.

□ _____　□ _____　□ _____　□ _____

□ _____　□ _____　□ _____　□ _____

□ _____　□ _____　□ _____　□ _____

19 알맞은 응답 찾기

대화를 듣고, 남자의 마지막 말에 이어질 여자의 응답으로 가장 적절한 것을 고르시오.

Woman: _____

① No, I haven't seen that picture yet.
② Here's a picture I took with my camera.
③ I'll probably start with pictures of fruit.
④ I've painted several pictures in the past week.
⑤ Yes, my mother painted that picture on the wall.

W: I just □ _____ □ _____ to take □ _____ □ _____.
M: That's interesting. Is the □ _____ going to □ _____ your □ _____?
W: No, I've got to go to her □ _____.
M: □ _____ □ _____ are you going to have lessons?
W: □ _____ □ _____ □ _____. I'll go there on □ _____ and □ _____.
M: I □ _____ □ _____ you liked painting.
W: I □ _____ □ _____, but I've never tried to do any painting.
M: □ _____ □ _____ □ _____ pictures are you going to make?
W: _____

20 알맞은 응답 찾기

대화를 듣고, 남자의 마지막 말에 이어질 여자의 응답으로 가장 적절한 것을 고르시오.

Woman: _____

① I wrote my paper earlier this morning.
② You should have written two pages by now.
③ Yes, I worked there for the past three years.
④ Yes, Ms. Durham works very hard every day.
⑤ Write down anything you think of on your paper.

M: This is so frustrating.
W: Are you □ _____ □ _____ your essay? How's it going?
M: Terribly. I haven't written a □ _____ □ _____ □ _____.
W: Why not? You need to □ _____ it □ _____ to Ms. Durham □ _____ □ _____.
M: But I can't □ _____ □ _____ □ _____ any □ _____.
W: Why don't you □ _____ □ _____? Then, you can write whatever □ _____ □ _____ □ _____.
M: I've □ _____ tried that □ _____. Please □ _____ □ _____ it works.
W: _____

✏️ **어휘복습** 잘 안 들리거나 몰라서 체크한 어휘를 써 놓고 복습해 보세요.

□ _____   □ _____   □ _____   □ _____
□ _____   □ _____   □ _____   □ _____
□ _____   □ _____   □ _____   □ _____

01 다음을 듣고, 수요일의 날씨로 가장 적절한 것을 고르시오.

① ② ③ ④ ⑤

02 대화를 듣고, 남자의 노트북 가방을 고르시오.

① ② ③

④ ⑤

03 대화를 듣고, 남자의 심정으로 가장 적절한 것을 고르시오.

① joyful ② angry ③ scared
④ curious ⑤ satisfied

04 대화를 듣고, 두 사람이 대화하는 장소로 가장 적절한 곳을 고르시오.

① 음식점 ② 학교 ③ 박물관
④ 문구점 ⑤ 도서관

05 대화를 듣고, 여자가 어제 한 일로 가장 적절한 것을 고르시오.

① 친구 만나기 ② 개 산책시키기
③ 엄마와 산책하기 ④ 관람객 안내하기
⑤ 공원에서 운동하기

06 대화를 듣고, 여자의 마지막 말의 의도로 가장 적절한 것을 고르시오.

① 동의 ② 축하 ③ 요청
④ 거절 ⑤ 충고

07 대화를 듣고, 역사 동아리에 등록한 학생의 수를 고르시오.

① 4 ② 8 ③ 12
④ 13 ⑤ 14

08 대화를 듣고, 남자가 대화 직후에 할 일로 가장 적절한 것을 고르시오.

① 호텔 예약하기
② 여행 안내서 사기
③ 여행 계획 세우기
④ 삼촌에게 연락하기
⑤ 비행기 표 예약하기

09 대화를 듣고, 여자가 가장 좋아한 공연으로 가장 적절한 것을 고르시오.

① 판소리 ② 인형극
③ 불꽃놀이 ④ 한국 전통 춤
⑤ 브레이크댄스

10 다음을 듣고, 남자가 하는 말의 내용으로 가장 적절한 것을 고르시오.

① 독서의 중요성
② 특별 수업 소개
③ 도서관 이용 방법
④ 어린이 안전 교육
⑤ 최신 컴퓨터 기능 안내

11 대화를 듣고, 남자에 관한 내용으로 일치하지 <u>않는</u> 것을 고르시오.

① 새로운 일을 시작했다.
② Chicken Heaven에서 일한다.
③ 가장 좋아하는 식당은 Chicken Heaven이다.
④ 몇 가지 실수를 저질렀다.
⑤ 손님들에게 사과를 했다.

12 대화를 듣고, 남자가 여자에게 전화한 목적으로 가장 적절한 것을 고르시오.

① 선물에 대해 감사하려고
② 실수에 대해 사과하려고
③ 학교에서 만나자고 말하려고
④ 아기 돌보는 것을 부탁하려고
⑤ 슈퍼마켓에 들를 것을 부탁하려고

13 다음을 듣고, 두 사람의 대화가 <u>어색한</u> 것을 고르시오.

①   ②   ③   ④   ⑤

14 다음을 듣고, 학생들이 가장 많이 빌리는 DVD를 고르시오.

① 공상과학 영화   ② 다큐멘터리
③ 액션 영화   ④ 만화 영화
⑤ 드라마

15 대화를 듣고, 남자가 대화 직후에 할 일로 가장 적절한 것을 고르시오.

① 전화하기   ② 명동에 가기
③ 영화 표 예매하기   ④ 공연 표 예매하기
⑤ 영화 시간 확인하기

16 대화를 듣고, 두 사람이 대화하는 장소로 가장 적절한 곳을 고르시오.

① museum   ② bookstore
③ library   ④ furniture store
⑤ electronics store

17 대화를 듣고, 여자가 병원에 가는 이유로 가장 적절한 것을 고르시오.

① 처방전을 받으려고
② 건강검진을 받으려고
③ 할아버지를 만나려고
④ 상처를 치료받으려고
⑤ 예방주사를 맞으려고

18 대화를 듣고, 상황을 가장 잘 표현한 속담을 고르시오.

① Don't judge a book by its cover.
② The early bird catches the worm.
③ Many hands make light work.
④ Absence makes the heart grow fonder.
⑤ The grass is always greener on the other side.

[19-20] 대화를 듣고, 남자의 마지막 말에 이어질 여자의 응답으로 가장 적절한 것을 고르시오.

19 Woman: _____

① That's my boy.
② Why did you do that?
③ What else did you do?
④ When did he move here?
⑤ Teach him how to speak Italian.

20 Woman: _____

① Why didn't you help me out at all?
② No, we haven't made any plans yet.
③ Thanks. I really appreciate your help.
④ All right. I'll do that in a few minutes.
⑤ But I told you my room is already clean.

01 날씨 파악

다음을 듣고, 수요일의 날씨로 가장 적절한 것을 고르시오.

① ② ③

④ ⑤

W: Here's the weather report for □ _____ □ _____. You're going to □ _____ your □ _____ on □ _____ since it's going to □ _____ □ _____ □ _____ □ _____. The □ _____ will □ _____ on □ _____, and we'll have □ _____ □ _____ weather. On □ _____, it's going to be very □ _____. The □ _____ is going to □ _____ much □ _____, too. We might get a little □ _____ on □ _____. It's definitely going to □ _____ on □ _____. Expect around three to five centimeters of snow then.

02 그림 정보 파악

대화를 듣고, 남자의 노트북 가방을 고르시오.

① ② ③

④ ⑤

W: Can I help you, sir?

M: Yes, I left my □ _____ □ _____ here in the □ _____, and I can't find it now.

W: What does it □ _____ □ _____?

M: It's □ _____ □ _____, and it has a □ _____ □ _____.

W: We have □ _____ □ _____ those. Is there anything on the □ _____? Is there a □ _____ on it?

M: No, but there is a □ _____ on it. The sticker shows a □ _____ □ _____ a □ _____.

W: Ah, I □ _____ that we have your bag.

M: You do?

W: Yes, I think □ _____ □ _____ the bag you're □ _____ □ _____.

✎ **어휘복습** 잘 안 들리거나 몰라서 체크한 어휘를 써 놓고 복습해 보세요.

□ _____   □ _____   □ _____   □ _____
□ _____   □ _____   □ _____   □ _____
□ _____   □ _____   □ _____   □ _____

03 심정 추론

대화를 듣고, 남자의 심정으로 가장 적절한 것을 고르시오.

① joyful   ② angry
③ scared   ④ curious
⑤ satisfied

W: Why aren't you eating your dinner, Minsu?

M: It □ _____ every time I □ _____ my □ _____.

W: Do you have a □ _____ □ _____?

M: Yes, I do. I think I □ _____ a □ _____.

W: Well, you need to □ _____ a □ _____ then.

M: But I □ _____ going to the dentist. It always hurts when I go there.

W: Don't □ _____ □ _____ □ _____ going there. The dentist can help you □ _____ □ _____.

M: I □ _____, □ _____ I still don't want to go.

W: If you don't go now, your tooth will hurt □ _____ □ _____.

04 장소 추론

대화를 듣고, 두 사람이 대화하는 장소로 가장 적절한 곳을 고르시오.

① 음식점   ② 학교   ③ 박물관
④ 문구점   ⑤ 도서관

W: □ _____ did you want to □ _____ □ _____?

M: I need to □ _____ a few □ _____.

W: Well, □ _____ □ _____. I'm □ _____ and need to get □ _____ □ _____ □ _____.

M: □ _____ □ _____ just a minute. Let me □ _____ □ _____.

W: What are you □ _____ □ _____?

M: I need an □ _____ and a □ _____.

W: Is that it?

M: No. I should also buy □ _____ □ _____ □ _____ red pens.

W: Okay. Get those items, □ _____ □ _____ let's go.

✎ **어휘복습** 잘 안 들리거나 몰라서 체크한 어휘를 써 놓고 복습해 보세요.

□ _____   □ _____   □ _____   □ _____
□ _____   □ _____   □ _____   □ _____
□ _____   □ _____   □ _____   □ _____

05 한 일 파악

대화를 듣고, 여자가 어제 한 일로 가장 적절한 것을 고르시오.

① 친구 만나기
② 개 산책시키기
③ 엄마와 산책하기
④ 관람객 안내하기
⑤ 공원에서 운동하기

M: Your dog is □ _____ □ _____ □ _____. Do you □ _____ her a lot?

W: Yes. We □ _____ □ _____ in the park every day.

M: Did you □ _____ her □ _____ □ _____ □ _____ yesterday?

W: No, I didn't. My mom did that □ _____ □ _____ me.

M: □ _____? Did something happen to you?

W: I was □ _____ □ _____, but I □ _____ □ _____ □ _____ all day long.

M: Where were you?

W: I was □ _____ at the □ _____. I □ _____ by □ _____ □ _____ there every weekend.

M: That's □ _____. I should go there and see you.

W: Visit there □ _____ □ _____, and I can give you a tour.

06 의도 파악

대화를 듣고, 여자의 마지막 말의 의도로 가장 적절한 것을 고르시오.

① 동의   ② 축하   ③ 요청
④ 거절   ⑤ 충고

W: Why do you □ _____ so □ _____ today?

M: I □ _____ □ _____ getting to sleep.

W: Were your □ _____ □ _____ being □ _____ again?

M: No, they were □ _____. I was just □ _____ □ _____ a few things.

W: □ _____ □ _____?

M: I was □ _____ about our upcoming □ _____. I really need to □ _____ □ _____.

W: You need to □ _____. If you don't, you □ _____ get any sleep □ _____ □ _____. And then you'll □ _____ really □ _____ □ _____ the tests.

✎ **어휘복습** 잘 안 들리거나 몰라서 체크한 어휘를 써 놓고 복습해 보세요.

□ _____   □ _____   □ _____   □ _____
□ _____   □ _____   □ _____   □ _____
□ _____   □ _____   □ _____   □ _____

대화를 듣고, 역사 동아리에 등록한 학생의
수를 고르시오.

① 4   ② 8   ③ 12
④ 13   ⑤ 14

W: Sam, are you really going to □ _____ a □ _____ □ _____?
M: That's right. I'm going to start a □ _____ club. Would you like to □ _____ it?
W: I don't know. What are you going to do?
M: We're going to □ _____ historical □ _____.
W: That sounds boring to me.
M: That's not it. We'll □ _____ history □ _____ and □ _____
□ _____ important □ _____ □ _____ □ _____
□ _____.
W: □ _____ □ _____ students □ _____ □ _____ yet?
M: Yes. □ _____ boys and □ _____ girls are going to join.
W: Does that □ _____ you?
M: No, it doesn't, and it doesn't include Kevin. I □ _____
□ _____ him.

대화를 듣고, 남자가 대화 직후에 할 일로
가장 적절한 것을 고르시오.

① 호텔 예약하기
② 여행 안내서 사기
③ 여행 계획 세우기
④ 삼촌에게 연락하기
⑤ 비행기 표 예약하기

M: How are your □ _____ □ _____ going?
W: Not bad. I've □ _____ the □ _____ □ _____ to fly to Jeju Island.
M: □ _____ □ _____ will you □ _____ there?
W: I'm planning to stay there □ _____ □ _____ □ _____.
M: That's a long time. You'll have a lot of fun.
W: The only □ _____ □ _____ that all of the □ _____ are □ _____. I □ _____ □ _____ any □ _____ □ _____ right now.
M: Would you like me to □ _____ my □ _____? He has a □ _____ □ _____ on Jeju Island. I'm sure he can □ _____ you □ _____.
W: Would you □ _____ that □ _____ □ _____? That would be great.
M: Sure. I'll do that □ _____ □ _____.

✎ **어휘복습** 잘 안 들리거나 몰라서 체크한 어휘를 써 놓고 복습해 보세요.

□ _____   □ _____   □ _____   □ _____

□ _____   □ _____   □ _____   □ _____

□ _____   □ _____   □ _____   □ _____

09 특정 정보 파악

대화를 듣고, 여자가 가장 좋아한 공연으로 가장 적절한 것을 고르시오.

① 판소리   ② 인형극
③ 불꽃놀이   ④ 한국 전통 춤
⑤ 브레이크댄스

M: Thanks for □ _____ □ _____ to the □ _____ today. I had a great time.
W: I'm glad you came with me.
M: We □ _____ so many □ _____. I □ _____ the □ _____ □ _____ by the students.
W: That was nice. I thought the breakdancing □ _____ were good □ _____ □ _____.
M: Were they your □ _____?
W: No, but I liked them a lot. The performance I □ _____ □ _____ □ _____ was the □ _____ □ _____ □ _____. It was very elegant.
M: Yes, it was pretty nice. It was □ _____ □ _____ □ _____ for me to □ _____ that kind of performance.
W: We should □ _____ □ _____ here □ _____ tomorrow.
M: Good idea.

10 화제 추론

다음을 듣고, 남자가 하는 말의 내용으로 가장 적절한 것을 고르시오.

① 독서의 중요성
② 특별 수업 소개
③ 도서관 이용 방법
④ 어린이 안전 교육
⑤ 최신 컴퓨터 기능 안내

M: Thank you for coming to the Eastside □ _____ today. This is the □ _____ □ _____ of a special □ _____ we're starting. We're going to □ _____ □ _____ □ _____ to young children. We □ _____ □ _____ computers very much □ _____ □ _____, so everyone needs to know □ _____ □ _____ □ _____ them. Today, we're going to learn how to do some □ _____ computer □ _____. All right, everyone, why don't you □ _____ □ _____ at a computer? It's time to begin.

✎ **어휘복습** 잘 안 들리거나 몰라서 체크한 어휘를 써 놓고 복습해 보세요.

□ _____   □ _____   □ _____   □ _____
□ _____   □ _____   □ _____   □ _____
□ _____   □ _____   □ _____   □ _____

11 내용 일치 파악

대화를 듣고, 남자에 관한 내용으로 일치하지 <u>않는</u> 것을 고르시오.

① 새로운 일을 시작했다.
② Chicken Heaven에서 일한다.
③ 가장 좋아하는 식당은 Chicken Heaven이다.
④ 몇 가지 실수를 저질렀다.
⑤ 손님들에게 사과를 했다.

W: You look □ _____, Jeff. What's up?
M: It was my □ _____ □ _____ of □ _____ at my □ _____ □ _____ today.
W: Did you □ _____ a job? □ _____ are you □ _____?
M: I'm working at Chicken Heaven.
W: Oh, that's my □ _____ fast-food □ _____. How was work?
M: It was hard. We got really □ _____ □ _____ □ _____, and I □ _____ a few □ _____ with customers' □ _____.
W: Did they □ _____ □ _____?
M: □ _____ □ _____ □ _____ them did. But I □ _____, so they were okay.
W: That's good to know.

12 전화 목적 파악

대화를 듣고, 남자가 여자에게 전화한 목적으로 가장 적절한 것을 고르시오.

① 선물에 대해 감사하려고
② 실수에 대해 사과하려고
③ 학교에서 만나자고 말하려고
④ 아기 돌보는 것을 부탁하려고
⑤ 슈퍼마켓에 들를 것을 부탁하려고

W: Hi, Dad. What's going on?
M: Hi, Kelly. Are you still □ _____ □ _____?
W: No, I'm □ _____ □ _____ □ _____ □ _____ now.
M: That's good. You need to get home □ _____ □ _____ □ _____ □ _____.
W: Why? Is □ _____ □ _____?
M: Your mother needs to go to the □ _____. But she can't □ _____ the □ _____ home □ _____.
W: Oh, okay. Do you need me to □ _____ her □ _____ Mom's □ _____?
M: Yes. Do you □ _____?
W: Not at all. I'll be home □ _____ about □ _____ □ _____.
M: Thanks. I really □ _____ your □ _____.

✎ **어휘복습** 잘 안 들리거나 몰라서 체크한 어휘를 써 놓고 복습해 보세요.

□ _____ □ _____ □ _____ □ _____
□ _____ □ _____ □ _____ □ _____
□ _____ □ _____ □ _____ □ _____

13 어색한 대화 찾기

다음을 듣고, 두 사람의 대화가 <u>어색한</u> 것을 고르시오.

①　　②　　③　　④　　⑤

①　M: Can I □ _____ my □ _____, please?
　　W: □ _____. What would you like?
②　M: □ _____ □ _____ are you going to meet your sister?
　　W: She's □ _____ □ _____ □ _____.
③　M: I got an A □ _____ my science □ _____.
　　W: That's great news. I'm □ _____ □ _____ you.
④　M: Have you □ _____ the □ _____ □ _____ yet?
　　W: I've got □ _____ □ _____ to do.
⑤　M: Did you remember to □ _____ an □ _____?
　　W: Yes, I've □ _____ □ _____ here in my bag.

14 특정 정보 파악

다음을 듣고, 학생들이 가장 많이 빌리는 DVD를 고르시오.

① 공상과학 영화
② 다큐멘터리
③ 액션 영화
④ 만화 영화
⑤ 드라마

W:　The public □ _____ has many DVDs, and students
　　□ _____ □ _____ lots of them. Most people believe that
　　□ _____ □ _____ are the most popular DVDs, but only
　　□ _____ □ _____ of the □ _____ □ _____ them.
　　□ _____ □ _____ of the DVDs the students borrow are
　　□ _____. Those are □ _____ □ _____ □ _____ ones.
　　□ _____ DVDs are □ _____ □ _____ most popular
　　after action movies, and □ _____ movies and □ _____
　　are popular as well.

✎ **어휘복습** 잘 안 들리거나 몰라서 체크한 어휘를 써 놓고 복습해 보세요.

□ _____　　　□ _____　　　□ _____　　　□ _____
□ _____　　　□ _____　　　□ _____　　　□ _____
□ _____　　　□ _____　　　□ _____　　　□ _____

15 할 일 파악

대화를 듣고, 남자가 대화 직후에 할 일로 가장 적절한 것을 고르시오.

① 전화하기
② 명동에 가기
③ 영화 표 예매하기
④ 공연 표 예매하기
⑤ 영화 시간 확인하기

M: Why don't we □ _____ a □ _____ tomorrow?

W: Hmm... How about doing □ _____ □ _____?

M: Why? You like watching movies □ _____ □ _____.

W: That's too □ _____ now.

M: Okay. What would you like to do then?

W: I'd like to see *Nanta*. It's □ _____ in Myeongdong every day.

M: Oh, my friends said it's a □ _____ □ _____. Let's □ _____ □ _____ now.

W: Should we □ _____ the □ _____?

M: No, we can do that □ _____ □ _____ □ _____.

16 장소 추론

대화를 듣고, 두 사람이 대화하는 장소로 가장 적절한 곳을 고르시오.

① museum
② bookstore
③ library
④ furniture store
⑤ electronics store

W: Hi. Can you □ _____ me some □ _____, please?

M: Sure. What do you □ _____?

W: I'm looking for a □ _____ □ _____ *The Ancient Egyptians* □ _____ Carl Weathers, but I can't find it.

M: Did you □ _____ □ _____ it □ _____ the □ _____?

W: Yes, I did. It's supposed to be □ _____, but I can't find it □ _____ the □ _____.

M: That's □ _____. I remember seeing it an hour ago.

W: □ _____ do you think □ _____?

M: Maybe □ _____ □ _____ is reading it or is going to □ _____ it □ _____ soon.

W: I hope not. I need it for a □ _____ □ _____.

✎ **어휘복습** 잘 안 들리거나 몰라서 체크한 어휘를 써 놓고 복습해 보세요.

□ _____   □ _____   □ _____   □ _____

□ _____   □ _____   □ _____   □ _____

□ _____   □ _____   □ _____   □ _____

17 이유 파악

대화를 듣고, 여자가 병원에 가는 이유로 가장 적절한 것을 고르시오.

① 처방전을 받으려고
② 건강검진을 받으려고
③ 할아버지를 만나려고
④ 상처를 치료받으려고
⑤ 예방주사를 맞으려고

M: Hi, Sue. What are you doing now?

W: I'm □ _____ □ _____ the □ _____.

M: Is your □ _____ still there? Are you going to □ _____ □ _____?

W: Actually, he □ _____ □ _____ □ _____ the hospital two weeks ago. He's much □ _____ now.

M: That's good to hear.

W: Yeah. Anyway, I'm going there to □ _____ a □ _____ □ _____.

M: Are you □ _____ now?

W: No, but □ _____ is □ _____. I want to be □ _____.

M: That's a good idea. I should do the □ _____ □ _____.

18 속담 추론

대화를 듣고, 상황을 가장 잘 표현한 속담을 고르시오.

① Don't judge a book by its cover.
② The early bird catches the worm.
③ Many hands make light work.
④ Absence makes the heart grow fonder.
⑤ The grass is always greener on the other side.

M: Are you ready to □ _____ □ _____ the □ _____?

W: Yes, I am.

M: We're going to be really busy □ _____ □ _____ the □ _____.

W: I know. But it will be □ _____ □ _____. I □ _____ seeing all the □ _____ □ _____ the □ _____.

M: Do you think we can clean much? □ _____ □ _____ □ _____ can we □ _____ □ _____ by ourselves?

W: We □ _____ □ _____ the □ _____ □ _____ there today.

M: Won't we? □ _____ □ _____ is going?

W: More than □ _____ students □ _____ □ _____ to help. We should all be able to make the mountain □ _____ □ _____.

M: That's wonderful. If we all □ _____ □ _____, we'll □ _____ a □ _____ □ _____.

✎ **어휘복습** 잘 안 들리거나 몰라서 체크한 어휘를 써 놓고 복습해 보세요.

□ _____   □ _____   □ _____   □ _____
□ _____   □ _____   □ _____   □ _____
□ _____   □ _____   □ _____   □ _____

19 알맞은 응답 찾기

대화를 듣고, 남자의 마지막 말에 이어질 여자의 응답으로 가장 적절한 것을 고르시오.

Woman: _____
① That's my boy.
② Why did you do that?
③ What else did you do?
④ When did he move here?
⑤ Teach him how to speak Italian.

W: Did you □ _____ a □ _____ □ _____ at school?

M: It was fun, Mom. We got a □ _____ □ _____ in our □ _____ .

W: □ _____ is the student □ _____ ?

M: He is from Italy. His family just □ _____ here □ _____ □ _____ .

W: Does he □ _____ □ _____ □ _____ ?

M: No, he only knows □ _____ □ _____ □ _____ .

W: You ought to □ _____ him □ _____ then. You should □ _____ a □ _____ □ _____ .

M: Don't worry, Mom. I □ _____ □ _____ a few □ _____ for him today.

W: _____

20 알맞은 응답 찾기

대화를 듣고, 남자의 마지막 말에 이어질 여자의 응답으로 가장 적절한 것을 고르시오.

Woman: _____
① Why didn't you help me out at all?
② No, we haven't made any plans yet.
③ Thanks. I really appreciate your help.
④ All right. I'll do that in a few minutes.
⑤ But I told you my room is already clean.

M: Did you remember to □ _____ your □ _____ today?

W: Sorry. I'll do it □ _____ .

M: You □ _____ the □ _____ □ _____ yesterday.

W: I want to clean my room, but I just □ _____ □ _____ □ _____ □ _____ .

M: But aren't you planning to □ _____ □ _____ □ _____ Lily this evening?

W: Yes. We're going to □ _____ □ _____ □ _____ together.

M: □ _____ you have time to go out, □ _____ you have time to clean your room.

W: _____

✎ **어휘복습** 잘 안 들리거나 몰라서 체크한 어휘를 써 놓고 복습해 보세요.

□ _____   □ _____   □ _____   □ _____
□ _____   □ _____   □ _____   □ _____
□ _____   □ _____   □ _____   □ _____

◄◼))) MP3 기출 01

점수

/ 20

01 다음을 듣고, 내일 대전의 날씨로 가장 적절한 것을 고르시오.

① ② ③ ④ ⑤

02 대화를 듣고, 두 사람이 보고 있는 사진으로 가장 적절한 것을 고르시오.

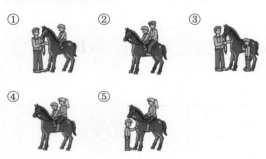

① ② ③
④ ⑤

03 대화를 듣고, 남자의 심정으로 가장 적절한 것을 고르시오.

① excited   ② relaxed   ③ bored
④ angry   ⑤ surprised

04 대화를 듣고, 여자가 어제 한 일로 가장 적절한 것을 고르시오.

① 가족 여행   ② 동물원 견학
③ 콘서트 관람   ④ 컴퓨터 게임
⑤ 축구 경기 관람

05 대화를 듣고, 두 사람이 대화하는 장소로 가장 적절한 곳을 고르시오.

① 경찰서   ② 도서관   ③ 은행
④ 식당   ⑤ 서점

06 대화를 듣고, 여자의 마지막 말의 의도로 가장 적절한 것을 고르시오.

① 축하   ② 허가   ③ 사과
④ 충고   ⑤ 감사

07 대화를 듣고, 두 사람이 보게 될 뮤지컬이 시작하는 시각을 고르시오.

① 1:00 P.M.   ② 3:00 P.M.   ③ 4:00 P.M.
④ 5:00 P.M.   ⑤ 7:00 P.M.

08 대화를 듣고, 남자가 대화 직후에 할 일로 가장 적절한 것을 고르시오.

① 기차표 가져오기
② 운동 계획 세우기
③ 약속 시간 정하기
④ 책상 서랍 정리하기
⑤ 기차 시간 확인하기

09 대화를 듣고, 남자가 주문할 음식을 고르시오.

① 치즈버거
② 피자와 콜라
③ 치킨 샐러드
④ 토마토 스파게티
⑤ 감자튀김과 콜라

10 다음을 듣고, 여자가 하는 말의 내용으로 가장 적절한 것을 고르시오.

① 어린이 병원 홍보
② 봉사상 수상 소감
③ 봉사상 시상 계획
④ 학교 홈페이지 소개
⑤ 봉사 동아리 회원 모집

11 대화를 듣고, 여자에 대한 내용으로 일치하지 <u>않는</u> 것을 고르시오.

① 여자의 성은 Woods이다.
② 캐나다 출신이다.
③ 1년 전에 한국에 왔다.
④ 세 명의 자녀가 있다.
⑤ 중국에서 영어를 가르쳤다.

12 대화를 듣고, 남자가 서점에 간 목적으로 가장 적절한 것을 고르시오.

① 문제집을 구입하기 위해서
② 퍼즐을 구입하기 위해서
③ 만화가를 만나기 위해서
④ 친구를 만나기 위해서
⑤ 책을 교환하기 위해서

13 대화를 듣고, 두 사람의 대화 내용과 일치하지 <u>않는</u> 것을 고르시오.

① Mike는 일본에 다녀왔다.
② Mike는 지난 금요일에 돌아왔다.
③ Julie는 영화클럽 회원이다.
④ 영화클럽 모임이 이번 토요일에 열린다.
⑤ 이번 영화클럽 모임 장소는 203호 교실이다.

14 대화를 듣고, 두 사람의 관계로 가장 적절한 것을 고르시오.

① 마술사 - 관객   ② 문구점 점원 - 학생
③ 은행직원 - 고객   ④ 택배 기사 - 고객
⑤ 인물화가 - 모델

15 대화를 듣고, 여자가 남자에게 요청한 일로 가장 적절한 것을 고르시오.

① 식사 후 설거지 돕기
② 점심식사에 늦지 않기
③ 전화로 음식 주문하기
④ 저녁상 차리는 일 돕기
⑤ 스마트폰으로 식당 예약하기

16 대화를 듣고, 남자가 Vincent van Gogh의 작품을 좋아하는 이유로 가장 적절한 것을 고르시오.

① 이해하기 쉬워서
② 소재가 다양해서
③ 세계적으로 유명해서
④ 밝은 색깔을 사용해서
⑤ 다양한 기법을 활용해서

17 대화를 듣고, <u>어색한</u> 것을 고르시오.

①   ②   ③   ④   ⑤

18 대화를 듣고, 여자가 학교 축제에서 참여할 활동을 고르시오.

① 사진 찍기   ② 비누 만들기
③ 로켓 만들기   ④ 페이스 페인팅
⑤ 단어 퀴즈 대회

[19-20] 대화를 듣고, 남자의 마지막 말에 이어질 여자의 말로 가장 적절한 것을 고르시오.

19 Woman: _____

① I'm looking forward to meeting you.
② Oh, thanks! I should talk to her.
③ You can't miss it.
④ Let me help you.
⑤ Here you are.

20 Woman: _____

① I don't know where to go shopping.
② How is everything going recently?
③ Are you going to watch it again?
④ Of course! You can keep it.
⑤ Don't miss it. You'll love it.

01 날씨 파악

다음을 듣고, 내일 대전의 날씨로 가장 적절한 것을 고르시오.

① ② ③
④ ⑤

W: Welcome to our □ _____ □ _____! The □ _____ on the streets will □ _____ because of a □ _____ □ _____ from the south. □ _____ □ _____ in the country will □ _____ □ _____ and □ _____ all day □ _____, but in a few cities like Daejeon and Cheongju, it will □ _____. So, □ _____ □ _____ in □ _____ if you travel to those cities.

02 그림 정보 파악

대화를 듣고, 두 사람이 보고 있는 사진으로 가장 적절한 것을 고르시오.

① ② ③
④ ⑤

W: How was your □ _____ □ _____?
M: Great. This is a □ _____ □ _____ my trip to *Horse Hill* on Jeju Island.
W: Wow! You are □ _____ a □ _____. Weren't you □ _____?
M: □ _____ □ _____ □ _____. Riding a horse was fantastic.
W: □ _____ is this man □ _____ □ _____ □ _____ the horse?
M: That's my □ _____. We had a wonderful time.
W: I'm sure you had many □ _____ □ _____ of your trip.

✎ **어휘복습** 잘 안 들리거나 몰라서 체크한 어휘를 써 놓고 복습해 보세요.

□ _____   □ _____   □ _____   □ _____
□ _____   □ _____   □ _____   □ _____
□ _____   □ _____   □ _____   □ _____

03 심정 추론

대화를 듣고, 남자의 심정으로 가장 적절한 것을 고르시오.

① excited
② relaxed
③ bored
④ angry
⑤ surprised

W: Hey, Kevin. What are you doing?
M: I'm planning a □ _____ □ _____ for my mom's □ _____.
W: You seem so happy. So what are you going to do?
M: My family will □ _____ a □ _____ □ _____ when she opens the door.
W: That's a good idea. □ _____ □ _____ your mom will □ _____ that.
M: I hope so. I □ _____ □ _____ to □ _____ the □ _____ on her face.

04 한 일 파악

대화를 듣고, 여자가 어제 한 일로 가장 적절한 것을 고르시오.

① 가족 여행
② 동물원 견학
③ 콘서트 관람
④ 컴퓨터 게임
⑤ 축구 경기 관람

M: You're late! The □ _____ game started □ _____ □ _____ □ _____.
W: I'm so sorry. I □ _____ □ _____ □ _____ this morning.
M: Why? □ _____ did you do □ _____?
W: I went on a □ _____ □ _____ □ _____ Black Water Mountain, so I was really □ _____.
M: I was □ _____ because you didn't □ _____ □ _____.
W: Sorry, I □ _____ not to be late □ _____ □ _____.
M: That's okay. Let's just watch the soccer game!

✎ **어휘복습** 잘 안 들리거나 몰라서 체크한 어휘를 써 놓고 복습해 보세요.

□ _____   □ _____   □ _____   □ _____
□ _____   □ _____   □ _____   □ _____
□ _____   □ _____   □ _____   □ _____

05 장소 추론

대화를 듣고, 두 사람이 대화하는 장소로 가
장 적절한 곳을 고르시오.

① 경찰서　② 도서관　③ 은행
④ 식당　⑤ 서점

M: Good morning. How may I help you?

W: Hi. I □ _____ this □ _____ □ _____ yesterday. But there's a problem with it.

M: What is it?

W: I found two □ _____ were □ _____.

M: □ _____ □ _____ □ _____ your book. Oh, we're very sorry. Could you show me your □ _____, please?

W: Yes, □ _____ □ _____ □ _____.

M: Okay, just a minute. I'll get you a new one.

W: Thank you.

06 의도 파악

대화를 듣고, 여자의 마지막 말의 의도로 가
장 적절한 것을 고르시오.

① 축하　② 허가　③ 사과
④ 충고　⑤ 감사

W: □ _____ □ _____ the baby □ _____! It is holding on to its mom so tight!

M: Yeah, that's so □ _____. I want to □ _____ it some □ _____.

W: No, you can't. The □ _____ □ _____ "□ _____ □ _____ the monkeys."

M: Really? □ _____ □ _____?

W: I think that's because it can □ _____ them □ _____.

M: Oh, is it □ _____ □ _____ their □ _____?

W: Yes. You □ _____ □ _____ give our snacks to animals.

✎ **어휘복습** 잘 안 들리거나 몰라서 체크한 어휘를 써 놓고 복습해 보세요.

□ _____　□ _____　□ _____　□ _____

□ _____　□ _____　□ _____　□ _____

□ _____　□ _____　□ _____　□ _____

07 숫자 정보 파악

대화를 듣고, 두 사람이 보게 될 뮤지컬이
시작하는 시각을 고르시오.

① 1:00 P.M.　② 3:00 P.M.
③ 4:00 P.M.　④ 5:00 P.M.
⑤ 7:00 P.M.

M: Sue, do you want to see the □ _____ *The Jungle Story*
　　with me □ _____ □ _____?
W: That □ _____ □ _____!
M: Then, I'll □ _____ □ _____ for the musical.
W: Thank you, Ted. □ _____ □ _____ does it □ _____?
M: There are shows at □ _____, □ _____, and □ _____
　　o'clock.
W: I'm going to □ _____ □ _____ with my family at one.
M: Then, □ _____ □ _____ the four o'clock show?
W: □ _____, I'll call you Saturday morning.

08 할 일 파악

대화를 듣고, 남자가 대화 직후에 할 일로
가장 적절한 것을 고르시오.

① 기차표 가져오기
② 운동 계획 세우기
③ 약속 시간 정하기
④ 책상 서랍 정리하기
⑤ 기차 시간 확인하기

W: David, □ _____ □ _____! It's time to leave.
M: All right, Mom. I'm □ _____ □ _____ my □ _____ now!
　　□ _____ is the □ _____ □ _____?
W: We need to get there □ _____ □ _____ P.M. We only
　　have one hour.
M: Okay, I'm done! Mom, do you have my train □ _____?
W: No, I gave it to you □ _____. Don't you have it?
M: Oh, no! It's still □ _____ my □ _____!
W: Go and get it.
M: I'll get it □ _____ □ _____, Mom.

✏ **어휘복습** 잘 안 들리거나 몰라서 체크한 어휘를 써 놓고 복습해 보세요.

□ _____　　□ _____　　□ _____　　□ _____
□ _____　　□ _____　　□ _____　　□ _____
□ _____　　□ _____　　□ _____　　□ _____

09 특정 정보 파악

대화를 듣고, 남자가 주문할 음식을 고르시오.

① 치즈버거
② 피자와 콜라
③ 치킨 샐러드
④ 토마토 스파게티
⑤ 감자튀김과 콜라

W: □ _____ are you going to □ _____?
M: I haven't □ _____ □ _____. I really want to □ _____ some □ _____ and □ _____. But I'm afraid it's not □ _____ □ _____ my □ _____.
W: Then, □ _____ □ _____ □ _____ spaghetti? Tomatoes are really □ _____. So, that would be □ _____ □ _____ you.
M: Okay, I will have that. What about you?
W: I'm going to □ _____ a □ _____ □ _____.
M: Sounds great.

10 화제 추론

다음을 듣고, 여자가 하는 말의 내용으로 가장 적절한 것을 고르시오.

① 어린이 병원 홍보
② 봉사상 수상 소감
③ 봉사상 시상 계획
④ 학교 홈페이지 소개
⑤ 봉사 동아리 회원 모집

W: Hello, students! May I □ _____ your □ _____, please? We're □ _____ □ _____ new □ _____ of our □ _____ □ _____. In this club, you will □ _____ old people and □ _____ □ _____ □ _____ children in the □ _____. If you're interested, please □ _____ your □ _____ □ _____ by October fifth. You can find more □ _____ □ _____ the school □ _____. Come and join us!

✎ 어휘복습 잘 안 들리거나 몰라서 체크한 어휘를 써 놓고 복습해 보세요.

□ _____ □ _____ □ _____ □ _____
□ _____ □ _____ □ _____ □ _____
□ _____ □ _____ □ _____ □ _____

11 내용 일치 파악

대화를 듣고, 여자에 대한 내용으로 일치하지 <u>않는</u> 것을 고르시오.

① 여자의 성은 Woods이다.
② 캐나다 출신이다.
③ 1년 전에 한국에 왔다.
④ 세 명의 자녀가 있다.
⑤ 중국에서 영어를 가르쳤다.

M: Hello, Ms. Woods. I'm Inho, a school □ _____ □ _____. May I □ _____ you, please?

W: Sure. □ _____ □ _____.

M: Thank you. □ _____ are you □ _____?

W: □ _____ □ _____ Canada.

M: □ _____ did you come to Korea?

W: I came here □ _____ □ _____ with my family. I have three children.

M: □ _____ did you □ _____ before coming to Korea?

W: I □ _____ □ _____ in China for five years.

12 목적 파악

대화를 듣고, 남자가 서점에 간 목적으로 가장 적절한 것을 고르시오.

① 문제집을 구입하기 위해서
② 퍼즐을 구입하기 위해서
③ 만화가를 만나기 위해서
④ 친구를 만나기 위해서
⑤ 책을 교환하기 위해서

W: Tom, where did you go after school yesterday?

M: I went to the Wisdom □ _____.

W: My friend told me the □ _____ were □ _____ □ _____ there. Did you buy any books?

M: No. In fact, I went there to □ _____ my □ _____ □ _____, Alex Parker. He □ _____ one of my □ _____ books.

W: Wow!

M: And I even □ _____ a great □ _____ of him.

W: Oh, you're so □ _____.

✎ **어휘복습** 잘 안 들리거나 몰라서 체크한 어휘를 써 놓고 복습해 보세요.

□ _____ □ _____ □ _____ □ _____
□ _____ □ _____ □ _____ □ _____
□ _____ □ _____ □ _____ □ _____

13 내용 일치 파악

대화를 듣고, 두 사람의 대화 내용과 일치하지 <u>않는</u> 것을 고르시오.

① Mike는 일본에 다녀왔다.
② Mike는 지난 금요일에 돌아왔다.
③ Julie는 영화클럽 회원이다.
④ 영화클럽 모임이 이번 토요일에 열린다.
⑤ 이번 영화클럽 모임 장소는 203호 교실이다.

M: Hey, Julie. Did you know Mike □ _____ □ _____?

W: No, Todd. I thought he was □ _____ □ _____.

M: He was. But he came back from Japan □ _____ □ _____.

W: Really? That's good! Then he can come back to our □ _____ □ _____!

M: Yes. He told me that he's going to □ _____ □ _____ □ _____.

W: That's great.

M: □ _____ are we going to □ _____ this Saturday?

W: The club meeting will be in □ _____ two oh three as usual.

14 관계 추론

대화를 듣고, 두 사람의 관계로 가장 적절한 것을 고르시오.

① 마술사 – 관객
② 문구점 점원 – 학생
③ 은행직원 – 고객
④ 택배 기사 – 고객
⑤ 인물화가 – 모델

W: Hi, I want to buy a twelve-color □ _____ □ _____.

M: No problem. Here you are. □ _____ □ _____?

W: I also need a □ _____ like that one.

M: Here you go. What about a □ _____ □ _____? Don't you need one?

W: You're right. I'll take this one. How much is all that?

M: □ _____ □ _____ it's □ _____ dollars.

W: Here you are.

M: Thanks.

✎ **어휘복습** 잘 안 들리거나 몰라서 체크한 어휘를 써 놓고 복습해 보세요.

□ _____   □ _____   □ _____   □ _____

□ _____   □ _____   □ _____   □ _____

□ _____   □ _____   □ _____   □ _____

15 부탁 파악

대화를 듣고, 여자가 남자에게 요청한 일로 가장 적절한 것을 고르시오.

① 식사 후 설거지 돕기
② 점심식사에 늦지 않기
③ 전화로 음식 주문하기
④ 저녁상 차리는 일 돕기
⑤ 스마트폰으로 식당 예약하기

W: Hojun! Are you still □ _____ that □ _____ on your □ _____? You've been playing for more than thirty minutes.

M: I know, Mom. But can I play for □ _____ □ _____ □ _____, please?

W: It's □ _____ □ _____ □ _____. And I need your help.

M: Just a minute, Mom. Okay, what do I need to do?

W: Please help me to □ _____ □ _____ □ _____.

M: Okay, Mom.

16 이유 파악

대화를 듣고, 남자가 Vincent van Gogh의 작품을 좋아하는 이유로 가장 적절한 것을 고르시오.

① 이해하기 쉬워서
② 소재가 다양해서
③ 세계적으로 유명해서
④ 밝은 색깔을 사용해서
⑤ 다양한 기법을 활용해서

W: Hey, Taeyong. What did you do □ _____?

M: I watched a □ _____ □ _____, *The Great Artist: Vincent van Gogh.*

W: □ _____ was that □ _____?

M: It was about Vincent van Gogh's □ _____ and his □ _____ □ _____ □ _____.

W: Was it interesting?

M: Yes! He is my □ _____ □ _____.

W: Oh, I see. It is not easy for me to □ _____ his □ _____. Why do you like him?

M: That's because he □ _____ □ _____ □ _____ in his paintings. I like bright colors.

✎ **어휘복습** 잘 안 들리거나 몰라서 체크한 어휘를 써 놓고 복습해 보세요.

□ _____ □ _____ □ _____ □ _____

□ _____ □ _____ □ _____ □ _____

□ _____ □ _____ □ _____ □ _____

17 어색한 대화 찾기

대화를 듣고, 어색한 것을 고르시오.

① ② ③ ④ ⑤

① W: □ _____ are you □ _____?
  M: I'm sorry. I □ _____ the □ _____.

② W: What are you going to do □ _____ □ _____?
  M: I □ _____ □ _____ □ _____ three years ago.

③ W: Sam, □ _____ you □ _____ met Jenny?
  M: No, I haven't.

④ W: □ _____ □ _____! There is a car coming!
  M: Oh, my! Thank you.

⑤ W: Tony! I □ _____ my □ _____. What should I do?
  M: Don't worry. Let's □ _____ it □ _____.

18 특정 정보 파악

대화를 듣고, 여자가 학교 축제에서 참여할 활동을 고르시오.

① 사진 찍기　　② 비누 만들기
③ 로켓 만들기　　④ 페이스 페인팅
⑤ 단어 퀴즈 대회

M: Nahyeon, □ _____ □ _____ are you going to do at the □ _____ □ _____?

W: I □ _____ □ _____ and □ _____ last year, so I will probably □ _____ that □ _____.

M: Really? Why don't you □ _____ □ _____ □ _____?

W: Like what?

M: Like □ _____ □ _____! Why don't you do it with me?

W: Face painting? But I'm not □ _____ □ _____ painting.

M: Don't worry. I can help you.

W: Well. Then, I'll do it with you. Thanks.

✎ **어휘복습** 잘 안 들리거나 몰라서 체크한 어휘를 써 놓고 복습해 보세요.

□ _____　　□ _____　　□ _____　　□ _____

□ _____　　□ _____　　□ _____　　□ _____

□ _____　　□ _____　　□ _____　　□ _____

19 알맞은 응답 찾기

대화를 듣고, 남자의 마지막 말에 이어질 여자의 말로 가장 적절한 것을 고르시오.

Woman: _____
① I'm looking forward to meeting you.
② Oh, thanks! I should talk to her.
③ You can't miss it.
④ Let me help you.
⑤ Here you are.

M: Hey, Mina. You □ _____ so □ _____. What's the matter?

W: I □ _____ my □ _____ □ _____ this morning.

M: Did you □ _____ your □ _____?

W: Yes, I did. But it wasn't there.

M: Hmm... Oh, □ _____ □ _____ you □ _____ □ _____ Ms. Kim, the English □ _____?

W: Why is that?

M: □ _____ □ _____ she □ _____ someone's English textbook this morning.

W: _____

20 알맞은 응답 찾기

대화를 듣고, 남자의 마지막 말에 이어질 여자의 말로 가장 적절한 것을 고르시오.

Woman: _____
① I don't know where to go shopping.
② How is everything going recently?
③ Are you going to watch it again?
④ Of course! You can keep it.
⑤ Don't miss it. You'll love it.

M: Susie! Have you seen the □ _____, *Brave Me*?

W: Yes. I saw it □ _____ my □ _____. It was □ _____.

M: I've heard many people have seen that movie. I want to see it, too.

W: You should! It's one of the □ _____ movies I □ _____ □ _____ seen.

M: Really? I am going to ask my brother to go and see it with me.

W: _____

✎ **어휘복습** 잘 안 들리거나 몰라서 체크한 어휘를 써 놓고 복습해 보세요.

□ _____   □ _____   □ _____   □ _____

□ _____   □ _____   □ _____   □ _____

□ _____   □ _____   □ _____   □ _____

01 다음을 듣고, 토요일의 날씨로 가장 적절한 것을 고르시오.

① ② ③ ④ ⑤

02 대화를 듣고, 남자가 구입할 티셔츠로 가장 적절한 것을 고르시오.

① ② ③

④ ⑤

03 대화를 듣고, 여자의 심정으로 가장 적절한 것을 고르시오.

① bored   ② proud   ③ excited
④ peaceful   ⑤ worried

04 대화를 듣고, 남자가 한 일로 가장 적절한 것을 고르시오.

① 방 청소하기
② 티셔츠 구입하기
③ 야구경기 관람하기
④ 학교 축제 연습하기
⑤ 벼룩시장에서 팔 물건 찾기

05 대화를 듣고, 두 사람이 대화하는 장소로 가장 적절한 곳을 고르시오.

① 공항   ② 세차장
③ 놀이공원   ④ 학교 운동장
⑤ 버스터미널

06 대화를 듣고, 여자의 마지막 말의 의도로 가장 적절한 것을 고르시오.

① 칭찬   ② 비난   ③ 충고
④ 사과   ⑤ 설득

07 대화를 듣고, 올해 Mina의 반을 고르시오.

① Class A   ② Class B   ③ Class C
④ Class D   ⑤ Class E

08 대화를 듣고, 남자가 대화 직후에 할 일로 가장 적절한 것을 고르시오.

① 목욕하기   ② 약 구입하기
③ 화장실 가기   ④ 날씨 확인하기
⑤ 간식 구입하기

09 다음을 듣고, 남자가 하는 말의 내용으로 가장 적절한 것을 고르시오.

① 점심 메뉴 소개
② 건강 회복 비결
③ 올바른 운동 순서
④ 건강 검진 절차
⑤ 물 절약 방법

10 대화를 듣고, 남자의 장래 희망으로 가장 적절한 것을 고르시오.

① 농부   ② 과학자   ③ 미용사
④ 요리사   ⑤ 회사원

11 다음을 듣고, The Purple Orange에 관한 정보로 일치하지 <u>않는</u> 것을 고르시오.

① 작가는 Monica Smith이다.
② 세계에서 가장 유명한 책 중 하나이다.
③ 우정과 사랑에 관한 이야기이다.
④ 10개의 다른 언어로 쓰였다.
⑤ 100개 이상의 나라에서 팔린다.

12 대화를 듣고, 여자가 전화를 건 목적으로 가장 적절한 것을 고르시오.

① 가족 숙소를 예약하기 위해서
② 객실 청소를 요청하기 위해서
③ 숙박 예약 날짜를 변경하기 위해서
④ 미용실 예약 시간을 확인하기 위해서
⑤ 헤어 드라이어가 있는지 확인하기 위해서

13 다음을 듣고, Fun Night에 관한 내용과 일치하는 것을 고르시오.

① 행사는 2층에서 열린다.
② 음식물을 가져올 수 없다.
③ 가족과 함께 올 수 있다.
④ 매주 목요일에 진행된다.
⑤ 오후 5시에 시작된다.

14 대화를 듣고, 두 사람의 관계로 가장 적절한 것을 고르시오.

① 과학자 - 기자 ② 요리사 - 손님
③ 체육 교사 - 학생 ④ 지휘자 - 연주자
⑤ 주치의 - 축구선수

15 대화를 듣고, 여자가 남자에게 부탁한 일로 가장 적절한 것을 고르시오.

① 인터넷으로 요리 강습 신청하기
② 할머니께 사과파이 갖다드리기
③ 도서관에 역사책 반납하기
④ 할머니께 안부전화 드리기
⑤ 역사 보고서 작성하기

16 대화를 듣고, 여자가 집에 걸어가는 이유로 가장 적절한 것을 고르시오.

① 날씨가 좋아서
② 서점에 들르려고
③ 수영장에 들르려고
④ 버스가 늦게 와서
⑤ 교통 카드를 잃어버려서

17 대화를 듣고, 두 사람의 대화가 <u>어색한</u> 것을 고르시오.

①   ②   ③   ④   ⑤

18 다음을 듣고, 여자가 학생 식당 이용에 대해 언급하지 <u>않은</u> 것을 고르시오.

① 식당 위치
② 식당 이용 시간
③ 식수대 위치
④ 학년별 식사 순서
⑤ 식사 후 주의 사항

[19-20] 대화를 듣고, 남자의 마지막 말에 이어질 여자의 말로 가장 적절한 것을 고르시오.

19 Woman: _____

① That's a good idea.
② Please help yourself.
③ Thank you for your help.
④ Don't worry. You can do it.
⑤ You've got the wrong number.

20 Woman: _____

① I wanted to go there again.
② Well, I want to buy more.
③ Yes! That's amazing.
④ All right! I will.
⑤ I ate bibimbap.

02회 DICTATION

다시 듣고, 빈칸에 알맞은 단어를 써 보세요.

◀)》 MP3 기출 02-1

01 날씨 파악

다음을 듣고, 토요일의 날씨로 가장 적절한 것을 고르시오.

① ② ③ ④ ⑤

W: Good morning! This is the □ _____ □ _____ for □ _____ □ _____. There has been lots of □ _____ these days. We will have more sunny days. It will be □ _____ on □ _____, □ _____, and □ _____. However, it will □ _____ on □ _____ and □ _____. On □ _____ and □ _____, it will be sunny □ _____. Have a wonderful week. Thank you.

02 그림 정보 파악

대화를 듣고, 남자가 구입할 티셔츠로 가장 적절한 것을 고르시오.

① ② ③ ④ ⑤

W: Good morning! May I help you?

M: I am □ _____ □ _____ a □ _____ with a □ _____ on it.

W: □ _____ □ _____ this one? There is a cute snowman □ _____ □ _____ □ _____ and one □ _____.

M: It looks nice. But I don't need the pocket.

W: Okay. Here's the □ _____ T-shirt □ _____ a pocket. How about this?

M: Great. Thanks. I will □ _____ it.

✎ **어휘복습** 잘 안 들리거나 몰라서 체크한 어휘를 써 놓고 복습해 보세요.

□ _____   □ _____   □ _____
□ _____   □ _____   □ _____
□ _____   □ _____   □ _____

03 심정 추론

대화를 듣고, 여자의 심정으로 가장 적절한 것을 고르시오.

① bored   ② proud
③ excited   ④ peaceful
⑤ worried

M: Hi, Sally. □ _____ □ _____ □ _____ □ _____. What's the matter with your □ _____?

W: Hello, Dr. Park. He doesn't □ _____ □ _____ □ _____.

M: Oh, I see. When did he stop eating?

W: Yesterday morning. And he □ _____ □ _____ much these days.

M: I'll give him a □ _____ □ _____.

W: Please do. I hope it's □ _____ □ _____.

04 한 일 파악

대화를 듣고, 남자가 한 일로 가장 적절한 것을 고르시오.

① 방 청소하기
② 티셔츠 구입하기
③ 야구경기 관람하기
④ 학교 축제 연습하기
⑤ 벼룩시장에서 팔 물건 찾기

W: Oh, no! Brian! □ _____ □ _____ to your room?

M: I'm sorry, Mom. I promise to □ _____ it □ _____.

W: Okay. Well, what were you doing?

M: I was looking for □ _____ □ _____ □ _____ at the school □ _____ □ _____.

W: Oh! □ _____ did you □ _____?

M: I found a □ _____ □ _____ and some □ _____. Why don't you come, Mom?

W: □ _____ is it?

M: It opens □ _____ at □ _____ in the afternoon.

✎ **어휘복습** 잘 안 들리거나 몰라서 체크한 어휘를 써 놓고 복습해 보세요.

□ _____   □ _____   □ _____   □ _____

□ _____   □ _____   □ _____   □ _____

□ _____   □ _____   □ _____   □ _____

05 장소 추론

대화를 듣고, 두 사람이 대화하는 장소로 가장 적절한 곳을 고르시오.

① 공항 ② 세차장
③ 놀이공원 ④ 학교 운동장
⑤ 버스터미널

M: I'm so □ _____!

W: Me, too. We're lucky. The □ _____ isn't so long.

M: Jane, look □ _____ □ _____. There's a big □ _____.

W: Yes, I can see some people □ _____ and □ _____ their □ _____.

M: Oh, look at that man. He's □ _____ an □ _____ □ _____ and riding a bike.

W: Wow! There are so many □ _____ things happening at this □ _____ □ _____.

M: Oh, it's our turn to □ _____ the □ _____ □ _____. Let's go.

06 의도 파악

대화를 듣고, 여자의 마지막 말의 의도로 가장 적절한 것을 고르시오.

① 칭찬 ② 비난 ③ 충고
④ 사과 ⑤ 설득

M: Mom, I'm home.

W: John, you're home already. How was today's □ _____ □ _____?

M: It was □ _____! We □ _____ the □ _____!

W: Oh, really? Tell me □ _____ □ _____ it.

M: We were □ _____ in the □ _____ by two points.

W: So, everyone was worried, right? Then, □ _____ did you □ _____?

M: Guess what? I □ _____ a □ _____ □ _____, and we got three points.

W: That's my boy! You □ _____ a □ _____ □ _____!

✎ **어휘복습** 잘 안 들리거나 몰라서 체크한 어휘를 써 놓고 복습해 보세요.

□ _____   □ _____   □ _____   □ _____

□ _____   □ _____   □ _____   □ _____

□ _____   □ _____   □ _____   □ _____

07 특정 정보 파악

대화를 듣고, 올해 Mina의 반을 고르시오.

① Class A   ② Class B
③ Class C   ④ Class D
⑤ Class E

M: Good morning, Kelly. □ _____ □ _____ are you □ _____?

W: Hi, Dohoon. □ _____ □ _____ □ _____ Class C. What about you?

M: Wow! We are in the □ _____ class this year.

W: That's great. Do you know which class Mina is in?

M: She is in Class D, □ _____ □ _____ □ _____ to our class.

W: □ _____ □ _____ she's not in the same class with us.

M: I know, but we can see each other every day.

08 할 일 파악

대화를 듣고, 남자가 대화 직후에 할 일로 가장 적절한 것을 고르시오.

① 목욕하기   ② 약 구입하기
③ 화장실 가기   ④ 날씨 확인하기
⑤ 간식 구입하기

W: Tom, did you finish □ _____ your □ _____ to □ _____ □ _____ tomorrow?

M: Yes, Mom. I packed □ _____, □ _____, □ _____, and my sleeping bag.

W: Oh, did you get your □ _____ □ _____ □ _____? It is in the bathroom closet.

M: Okay. Mom, there is □ _____ □ _____ at all in the box.

W: Really? Then, you should □ _____ and □ _____ some medicine.

M: Okay. I will go now.

✎ **어휘복습** 잘 안 들리거나 몰라서 체크한 어휘를 써 놓고 복습해 보세요.

□ _____   □ _____   □ _____   □ _____

□ _____   □ _____   □ _____   □ _____

□ _____   □ _____   □ _____   □ _____

09 화제 추론

다음을 듣고, 남자가 하는 말의 내용으로 가장 적절한 것을 고르시오.

① 점심 메뉴 소개   ② 건강 회복 비결
③ 올바른 운동 순서 ④ 건강 검진 절차
⑤ 물 절약 방법

M: Hello, listeners! Welcome to *Health 24*. I am Andy Brown. □ _____ I was □ _____, I was very □ _____ for a long time. Do you want to know how I □ _____ □ _____ it? First, I □ _____ one hour every day. Second, I □ _____ two liters of □ _____ a day. It sounds □ _____, but it □ _____ a huge □ _____ in my life.

10 장래 희망 파악

대화를 듣고, 남자의 장래 희망으로 가장 적절한 것을 고르시오.

① 농부   ② 과학자   ③ 미용사
④ 요리사 ⑤ 회사원

M: Would you like to □ _____ one of these □ _____? They're from my grandma's □ _____.
W: Thanks. Mmm... They're □ _____. Did she □ _____ these □ _____?
M: Yes, she grows lots of things. I want to be a □ _____ and □ _____ in the □ _____ like her someday.
W: Really? Living in the country is not easy. I think it's □ _____ to live in a city as an □ _____ □ _____.
M: It may be difficult, but I still like the country life.

✎ **어휘복습** 잘 안 들리거나 몰라서 체크한 어휘를 써 놓고 복습해 보세요.

□ _____   □ _____   □ _____   □ _____
□ _____   □ _____   □ _____   □ _____
□ _____   □ _____   □ _____   □ _____

11 내용 일치 파악

다음을 듣고, The Purple Orange에 관한 정보로 일치하지 <u>않는</u> 것을 고르시오.

① 작가는 Monica Smith이다.
② 세계에서 가장 유명한 책 중 하나이다.
③ 우정과 사랑에 관한 이야기이다.
④ 10개의 다른 언어로 쓰였다.
⑤ 100개 이상의 나라에서 팔린다.

W: Hello, everyone. □ _____ □ _____ Susan from Book Talk. I am going to □ _____ □ _____ *The Purple Orange* □ _____ □ _____ Monica Smith. It is one of the most □ _____ □ _____ in the world. She tells us about □ _____ and □ _____ in this book. This book was written in □ _____ different □ _____. It is □ _____ in more than one hundred countries.

12 전화 목적 파악

대화를 듣고, 여자가 전화를 건 목적으로 가장 적절한 것을 고르시오.

① 가족 숙소를 예약하기 위해서
② 객실 청소를 요청하기 위해서
③ 숙박 예약 날짜를 변경하기 위해서
④ 미용실 예약 시간을 확인하기 위해서
⑤ 헤어 드라이어가 있는지 확인하기 위해서

M: Flower Guest House. How may I help you?
W: Hi. I am Sujin Park and I have □ _____ a □ _____ for □ _____.
M: Hi, Sujin. We are □ _____ you. Do you need anything?
W: Yes. Do you have a □ _____ □ _____ in the room?
M: We have a hair dryer in every room. Do you need anything else?
W: No, thank you. □ _____ □ _____. See you tomorrow.

✎ **어휘복습** 잘 안 들리거나 몰라서 체크한 어휘를 써 놓고 복습해 보세요.

□ _____   □ _____   □ _____   □ _____

□ _____   □ _____   □ _____   □ _____

□ _____   □ _____   □ _____   □ _____

13 내용 일치 파악

다음을 듣고, Fun Night에 관한 내용과 일치하는 것을 고르시오.

① 행사는 2층에서 열린다.
② 음식물을 가져올 수 없다.
③ 가족과 함께 올 수 있다.
④ 매주 목요일에 진행된다.
⑤ 오후 5시에 시작된다.

M: □ _____ □ _____ □ _____ □ _____ ABC Library. Today, we'll have *Fun Night* on the □ _____ □ _____. Our story lady will read you an interesting story. You can □ _____ □ _____ or □ _____. You can come □ _____ your □ _____ and □ _____. *Fun Night* is on □ _____ □ _____. It □ _____ at □ _____ □ _____ P.M. Come and have fun together at ABC Library!

14 관계 추론

대화를 듣고, 두 사람의 관계로 가장 적절한 것을 고르시오

① 과학자 – 기자
② 요리사 – 손님
③ 체육 교사 – 학생
④ 지휘자 – 연주자
⑤ 주치의 – 축구선수

M: Jisu, you are □ _____ really □ _____ in my P.E. class.
W: Thank you, Mr. Song. I □ _____ □ _____ on the □ _____ every day.
M: Great. You're beginning to □ _____ □ _____ a real □ _____ □ _____.
W: Really? Do you think I'm □ _____ □ _____?
M: Yes. □ _____ □ _____, and you'll □ _____ □ _____ □ _____ the □ _____ next week.
W: Okay, I'll do that.
M: □ _____ □ _____ to you.

✎ **어휘복습** 잘 안 들리거나 몰라서 체크한 어휘를 써 놓고 복습해 보세요.

□ _____ □ _____ □ _____ □ _____

□ _____ □ _____ □ _____ □ _____

□ _____ □ _____ □ _____ □ _____

15 부탁 파악

대화를 듣고, 여자가 남자에게 부탁한 일로 가장 적절한 것을 고르시오.

① 인터넷으로 요리 강습 신청하기
② 할머니께 사과파이 갖다드리기
③ 도서관에 역사책 반납하기
④ 할머니께 안부전화 드리기
⑤ 역사 보고서 작성하기

W: □ _____ are you □ _____, Taeho?

M: I'm going to the □ _____ to do a □ _____ □ _____ with my friends.

W: Okay. Then, would you □ _____ □ _____ □ _____ □ _____?

M: Sure, Mom. What is it?

W: I made an apple pie for your □ _____. Please take it to her □ _____ □ _____ □ _____ □ _____ the library.

M: No problem. Apple pies are her □ _____. She will love it.

W: Thank you.

16 이유 파악

대화를 듣고, 여자가 집에 걸어가는 이유로 가장 적절한 것을 고르시오.

① 날씨가 좋아서
② 서점에 들르려고
③ 수영장에 들르려고
④ 버스가 늦게 와서
⑤ 교통 카드를 잃어버려서

M: Good afternoon, Katie. Where are you going?

W: Hi, Jason. I'm □ _____ □ _____ □ _____ home.

M: Then, let's □ _____ the □ _____ together.

W: Sorry, but I'd like to □ _____ □ _____ today.

M: Why?

W: I am walking home because the □ _____ is so □ _____. Do you want to □ _____ me?

M: I'd □ _____ □ _____, □ _____ I can't. I have a □ _____ □ _____ this afternoon.

W: All right. See you tomorrow.

✎ **어휘복습** 잘 안 들리거나 몰라서 체크한 어휘를 써 놓고 복습해 보세요.

□ _____ □ _____ □ _____ □ _____

□ _____ □ _____ □ _____ □ _____

□ _____ □ _____ □ _____ □ _____

17 어색한 대화 찾기

대화를 듣고, 두 사람의 대화가 <u>어색한</u> 것을 고르시오.

① ② ③ ④ ⑤

① W: □ _____ did you □ _____ □ _____?

M: □ _____ about □ _____ □ _____ A.M.

② W: Did you □ _____ a □ _____ □ _____ at the park?

M: Sounds great!

③ W: Thank you for □ _____ me.

M: Make yourself at home.

④ W: Do you know □ _____ □ _____ □ _____ a paper flower?

M: I have □ _____ □ _____.

⑤ W: □ _____ □ _____ will you □ _____ there?

M: Maybe □ _____ □ _____ days.

18 미언급 파악

다음을 듣고, 여자가 학생 식당 이용에 대해 언급하지 <u>않은</u> 것을 고르시오.

① 식당 위치
② 식당 이용 시간
③ 식수대 위치
④ 학년별 식사 순서
⑤ 식사 후 주의 사항

W: Hello, new Hillside Middle School students! I want to explain our □ _____ □ _____. Our □ _____ is on the □ _____ □ _____ of the □ _____ □ _____. Lunch starts at □ _____ □ _____, and it's open for one hour. The □ _____ □ _____ will use the cafeteria □ _____, □ _____ □ _____ the □ _____ graders, and □ _____ the □ _____ graders. After eating, please be sure to □ _____ your □ _____. Thank you.

✎ **어휘복습** 잘 안 들리거나 몰라서 체크한 어휘를 써 놓고 복습해 보세요.

□ _____ □ _____ □ _____ □ _____

□ _____ □ _____ □ _____ □ _____

□ _____ □ _____ □ _____ □ _____

19 알맞은 응답 찾기

대화를 듣고, 남자의 마지막 말에 이어질 여자의 말로 가장 적절한 것을 고르시오.

Woman: _____
① That's a good idea.
② Please help yourself.
③ Thank you for your help.
④ Don't worry. You can do it.
⑤ You've got the wrong number.

W: What are these □ _____ about?
M: They are for our first □ _____ □ _____.
W: Really? □ _____ are you going to have the performance?
M: This □ _____ at □ _____.
W: □ _____ do you □ _____ in the band?
M: I play the □ _____. You should □ _____ □ _____ □ _____.
W: Of course, I will. I really want to see you playing the drums on the stage.
M: Well, I've □ _____ a lot, but also I'm very □ _____ now.
W: _____

20 알맞은 응답 찾기

대화를 듣고, 남자의 마지막 말에 이어질 여자의 말로 가장 적절한 것을 고르시오.

Woman: _____
① I wanted to go there again.
② Well, I want to buy more.
③ Yes! That's amazing.
④ All right! I will.
⑤ I ate bibimbap.

M: Cindy! You □ _____ □ _____. What did you do for the □ _____?
W: I went to Jeonju with my family.
M: That □ _____ □ _____. How was it?
W: It was wonderful. I think you should go there.
M: Really? What did you do there?
W: I □ _____ the □ _____ Korean □ _____, and ate □ _____ □ _____.
M: I'm sure you really enjoyed that. □ _____ did you □ _____ there?
W: _____

✎ **어휘복습** 잘 안 들리거나 몰라서 체크한 어휘를 써 놓고 복습해 보세요.

□ _____ □ _____ □ _____ □ _____
□ _____ □ _____ □ _____ □ _____
□ _____ □ _____ □ _____ □ _____

01 대화를 듣고, 탁자 위 물건 배치로 가장 적절한 것을 고르시오.

① ② ③

④ ⑤

02 대화를 듣고, 여자의 심정으로 가장 적절한 것을 고르시오.

① satisfied　② nervous　③ alarmed
④ relaxed　⑤ bored

03 대화를 듣고, 남자가 한 일로 가장 적절한 것을 고르시오.

① 책 주문　　　　② 치과 예약
③ 식탁 구입　　　④ 휴대폰 구입
⑤ 저녁 식사 예약

04 대화를 듣고, 두 사람이 대화하는 장소로 가장 적절한 곳을 고르시오.

① library　　　② theater
③ bookstore　　④ restaurant
⑤ bank

05 대화를 듣고, 여자의 마지막 말의 의도로 가장 적절한 것을 고르시오.

① 감사　　② 허가　　③ 사과
④ 동의　　⑤ 충고

06 대화를 듣고, 여자가 지불할 금액을 고르시오.

① $2　　　② $3　　　③ $4
④ $5　　　⑤ $6

07 대화를 듣고, 여자가 대화 직후에 할 일로 가장 적절한 것을 고르시오.

① 문화재 조사하기　② 전통시장 방문하기
③ 웹사이트 살펴보기　④ 여행사에 문의하기
⑤ 친구에게 답장쓰기

08 대화를 듣고, 두 사람이 가기로 한 장소로 가장 적절한 곳을 고르시오.

① 영화관　　② 수영장　　③ 동물원
④ 백화점　　⑤ 야구 경기장

09 다음을 듣고, 남자가 하는 말의 내용으로 가장 적절한 것을 고르시오.

① 경기 일정　　　　② 동료 소개
③ 수상 소감　　　　④ 출판 기념회 초대
⑤ 학부모의 날 행사 개최

10 대화를 듣고, Susan에 대한 내용으로 일치하지 않는 것을 고르시오.

① Rachel에게 엽서를 보냈다.
② 중국에서 어제 돌아왔다.
③ 남자 형제가 있다.
④ 조부모는 중국에 있다.
⑤ 이번 달에는 독서 동아리에 나오지 않았다.

11 대화를 듣고, 여자가 전화를 건 이유로 가장 적절한 것을 고르시오.

① 상품을 환불받기 위해서
② 잔돈을 돌려받지 못해서
③ 환전방법을 문의하기 위해서
④ 자판기의 위치를 확인하기 위해서
⑤ 도서관 열람시간을 알아보기 위해서

12 대화를 듣고, 대화의 내용과 일치하지 <u>않는</u> 것을 고르시오.

① 남자의 직업은 소설가이다.
② 여자는 잡지사에서 근무한다.
③ Blue Ocean은 남자의 최근 작품이다.
④ 남자는 야생 돌고래와 수영한 적이 있다.
⑤ 남자는 호주에 가 본 경험이 없다.

13 대화를 듣고, 두 사람의 관계로 가장 적절한 것을 고르시오.

① 약사 – 환자
② 교사 – 학생
③ 의사 – 간호사
④ 서점 주인 – 손님
⑤ 우체국 직원 – 고객

14 대화를 듣고, 남자가 여자에게 요청한 일로 가장 적절한 것을 고르시오.

① 주문 취소
② 재고 확보
③ 배송지 변경
④ 주문 내역 조회
⑤ 홈페이지 주소 확인

15 대화를 듣고, 남자가 슈퍼마켓에 가는 이유로 가장 적절한 것을 고르시오.

① 우산을 사려고
② 준비물을 사려고
③ 친구를 데려오려고
④ 식료품을 구입하려고
⑤ 엄마의 심부름을 하려고

16 대화를 듣고, 두 사람의 대화가 <u>어색한</u> 것을 고르시오.

① ② ③ ④ ⑤

17 대화를 듣고, 대화의 상황에 어울리는 속담으로 가장 적절한 것을 고르시오.

① 빈 수레가 요란하다.
② 소 잃고 외양간 고친다.
③ 발 없는 말이 천 리 간다.
④ 사공이 많으면 배가 산으로 간다.
⑤ 자라 보고 놀란 가슴 솥뚜껑 보고 놀란다.

18 다음을 듣고, 금요일 밤의 날씨로 가장 적절한 것을 고르시오.

① ② ③ ④ ⑤

[19-20] 대화를 듣고, 남자의 마지막 말에 이어질 여자의 말로 가장 적절한 것을 고르시오.

19 Woman: _____

① Please help yourself.
② I'm sure he can do it.
③ I had a very good time.
④ Thank you for your advice.
⑤ I'm pleased to meet you, too.

20 Woman: _____

① In fact, I prefer science to history.
② Well, I haven't found a good one yet.
③ Okay. I'm sure I turned off the computer.
④ Right! We should respect inventors' ideas.
⑤ The deadline for the report has already passed.

01 그림 정보 파악

대화를 듣고, 탁자 위 물건 배치로 가장 적절한 것을 고르시오.

① ② ③
④ ⑤

W: Tony, why don't we □ _____ this □ _____ □ _____ the □ _____?

M: Sounds good. How about □ _____ □ _____ □ _____, □ _____ □ _____ the clock?

W: Okay. Then let's put the □ _____ □ _____ □ _____ the picture and the clock.

M: Wait. I don't think that's a good idea. □ _____ □ _____ put the teddy bear on the table.

W: Okay. I □ _____.

02 심정 추론

대화를 듣고, 여자의 심정으로 가장 적절한 것을 고르시오.

① satisfied   ② nervous
③ alarmed   ④ relaxed
⑤ bored

M: Rachel, what are you doing? It's already ten thirty.

W: I'm □ _____ my □ _____. I'm almost done.

M: You should □ _____ □ _____ □ _____. Tomorrow is your □ _____ □ _____ at your new □ _____.

W: I know, but I want to □ _____ □ _____ I have □ _____ □ _____.

M: Don't worry. Everything will be fine.

W: Thanks, Dad. But □ _____ □ _____ □ _____ I'll be able to □ _____ good □ _____ there.

✎ 어휘복습 잘 안 들리거나 몰라서 체크한 어휘를 써 놓고 복습해 보세요.

□ _____   □ _____   □ _____   □ _____
□ _____   □ _____   □ _____   □ _____
□ _____   □ _____   □ _____   □ _____

03 한 일 파악

대화를 듣고, 남자가 한 일로 가장 적절한 것을 고르시오.

① 책 주문 ② 치과 예약
③ 식탁 구입 ④ 휴대폰 구입
⑤ 저녁 식사 예약

W: Dr. Benson's □ _____ □ _____. How may I help you?

M: Can I □ _____ □ _____ Dr. Benson? This is Tom, Dr. Benson's friend.

W: I'm □ _____, □ _____ she's busy right now.

M: Then, can I □ _____ a □ _____?

W: Of course.

M: Please tell her that I □ _____ a □ _____ for □ _____ at seven P.M.

W: Okay, I'll □ _____ her □ _____.

04 장소 추론

대화를 듣고, 두 사람이 대화하는 장소로 가장 적절한 곳을 고르시오.

① library ② theater
③ bookstore ④ restaurant
⑤ bank

M: Excuse me. Is it possible to □ _____ □ _____ □ _____ with a student ID card?

W: No, you need a □ _____ □ _____.

M: I see. Actually, I don't have one. Can I get a new card here?

W: Sure. Just □ _____ □ _____ this □ _____.

M: Okay. □ _____ □ _____ will it □ _____ to make it?

W: About an hour.

M: All right.

✎ **어휘복습** 잘 안 들리거나 몰라서 체크한 어휘를 써 놓고 복습해 보세요.

□ _____ □ _____ □ _____ □ _____

□ _____ □ _____ □ _____ □ _____

□ _____ □ _____ □ _____ □ _____

05 의도 파악

대화를 듣고, 여자의 마지막 말의 의도로 가장 적절한 것을 고르시오.

① 감사   ② 허가   ③ 사과
④ 동의   ⑤ 충고

W: Is □ _____ □ _____, John? You don't look so good.

M: I □ _____ my □ _____ while moving a desk into the classroom.

W: Did you go see the □ _____ □ _____?

M: No, I didn't think it was □ _____.

W: But it □ _____ □ _____ you're □ _____ □ _____.

M: Don't worry. It'll be okay tomorrow.

W: I think □ _____ □ _____ go and see the nurse.

06 숫자 정보 파악

대화를 듣고, 여자가 지불할 금액을 고르시오.

① $2   ② $3   ③ $4
④ $5   ⑤ $6

M: Hello. How can I help you?

W: Hi. □ _____ □ _____ are these □ _____?

M: The cookies are □ _____ □ _____ each.

W: And how much is a □ _____ □ _____ □ _____?

M: It's □ _____ dollars.

W: Okay. I'll take two cookies and a cup of coffee.

M: Please wait a moment. I'll be □ _____ □ _____ with your order.

✎ **어휘복습** 잘 안 들리거나 몰라서 체크한 어휘를 써 놓고 복습해 보세요.

□ _____   □ _____   □ _____   □ _____
□ _____   □ _____   □ _____   □ _____
□ _____   □ _____   □ _____   □ _____

대화를 듣고, 여자가 대화 직후에 할 일로
가장 적절한 것을 고르시오.

① 문화재 조사하기
② 전통시장 방문하기
③ 웹사이트 살펴보기
④ 여행사에 문의하기
⑤ 친구에게 답장쓰기

W: Guess what! My friend from the Philippines is going to visit me.

M: Oh, really? You must be □ _____ .

W: Yes. But I don't know □ _____ to □ _____ him.

M: You should take your friend to a □ _____ Korean □ _____ or □ _____ .

W: □ _____ . Do you know any good Korean restaurants?

M: Yes. The Seoul restaurant is very □ _____ . Their □ _____ is on their □ _____ .

W: Oh, I'll □ _____ □ _____ □ _____ □ _____ the website.

대화를 듣고, 두 사람이 가기로 한 장소로
가장 적절한 곳을 고르시오.

① 영화관 ② 수영장 ③ 동물원
④ 백화점 ⑤ 야구 경기장

W: We have a □ _____ □ _____ . Do you want to go to the swimming pool with me?

M: It's too cold to □ _____ □ _____ . How about going to a □ _____ □ _____ ?

W: Well, I don't like baseball that much. □ _____ □ _____ going to the □ _____ or going □ _____ ?

M: Come on, Chicago Bears has a very important game coming up. □ _____ □ _____ you'll like it.

W: Okay, □ _____ □ _____ □ _____ □ _____ , let's go!

✎ **어휘복습** 잘 안 들리거나 몰라서 체크한 어휘를 써 놓고 복습해 보세요.

□ _____ □ _____ □ _____ □ _____

□ _____ □ _____ □ _____ □ _____

□ _____ □ _____ □ _____ □ _____

09 화제 추론

다음을 듣고, 남자가 하는 말의 내용으로 가장 적절한 것을 고르시오.

① 경기 일정
② 동료 소개
③ 수상 소감
④ 출판 기념회 초대
⑤ 학부모의 날 행사 개최

M: Hello, everyone. I'm very happy to □ _____ the □ _____ for Player of the Year. I can't □ _____ how much I □ _____ this □ _____. I'd especially like to □ _____ my parents □ _____ their □ _____ during the difficult times. Whenever I wanted to □ _____ □ _____, they □ _____ me □ _____. I really thank them for all their help. This award is also for them.

10 미언급 파악

대화를 듣고, Susan에 대한 내용으로 일치하지 <u>않는</u> 것을 고르시오.

① Rachel에게 엽서를 보냈다.
② 중국에서 어제 돌아왔다.
③ 남자 형제가 있다.
④ 조부모는 중국에 있다.
⑤ 이번 달에는 독서 동아리에 나오지 않았다.

M: Rachel, is this □ _____ □ _____ □ _____?
W: Yes, I got it from Susan □ _____.
M: Oh, is she in China?
W: Yes. She went there □ _____ her □ _____ to □ _____ their □ _____.
M: I see, that's why she couldn't come to the □ _____ □ _____ this month.
W: Yeah, but she'll □ _____ □ _____ next month.

✎ **어휘복습** 잘 안 들리거나 몰라서 체크한 어휘를 써 놓고 복습해 보세요.

□ _____ □ _____ □ _____ □ _____
□ _____ □ _____ □ _____ □ _____
□ _____ □ _____ □ _____ □ _____

11 전화 목적 파악

대화를 듣고, 여자가 전화를 건 이유로 가장 적절한 것을 고르시오.

① 상품을 환불받기 위해서
② 잔돈을 돌려받지 못해서
③ 환전방법을 문의하기 위해서
④ 자판기의 위치를 확인하기 위해서
⑤ 도서관 열람시간을 알아보기 위해서

M: Hello. Grab and Go □ _____ □ _____.

W: Hi. There's a □ _____ □ _____ the vending machine in Greenwood Library.

M: All right. What's the problem?

W: The vending machine didn't □ _____ me my □ _____.

M: Sorry about that. I'll come and □ _____. I'll be there □ _____ about □ _____ □ _____.

W: Okay. Thanks.

12 내용 일치 파악

대화를 듣고, 대화의 내용과 일치하지 <u>않는</u> 것을 고르시오.

① 남자의 직업은 소설가이다.
② 여자는 잡지사에서 근무한다.
③ Blue Ocean은 남자의 최근 작품이다.
④ 남자는 야생 돌고래와 수영한 적이 있다.
⑤ 남자는 호주에 가 본 경험이 없다.

W: Hello, Mr. Smith. I'm so glad to meet a world □ _____ □ _____. I'm Kate from ABC □ _____.

M: Glad to meet you, Kate.

W: I know your □ _____ □ _____, *Blue Ocean*, is very □ _____ all over the world. How did you □ _____ □ _____ □ _____ for the novel?

M: Well, I had an amazing chance to □ _____ □ _____ wild □ _____.

W: Really? Where was that?

M: It was in Australia.

W: I see. So that's □ _____ the □ _____ □ _____.

✏ **어휘복습** 잘 안 들리거나 몰라서 체크한 어휘를 써 놓고 복습해 보세요.

□ _____ □ _____ □ _____ □ _____

□ _____ □ _____ □ _____ □ _____

□ _____ □ _____ □ _____ □ _____

13 관계 추론

대화를 듣고, 두 사람의 관계로 가장 적절한 것을 고르시오.

① 약사-환자
② 교사-학생
③ 의사-간호사
④ 서점 주인-손님
⑤ 우체국 직원-고객

M: Good morning. How may I help you?

W: I've had a □ _____ □ _____ since yesterday.

M: Do you also have a sore throat?

W: No, but I □ _____ a little □ _____ too. Do you have anything I can take?

M: This aspirin will □ _____ your □ _____. But if you don't □ _____ □ _____ soon, please □ _____ □ _____ the □ _____.

W: Thank you. How much is it?

M: It's two thousand won.

14 부탁 파악

대화를 듣고, 남자가 여자에게 요청한 일로 가장 적절한 것을 고르시오.

① 주문 취소
② 재고 확보
③ 배송지 변경
④ 주문 내역 조회
⑤ 홈페이지 주소 확인

M: Hello.

W: Hello. This is Jenny from Alice □ _____ □ _____. Are you Bradley Smith?

M: Yes, I am.

W: I'm calling to □ _____ □ _____ □ _____ that the □ _____ you ordered, *Fantastic Fox*, is currently □ _____ □ _____.

M: Hmm... □ _____ are my □ _____ then?

W: If you want to, you can □ _____ □ _____ we get more books.

M: Well, can I just □ _____ my □ _____?

W: Okay, □ _____ □ _____. I'll do it for you.

✏ **어휘복습** 잘 안 들리거나 몰라서 체크한 어휘를 써 놓고 복습해 보세요.

□ _____   □ _____   □ _____   □ _____

□ _____   □ _____   □ _____   □ _____

□ _____   □ _____   □ _____   □ _____

대화를 듣고, 남자가 슈퍼마켓에 가는 이유로 가장 적절한 것을 고르시오.

① 우산을 사려고
② 준비물을 사려고
③ 친구를 데려오려고
④ 식료품을 구입하려고
⑤ 엄마의 심부름을 하려고

W: Jim, where are you going?

M: Mom, I'm going to the □ _____ to □ _____ □ _____ a friend of mine, Minho.

W: Oh, I thought he knew □ _____ □ _____ □ _____ □ _____ .

M: He does, but it's □ _____ really □ _____ □ _____ and he doesn't have an □ _____ .

W: So, is he □ _____ □ _____ you □ _____ □ _____ □ _____ the supermarket?

M: Yes. I'll □ _____ □ _____ □ _____ with him.

W: All right.

대화를 듣고, 두 사람의 대화가 <u>어색한</u> 것을 고르시오.

①   ②   ③   ④   ⑤

① W: Long time no see.
   M: I've been □ _____ □ _____ □ _____ for a month.

② W: I think you should □ _____ some □ _____ .
   M: I think I should, too.

③ W: Will you □ _____ me □ _____ □ _____ ?
   M: Sure. What is it?

④ W: Are you □ _____ □ _____ singing?
   M: Good □ _____ !

⑤ W: □ _____ □ _____ shall we meet?
   M: □ _____ □ _____ at five?

✏ **어휘복습** 잘 안 들리거나 몰라서 체크한 어휘를 써 놓고 복습해 보세요.

□ _____   □ _____   □ _____   □ _____

□ _____   □ _____   □ _____   □ _____

□ _____   □ _____   □ _____   □ _____

17 속담 추론

대화를 듣고, 대화의 상황에 어울리는 속담으로 가장 적절한 것을 고르시오.

① 빈 수레가 요란하다.
② 소 잃고 외양간 고친다.
③ 발 없는 말이 천 리 간다.
④ 사공이 많으면 배가 산으로 간다.
⑤ 자라 보고 놀란 가슴 솥뚜껑 보고 놀란다.

M: Hey, Minju. What are you doing?

W: I'm retyping my □ _____.

M: Why? You told me that you □ _____ it □ _____.

W: I did, but I □ _____ my □ _____. My □ _____ got a □ _____.

M: What? I told you to □ _____ your virus □ _____ as often as possible.

W: Oh, I just updated it.

M: Come on. You should be more □ _____ to prevent □ _____ □ _____ from □ _____.

18 날씨 파악

다음을 듣고, 금요일 밤의 날씨로 가장 적절한 것을 고르시오.

① ② ③
④ ⑤

W: Hello. Here's Wednesday night's weather report. We had some □ _____ this □ _____ and it □ _____ □ _____ and □ _____. □ _____ will be perfect for □ _____ □ _____ because it will be □ _____ all day. However, it's very likely to rain again □ _____ in the □ _____, which is expected to □ _____ □ _____ □ _____ on Friday □ _____. Please be sure to □ _____ yourselves □ _____ because the □ _____ are quite □ _____ these days. Thank you.

✏ **어휘복습** 잘 안 들리거나 몰라서 체크한 어휘를 써 놓고 복습해 보세요.

□ _____ □ _____ □ _____ □ _____
□ _____ □ _____ □ _____ □ _____
□ _____ □ _____ □ _____ □ _____

대화를 듣고, 남자의 마지막 말에 이어질 여
자의 말로 가장 적절한 것을 고르시오.

Woman: _____

① Please help yourself.
② I'm sure he can do it.
③ I had a very good time.
④ Thank you for your advice.
⑤ I'm pleased to meet you, too.

M: Hey, Sarah. □ _____ □ _____ □ _____ □ _____?
W: I'm worried that Jaeho might be □ _____ □ _____ me.
M: Why?
W: We □ _____ a □ _____ together this morning, but I
   didn't go.
M: Did something happen?
W: No. I just □ _____ □ _____ about it. What should I do?
M: You should □ _____ □ _____ that □ _____ □ _____.
   I'm sure that's the best thing to do.
W: _____

대화를 듣고, 남자의 마지막 말에 이어질 여
자의 말로 가장 적절한 것을 고르시오.

Woman: _____

① In fact, I prefer science to
   history.
② Well, I haven't found a good one
   yet.
③ Okay. I'm sure I turned off the
   computer.
④ Right! We should respect
   inventors' ideas.
⑤ The deadline for the report has
   already passed.

M: Kelly, why are you still here in the □ _____ □ _____?
W: Oh, I'm □ _____ the □ _____ for my □ _____
   □ _____.
M: You mean the □ _____ for Mr. Kim's class?
W: Yes, that's right. I need to □ _____ an □ _____ □ _____
   and write a report about it.
M: I see. So, □ _____ invention did you □ _____?
W: _____

✎ **어휘복습** 잘 안 들리거나 몰라서 체크한 어휘를 써 놓고 복습해 보세요.

□ _____ □ _____ □ _____ □ _____

□ _____ □ _____ □ _____ □ _____

□ _____ □ _____ □ _____ □ _____

01 대화를 듣고, 남자가 만든 카드로 가장 적절한 것을 고르시오.

①   ②   ③

④   ⑤

02 대화를 듣고, 남자의 심정으로 가장 적절한 것을 고르시오.

① angry　② bored　③ excited
④ relaxed　⑤ worried

03 대화를 듣고, 남자가 지난 주말에 한 일로 가장 적절한 것을 고르시오.

① 승마 체험　② 자전거 타기
③ 콘서트 관람　④ 박물관 견학
⑤ 할머니 댁 방문

04 대화를 듣고, 두 사람이 대화하는 장소로 가장 적절한 곳을 고르시오.

① 은행　② 우체국　③ 농구장
④ 영화관　⑤ 기차역

05 대화를 듣고, 남자의 마지막 말의 의도로 가장 적절한 것을 고르시오.

① 기원　② 허가　③ 사과
④ 동의　⑤ 감사

06 대화를 듣고, 저녁 식사에 참석할 인원수를 고르시오.

① 4　② 5　③ 6
④ 7　⑤ 8

07 대화를 듣고, 여자가 대화 직후에 할 일로 가장 적절한 것을 고르시오.

① 축구공 구입하기
② 친구에게 전화하기
③ 축구 경기 관람하기
④ 체육 선생님 찾아가기
⑤ 탁구 동아리 가입하기

08 대화를 듣고, 두 사람이 수강할 방과 후 수업을 고르시오.

① 기타반　② 미술반　③ 서예반
④ 댄스반　⑤ 테니스반

09 다음을 듣고, 여자가 하는 말의 내용으로 가장 적절한 것을 고르시오.

① 운동 경기 소개
② 축하 행사 안내
③ 동아리 가입 홍보
④ 경기 일정 변경 공지
⑤ 배구 선수 모집 공고

10 대화를 듣고, 여자가 구입한 물건이 <u>아닌</u> 것을 고르시오.

① 머리핀　② 허리띠　③ 운동화
④ 책　⑤ 귀걸이

11 대화를 듣고, 남자가 도서관에 전화를 건 목적으로 가장 적절한 것을 고르시오.

① 위치를 물어보려고
② 이용 시간을 알아보려고
③ 대출 기간을 연장하려고
④ 봉사 활동에 대해 문의하려고
⑤ 도서 대출 가능 여부를 확인하려고

12 다음을 듣고, 방송의 내용과 일치하지 않는 것을 고르시오.

① 기장의 이름은 Brian이다.
② 폭설로 출발이 늦어졌다.
③ 비행기는 New York행이다.
④ 목적지까지는 약 12시간 걸린다.
⑤ 출발 시간은 오전 9시이다.

13 대화를 듣고, 두 사람의 관계로 가장 적절한 것을 고르시오.

① 시민 – 교통 경찰관
② 투숙객 – 호텔 주방장
③ 승객 – 버스 운전기사
④ 고객 – 자동차 정비사
⑤ 관광객 – 기념품 가게 주인

14 대화를 듣고, 남자가 여자에게 요청한 일로 가장 적절한 것을 고르시오.

① 물 가져다주기
② 담요 가져다주기
③ 감기약 가져다주기
④ 도착시간 알려주기
⑤ 안전벨트 점검해주기

15 대화를 듣고, 남자가 영화를 볼 수 없는 이유로 가장 적절한 것을 고르시오.

① 부모님이 아프셔서
② 생일파티에 가야 해서
③ 체험활동을 가야 해서
④ 가족여행을 가야 해서
⑤ 여동생을 돌보아야 해서

16 대화를 듣고, 두 사람의 대화가 어색한 것을 고르시오.

①   ②   ③   ④   ⑤

17 대화를 듣고, 대화의 상황에 어울리는 속담으로 가장 적절한 것을 고르시오.

① 노력은 성공의 어머니다.
② 하나를 듣고 열을 안다.
③ 낫 놓고 기역 자도 모른다.
④ 닭 쫓던 개 지붕 쳐다본다.
⑤ 안에서 새는 바가지 밖에서도 샌다.

18 다음을 듣고, 내일 오후의 날씨로 가장 적절한 것을 고르시오.

①   ②   ③   ④   ⑤

[19-20] 대화를 듣고, 남자의 마지막 말에 이어질 여자의 말로 가장 적절한 것을 고르시오.

19 Woman: _____

① You did a good job!
② Sure, let's go together.
③ Make yourself at home.
④ Wow, you're so lucky.
⑤ Cheer up! You can do it.

20 Woman: _____

① Really? Let's go there some time.
② They won't like the restaurant, either.
③ Oh, I'm glad to hear that you like this place.
④ Well, there isn't any Indian restaurant in this mall.
⑤ Hmm... Many people prefer to eat out on weekends.

04회 DICTATION

다시 듣고, 빈칸에 알맞은 단어를 써 보세요.

◀◗》 MP3 기출 04-1

01 그림 정보 파악

대화를 듣고, 남자가 만든 카드로 가장 적절한 것을 고르시오.

① ② ③
④ ⑤

W: Tomorrow is Mom's □ _____. Did you get a □ _____ for her?
M: Yes, and I □ _____ a birthday □ _____ for her, too. Look! This is the card.
W: Oh, you wrote '□ _____ □ _____' on the card.
M: Yes, I did. □ _____ do you □ _____ about this □ _____ □ _____ □ _____?
W: It's □ _____. Mom will like it.

02 심정 추론

대화를 듣고, 남자의 심정으로 가장 적절한 것을 고르시오.

① angry   ② bored
③ excited   ④ relaxed
⑤ worried

W: Hey, John. You're still □ _____.
M: Yes, Mom. I □ _____ □ _____ because of the □ _____ □ _____.
W: Why? Is there □ _____ □ _____?
M: No. I'm just so □ _____. This is my □ _____ □ _____ to Gyeongju.
W: I know. You'll □ _____ □ _____ □ _____ from this trip.
M: Yeah. I'm really □ _____ □ _____ □ _____ seeing Cheomseongdae the most. I heard it's beautiful.

03 한 일 파악

대화를 듣고, 남자가 지난 주말에 한 일로 가장 적절한 것을 고르시오.

① 승마 체험
② 자전거 타기
③ 콘서트 관람
④ 박물관 견학
⑤ 할머니 댁 방문

M: What are you going to do □ _____ □ _____, Susan?
W: I'm going to □ _____ my □ _____ on Jeju Island.
M: Wow, Jeju Island! I □ _____ □ _____ last weekend.
W: Really? What did you do there?
M: I went □ _____ □ _____. It was great!
W: Horseback riding? That □ _____ □ _____!

✎ 어휘복습 잘 안 들리거나 몰라서 체크한 어휘를 써 놓고 복습해 보세요.

□ _____   □ _____   □ _____   □ _____
□ _____   □ _____   □ _____   □ _____
□ _____   □ _____   □ _____   □ _____

04 장소 추론

대화를 듣고, 두 사람이 대화하는 장소로 가장 적절한 곳을 고르시오.

① 은행   ② 우체국   ③ 농구장
④ 영화관   ⑤ 기차역

W: Two □ _____ □ _____ *Titanic* at five o'clock, please.
M: Sorry, the tickets are all □ _____ □ _____.
W: □ _____ are the □ _____ □ _____?
M: At □ _____ □ _____ or six □ _____ □ _____. The six forty five showing is in □ _____.
W: I see. Then □ _____ □ _____ tickets for the 3D movie.
M: Okay. Please take a look at the □ _____ □ _____ and □ _____ your □ _____.

05 의도 파악

대화를 듣고, 남자의 마지막 말의 의도로 가장 적절한 것을 고르시오.

① 기원   ② 허가   ③ 사과
④ 동의   ⑤ 감사

M: Are you doing anything for your school's □ _____?
W: Well, my friends and I are going to □ _____ a □ _____ □ _____.
M: A dance performance? That's □ _____!
W: You know, this is my □ _____ □ _____. I □ _____ really □ _____.
M: Don't worry. I know you'll □ _____ □ _____.
W: Thanks a lot.
M: I wish you □ _____ □ _____!

06 숫자 정보 파악

대화를 듣고, 저녁 식사에 참석할 인원수를 고르시오.

① 4   ② 5   ③ 6
④ 7   ⑤ 8

M: Honey, I'm going to □ _____ a □ _____ □ _____ now.
W: Are we going to the □ _____ □ _____?
M: Yes. There are □ _____ □ _____ □ _____, right?
W: Oh, Mr. and Mrs. Brown □ _____ and said they can't come.
M: Okay. Hmm... There will be □ _____, □ _____.
W: Yes, □ _____ □ _____.
M: Okay. I'll make a reservation □ _____ □ _____.

✏️ **어휘복습** 잘 안 들리거나 몰라서 체크한 어휘를 써 놓고 복습해 보세요.

□ _____   □ _____   □ _____   □ _____
□ _____   □ _____   □ _____   □ _____
□ _____   □ _____   □ _____   □ _____

07 할 일 파악

대화를 듣고, 여자가 대화 직후에 할 일로
가장 적절한 것을 고르시오.

① 축구공 구입하기
② 친구에게 전화하기
③ 축구 경기 관람하기
④ 체육 선생님 찾아가기
⑤ 탁구 동아리 가입하기

W: Daniel, □ _____ do you usually □ _____ □ _____
□ _____?
M: I usually □ _____ □ _____ with the school soccer club.
How about you?
W: I play □ _____ □ _____ . But I □ _____ □ _____
□ _____ play soccer.
M: We play soccer □ _____ □ _____ . Why don't you
□ _____ the □ _____?
W: Wonderful! □ _____ can I join?
M: Just go and ask Mr. Kim, our □ _____ □ _____ .
W: Okay! I'll go to see him □ _____ □ _____ . Thanks.

08 특정 정보 파악

대화를 듣고, 두 사람이 수강할 방과 후 수
업을 고르시오.

① 기타반   ② 미술반
③ 서예반   ④ 댄스반
⑤ 테니스반

W: You know what? There will be an □ _____ □ _____
□ _____ this summer!
M: Great. I heard there will be a □ _____ class, □ _____ .
W: I know. □ _____ □ _____ do you □ _____ □ _____?
M: I'd really like to learn □ _____ □ _____ □ _____ the
guitar this summer. What about you?
W: Well, □ _____ □ _____ I wanted the tennis class.
□ _____ I'll take the guitar class, if you take it.
M: Okay. Let's go and □ _____ □ _____ □ _____ it.

✎ **어휘복습** 잘 안 들리거나 몰라서 체크한 어휘를 써 놓고 복습해 보세요.

□ _____   □ _____   □ _____   □ _____

□ _____   □ _____   □ _____   □ _____

□ _____   □ _____   □ _____   □ _____

다음을 듣고, 여자가 하는 말의 내용으로 가장 적절한 것을 고르시오.

① 운동 경기 소개
② 축하 행사 안내
③ 동아리 가입 홍보
④ 경기 일정 변경 공지
⑤ 배구 선수 모집 공고

W: Good morning, everyone! I have wonderful news. Our girl's □ _____ team □ _____ the local □ _____ last night. To □ _____ the □ _____, we've □ _____ afternoon □ _____ today. □ _____, we're planning to □ _____ a special □ _____ at two o'clock this afternoon. Please come to the □ _____ and enjoy free snacks and drinks. Thank you.

대화를 듣고, 여자가 구입한 물건이 <u>아닌</u> 것을 고르시오.

① 머리핀　　② 허리띠
③ 운동화　　④ 책
⑤ 귀걸이

M: How was the new □ _____ □ _____?
W: It was □ _____ and very □ _____.
M: What did you buy there?
W: I bought a □ _____, a □ _____, and □ _____ for Parents' Day.
M: You mean presents for your □ _____?
W: Yes, I bought a □ _____ my □ _____ and □ _____ for my □ _____.
M: Oh, you're so sweet.

대화를 듣고, 남자가 도서관에 전화를 건 목적으로 가장 적절한 것을 고르시오.

① 위치를 물어보려고
② 이용 시간을 알아보려고
③ 대출 기간을 연장하려고
④ 봉사 활동에 대해 문의하려고
⑤ 도서 대출 가능 여부를 확인하려고

W: Hello. Green Star □ _____. How may I help you?
M: Hi. □ _____ □ _____ □ _____ to □ _____ at your library?
W: Yes. We always welcome volunteers.
M: That's great.
W: If you're □ _____, □ _____ our □ _____. On the website, you'll find □ _____ about volunteering.
M: Oh, I see. Thank you for the information.

✎ **어휘복습** 잘 안 들리거나 몰라서 체크한 어휘를 써 놓고 복습해 보세요.

□ _____	□ _____	□ _____	□ _____
□ _____	□ _____	□ _____	□ _____
□ _____	□ _____	□ _____	□ _____

12 내용 일치 파악

다음을 듣고, 방송의 내용과 일치하지 <u>않는</u> 것을 고르시오.

① 기장의 이름은 Brian이다.
② 폭설로 출발이 늦어졌다.
③ 비행기는 New York행이다.
④ 목적지까지는 약 12시간 걸린다.
⑤ 출발 시간은 오전 9시이다.

M: Hello, everyone. My □ _____ is Brian Smith, and I'm the □ _____ of this □ _____. We're sorry that we □ _____ a little □ _____ because of the □ _____ □ _____ this morning. This flight is □ _____ New York. It'll □ _____ about □ _____ hours to get there. We'll □ _____ in New York □ _____ □ _____ o'clock in the morning. Please enjoy the flight. Thank you.

13 관계 추론

대화를 듣고, 두 사람의 관계로 가장 적절한 것을 고르시오.

① 시민 – 교통 경찰관
② 투숙객 – 호텔 주방장
③ 승객 – 버스 운전기사
④ 고객 – 자동차 정비사
⑤ 관광객 – 기념품 가게 주인

W: Excuse me. Does this □ _____ go to Victoria □ _____?
M: Yes, it does. We're □ _____ □ _____ leave. If you want to take this bus, you'd better □ _____ □ _____ now.
W: Okay, thanks. □ _____ □ _____ will it □ _____ to get there?
M: About □ _____ □ _____ □ _____.
W: Okay. Can you tell me when we get there please? I'm not □ _____ □ _____ □ _____.
M: Sure, no problem. □ _____ □ _____ □ _____ please.

14 부탁 파악

대화를 듣고, 남자가 여자에게 요청한 일로 가장 적절한 것을 고르시오.

① 물 가져다주기
② 담요 가져다주기
③ 감기약 가져다주기
④ 도착시간 알려주기
⑤ 안전벨트 점검해주기

W: Excuse me, sir. Please □ _____ □ _____ □ _____. We'll □ _____ □ _____ soon.
M: Sure. But, can I get a □ _____? I □ _____ a little □ _____.
W: Of course. Can I bring you some □ _____ □ _____, too?
M: That's okay.
W: Please wait a moment. I'll be □ _____ □ _____.
M: Thank you so much.

✏ **어휘복습** 잘 안 들리거나 몰라서 체크한 어휘를 써 놓고 복습해 보세요.

□ _____   □ _____   □ _____   □ _____

□ _____   □ _____   □ _____   □ _____

□ _____   □ _____   □ _____   □ _____

15 이유 파악

대화를 듣고, 남자가 영화를 볼 수 없는 이유로 가장 적절한 것을 고르시오.

① 부모님이 아프셔서
② 생일파티에 가야 해서
③ 체험활동을 가야 해서
④ 가족여행을 가야 해서
⑤ 여동생을 돌보아야 해서

M: Hi, Nancy.

W: Hi, Henry. Can you □ _____ □ _____ the □ _____ with me tomorrow?

M: I'd □ _____ □ _____, □ _____ I can't.

W: Why? Do you have □ _____ □ _____?

M: I have to stay home and □ _____ □ _____ □ _____ my younger □ _____.

W: Really? Aren't your parents home?

M: No, they're □ _____ □ _____ □ _____ on a trip.

W: Then, □ _____ □ _____ □ _____.

16 어색한 대화 찾기

대화를 듣고, 두 사람의 대화가 어색한 것을 고르시오.

①   ②   ③   ④   ⑤

① W: □ _____ □ _____ do you play soccer?

　 M: □ _____ a week.

② W: □ _____ do you want □ _____ □ _____?

　 M: I want to wear □ _____ □ _____.

③ W: Can you □ _____ my skateboard?

　 M: Let me see. □ _____ □ _____.

④ W: □ _____ do you □ _____ □ _____ the library?

　 M: I don't □ _____ □ _____.

⑤ W: Thank you for your help.

　 M: Sure, □ _____!

✎ **어휘복습** 잘 안 들리거나 몰라서 체크한 어휘를 써 놓고 복습해 보세요.

□ _____　　□ _____　　□ _____　　□ _____

□ _____　　□ _____　　□ _____　　□ _____

□ _____　　□ _____　　□ _____　　□ _____

17 속담 추론

대화를 듣고, 대화의 상황에 어울리는 속담
으로 가장 적절한 것을 고르시오.

① 노력은 성공의 어머니다.
② 하나를 듣고 열을 안다.
③ 낫 놓고 기역 자도 모른다.
④ 닭 쫓던 개 지붕 쳐다본다.
⑤ 안에서 새는 바가지 밖에서도 샌다.

W: □ _____ □ _____ winning the MVP award, Mr. Park.

M: Thank you.

W: □ _____ did you □ _____ such a □ _____ □ _____?

M: □ _____, I was not really good when I first started
□ _____ □ _____, but I □ _____ a lot.

W: What did you do?

M: When my team practiced, I was always the □ _____ player
□ _____ □ _____ and the □ _____ player □ _____
□ _____.

W: Oh, I see. □ _____ □ _____ you became such a good
player.

18 날씨 파악

다음을 듣고, 내일 오후의 날씨로 가장 적절
한 것을 고르시오.

① ② ③
④ ⑤

W: Hello. This is the □ _____ □ _____ for tonight and
tomorrow. The □ _____ that started □ _____ □ _____
has □ _____ for the moment. And it's very likely to be
□ _____ □ _____ morning. In the □ _____, it'll be
partly □ _____ with □ _____ strong □ _____. Still, the
□ _____ will be □ _____ □ _____ □ _____ all day
tomorrow. Thank you.

✏ **어휘복습** 잘 안 들리거나 몰라서 체크한 어휘를 써 놓고 복습해 보세요.

□ _____ □ _____ □ _____ □ _____

□ _____ □ _____ □ _____ □ _____

□ _____ □ _____ □ _____ □ _____

19 알맞은 응답 찾기

대화를 듣고, 남자의 마지막 말에 이어질 여자의 말로 가장 적절한 것을 고르시오.

Woman: _____

① You did a good job!
② Sure, let's go together.
③ Make yourself at home.
④ Wow, you're so lucky.
⑤ Cheer up! You can do it.

W: Hey, Mike. How is it going?

M: Good. Oh, have you □ _____ □ _____ James?

W: No. Did something happen to him?

M: He □ _____ his □ _____ yesterday. He's □ _____ the □ _____ now.

W: Really? That's □ _____.

M: □ _____ □ _____ going to □ _____ him after school?

W: _____

20 알맞은 응답 찾기

대화를 듣고, 남자의 마지막 말에 이어질 여자의 말로 가장 적절한 것을 고르시오.

Woman: _____

① Really? Let's go there some time.
② They won't like the restaurant, either.
③ Oh, I'm glad to hear that you like this place.
④ Well, there isn't any Indian restaurant in this mall.
⑤ Hmm... Many people prefer to eat out on weekends.

M: Helen, this is □ _____ □ _____ □ _____ dinner.

W: Yes, it is. This □ _____ is really great.

M: □ _____ is your □ _____?

W: It is so □ _____. I really love □ _____ □ _____.

M: Oh, do you? □ _____, there's □ _____ nice Indian restaurant in this □ _____.

W: _____

✎ **어휘복습** 잘 안 들리거나 몰라서 체크한 어휘를 써 놓고 복습해 보세요.

□ _____   □ _____   □ _____   □ _____
□ _____   □ _____   □ _____   □ _____
□ _____   □ _____   □ _____   □ _____

01 대화를 듣고, 남자가 벼룩시장에 가져갈 물건을 고르시오.

①   ②   ③

④   ⑤

02 대화를 듣고, 여자가 방문한 곳의 날씨로 가장 적절한 것을 고르시오.

①   ②   ③   ④   ⑤

03 대화를 듣고, 여자의 마지막 말에 드러난 심정으로 가장 적절한 것을 고르시오.

① proud   ② bored   ③ sorry
④ scared   ⑤ relaxed

04 대화를 듣고, 두 사람이 대화하는 장소로 가장 적절한 곳을 고르시오.

① 병원   ② 호텔   ③ 은행
④ 영화관   ⑤ 도서관

05 대화를 듣고, 여자가 묘사하는 사람을 고르시오.

①   ②   ③

④   ⑤

06 대화를 듣고, 여자가 지불한 금액을 고르시오.

① $3   ② $6   ③ $15
④ $18   ⑤ $20

07 대화를 듣고, 남자가 전화를 건 목적으로 가장 적절한 것을 고르시오.

① 주문을 취소하려고
② 배송 날짜를 변경하려고
③ 방문 약속을 확인하려고
④ 상품의 색을 선택하려고
⑤ 불만 사항을 건의하려고

08 대화를 듣고, 남자가 할 일로 가장 적절한 것을 고르시오.

① 충고해주기   ② 휴식 취하기
③ 약속 정하기   ④ 병원에 가기
⑤ 수학 숙제하기

09 대화를 듣고, 두 사람의 관계로 가장 적절한 것을 고르시오.

① 약사 – 고객   ② 교사 – 학생
③ 승무원 – 승객   ④ 심판 – 운동선수
⑤ 관광 안내원 – 관광객

10 다음을 듣고, 학생들이 가장 많이 빌리는 책의 종류를 고르시오.

① novels   ② magazines
③ dictionaries   ④ comic books
⑤ cooking books

11 대화를 듣고, 여자가 남자를 위해 할 일로 가장 적절한 것을 고르시오.

① 교실 청소하기   ② 노트 빌려주기
③ 보고서 도와주기   ④ 숙제 제출해주기
⑤ 영어 선생님 모셔오기

12 다음을 듣고, 오늘 오후 4시에 열릴 행사로 가장 적절한 것을 고르시오.

① 동아리 소개   ② 동영상 시청
③ 그림 그리기   ④ 글짓기 대회
⑤ 글쓰기 수업

13 대화를 듣고, 여자가 할 일로 가장 적절한 것을 고르시오.

① 연극 보기
② 책 구입하기
③ 영어 대본 읽기
④ 연극 포스터 만들기
⑤ 영어 선생님께 여쭤보기

14 다음을 듣고, 도표의 내용과 다른 것을 고르시오.

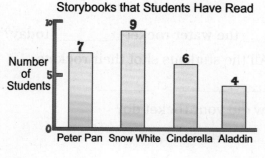

Storybooks that Students Have Read

①   ②   ③   ④   ⑤

15 대화를 듣고, 남자의 휴대전화에 대한 설명으로 일치하지 않는 것을 고르시오.

① 생일 선물로 받았다.
② 책을 읽을 수 있다.
③ 목소리를 녹음할 수 있다.
④ 사진을 찍을 수 있다.
⑤ 영화를 볼 수 있다.

16 다음을 듣고, 두 사람의 대화가 어색한 것을 고르시오.

①   ②   ③   ④   ⑤

17 다음을 듣고, 학교 방송의 내용과 일치하지 않는 것을 고르시오.

① 운동회 날은 다음 주 금요일이다.
② 자원 봉사 모집 인원은 30명이다.
③ 모두에게 신청 기회가 주어진다.
④ 지원자는 체육관에서 신청할 수 있다.
⑤ 모집 기간은 다음 주 화요일까지이다.

[18~19] 대화를 듣고, 여자의 마지막 말에 이어질 남자의 응답으로 가장 적절한 것을 고르시오.

18 Man: _____

① I've been there, too.
② That's a great idea!
③ I'm going with my family.
④ Last time, Mike and I went hiking.
⑤ The mountain is great this time of the year.

19 Man: _____

① I'm going to bake a cake.
② I'll finish it as soon as I can.
③ I can't go to the market now.
④ I like taking pictures very much.
⑤ I don't want to go to the party.

20 다음을 듣고, James가 민지에게 할 말로 가장 적절한 것을 고르시오.

James: _____

① I like badminton the most.
② I want to win every game.
③ Congratulations! You won the game!
④ Hurry up! I need to do my homework.
⑤ Don't be disappointed. You will do better next time.

01 그림 정보 파악

대화를 듣고, 남자가 벼룩시장에 가져갈 물건을 고르시오.

① ② ③
④ ⑤

W: Chris, what will you take to the ☐ _____ ☐ _____?
M: Well Mom, I haven't ☐ _____ ☐ _____.
W: ☐ _____ ☐ _____ this ☐ _____ ☐ _____?
M: I'm still playing with it. Can I take this ☐ _____?
W: Sure. I'll ☐ _____ it for you.
M: Thanks. I'm also thinking of ☐ _____ these ☐ _____ at the market.
W: They're ☐ _____ ☐ _____. This jacket will be ☐ _____.

02 날씨 파악

대화를 듣고, 여자가 방문한 곳의 날씨로 가장 적절한 것을 고르시오.

① ② ③
④ ⑤

M: ☐ _____ did you go on your ☐ _____ ☐ _____?
W: I ☐ _____ my uncle's house in Los Angeles.
M: ☐ _____ was the ☐ _____ ☐ _____ there?
W: We had ☐ _____ days.
M: Really? We ☐ _____ a lot of ☐ _____ here in Korea.

03 심정 추론

대화를 듣고, 여자의 마지막 말에 드러난 심정으로 가장 적절한 것을 고르시오.

① proud   ② bored
③ sorry   ④ scared
⑤ relaxed

W: ☐ _____ ☐ _____ the water rocket ☐ _____ today?
M: Fantastic, Mom! All the students shot their rockets ☐ _____ ☐ _____ ☐ _____ ☐ _____.
W: Sounds great! How did your rocket do?
M: It flew about ☐ _____ ☐ _____!
W: That's ☐ _____!
M: Yeah. I ☐ _____ ☐ _____ ☐ _____.
W: You ☐ _____ a ☐ _____ ☐ _____!

✏️ 어휘복습 잘 안 들리거나 몰라서 체크한 어휘를 써 놓고 복습해 보세요.

☐ _____   ☐ _____   ☐ _____   ☐ _____
☐ _____   ☐ _____   ☐ _____   ☐ _____
☐ _____   ☐ _____   ☐ _____   ☐ _____

04 장소 추론

대화를 듣고, 두 사람이 대화하는 장소로 가장 적절한 곳을 고르시오.

① 병원　② 호텔　③ 은행
④ 영화관　⑤ 도서관

M: Excuse me, may I □ _____ you □ _____?
W: Sure. What is it?
M: I □ _____ two □ _____ last week, but I □ _____ them.
W: Oh, that's too bad. Do you have your □ _____ □ _____?
M: Here it is.
W: Your name is Andrew Smith, right?
M: Yes. What should I do?
W: I'm sorry, but you have to □ _____ □ _____ the books you lost.

05 그림 정보 파악

대화를 듣고, 여자가 묘사하는 사람을 고르시오.

①　②　③
④　⑤

M: I'm □ _____ Jones. I heard you □ _____ the □ _____ last night.
W: Yes. I saw him □ _____ □ _____ □ _____ the house.
M: □ _____ did he □ _____ □ _____?
W: He was very □ _____. And he was □ _____ a □ _____ □ _____.
M: Oh, I see. Was he wearing a □ _____?
W: Yes, he was.

✎ **어휘복습** 잘 안 들리거나 몰라서 체크한 어휘를 써 놓고 복습해 보세요.

□ _____　□ _____　□ _____　□ _____
□ _____　□ _____　□ _____　□ _____
□ _____　□ _____　□ _____　□ _____

06 숫자 정보 파악

대화를 듣고, 여자가 지불한 금액을 고르시오.

① $3　　② $6　　③ $15
④ $18　　⑤ $20

M: Welcome to the □ _____ □ _____.

W: □ _____ □ _____ is a □ _____ for a student?

M: It's □ _____ dollars, but we □ _____ □ _____ one-dollar □ _____ per ticket after six o'clock.

W: That's great! It's six thirty. I need □ _____ tickets.

M: All right. The □ _____ is □ _____ dollars.

W: Here you are.

07 전화 목적 파악

대화를 듣고, 남자가 전화를 건 목적으로 가장 적절한 것을 고르시오.

① 주문을 취소하려고
② 배송 날짜를 변경하려고
③ 방문 약속을 확인하려고
④ 상품의 색을 선택하려고
⑤ 불만 사항을 건의하려고

W: Hello, ABC Carpet. How may I help you?

M: I'm calling to □ _____ my □ _____.

W: May I □ _____ your □ _____, please?

M: This is David Miller. I ordered a blue □ _____ for my □ _____ □ _____ yesterday.

W: Yes, I found your order. What do you want to change?

M: The □ _____ □ _____. I want to get it on October seventh.

W: Okay. You want to change your delivery date from □ _____ □ _____ to October □ _____, right?

M: That's right. Thanks.

✎ **어휘복습** 잘 안 들리거나 몰라서 체크한 어휘를 써 놓고 복습해 보세요.

□ _____　　□ _____　　□ _____　　□ _____

□ _____　　□ _____　　□ _____　　□ _____

□ _____　　□ _____　　□ _____　　□ _____

08 할 일 파악

대화를 듣고, 남자가 할 일로 가장 적절한 것을 고르시오.

① 충고해주기
② 휴식 취하기
③ 약속 정하기
④ 병원에 가기
⑤ 수학 숙제하기

W: You □ _____ □ _____. What's the matter?

M: I think I □ _____ a □ _____.

W: Why don't you go home and □ _____ some □ _____?

M: I want to, but I have to □ _____ □ _____ my □ _____ □ _____. It's on Friday.

W: You have three days before the test. You should go and □ _____ □ _____ □ _____.

M: Okay, I'll do that. □ _____ □ _____ for your □ _____.

09 관계 추론

대화를 듣고, 두 사람의 관계로 가장 적절한 것을 고르시오.

① 약사 – 고객
② 교사 – 학생
③ 승무원 – 승객
④ 심판 – 운동선수
⑤ 관광 안내원 – 관광객

M: How may I help you?

W: I need to □ _____ the □ _____ my doctor ordered for me.

M: Please □ _____ □ _____ □ _____.

W: Okay.

M: Here's your medicine. □ _____ one □ _____ □ _____ □ _____ □ _____ □ _____ after each meal.

W: All right. □ _____ □ _____ is it?

M: It's □ _____ dollars.

W: Here you are.

✎ **어휘복습** 잘 안 들리거나 몰라서 체크한 어휘를 써 놓고 복습해 보세요.

□ _____   □ _____   □ _____   □ _____

□ _____   □ _____   □ _____   □ _____

□ _____   □ _____   □ _____   □ _____

10 특정 정보 파악

다음을 듣고, 학생들이 가장 많이 빌리는 책의 종류를 고르시오.

① novels
② magazines
③ dictionaries
④ comic books
⑤ cooking books

W: We have more than □ _____ □ _____ □ _____ in our school □ _____. A lot of students □ _____ various kinds of books there. □ _____ those books, □ _____ are □ _____ □ _____ □ _____ books. The □ _____ most popular books are □ _____ books, and then □ _____, followed by □ _____.

11 할 일 파악

대화를 듣고, 여자가 남자를 위해 할 일로 가장 적절한 것을 고르시오.

① 교실 청소하기
② 노트 빌려주기
③ 보고서 도와주기
④ 숙제 제출해주기
⑤ 영어 선생님 모셔오기

M: Hi, Sumi! □ _____ are you □ _____?
W: I'm going to the English □ _____ □ _____.
M: Oh, good. Will you □ _____ me □ _____ □ _____?
W: Sure, what is it?
M: Could you □ _____ my □ _____ □ _____ Mr. Kim? I have to go to my music class now.
W: Sure, Minsu.
M: Thanks a lot.

12 특정 정보 파악

다음을 듣고, 오늘 오후 4시에 열릴 행사로 가장 적절한 것을 고르시오.

① 동아리 소개
② 동영상 시청
③ 그림 그리기
④ 글짓기 대회
⑤ 글쓰기 수업

M: Hello, everyone! Today is Hangul Day. Let me tell you about today's □ _____. At □ _____ o'clock, there will be a class about □ _____ □ _____ □ _____ an □ _____. At □ _____, we will have a □ _____ □ _____. And at □ _____, we will □ _____ a □ _____ about King Sejong. I hope all of you will have a great time! Thank you.

✏ **어휘복습** 잘 안 들리거나 몰라서 체크한 어휘를 써 놓고 복습해 보세요.

□ _____   □ _____   □ _____   □ _____
□ _____   □ _____   □ _____   □ _____
□ _____   □ _____   □ _____   □ _____

13 할 일 파악

대화를 듣고, 여자가 할 일로 가장 적절한 것을 고르시오.

① 연극 보기
② 책 구입하기
③ 영어 대본 읽기
④ 연극 포스터 만들기
⑤ 영어 선생님께 여쭤보기

W: Did you hear the news? The □ _____ □ _____ is looking for □ _____.
M: Yes, I heard about it. They are going to □ _____ *Beauty and the Beast* at the □ _____ □ _____.
W: I really want to be □ _____ □ _____.
M: That would be □ _____!
W: Do you know how I can □ _____ □ _____ □ _____ it?
M: I have □ _____ □ _____. You should □ _____ your □ _____ □ _____ about it.
W: Okay, I will. Thanks.

14 도표 · 실용문 파악

다음을 듣고, 도표의 내용과 <u>다른</u> 것을 고르시오.

Storybooks that Students Have Read

Number of Students

Peter Pan 7, Snow White 9, Cinderella 6, Aladdin 4

① ② ③ ④ ⑤

① *Peter Pan* was □ _____ □ _____ seven students.
② *Snow White* was read by □ _____ □ _____ □ _____ □ _____ students.
③ *Cinderella* was read by □ _____ students □ _____ *Aladdin*.
④ *Cinderella* was read by six students.
⑤ *Aladdin* was read by nine students.

15 내용 일치 파악

대화를 듣고, 남자의 휴대전화에 대한 설명으로 일치하지 <u>않는</u> 것을 고르시오.

① 생일 선물로 받았다.
② 책을 읽을 수 있다.
③ 목소리를 녹음할 수 있다.
④ 사진을 찍을 수 있다.
⑤ 영화를 볼 수 있다.

W: David, did you get a new □ _____?
M: Yes! It was my □ _____ □ _____.
W: Wow! I really □ _____ you. What can you do with it?
M: I can □ _____ □ _____ with it.
W: That's great! Can you □ _____ your □ _____?
M: □ _____, I can't. But I can □ _____ □ _____.
W: What else can you do with it?
M: I can also □ _____ □ _____.

✏ **어휘복습** 잘 안 들리거나 몰라서 체크한 어휘를 써 놓고 복습해 보세요.

□ _____ □ _____ □ _____ □ _____

□ _____ □ _____ □ _____ □ _____

□ _____ □ _____ □ _____ □ _____

16 어색한 대화 찾기

다음을 듣고, 두 사람의 대화가 어색한 것을 고르시오.

①   ②   ③   ④   ⑤

① M: □ _____ you ever □ _____ □ _____ Seoul Tower?

    W: Yes, I have.

② M: □ _____ □ _____ does it □ _____ to get to school?

    W: I go to school □ _____ □ _____.

③ M: Did you see the TV show, *Quiz King*, last night?

    W: Yes, it was great!

④ M: Don't forget to □ _____ your □ _____.

    W: I won't, Dad.

⑤ M: What do you like to do □ _____ your □ _____

       □ _____?

    W: I like to □ _____ □ _____.

17 내용 일치 파악

다음을 듣고, 학교 방송의 내용과 일치하지 <u>않는</u> 것을 고르시오.

① 운동회 날은 다음 주 금요일이다.
② 자원 봉사 모집 인원은 30명이다.
③ 모두에게 신청 기회가 주어진다.
④ 지원자는 체육관에서 신청할 수 있다.
⑤ 모집 기간은 다음 주 화요일까지이다.

M: Hello, everyone. The school □ _____ □ _____ is coming up □ _____ □ _____! We need □ _____ □ _____ for that day. Everyone is welcomed. If you're □ _____, please □ _____ your □ _____ on the □ _____ in the school office. You can do it □ _____ next □ _____. Don't □ _____ your □ _____ to become a volunteer!

✎ **어휘복습**   잘 안 들리거나 몰라서 체크한 어휘를 써 놓고 복습해 보세요.

□ _____   □ _____   □ _____   □ _____

□ _____   □ _____   □ _____   □ _____

□ _____   □ _____   □ _____   □ _____

18 알맞은 응답 찾기

대화를 듣고, 여자의 마지막 말에 이어질 남자의 응답으로 가장 적절한 것을 고르시오.

Man: _____
① I've been there, too.
② That's a great idea!
③ I'm going with my family.
④ Last time, Mike and I went hiking.
⑤ The mountain is great this time of the year.

M: □ _____ □ _____ vacation □ _____ do we have □ _____?
W: Four days. What are you going to do?
M: I'm planning to □ _____ □ _____.
W: Where?
M: Halla □ _____.
W: Really? □ _____ are you going □ _____?
M: _____

19 알맞은 응답 찾기

대화를 듣고, 여자의 마지막 말에 이어질 남자의 응답으로 가장 적절한 것을 고르시오.

Man: _____
① I'm going to bake a cake.
② I'll finish it as soon as I can.
③ I can't go to the market now.
④ I like taking pictures very much.
⑤ I don't want to go to the party.

M: What are you doing □ _____ □ _____ □ _____?
W: I'm □ _____ □ _____ □ _____ of our family.
M: What will you do with them?
W: I'm planning to make a CD for Mom and Dad's □ _____ □ _____.
M: That's great! □ _____ □ _____ they'll like it.
W: I hope so. What are you going to do for them?
M: _____

20 상황에 적절한 말 찾기

다음을 듣고, James가 민지에게 할 말로 가장 적절한 것을 고르시오.

James: _____
① I like badminton the most.
② I want to win every game.
③ Congratulations! You won the game!
④ Hurry up! I need to do my homework.
⑤ Don't be disappointed. You will do better next time.

W: Minji and James like playing badminton. Every Sunday, they □ _____ □ _____ at a □ _____ together. Today, they went to the park to play badminton. Minji wanted to □ _____ □ _____ this time. □ _____, she □ _____ the game. In this situation, what could James say to Minji to encourage her?
James: _____

✎ **어휘복습** 잘 안 들리거나 몰라서 체크한 어휘를 써 놓고 복습해 보세요.

□ _____ □ _____ □ _____ □ _____
□ _____ □ _____ □ _____ □ _____
□ _____ □ _____ □ _____ □ _____

그림 정보 파악

1. 대화를 듣고, 남자가 구입할 티셔츠로 가장 적절한 것을 고르시오.

🔊MP3 유형 01

① 　② 　③ 　④✓　⑤

● 정답 근거 ● 오답 함정

W: Good morning! May I help you?
M: I am looking for a T-shirt with a snowman on it.
W: How about this one? There is a cute snowman in the middle and one pocket.
M: It looks nice. But I don't need the pocket.
W: Okay. Here's the same T-shirt without a pocket. How about this?
M: Great. Thanks. I will take it.

> ❶ 선택지의 그림을 보며 각 특징을 확인하세요.
> → pocket, number 1, snowman
> ❷ 사물을 묘사하는 표현이 여러 개 등장하지만, 주로 앞의 내용을 뒤집는 But 뒤에 정답이 등장해요.
> ❸ 구입을 결정하는 긍정의 대사까지 확인한 후 고르세요.

여: 안녕하세요! 무엇을 도와드릴까요?
남: 저는 눈사람이 그려진 티셔츠를 찾고 있어요.
여: 이것은 어때요? 가운데에 귀여운 눈사람이 있고, 주머니가 하나 있어요.
남: 멋져 보여요. 하지만 저는 주머니가 필요 없어요.
여: 알겠어요. 여기 주머니가 없는 같은 티셔츠가 있어요. 이건 어때요?
남: 멋져요. 고마워요. 그것으로 할게요.

2. 대화를 듣고, 탁자 위 물건 배치로 가장 적절한 것을 고르시오.

🔊MP3 유형 02

① 　② 　③ 　④✓　⑤

● 정답 근거 ● 오답 함정

W: Tony, why don't we put this picture on the table?
M: Sounds good. How about on the left, next to the clock?
W: Okay. Then let's put the teddy bear between the picture and the clock.
M: Wait. I don't think that's a good idea. Let's not put the teddy bear on the table.
W: Okay. I agree.

> ❶ 그림에서 어떤 물건이 있는지 확인하세요.
> → picture, teddy bear, clock
> ❷ 위치에 관한 어휘를 듣고 선택지와 대조해 보세요.
> ❸ 앞의 내용을 뒤집는 I don't think 뒤에 정답이 등장해요.

여: 토니, 우리 이 사진을 탁자 위에 놓는 게 어때?
남: 좋아. 시계 옆으로 왼쪽은 어때?
여: 그래. 그럼 사진과 시계 사이에 곰 인형을 놓자.
남: 잠깐만. 그건 좋은 생각이 아닌 것 같아. 곰 인형은 탁자 위에 놓지 말자.
여: 알겠어. 나도 찬성이야.

📖 **필수어휘**

모양	round 둥근　circle 동그라미, 원　triangle 삼각형　square 정사각형　rectangle 직사각형　heart-shaped 하트 모양의
무늬	striped 줄무늬의　checked 체크무늬의　plain 무늬가 없는　bird print 새 그림의　flower pattern 꽃무늬의
위치	on the left 왼쪽에　on the right 오른쪽에　between ~사이에　in front of ~앞에　behind ~뒤에

다음을 듣고, 토요일의 날씨로 가장 적절한 것을 고르시오.

🔊 MP3 유형 03

① 　② 　③ 　④ 　⑤

❶ 지시문에서 무슨 요일의 날씨인지, 오후인지, 밤인지, 들어야 할 정보를 확인하세요.

❷ 날씨는 시간 순서대로 나와요. 예를 들어 토요일의 날씨는 금요일 날씨 뒤에 나와요. 금요일 날씨가 나오면, 토요일 날씨를 기대하며 집중하세요.
Monday → Friday → Saturday

●정답 근거 ●오답 함정

Good morning! This is the weather forecast for this week. There has been lots of sunshine these days. We will have more sunny days. It will be sunny on Monday, Tuesday, and Wednesday. However, it will rain on Thursday and Friday. On Saturday and Sunday, it will be sunny again. Have a wonderful week. Thank you.

안녕하세요! 이번 주 일기 예보입니다. 요즘은 일조량이 많았는데요. 앞으로도 화창한 날씨가 이어질 것입니다. 월요일, 화요일 그리고 수요일에는 화창하겠습니다. 그러나 목요일과 금요일에는 비가 내리겠습니다. 토요일과 일요일에는 다시 화창하겠습니다. 즐거운 한 주 보내세요. 감사합니다.

 주요표현

It will be sunny / **on** Saturday. 토요일에는 화창할 거예요.

It's very likely to rain / **on** Friday night. 금요일 밤에 비올 확률이 높아요.

Tuesday **through** Friday, / it**'s going to** rain. 화요일에서 금요일까지 비가 올 거예요.

We **are expecting** rain showers / tomorrow. 내일 소나기가 내릴 예정입니다.

The rain **is expected to** turn into snow / tonight. (= The rain will change to snow tonight.)
오늘 밤에 비가 눈으로 바뀔 것으로 예상됩니다.

The snowy weather **will continue** / **until** Sunday. 일요일까지 눈이 계속 내릴 거예요.

 필수어휘

sunny 화창한	warm 따뜻	(partly) cloudy (부분적으로) 흐린	windy 바람 부는
snowy 눈 오는	rainy 비 오는	heavy rain 폭우	shower 소나기
sunshine 햇빛	temperature 온도	a chance of rain 비올 확률	freezing 매우 추운
foggy 안개 낀	humid 습한	weather forecast 일기 예보	

대화를 듣고, 여자의 심정으로 가장 적절한 것을 고르시오.

🔊 MP3 유형 04

① satisfied   ✓② nervous   ③ alarmed

④ relaxed   ⑤ bored

❶ 지시문에서 누구의 심정인지 확인하세요.

❷ 초반부에 여자가 처한 상황이 나와요. 그 상황에 대해 여자가 느끼는 감정이 긍정적인지 부정적인지 파악하세요.

❸ 결정적인 단서는 주로 대화 마지막 부분에 나와요.

●정답 근거 ●오답 함정

M: Rachel, what are you doing? It's already 10:30.

W: I'm checking my bag. I'm almost done.

M: You should go to bed. Tomorrow is your first day at your new school.

W: I know, but I want to make sure I have everything ready.

M: Don't worry. Everything will be fine.

W: Thanks, Dad. But I'm not sure I'll be able to make good friends there.

남: 레이첼, 너 뭐 하고 있니? 벌써 10시 30분이야.

여: 제 가방을 확인하고 있어요. 거의 다 했어요.

남: 넌 잠자리에 들어야 한다. 내일이 새로운 학교에서의 첫날이잖니.

여: 저도 알지만, 모든 준비가 다 됐는지 확인하고 싶어요.

남: 걱정하지 마. 다 괜찮을 거야.

여: 고마워요, 아빠. 하지만 그곳에서 좋은 친구들을 사귈 수 있을지 잘 모르겠어요.

💡 **주요표현**

worried 걱정하는	I hope it's **nothing serious**. 심각한 일이 아니길 바라요.
excited 신난	I'm really **looking forward to** seeing Cheomseongdae the most. 저는 정말로 첨성대를 보는 게 제일 기대돼요.
proud 자랑스러운	You did **a great job**! 매우 잘했어요!
thankful 감사하는	Good job! **I'm impressed.** This is the best spaghetti I've ever had! 잘했어요. 감명을 받았습니다. 제가 먹어본 스파게티 중에 최고예요.

📖 **필수어휘**

pleased 기쁜	satisfied 만족한	excited 신난
moved 감동받은	relaxed 느긋한	relieved 안도한
disappointed 실망한	nervous 초조한	worried 걱정하는
bored 지루한	regretful 후회하는	shocked 충격 받은

장소 추론

1. 대화를 듣고, 두 사람이 대화하는 장소로 가장 적절한 곳을 고르시오.

🔊 MP3 유형 05

① library   ② theater   ③ bookstore

④ restaurant   ⑤ bank

❶ 선택지에 비슷한 역할을 하는 장소가 있는지 확인하세요.
→ 도서관 vs. 서점

❷ 장소를 추론할 수 있는 힌트가 나와요. 들리는 힌트를 종합하여 정답을 고르세요.
→ check out books, library card

●정답 근거 ●오답 함정

M: Excuse me. Is it possible to check out books with a student ID card?
W: No, you need a library card.
M: I see. Actually, I don't have one. Can I get a new card here?
W: Sure. Just fill out this form.
M: Okay. How long will it take to make it?
W: About an hour.
M: All right.

남: 실례합니다. 학생증으로 책을 대출하는 것이 가능한가요?
여: 아니요. 도서관 카드가 필요합니다.
남: 그렇군요. 사실, 제가 도서관 카드가 없거든요. 여기서 새 카드를 받을 수 있나요?
여: 물론입니다. 이 양식만 작성해 주시면 됩니다.
남: 네. 만드는 데 얼마나 걸리죠?
여: 약 한 시간 정도요.
남: 알겠습니다.

2. 다음을 듣고, 방송이 이루어지고 있는 장소로 가장 적절한 곳을 고르시오. 🔊 MP3 유형 06

① 백화점   ② 놀이공원   ③ 동물원

④ 야구경기장   ⑤ 영화관

❶ 장소를 추론할 수 있는 힌트가 나와요. 들리는 힌트를 종합하여 정답을 고르세요.
→ shoppers, toy section, our department store

●정답 근거 ●오답 함정

Hello, shoppers. We have a lost child. His name is Kim Min-su and he was found near the toy section of our department store. He is looking for his mom. He is 5 years old. He is wearing a red baseball cap, a white T-shirt and blue jeans. You can find him at the information desk. Once again! A 5-year-old boy named Kim Min-su is waiting for his mom at the information desk on the first floor.

쇼핑객 여러분, 안녕하세요. 저희가 미아를 보호하고 있습니다. 이름은 김민수라고 하고 저희 백화점의 장난감 코너 근처에서 발견했습니다. 아이는 엄마를 찾고 있어요. 5살입니다. 빨간 야구 모자, 하얀 티셔츠, 그리고 청바지를 입고 있습니다. 안내 데스크로 오시면 그를 찾을 수 있습니다. 다시 한 번 말씀드립니다! 김민수라는 이름의 5살 남자아이가 1층 안내 데스크에서 엄마를 기다리고 있습니다.

📖 **장소 관련 힌트 어휘**

① **library** 도서관   library card 도서관 카드   check out a book 책을 대출하다 (= borrow a book)   overdue charge 연체료

② **amusement park** 놀이공원   parade 퍼레이드   ride 타다; 놀이 기구   roller coaster 롤러 코스터

③ **theater** 극장, 영화관   ticket 티켓   showing 상영   3D movie 3D 영화   seat 좌석

④ **post office** 우체국   send a package 소포를 보내다 (= send a parcel)   by airmail 항공 우편으로   express mail 속달 우편

⑤ **train station** 기차역   station 역   platform 승강장

⑥ **travel agency** 여행사   tour 여행(하다)   tour packages 여행 패키지

대화를 듣고, 두 사람의 관계로 가장 적절한 것을 고르시오.

◀)MP3 유형 07

✔① 약사 – 환자
② 교사 – 학생
③ 의사 – 간호사
④ 서점 주인 – 손님
⑤ 우체국 직원 – 고객

❶ 선택지를 읽으면서 어떤 공간에서 대화가 이루어질지 생각해 보세요. (약국, 교실, 병원, 서점, 우체국)

❷ headache, sore throat, fever 등을 통해 병원이나 약국임을 알 수 있어요.

❸ 두 개의 선택지 중에 헷갈린다면, 결정적인 힌트를 기다리면서 끝까지 집중하세요. (→ 'if you don't feel better soon, please go to the doctor.'를 통해 말하는 사람이 의사가 아니라 약사임을 알 수 있어요.)

● 정답 근거

M: Good morning. How may I help you?

W: I've had a terrible headache since yesterday.

M: Do you also have a sore throat?

W: No, but I have a little fever too. Do you have anything I can take?

M: This aspirin will ease your pain. But if you don't feel better soon, please go to the doctor.

W: Thank you. How much is it?

M: It's 2,000 won.

남: 안녕하세요. 무엇을 도와드릴까요?
여: 어제부터 두통이 너무 심하네요.
남: 목도 아프신가요?
여: 아니요. 하지만 열이 조금 있어요. 제가 먹을 만한 약이 있나요?
남: 이 아스피린이 아픈 것을 덜어줄 겁니다. 하지만 금방 나아지지 않으면 병원에 가 보세요.
여: 감사합니다. 얼마죠?
남: 2천 원입니다.

💡 **관계를 예상할 수 있는 표현**

① **체육교사-학생**   Jisu, you are doing really well in my P.E. class.
지수야, 내 체육 시간에 네가 무척 잘하는구나.

② **승객-버스 기사**   We're about to leave. If you want to take this bus, you'd better get on now.
이제 곧 출발합니다. 이 버스를 타시려면, 지금 탑승하시는 편이 좋습니다.

③ **교사-학부모**   Hello. This is Yuna's mother. Can I talk to you for a moment?
안녕하세요. 저는 유나 엄마예요. 잠깐 이야기 좀 할 수 있을까요?

④ **서점 점원-손님**   Then, can I order the book and get it later?
그렇다면, 그 책을 주문해서 나중에 받을 수 있을까요?

⑤ **입국 심사관-여행자**   What is the purpose of your visit to our country?
우리나라를 방문한 목적이 무엇입니까?

특정 정보 파악

1. 대화를 듣고, 올해 Mina의 반을 고르시오.

🔊 MP3 유형 08

① Class A ② Class B ③ Class C

④ Class D ⑤ Class E

●정답 근거 ●오답 함정

M: Good morning, Kelly. What class are you in?

W: Hi, Dohoon. I am in Class C. What about you?

M: Wow! We are in the same class this year.

W: That's great. Do you know which class Mina is in?

M: She is in Class D, right next door to our class.

W: I'm sorry she's not in the same class with us.

M: I know, but we can see each other every day.

❶ 지시문에서 요구하는 특정 정보가 무엇인지 확인하세요.
   → 대화 소재는 반 배정임을 알 수 있으며, Mina의 반이 언급될 때 집중해야 해요.
❷ 정답은 주로 특정 정보를 직접적으로 묻는 질문 뒤에 나와요.

남: 안녕, 켈리. 너는 어느 반이야?
여: 안녕, 도훈아. 나는 C반이야. 너는?
남: 와! 우린 올해 같은 반이야.
여: 좋아. 미나는 어느 반인지 알아?
남: 그 애는 우리 반 바로 옆에 D반이야.
여: 그 애가 우리랑 같은 반이 되지 않아서 아쉽다.
남: 맞아, 그렇지만 우리는 서로 매일 볼 수 있잖아.

2. 대화를 듣고, 두 사람이 수강할 방과 후 수업을 고르시오.

🔊 MP3 유형 09

① 기타반 ② 미술반 ③ 서예반

④ 댄스반 ⑤ 테니스반

●정답 근거 ●오답 함정

W: You know what? There will be an after-school tennis class this summer!

M: Great. I heard there will be a guitar class, too.

W: I know. Which one do you like more?

M: I'd really like to learn how to play the guitar this summer. What about you?

W: Well, at first I wanted the tennis class. But I'll take the guitar class, if you take it.

M: Okay. Let's go and sign up for it.

❶ 지시문에서 요구하는 특정 정보가 무엇인지 확인하세요.
❷ 두 사람이 하기로 한 것을 고르는 유형은 두 가지 이상이 언급되며, 의견을 조율하는 과정이 나와요.
   → tennis class vs. guitar class
❸ 주로 대화의 끝부분에 두 사람의 선택이 결정되므로 끝까지 집중하세요.

여: 너 그거 아니? 이번 여름에 방과 후 테니스 수업이 개설될 거래!
남: 좋아. 기타 수업도 개설될 거라고 들었어.
여: 나도 알아. 넌 어떤 게 더 좋니?
남: 나는 이번 여름에 정말 기타 연주를 배우고 싶어. 너는 어때?
여: 음, 난 처음에는 테니스 수업을 듣고 싶었어. 하지만 네가 기타 수업을 듣는다면 나도 그 수업을 들을래.
남: 그래. 같이 가서 등록하자.

💡 기타 특정 정보 파악 문제

- 오늘 오후 4시에 열릴 행사
- 남자가 가장 좋았다고 생각한 운동 경기
- 한국 아트센터의 제 2관에서 할 수 있는 일
- 학생들이 가장 많이 빌리는 책의 종류

1. 대화를 듣고, 남자가 대화 직후에 할 일로 가장 적절한 것을 고르시오.

🔊 MP3 유형 10

① 목욕하기
② 약 구입하기 ✓
③ 화장실 가기
④ 날씨 확인하기
⑤ 간식 구입하기

❶ 지시문에서 누가 할 일을 묻고 있는지 확인하세요.
→ 오답함정으로 다른 대화자(상대방)가 할 일이 나올 수 있어요.

❷ 초반부는 '할 일'에 대한 상황이 나와요.
→ 캠핑 갈 준비

❸ 정답은 대화의 후반부에서 상대방의 제안이나 부탁 뒤에 나오는 경우가 많아요.
→ You should ~
Why don't you ~
명령문 ~

● 정답 근거 ● 오답 함정

W: Tom, did you finish packing your bag to go camping tomorrow?
M: Yes, Mom. I packed snacks, water, clothes, and my sleeping bag.
W: Oh, did you get your first aid kit? It is in the bathroom closet.
M: Okay. Mom, there is no medicine at all in the box.
W: Really? Then, you should go and buy some medicine.
M: Okay. I will go now.

여: 톰, 넌 내일 캠핑에 가져갈 가방을 다 쌌니?
남: 네, 엄마. 저는 간식, 물, 옷, 그리고 제 침낭을 챙겼어요.
여: 아, 네 구급상자는 챙겼니? 그건 화장실 서랍장에 있단다.
남: 알겠어요. 엄마, 상자 안에 약이 하나도 없어요.
여: 정말이니? 그럼, 네가 가서 약을 좀 사오렴.
남: 네. 제가 지금 갈게요.

2. 대화를 듣고, 남자가 지난 주말에 한 일로 가장 적절한 것을 고르시오.

🔊 MP3 유형 11

① 승마 체험 ✓
② 자전거 타기
③ 콘서트 관람
④ 박물관 견학
⑤ 할머니 댁 방문

❶ 지시문에서 누가 언제 한 일을 묻고 있는지 확인하세요.
→ 오답함정: 여자가 이번 주에 할 일

❷ 정답은 주로 무엇을 했는지를 직접적으로 묻는 질문 뒤에 나와요. 또는 과거시점을 나타내는 표현(last weekend, yesterday 등)과 함께 나와요.

● 정답 근거 ● 오답 함정

M: What are you going to do this weekend, Susan?
W: I'm going to visit my grandmother on Jeju Island.
M: Wow, Jeju Island! I went there last weekend.
W: Really? What did you do there?
M: I went horseback riding. It was great!
W: Horseback riding? That sounds wonderful!

남: 이번 주말에 무엇을 할 계획이니, 수잔?
여: 난 제주도에 있는 할머니 댁을 방문할 거야.
남: 우와, 제주도! 난 지난 주말에 거기에 갔었어.
여: 정말? 거기서 뭐 했어?
남: 말 타기를 했어. 정말 재미있었어!
여: 말 타기? 멋진데!

부탁·이유 파악

1. 대화를 듣고, 여자가 남자에게 부탁한 일로 가장 적절한 것을 고르시오.

🔊 MP3 유형 12

① 인터넷으로 요리 강습 신청하기
② 할머니께 사과파이 갖다 드리기
③ 도서관에 역사책 반납하기
④ 할머니께 안부전화 드리기
⑤ 역사 보고서 작성하기

● 정답 근거 ● 오답 함정

W: Where are you going, Taeho?
M: I'm going to the library to do a history project with my friends.
W: Okay. Then, would you do me a favor?
M: Sure, Mom. What is it?
W: I made an apple pie for your grandmother. Please take it to her on your way to the library.
M: No problem. Apple pies are her favorite. She will love it.
W: Thank you.

> ❶ 지시문에서 누가 누구에게 부탁하는 것인지 확인하세요.
>
> ❷ 초반부는 어떤 상황인지 확인하세요. 부탁한 일은 주로 후반부에 등장해요.
>
> ✪ 부탁을 할 때 쓰이는 표현
> Please 명령문
> Can I ~?
> Can you ~? / Could you ~?
> Would you mind ~?

여: 태호야, 어디에 가니?
남: 저는 도서관에 가서 친구들과 역사 숙제를 할 거예요.
여: 그렇구나. 그럼 내 부탁 좀 들어주겠니?
남: 물론이죠, 엄마. 부탁이 뭐예요?
여: 내가 할머니께 드리려고 애플 파이를 만들었어. 네가 도서관 가는 길에 할머니께 그것을 갖다 드리렴.
남: 그럼요. 애플 파이는 할머니께서 가장 좋아하시는 거잖아요. 무척 좋아하실 거예요.
여: 고맙구나.

2. 대화를 듣고, 남자가 영화를 볼 수 없는 이유로 가장 적절한 것을 고르시오. 🔊 MP3 유형 13

① 부모님이 아프셔서
② 생일파티에 가야 해서
③ 체험활동을 가야 해서
④ 가족여행을 가야 해서
⑤ 여동생을 돌보아야 해서

● 정답 근거 ● 오답 함정

M: Hi, Nancy.
W: Hi, Henry. Can you go to the movies with me tomorrow?
M: I'd love to, but I can't.
W: Why? Do you have other plans?
M: I have to stay home and take care of my younger sister.
W: Really? Aren't your parents home?
M: No, they're out of town on a trip.
W: Then, maybe next time.

> ❶ 지시문에서 '누구의', '무엇'에 대한 이유인지 확인하세요.
>
> ❷ 정답은 주로 Why ~?나 What for ~?에 대한 대답으로 제시되며, because 또는 질문 없이 바로 to 부정사(~하기 위해서)로 이유를 표현하기도 해요.

남: 안녕, 낸시.
여: 안녕, 헨리. 내일 나랑 영화 보러 갈 수 있니?
남: 나도 가고 싶지만 갈 수 없어.
여: 왜? 다른 계획이 있니?
남: 집에 있으면서 내 여동생을 돌봐야 해.
여: 정말? 너희 부모님이 집에 안 계시니?
남: 응, 시골로 여행 가셨어.
여: 그럼, 다음에 보자.

대화를 듣고, 여자가 전화를 건 목적으로 가장 적절한 것을 고르시오.

🔊 MP3 유형 14

① 가족 숙소를 예약하기 위해서
② 객실 청소를 요청하기 위해서
③ 숙박 예약 날짜를 변경하기 위해서
④ 미용실 예약 시간을 확인하기 위해서
✓⑤ 헤어 드라이어가 있는지 확인하기 위해서

❶ 지시문에서 누가 전화를 걸었는지 확인하세요.

❷ 선택지를 읽으면서 어디에 전화를 걸었는지 예상해 보세요.

→ 호텔 또는 미용실

❸ 주로 How may I help you?, What's up?, Do you need anything?, What's the problem? 등의 질문 뒤에 전화를 건 목적이 나와요.

● 정답 근거 ● 오답 함정

M: Flower Guest House. How may I help you?
W: Hi. I am Sujin Park and I have booked a room for tomorrow.
M: Hi, Sujin. We are expecting you. Do you need anything?
W: Yes. Do you have a hair dryer in the room?
M: We have a hair dryer in every room. Do you need anything else?
W: No, thank you. That's all. See you tomorrow.

남: 플라워 게스트 하우스입니다. 무엇을 도와드릴까요?
여: 안녕하세요. 저는 박수진이라고 하는데요, 내일 객실 하나를 예약했어요.
남: 네, 수진 씨. 기다리고 있었습니다. 필요한 것이 있습니까?
여: 네. 객실에 헤어드라이어가 있나요?
남: 저희는 모든 객실에 헤어드라이어가 구비되어 있습니다. 더 필요한 것이 있나요?
여: 아니요, 감사합니다. 그게 전부예요. 내일 뵐게요.

💡 전화를 건 목적

① **문의** **Is it possible to** volunteer at your library? 도서관에서 봉사활동을 할 수 있을까요?

② **부탁(요청)** **Can you** buy some on your way home? 집에 오는 길에 뭐 좀 사줄 수 있어요?

③ **제안** **Why don't we** visit him? 그를 방문하는 것이 어때요?

④ **문제점 신고** **The vending machine didn't give me my change.** 자판기에서 잔돈이 나오지 않았어요.

⑤ **변경 (약속 관련, 주문 관련)** **I'm calling to** change my order. 주문을 변경하려고 전화했어요.

How about meeting at six o'clock? 여섯 시에 만나는 것이 어때요?

I'm afraid I can't come to your party. 죄송하지만 당신의 파티에 갈 수 없을 것 같아요.

의도 파악

대화를 듣고, 여자의 마지막 말의 의도로 가장 적절한 것을 고르시오.

🔊 MP3 유형 15

① 감사　　　② 허가　　　③ 사과
④ 동의　　　⑤ 충고

① 마지막 말을 하는 사람이 누구인지 확인하세요.

② 마지막 말을 하는 사람이 여자이므로 남자가 처해진 상황이 무엇인지 파악하세요.
→ 남자가 허리를 다친 상황

③ 마지막 말의 의미를 파악하며 정답을 고르세요.

● 정답 근거

W: Is something wrong, John? You don't look so good.
M: I hurt my back while moving a desk into the classroom.
W: Did you go see the school nurse?
M: No, I didn't think it was serious.
W: But it looks like you're in pain.
M: Don't worry. It'll be okay tomorrow.
W: I think you'd better go and see the nurse.

여: 무슨 문제 있니, 존? 몸이 좀 안 좋아 보여.
남: 교실 안으로 책상을 옮기다가 허리를 다쳤어.
여: 양호 선생님께 가 봤니?
남: 아니, 난 그게 심각하지 않다고 생각했어.
여: 하지만 넌 아픈 것처럼 보여.
남: 걱정하지 마. 내일이면 괜찮을 거야.
여: 내 생각에는 양호 선생님께 가보는 게 좋을 것 같아.

💡 **의도가 드러나는 표현**

① **칭찬**　　You did a great job. 참 잘했어요.
　　　　　　Good for you! 잘했구나!

② **충고**　　I think you'd better go and see the doctor. 병원에 가는 것이 좋을 것 같아.

③ **기원**　　I wish you good luck! 행운을 빌어!
　　　　　　(= I'll keep my fingers crossed for you.)

④ **동의**　　I agree. 동의해.
　　　　　　You can say that again. 네 말이 맞아.

⑤ **반대**　　I'm against it. 그것에 반대해요.

⑥ **제안**　　Let's visit her and sing the song together. 그녀를 방문해서 같이 노래를 부르자.
　　　　　　How about going together? 같이 가는 게 어때?

⑦ **위로/격려**　You'll do better next time. 넌 다음에 잘할 거야.
　　　　　　I hope you do better next time. 다음에 잘하길 바라.
　　　　　　Don't worry. 걱정하지 마.
　　　　　　Come on, cheer up. 힘내.

숫자 정보 파악

1.
대화를 듣고, 여자가 지불할 금액을 고르시오.

🔊 MP3 유형 16

① $2   ② $3   ✓③ $4

④ $5   ⑤ $6

❶ 물건의 가격과 구입할 개수가 나오므로 메모하세요.

❷ 가격과 개수를 곱하여 계산하세요.
→ 쿠키 $1 × 2 + 커피 $2 = $4

● 정답 근거 ● 오답 함정

M: Hello. How can I help you?
W: Hi. How much are these cookies?
M: The cookies are one dollar each.
W: And how much is a cup of coffee?
M: It's two dollars.
W: Okay. I'll take two cookies and a cup of coffee.
M: Please wait a moment. I'll be right back with your order.

남: 안녕하세요. 무엇을 도와드릴까요?
여: 안녕하세요. 이 쿠키들은 얼마죠?
남: 그 쿠키는 개당 1달러입니다.
여: 그리고 커피 한 잔에 얼마죠?
남: 2달러입니다.
여: 알겠어요. 쿠키 두 개와 커피 한 잔 주세요.
남: 잠시만 기다려 주세요. 주문하신 것을 가지고 바로 오겠습니다.

2.
대화를 듣고, 두 사람이 만날 시각으로 가장 적절한 것을 고르시오.

🔊 MP3 유형 17

① 6:00 P.M.   ✓② 6:30 P.M.

③ 7:00 P.M.   ④ 7:30 P.M.

❶ 지시문에서 '현재 시각'인지 '만날 시각'인지 어느 때의 시각을 묻는지 확인하세요.

❷ 대화에 처음 제시된 시각을 메모하세요.
→ seven

❸ 몇 시간 후나 전에 볼지 시간을 조율하는 것을 잘 듣고 계산하여 답을 고르세요.
→ 07:00 - 00:30 = 06:30

● 정답 근거 ● 오답 함정

W: Hello.
M: Hello, Judy! This is Brian. Do you have some time tomorrow?
W: Yes. Why?
M: I have two movie tickets for *Dancing Princess*. Do you want to come with me?
W: Of course! What time does it start?
M: It starts at seven P.M. Let's meet thirty minutes earlier at ABC Cinema.
W: Okay. See you tomorrow.

여: 여보세요.
남: 안녕, 주디! 나 브라이언이야. 내일 시간 있어?
여: 응. 왜?
남: 내일 '댄싱 프린세스' 영화 티켓이 두 장 있거든. 나랑 같이 갈래?
여: 물론이지! 몇 시에 시작해?
남: 오후 7시에 시작해. ABC 시네마에서 30분 일찍 보자.
여: 좋아. 내일 보자.

3. 대화를 듣고, 저녁 식사에 참석할 인원수를 고르시오. ◀)) **MP3 유형 18** ◀

① 4 　　　② 5 　　　③ 6
④ 7 　　　⑤ 8

❶ 인원수를 묻는 문제 유형은 초반부에 참석하기로 예정된 수와 못 오는 사람의 수를 언급해요.

❷ 최종적으로 참석할 인원수를 말해주기도 하지만 그렇지 않을 경우를 대비해서 숫자가 나올 때 메모하세요.
→ 8-2= 6

●정답 근거 ●오답 함정

M: Honey, I'm going to make a dinner reservation now.
W: Are we going to the Chinese restaurant?
M: Yes. There are eight of us, right?
W: Oh, Mr. and Mrs. Brown called and said they can't come.
M: Okay. Hmm... there will be six, then.
W: Yes, that's right.
M: Okay. I'll make a reservation right away.

남: 여보, 내가 지금 저녁 예약을 하려고 해요.
여: 우리는 중국 음식점에 가는 건가요?
남: 네, 우리는 8명이죠, 그렇죠?
여: 아, 브라운 씨와 브라운 부인이 전화가 왔는데 못 오신다고 하셨어요.
남: 알겠어요. 음, 그럼 6명이겠네요.
여: 네, 맞아요.
남: 알겠어요. 지금 바로 예약할게요.

💡 **금액 관련 표현**

가격 물어보기	**How much** is it? 얼마입니까? (= How much would that cost?)
가격 대답하기	Sodas are two dollars **each**. 탄산음료는 각각 2달러입니다. / Twenty-five dollars **a person**. 일인 당 25달러입니다.
	The **regular price** is 60 dollars. 정가는 60달러입니다. / Two **for** 3,000 won. 두 개에 3천 원입니다.
	1,000 won **for students** and 1,500 won **for adults**. 학생은 천 원이고 어른은 천오백 원입니다.
구입 물건의 개수	I need **three** tickets. 티켓 세 장이 필요합니다.
할인 조건	Everything is **50% off**. 모든 제품은 50퍼센트 할인됩니다.
	We give **a one-dollar discount** per ticket after six o'clock. 여섯 시 이후에 티켓 하나당 1달러를 할인해 드립니다.
총 지불 금액	**The total** is fifteen dollars. 총 15달러입니다.

💡 **시간 관련 표현**

It's quarter **past** three. 3시 15분이야. (= It's three fifteen.)

It's quarter **to** three. 2시 45분이야. (= It's two forty-five.)

It's half **past** two. 2시 30분이야. (= It's two thirty.)

We **have** ten minutes **left**. 10분 남았어.

Let's meet **thirty minutes earlier**. 30분 일찍 만나자. (= Let's meet half an hour earlier.)

How about **thirty minutes later**? 30분 후에 보는 것이 어때?

How about four o'clock, **two hours before** the concert starts? 콘서트 시작하기 두 시간 전인 4시는 어때?

화제 추론

1. 다음을 듣고, 남자가 하는 말의 내용으로 가장 적절한 것을 고르시오.

🔊 MP3 유형 19

① 점심 메뉴 소개　　　✔️ ② 건강 회복 비결

③ 올바른 운동 순서　　　④ 건강 검진 절차

⑤ 물 절약 방법

◀ ❶ 선택지에서 키워드를 확인하세요.

❷ 담화의 화제를 추론하는 유형은 전반부에 직접적으로 힌트가 제시되는 경우가 많으므로 전반부에 집중하세요.

●정답 근거 ●오답 함정

Hello, listeners! Welcome to Health 24. I am Andy Brown. When I was young, I was very sick for a long time. Do you want to know how I got over it? First, I exercised one hour every day. Second, I drank two liters of water a day. It sounds simple, but it made a huge difference in my life.

청취자 여러분, 안녕하세요! '건강 24시간'에 오신 것을 환영합니다. 저는 앤디 브라운입니다. 저는 어렸을 때 오랫동안 매우 아팠습니다. 제가 어떻게 병을 극복했는지 아십니까? 첫째, 저는 매일 한 시간씩 운동했습니다. 둘째, 저는 하루에 물 2리터를 마셨습니다. 그것은 간단해 보이지만 제 삶에 엄청난 변화를 가져왔습니다.

2. 대화를 듣고, 무엇에 관한 내용인지 고르시오.

🔊 MP3 유형 20

✔️ ① 지진　　　② 홍수　　　③ 가뭄

④ 태풍　　　⑤ 산불

◀ ❶ 선택지에서 키워드를 확인하세요.

❷ 대화의 소재를 직접 언급하기도 하고, 주제와 관련된 단어들이 언급되므로 종합하여 추론하세요.

●정답 근거

W: Did you watch the news last night?

M: No. Did I miss anything important?

W: There was an earthquake in New Zealand.

M: That's terrible. It's only been about 6 months since the last one.

W: That's true. The news said many people died and many buildings were destroyed.

M: Sorry to hear that. I hope it doesn't happen again.

여: 어젯밤에 뉴스 봤어?

남: 아니. 내가 무슨 중요한 거라도 놓쳤니?

여: 뉴질랜드에서 지진이 있었어.

남: 끔찍하네. 지난 지진이 발생한 지 여섯 달밖에 안 됐는데.

여: 맞아. 뉴스에 의하면 많은 사람이 죽고, 많은 건물이 붕괴됐다고 하더라.

남: 유감이야. 다시는 이런 일이 발생하지 않았으면 좋겠어.

💡 출제된 담화 화제

① **수상 소감 발표**　I'm very happy to receive the award for Player of the Year. I can't express how much I appreciate this honor. 제가 올해의 선수상을 받게 되어 매우 기쁩니다. 이 영광에 대한 감사를 어떻게 표현해야 할지 모르겠네요.

② **행사 안내**　To celebrate the victory, we've cancelled afternoon classes today. Instead, we're planning to have a special party at 2 o'clock this afternoon. 승리를 축하하기 위해 오늘 오후 수업을 취소했습니다. 대신, 오늘 오후 2시에 특별 파티를 열 계획입니다.

③ **일정 안내**　Let me tell you about today's schedule. 오늘 일정에 대해서 말씀 드릴게요.

속담 추론

대화를 듣고, 대화의 상황에 어울리는 속담으로 가장 적절한 것을 고르시오. ◀ 🔊 MP3 유형 21

① 노력은 성공의 어머니다.
② 하나를 듣고 열을 안다.
③ 낫 놓고 기역 자도 모른다.
④ 닭 쫓던 개 지붕 쳐다본다.
⑤ 안에서 새는 바가지 밖에서도 샌다.

● 선택지에 나온 속담의 의미를 파악하세요.
→ ① → 노력, ② → 똑똑함 ③ → 무식함, ④ → 열심히 한 것이 수포로 돌아감, ⑤ → 본성은 감출 수 없음
❷ 대화의 주제와 관련된 속담을 고르세요.

●정답 근거 ●오답 함정

W: Congratulations on winning the MVP award, Mr. Park.
M: Thank you.
W: How did you become such a great player?
M: Actually, I was not really good when I first started playing baseball, but I practiced a lot.
W: What did you do?
M: When my team practiced, I was always the first player to arrive and the last player to leave.
W: Oh, I see. That's why you became such a good player.

여: MVP 상을 받은 것을 축하합니다, 박 선수.
남: 감사합니다.
여: 어떻게 그렇게 훌륭한 선수가 되었죠?
남: 사실, 제가 처음 야구를 시작했을 때는 정말 잘하지는 못했어요. 하지만 연습을 많이 했죠.
여: 무엇을 하셨나요?
남: 저희 팀이 연습을 할 때, 저는 항상 제일 먼저 오고 제일 늦게 가는 선수였습니다.
여: 아, 그렇군요. 그래서 이렇게 훌륭한 선수가 되셨군요.

💡 기출 속담

No pain, no gain. 고통 없이는 얻는 것도 없다.

A friend in need is a friend indeed. 어려울 때 돕는 친구가 진정한 친구이다.

Practice makes perfect. 연습이 완벽을 만든다.

Lock the stable door when the steed is stolen. 소 잃고 외양간 고친다.
→ 일이 이미 잘못된 뒤에는 손을 써도 소용이 없다.

💡 출제 가능한 속담

Well begun is half done. 시작이 반이다.

The early bird catches the worm. 일찍 일어나는 새가 벌레를 잡는다.

Better late than never. 늦게라도 하는 것이 아예 안 하는 것보다 낫다.

Don't judge a book by its cover. 외모로 사람을 판단하지 마라.

When in Rome, do as the Romans do. 로마에 가면 로마법을 따르라.

Actions speak louder than words. 말보다 행동이 중요하다. (= Easier said than done. 행동하는 것보다 말하는 것이 쉽다.)

Two heads are better than one. 백지장도 맞들면 낫다. (= Many hands make light work.)
→ 아무리 쉬운 일이라도 함께 협력해서 하면 훨씬 더 쉽고 효과적이다.

Look before you leap. 돌다리도 두들겨 보고 건너라.
→ 비록 잘 아는 일이라도 세심한 주의를 기울여서 실수가 없도록 해야 한다.

미언급·내용 일치 파악

1) 미언급 파악

대화를 듣고, 여자가 구입한 물건이 <u>아닌</u> 것을 고르시오.

◀)) MP3 유형 22

① 머리핀   ② 허리띠   ✔️ 운동화

④ 책   ⑤ 귀걸이

---

❶ ~한 것이 '아닌' 것을 찾는 유형은 스크립트에서 언급된 4개의 선택지를 지우고 언급되지 않는 것을 고르는 거예요.

❷ 주로 무엇을 구입했는지를 묻는 질문 뒤에 구입한 물건이 등장해요.

❸ 선택지의 순서대로 대화나 담화가 진행되므로 들리는 선택지를 지워나가세요.

● 정답 근거 ● 오답 함정

M: How was the new shopping mall?

W: It was huge and very crowded.

M: What did you buy there?

W: I bought a hairpin, a belt, and presents for Parents' Day.

M: You mean presents for your parents?

W: Yes, I bought a book for my dad and earrings for my mom.

M: Oh, you're so sweet.

남: 새로 생긴 쇼핑몰은 어땠어?

여: 엄청 크고 사람이 무척 많았어.

남: 넌 거기서 뭘 샀니?

여: 머리핀, 벨트, 그리고 어버이날 선물을 샀어.

남: 너희 부모님께 드릴 선물을 말하는 거야?

여: 응, 아빠에게 드릴 책과 엄마에게 드릴 귀걸이를 샀어.

남: 아, 넌 정말 착하구나.

📖 기타 미언급 문제 예시

- 여자가 학생 식당 이용에 대해 언급하지 <u>않은</u> 것
- 여자가 아이들을 위해 한 일이 <u>아닌</u> 것
- 남자가 주문한 것으로 언급하지 <u>않은</u> 것
- 두 사람이 요리 재료로 사용하지 <u>않은</u> 것

2) 내용 일치 파악

1. 다음을 듣고, The Purple Orange에 관한 정보로 일치하지 <u>않는</u> 것을 고르시오. ◀)) MP3 유형 23

① 작가는 Monica Smith이다.

② 세계에서 가장 유명한 책 중 하나이다.

③ 우정과 사랑에 관한 이야기이다.

✔️ 10개의 다른 언어로 쓰였다.

⑤ 100개 이상의 나라에서 팔린다.

---

❶ 지시문과 선택지를 먼저 읽어보고 들어야 할 정보가 무엇인지 확인하세요.
→ 작가, 책의 주제 등

❷ 선택지의 순서대로 들리므로 일치하는 선택지를 지워나가세요.

❸ 오답 함정은 숫자를 다르게 바꾸거나 '있다'를 '없다'로, '없다'를 '있다'로 바꿔놓으므로 주의하세요.
→ 지문: 12 → 선택지: 10

● 정답 근거 ● 오답 함정

Hello, everyone. This is Susan from Book Talk. I am going to talk about The *Purple Orange* written by Monica Smith. It is one of the most famous books in the world. She tells us about friendship and love in this book. This book was written in 12 different languages. It is sold in more than 100 countries.

안녕하세요, 여러분. 북 토크의 수잔입니다. 저는 모니카 스미스가 쓴 '퍼플 오렌지'에 대해 이야기하려고 합니다. 그것은 세계에서 가장 유명한 책 중 하나죠. 그녀는 이 책에서 우리에게 우정과 사랑에 관해서 이야기합니다. 이 책은 12개의 다른 언어로 쓰였습니다. 그것은 100개 이상의 나라에서 팔립니다.

---

2. 다음을 듣고, Fun Night에 관한 내용과 일치하는 것을 고르시오.

🔊 MP3 유형 24

① 행사는 2층에서 열린다.
② 음식물을 가져 올 수 없다.
✓③ 가족과 함께 올 수 있다.
④ 매주 목요일에 진행된다.
⑤ 오후 5시에 시작된다.

❶ 지시문과 선택지를 먼저 읽으면서 어떤 부분을 틀리게 바꿀지 예상해 보세요.
→ 2층?, 없다?, 있다?, 목요일?, 5시?

❷ 선택지의 순서대로 담화가 진행되므로 일치하지 않는 선택지는 듣고 바로 지워나가세요.
→ on the first floor → 2층,
You can bring → 가져올 수 없다,
on every Friday → 매주 목요일,
starts at 6:30 p.m. → 5시

●정답 근거 ●오답 함정

Thank you for visiting ABC Library. Today, we'll have *Fun Night* on the first floor. Our story lady will read you an interesting story. You can bring snacks or drinks. You can come with your family. *Fun Night* is on every Friday. It starts at 6:30 P.M. Come and have fun together at ABC Library!

ABC 도서관을 방문해 주셔서 감사합니다. 오늘 우리는 1층에서 '펀 나이트' 시간을 가지려고 합니다. 저희 이야기꾼 아가씨가 여러분께 재미있는 이야기를 읽어 드릴 것입니다. 여러분은 간식이나 음료수를 가져와도 됩니다. 여러분의 가족과 함께 오셔도 됩니다. '펀 나이트'는 매주 금요일에 있습니다. 그것은 오후 6시 30분에 시작합니다. ABC 도서관에 오셔서 함께 즐거운 시간을 보내세요.

3. 대화를 듣고, Susan에 대한 내용으로 일치하지 <u>않는</u> 것을 고르시오.

🔊 MP3 유형 25

① Rachel에게 엽서를 보냈다.
✓② 중국에서 어제 돌아왔다.
③ 남자 형제가 있다.
④ 조부모는 중국에 있다.
⑤ 이번 달에는 독서 동아리에 나오지 않았다.

❶ 선택지를 읽으며 대화의 내용을 짐작해 보세요.

❷ 선택지의 순서대로 대화가 진행되므로 일치하지 않는 선택지는 듣고 바로 지워나가세요. (대화 내용 불일치 유형은 담화처럼 직접적으로 내용이 언급되지 않아요.)

⭐ 선택지 1번 확인

⭐ 선택지 2번 오류
→ 어제 수잔에게서 엽서를 받은 것을 '어제 중국에서 돌아왔다'로 바꿈

⭐ 선택지 3번과 4번, 5번 확인

●정답 근거 ●오답 함정

M: Rachel, is this postcard from China?
W: Yes, I got it from Susan yesterday.
M: Oh, is she in China?
W: Yes. She went there with her brother to visit their grandparents.
M: I see, that's why she couldn't come to the book club this month.
W: Yeah, but she'll come back next month.

남: 레이첼, 이게 중국에서 온 엽서니?
여: 응, 어제 그걸 수잔에게서 받았어.
남: 아, 수잔이 중국에 있니?
여: 응. 조부모님을 뵈러 그녀의 오빠랑 중국에 갔어.
남: 그렇구나, 그래서 이번 달에 독서 동아리에 못 온 거구나.
여: 응. 그렇지만 다음 달에는 다시 올 거야.

1) 도표 파악

다음을 듣고, 도표의 내용과 <u>다른</u> 것을 고르시오.

🔊 MP3 유형 26

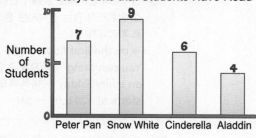

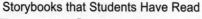

① ② ③ ④ ⑤

●정답 근거 ●오답 함정

① *Peter Pan* was read by seven students.
② *Snow White* was read by the largest number of students.
③ *Cinderella* was read by more students than *Aladdin*.
④ *Cinderella* was read by six students.
⑤ *Aladdin* was read by nine students.

> ❶ 도표가 무엇을 나타내는지 확인하세요.
> → 이야기책을 읽은 학생의 수
> ❷ 도표는 왼쪽부터 읽으세요. 도표의 순서는 선택지의 순서와 일치하므로 들으면서 맞는 내용은 지워나가세요.
> ❸ 비교급이나 최상급으로 난이도를 높일 수 있어요.
> → Snow White를 읽은 학생의 수를 nine으로 해도 되지만, 최상급으로 표현했고 두 책을 읽은 학생의 수를 비교급으로 비교했어요.
> ❹ 숫자나 비교급에서 오답을 만드므로 주의하세요.

① '피터팬'은 7명의 학생들이 읽었다.
② '백설공주'는 가장 많은 학생들이 읽었다.
③ '알라딘'보다 '신데렐라'를 더 많은 학생들이 읽었다.
④ '신데렐라'는 6명의 학생들이 읽었다.
⑤ '알라딘'은 9명의 학생들이 읽었다.

2) 실용문 파악

다음을 듣고, 광고문의 내용과 일치하지 <u>않는</u> 것을 고르시오.

🔊 MP3 유형 27

2012 Weekend Classes		
Title	Day&Hours	Fee
Family Newspaper	Sat. 09:00~12:00	$15
Cake Baking	Sat. 14:00~16:00	$24
Card Magic	Sat. 09:00~11:30	$30

●정답 근거 ●오답 함정

① These three classes are for Saturdays or Sundays.
② You can take the Family Newspaper class in the morning.
③ The Cake Baking class fee is $24.
④ You have to pay $15 for the Card Magic class.

> ❶ 광고문이 무엇을 나타내는지 확인하세요.
> ❷ 광고문 또한 스크립트를 읽는 순서는 선택지의 순서와 일치하므로 들으면서 맞는 내용을 지워나가세요.
> ✪ 수업 전체
> ↓
> Family Newspaper 수업
> ↓
> Cake Baking 수업
> ↓
> Card Magic 수업

① 이 세 강좌는 토요일 또는 일요일에 있다.
② 오전에 가족 신문 강좌를 들을 수 있다.
③ 케이크 만들기 강좌의 수강료는 24달러이다.
④ 카드 매직 강좌를 들으려면 15달러를 내야 한다.

어색한 대화 찾기

대화를 듣고, 두 사람의 대화가 <u>어색한</u> 것을 고르시오.

🔊 MP3 유형 28

①   ②   ③   ✔④   ⑤

❶ 대화의 처음 두세 개 단어를 놓치지 말고 들어야 해요.

❷ 들으면서 자연스러운 대화는 O, 헷갈리는 대화는 △, 확실히 어색한 것은 X를 표시하세요.

❸ I don't feel well.은 How are you feeling?에 대한 대답으로 적절해요.

●정답 근거 ●오답 함정

① W: How often do you play soccer?
   M: Once a week.
② W: What do you want to wear?
   M: I want to wear blue jeans.
③ W: Can you fix my skateboard?
   M: Let me see. I'll try.
④ W: How do you get to the library?
   M: I don't feel well.
⑤ W: Thank you for your help.
   M: Sure, anytime!

① 여: 넌 얼마나 자주 축구를 하니?
   남: 일주일에 한 번 해.
② 여: 넌 무엇을 입고 싶니?
   남: 난 청바지를 입고 싶어.
③ 여: 네가 내 스케이트보드를 고칠 수 있니?
   남: 한번 볼게. 내가 해볼게.
④ 여: 넌 도서관에 어떻게 가니?
   남: 난 몸이 좋지 않아.
⑤ 여: 도와줘서 고마워.
   남: 응, 언제든지!

💡 의문문과 대답 패턴

1) 의문사 의문문

- W : **What time** shall we meet? 우리 몇 시에 만날까?
  M : I met him yesterday. 난 어제 그를 만났어. (X) → M: How about at 5? 5시는 어때? (O)

- W : **How long** will you stay there? 거기에 얼마나 머무르실 거예요?
  M : I will go there by airplane. 비행기를 타고 그곳에 갈 거예요. (X) → M: Maybe about five days. 아마도 5일 정도요. (O)

- W : **How often** do you visit your grandparents? 얼마나 자주 조부모님을 뵈러 가세요?
  M : At 7 P.M. 오후 7시예요. (X) → Once a month. 한 달에 한 번이요. (O)
  c.f. 오답 함정: 의문사 의문문은 Yes, No로 대답하지 않는다.

- M : **How** is it going? 요즘 어떠세요?
  W : Yes, I'm very busy now. 네, 저는 지금 매우 바빠요. (X) → Not bad. 나쁘지 않아요. (O)

- W : **When** will you come back home? 언제 집에 돌아오실 거예요?
  M : Yes, I came back yesterday. 네, 저는 어제 돌아왔어요. (X) → Tomorrow. 내일요. (O)

2) 기타 의문문

- M : **Have** you ever **heard of** Seoul Tower? 서울 타워에 대해 들어본 적이 있어요?
  W : Yes, I have. 네, 들어봤어요.

- W : **Do you know** how to make a paper flower? 종이꽃을 만드는 방법을 아세요?
  M : I have no idea. 몰라요.

- W : **Can I** use your phone for a minute? 잠깐 당신의 전화를 써도 될까요?
  M : Sorry, but I'm busy right now. 미안하지만 저는 지금 바빠요.

1. 대화를 듣고, 남자의 마지막 말에 이어질 여자의 말로 가장 적절한 것을 고르시오. ◀)) MP3 유형 29

W: _____

① I wanted to go there again.
② Well, I want to buy more.
③ Yes! That's amazing.
④ All right! I will.
⑤ I ate bibimbap. ✓

● 정답 근거 ● 오답 함정

M: Cindy! You look happy. What did you do for the holiday?
W: I went to Jeonju with my family.
M: That sounds interesting. How was it?
W: It was wonderful. I think you should go there.
M: Really? What did you do there?
W: I visited the traditional Korean village, and ate delicious food.
M: I'm sure you really enjoyed that. What did you eat there?
W: _____

❶ 지시문에서 누가 마지막 말을 하게 되는지 확인하세요.
❷ 남자의 말이 언제 끝날지 모르기 때문에 대화쌍 단위로 들으면서 흐름을 파악하세요.
❸ 마지막 말이 의문문일 경우에 의문사에 적절한 답을 고르세요.

남: 신디! 너 기분이 좋아 보여. 너는 휴가 때 뭘 했니?
여: 나는 가족과 함께 전주에 갔어.
남: 그거 재미있었겠다. 어땠어?
여: 굉장했어. 너도 그곳에 꼭 가 봐.
남: 정말? 너는 거기서 무엇을 했어?
여: 나는 전통 한옥 마을에 가 봤고, 맛있는 음식도 먹었어.
남: 굉장히 좋았나 보다. 넌 거기서 뭘 먹었니?
여: _____

① 나는 그곳에 다시 가고 싶었어.
② 글쎄, 나는 좀 더 사고 싶어.
③ 응! 그건 멋져.
④ 알겠어. 그렇게 할게.
⑤ 난 비빔밥을 먹었어.

2. 다음을 듣고, James가 민지에게 할 말로 가장 적절한 것을 고르시오.
◀)) MP3 유형 30

James: _____

① I like badminton the most.
② I want to win every game.
③ Congratulations! You won the game!
④ Hurry up! I need to do my homework.
⑤ Don't be disappointed. You will do better next time. ✓

● 정답 근거 ● 오답 함정

Minji and James like playing badminton. Every Sunday, they play badminton at a park together. Today, they went to the park to play badminton. Minji wanted to win the game this time. However, she lost the game. In this situation, what could James say to Minji to encourage her?

❶ 지시문에서 누구에게 하는 말인지 확인하세요.
❷ '민지'의 상황을 들어보세요.
❸ 스크립트에 나오는 badminton, win the game을 활용한 선택지로 오답함정을 만드므로 주의하세요.

민지와 제임스는 배드민턴 치는 것을 좋아합니다. 매주 일요일, 그들은 공원에서 함께 배드민턴을 칩니다. 오늘, 그들은 배드민턴을 치러 공원에 갔습니다. 민지가 이번에는 경기에서 이기고 싶었습니다. 하지만 민지는 경기에서 졌습니다. 이런 상황에서 제임스가 민지를 격려하기 위해 할 수 있는 말은 무엇일까요?
James: _____

① 나는 배드민턴을 가장 좋아해.
② 나는 모든 경기에서 이기고 싶어.
③ 축하해! 네가 경기에서 이겼어!
④ 서둘러! 난 숙제를 해야 해.
⑤ 실망하지 마. 너는 다음에 더 잘할 거야.

중학 서술형이 **만만해지는 문장연습**

쓰기 + 작문

교과서 맞춤형 **본 책** + 탄탄해진 **워크북** + 맞춤형 **부가자료**

내가 **쓰**는 대로
작문이 완성된다!

❶ 중학 교과서 진도 맞춤형 내신 서술형 대비

❷ 한 페이지로 끝내는 핵심 영문법 포인트별 정리 + 문제 풀이

❸ 효과적인 3단계 쓰기 훈련 :
   순서배열 → 빈칸 완성 → 내신 기출

❹ 최신 서술형 100% 반영된 문제와 추가 워크북으로 서술형 완벽 대비

❺ 13종 교과서 문법 분류표·연계표 등 특별 부록 수록

쎄듀북닷컴(www.cedubook.com)에서 부가 자료를 무료로 다운로드할 수 있습니다.

쎄듀

천일문·어법끝 온라인 복습테스트를 찾는다면?

쎄듀런 OPEN

쎄듀가 직접 제작한 온라인 학습 콘텐츠와 선생님 인강이 합쳐져
학습은 더 쉽게, 실력은 더 높게!

9만 5천
문법·서술형
문항

2만 3천
구문 문장

2만 5천
어휘

총 **143,000 DB**를
쎄듀런에서!

www.cedulearn.com

쎄듀런은 PC & Moblie APP 모두 사용 가능합니다.
콘텐츠를 제작하는 콘텐츠팩토리 및 서비스 결제 기능은 **PC버전**에서만 이용 가능합니다.

쎄듀런 모바일 앱 설치

GET IT ON
Google Play

Download on the
App Store

쎄듀런 홈페이지 상단의 쎄듀캠퍼스에서 똑똑한 온라인 영어학습을 시작해보세요!

쎄듀런

1 구문

판매 1위 '천일문' 콘텐츠를 활용하여 정확하고 다양한 구문 학습

(끊어읽기) (해석하기) (문장 구조 분석) (해설·해석 제공) (단어 스크램블링) (영작하기)

2 문법·서술형

쎄듀의 모든 문법 문항을 활용하여 내신까지 해결하는 정교한 문법 유형 제공

(객관식과 주관식의 결합) (문법 포인트별 학습) (보기를 활용한 집합 문항) (내신대비 서술형) (어법+서술형 문제)

3 어휘

초·중·고·공무원까지 방대한 어휘량을 제공하며 오프라인 TEST 인쇄도 가능

(영단어 카드 학습) (단어 ↔ 뜻 유형) (예문 활용 유형) (단어 매칭 게임)

4 선생님 보유 문항 이용

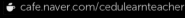

(Online Test) (OMR Test)

🐾 cafe.naver.com/cedulearnteacher

쎄듀런 학습 정보가 궁금하다면?

쎄듀런 Cafe

· 쎄듀런 사용법 안내 & 학습법 공유
· 공지 및 문의사항 QA
· 할인 쿠폰 증정 등 이벤트 진행

1001개 문장으로 완성하는 중등 필수 영단어

천일문

중등 시리즈

VOCA

하루 20개,
40일 완성
800개

하루 25개,
40일 완성
1,000개

하루 25개,
40일 완성
1,000개

1001개 문장으로 완성하는 중등 필수 영단어

천일문 VOCA

40 DAYS × 20단어

중등 스타트

대상: 예비중 ~ 중1

1001개 문장으로 완성하는 중등 필수 영단어

천일문 VOCA

40 DAYS × 25단어

중등 필수

대상: 중2~중3

1001개 문장으로 완성하는 중등 필수 영단어

천일문 VOCA

40 DAYS × 25단어

중등 마스터

대상: 중3 ~ 예비고

휴대용
암기장 제공

천일문 VOCA
단어
암기장

편리하게 반복 학습 가능해요!

편리한
MP3 player
제공

DAY 01

1001 Sentences
Day 01 - 02

MP3를 직접 들어보세요!

① 중등 교과서 및 교육부 지정 필수 어휘 반영

② 주제별 중등 단어+빈출 표현 수록

③ 쉬운 우리말 풀이와 관련 다양한 tip 제공

④ 문장을 통한 자연스러운 누적 학습

⑤ 쎄듀런을 통한 온라인 단어 암기 서비스

쎄듀북닷컴(www.cedubook.com)에서 부가 자료를 무료로 다운로드할 수 있습니다.

쎄듀

쎄듀 빠르게

중학영어듣기
모의고사 20회

쎄듀 '빠르게' 중학영어듣기 모의고사 시리즈

정답 및 해설

2

실전 모의고사 20회
기출 듣기평가 5회
문제 유형 공략 및 필수 표현 익히기

QR코드 방식의 편리한 음원 제공
MP3 파일 무료 다운로드
모의고사, 딕테이션, 문항별 음원 제공

쎄듀 빠르게
중학영어듣기
모의고사 20회

정답 및 해설

2

01 ④	02 ④	03 ⑤	04 ⑤	05 ③
06 ①	07 ⑤	08 ③	09 ⑤	10 ②
11 ⑤	12 ①	13 ④	14 ⑤	15 ④
16 ④	17 ④	18 ④	19 ③	20 ③

01 ④

M: Good morning, everyone. It's Monday, so it's time for the weekly weather forecast. We're going to get a lot of rain today and on Tuesday. On Wednesday, it's going to be a beautiful, sunny day. Thursday will be pleasant but windy. Clouds will start appearing on Friday, and it's going to rain on both Saturday and Sunday.

안녕하세요, 여러분. 오늘은 월요일이니 주간 일기예보를 알려 드릴 시간입니다. 오늘과 화요일은 비가 많이 오겠습니다. 수요일은 맑고 화창한 날씨가 되겠습니다. 목요일은 쾌적하지만 바람이 불겠습니다. 금요일부터 구름이 끼기 시작하여 토요일과 일요일에는 모두 비가 오겠습니다.

어휘 weekly 주간의 weather forecast 일기예보 pleasant 쾌적한, 맑은 appear 나타나다 both 둘 다

02 ④

W: Hello, sir. May I help you?
안녕하세요, 손님. 무엇을 도와드릴까요?

M: I'm looking for a T-shirt for my son. He likes stripes.
제 아들에게 줄 티셔츠를 찾고 있어요. 아들은 줄무늬를 좋아해요.

W: Here's one with stripes. What do you think of it?
여기 줄무늬 티셔츠가 있어요. 어떻게 생각하세요?

M: Those stripes go up and down. He wants ones that go from left to right. 그 줄무늬는 세로로 나 있네요. 제 아들은 가로 줄무늬를 원해요.

W: Should the T-shirt have a pocket or not? We have both right here. 티셔츠에 주머니가 있어야 하나요, 없어야 하나요? 저희는 두 종류 모두 여기 보유하고 있습니다.

M: The one with the pocket would be great. I'll take it.
주머니가 있는 게 좋겠네요. 그걸로 살게요.

해설 남자는 가로 줄무늬에 주머니가 있는 티셔츠를 살 것이다.

어휘 look for ~을 찾다 stripe 줄무늬 up and down 아래위로 left to right 왼쪽에서 오른쪽으로 pocket 주머니 right here 바로 이곳에

03 ⑤

W: How are you feeling today? Are you still sick?
넌 오늘 기분이 어떠니? 여전히 아프니?

M: I'm not sick anymore. But I'm really concerned about our test.

난 더 이상 아프지 않아. 하지만 우리 시험이 정말 걱정이야.

W: Why are you nervous? Didn't you study?
넌 왜 긴장하고 있니? 공부하지 않니?

M: I studied, but I need to do well on the test. I don't want to get a low grade in the class. 공부했는데, 난 시험을 잘 봐야 해. 반에서 낮은 점수를 받고 싶지 않아.

W: Just relax. I'm sure that you will do great.
편하게 생각해. 넌 분명히 아주 잘할 거야.

M: I hope so. I don't want to get a poor grade.
나도 그랬으면 좋겠어. 난 형편없는 성적을 받고 싶지 않아.

해설 남자의 'concerned about'에서 걱정하는 심정을 확인할 수 있다.

어휘 still 여전히 sick 아픈 anymore 더 이상 be concerned about ~에 대해 걱정하다 nervous 긴장하는 do well 잘하다 grade 점수; 학년; 등급 poor 형편없는 hopeful 희망찬 relaxed 느긋한

04 ⑤

M: Linda, what happened to the magazines on the table? 린다, 식탁 위에 있던 잡지는 어떻게 된 거니?

W: Oh, I moved them, Dad. I put them in the living room. 아, 제가 그걸 옮겼어요, 아빠. 제가 거실에 갖다 놓았어요.

M: Why did you put them there? 왜 거기 갖다 놓았니?

W: I needed to work on the table. I was making a project for art class. 제가 식탁에서 할 일이 있었어요. 미술 수업을 위한 과제를 했거든요.

M: Can you put them back on the table, please?
그걸 다시 식탁으로 가져다 놓을 수 있니?

W: I can't. Mom wants me to set the table now. We're going to eat soon. 그럴 수 없어요. 엄마가 지금 식탁을 차리라고 하셨거든요. 곧 식사를 한대요.

M: That's fine. 그럼 괜찮단다.

W: Thanks, Dad. 고마워요, 아빠.

어휘 What happened to ~? ~은 어떻게 되었니? magazine 잡지 living room 거실 put something back ~을 제자리에 갖다 놓다 set the table 식탁을 차리다

05 ③

W: Is there something I can help you with?
제가 도와드릴 것이 있나요?

M: I hope so. I've been coughing a lot lately.
그래 주셨으면 좋겠어요. 요즘 기침을 많이 하고 있거든요.

W: Do you have any other symptoms? Do you have a sore throat? 다른 증상이 있나요? 목이 아프세요?

M: No, I feel fine. The only problem is that I can't stop coughing.
아니요, 괜찮습니다. 기침을 멈출 수가 없는 게 유일한 문제에요.

W: Why don't you buy a bottle of this? Take it three times a day.
이걸 한 병 구입하시는 게 어떤가요? 하루에 세 번 복용하세요.

M: How long should I take it for?

얼마나 오랫동안 복용해야 하죠?

W: Three days. If you don't get better, then you'd better see a doctor. 3일입니다. 만약 상태가 나아지지 않으면 그때는 병원을 가보시는 게 좋겠습니다.

어휘 cough 기침하다 lately 최근에, 요즘에 symptom 증상 have a sore throat 목이 아프다 bottle 병 three times a day 하루에 세 번 get better (상태가) 나아지다 see a doctor 병원에 가다

06 ①

W: Jack, happy birthday. 잭, 생일 축하해.

M: You actually remembered. I think everyone else forgot.
너는 정말 기억하고 있었구나. 나는 모두가 잊어버렸다고 생각했어.

W: How could I forget your birthday? You're my best friend.
내가 어떻게 네 생일을 잊을 수 있겠니? 넌 내 제일 친한 친구잖아.

M: Thanks for saying that. It really means a lot to me.
그렇게 말해줘서 고마워. 그건 정말 나한테 큰 의미가 있어.

W: So what are you going to do tonight?
그래서 넌 오늘 밤에 뭐 할 거니?

M: My mom is making my favorite meal. And we're going to have cake and ice cream, too.
우리 엄마가 내가 제일 좋아하는 음식을 해주실 거야. 그리고 우리는 케이크와 아이스크림도 먹을 거야.

W: That sounds great. By the way, here's something for you. I hope you like it. 멋지네. 그건 그렇고, 여기 널 위해 준비했어. 네가 그걸 좋아하면 좋겠어.

M: You shouldn't have, Tina. I really appreciate it.
이럴 필요는 없었는데, 티나. 정말 너무 고마워.

어휘 actually 정말로, 실제로 remember 기억하다 forget 잊다(forget-forgot-forgotten) mean a lot 많은 것을 의미하다 favorite 가장 좋아하는 meal 음식, 식사 appreciate 감사하다

07 ⑤

W: I finished reading another book today.
나는 오늘 다른 책을 다 읽었어.

M: You seem to be reading lots of books these days.
넌 요즘 정말 책을 많이 읽는 것 같아.

W: That's true. This was a biography. I have also read history books, storybooks, poetry books, and novels. 맞아. 이번에는 전기였어. 그리고 나는 역사책, 동화책, 시집, 그리고 소설도 읽었어.

M: Which one did you like the most?
어떤 게 가장 좋았니?

W: I read an outstanding novel. It was written by my favorite author. 나는 정말 대단한 소설을 읽었어. 그건 내가 제일 좋아하는 작가가 쓴 책이었어.

M: Can you lend it to me sometime?
나한테 그걸 언제 한 번 빌려줄 수 있니?

W: I got it from the library. You'll have to go there to borrow it.

난 그걸 도서관에서 빌렸어. 너도 도서관에 가서 빌려야 할 거야.

어휘 another 또 하나의, 다른 seem ~인 것처럼 보이다 biography 전기 history 역사 storybook 동화책, 이야기책 poetry 시 outstanding 뛰어난, 두드러진 favorite 가장 좋아하는 author 작가 lend 빌려주다 borrow 빌리다

08 ③

W: Are you going to clean your room soon? It's such a mess. 넌 금방 네 방을 청소할 거니? 방이 너무 엉망이구나.

M: I can't, Mom. I've got to leave the house in a few minutes. 못해요, 엄마. 몇 분 후에 집에서 나가야 해요.

W: But you don't have soccer practice today. That's tomorrow.
하지만 넌 오늘은 축구 연습이 없잖니. 연습은 내일이잖아.

M: Right. I've got my piano lesson instead.
맞아요. 대신 피아노 레슨이 있어요.

W: Oh, I totally forgot about that. Do I need to pick you up after it's finished?
아, 그걸 완전히 잊고 있었네. 레슨이 끝나면 내가 데리러 갈까?

M: You don't need to do that. I'm going to John's house to do some homework afterward. 그러실 필요 없어요. 저는 레슨 후에 숙제를 하러 존의 집으로 갈 거예요.

어휘 mess 엉망인 상태 in a few minutes 몇 분 후에 practice 연습(하다) instead 대신에 totally 완전히 pick somebody up ~을 데리러 가다 afterward 그 이후에

09 ⑤

W: Everyone, listen closely, please. The school has finally added some recycling bins. So don't throw cans, glass, paper, or plastic items in the trashcans anymore. You need to put them in the recycling bins. You can find them by the front door, next to the library, and in front of room one oh seven. Let's all take good care of the environment.

여러분, 잘 들어 주시기 바랍니다. 학교에서 마침내 재활용 수거함을 몇 개 추가했습니다. 그러니 캔, 유리, 종이, 혹은 플라스틱으로 된 물품을 더 이상 쓰레기통에 버리지 마시기 바랍니다. 여러분은 그런 것들을 재활용 수거함에 넣으셔야 합니다. 수거함은 정문 옆, 도서관 옆, 그리고 107호실 앞에서 찾을 수 있습니다. 다 함께 환경을 보호하도록 합시다.

어휘 listen closely 자세히 듣다 finally 마침내 add 더하다, 추가하다 recycling bins 재활용 수거함 throw 버리다, 던지다 item 물건 trashcan 쓰레기통 by ~옆에(= next to) in front of ~앞에 take good care of ~을 잘 돌보다 environment 환경

10 ②

W: Here, try some of this and tell me how you think it tastes. 여기, 이것 좀 맛보고 맛이 어떤지 좀 말해 줘.

M: Wow, this cookie tastes delicious. Did you make it yourself? 우와, 이 쿠키는 정말 맛있어. 네가 직접 만들었니?

W: Yes, I did. I want to be a cook when I grow up, so I practice making all kinds of foods.
응, 내가 만들었어. 난 커서 요리사가 되고 싶어서 온갖 종류의 음식을 만드는 연습을 하지.

M: Which food can you cook the best?
넌 어떤 음식을 제일 잘 만들 수 있니?

W: I make a really good dish with chicken and mushrooms. You should try it sometime. 난 치킨과 버섯으로 정말 맛있는 음식을 만들 수 있어. 언제 한번 먹어봐.

M: I'd love to. Tell me the next time you're planning to make it. 나도 그러고 싶어. 다음에 음식을 만드는 날이 있으면 나한테 말해줘.

어휘 try (음식을) 맛보다 taste ~한 맛이 나다 delicious 맛있는 grow up 성장하다, 어른이 되다 mushroom 버섯 sometime 언젠가

11 ⑤

M: In just a moment, we're going to speak with Eric Hampton. He's one of the top movie stars in the world. He has a new movie coming out this Friday. The title is *Galaxy War*. He has the lead role in the action movie, and it's sure to be a blockbuster. Critics are calling it one of the best movies of the year.

잠시 후에 우리는 에릭 햄튼 씨와 이야기를 나눌 것입니다. 그는 세계적으로 가장 유명한 영화배우 중 한 명입니다. 이번 주 금요일에 그의 신작 영화가 개봉합니다. 제목은 '갤럭시 전쟁'입니다. 그는 이 액션 영화에서 주인공 역할을 맡았고, 이 영화는 분명히 블록버스터가 될 것입니다. 비평가들은 이 영화를 올해 최고의 영화 중 하나라고 부르고 있습니다.

어휘 in just a moment 곧, 잠시 후에 speak with ~와 이야기를 나누다 come out (영화가) 개봉하다 title 제목 lead role 주인공 역할 blockbuster 블록버스터, 크게 성공한 영화 critic 비평가, 평론가

12 ①

[*Phone rings.*] [전화벨이 울린다.]

M: Hello. This is David's Bookstore.
여보세요. 데이비드 서점입니다.

W: Hello. My name is Soyun Park. I ordered a couple of books at your store yesterday. 안녕하세요. 제 이름은 박소윤입니다. 제가 어제 그곳 서점에서 책 두 권을 주문했어요.

M: Yes, I remember you. Is everything okay?
네. 기억합니다. 별문제 없으시죠?

W: Actually, I want to change something. I need to add one more book to the list. It's *Daytime Troubles* by Linda Matters.
사실은, 변경하고 싶은 게 있어요. 목록에 책 한 권을 추가하고 싶거든요. 그건 린다 매터스가 쓴 '데이타임 트러블스'예요.

M: I know that book. I'll add it to your order. They will all be here tomorrow. 제가 그 책을 알고 있습니다. 주문에 추

가해 드릴게요. 책은 모두 내일 들어올 겁니다.

W: Great. I'll pick them up in the evening.
좋네요. 저녁에 책을 찾으러 갈게요.

어휘 order 주문하다 a couple of 둘의 actually 사실은 add something to the list 목록에 ~을 추가하다 pick something up ~을 가지러 가다

13 ④

M: We're going to have our first soccer game of the season this weekend. The game will be at two in the afternoon on Saturday. We're going to play at Bell Park. We're going to play against a team from Morristown. Please arrive at the park at one P.M. We need to warm up and get ready for the game.

우리는 이번 주말에 시즌 첫 번째 축구 경기를 가질 예정입니다. 경기는 토요일 오후 2시에 있을 것입니다. 우리는 벨 파크에서 경기를 할 것입니다. 우리는 모리스타운에서 온 팀과 경기를 하게 됩니다. 공원에 오후 1시까지 도착해 주시기 바랍니다. 우리는 경기를 위해 몸을 풀고 준비를 해야 합니다.

해설 축구 경기가 몇 시간 동안 진행되는지는 나와 있지 않다.

어휘 weekend 주말 against ~에 맞서서 warm up 몸을 풀다 get ready for ~에 대비하다

14 ⑤

W: Thank you for coming to this meeting today.
오늘 회의에 와주셔서 감사합니다.

M: It's no problem. My boss let me leave work early. So what do you want to talk about?
아닙니다. 제 상사가 일찍 퇴근할 수 있게 해 주셨습니다. 그런데 무슨 이야기를 하고 싶으신가요?

W: We need to talk about Minho. His homework isn't very good these days. 우리는 민호에 대해서 이야기를 해야 할 것 같아요. 요즘 민호의 숙제가 별로 좋지 않거든요.

M: It's not? What's the problem? 안 좋아요? 무엇이 문제죠?

W: He makes a lot of mistakes on it.
숙제에 실수가 너무 많아요.

M: I'll start checking his homework at home after he finishes it. 이제부터는 집에서 민호가 숙제를 마치면 제가 확인을 하도록 하겠습니다.

W: That would be great. I want his work to improve.
그게 좋을 것 같아요. 저는 민호의 숙제가 나아졌으면 좋겠습니다.

어휘 boss 상사 let (~하도록) 허락하다(let-let-let) leave work 퇴근하다 homework 숙제 mistake 실수 check 확인하다 improve 향상하다

15 ④

W: Are you going out now, Jaehwan?
넌 지금 나가니, 재환아?

M: Yes, I am. I'm going out to play basketball with my friends. 네, 그래요. 저는 친구들이랑 농구하러 갈 거예요.

W: I see. But I need you to do a favor for me, please.
알았다. 그런데 내 부탁을 들어 주었으면 좋겠구나.

M: Okay. What do you want me to do?
네. 무슨 일을 시키고 싶으세요?

W: On your way home, stop by the grocery store and buy some milk, will you?
집에 오는 길에, 식료품점에 들려서 우유 좀 사 올 수 있겠니?

M: All right. Should I buy anything else?
알겠어요. 또 다른 것을 살 게 있나요?

W: No. Here's some money for you.
아니야. 여기 돈을 가져가렴.

어휘 do somebody a favor ~의 부탁을 들어주다(= do a favor for somebody) on one's way home 집으로 오는 길에 stop by 잠깐 들르다 grocery store 식료품점

16 ④

W: Do you have any plans right now, Tom?
너 지금 무슨 계획이 있니, 톰?

M: Yes, I do. I'm on my way to the park.
응, 있어. 난 공원에 가는 길이야.

W: That's great. I'm riding my bike there, too. Shall we go together?
잘됐다. 나도 거기서 자전거 탈 거야. 같이 가도 될까?

M: Sure. Why not? 응. 그거 좋지.

W: I'm going there to take a walk. How about you?
나는 산책하려고 공원에 가는 거야. 너는?

M: I'm going to go skateboarding with some of my friends. Do you know how to skateboard?
난 친구 몇 명이랑 스케이트보드를 타러 갈 거야. 넌 스케이트보드를 탈 줄 아니?

W: No, but I can rollerblade. That's a lot of fun.
아니, 하지만 롤러블레이드는 탈 수 있어. 그건 정말 재미있어.

M: You're right. I enjoy doing it, too.
네 말이 맞아. 나도 롤러블레이드 타는 걸 좋아해.

어휘 on one's way to ~로 가는 중인 why not? (동의를 나타내며) 왜 아니겠어? take a walk 산책하다

17 ④

① W: What time do you go to bed? 넌 몇 시에 잠을 자니?
　 M: At ten P.M. every night. 매일 밤 10시에.

② W: Why did you call your classmate?
　　 너희 반 친구한테 왜 전화했니?
　 M: To ask about our homework.
　　 우리 숙제에 대해서 물어보려고.

③ W: How about having a snack? 간식을 먹는 게 어때?
　 M: Good idea. 좋은 생각이야.

④ W: What are you planning to do this weekend?
　　 이번 주말에 뭘 할 계획이니?
　 M: On Saturday or Sunday. 토요일 아니면 일요일이야.

⑤ W: Do you know how to find Mark's house?
　　 마크의 집을 어떻게 찾을 수 있는지 아니?
　 M: Yes, I have been there before. 응, 난 전에 가봤어.

어휘 go to bed 잠자리에 들다 classmate 학급 친구 have a snack 간식을 먹다 find 찾다

18 ④

W: Good morning, everyone. Thank you for coming to the museum. You can see many items from ancient Greece, Rome, and China at the museum. We have three exhibit halls here. We will visit the first two exhibit halls before lunch. Then, we'll eat in the cafeteria for an hour. Next, we'll go to the third exhibit hall. After that, we'll go to the museum's outdoor exhibits. The tour will end around two. Let's get started right now.

안녕하세요, 여러분. 박물관에 와 주셔서 감사합니다. 여러분은 박물관에서 고대 그리스, 로마, 중국에서 온 많은 전시품을 볼 수 있습니다. 이곳에는 세 곳의 전시관이 있습니다. 우리는 점심식사 전에 처음 두 곳의 전시관을 방문할 것입니다. 그리고 한 시간 동안 구내식당에서 식사를 할 것입니다. 그다음에 우리는 세 번째 전시관에 갈 것입니다. 그 이후에 박물관의 야외 전시를 보러 갈 것입니다. 관람은 2시쯤 끝날 것입니다. 지금부터 시작하겠습니다.

어휘 museum 박물관 exhibit hall 전시관 cafeteria 구내식당, 카페테리아 outdoor 야외의 get started 시작하다

19 ③

W: We should stop working on this project for a while.
우리는 이 과제를 하는 걸 잠시 중단해야겠어.

M: Why do you want to do that? 왜 그렇게 하고 싶니?

W: I'm starving. I need some food.
난 너무 배고파. 음식이 좀 필요해.

M: Didn't you eat breakfast this morning?
오늘 아침에 아침을 안 먹었니?

W: I didn't have any time to eat. I woke up late, so I ran to the library to meet you. 먹을 시간이 없었어. 늦게 일어났기 때문에 널 만나려고 도서관에 달려와야 했거든.

M: Oh, I didn't realize that. You should have told me.
아, 난 그걸 몰랐네. 나한테 말했어야지.

W: I didn't want to bother you. 널 신경 쓰게 하고 싶지 않았어.

M: So what would you like to have? 그럼 뭘 먹고 싶니?

W: Let's get some sandwiches. 샌드위치를 좀 먹자.

① Yes, I have it with me. 응, 내가 그걸 갖고 있어.
② It's almost dinnertime now. 이제 거의 저녁 식사 시간이야.
③ Let's get some sandwiches. 샌드위치를 좀 먹자.
④ Sure, we can study a bit longer.
　 물론이지. 우린 좀 더 공부할 수 있어.
⑤ I don't have my books with me.
　 난 지금 내 책을 갖고 있지 않아.

어휘 for a while 잠시 동안 starving 배고픈, 굶주린 wake (잠에서) 깨다(wake-woke-woken) realize 깨닫다, 알아차리다 should have p.p. ~했어야 했다(사실은 하지 않았다) bother 성가시게 하다, 괴롭히다 dinnertime 저녁 식사 시간 a bit 조금 longer 더 오래

20 ③

M: Jean, it's good to see you. Did you have a good weekend? 진, 만나서 반가워. 좋은 주말을 보냈니?

W: Yes, I did. I went to the <u>beach</u> with my family. 응, 잘 보냈어. 난 가족들과 바닷가에 갔어.

M: That <u>sounds fun</u>. What did you do there? 재미있었겠다. 거기서 뭐 했니?

W: I <u>went swimming</u> in the <u>ocean</u>. I also went <u>snorkeling</u>. 난 바다에서 수영을 했어. 그리고 스노클링도 했어.

M: I didn't know you enjoyed the ocean so much. 난 네가 그렇게 바다를 좋아하는지 몰랐어.

W: It was my <u>first time</u> to go there. I want to <u>go back</u> soon. 거기 가본 건 이번이 처음이었어. 곧 다시 가고 싶어.

M: My family is going there next week. You can go with us. 우리 가족은 다음 주에 거기 갈 거야. 너도 같이 갈 수 있어.

W: Thanks for the invitation. 초대해 줘서 고마워.

① I'm sure you'll have fun. 넌 분명히 재미있는 시간을 보낼 거야.

② Not really. I didn't like it. 사실은 아니야. 난 그걸 좋아하지 않았어.

③ Thanks for the invitation. 초대해 줘서 고마워.

④ I saw lots of fish in the water. 난 물속에서 물고기를 많이 봤어.

⑤ Yes, we were there for one week. 응, 우린 일주일 동안 그곳에 있었어.

어휘 ocean 바다 go snorkeling 스노클링을 하다 invitation 초대

02회 실전모의고사
본문 p.18-19

01 ②	**02** ①	**03** ④	**04** ③	**05** ⑤
06 ④	**07** ③	**08** ①	**09** ④	**10** ③
11 ①	**12** ④	**13** ③	**14** ④	**15** ④
16 ①	**17** ②	**18** ②	**19** ③	**20** ②

---

01 ②

W: I'm thinking about putting this <u>flower vase on</u> the <u>table</u>. 난 테이블 위에 이 꽃병을 올려 놓으려고 생각하고 있어.

M: That's a good idea. We can put it <u>on the left</u>. It should go <u>beside</u> the <u>clock</u>. 좋은 생각이야. 우리는 그걸 왼쪽에 놓을 수 있어. 꽃병은 시계 옆으로 가야 해.

W: I think that looks nice. Do you think we should <u>put</u> the <u>telephone between</u> the flower vase and the clock? 그러면 보기 좋을 것 같아. 꽃병과 시계 사이에 전화기를 놓아야 할까?

M: No, I don't like that. <u>Let's not</u> put the telephone on the table. 아니, 난 그건 별로야. 테이블 위에 전화기는 놓지 말자.

W: Sure. That's fine with me. 알았어. 나도 좋아.

어휘 flower vase 꽃병 on the left 왼쪽에 beside ~옆에 between A and B A와 B 사이에

---

02 ①

M: Sarah, <u>why</u> are you still <u>awake</u>? It's <u>getting late</u>. 사라, 넌 왜 아직 안 자니? 시간이 늦었어.

W: I want to <u>make sure</u> I'm <u>ready for</u> the school field trip tomorrow. 저는 내일 있을 학교 수학여행에 대한 준비를 확실히 하고 싶어요.

M: You need to <u>get</u> some <u>sleep</u>. You're going to be really busy on your <u>trip to</u> the <u>zoo</u>. 넌 잠을 좀 자야 한다. 동물원으로 가는 수학여행 길은 정말 바쁠 거야.

W: I know. <u>That's why</u> I am <u>checking</u> my <u>bag</u>. I don't want to forget anything. 저도 알아요. 그래서 제가 제 가방을 확인하는 거예요. 저는 아무 것도 빠뜨리고 싶지 않거든요.

M: I know you're <u>looking forward to</u> going there, but you really have to <u>go to bed</u>. 네가 거기 가는 걸 기대하고 있다는 건 알겠는데, 하지만 정말로 잠은 자야 해.

W: But I can't sleep. All I'm doing is <u>thinking about</u> the trip. 하지만 저는 잠을 잘 수 없어요. 제가 하고 있는 건 여행에 관해 생각하는 것뿐이라고요.

해설 남자의 대사 'I know you're looking forward to ~'를 통해 내일 있을 수학여행으로 신이 난 여자의 심정을 읽을 수 있다.

어휘 awake 깨어 있는 make sure 확실히 하다 ready for ~에 대한 준비가 된 field trip 수학여행, 현장학습 get sleep 잠을 자다 zoo 동물원 check 점검하다, 확인하다 look forward to ~을 기대하다 go to bed 잠을 자다 excited 흥분한, 신이 난 upset 속상한, 화가 난 nervous 불안한 scared 무서운 proud 자랑스러운

---

03 ④

[Telephone rings.] [전화벨이 울린다.]

W: Hello. <u>This is</u> Mr. Bradbury's office. How may I help you? 여보세요. 브래드베리 씨의 사무실입니다. 무엇을 도와드릴까요?

M: Hi. This is Jim Phillips. I'm Mr. Bradbury's friend. Can I <u>speak to</u> him, please? 안녕하세요. 짐 필립스입니다. 저는 브래드베리 씨의 친구예요. 그와 통화할 수 있을까요?

W: I'm sorry, but he's <u>in a meeting</u> right now. 죄송합니다만, 그분은 지금 회의 중이에요.

M: Okay. Can I <u>leave a message</u> then? 알겠습니다. 그럼 메시지를 남길 수 있을까요?

W: Yes. Go ahead. 네, 그러세요.

M: Please tell him that we're going to <u>play golf tomorrow</u> at <u>nine</u> in the morning. He should be at the golf course <u>by eight thirty</u>. 그에게 우리가 내일 오전 9시에 골프를 칠 거라고 말해 주세요. 그는 골프장에 8시 반까지 나와야 합니다.

W: Okay. I'll give him the message.

네. 그분에게 메시지를 전해 드릴게요.

어휘 office 사무실 leave a message 메시지를 남기다 go ahead 계속 진행하다 golf course 골프장

04 ③

M: Good afternoon. I'd like to check out these books.
안녕하세요. 이 책들을 대출하고 싶습니다.

W: Okay. I need to see your library card.
네. 제가 당신의 도서관 카드를 봐야 합니다.

M: I don't have one. Can I use my student ID card instead?
저는 도서관 카드가 없어요. 대신 학생증을 사용할 수 있을까요?

W: Sorry, but you must have a library card.
죄송합니다만, 도서관 카드를 지참하셔야 합니다.

M: Oh, I didn't know that. I just moved here.
아, 그건 몰랐어요. 이제 막 이사 왔거든요.

W: You can make one right now if you want.
원하신다면 지금 바로 만드실 수 있어요.

M: Okay. What should I do? 좋아요. 어떻게 해야 하죠?

W: Please fill out this form. 이 양식을 작성해 주세요.

해설 'check out these books', 'library card' 등을 통해 정답을 유추할 수 있다.

어휘 check out (책을) 대출하다 library card 도서관 카드 student ID card 학생증 instead 대신에 move 이사하다 fill out 작성하다 form 양식

05 ⑤

W: What's wrong with you, Eric? You look like you're hurt. 무슨 일이니 에릭? 다친 것 같아 보여.

M: I injured my back while I was playing volleyball during gym class.
체육시간에 배구를 하다가 허리를 다쳤어.

W: Did you visit the school nurse?
양호 선생님에게 가봤니?

M: No, I didn't. I don't think it's very serious.
아니, 안 갔어. 심각하지 않은 것 같아서.

W: But you appear to be in pain. 하지만 넌 아픈 것처럼 보여.

M: I'm okay. Don't worry about me. 괜찮아. 내 걱정 마.

W: I hope you feel better soon. 네가 얼른 나았으면 좋겠다.

어휘 hurt 다치다 injure 부상을 입다 back 허리, 등 while ~하는 동안에 volleyball 배구 school nurse 양호 선생님 serious 심각한 appear ~인 것 같다; 나타나다 be in pain 아파하다, 괴로워하다

06 ④

M: Good evening. Can I help you?
안녕하세요. 제가 도와드릴까요?

W: Yes, please. How much are these cupcakes?
네. 이 컵케이크는 얼마죠?

M: Each cupcake costs two dollars.
컵케이크는 개당 2달러입니다.

W: And how much does a glass of apple juice cost?
그럼 사과 주스 한 잔은 얼마죠?

M: It costs one dollar and fifty cents. 1달러 50센트입니다.

W: Okay. I'd like two cupcakes and one glass of apple juice, please.
알겠어요. 컵케이크 두 개랑 사과 주스 한 잔 주세요.

M: All right. Hold on one moment, please.
알겠습니다. 잠시만 기다려 주세요.

해설 컵케이크 2개($2×2=$4) + 주스 1잔($1.50) = $5.50

어휘 cupcake 컵케이크 each 각각 cost 비용이 들다, (값이) ~이다 a glass of ~의 한 잔 hold on 기다리다

07 ③

W: I'm so excited. My friend from the United States is coming to visit Korea next week. 난 정말 신나. 다음 주에 미국에 있는 내 친구가 한국에 오기로 했어.

M: That's wonderful news. What are you going to do when your friend is here?
정말 좋은 소식이네. 친구가 여기 오면 뭘 할 거니?

W: I'm not sure where I should take her.
그녀를 어디로 데려가야 할지 아직 모르겠어.

M: You should definitely take her to a traditional Korean restaurant.
그녀를 전통 한국 식당에 꼭 데려가도록 해.

W: That's a good idea. Do you know any good ones?
좋은 생각이야. 좋은 식당을 알고 있니?

M: No, I don't. But I'm sure you can find some on the Internet. 아니, 몰라. 하지만 넌 분명히 인터넷에서 식당을 찾을 수 있을 거야.

W: I think you're right. I'm going to do that right now.
네 말이 맞는 것 같아. 지금 바로 찾아볼게.

해설 남자의 대사 'I'm sure you can ~'에 여자가 할 일이 나온다.

어휘 visit 방문하다 wonderful 훌륭한, 멋진 sure 확실한 take (사람을) 데리고 가다 definitely 분명히, 반드시 traditional 전통의 on the Internet 인터넷에서

08 ①

W: There is a holiday on Friday. Do you want to come to my house then? 금요일이 휴일이야. 그때 우리 집에 올래?

M: What do you want to do there?
너희 집에서 뭘 하고 싶니?

W: How about solving some puzzles? We could also watch a movie.
퍼즐 맞추기를 하는 게 어때? 우리는 영화를 볼 수도 있어.

M: Sorry, but I'd rather do something outdoors. Why don't we go to the park and play there? 미안하지만 나는 야외 활동을 하고 싶어. 공원에 가서 노는 게 어때?

W: Well, I guess it's okay. We can do that.
글쎄, 그것도 괜찮을 것 같아. 그렇게 하자.

해설 남자의 대사 'Why don't we ~?'에 제안 내용이 나오고, 여자

도 이에 동의했다.

어휘 holiday 휴일 solve 풀다, 해결하다 watch a movie 영화를 보다 would rather ~하고 싶다; ~하는 게 낫다 outdoors 야외에서

09 ④

M: Listen carefully, everyone. We're going to do some work in the garden now. All of you should have a pot with a tomato plant in it. Take your pot and go to a spot in the garden. Then, remove the tomato plant and the dirt in the pot and put it in the ground. Put dirt around the entire plant and then water it well. When you're finished, come back here. I have some more work for you to do.

잘 들으세요, 여러분. 우리는 이제 정원에서 어떤 일을 하게 될 겁니다. 여러분 모두는 토마토 모종이 심어진 화분을 갖고 있어야 합니다. 화분을 가지고 정원의 한 장소로 가시기 바랍니다. 그리고 나서, 화분에서 토마토 모종과 흙을 꺼내서 땅에 심으세요. 모종 주변에 전체적으로 흙을 덮어 주시고, 물을 충분히 주세요. 끝나고 나면 이곳으로 돌아오세요. 여러분이 해야 할 일이 더 있습니다.

어휘 carefully 신중하게 pot 화분 plant 모종; 식물 spot 장소, 자리 remove 제거하다; 떼어내다 dirt 흙; 먼지 ground 땅 entire 전체의 water 물을 주다; 물

10 ③

M: What are you looking at? 넌 뭘 보고 있니?
W: It's a letter from Lisa. She sent it to me from Italy. 이건 리사한테서 온 편지야. 그 애가 이탈리아에서 나한테 이걸 보냈어.
M: Is she in Italy now? 그 애가 지금 이탈리아에 있니?
W: Yes, she's spending the summer there. She is there with her sister and aunt. 응, 거기서 여름을 보내고 있어. 그녀는 그곳에 여동생이랑 이모랑 함께 있어.
M: I didn't know that. Now I understand why I haven't seen her at the park this month. When is she going to come back? 그건 몰랐네. 이제야 왜 이번 달에 공원에서 리사를 못 봤는지 이해가 되네. 그 애는 언제 돌아오니?
W: She'll be back at the end of August. 8월 말에 돌아올 거야.

어휘 letter 편지 spend (시간을) 보내다 come back 돌아오다 (= be back)

11 ①

[*Telephone rings.*] [전화벨이 울린다.]
M: Hello. Customer Service. How may I help you? 안녕하세요. 고객 서비스입니다. 무엇을 도와 드릴까요?
W: Hi. There's a problem with the copy machine at Vernon Library. 안녕하세요. 버논 도서관에 있는 복사기에 문제가 있어요.
M: What's the problem? 무슨 문제죠?
W: It won't make any copies. I think there's some

paper stuck in it. 복사가 안 돼요. 복사기에 종이가 걸린 것 같아요.
M: I see. I'll send a repairman over right away. He should be there in thirty minutes. 그렇군요. 지금 바로 수리기사를 보내겠습니다. 30분 후면 도착할 겁니다.
W: Thank you very much. 정말 감사합니다.

어휘 customer service 고객 서비스 copy machine 복사기 make copies 복사하다 stuck 갇힌; 꼼짝 못하는 repairman 수리 기사 right away 즉시

12 ④

W: Good evening, Mr. Jefferson. My name is Cathy Powers. I'm from World News Magazine. It's a pleasure to meet such a famous actor. 안녕하세요, 제퍼슨 씨. 제 이름은 캐시 파워스입니다. 월드 뉴스 매거진에서 나왔어요. 이렇게 유명한 배우 분을 만나게 돼서 반갑습니다.
M: It's a pleasure to meet you, too. 저도 만나게 되어 반갑습니다.
W: Your latest movie is a big success. Why do you think so many people like it? 당신의 최신 영화가 아주 성공적이에요. 왜 많은 사람들이 그 영화를 좋아한다고 생각하세요?
M: All of the performers did a great job, and the story is amazing, too. 모든 연기자들이 훌륭한 연기를 했고 줄거리도 훌륭했어요.
W: That's interesting. How did you like acting in the movie? 흥미로운 얘기네요. 영화에서의 연기는 어땠나요?
M: It was difficult at times, but I really enjoyed it overall. 어려운 점도 가끔 있었지만 전반적으로 정말 즐겁게 연기를 했습니다.
W: That's good to hear. How about telling us something interesting that happened when you were filming? 그 말씀을 들으니 좋네요. 영화 촬영 도중 있었던 재미있는 이야기가 있으면 말씀해 주시겠어요?

어휘 magazine 잡지 actor 배우 pleasure 기쁨, 즐거움 latest 가장 최근의(late - later - latest) performer 연기자, 배우 do a great job 일을 아주 잘하다 amazing 놀라운 acting 연기 at times 때로는, 가끔 overall 전반적으로 interesting 재미있는 happen 발생하다, 벌어지다 film 영화를 찍다

13 ③

M: Hello. Are you looking for something? 안녕하세요. 뭔가를 찾고 계세요?
W: Yes, I am. My knee really hurts. I hurt it playing soccer yesterday. 네. 제 무릎이 너무 아파요. 어제 축구를 하다가 다쳤거든요.
M: You should use this knee brace. It will help you walk better. 이 무릎 보호대를 사용하셔야 합니다. 좀 더 편하게 걷는 걸 도와줄 거예요.
W: Can you recommend any medicine for me? 약을 권해 주실 수 있나요?
M: This aspirin will make the pain go away. Take two

of these a day. 이 아스피린이 통증을 사라지게 할 겁니다. 하루에 이걸 두 개 드세요.

W: What should I do if it still hurts in a couple of days? 이틀이 지나도 여전히 아프면 제가 어떻게 해야 하죠?

M: You should go to see a doctor at once then. 그때는 바로 병원에 가셔야 해요.

어휘 look for ~을 찾다 knee 무릎 hurt 다치다(hurt-hurt-hurt) brace 보호대; 버팀대 recommend 추천하다 medicine 약 pain 통증 go away 사라지다 take (약을) 복용하다 still 여전히 a couple of 둘의 go to see a doctor 병원에 가다 at once 즉시

14 ④

[Telephone rings.] [전화벨이 울린다.]

M: Hello. 여보세요.

W: Hello. I'm calling from Orion Books. May I speak with Mark Sullivan? 여보세요. 오리온 북스에서 전화 드렸습니다. 마크 설리반 씨와 통화할 수 있을까요?

M: This is Mark. 제가 마크인데요.

W: Hi, I'd like to let you know that the book you requested has just arrived. 안녕하세요, 손님께서 요청하신 책이 방금 도착했다는 것을 알려 드리려고요.

M: Oh, that's good news. I've been waiting for you to call me for over a week. 아, 그거 좋은 소식이네요. 일주일 넘게 전화 오기를 기다리고 있었거든요.

W: Really? Why don't you come here to pick it up? 정말요? 이곳으로 오셔서 책을 찾아가시겠습니까?

M: Can you send the book to me by mail? I don't have time to visit the store this week. 책을 우편으로 보내주실 수 있나요? 이번 주에는 가게를 찾아갈 시간이 없어서요.

해설 남자의 대사 'Can you ~?'에 남자의 요청 내용이 나온다.

어휘 let somebody know ~에게 알리다 request 요청하다 arrive 도착하다 over a week 일주일 넘게 pick up 가져가다, 찾아가다 by mail 우편으로

15 ④

M: Alice, where are you going now? 앨리스, 지금 어디 가고 있니?

W: I have to go to the shopping mall. 쇼핑몰에 가야 해.

M: Why are you doing that? 왜 가야 해?

W: I'm going there to meet my mom. She just called me. 난 우리 엄마를 만나러 거기 가는 거야. 방금 전화가 왔어.

M: Is she all right? 어머니는 괜찮으시니?

W: She went to buy some clothes, but she forgot her purse. She asked me to bring it there to her. 엄마가 옷을 사러 가셨는데, 지갑을 깜빡하셨어. 나더러 지갑을 가져다 달라고 부탁하셨어.

M: I see. 그렇구나.

어휘 clothes 옷 forget 잊어버리다(forget-forgot-forgotten) purse 지갑 bring 가져오다

16 ①

① W: How have you been lately? 요즘 어떻게 지냈니?
   M: Yes, I've been there before. 응, 난 전에 거기 가봤어.
② W: I think you should speak more loudly. 넌 좀 더 크게 말해야 할 것 같아.
   M: Okay. I'll try to do that. 알았어. 그렇게 해볼게.
③ W: Will you do me a favor? 내 부탁을 들어줄 수 있니?
   M: Okay. What do you need? 그래. 뭐가 필요하니?
④ W: Are you good at cooking? 넌 요리를 잘하니?
   M: Not really. 아니.
⑤ W: What time does the game start? 경기는 몇 시에 시작하니?
   M: It should begin at seven. 7시에 시작할 거야.

어휘 loudly (소리를) 크게 do somebody a favor ~의 부탁을 들어주다 good at 잘하는

17 ②

M: Who were you talking to on the phone? 누구랑 전화하고 있었니?

W: Eric. I was asking him about our science homework. 에릭. 난 그 애한테 우리 과학 숙제에 대해서 물어보고 있었어.

M: Why did you call him? You asked me about it ten minutes ago. 왜 그 애한테 전화했니? 넌 10분 전에 나한테 그걸 물어봤잖아.

W: Yeah, but I wanted to check. 응, 하지만 난 확인해 보고 싶었어.

M: How come? 왜?

W: One time, I asked a friend, and she gave me the wrong answer. So now I always ask two people the same question. I don't want to get in trouble like I did that time. 한 번은, 내가 친구한테 물어봤는데, 그 애가 나한테 틀린 답을 알려줬어. 그래서 난 지금은 항상 같은 질문을 두 사람에게 물어봐. 그때 그랬던 것처럼 문제를 겪고 싶지 않거든.

① All's well that ends well. 끝이 좋으면 모두 좋다.
② Better safe than sorry. 나중에 후회하는 것보다 조심하는 것이 낫다.
③ Bad news travels quickly. 나쁜 소문은 빨리 퍼진다.
④ A rolling stone gathers no moss. 구르는 돌은 이끼가 끼지 않는다.
⑤ A bird in the hand is worth two in the bush. 손 안에 든 새 한 마리는 풀 숲에 있는 두 마리 새의 가치가 있다.

해설 'Better safe than sorry.'는 'Look before you leap.(돌다리도 두드려 보고 건너라.)'와 일맥상통하는 속담이다.

어휘 on the phone 전화로 check 확인하다 how come 왜, 어째서 wrong 잘못된, 틀린 same 같은 get in trouble 곤란한 상황에 처하다 safe 안전한 sorry 후회하는, 유감스러운 rolling 구르는 gather 모으다 moss 이끼 worth 가치 있는

18 ②

W: It's time for the weather report for this week. We're

going to have cold and snowy weather on Monday. On Tuesday, it will warm up a bit, but it will rain as well. It will be sunny on Wednesday morning, but it's going to become very windy in the evening. It will start snowing again on Thursday, and the weather will be cold and cloudy on Saturday. I'll be back in one hour with another update.

이번 주 날씨를 알려드릴 시간입니다. 월요일 날씨는 춥고 눈이 오겠습니다. 화요일에는 살짝 포근해지겠고 비도 오겠습니다. 수요일 오전에는 맑겠지만 저녁이 되면 바람이 무척 세게 불 것입니다. 목요일에는 다시 눈이 내리겠습니다. 그리고 토요일에는 춥고 흐리겠습니다. 한 시간 뒤에 다른 최신 정보를 가지고 돌아오겠습니다.

어휘 snowy 눈이 오는 warm up 따뜻해지다 a bit 약간 windy 바람이 부는 cloudy 구름 낀, 흐린 update 최신 정보(를 알려주다)

19 ③

M: Would you like to try some of this cake?
이 케이크의 맛 좀 볼래?

W: Sure. It looks good. Who made it?
물론이지. 맛있어 보이네. 누가 만들었니?

M: I did. 내가 만들었어.

W: You made this all by yourself? Why?
너 혼자 이걸 다 만들었어? 왜?

M: I'd like to become a chef one day. So how does it taste? 난 언젠가는 요리사가 되고 싶어. 그래서, 맛이 어때?

W: It's amazing. I'd love to be able to cook like this.
굉장해. 나도 이렇게 요리할 수 있으면 좋겠다.

M: I can show you how to do it if you want.
네가 원하면 어떻게 만드는지 보여줄게.

W: Okay. I think I'd like that. 응, 그러고 싶어.

① Who helped you make it? 누가 그걸 만드는 걸 도와줬니?
② No, I haven't tasted it yet. 아니, 아직 맛보지 않았어.
③ Okay. I think I'd like that. 응, 그러고 싶어.
④ Where did you buy this cake? 이 케이크를 어디서 샀니?
⑤ I want one more piece, please. 한 조각 더 줘.

어휘 try (음식을) 맛보다, 먹어보다 by oneself 스스로, 혼자 chef 요리사 one day 언젠가, 어느 날 taste ~한 맛이 나다 piece 조각

20 ②

M: Are you going camping with your family this weekend? 이번 주말에 가족이랑 캠핑을 가니?

W: No, I'm not going to do that.
아니, 난 그걸 하지 않을 거야.

M: Did your family cancel the trip?
너희 가족이 여행을 취소했니?

W: No, my parents and little brother are still going.
아니, 우리 부모님이랑 남동생은 그대로 갈 거야.

M: But you're not? Why not?
하지만 너는 안 가잖아? 왜 안 가니?

W: I've got to finish a report for class by Monday morning. 난 월요일 아침까지 수업 리포트를 끝내야 해.

M: Are you going to stay at your home all alone?
넌 집에 혼자 있을 거니?

W: No, I'm going to be at my grandmother's house instead. 아니, 대신 할머니 댁에 있을 거야.

① Sure. We can get together and do some work on the weekend. 물론이지. 우리는 주말에 모여서 일을 같이 할 수 있어.
② No, I'm going to be at my grandmother's house instead. 아니, 대신 할머니 댁에 있을 거야.
③ We need to hurry up and finish the assignment.
우리 서둘러서 과제를 끝내야 해.
④ Why don't we work on our reports together?
우리가 함께 리포트를 쓰는 게 어때?
⑤ No, I'm not going to my house right now.
아니, 지금은 집에 가지 않을 거야.

어휘 go camping 캠핑 가다 cancel 취소하다 still 여전히 report 보고서, 리포트 alone 혼자 get together 모이다 instead 대신에 hurry up 서두르다 assignment 과제 work on ~을 작업하다

<table>
<tr><td colspan="5">03회 실전모의고사   본문 p.30-31</td></tr>
<tr><td>01 ⑤</td><td>02 ④</td><td>03 ②</td><td>04 ①</td><td>05 ③</td></tr>
<tr><td>06 ②</td><td>07 ②</td><td>08 ①</td><td>09 ①</td><td>10 ⑤</td></tr>
<tr><td>11 ⑤</td><td>12 ⑤</td><td>13 ②</td><td>14 ⑤</td><td>15 ④</td></tr>
<tr><td>16 ④</td><td>17 ④</td><td>18 ②</td><td>19 ⑤</td><td>20 ④</td></tr>
</table>

01 ⑤

W: You should send a postcard to your friend in Korea.
넌 한국에 있는 네 친구에게 엽서를 한 장 보내는 게 좋을 것 같아.

M: That's a good idea. How about this postcard of the beach? 그거 좋은 생각이야. 이 바닷가 엽서는 어떠니?

W: I don't like that one. This one with the ship on it looks better.
나는 그게 마음에 안 들어. 배가 있는 이게 더 보기 좋아.

M: It's nice, but I think the postcard with the bird on it is the best one. 그것도 좋긴 한데, 내 생각엔 새가 나와 있는 것이 제일 좋은 것 같아.

W: I agree. You should get it.
나도 그렇게 생각해. 저 엽서를 사도록 해.

M: Okay. I will. 알았어. 그렇게 할게.

어휘 postcard 엽서 beach 해변, 바닷가 ship 배 better 더 나은(good – better – best)

02 ④

W: It's late. Why haven't you gone to bed yet?
시간이 늦었어. 넌 왜 아직 안 자고 있니?

M: I can't sleep. I can't stop thinking about tomorrow.

잠을 잘 수가 없어요. 내일에 대한 생각을 멈출 수가 없어요.

W: Why? Do you have a test tomorrow?
왜? 내일 시험이 있니?

M: No. It's my first soccer game. I'm really looking forward to playing.
아니요. 제 첫 번째 축구 시합이 있거든요. 경기가 정말 기대돼요.

W: Right. You must be excited. 맞아. 정말 흥분되겠구나.

M: I am. I hope we win. 네. 우리가 이겼으면 좋겠어요.

어휘 yet 아직 stop -ing ~을 멈추다 look forward to -ing ~을 기대하다 excited 들뜬, 신이 난 nervous 긴장한 upset 속상한 surprised 놀란 thankful 감사한

03 ②

M: How was your weekend, Mina?
주말을 어떻게 보냈니, 미나?

W: I met a friend and went shopping with her. What about you? 친구를 만나서 같이 쇼핑하러 갔어. 너는 어땠니?

M: I went on a trip to the forest. 나는 숲으로 여행을 갔었어.

W: The forest? What did you do there?
숲? 거기서 뭘 했니?

M: My father and I went camping for two days. We had lots of fun.
우리 아버지와 나는 이틀 동안 야영을 했어. 정말 재미있었어.

W: That sounds amazing. 정말 대단하구나.

해설 남자와 여자의 한 일을 구분해서 듣는다. ①과 ⑤는 여자가 주말에 한 일이다.

어휘 weekend 주말 go shopping 쇼핑하러 가다 go on a trip to ~로 여행가다 forest 숲 go camping 캠핑을 가다 have fun 재미있는 시간을 보내다 amazing 멋진

04 ①

W: I'd like to open an account, please.
계좌를 하나 만들고 싶습니다.

M: No problem. Do you have your ID card?
네. 신분증을 갖고 오셨나요?

W: Yes, I do. Here you are. 네, 가져 왔습니다. 여기 있어요.

M: Thank you. Do you want to open a savings account? 감사합니다. 예금 계좌를 만들고 싶으신 건가요?

W: Yes, and I will deposit one hundred dollars in it.
네. 그리고 계좌에 100달러를 예금할 겁니다.

M: Okay. Fill out this form, please.
알겠습니다. 이 양식을 작성해 주십시오.

어휘 open an account 계좌를 개설하다 ID card 신분증 savings account 예금 계좌 deposit 예금하다; 보증금 fill out 작성하다; 기입하다

05 ③

M: Mom, some of my friends are going out on Saturday night.
엄마, 제 친구들 몇 명이 토요일 밤에 외출을 한대요.

W: Where are they going to go?
그 애들은 어디로 간다고 하니?

M: They're going to watch the baseball game at the stadium. 그 애들은 경기장에서 야구 경기를 볼 거예요.

W: Do you want to go with them?
너도 그 애들과 함께 가고 싶니?

M: Yes, I'd like to. 네, 가고 싶어요.

W: Have you finished all your homework?
숙제는 전부 끝냈니?

M: Yes, I have. I finished it after school today.
네, 끝냈어요. 오늘 방과 후에 숙제를 끝냈어요.

W: Then I will allow you to go with them.
그럼 그 애들과 같이 가는 것을 허락하마.

어휘 go out 외출하다, 나가다 stadium 경기장 would like ~하고 싶다 finish 끝내다 after school 방과 후에 allow 허락하다

06 ②

M: Did you give out the invitations to your birthday party? 넌 생일파티 초대장을 나눠 줬니?

W: Yes. I gave them out at school today.
네. 오늘 학교에서 나눠 줬어요.

M: How many of your friends can come?
네 친구들이 몇 명이나 올 수 있니?

W: Everyone said they will be there.
모든 애들이 올 거라고 말했어요.

M: So ten people are coming, right?
그럼 10명이 오는 거지, 그렇지?

W: Oh, wait. Elizabeth can't come. She has a piano lesson that day. 아, 잠시만요. 엘리자베스는 올 수 없어요. 그날 피아노 수업이 있거든요.

M: Okay. I'll make sure there is enough food for everyone. 알았다. 모두에게 충분한 음식을 준비하도록 하마.

어휘 give out 나눠 주다 invitation 초대(장) make sure 확실히 하다 enough 충분한

07 ②

W: Joe, are you free right now? 조, 지금 시간 있니?

M: No, I'm going to go to the swimming pool.
아니, 난 수영장에 갈 거야.

W: The pool? I didn't know you could swim.
수영장? 난 네가 수영을 할 수 있는지 몰랐어.

M: I can't, but I'm taking swimming lessons now. You should learn with me. 난 수영을 못하지만 지금 수영 레슨을 받고 있어. 넌 나랑 같이 배워야 해.

W: I'd like to. It sounds fun.
나도 그렇게 하고 싶어. 재미있겠다.

M: Let's go together today. You can watch people swim and sign up later.
오늘 같이 가자. 사람들이 수영하는 걸 보고 등록은 나중에 해도 돼.

W: Okay. I'll do that. 알았어. 그렇게 할게.

어휘 free 한가한, 시간이 있는 right now 지금 당장 swimming

pool 수영장 take (수업을) 듣다, 수강하다 sign up 등록하다 later 나중에

08 ①

W: Are you going to sign up for an after-school class?
넌 방과 후 수업에 등록할 거니?

M: Yes. But there are so many good classes. I can't choose one.
응. 하지만 좋은 수업들이 너무 많아. 하나를 고를 수가 없어.

W: I'd like to take the music class.
나는 음악 수업을 듣고 싶어.

M: That one looks okay. But the art class and cycling class look better for me. 그것도 좋겠다. 하지만 미술 수업과 자전거 수업이 나한테는 더 좋은 것 같아.

W: I didn't know there's an art class. I'd love to study art. Shall we take it together? 난 미술 수업이 있는지 몰랐어. 난 미술을 공부하고 싶어. 우리 같이 미술 수업 들을래?

M: Okay. Let's sign up for it now.
그래. 지금 등록하러 가자.

어휘 sign up for ~을 신청하다 after-school class 방과 후 수업 choose 선택하다 cycling 자전거 타기

09 ①

W: Listen carefully, everybody. We're not going to have classes in the afternoon. Instead, we're going to have a special event. Dr. Douglas from the local hospital is going to come here. He's going to speak about his job. Then, you can ask him questions about his life as a doctor. I think this will be a lot of fun. Please go to the auditorium after lunch. Thank you.

경청해 주시기 바랍니다, 여러분. 우리는 오후에 수업이 없을 겁니다. 대신, 우리는 특별한 행사를 열 것입니다. 지역 병원에서 나오신 더글라스 박사님께서 이곳에 오실 겁니다. 박사님께서 그의 직업에 대해서 말씀해 주실 것입니다. 그리고 나면 여러분은 그분에게 의사로서의 삶에 대해 질문하실 수 있습니다. 이건 아주 재미있는 시간이 될 것으로 생각됩니다. 점심 후에 강당으로 가 주시기 바랍니다. 감사합니다.

어휘 have a class 수업이 있다 instead 대신에 special event 특별 행사 local 지역의 job 직업 auditorium 강당

10 ⑤

M: How was shopping at the new store?
새로운 가게에서의 쇼핑은 어땠어?

W: It was great. The store was having a big sale.
아주 좋았어. 가게에서 큰 세일을 하고 있었거든.

M: What did you buy? 넌 뭘 샀니?

W: I got a sweater, shorts, and pants for myself.
내가 입을 스웨터, 반바지, 그리고 긴 바지를 샀어.

M: Did you buy anything for your sister?
여동생에게 줄 것은 샀니?

W: Yes, I did. I bought her a T-shirt and some earrings.
응, 샀어. 여동생에게 티셔츠와 귀걸이 몇 개를 사줬어.

M: Wow. That was nice of you.
와. 너 정말 좋은 일을 했구나.

어휘 have a sale 세일을 하다 shorts 반바지 pants (긴) 바지 earrings 귀걸이 nice 친절한, 다정한

11 ⑤

[Telephone rings.] [전화벨이 울린다.]

W: Hello. This is Johnny's Steakhouse. How can I help you?
여보세요. 조니 스테이크하우스입니다. 무엇을 도와드릴까요?

M: Hi. I read your job posting online.
안녕하세요. 제가 인터넷에서 그곳의 채용 공고를 읽었거든요.

W: Are you talking about the job for assistant chef?
보조 요리사 자리에 대한 이야기를 하고 계신 건가요?

M: Yes, that's the one. Is it still available?
네, 그겁니다. 그 자리가 여전히 남아 있나요?

W: Yes, it is. Would you like to come for an interview?
네, 있습니다. 면접을 보러 오시겠어요?

M: I'd love to. What's a good time to go there?
그럴게요. 언제 가면 좋을까요?

W: Why don't you come here today at around three?
오늘 3시쯤 여기 오시는 건 어떨까요?

M: All right. I'll be there then. 좋습니다. 그때 가겠습니다.

어휘 job posting 구인 공고 assistant 조수, 보조원 chef 요리사 available 이용 가능한 interview 면접 around ~쯤

12 ⑤

M: Hello. My name is Jake Sullivan, and I'll be your tour guide today. We're going to visit several places for the next few hours. First, we'll visit the museum, and then we'll go to the aquarium. At noon, we'll have lunch together. After lunch, we'll walk around parts of the city. Please ask me questions anytime. I hope you have fun. Let's get started.

안녕하세요. 제 이름은 제이크 설리반이고, 오늘 여러분의 여행 가이드를 맡을 겁니다. 우리는 앞으로 몇 시간 동안 몇 개의 장소를 방문하게 될 겁니다. 처음에 우리는 박물관을 방문하고, 그 다음에는 수족관에 갈 것입니다. 정오에는 함께 점심식사를 할 겁니다. 점심식사 후에는 도시의 몇몇 지역을 걸어서 돌아다니게 됩니다. 제게 언제든지 질문하세요. 즐거운 시간이 되시길 바랍니다. 이제 시작하겠습니다.

어휘 tour guide 여행 가이드 several 몇몇의 aquarium 수족관, 아쿠아리움 noon 정오, 오후 12시 walk around 걸어서 돌아다니다 anytime 언제든지

13 ②

W: Thanks so much for the meal.

식사를 정말 잘했습니다.

M: Did you enjoy it? Were there any problems with it?
식사는 맛있게 하셨나요? 식사에 무슨 문제라도 있었나요?

W: No, not at all. This was the best meal I've had in a long time.
아니요, 전혀요. 오랜만에 먹어보는 최고의 음식이었어요.

M: Thank you for saying that. I'll let the chef know you said that. 그렇게 말씀해 주셔서 감사합니다. 제가 주방장에게 그 말씀을 전하도록 하겠습니다.

W: I'll definitely come back to this restaurant in the future. 앞으로도 이 음식점에 꼭 다시 오도록 할게요.

M: I'm glad to hear that. 그 말씀을 들으니 기쁘네요.

해설 손님이 식사 소감을 묻는 웨이터에게 대답하는 상황이다.

어휘 meal 식사 not at all 전혀 아니다 in a long time 오랜만에, 오랫동안 chef 주방장 definitely 반드시 in the future 앞으로, 미래에

14 ⑤

W: Hello. Are you looking for a book?
안녕하세요. 책을 찾고 계신가요?

M: Yes, I'm trying to find the history section.
네, 저는 역사 코너를 찾고 있어요.

W: It's on another floor. You need to go to the fourth floor. 그건 다른 층에 있어요. 4층으로 가셔야 합니다.

M: Can you tell me how I can get there?
제가 거기에 어떻게 갈 수 있는지 알려 주시겠어요?

W: Sure. Just take the escalator to the fourth floor. You'll find it there. 물론이죠. 에스컬레이터를 타시고 4층으로 가시면 됩니다. 거기서 찾으실 수 있을 겁니다.

M: Thanks for your help. 도와주셔서 감사합니다.

어휘 section 구역, 코너 another 다른 floor 층; 바닥 fourth 네 번째의 take the escalator 에스컬레이터를 타다

15 ④

[Cellphone rings.] [휴대폰이 울린다.]

M: Hello. 여보세요.

W: Hi, Rick. Would you like to go on a picnic tomorrow? 안녕, 릭. 내일 소풍을 가는 게 어때?

M: That sounds great, but I can't go.
재미있겠지만, 난 못 가.

W: Why not? Are you busy? 왜 못 가? 바쁘니?

M: Yes. I'm going to help my dad paint the house.
응. 난 아빠가 집에 페인트를 칠하시는 걸 도울 거야.

W: Will that take a long time? 그 일이 오래 걸리니?

M: It will take almost half a day. 거의 반나절이 걸릴 거야.

W: Okay. We can do that next weekend then.
알았어. 그럼 다음 주말에 가면 되겠다.

어휘 go on a picnic 소풍을 가다 paint 페인트칠하다 take (시간이) 걸리다 almost 거의 half a day 반나절

16 ④

① W: How often do you call your grandmother?
너는 얼마나 자주 할머니께 전화를 드리니?

M: At least twice a week. 적어도 일주일에 두 번.

② W: What do you want to eat for dinner?
저녁으로 뭘 먹고 싶니?

M: I want steak and potatoes.
스테이크와 감자를 먹고 싶어.

③ W: Can you book tickets for the concert?
콘서트 표를 예약해 줄 수 있니?

M: Sorry. They are all sold out. 미안해. 매진됐어.

④ W: How long does it take to get to your home?
너희 집까지 가는 데 얼마나 걸리니?

M: About two meters. 약 2미터 정도야.

⑤ W: Thank you for giving me some advice.
충고해 줘서 고마워.

M: It's my pleasure. 내가 더 고맙지.

해설 집까지 가는 데 걸리는 시간으로 답하는 것이 적절하다.

어휘 at least 적어도 twice 두 번 book 예약하다 sold out 매진된 advice 충고 pleasure 기쁨

17 ④

W: You look unhappy, Phil. What's the matter?
넌 기분이 안 좋아 보여, 필. 무슨 일 있니?

M: I bought a new smartphone yesterday, but it already broke.
내가 어제 새로운 스마트폰을 샀는데, 벌써 고장 났어.

W: What's wrong? 뭐가 문제야?

M: I don't know. I tried to turn on the phone, but it doesn't work. 모르겠어. 휴대폰을 켜 봤는데, 작동하지 않아.

W: Did you buy a cheap one? 저렴한 것으로 샀니?

M: Yes, it was cheap. But I chose it because it looks fancy and shiny.
응, 저렴했어. 하지만 화려하고 반짝거려 보여서 골랐지.

W: Don't buy things because they look nice and shiny.
멋있고 반짝거려 보인다고 물건을 사면 안 돼.

① No pain, no gain. 고통 없이는 얻는 것도 없다.

② Look before you leap. 돌다리도 두드려 보고 건너라.

③ A stitch in time saves nine.
제때의 한 땀은 나중의 열 땀을 덜어준다.

④ All that glitters is not gold. 반짝인다고 모두가 금은 아니다.

⑤ There is no royal road to learning. 학문에는 왕도가 없다.

어휘 break 고장 나다(break-broke-broken) turn on (전원을) 켜다 work 작동하다 cheap 저렴한, 싼 choose 선택하다 (choose-chose-chosen) fancy 화려한 shiny 빛나는 leap 뛰다 stitch 바늘땀 glitter 반짝거리다 royal road 왕도, 쉬운 방법

18 ②

M: Good afternoon. I'm Bud Samuels, and I'm here with this week's weather report. You need to wear your jackets today since it's cold and cloudy. But the clouds will disappear tomorrow, so we'll enjoy sunny skies all day long. We'll keep having sunny weather on Wednesday and Thursday, and the temperature will increase, too. But the weather will be cold on Friday and Saturday. Expect both heavy rain and wind on those two days.

안녕하세요. 저는 버드 새뮤얼스이고, 이번 주의 날씨를 가지고 나왔습니다. 오늘은 날씨가 춥고 흐리기 때문에 재킷을 입으셔야 합니다. 하지만 내일은 구름이 걷혀 하루 종일 화창한 날씨를 즐길 수 있을 겁니다. 수요일과 목요일까지 화창한 날씨가 계속될 것이며, 기온도 올라갈 것입니다. 하지만 날씨는 금요일과 토요일에 추워질 것입니다. 이틀 동안에는 폭우와 바람을 예상하셔야 합니다.

어휘 disappear 사라지다 all day long 하루 종일 temperature 기온 increase 올라가다, 상승하다 expect 기대하다, 예상하다 heavy rain 폭우

19 ⑤

W: Steve, did you remember to clean your room?
스티브, 네 방을 청소하는 걸 기억하고 있지?

M: I didn't forget, but I don't have time to do that now.
잊지 않았지만, 지금은 그걸 할 시간이 없어요.

W: Why not? What are you doing now?
왜 없어? 지금 뭐 하고 있니?

M: I need to finish my math homework.
수학 숙제를 끝내야 해요.

W: When are you planning to clean your room?
넌 언제 네 방 청소를 할 계획이니?

M: After I finish my homework, I'm going out to play basketball. So I'll clean my room tonight. Is that okay? 숙제를 끝낸 후에 농구를 하러 갈 거예요. 그러니까 오늘 밤에 제 방을 청소할게요. 됐죠?

W: Okay, but clean your room once you're finished.
좋아, 하지만 끝나고 나면 네 방 청소를 하거라.

① What kind of homework is it? 어떤 종류의 숙제니?
② Yes, you're doing your homework.
그래. 넌 숙제를 하고 있구나.
③ You need to prepare for your test next.
다음에 넌 시험 준비를 해야 한단다.
④ Why didn't you clean your room today?
왜 오늘 네 방 청소를 하지 않았니?
⑤ Okay, but clean your room once you're finished.
좋아, 하지만 끝나고 나면 네 방 청소를 하거라.

어휘 remember 기억하다 forget 잊어버리다 finish 끝내다 plan 계획하다 chore (하기 싫은 따분한)일 prepare 준비하다 once 일단 ~하면, ~하자마자

20 ④

M: How are you enjoying your lunch?
점심은 맛있게 먹고 있니?

W: It's delicious. Thanks for taking me here.
맛있어. 날 여기 데려와 줘서 고마워.

M: I'm glad you like it. 네가 마음에 들어 하니 나도 기뻐.

W: Are you going to get some dessert?
디저트를 먹으러 갈 거니?

M: I think I will. What would you like?
가려고 생각 중이야. 어떤 것이 좋겠니?

W: A piece of cake would be nice.
케이크 한 조각이 좋을 것 같아.

① Sure, we can go now. 물론이지, 우린 지금 갈 수 있어.
② No, I didn't like the meal.
아니, 난 식사가 마음에 들지 않았어.
③ Yes, I've been here before. 응, 난 전에 여기 와 봤어.
④ A piece of cake would be nice.
케이크 한 조각이 좋을 것 같아.
⑤ That's right. This place has dessert.
맞아. 여기는 디저트가 있어.

어휘 dessert 디저트 meal 식사, 음식

04회 실전모의고사   본문 p.42-43

01 ⑤	**02** ④	**03** ②	**04** ③	**05** ①
06 ③	**07** ⑤	**08** ②	**09** ②	**10** ①
11 ①	**12** ③	**13** ④	**14** ⑤	**15** ③
16 ②	**17** ②	**18** ③	**19** ⑤	**20** ①

01 ⑤

M: Nancy, have you packed your bag?
낸시, 네 가방은 챙겼니?

W: Not yet. Can you help me pack my clothes, Dad?
아직이요. 제 옷을 싸는 걸 도와주실래요, 아빠?

M: Okay. What do you need to bring? Do you need a jacket and some sweaters? 알겠어. 무엇을 가져가야 하니? 재킷이랑 스웨터가 필요하니?

W: No, I don't. Brazil will be hot and sunny.
아니요, 필요 없어요. 브라질은 덥고 화창할 거예요.

M: Okay. Then you don't need any long-sleeved shirts either. 알았다. 그럼 긴팔 셔츠도 필요 없겠구나.

W: I think I should take my swimsuit with me.
제 생각에는 수영복을 챙겨야 할 것 같아요.

M: Okay. Let me get it for you.
그래. 내가 수영복을 챙겨 줄게.

어휘 pack 짐을 싸다 long-sleeved 긴팔의 either 역시, 또한 swimsuit 수영복

02 ④

M: How was your trip to Vietnam? 베트남 여행은 어땠니?

W: I had a great time there. It was my first overseas trip.
거기서 정말 좋은 시간을 보냈어. 그건 내 첫 해외 여행이었어.

M: Was it really sunny there? 그곳의 날씨는 정말 화창했지?

W: No, it wasn't. It rained a lot. I had to carry my umbrella at all times. 아니, 그렇지 않았어. 비가 많이 왔어. 난 항상 우산을 갖고 다녀야 했어.

M: I'm sorry to hear that. 그 말을 들으니 유감이구나.

W: It's okay. I like rainy weather, so I still had a good time there. 괜찮아. 나는 비 오는 날씨를 좋아해서 그곳에서 좋은 시간을 보냈어.

어휘 overseas trip 해외 여행 carry 가지고 다니다 umbrella 우산 at all times 항상

03 ②

W: Did you have a good time at the science fair today? 오늘 과학 박람회에서 즐거운 시간을 보냈니?

M: Yes. It was amazing. There were so many good science projects. 응, 정말 대단했어. 정말 굉장한 과학 프로젝트들이 많았어.

W: How did your robot do? 네 로봇은 어땠니?

M: Everyone there liked it a lot. 거기 모인 모든 사람들이 그걸 굉장히 좋아했어.

W: I'm glad to hear that. 정말 잘됐구나.

M: The judges gave me a silver medal. 심사위원들이 나에게 은메달을 줬어.

W: Wow. You did an amazing job. 우와. 넌 놀라운 일을 해냈구나.

어휘 fair 박람회 amazing 놀라운, 멋진 science project 과학 프로젝트 judge 심사위원 silver medal 은메달 unpleasant 불쾌한 proud 자랑스러운 regretful 후회하는 disappointed 실망한

04 ③

M: Excuse me. Can I get some help? 실례합니다. 좀 도와주실 수 있나요?

W: Sure. What do you need? 물론이죠. 무엇이 필요하세요?

M: Today is my wife's birthday, so I need a cake. 오늘이 제 아내의 생일이라서 케이크가 필요해요.

W: Does she prefer chocolate or vanilla? 아내분이 초콜릿을 좋아하시나요, 아니면 바닐라를 좋아하시나요?

M: She loves chocolate. 아내는 초콜릿을 좋아해요.

W: We have many chocolate cakes here. Do you like any of them? 여기에 초콜릿 케이크가 많이 있습니다. 마음에 드시는 게 있나요?

M: That heart-shaped one looks nice. I'll take it. 하트 모양 케이크가 예쁘네요. 저걸로 살게요.

W: That's a great choice. It's the bestselling item in our store. 훌륭한 선택입니다. 저게 저희 가게에서 제일 잘 팔리는 상품이거든요.

어휘 prefer 선호하다 vanilla 바닐라 heart-shaped 하트 모양의 choice 선택 bestselling 가장 많이 팔리는

05 ①

M: Which one is the new math teacher?

누가 새로 오신 수학 선생님이니?

W: He's standing over there with the other men. 그분은 저쪽에 다른 사람들과 함께 서 계셔.

M: Many of those guys over there are wearing glasses. Is he wearing glasses, too? 저기 있는 많은 남자들은 안경을 쓰고 있어. 선생님도 안경을 쓰고 계시니?

W: Yes, he is. But he isn't wearing a cap. Can you find him? 응, 쓰고 계셔. 하지만 모자는 쓰고 계시지 않아. 네가 찾을 수 있겠니?

M: I'm not quite sure. Is he tall or short? 아직 잘 모르겠어. 키가 크시니, 아니면 작으시니?

W: He's shorter than the other men. 다른 남자들보다 키가 작으셔.

어휘 math 수학 stand 서다 over there 저 쪽에 wear 입다; 쓰다 glasses 안경 find 찾다 shorter 더 작은(short – shorter – shortest)

06 ③

M: Hello. How can I help you? 안녕하세요. 무엇을 도와드릴까요?

W: Hi. I'd like to have one ticket for the photo exhibition. How much does it cost? 안녕하세요. 사진 전시회 티켓 한 장을 사고 싶어요. 얼마죠?

M: Each ticket costs eight dollars. Do you have a discount card? 한 장에 8달러입니다. 할인 카드를 갖고 계신가요?

W: No, I don't. But I have a student ID. Can I get a discount with it? 아니요, 없어요. 하지만 학생증이 있어요. 이걸로 할인 받을 수 있나요?

M: Yes, you can get a two-dollar discount. 네, 2달러를 할인 받으실 수 있습니다.

W: Great. Here you are. 좋네요. 여기 있습니다.

어휘 exhibition 전시회 each 각각의 cost 비용이 들다 student ID 학생증 get a discount 할인을 받다

07 ⑤

[Telephone rings.] [전화벨이 울린다.]

W: Hello. This is Fine Furniture. May I help you? 여보세요. 파인 가구입니다. 무엇을 도와드릴까요?

M: Hello. My name is Dave Thomas. I bought a sofa there yesterday. 안녕하세요. 제 이름은 데이브 토마스입니다. 어제 거기서 소파를 샀어요.

W: Yes, Mr. Thomas. What can I do for you? 네, 토마스 씨. 무엇을 도와드릴까요?

M: Can I change the color? I don't want brown. 제가 색상을 바꿀 수 있을까요? 갈색을 원하지 않거든요.

W: What color do you want? 무슨 색상을 원하시나요?

M: I'd like a black sofa. The black one would go well with the other furniture in my house. 저는 검정색 소파를 원해요. 검정색 소파가 저희 집에 있는 다른 가구들과 잘 어울릴 것 같아요.

W: No problem. We will deliver a black sofa to you this

weekend.
문제 없습니다. 이번 주말에 검정색 소파로 배송해 드리겠습니다.

어휘 furniture 가구 brown 갈색 go well with ~와 잘 어울리다 deliver 배송하다, 배달하다

08 ②

W: Hi, John. What's wrong with your leg?
안녕, 존. 네 다리가 왜 그러니?

M: I hurt it while I was running early this morning.
오늘 아침 일찍 달리기를 하다가 다쳤어.

W: You should get some rest then.
그럼 넌 좀 쉬어야겠다.

M: I can't. I have baseball practice today. I really can't miss it. 그럴 수 없어. 오늘 야구 연습이 있거든. 그건 정말 빠지고 싶지 않아.

W: Don't go to it. Go to see a doctor instead. I'm worried about your health.
가지 마. 대신 병원에 가봐. 난 네 건강이 걱정돼.

M: Okay. I'll do that. Thanks for your concern.
알았어. 그렇게 할게. 걱정해 줘서 고마워.

어휘 leg 다리 hurt 다치게 하다, 아프다 get some rest 휴식을 취하다 practice 연습 miss 놓치다, 빠지다 see a doctor 병원에 가다 instead 대신에 worried 걱정하는 concern 걱정, 관심

09 ②

M: Ms. Kim, can I ask a question?
김 선생님, 질문 하나 해도 될까요?

W: Sure, Minsu. What is it? 물론이지, 민수야. 뭔데 그러니?

M: Can you tell me why I got a C on my paper? I don't understand. 제가 보고서에서 C를 받은 이유를 말씀해 주실 수 있나요? 이해가 되지 않아요.

W: You made a lot of mistakes on it.
넌 보고서에 많은 실수를 했단다.

M: Can I write it again and then turn it in to you?
보고서를 다시 써서 제출해도 될까요?

W: Sorry, but you can't. Just do better on the next class assignment.
안타깝지만 그럴 수 없단다. 다음 번 수업 과제를 더 열심히 하렴.

M: Okay. I understand. 알았어요. 이해했습니다.

어휘 paper 보고서, 리포트 make a mistake 실수를 하다 turn something in ~을 제출하다 assignment 과제

10 ①

W: Students at our school enjoy playing many different sports. The boys love some sports while the girls enjoy playing other ones. For example, volleyball and softball are popular girls' sports. Baseball and basketball are two of the favorite sports for boys. However, the most popular sport at the school is soccer. Both boys and girls like it very much.

우리 학교의 학생들은 많은 다양한 스포츠를 즐겨 합니다. 남학생들은 몇몇 스포츠를 좋아하는 반면 여학생들은 다른 것들을 좋아합니다. 예를 들면, 배구와 소프트볼은 인기 있는 여학생의 스포츠입니다. 야구와 농구는 남학생들이 가장 좋아하는 두 가지 스포츠입니다. 하지만 학교에서 가장 인기 있는 스포츠는 축구입니다. 남학생과 여학생 모두 축구를 좋아합니다.

어휘 play sports 스포츠를 하다 while 반면에 for example 예를 들어 volleyball 배구 softball 소프트볼 popular 인기 있는 basketball 농구 favorite 가장 좋아하는 both A and B A와 B 둘 다

11 ①

M: Julie, where are you going now?
줄리, 너 지금 어디 가니?

W: I'm going to the cafeteria. I'm hungry.
구내식당에 가고 있어. 난 배고파.

M: Can you do me a favor then?
그럼 내 부탁 좀 들어 줄 수 있니?

W: Sure. What do you need? 물론이지. 뭐가 필요하니?

M: Can you bring me a sandwich when you come back? 돌아올 때 나한테 샌드위치 좀 갖다 줄래?

W: Okay. But why can't you go there?
알았어. 그런데 넌 왜 못 가니?

M: I am busy working on this paper. I need to give it to Mr. Smith by one. 이 보고서를 작성하느라 바쁘거든. 1시까지 스미스 선생님께 제출해야 해.

어휘 cafeteria 구내식당 do somebody a favor ~의 부탁을 들어주다 bring 가져다 주다 sandwich 샌드위치 work on ~에 대한 작업을 하다

12 ③

M: Good morning, everyone. Today is our school's sports day. We're going to have lots of fun today. From nine to eleven, we'll play soccer. After that, we're going to have lunch. At one, we're going to play tug of war. And at three, we will have a baseball game. When the game ends, we'll have an awards ceremony as the final event. I hope everyone has fun.

안녕하세요, 여러분. 오늘은 우리 학교의 체육대회 날입니다. 오늘은 즐거운 하루가 될 겁니다. 9시부터 11시까지 우리는 축구 경기를 할 겁니다. 그 후에는 점심 식사를 할 겁니다. 1시에는 줄다리기가 있을 예정입니다. 그리고 3시에는 야구 경기를 합니다. 경기가 끝나면 마지막 행사로 시상식이 있을 예정입니다. 모두 즐거운 시간을 보내기를 바랍니다.

어휘 sports day 체육대회 tug of war 줄다리기 awards ceremony 시상식 final 마지막 event 행사

13 ④

W: I talked to Ms. Lee today. The school needs

volunteers for the festival. 내가 오늘 이 선생님과 이야기를 나누었어. 학교에서는 축제 때 일할 자원봉사자가 필요하대.

M: Are you going to help? 넌 그 행사를 도울 거니?

W: Yes. I'm going to volunteer at the school play.
응. 학교 연극에서 자원봉사를 할 거야.

M: That's good. How can I help the school have a good festival? 좋은 생각이네. 학교가 축제를 잘 치를 수 있도록 내가 어떤 도움을 줄 수 있지?

W: You should speak with Ms. Lee. She can tell you what to do. 이 선생님께 말씀드려 봐. 네가 할 수 있는 것을 말씀해 주실 수 있을 거야.

M: Okay. I'll visit her office after music class ends.
알았어. 음악 수업이 끝난 다음에 사무실로 찾아 뵈어야겠어.

어휘 volunteer 자원봉사(자) festival 축제 play 연극 visit 방문하다

14 ⑤

① Cats are owned by seven students.
7명의 학생들이 고양이를 가지고 있다.

② Dogs are owned by nine students.
9명의 학생들이 개를 가지고 있다.

③ Birds are owned by three students.
3명의 학생들이 새를 가지고 있다.

④ Birds are owned by the fewest students.
가장 적은 학생들이 새를 가지고 있다.

⑤ Hamsters are owned by more students than cats are. 햄스터를 가진 학생들이 고양이를 가진 학생들보다 더 많다.

해설 고양이를 가진 학생이 햄스터를 가진 학생보다 한 명 더 많다.

어휘 pet 애완동물 own 소유하다 few 적은(few – fewer – fewest)

15 ③

W: You'll never guess what I did today.
오늘 내가 뭘 했는지 넌 절대 알 수 없을 거야.

M: I give up. Go ahead and tell me.
난 포기했어. 그냥 말해 줘.

W: Jenny and I went to the Sandstone Mall and had lunch at the new Indian restaurant.
제니랑 내가 샌드스톤 몰에 가서 새로 생긴 인도 식당에서 점심을 먹었어.

M: Are you serious? I've heard so much about it. How was the food?
정말이니? 난 그 식당에 대해서 정말 많이 들었어. 음식은 어땠니?

W: It was incredible. Some of it was spicy, but it wasn't so hot that you couldn't eat it. 정말 놀라웠어. 몇 가지 음식은 매웠지만, 먹지 못할 정도로 너무 맵지는 않았어.

M: Were the prices reasonable? 가격은 적당했니?

W: Yes, they were. And the restaurant was having a special offer to celebrate its opening. So we only paid half price. 응, 적당했어. 그리고 식당에서 개업을 축하하는 특가 판매도 있었어. 그래서 우리는 반값만 냈어.

M: Wow. I really envy you. I'd love to go there.
우와. 정말 부럽다. 나도 거길 가보고 싶어.

어휘 guess 추측하다 give up 포기하다 go ahead 밀고 나가다, 시작하다 serious 진지한, 심각한 incredible 놀라운, 믿을 수 없는 spicy 매운 reasonable 적당한, 합리적인 special offer 특가 판매 celebrate 축하하다, 기념하다 opening 개업, 개장 half 절반 envy 부러워하다

16 ②

① M: Have you ever eaten Mexican food?
넌 멕시코 음식을 먹어본 적이 있니?

W: Yes, but I did not like it.
응, 하지만 별로 마음에 들지는 않았어.

② M: How long is your flight to Jeju Island?
제주도까지 비행기로 얼마나 걸리니?

W: I will be there for one week.
난 일주일 동안 그곳에 있을 거야.

③ M: Did you remember to call your brother?
네 오빠한테 전화하는 걸 기억했니?

W: No, I forgot to do that.
아니. 전화하는 걸 잊어버렸어.

④ M: What's the weather like now? 지금은 날씨가 어떻니?

W: It's cold and rainy. 춥고 비가 와.

⑤ M: What do you usually do on the weekend?
주말에는 보통 뭘 하니?

W: I visit my grandparents and stay at their home.
조부모님 댁을 방문에서 그곳에 있어.

어휘 eat 먹다(eat – ate – eaten) flight 비행 remember 기억하다 forget 잊어버리다(forget – forgot – forgotten) usually 보통은

17 ②

[Chime rings.] [차임벨이 울린다.]

M: Good morning, students. Today, we will not have lunch in the cafeteria. Instead, we will have a picnic outside on the school grounds. At twelve, everyone should go outside. We will provide food and drinks for all of you. After lunch, we will play some games, too.

안녕하세요, 학생 여러분. 우리는 오늘 구내식당에서 점심식사를 먹지 않을 것입니다. 대신 학교 운동장에서 야외 소풍을 할 예정입니다. 12시가 되면 모두 밖으로 나오시기 바랍니다. 모든 학생들에게 음식과 음료를 제공할 것입니다. 점심 식사 후에는 게임도 할 것입니다.

어휘 cafeteria 구내식당 instead 대신에 have a picnic 소풍을 하다 ground 운동장 outside 야외에, 밖에 provide 제공하다

18 ③

M: Vacation is almost over. We start school next week.
방학이 거의 끝났어. 우리는 다음 주에 학기가 시작해.

W: What are you going to do before school starts?
너 학기가 시작하기 전에 뭘 할 거니?
M: I'm going to go shopping. 난 쇼핑하러 갈 거야.
W: What for? 뭘 사려고?
M: I need some school supplies. 난 학용품이 좀 필요해.
W: When are you going to visit the stationery store then? 그럼 언제 문구점에 갈 거니?
M: I'll do that on Thursday or Friday.
목요일이나 금요일에 할 거야.

① Yes, I'm all ready for school.
  응, 나는 학교 갈 준비가 다 됐어.
② I went to the park last week.
  난 지난주에 공원에 갔어.
③ I'll do that on Thursday or Friday.
  목요일이나 금요일에 할 거야.
④ I'm going shopping with my family.
  난 가족과 함께 쇼핑을 갈 거야.
⑤ No, I don't need any school supplies.
  아니, 나는 아무 학용품도 필요 없어.

어휘 vacation 방학 be over 끝나다 almost 거의 what for? 뭐하러?, 왜? (목적·이유를 물음) school supplies 학용품 stationery store 문구점 be ready for ~할 준비가 되다

19 ⑤

M: Mom's birthday is tomorrow.
엄마 생신이 내일이야.
W: Oh, I almost forgot. What should we do?
아, 거의 잊어버릴 뻔했어. 우리가 뭘 해야 하지?
M: We should have a party for her.
우리는 엄마를 위해 파티를 열어야 해.
W: Okay. That's a good idea. What are you planning to do for it? 알겠어. 좋은 생각이야. 넌 뭘 계획하고 있니?
M: We need a cake and a card. I can bake a cake.
우리는 케이크와 카드가 필요해. 내가 케이크를 만들 수 있어.
W: What do you want me to do?
나는 무엇을 하면 좋겠니?
M: You should make a card for Mom.
넌 엄마에게 드릴 카드를 만들어야 해.

① Let's buy one at the bakery. 제과점에서 하나 사자.
② No, you don't have to do that.
  아니, 넌 그럴 필요는 없어.
③ I want a cake with vanilla icing.
  난 바닐라 당의가 있는 케이크를 원해.
④ How about buying me a present?
  내게 선물을 사주는 게 어때?
⑤ You should make a card for Mom.
  넌 엄마에게 드릴 카드를 만들어야 해.

어휘 almost 거의 have a party 파티를 열다 bake a cake 케이크를 굽다 bakery 빵집 icing (케이크 위에 올리는) 당의 present 선물

20 ①

W: Tom and Amy are planning to see a movie together on Saturday. However, on Saturday, Amy's father tells her she can't go out. She has to clean her room and do some other chores. Amy is very unhappy, but she calls Tom and tells him the news. In this situation, what could Tom say to make Amy feel better?

톰과 에이미는 토요일에 함께 영화를 보기로 계획 중이다. 그러나, 토요일에 에이미의 아버지가 에이미에게 밖에 나가지 말라고 말씀하신다. 에이미는 방 청소를 해야 하고 다른 집안일을 해야 한다. 에이미는 매우 속상하지만 톰에게 전화하여 그 소식을 알린다. 이런 상황에서 톰이 에이미의 기분을 풀어주기 위해 할 수 있는 가장 적절한 말은 무엇인가?

Tom: We can go another time. 우리는 다음에 갈 수 있어.

① We can go another time. 우리는 다음에 갈 수 있어.
② I'm so glad you feel that way.
  네가 그렇게 느낀다니 정말 기뻐.
③ I helped you clean your room.
  나는 네가 방 청소를 하는 것을 도왔어.
④ I had a great time at the movie.
  나는 영화관에서 정말 즐거운 시간을 보냈어.
⑤ Of course, your father must be proud.
  물론 너희 아버지는 자랑스러워 하실 거야.

어휘 go out 나가다, 외출하다 chore (자질구레한) 집안일 unhappy 속상한, 슬픈 news 소식, 정보 situation 상황

05회 실전모의고사

01 ③	02 ④	03 ①	04 ①	05 ⑤
06 ①	07 ①	08 ②	09 ⑤	10 ③
11 ③	12 ③	13 ⑤	14 ②	15 ⑤
16 ③	17 ③	18 ③	19 ⑤	20 ⑤

01 ③

M: Good evening. It's time for the Friday weather report. It finally stopped raining this morning. So we had a bright, sunny day today. The sunshine is going away tomorrow. We will have cloudy skies all day on Saturday. But it will be sunny again on Sunday. You'll need your umbrellas on Monday. It's going to start raining again.

안녕하세요. 금요일 일기예보 시간입니다. 오늘 아침 마침내 비가 그쳤습니다. 그래서 오늘은 맑고 화창한 날씨였습니다. 햇빛은 내일 사라질 것입니다. 토요일은 하루 종일 구름 낀 하늘을 보게 될 것입니다. 하지만 날씨는 일요일에 다시 맑아질 것입니다. 월요일에는 우산을 챙기시기 바랍니다. 다시 비가 올 것입니다.

어휘 finally 마침내 stop –ing ~을 멈추다 bright 화창한 sunshine 햇빛 go away 사라지다 all day 하루 종일

02 ④

M: Hello. How may I help you?
안녕하세요. 무엇을 도와드릴까요?

W: Hi. I'd like to buy a sweater for my daughter.
제 딸에게 줄 스웨터를 하나 사고 싶어요.

M: How about this one with stripes?
줄무늬가 들어간 이건 어떠세요?

W: No, I don't think she'll like that. She likes clothes with pictures on them. 아니요, 그건 제 딸이 좋아하지 않을 것 같네요. 그 애는 그림이 그려져 있는 옷을 좋아해요.

M: How about this one with a dolphin on it?
돌고래 한 마리가 있는 이건 어떠세요?

W: She loves dolphins. I'll take it.
그 애는 돌고래를 좋아해요. 그걸로 할게요.

어휘 sweater 스웨터 daughter 딸 stripe 줄무늬 clothes 옷 picture 그림, 사진 dolphin 돌고래

03 ①

M: What's the matter, Karen? 무슨 일 있니 카렌?

W: Jason just broke my MP3 player.
제이슨이 제 MP3플레이어를 망가뜨렸어요.

M: Don't be mad. He's only six years old.
화내지 마. 제이슨은 겨우 6살밖에 안됐잖아.

W: But it cost a lot of money. I can't buy a new one.
하지만 이건 정말 비싼 거예요. 저는 새것을 살 여유가 없어요.

M: I understand. I'll buy a new one for you.
이해한단다. 아빠가 너한테 새것을 사 줄게.

어휘 break 망가뜨리다(break – broke-broken) mad 화가 난 cost 비용이 들다(cost-cost-cost) understand 이해하다 proud 자랑스러운 regretful 후회하는 bored 지루한 pleased 기쁜

04 ①

M: Sarah, you're wearing a nice dress today.
사라, 넌 오늘 예쁜 드레스를 입었구나.

W: Thanks. I just got it yesterday. 고마워. 바로 어제 생겼어.

M: Was it a birthday present from someone?
누군가한테 생일 선물로 받은 거니?

W: No, my birthday is next week. I went shopping with my mom yesterday.
아니, 내 생일은 다음 주야. 어제 엄마랑 같이 쇼핑을 갔었어.

M: I see. Tell me when your birthday is. Then, I'll get you a present on your birthday. 그렇구나. 네 생일이 언제인지 말해 줘. 그러면 내가 생일 선물을 사줄게.

어휘 birthday present 생일 선물

05 ⑤

W: Hello. Can I help you, sir?
안녕하세요. 제가 도와드릴까요, 손님?

M: Yes, please. There's a problem with my phone.
네. 제 전화기에 문제가 있어요.

W: What's wrong with it? 무슨 문제가 있죠?

M: I can't hear anything when people call me.
사람들이 저에게 전화를 걸 때 아무 소리도 들을 수가 없어요.

W: There must be a problem with it. Let me take a look. 전화기에 문제가 있는 게 확실하군요. 제가 한번 볼게요.

M: Here it is. Can you fix it? 여기 있어요. 고칠 수 있나요?

W: Yes, we can. It will take about one hour.
네, 고칠 수 있습니다. 약 한 시간 정도 걸릴 거예요.

어휘 problem 문제 take a look 한번 보다 fix 고치다, 수리하다 take (시간이) 걸리다 repair center 수리센터

06 ①

W: You look pleased today. What's going on?
너 오늘 기분이 좋아 보이는구나. 무슨 일이니?

M: I think I got an A on my history test.
난 역사 시험에서 A를 받은 것 같아.

W: Really? Good for you. Did you think it was easy?
정말? 잘됐다. 시험이 쉬웠다고 생각했니?

M: Yes, I did. The teacher didn't ask many difficult questions.
응, 그랬어. 선생님이 어려운 문제를 많이 내지 않으셨어.

W: I feel just about the same as you do. I think I did pretty well, too.
나도 네가 생각한 것처럼 생각해. 나도 꽤 잘 본 것 같아.

어휘 pleased 기쁜 history 역사 good for you 잘됐구나 do well 잘하다 pretty 꽤, 아주

07 ①

W: Are you ready for tonight's Halloween party?
오늘 밤 핼러윈 파티에 대한 준비가 됐니?

M: Yes. It's going to be a lot of fun.
네. 정말 재미있을 것 같아요.

W: Everyone from your class is coming, right? That's twenty people.
너희 반 친구들 모두 오는 게 맞지? 모두 20명이잖아.

M: No. Sarah and Jay can't make it. They're both sick.
아니요. 사라와 제이는 올 수 없어요. 둘 다 아프거든요.

W: So eighteen of your friends are going to come?
그럼 친구들 중 18명이 오는 거니?

M: That's right.
네 맞아요.

어휘 be ready for ~을 준비하다 make it 참석하다; 해내다 sick 아픈

08 ②

M: Did you buy a new smartphone yet?
넌 새 스마트폰을 샀니?

W: No. I don't know which one I should buy.
아니, 어떤 것을 사야 할지 잘 모르겠어.

M: Why don't you talk to Jeff?
제프랑 얘기해 보는 게 어때?

W: Jeff? Why should I speak with him?
제프? 왜 내가 제프랑 얘기를 해야 하지?

M: His father owns an electronics store. He knows all the good smartphones.
제프의 아버지가 전자제품 상점을 운영하시잖아. 그 애는 모든 좋은 스마트폰을 알고 있어.

W: Thanks for the advice. I'll give him a call right now.
충고해 줘서 고마워. 지금 제프한테 전화해 볼게.

어휘 why don't you ~? ~하는 게 어때? own 운영하다, 소유하다 electronics store 전자제품 매장 advice 조언, 충고 give somebody a call ~에게 전화하다 right now 지금 당장

09 ⑤

W: Did you have fun at the community center today?
오늘 문화센터에서 재미있었니?

M: Yes, I did. My friends and I played lots of games there.
응, 재미있었어. 내 친구들이랑 나는 거기서 많은 경기를 했어.

W: What games did you play?
너희는 어떤 경기를 했니?

M: We played basketball, ping-pong, tennis, and baseball.
우리는 농구, 탁구, 테니스, 그리고 야구를 했어.

W: That sounds fun. Which game did you like the most?
재미있었겠다. 어떤 게임이 가장 좋았니?

M: Baseball was the best. My team won the game.
야구가 최고였어. 우리 팀이 경기에서 이겼거든.

어휘 community center 문화센터, 주민센터 ping pong 탁구 win 이기다(win – won – won)

10 ③

W: Hello, shoppers. Let me tell you about a special sale we are having. All fruits and vegetables in the store are now half off. Please go to the back of the store. Our workers will help you find the freshest fruits and vegetables. This sale will end when the store closes tonight. Enjoy your shopping.

안녕하세요, 쇼핑객 여러분. 현재 진행 중인 특별 할인판매에 대해서 말씀드리겠습니다. 매장 내에 있는 모든 과일과 채소가 현재 반값입니다. 매장 뒤쪽으로 가주시기 바랍니다. 저희 직원들이 신선한 과일과 채소를 찾을 수 있도록 도울 것입니다. 이 할인판매는 오늘 밤 매장이 문을 닫을 때 끝날 예정입니다. 즐거운 쇼핑 되시기 바랍니다.

어휘 shopper 쇼핑객 let me tell you about ~에 대해 말씀드리겠습니다 sale 세일, 할인판매 half off 반값의(= 50% off) freshest 가장 신선한(fresh – fresher – freshest)

11 ③

W: Good evening. May I take your order, please?
안녕하세요. 제가 주문을 받아도 될까요?

M: Yes, I'd like to have the fried chicken and a salad.
네, 저는 프라이드 치킨과 샐러드를 먹을게요.

W: Would you like anything else?
또 다른 것이 필요하신가요?

M: I'd love to have a baked potato, please.
구운 감자도 주세요.

W: Okay, and do you want something to drink?
알겠습니다. 마실 것도 드릴까요?

M: Yes. I'd like a glass of iced tea.
네. 아이스티 한 잔 주세요.

W: Very good. Just a moment, please.
알겠습니다. 잠시만 기다려 주세요.

어휘 take one's order ~의 주문을 받다 anything else 그 밖의 다른 것 baked 구워진 something to drink 마실 것 iced tea 아이스티 moment 잠깐, 잠시

12 ③

[*Cellphone rings.*] [휴대폰이 울린다.]

M: Hi, Julie. How are you?
안녕, 줄리. 잘 지내니?

W: Hi, Steve. I'm good. By the way, do you have my science book?
안녕, 스티브. 난 잘 지내. 그런데, 네가 내 과학책을 갖고 있니?

M: Do you mean the science book you lent me?
네가 나한테 빌려준 과학책을 말하는 거니?

W: Yes, that one. I need it to do my homework.
응, 그 과학책. 숙제를 하기 위해 그게 필요하거든.

M: Do you need it right now?
지금 당장 필요하니?

W: Yes. Can you please bring it to my house?
응. 우리 집으로 가져다 줄 수 있니?

M: Oh, okay. I'll be at your house in a few minutes.
아, 알았어. 난 몇 분 안에 너희 집에 도착할 거야.

어휘 by the way (화제 전환) 그런데 science 과학 lend 빌려주다(lend – lent – lent) in a few minutes 몇 분 안에

13 ⑤

M: What are you making, Mom?
뭘 만들고 계세요, 엄마?

W: I'm baking cookies. Do you want to help?
난 쿠키를 굽고 있어. 네가 좀 도와줄래?

M: Sure. Do we need flour?
물론이죠. 우리는 밀가루가 필요한가요?

W: Yes, we do. We also need butter, eggs, and sugar.
응, 필요해. 버터, 달걀, 그리고 설탕도 필요하단다.

M: How about chocolate chips?
초콜릿칩은요?

W: No. I'm not making chocolate chip cookies. I'm making sugar cookies.
아니. 난 초콜릿칩 쿠키를 만들고 있는 게 아니야. 난 설탕 쿠키를 만들고 있단다.

어휘 bake 굽다 cookie 쿠키 flour 밀가루 butter 버터 egg 달걀 sugar 설탕

14 ②

[Cellphone rings.] [휴대폰이 울린다.]
M: Hello. This is Coach Young speaking.
안녕하세요. 영 감독입니다.
W: Hello, Coach Young. This is Tim's mother. Do you have some time to talk?
안녕하세요, 영 감독님. 저는 팀의 엄마예요. 이야기를 나눌 시간이 있으신가요?
M: Sure. What can I do for you?
물론입니다. 무엇을 도와드릴까요?
W: I'm sorry to say this, but Tim can't go to baseball practice today.
이런 말씀을 드리게 되어 죄송하지만, 팀이 오늘 야구 연습에 못 가게 되었어요.
M: Is he sick? What's the matter?
팀이 아픈가요? 무슨 문제가 있죠?
W: No, he's not sick, so please don't worry. I have to take him to see his grandfather.
아니요, 아프지 않으니까 걱정 마세요. 제가 팀을 데리고 그 애의 할아버지를 뵈러 가야 하거든요.
M: I understand. Do you think he'll be at practice tomorrow? 알겠습니다. 팀은 내일 연습에 나올 수 있나요?
W: Yes, he will. 네, 나갈 거예요.

어휘 coach 감독, 코치 practice 연습(하다) sick 아픈 take 데려가다 understand 이해하다

15 ⑤

[Cellphone rings.] [휴대폰이 울린다.]
M: Hi, Mom. 안녕, 엄마.
W: Hi, Joe. Where are you? 안녕, 조. 너 어디니?
M: I'm at home. I'm watching TV.
저는 집에 있어요. TV를 보고 있어요.
W: Can you do something for me, please?
엄마 부탁 좀 들어줄 수 있니?
M: Sure. What is it? 물론이죠. 뭐예요?
W: Can you turn the washing machine on? I forgot. The clothes are already in it. 네가 세탁기를 작동시킬 수 있니? 내가 깜박했어. 옷은 이미 세탁기 안에 있어.
M: No problem. I'll do that. 문제 없어요. 제가 할게요.

어휘 turn something on ~의 전원을 켜다, 작동시키다 washing machine 세탁기 already 이미

16 ③

W: Where are you going now, Jeff?

넌 어디 가고 있니, 제프?
M: I'm going to the bus terminal.
난 버스 터미널에 가고 있어.
W: Yeah? Are you taking a trip? 그래? 여행 가는 거니?
M: No, I'm not. My best friend is coming to visit me. So I'm going there to pick him up. 아니, 여행은 안 가. 내 친한 친구가 나를 찾아오거든. 그래서 데리러 가는 거야.
W: What time will his bus arrive?
친구가 탄 버스가 몇 시에 도착하니?
M: In about thirty minutes. So I need to hurry.
약 30분 후에 도착해. 그래서 서둘러야 해.

어휘 terminal (철도·버스의) 터미널 take a trip 여행하다 best friend 가장 친한 친구 pick somebody up ~을 (차로) 데리러 가다 hurry 서두르다

17 ③

① M: Have you met the new teacher?
새로 온 선생님은 만나 봤니?
W: Yes, I have. He's a very humorous person.
응, 만나 봤어. 굉장히 유머러스한 분이셔.
② M: How was the movie you saw?
네가 봤던 영화는 어땠니?
W: I liked it a lot. 엄청 재미있었어.
③ M: This was a delicious meal, wasn't it?
정말 맛있는 식사였어, 그렇지 않니?
W: I haven't had lunch yet. 난 아직 점심을 먹지 못했어.
④ M: Do you usually go hiking on weekends?
넌 보통 주말마다 하이킹을 하러 가니?
W: Yes, I enjoy doing that. 응, 나는 그걸 즐겨 해.
⑤ M: Why didn't you call me last night?
왜 어젯밤에 나한테 전화하지 않았니?
W: Sorry. I forgot. 미안해. 잊어버렸어.

어휘 humorous 유머러스한, 재미있는 delicious 맛있는 meal 식사 have lunch 점심을 먹다 usually 보통 go hiking 하이킹을 가다 on weekends 주말마다

18 ③

W: How is your Chinese class going, Tom?
네 중국어 수업은 어떻게 되어 가고 있니, 톰?
M: Terrible. I can't speak Chinese at all.
끔찍해. 난 중국어를 전혀 말할 수 없어.
W: Didn't you just start learning it last week?
넌 고작 지난주에 중국어를 배우기 시작하지 않았니?
M: Yes, and I still don't know much.
응. 그리고 지금도 많이 알지 못해.
W: Relax. You're just a beginner. You need to spend a lot more time learning it. 편하게 마음 먹어. 넌 초보자일 뿐이야. 그걸 배우려면 많은 시간을 들여야 할 거야.
M: What do you mean? 무슨 뜻이니?
W: It takes time to learn a new language. You need to be patient. 새로운 언어를 배우는 데는 시간이 필요해. 넌 인내심을 가질 필요가 있어.

① Better late than never.
늦게라도 하는 것이 아예 안 하는 것보다 낫다.

② Look before you leap. 돌다리도 두드려 보고 건너라.

③ Rome wasn't built in a day.
로마는 하루아침에 이루어진 것이 아니다.

④ After a storm comes a calm. 비 온 뒤에 땅이 굳어진다.

⑤ All work and no play makes Jack a dull boy.
공부만 하고 놀지 않으면 바보가 된다.

어휘 Chinese 중국어 beginner 초급자, 초보자 spend time -ing ~하면서 시간을 보내다[들이다] language 언어 patient 인내심이 있는, 참을성 있는 leap 뛰다 build 짓다(build-built-built) storm 폭풍우 calm 평온; 차분한 dull 둔한

19 ⑤

W: Hi, Jay. Are you looking for someone?
안녕, 제이. 누구를 찾고 있니?

M: Yes. I need to find Mr. Stephens.
응, 나는 스티븐스 씨를 찾아야 해.

W: Do you mean the math teacher? Why do you want to see him?
수학 선생님을 말하는 거니? 왜 그 분을 봐야 하는 거니?

M: I have some questions about the math homework he assigned. Do you know where he is? 선생님이 내주신 숙제에 대해서 질문이 몇 개 있거든. 어디 계신지 알고 있니?

W: No, I haven't seen him all day.
아니, 하루 종일 그분을 못 봤어.

① Yes, his class is fun. 응, 그분의 수업은 재미있어.

② Thanks for your help. 도와줘서 고마워.

③ I love his math class. 난 그분의 수학 수업이 좋아.

④ No, I don't have any homework. 아니, 난 숙제 없어.

⑤ No, I haven't seen him all day.
아니, 하루 종일 그분을 못 봤어.

어휘 look for ~을 찾다 assign (일, 숙제 등을) 부과하다, 맡기다 all day 하루 종일

20 ⑤

M: Do you still exercise a lot, Amy?
넌 여전히 운동을 많이 하니, 에이미?

W: Yes. I go jogging every day. 응. 난 매일 조깅해.

M: How long do you jog for? 얼마나 오래 조깅하니?

W: I jog at least one hour every day.
난 매일 적어도 한 시간씩은 조깅해.

M: Wow, that's amazing. Where do you go jogging?
와, 놀라운데. 어디서 조깅하니?

W: I usually run in the park. 난 주로 공원에서 뛰어.

M: Do you mind if I do that with you sometime?
나도 언젠가 너랑 같이 조깅해도 될까?

W: Not at all. You can meet me at six in the morning.
물론이지. 아침 6시에 나랑 만나면 돼.

① Have you been to the park? 넌 공원에 가봤니?

② I jog around ten kilometers. 난 약 10킬로미터를 조깅해.

③ I'm trying to get in good shape.
난 좋은 몸매를 가꾸려고 노력 중이야.

④ I go jogging at six in the morning.
나는 아침 6시에 조깅하러 가.

⑤ Not at all. You can meet me at six in the morning.
물론이지. 아침 6시에 나랑 만나면 돼.

해설 'Do you mind ~?'로 묻는 질문에 '승낙'을 하려면 'No', 'Not at all' 등의 표현을 사용한다.

어휘 exercise 운동하다 go jogging 조깅하다(= jog) at least 적어도 Do you mind if ~? ~해도 될까요? in good shape 몸매가 좋은, 몸 상태가 좋은

06회 실전모의고사
본문 p.64-65

01 ②	02 ①	03 ②	04 ④	05 ③
06 ①	07 ①	08 ②	09 ②	10 ①
11 ⑤	12 ⑤	13 ②	14 ②	15 ④
16 ④	17 ③	18 ②	19 ④	20 ①

01 ②

M: We need to make a card for Mom since it's her birthday.
오늘이 엄마 생신이니까 우리는 카드를 만들어야 해.

W: Okay. What kind of card should we make?
그래. 어떤 종류의 카드를 만들어야 할까?

M: Let's make a square card that has some flowers on it. 꽃 몇 송이가 있는 정사각형의 카드를 만들자.

W: How about a heart instead of flowers? Won't that be better?
꽃 대신에 하트는 어때? 그게 더 낫지 않을까?

M: Good thinking. We can draw that and put "Happy Birthday, Mom" on the card. 좋은 생각이야. 우리가 하트를 그린 다음에 "엄마, 생신 축하드려요" 라고 쓰자.

W: All right. Let's start making it.
좋아. 이제 만들기 시작하자.

어휘 what kind of 어떤 종류의 square 정사각형(의) instead of ~대신에 better 더 나은(good-better-best) draw 그리다

02 ①

M: It's time for the weather forecast for California. There will be hot, sunny weather in San Francisco today. It's going to be cloudy in Los Angeles. There will be fog in San Diego. In Sacramento, it will be hot and sunny. Most of the state is going to get really nice weather today.

캘리포니아의 날씨를 전해 드릴 시간입니다. 오늘 샌프란시스코는 덥고 화창하겠습니다. 로스앤젤레스는 구름이 끼겠습니다. 샌디에이고는 안개가 끼겠습니다. 새크라멘토는 해가 나고 더워지겠습니

다. 주의 대부분의 지역은 오늘 정말 좋은 날씨가 예상됩니다.

어휘 fog 안개 most of ~의 대부분 state 주

03 ②

W: Pardon me. Can you <u>hold</u> the <u>door</u> <u>open</u>, please?
실례합니다. 문 좀 잡아 주시겠어요?

M: <u>No problem</u>. Where are you going?
물론이죠. 어디 가세요?

W: I'm going up to the <u>health</u> <u>club</u>.
저는 헬스클럽으로 올라가는 중이에요.

M: I believe that's the <u>tenth</u> <u>floor</u>. Let me <u>press</u> the <u>button</u>.
제 생각에 헬스클럽은 10층에 있어요. 버튼을 눌러 드릴게요.

W: Thanks a lot. Where are you going?
정말 고맙습니다. 어디 가세요?

M: I'm going to <u>have lunch</u> at a restaurant.
저는 식당에 점심을 먹으러 가요.

W: Is it on the <u>sixth</u> floor? 식당은 6층에 있나요?

M: That's right. It's an Italian restaurant. You should <u>go</u> there <u>sometime</u>.
맞아요. 이탈리아 식당이에요. 언젠가 꼭 가보세요.

W: Thanks. I will. 고마워요. 그럴게요.

어휘 hold the door open 문을 열어 놓다 believe 생각하다, 믿
다 floor 층, 바닥 press 누르다 Italian 이탈리아의

04 ④

M: How about <u>going to</u> the <u>park</u> this weekend?
이번 주말에 공원을 가는 게 어때?

W: Sure. We can <u>play tennis</u> there.
그래. 우린 거기서 테니스를 칠 수 있어.

M: Why don't we <u>pick up</u> <u>garbage</u> there? 우리는 거기서 쓰레기를 줍는 게 어때?

W: What do you mean? 무슨 뜻이야?

M: The park is really <u>dirty</u> these days. So I want to help <u>clean</u> <u>it</u> <u>up</u>. 공원이 요즘 정말 더러워. 그래서 나는 공원을 청소하는 것을 돕고 싶어.

W: <u>How nice</u> of you! Do you do that <u>often</u>?
넌 참 착하구나! 그걸 자주 하니?

M: No. It's my <u>first</u> <u>time</u>. You can go with me if you want. 아니. 이번이 처음이야. 네가 원하면 같이 갈 수 있어.

W: Sure, <u>I'd love to</u>. 응. 나도 그러고 싶어.

어휘 weekend 주말 pick up 줍다 garbage 쓰레기 dirty 더러
운 clean up 청소하다, 치우다 nice 친절한

05 ③

[*Telephone rings.*] [전화벨이 울린다.]

M: Hi, Tina. 안녕, 티나.

W: Hey, Chris. Do you know Eric?
안녕, 크리스. 넌 에릭을 아니?

M: <u>Of course</u> I know him. He's one of my friends.
당연히 알지. 그 애는 내 친구 중 한 명이야.

W: That's great. Do you know his <u>phone</u> <u>number</u>?
잘됐다. 너 에릭의 전화번호를 아니?

M: Yes, <u>what</u> do you need it <u>for</u>?
응, 무슨 일 때문에 필요한데?

W: I have to <u>ask</u> him about our <u>group</u> <u>project</u>.
그 애한테 우리의 조별 과제에 대해서 물어볼 게 있어.

M: Oh, okay. It's four zero nine, five four zero five.
아, 알았어. 409-5405번이야.

W: Thanks a lot. See you at school tomorrow.
정말 고마워. 내일 학교에서 보자.

어휘 phone number 전화번호 group project 조별 과제

06 ①

M: Kate, what's the matter? 케이트, 무슨 일이니?

W: I can't find my new <u>ring anywhere</u>.
내 새 반지를 어디서도 못 찾겠어.

M: That's too bad. <u>Where</u> do you think you <u>lost</u> it?
정말 안됐구나. 어디서 그걸 잃어버린 것 같아?

W: I'm sure it's <u>somewhere</u> here in the <u>classroom</u>. I have been looking but can't find it. 여기 교실 어딘가에 있는 게 확실해. 계속 찾아봤는데 찾을 수가 없어.

M: Let me help you. Where did you look?
내가 도와줄게. 어디를 찾아봤어?

W: I <u>looked</u> <u>around</u> my desk. 내 책상 근처를 찾아봤어.

M: Oh, is it a <u>gold</u> ring? 아, 그게 금반지니?

W: That's right. 맞아.

M: Here it is. It's under this desk <u>over</u> <u>here</u>.
여기 있어. 이쪽에 있는 이 책상 밑에 있었어.

W: Seriously? Thank you very much.
정말이야? 정말 고마워.

해설 여자는 반지를 찾지 못해 초조해 하다가, 남자가 반지를 찾자 기뻐하고 있다.

어휘 ring 반지 lose 잃어버리다(lose-lost-lost) somewhere 어딘가에 around 주위에, 사방에 over here 이쪽에 seriously 정말, 진지하게 nervous 초조한 concerned 걱정하는 relieved 안도하는

07 ①

W: Would you like to <u>go</u> <u>out</u> to <u>dinner</u> tonight?
오늘 밤에 나가서 저녁 먹을래?

M: <u>What</u> <u>time</u> do you want to do that?
넌 몇 시에 가기를 원하는데?

W: <u>How</u> <u>about</u> at seven? 7시쯤 어때?

M: I'd rather not. My <u>favorite</u> TV <u>show</u> is coming on at that time.
난 안 되겠어. 내가 제일 좋아하는 TV 프로그램이 그 시간에 나와.

W: <u>Why</u> <u>don't</u> we go out after the show ends?
프로그램이 끝난 다음에 나가는 건 어때?

M: Okay. It will <u>finish</u> at <u>eight</u> since it's an <u>hour</u> <u>long</u>.
좋아. 그건 한 시간 정도 하니까 8시에 끝날 거야.

W: All right. We can leave around <u>eight</u> <u>fifteen</u> then.

좋아. 그럼 우리는 8시 15분쯤에 나갈 수 있겠다.

해설 ③은 프로그램이 끝나는 시각이고, ④는 두 사람이 저녁을 먹으러 나가는 시각이다.

어휘 go out 나가다, 외출하다 TV show 텔레비전 프로그램 come on 시작하다 at that time 그때 since ~이므로 around ~쯤, 대략

08 ③

W: Good afternoon, Tom. 안녕하세요, 톰.

M: Good afternoon. How are you?
안녕하세요. 잘 지냈어요?

W: I'm great. How should I cut your hair today?
저는 잘 지냈어요. 오늘은 머리를 어떻게 자를까요?

M: Take a look at this picture. 이 사진 좀 봐주세요.

W: I know him. He's a famous movie star.
저는 그 사람을 알아요. 유명한 영화배우잖아요.

M: Yeah. I love his hairstyle. Can you cut my hair the same way? 네. 저는 그의 헤어스타일을 좋아해요. 제 머리를 똑같이 잘라줄 수 있어요?

W: Sure. That won't be a problem. Have a seat in the chair. 그럼요. 문제 없어요. 의자에 앉으세요.

M: Thanks. 고마워요.

어휘 cut one's hair ~의 머리를 자르다 take a look at ~을 한번 보다 famous 유명한 the same way 똑같이 have a seat 자리에 앉다

09 ②

W: Pardon me. I'm trying to get to the public library. Where is it? 실례합니다. 제가 공립 도서관을 가려고 하는데요. 그게 어디에 있죠?

M: You need to cross the street first. You have to take a bus at the bus stop over there. 먼저 길을 건너셔야 해요. 저쪽에 있는 버스 정류장에서 버스를 타셔야 해요.

W: All right. Which bus goes to the library?
그렇군요. 어느 버스가 도서관에 가나요?

M: You should take the number seven bus. Get off the bus at Western Station. Then, take the subway.
7번 버스를 타셔야 해요. 웨스턴 역에서 버스에서 내리세요. 그런 다음, 지하철을 타세요.

W: Which subway station should I get off at?
저는 어떤 지하철역에서 내려야 하나요?

M: Go three stops to Main Street Station. After that, just walk to the library. 메인스트리트 역까지 세 정거장을 가세요. 그런 다음에 도서관까지 걸어가면 됩니다.

W: Thanks a lot for your help. 도와주셔서 정말 감사합니다.

M: It's my pleasure. 천만에요.

어휘 public library 공립 도서관 cross the street 길을 건너다 bus stop 버스 정류장 over there 저쪽에 get off 내리다

10 ①

[Phone rings.] [전화벨이 울린다.]

W: Hello. May I speak with Jim?
여보세요. 짐과 통화할 수 있을까요?

M: This is he. 전데요.

W: Hi, Jim. It's Wendy. Do you want to go to the amusement park with me today?
안녕, 짐. 나 웬디야. 오늘 나랑 같이 놀이공원에 갈래?

M: Yeah, that sounds like fun. What time shall we meet? 응, 재미있겠다. 우리 몇 시에 만날까?

W: How about going there now? 지금 가는 건 어때?

M: I'm eating lunch. Can we go there in thirty minutes?
난 점심을 먹는 중이야. 30분 후에 가도 될까?

W: Okay. That's fine. 응. 좋아.

M: Should we invite Eric, too? I can call him now and ask him. 우리, 에릭도 부를까? 내가 지금 그 애한테 전화해서 물어볼 수 있어.

W: Sure. I know he loves amusement parks.
그래. 난 에릭이 놀이공원을 좋아한다는 걸 알아.

어휘 amusement part 놀이공원 invite 초대하다

11 ⑤

M: Jane, I'm going to go jogging with Chris. Do you want to work out with us?
제인, 난 크리스랑 같이 조깅을 가려고 해. 우리랑 같이 운동할래?

W: No, thanks. 아니, 괜찮아.

M: Would you prefer to go cycling instead?
대신 자전거를 타고 싶니?

W: No. I don't really like exercising at all.
아니. 나는 정말 운동을 전혀 좋아하지 않아.

M: Why not? Do you think it's boring?
왜 안 좋아해? 운동이 지루하다고 생각하니?

W: My body always hurts after I finish exercising.
난 운동이 끝난 후에 몸이 항상 아파.

M: I see. Let's do something else together next time then. 그렇구나. 그럼, 다음에 다른 걸 같이 하자.

어휘 go jogging 조깅하러 가다 work out 운동하다(= exercise) prefer 선호하다 cycling 자전거 타기 boring 지루한 hurt 아프다 something else 다른 것

12 ⑤

W: Did you hear that Tina is moving to another country? 티나가 다른 나라로 이사 간다는 소식을 들었니?

M: Yes, I know. She's moving to Tokyo this Friday.
응, 알아. 이번 주 금요일에 도쿄로 이사 간대.

W: I'm really going to miss her. She's one of my best friends. 나는 그 애가 무척 그리울 거야. 그 애는 내 가장 친한 친구 중 한 명이잖아.

M: Yeah, I'm going to miss her, too. We often flew kites together at the park.
응, 나도 그 애가 그리울 거야. 우리는 공원에서 자주 연을 날렸어.

W: I know. Flying kites is one of her hobbies.
나도 알아. 연날리기는 그 애의 취미 중 하나지.

M: We should have a going-away party for her.
우리는 티나를 위해서 송별회를 열어줘야 해.

W: You're right. Let's talk to some of our friends about that. 네 말이 맞아. 우리 친구들 몇 명하고 그 문제에 관해 이야기해 보자.

M: Okay. We should prepare for it before Friday.
그래. 우리는 금요일 전에 송별회를 준비해야 해.

해설 Tina는 금요일에 이사를 가므로, 그 전에 송별회를 할 것이다.

어휘 move to ~로 이사하다 miss 그리워하다 fly 날리다(fly-flew-flown) kite 연 hobby 취미 going-away party 송별회

13 ②

W: Can I help you, sir? 제가 도와드릴까요, 손님?

M: Yes, please. Tomorrow is my mother's birthday. Can you recommend something for a woman in her fifties? 네. 내일이 저희 어머니의 생신이에요. 50대 여성을 위해서 추천해 주실 것이 있나요?

W: She might like this perfume.
어머님은 아마도 이 향수를 좋아하실 거예요.

M: It smells good. How much does it cost?
향기가 좋네요. 이건 얼마죠?

W: It's sixty dollars for one bottle. 한 병에 60달러예요.

M: Oh, that's too expensive for me. How about these gloves? 아, 저한테는 너무 비싸네요. 이 장갑은 얼마예요?

W: The gloves cost twenty-five dollars.
그 장갑은 25달러예요.

M: Okay, and what about the silver necklace?
알겠습니다. 그럼 은목걸이는 얼마예요?

W: It costs forty dollars. Which would you like?
그건 40달러예요. 어떤 걸 사고 싶으세요?

M: I'll take the gloves. I think she'll like them.
장갑을 살게요. 어머니가 좋아하실 것 같네요.

W: I think so as well. Let me gift-wrap them for you.
저도 그렇게 생각해요. 제가 선물 포장을 해드릴게요.

어휘 recommend 추천하다 perfume 향수 bottle 병 gloves 장갑 necklace 목걸이 as well 또한, 역시 gift-wrap 선물 포장하다

14 ②

W: Look outside. It's raining heavily.
밖을 좀 봐. 비가 많이 오네.

M: That's too bad. I'm going to the museum to meet Steve. 큰일이다. 난 스티브를 만나러 박물관에 가야 하거든.

W: How are you going to get there?
거기엔 어떻게 가려고?

M: I'm planning to take the bus. 버스를 타려고.

W: You need to take the subway instead.
넌 그 대신에 전철을 타야 할 것 같은데.

M: Why? The bus stop is closer to here than the subway station is.
왜? 버스 정류장은 지하철역보다 여기서 가까워.

W: That's true. But traffic always moves slowly in the rain. 맞아. 하지만 빗속에서는 교통이 항상 느리게 움직이잖아.

M: You're right about that. I'll take the subway then.
그건 네 말이 맞아. 그럼 전철을 탈게.

해설 'You're right about that'이라고 말하며 동의를 나타냈다.

어휘 rain heavily 폭우가 쏟아지다 museum 박물관 take (교통수단을) 타다 instead 대신에 closer 더 가까운(close-closer-closest) traffic 교통(량)

15 ④

M: What are you doing now, Jean?
지금 뭐 하고 있니, 진?

W: I'm reading this book for English class.
난 영어 수업 때문에 이 책을 읽고 있어.

M: Oh, right. I haven't started reading it yet.
아, 맞아. 난 책 읽는 걸 시작도 못 했어.

W: Why not? We have to read the book by tomorrow.
왜 안 했어? 우린 내일까지 책을 읽어야 해.

M: Are you sure about that? 그게 확실해?

W: Yes, I am. Mr. Bennett told us that in class today.
응, 확실해. 베넷 선생님이 오늘 수업에서 그렇게 말씀하셨어.

M: I'd better go to the library. I need a copy of it.
나는 도서관에 가는 게 낫겠어. 그 책 한 권이 필요해.

W: Don't worry. You can borrow mine. I'm almost finished reading it.
걱정 마. 내 책을 빌리면 돼. 난 그걸 거의 다 읽었어.

M: Great. Thanks a lot. 좋아. 고마워.

어휘 by ~까지(기한); ~ 옆에 sure 확실한 copy (책) 한 부 borrow 빌리다 mine 내 것

16 ④

W: Did you read the notice about basketball practice, son? 농구 연습에 대한 공지는 읽었니, 아들아?

M: Yes, I did. The first practice is on October twentieth. Can you take me to the gym at ten A.M. then? 네, 읽었어요. 첫 번째 연습은 10월 20일이에요. 그날 오전 10시까지 저를 농구장에 데려다 줄 수 있어요?

W: Yes, I can do that. You're going to the gym on Pine Street, right? 그럼, 그렇게 할 수 있지. 파인 스트리트에 있는 체육관으로 가는 거지, 그렇지?

M: That's right. Practice is going to finish at noon. Can you pick me up then? 맞아요. 연습은 정오에 끝날 거예요. 그때 저를 데리러 오실 수 있어요?

W: Sure. Do you need any snacks for practice?
물론이지. 연습할 때 간식이 필요하니?

M: Yes. I should bring some oranges and a sports drink. Thanks. 네. 오렌지 몇 개랑 스포츠 음료를 가져가야 할 것 같아요. 고마워요.

어휘 notice 공지 practice 연습 gym 체육관, 헬스클럽 then 그때, 그 다음에 pick somebody up ~을 (차로) 데리러 가다 snack 간식

17 ③

① W: I never knew we had a test today.
　 난 우리가 오늘 시험을 보는지 전혀 몰랐어.

　 M: Me neither. 나도 몰랐어.

② W: How do you go to your uncle's house?
　 너희 삼촌댁은 어떻게 가니?

　 M: I always take the bus. 난 항상 버스를 타.

③ W: Can you show me how to answer this problem?
　 이 문제를 어떻게 풀 수 있는지 내게 보여줄 수 있니?

　 M: No, I can't answer the phone now.
　 아니, 난 지금 전화를 받을 수 없어.

④ W: What time does your father come home?
　 너희 아버지는 몇 시에 집에 돌아오시니?

　 M: Around seven in the evening. 저녁 7시쯤이야.

⑤ W: What did you get for your birthday? 네 생일에 뭘 받았니?

　 M: Some clothes and money. 옷 몇 벌과 돈을 받았어.

어휘 have a test 시험을 보다 uncle 삼촌 answer a problem 문제를 풀다 answer the phone 전화를 받다

18 ②

W: Aren't you hungry? Why aren't you eating much for dinner? 넌 배고프지 않니? 왜 저녁을 많이 안 먹는 거니?

M: I'm trying to lose weight.
저는 체중을 줄이려고 노력 중이에요.

W: You're not overweight. Why do you want to get slimmer? 넌 과체중이 아니야. 왜 더 날씬해지고 싶은 거니?

M: My baseball coach thinks I weigh too much. He wants me to lose weight to run faster.
제 농구 감독님은 제가 몸무게가 무겁다고 생각하세요. 제가 더 빨리 뛸 수 있도록 체중을 빼는 걸 원하세요.

W: How much weight do you want to lose?
넌 체중을 얼마나 빼고 싶니?

M: I was seventy-five kilograms, but now I'm down to seventy-two kilograms. I'd like to lose six more kilograms though. 전에는 75kg이었는데 지금은 72kg까지 내려갔어요. 하지만 6kg을 더 빼고 싶어요.

W: Try jogging every day. That will help you lose weight. 매일 조깅을 해봐. 체중을 빼는 데 도움이 될 거야.

해설 72kg(현재 체중) – 6kg(추가 감량) = 66kg

어휘 lose weight 체중을 줄이다 overweight 과체중의 slim 날씬한 weigh (몸)무게가 나가다

19 ④

W: Do you have any special plans for the weekend?
주말에 무슨 특별한 계획이 있니?

M: No, I don't. What about you? 아니, 난 없어. 넌 어때?

W: My parents and I are going to the new shopping center. 우리 부모님과 나는 새로 생긴 쇼핑센터에 갈 거야.

M: Ah, I've heard about that place. What are you going to buy there?

아, 나도 그곳에 대해 들었어. 거기 가서 뭐 살 거야?

W: I need some clothes, and my parents want a new refrigerator.
난 옷이 몇 벌 필요하고, 우리 부모님은 새로운 냉장고를 원하셔.

M: Is it far away? How long will it take to get there?
그게 멀리 있니? 거기 가는 데 얼마나 걸려?

W: It's about an hour away from here.
여기서 한 시간 정도 거리야.

① No, I've never been there before.
아니, 나는 전에 그곳에 가본 적이 없어.

② Every store there is having a sale.
거기 있는 모든 상점이 세일 중이야.

③ Yes, it opens at ten in the morning.
맞아, 거기는 오전 10시에 문을 열어.

④ It's about an hour away from here.
여기서 한 시간 정도 거리야.

⑤ There are more than 200 stores in it.
거기에는 200개 이상의 상점이 있어.

어휘 refrigerator 냉장고 far away 멀리 떨어진 have a sale 세일을 하고 있다

20 ①

W: Sarah is going to a park to meet her friend. She takes the bus and gets off after seven stops. She walks for a while, but she thinks she is lost. She sees a policeman, so she asks him for directions. The policeman tells her to take a right at the light and to walk straight for five minutes. Sarah doesn't know the area well, so she is not sure about the directions. In this case, what would Sarah most likely say to the policeman?

사라는 그녀의 친구를 만나기 위해 공원에 가는 중이다. 그녀는 버스를 타고 일곱 정거장 후에 내린다. 그녀는 잠시 걷지만, 길을 잃었다고 생각한다. 그녀는 경찰관을 보고, 그에게 방향을 묻는다. 경찰관은 그녀에게 신호등에서 우회전해서 5분 동안 곧장 걸어가라고 말한다. 사라는 그 지역을 잘 알지 못해서 방향을 확신할 수 없다. 이 상황에서, 사라는 경찰관에게 뭐라고 말하겠는가?

Sarah: Could you repeat that one more time, please?
한 번만 더 말씀해 주시겠어요?

① Could you repeat that one more time, please?
한 번만 더 말씀해 주시겠어요?

② Yes, I'm going there to meet my friend.
네, 저는 친구를 만나러 그곳에 가는 중이에요.

③ Thanks for your help. I appreciate it.
도와주셔서 감사합니다. 정말 고맙습니다.

④ Okay, so I'll take a left at the light.
알겠어요, 그러니까 신호등에서 왼쪽으로 갈게요.

⑤ How far away is it by bus?
그곳은 버스로는 얼마나 걸리나요?

어휘 get off (교통수단에서) 내리다 stop 정거장 for a while

잠시 동안 be lost 길을 잃다 policeman 경찰관 direction 방향, 길 straight 똑바로, 곧장 area 지역 repeat 반복하다, 되풀이하다 appreciate 감사하다 far (거리가) 먼

01 ①	02 ⑤	03 ②	04 ③	05 ①
06 ②	07 ④	08 ⑤	09 ②	10 ②
11 ①	12 ③	13 ③	14 ①	15 ⑤
16 ③	17 ①	18 ⑤	19 ④	20 ①

01 ①

W: I'd like everyone to draw a picture right now. First, draw a large triangle. Inside the triangle, draw a circle. Be sure that the circle touches all three sides of the triangle. After that, I want you to draw two squares inside the circle. One square should be on top of the other.

여러분 지금 그림을 그리세요. 첫째, 큰 삼각형을 그리세요. 삼각형 안에는 원 하나를 그리세요. 그 원이 삼각형의 세 변에 닿도록 하세요. 그 다음에, 원 안에 두 개의 정사각형을 그리세요. 한 개의 정사각형이 다른 정사각형의 위에 있어야 합니다.

어휘 draw 그리다 triangle 삼각형 inside 안쪽에 circle 원 touch 닿다, 건드리다 square 정사각형

02 ⑤

W: Happy new year, everybody. It's New Year's Eve today, and it's time for the updated weather forecast. It's afternoon now, and the temperature is starting to go down. It's still sunny, but it will be cloudy and windy this evening. On New Year's Day, we're going to get lots of snow. The day after, it will clear up and be sunny again. But there will be cold temperatures all week long.

모두 새해 복 많이 받으세요. 오늘은 섣달 그믐이고, 최신 일기예보를 알려드릴 시간입니다. 현재는 오후인데, 기온이 떨어지기 시작했습니다. 아직 해가 나 있지만, 오늘 저녁이 되면 구름이 끼고 바람이 불겠습니다. 새해 첫날에는 눈이 많이 오겠습니다. 그 다음 날은 날씨가 개고 다시 화창해지겠습니다. 하지만 일주일 내내 기온이 낮을 것으로 보입니다.

어휘 new year's day 새해 첫날 new year's eve 섣달 그믐, 새해 전날 temperature 기온 go down 떨어지다 clear up (날씨가) 개다 all week long 일주일 내내

03 ②

W: Can I help you with something?
제가 무엇을 도와드릴까요?

M: Yes. I found this bag at the park.
네. 제가 공원에서 이 가방을 발견했어요.

W: Where in the park did you find it?
공원 어디에서 그걸 발견하셨나요?

M: It was on a bench. 벤치 위에 있었어요.

W: Did you see anyone leave it there?
누군가 그곳에 가방을 두고 가는 것을 보셨나요?

M: No, I didn't. I saw it when I arrived at the park. Half an hour later, it was still there.
아니요, 못 봤어요. 제가 공원에 도착했을 때 가방을 봤어요. 30분이 지난 후에도 가방은 계속 그곳에 있었어요.

W: Okay. Thanks for bringing it here. We'll try to return it to its owner. 알겠습니다. 가방을 이곳으로 가져와 주셔서 감사합니다. 가방을 주인에게 돌려줄 수 있도록 노력하겠습니다.

M: All right. Have a great day, Officer.
알겠습니다. 좋은 하루 보내세요, 경관님.

해설 남자의 마지막 말에 있는 'Officer'는 경찰관에 대한 호칭이다.

어휘 find 찾다(find-found-found) park 공원 leave 놓다, 두다 half an hour 30분 still 여전히 return 돌려주다, 돌아오다 owner 주인

04 ③

M: This place is really crowded.
이곳은 정말 붐비는구나.

W: Yeah, everyone wants to enjoy the beautiful weather. 응, 모두가 좋은 날씨를 즐기고 싶어하는구나.

M: It is a great day. And the water is so calm, too.
정말 날씨가 좋아. 그리고 물도 정말로 고요해.

W: Do you want to go swimming? 넌 수영하러 가고 싶니?

M: Not now. I want to lie here on the sand.
지금은 아니야. 난 여기 모래 위에 눕고 싶어.

W: Okay. I'm going to go into the water.
알겠어. 나는 물에 들어갈 거야.

M: Sounds good. I'll join you in a few minutes.
좋아. 몇 분만 있다가 나도 갈게.

해설 'lie here on the sand'가 있기 때문에 수영장이 아닌 해변이 정답이다.

어휘 place 장소 crowded 붐비는 calm 고요한, 차분한 lie 눕다 sand 모래 join 함께하다

05 ①

M: I can't believe it. I got the worst grade in math class.
정말 믿을 수가 없어. 난 수학 시간에 가장 안 좋은 점수를 받았어.

W: Don't be upset. These things happen sometimes.
속상해 하지 마. 그런 일은 가끔 일어나기 마련이야.

M: But I always get bad grades in math. I don't think I'll ever get better. 하지만 난 항상 수학에서 나쁜 점수를 받아. 아무리 해도 더 잘하지 못할 것 같아.

W: You shouldn't think that way. Think positively.
그렇게 생각하지 마. 긍정적으로 생각해 봐.

M: Why do you say that? 왜 그렇게 말하니?

W: You can learn from your mistakes. Keep studying hard, and you will definitely get better. 넌 실수를 통해 배울 수 있어. 계속 열심히 공부하면 분명히 나아질 거야.

M: Yeah, I guess you're right. I'll do what you suggest. 그래. 네 말이 맞는 것 같아. 네가 제안한 대로 해볼게.

해설 여자의 조언에 남자는 동의했다.

어휘 worst 가장 안 좋은(bad-worse-worst) grade 성적 upset 화난, 속상한 sometimes 가끔 get better 향상되다, 나아지다 positively 긍정적으로 mistake 실수 keep -ing 계속해서 ~하다 definitely 분명히 suggest 제안하다

06 ②

W: In spring, I planted some sunflowers outside my house. I took very good care of them. I was so excited to see them come up above the ground. But they grew so slowly. It was really disappointing to me. However, I was patient, so I waited. I kept taking good care of the flowers. Suddenly, they began to grow quickly. Now, they are taller than me, and the flowers are huge. I'm so pleased with how well they have grown.

저는 봄에 집 밖에 해바라기를 심었습니다. 저는 해바라기를 아주 잘 보살폈습니다. 땅 위로 올라오는 꽃을 보는 것이 정말 신이 났습니다. 하지만 그건 너무 느리게 자랐습니다. 저는 너무나 실망스러웠죠. 하지만 저는 참을성을 갖고 기다렸습니다. 계속해서 그것들을 잘 보살폈습니다. 갑자기 해바라기가 빠르게 자라기 시작했습니다. 이제 그건 제 키보다 크게 자랐고, 꽃도 아주 큽니다. 저는 해바라기가 잘 자라주어서 너무 기쁩니다.

해설 해바라기가 자람에 따라 여자의 심정은 실망에서 기쁨으로 바뀌었다.

어휘 plant (식물을) 심다 sunflower 해바라기 take care of ~을 돌보다 come up (땅을 뚫고) 나오다 above ~위로 ground 땅 slowly 느리게 disappointing 실망스러운 patient 참을성 있는 suddenly 갑자기 grow 자라다(grow-grew-grown) quickly 빠르게 huge 큰, 거대한 pleased 기쁜 satisfied 만족한 disappointed 실망한 worried 걱정하는 upset 화난

07 ④

[Telephone rings.] [전화벨이 울린다.]

M: Hello. 여보세요.

W: Hello. Who am I speaking with?
여보세요. 전화 받으시는 분은 누구시죠?

M: I'm sorry. Who are you? 죄송합니다. 누구세요?

W: You called me an hour ago, but I missed the call.
당신이 한 시간 전에 저에게 전화를 했는데 제가 전화를 못 받았어요.

M: Oh, do you live at forty-nine Watson Street?
아, 왓슨 스트리트 49번지에 살고 계시죠?

W: That's correct. 맞습니다.

M: I'm a deliveryman. I have a package for you.
저는 배달원입니다. 제가 당신에게 드릴 소포가 있어요.

W: That's great. I am home now, so you can come here anytime. 좋은 소식이네요. 저는 지금 집에 있으니까 언제든지 오셔도 됩니다.

M: Thank you. 감사합니다.

어휘 miss a call 전화를 받지 못하다 correct 정확한, 맞는 deliveryman 배달원 package 소포 anytime 언제든지

08 ⑤

W: What's wrong, Dave? 무슨 일이니, 데이브?

M: I think I failed my history test today.
오늘 역사 시험을 통과하지 못한 것 같아.

W: I'm sorry. Was the test hard? 안됐구나. 시험이 어려웠니?

M: Yes, it was really hard for me. 응, 나에게는 정말 어려웠어.

W: I can help you the next time. History is my favorite subject.
다음에는 내가 널 도와줄게. 역사는 내가 제일 좋아하는 과목이야.

M: I like history, too. But I studied the wrong information.
나도 역사를 좋아해. 하지만 난 잘못된 내용을 공부했어.

W: What do you mean by that? 그게 무슨 말이니?

M: The test was on chapter two, but I studied chapter three. 시험은 2장에서 나왔는데, 나는 3장을 공부했어.

W: Oh, you need to be careful the next time.
아, 넌 다음에는 좀 더 조심해야겠구나.

어휘 fail a test 시험에 낙제하다 hard 어려운 subject 과목 wrong 잘못된 information 정보, 내용 careful 신중한, 조심하는

09 ②

M: Tomorrow is Jane's birthday. We should buy her a present.
내일이 제인의 생일이야. 우리는 그녀에게 생일 선물을 사줘야 해.

W: That's a good idea. Why don't we buy her a dress? I saw a good one at the department store.
그거 좋은 생각이다. 그녀에게 옷을 사주는 게 어때? 내가 백화점에서 예쁜 옷을 봤어.

M: How much did it cost? 가격이 얼마였니?

W: The tag said it was eighty dollars. But it's on sale, so it's only fifty dollars now. 가격표에는 80달러라고 되어 있었어. 하지만 할인 중이라 지금은 고작 50달러야.

M: That's a lot of money. But we could buy it for her together. 그것도 무척 비싸네. 하지만 우리가 같이 살 수 있겠다.

W: Yeah. Let's each pay half. 응. 각자 절반씩 내자.

해설 할인가인 50달러를 절반씩 내면 25달러이다.

어휘 buy somebody a present ~에게 선물을 사주다 dress 옷, 드레스 department store 백화점 cost 비용이 들다 tag 가격표, 상표 on sale 할인 중인 each 각각 pay 지불하다 half 절반, 반값

10 ②

W: Good morning. Is this your first time at Hamilton Park? 안녕하세요. 해밀턴 공원에는 처음 오셨나요?

M: Yes, it is. I'm here to go jogging.
네, 처음입니다. 이곳에 조깅하러 왔어요.

W: There are many great places for jogging.
조깅하기에 아주 좋은 장소들이 많이 있어요.

M: Really? Where do most people do that?
정말요? 대부분의 사람들이 어디서 조깅하죠?

W: A lot of them run on the trails in the park.
많은 사람들이 공원 안에 있는 산책로를 따라서 뛰어요.

M: How about you? 당신은 어때요?

W: I prefer to run by the lake. It's very nice there.
저는 호숫가에서 달리는 걸 좋아해요. 거기가 굉장히 좋아요.

M: Thanks. I think I'll do that.
고마워요. 저도 그렇게 해야겠어요.

어휘 trail 산책로, 오솔길 prefer 선호하다 by ~옆에 lake 호수

11 ①

W: According to the weather forecast, it will be sunny today. 일기예보대로라면, 오늘은 날씨가 화창할 거야.

M: That's good news. We can go on a picnic like we planned.
좋은 소식이네. 우리가 계획한 대로 소풍을 갈 수 있겠어.

W: That's right. Did we buy everything we need?
맞아. 우리가 필요한 것을 다 샀니?

M: I think so. We have sandwiches, potato chips, and sodas.
그런 것 같아. 우리는 샌드위치, 감자칩, 그리고 탄산음료가 있어.

W: I have some paper plates and napkins. And Tina is going to bring some cookies for dessert.
나한테는 종이 접시와 냅킨이 있어. 그리고 티나가 디저트로 쿠키를 좀 가져올 거야.

M: It seems like we have everything already then. Let's go. 그럼 우리는 이미 모든 걸 가지고 있는 것 같네. 출발하자.

어휘 according to ~에 따르면 weather forecast 일기예보 go on a picnic 소풍을 가다 paper plate 종이 접시 napkin 냅킨, 휴지

12 ③

W: Did you read this article in the newspaper? It's about Eric Lee. He's a famous businessman from Korea. 신문에 난 이 기사를 읽었니? 에릭 리에 관한 기사였어. 그는 한국 출신의 유명한 사업가야.

M: No, I didn't read it. What information does it have about him?
아니, 읽지 않았어. 그 사람에 관한 어떤 정보가 실려 있니?

W: He is only twenty-five, but he owns three companies.
그는 고작 25살밖에 되지 않았는데, 세 개의 회사를 가지고 있어.

M: That's impressive. 정말 인상적이구나.

W: He can speak three languages, too. He knows Korean, English, and Japanese. 그는 또 세 개의 언어를

구사할 수 있어. 한국어, 영어, 그리고 일본어를 할 수 있어.

M: Wow. I guess he studied hard at school.
와. 그는 학교 다닐 때 정말 열심히 공부했을 거야.

어휘 article 기사 newspaper 신문 businessman 사업가 information 정보, 내용 own 소유하다 impressive 인상적인, 감명 깊은 language 언어 guess 추측하다

13 ③

W: Hi, Kevin. It's Wendy. 안녕, 케빈. 나 웬디야.

M: Hi, Wendy. How are you doing? 안녕, 웬디. 잘 지냈니?

W: I'm okay, but I have a problem with my printer.
잘 지냈어, 하지만 내 프린터에 문제가 있어.

M: What's going on? 무슨 일이야?

W: It has a paper jam. I don't know how to fix it.
종이가 걸려. 난 그걸 어떻게 고쳐야 하는지 모르겠어.

M: It's really easy. First, you need to lift up the lid of the printer. Then, you should be able to see some paper in it. 그건 정말 쉬워. 처음에 너는 프린터 덮개를 들어올려야 해. 그리고 나면, 그 안에 있는 종이를 볼 수 있을 거야.

W: What should I do with the paper?
내가 종이를 어떻게 해야 하니?

M: Take it out. Then, the printer should work well again. 그걸 꺼내야 해. 그리고 나면, 프린터가 다시 작동할 거야.

W: Thanks a lot for your help. 도와줘서 정말 고마워.

어휘 printer 프린터 paper jam 종이 걸림 fix 고치다 lift up 들어 올리다 lid 뚜껑, 덮개 work 작동하다

14 ①

M: Janet, did you have a good time at your aunt's birthday party?
재닛, 너희 이모 생일 파티에서 즐거운 시간을 보냈니?

W: I did. We went to a restaurant and celebrated her birthday there.
응. 우리는 음식점에 가서 이모의 생신을 축하했어.

M: Wow. I bet she was really happy.
우와. 이모가 정말로 행복하셨겠다.

W: Yeah. How about you? Did you go to the beach?
응. 너는 어땠니? 바닷가에 갔니?

M: We planned to go there, but we had to cancel our plans. My brother had a bike accident.
우리는 바닷가에 가려고 했는데, 계획을 취소해야 했어. 우리 형이 자전거 사고가 났거든.

W: Oh, no. Is he all right? 아, 이런. 형은 괜찮니?

M: My parents took him to the hospital, and I visited him in the hospital. He's getting better now. 부모님이 형을 병원에 데리고 갔고 나도 형을 보러 병원에 갔어. 그는 지금 회복 중이야.

해설 ②, ⑤는 여자가 한 일이며, ④는 남자의 취소된 계획이므로 오답이다.

어휘 aunt 이모; 고모, 숙모 celebrate 축하하다 cancel 취소하다 bike accident 자전거 사고 get better 회복하다, (상태가) 좋아지

다

15 ⑤

① Tony studies less than Greg.
토니는 그레그보다 공부를 적게 한다.
② Amy studies the same amount as Greg.
에이미는 그레그만큼 공부한다.
③ Mina studies the most. 미나가 가장 많이 공부한다.
④ Greg studies more than Tony.
그레그는 토니보다 공부를 많이 한다.
⑤ Amy studies more than Tony and Mina.
에이미는 토니와 미나보다 공부를 많이 한다.

어휘 less 더 적게(little-less-least) more 더 많이(much/many-more-most) amount 분량

16 ③

① M: May I sit in this seat? 이 자리에 앉아도 될까요?
W: Sorry, but that seat is already taken.
죄송합니다만, 그 자리는 이미 찼어요.
② M: How many pencils are in your pencil case?
네 필통에는 연필이 몇 자루나 있니?
W: None, but I have a few pens.
하나도 없고 펜만 몇 자루 있어.
③ M: I'm so sleepy right now. 난 지금 너무 졸려.
W: I'm glad I just ate dinner.
난 방금 저녁을 먹어서 기분이 좋아.
④ M: Can I have your number?
당신의 전화번호를 알 수 있을까요?
W: Sure. It's six oh four, three oh four three.
물론이죠. 604-3043 입니다.
⑤ M: Have you ever taken the subway to get there?
그곳에 가려고 지하철을 타본 적이 있니?
W: Sure. It takes about fifteen minutes.
네. 약 15분 정도 걸립니다.

어휘 seat 좌석 already 이미 pencil case 필통 none 아무도, 하나도 sleepy 졸린 eat 먹다(eat-ate-eaten)

17 ①

W: Tim, which student is the tallest in our class?
팀, 우리 반에서 누가 제일 키가 크니?
M: Let me think, Sue. Joe, Paul, and Mary are all very tall. 생각 좀 해볼게, 수. 조, 폴, 그리고 메리는 모두 키가 커.
W: But you're taller than Paul, aren't you?
하지만 네가 폴보다 키가 크지, 그렇지 않니?
M: Yes. That's right. 응. 맞아.
W: Are you taller than Joe? 네가 조보다 키가 크니?
M: No, I'm not. He's a bit taller than me.
아니, 그렇지 않아. 조가 나보다 조금 더 커.
W: And Joe is also taller than Mary, isn't he?
그리고 조가 메리보다 더 크지, 그렇지 않니?
M: Yes, that's correct. 응, 맞아.

해설 남자(Tim)는 Paul보다 키가 크고 Joe보다 키가 작다. 그리고 Joe는 Mary보다 더 크므로 Joe가 반에서 가장 크다.

어휘 tallest 가장 키가 큰(tall-taller-tallest) a bit 약간, 조금 correct 정확한

18 ⑤

M: Do you have a lot of things to do today?
넌 오늘 해야 할 일이 많니?
W: Yes, I do. I need to feed my cat in the morning and then go to the hair salon. 응, 많아. 아침에는 고양이 밥을 줘야 하고, 그 다음에는 미용실에 가야 해.
M: Don't you have a doctor's appointment, too?
병원 예약도 있지 않니?
W: That's right. I'm going there after I have lunch with Sue. Then, I'll go to the post office to mail a package. 맞아. 수랑 같이 점심을 먹은 후에 갈 거야. 그리고 나서 소포를 부치러 우체국에 갈 거야.
M: Do you have time to go to the library?
도서관에 갈 시간은 있니?
W: Not today. I can go there tomorrow.
오늘은 없어. 내일 갈 수 있어.

어휘 feed 먹이를 주다 hair salon 미용실 doctor's appointment 병원 진료 예약 post office 우체국 mail 우편으로 보내다 package 소포 library 도서관

19 ④

W: It's almost dinnertime. Are you ready to eat?
곧 저녁 먹을 시간이야. 저녁 먹을 준비는 됐니?
M: I'll eat later. I'm a bit busy now.
나중에 먹을 거예요. 지금은 좀 바빠요.
W: What are you doing? 넌 뭘 하고 있니?
M: I'm writing a book report for English class.
영어 수업을 위한 독후감을 쓰고 있어요.
W: When do you have to give it to the teacher?
선생님께 언제 그걸 제출해야 하니?
M: It's due tomorrow. 내일까지예요.
W: Tomorrow? Are you almost finished?
내일? 거의 다 끝냈니?
M: No, I just started a while ago.
아니요, 방금 전에 시작했어요.
W: Why didn't you start working on it earlier?
왜 더 일찍 시작하지 않았니?
M: I thought I could finish it soon.
그걸 빨리 끝낼 수 있을 거라고 생각했어요.

① It's a ten-page report. 그건 10쪽 분량의 보고서예요.
② I'm looking forward to dinner.
저는 저녁식사를 기대하고 있어요.
③ It's still only 6:00 in the evening.
아직 저녁 6시밖에 안 됐어요.
④ I thought I could finish it soon.
그걸 빨리 끝낼 수 있을 거라고 생각했어요.

⑤ Yes, the teacher needs it tomorrow.
네, 선생님께서 내일 그걸 필요로 하실 거예요.

어휘 dinnertime 저녁식사 시간 ready 준비된 later 나중에 a bit 약간 book report 독후감 due 마감인 a while ago 조금 전에 earlier 좀 더 일찍(early-earlier-earliest)

20 ①

M: Julie and her little sister are going to the park. They walk from their house to the park. Before they get to the park, they have to cross the street. It's a big street, and there are many cars on it. Julie's little sister is excited to go to the park, so she starts running toward it. However, the light in the crosswalk has not turned green yet. In this situation, what would Julie most likely say to her little sister?

줄리와 여동생은 공원에 가는 길이다. 그들은 집에서 공원으로 걸어 간다. 그들이 공원에 도착하기 전에 그들은 도로를 건너야 한다. 큰 도로이고, 차가 많이 있다. 줄리의 여동생은 공원 간다는 사실에 신이 나서 공원을 향해서 달리기 시작한다. 하지만 횡단보도의 신호등 은 아직 녹색불로 바뀌지 않았다. 이런 상황에서 줄리는 여동생에게 뭐라고 말할 것인가?

Julie: Don't cross the street yet. 아직 길을 건너지 마.

① Don't cross the street yet. 아직 길을 건너지 마.
② Please stop bothering me so much.
   나를 귀찮게 하지 말아줘.
③ We're going to have fun at the park.
   우리는 공원에서 재미있는 시간을 보낼 거야.
④ I think the park is closed for the day.
   공원은 오늘 문을 닫은 것 같아.
⑤ How about playing a game at the park?
   공원에서 게임을 하는 게 어때?

어휘 get to ~에 도착하다 cross the street 길을 건너다 excited 신이 난, 흥분한 toward ~을 향해 crosswalk 횡단보도 turn 바뀌다 bother 귀찮게 하다, 성가시게 하다 for the day 그날 은, 오늘은

08회 실전모의고사
본문 p.88-89

01 ④	02 ⑤	03 ⑤	04 ①	05 ②
06 ④	07 ③	08 ③	09 ⑤	10 ④
11 ④	12 ①	13 ①	14 ②	15 ①
16 ①	17 ①	18 ④	19 ⑤	20 ⑤

01 ④

W: Good evening. Can I help you find something?
안녕하세요. 제가 찾는 걸 도와드릴까요?
M: Yes, please. I'd like to buy a jacket.

네, 도와주세요. 저는 재킷을 사고 싶어요.
W: How about this jacket with a hood? It's a popular item these days.
모자가 달린 이 재킷은 어때요? 요새 제일 인기 있는 품목이에요.
M: No, thanks. That's not my style.
아니요, 괜찮아요. 그건 제 취향이 아니에요.
W: Would you like this jacket with two pockets on it?
주머니 두 개가 달려 있는 이 재킷은 어때요?
M: No. I want a jacket without any pockets. Oh, this jacket with fur around the neck looks great.
아뇨. 저는 주머니가 없는 재킷을 원해요. 아, 목에 털이 달린 이 재 킷이 멋지네요.
W: Good choice. It's perfect for cold weather.
훌륭한 선택이세요. 그건 추운 날씨에 딱이죠.
M: I love it. I'll take it. 이게 좋네요. 이걸로 살게요.

어휘 hood (외투에 달린) 모자 popular 인기 있는 item 품목, 물 품 pocket 주머니 without ~이 없는 fur 털 perfect 완벽한

02 ⑤

W: If you have plans to go outside tomorrow, you'd better do that in the morning. The morning will be bright and sunny. However, around one in the afternoon, it's going to rain heavily. The rain will stop in the evening, but it's going to be quite cool the rest of the night. Expect heavy fog the next morning. In addition, the weather will get warmer throughout the day.

내일 외출하실 계획이 있으시다면, 아침에 나가시는 것이 좋겠습니 다. 아침에는 밝고 맑겠습니다. 하지만 오후 1시쯤에는 비가 많이 내리기 시작하겠습니다. 비는 저녁에 그치겠지만 비가 그친 밤에는 무척 선선해지겠습니다. 그 다음 날 아침에는 짙은 안개가 예상됩니 다. 그리고 날씨는 하루 종일 점점 따뜻해지겠습니다.

어휘 outside 밖에 bright 밝은 rain heavily 폭우가 내리다 quite 꽤 cool 시원한, 선선한 the rest of the night 남은 밤 (시 간) expect 예상하다 in addition 게다가, 또한 warmer 더 따뜻한 (warm-warmer-warmest) throughout the day 하루 종일

03 ⑤

W: Steve, I haven't seen you in a while.
스티브, 오랜만에 보는구나.
M: I've been busy. I've been practicing by myself.
난 그동안 바빴어. 나 혼자 연습하는 중이야.
W: What have you been doing? 뭘 연습하고 있니?
M: Playing the piano. I'd love to become a pianist in the future. 피아노 치는 거. 난 앞으로 피아니스트가 되고 싶어.
W: Are you serious? I thought you wanted to be a basketball player.
정말이니? 나는 네가 농구선수가 되고 싶어한다고 생각했어.
M: That would be fun, but I don't think I'm good enough. 그것도 재미있을 것 같은데, 난 내가 충분히 잘한다고 생각하지 않아.

W: Be sure to practice singing, too. That might be helpful. 노래도 연습해 봐. 그것은 도움이 될 거야.

M: Thanks for the advice. 충고 고마워.

어휘 in a while 오랜만에 practice 연습하다 by oneself 스스로, 혼자 pianist 피아니스트 in the future 앞으로, 미래에 serious 진지한, 심각한 good enough 충분한, 만족스러운 helpful 도움이 되는 advice 조언

04 ①

M: Do we have reservations for dinner tomorrow?
우리는 내일 저녁식사를 예약했나요?

W: Yes, and we're going to see an opera after that.
네, 그리고 우리는 저녁을 먹은 후에 오페라를 보러 갈 거예요.

M: What time does everything begin?
그 모든 게 몇 시에 시작하죠?

W: We'll have dinner at six P.M. And the show starts at seven thirty P.M. 우리는 오후 6시에 저녁을 먹을 거예요. 그리고 공연은 오후 7시 30분에 시작해요.

M: How long will it take to get to the restaurant?
식당까지 가는데 얼마나 걸리죠?

W: It will take around forty-five minutes.
45분 정도 걸릴 거예요.

M: We'd better leave an hour early just in case.
만약의 경우에 대비해서 1시간 일찍 떠나는 게 좋겠어요.

W: All right. I can be ready to go at five.
알겠어요. 5시에 떠날 준비를 할 수 있어요.

M: Great. I can't wait. 좋아요. 빨리 가고 싶네요.

해설 두 사람은 5시에 출발해서 5시 45분에 식당에 도착하고, 6시부터 저녁을 먹고 7시 30분 공연을 볼 것이다.

어휘 reservation 예약 opera 오페라 leave 떠나다 show 공연, 쇼 just in case 만일에 대비해서 I can't wait 빨리 하고 싶다

05 ②

W: Did you enjoy the amusement park?
놀이공원은 재미있었니?

M: Yes, it was great. Why didn't you go with us?
응, 정말 재미있었어. 넌 왜 우리랑 같이 안 갔니?

W: I wanted to stay home to get some rest.
난 집에서 쉬고 싶었어.

M: I see. Well, guess what happened while we were there?
그랬구나. 음, 우리가 거기 있는 동안 무슨 일이 있었는지 알아?

W: I don't know. What? 모르겠어. 뭔데?

M: They were filming a movie at the amusement park.
놀이공원에서 영화를 찍고 있었어.

W: A movie? Seriously? 영화? 정말이야?

M: Yeah, and we got to be in a scene.
응. 그리고 우리는 한 장면에 등장하게 됐어.

W: No way. I wish I had gone there with you.
말도 안돼. 나도 너희랑 같이 갔으면 좋았을 텐데.

해설 'I wish I had gone there with you.'는 가정법 과거완료

문장이며, 과거 사실과 반대되는 일을 소망할 때 사용된다.

어휘 amusement park 놀이공원 stay 머무르다 get rest 휴식을 취하다 guess 추측하다 happen 일어나다 while ~하는 동안에 film a movie 영화를 찍다 seriously 진지하게, 진심으로 no way (놀랐을 때) 말도 안돼; 절대로 안돼 regretful 후회하는 proud 자랑스러운

06 ④

M: Hello, everyone. Thank you for shopping at Sullivan's Department Store. A customer just turned in a bag. It's a black leather bag with a cellphone and some cash in it. If you lost your bag, please talk to a salesperson right now. The salesperson will help you come down here and get your bag back.

안녕하세요, 여러분. 설리번 백화점에서 쇼핑해 주셔서 감사합니다. 고객 한 분이 방금 전에 가방을 돌려주셨습니다. 검정색 블랙 가죽 가방이며, 안에 휴대폰과 약간의 돈이 들어 있습니다. 가방을 잃어버리셨다면, 지금 바로 판매원에게 말씀해 주세요. 판매원이 여러분을 이곳으로 모시고 와서 가방을 찾을 수 있도록 도울 것입니다.

어휘 customer 손님 turn in ~을 돌려주다, 반납하다 leather 가죽 cash 현금 lose 잃어버리다(lose-lost-lost) salesperson 점원, 판매원

07 ③

W: What do you like doing in your free time, Fred?
넌 여가 시간에 뭘 하는 걸 좋아하니, 프레드?

M: I love spending time in the water. Swimming and snorkeling are lots of fun. 나는 물속에서 시간을 보내는 걸 좋아해. 수영하고 스노클링은 정말 재미있어.

W: I enjoy swimming, too. I go to the pool a lot, but I have never gone snorkeling before. 나도 수영을 좋아해. 난 수영장에 많이 가지만 스노클링은 전에 해본 적이 없어.

M: Do you want me to teach you? 내가 널 가르쳐 줄까?

W: Can you do that? That would be great.
그럴 수 있어? 그러면 정말 좋겠어.

M: Sure. We can go to the beach on Saturday.
물론이지. 우리는 토요일에 해변에 갈 수 있어.

어휘 free time 여가 시간 snorkeling 스노클링 pool 수영장

08 ③

W: Joe, it's nice to see you. What have you been doing lately? 조, 만나서 반가워. 최근에 뭐하고 지냈니?

M: I was at summer camp all last week. I had a great time there. 난 지난주 내내 여름 캠프에 있었어. 거기서 아주 좋은 시간을 보냈지.

W: That's good. 좋았겠다.

M: What are you doing here? 넌 여기서 뭘 하는 거니?

W: I'm going to do some shopping. Would you like to go to some stores with me?

쇼핑을 좀 하려고 해. 나랑 같이 가게를 좀 다닐래?

M: I'd love to, but I can't. My friend Jina is coming soon. We're going to see a movie. 그러고 싶은데, 안 돼. 내 친구 지나가 곧 올 거야. 우리는 영화를 볼 거야.

W: That sounds like fun. Let's have lunch together later. 재미있겠다. 나중에 같이 점심 먹자.

해설 남자가 한 일, 여자가 할 일, 그리고 여자가 남자에게 제안하는 일과 헷갈리지 말아야 한다.

어휘 lately 최근에 all last week 지난주 내내 do shopping 쇼핑을 하다, 물건을 사다 see a movie 영화를 보다

09 ⑤

W: Good evening, sir. 안녕하세요, 손님.

M: Hello. I'd like to return this DVD I rented. 안녕하세요. 제가 빌린 이 DVD를 반납하려고 해요.

W: No problem. How did you like the movie? 알겠습니다. 영화는 어떠셨어요?

M: It was nice. My entire family liked it. 좋았어요. 저희 모든 가족이 좋아했답니다.

W: That's good to hear. Hmm... It looks like you're returning this DVD late. You needed to return it three days ago. 그 말씀을 들으니 좋네요. 음, 이 DVD는 반납을 늦게 하신 것 같은데요. 손님은 3일 전에 반납하셨어야 해요.

M: Three days ago? Really? 3일 전이요? 정말요?

W: Yes. So you need to pay a late fee. 네. 그래서 연체료를 내셔야 합니다.

M: How much does that cost? 그건 얼마죠?

W: It's two dollars per day. And you have to pay a fine for three days. 하루에 2달러예요. 그리고 손님은 3일치에 대한 벌금을 내셔야 합니다.

M: Okay. Here's the money. 알겠어요. 여기 있어요.

어휘 return 반납하다 rent 빌리다 entire 전체의 pay 지불하다 late fee 연체료 per ~마다, ~당 fine 벌금

10 ④

W: I'd like to buy a new pair of shoes. They need to be jogging shoes since I run a lot. I wear a size seven shoe, and I don't want to spend more than sixty dollars on them. They need to be at the store now since I have to wear them tomorrow morning when I go running.

저는 새 신발을 사고 싶어요. 제가 많이 달리기 때문에, 조깅화여야 해요. 저는 사이즈가 7인 신발을 신고, 신발에 60달러 이상은 쓰고 싶지 않아요. 내일 아침에 달리기를 하러 나갈 때 신어야 하니까 새 신발은 지금 가게에 있어야 해요.

어휘 a pair of 한 쌍의, 한 켤레의 jogging shoes 조깅화 since ~때문에, ~이므로

11 ④

M: I'm sorry I'm late. How is the game going?

늦어서 미안해. 경기는 어떻게 되고 있니?

W: Have a seat. You've missed an exciting game. 앉아. 넌 아주 흥미진진한 경기를 놓쳤어.

M: Oh, yeah? That's too bad. What's the score? 아, 그래? 정말 아쉽네. 점수는 어떻게 돼?

W: It's four to three. 4대 3이야.

M: Who's winning? 누가 이기고 있어?

W: Our school's team is. Jeff Baker hit a homerun a few minutes ago. 우리 학교 팀이 이기고 있어. 제프 베이커가 몇 분 전에 홈런을 쳤어.

M: Yeah? I can't believe I missed it. 그래? 내가 그걸 놓쳤다는 게 믿어지지 않네.

W: You should have seen it. It went really far. 넌 그걸 봐야 했어. 공이 정말 멀리 갔어.

해설 두 사람은 야구 경기장에 있다.

어휘 have a seat 자리에 앉다 miss 놓치다 exciting 흥미진진한, 재미있는 score 점수 hit a homerun 홈런을 치다 far (거리가) 먼

12 ①

M: How do you feel today, Cindy? 오늘은 기분이 어때, 신디?

W: I'm doing much better than I was. I think I'm getting over my cold. 예전보다는 훨씬 나아. 감기가 낫고 있는 것 같아.

M: That's good to hear. 그 말을 들으니 다행이다.

W: I had to stay in bed for almost a week. 난 거의 한 주 동안이나 침대에 누워 있어야만 했어.

M: I bet that was hard. 정말 힘들었겠다.

W: It was. I feel like going out and playing at the park. 그랬어. 난 나가서 공원에서 놀고 싶어.

M: Don't do that. You're still not well. You can go for a walk if you really want to be outside. Just make sure you put on a warm jacket. 그럼 안돼. 넌 아직 다 낫지 않았어. 네가 정말 나가고 싶으면, 산책을 할 수는 있을 거야. 하지만 꼭 따뜻한 잠바를 입도록 해.

W: Okay. I think I'll do that. 알았어. 그렇게 해야 할 것 같아.

어휘 get over (병에서) 회복하다 cold 감기 stay in bed 침대에 누워 있다 bet 확신하다 well 건강한 feel like –ing ~을 하고 싶다 go for a walk 산책하다 outside 밖에 put on 입다 jacket 잠바, 재킷

13 ①

M: Where are you going? 어디로 가시나요?

W: I'd like to visit the stadium. 저는 경기장을 방문하고 싶어요.

M: No problem. 문제 없어요.

W: How long will it take to get there? 거기까지 가는데 얼마나 걸릴까요?

M: It's about ten minutes away from here if traffic is okay. 교통이 괜찮으면 여기서 10분 정도 걸릴 거예요.

W: That's great. I'm glad I got a taxi. There was no bus

stop on Pine Street. 좋네요. 택시를 타길 잘했어요. 파인 스트리트에는 버스 정류장이 없었거든요.

M: Have you ever been in this city before?
전에 이 도시에 와본 적이 있으세요?

W: No, I haven't. I just flew here to see the big game.
아뇨, 없어요. 큰 경기를 보러 비행기를 타고 이곳에 왔어요.

M: I hope you have a good time.
좋은 시간을 보내시길 바랄게요.

어휘 stadium 경기장 traffic 교통(량) bus stop 버스 정류장 fly (비행기 등을) 타고 가다(fly-flew-flown)

14 ②

제 개를 찾는 걸 도와주세요.
① 개를 공원에서 잃어버렸어요.
② 검은색과 흰색의 털이 있어요.
③ 개의 이름은 샐리예요.
④ 사람을 좋아해요.
⑤ 개를 찾으시면 631-9054로 전화 주세요.

M: Are you all right? 너 괜찮아?

W: No, I'm not. I lost my dog at the park two days ago. 아니, 안 괜찮아. 이틀 전에 공원에서 내 개를 잃어버렸어.

M: That's too bad. Can I help you look for her?
정말 안됐다. 내가 개를 찾는 걸 도와줄까?

W: Yes, please. She has black fur.
응, 그렇게 해줘. 내 개는 까만 털을 갖고 있어.

M: What's her name? 개 이름이 뭐야?

W: Sally. She will come to you if you call her. She loves people. 샐리. 네가 이름을 부르면 너한테 올 거야. 그 개는 사람들을 좋아해.

M: If I find her, how can I contact you?
내가 개를 찾으면, 너에게 어떻게 연락해야 하지?

W: Call me at six three one, nine oh five four, please.
631-9054로 전화해 줘.

어휘 fur 털, 모피 contact 연락하다

15 ①

[*Telephone rings.*] [전화벨이 울린다.]

W: Hello. 여보세요.

M: Hi, this is Joe. Is Sam there?
안녕하세요, 저, 조예요. 샘이 거기 있나요?

W: I'm sorry, Joe, but Sam isn't here now. He's out with his father.
조, 미안하지만, 샘은 지금 여기 없어. 아빠랑 밖에 나갔단다.

M: When are they going to be back?
그들은 언제 돌아오나요?

W: They'll be back very late tonight.
그들은 오늘 밤 아주 늦게 돌아올 거야.

M: Oh... I guess he can't come to my house for dinner this evening.
아, 그럼 샘은 오늘 저녁에 저녁을 먹으러 우리 집에 못 오겠네요.

W: No, he can't. Why don't you call again in the morning? 응, 못 갈 거야. 아침에 다시 전화하는 게 어때?

어휘 be back 돌아오다 guess 추측하다

16 ①

W: Are you all right, Sean? 너, 괜찮니, 션?

M: No, I'm not. I got in a fight with my friend John today. 아니요, 안 괜찮아요. 오늘 제 친구 존과 싸웠어요.

W: Why did you have a fight with him? 왜 그 애와 싸웠니?

M: I told him that we shouldn't be friends anymore.
제가 존에게 우리는 더 이상 친구가 될 수 없다고 말했어요.

W: Why did you tell him that? 왜 그 애한테 그렇게 말했니?

M: He wouldn't lend his baseball glove to me. I feel bad about that now though.
그 애가 저에게 야구 글러브를 빌려주려고 하지 않았어요. 하지만 지금은 그렇게 말한 게 마음에 걸려요.

W: You should give him a call and apologize to him right now. 넌 당장 그 애한테 전화해서 사과해야 해.

어휘 get in a fight 싸움을 하다(= have a fight) anymore 더 이상 lend 빌려주다 apologize 사과하다 feel bad 기분이 안 좋다, (잘못을) 후회하다

17 ①

① W: My brother was in an accident. 내 동생이 사고를 당했어.
　 M: I saw you riding a new bicycle.
　　나는 네가 새 자전거를 타는 걸 봤어.

② W: What would you like to do? 넌 뭘 하고 싶니?
　 M: Why don't we play computer games?
　　우리 컴퓨터 게임을 하는 게 어때?

③ W: You need to take a right at the stoplight.
　　넌 신호등에서 우회전을 해야 해.
　 M: Thanks for the tip. 알려 줘서 고마워.

④ W: The coach told me I'm on the soccer team.
　　감독님이 내가 축구팀에 들어갔다고 말씀하셨어.
　 M: Congratulations. I'm so proud of you.
　　축하해. 난 네가 무척 자랑스러워.

⑤ W: What's our assignment for today? 오늘 우리 과제가 뭐지?
　 M: We need to read the rest of the chapter.
　　우리는 나머지 챕터를 읽어야 해.

어휘 be in an accident 사고를 당하다 ride a bicycle 자전거를 타다 take a right 우회전하다 stoplight 정지 신호, 빨간 불 tip 정보, 힌트 proud 자랑스러운 assignment 과제 rest 나머지 chapter (책의) 챕터, 장

18 ④

M: You're finally here. Why are you late?
마침내 왔구나. 왜 늦었어?

W: Sorry. The bus got caught in bad traffic.
미안해. 버스가 교통 체증에 갇혔었어.

M: You were late the last time, too. 넌 지난번에도 늦었잖아.

W: I know. I forgot my purse that time and had to go

<u>back home</u> to get it. 알아. 그때는 내 지갑을 잊어서 그것을 가지러 집으로 돌아가야 했어.

M: Well, let's go to the <u>restaurant</u>. I'm <u>starving</u>.
그래, 식당으로 가자. 난 너무 배고파.

W: Okay. I'll <u>pay for</u> the pizza since I was late.
알았어. 내가 늦었으니까 피자를 살게.

해설 ⑤는 지난번에 늦은 이유이다.

어휘 finally 마침내, 결국 late 늦은 get caught in bad traffic 교통 체증에 갇히다 purse 지갑 starving 배가 몹시 고픈

19 ⑤

W: Hello. Daydream Travel. This is Linda speaking.
안녕하세요, 데이드림 여행사입니다. 저는 린다예요.

M: Hi. This is Mr. Jacobs. I <u>reserved</u> a <u>flight</u> to New York with you. 안녕하세요. 저는 제이콥스입니다. 제가 당신을 통해 뉴욕행 항공기를 예약했어요.

W: Yes, Mr. Jacobs. I remember. How can I help you?
네, 제이콥스 씨. 기억납니다. 제가 어떻게 도와드릴까요?

M: I reserved a <u>room</u> at the Westside Hotel. Do you know it?
제가 웨스트사이드 호텔에 방을 예약했어요. 알고 계시죠?

W: Yes, I do. 네, 그럼요.

M: I don't know <u>how to get there</u>. Should I <u>take</u> a <u>bus</u> or a <u>taxi</u> to the hotel? 그곳에 어떻게 가야 하는지 모르겠어요. 호텔에 가려면 버스나 택시를 타야 하나요?

W: A taxi would be <u>better</u>. The bus <u>doesn't go</u> there.
택시가 좋을 거예요. 버스는 거기에 가지 않아요.

M: Okay. <u>Thanks for the information.</u>
알겠습니다. 알려 주셔서 감사합니다.

① What's my flight number? 제 항공편 번호가 뭔가요?
② Great. Then I'll take the subway.
좋아요. 그럼 지하철을 타야겠어요.
③ So I should cancel my reservation.
그래서 제 예약을 취소해야겠어요.
④ No, I've never been there before.
아니요, 전에는 그곳에 가본 적이 없어요.
⑤ Okay. Thanks for the information.
알겠습니다. 알려 주셔서 감사합니다.

어휘 reserve 예약하다 flight 항공편, 비행기 take (교통편을) 타다 information 정보

20 ⑤

W: Tina and two of her friends are at her house. They are going to <u>watch</u> a <u>movie</u>, but they want to <u>order</u> some <u>food</u> first. Tina <u>calls</u> a pizza <u>restaurant</u> and orders a pepperoni pizza and spaghetti. When the <u>deliveryman</u> arrives, Tina looks at the order. She sees a pepperoni pizza and breadsticks. In this situation, what would Tina most likely say to the deliveryman?

티나는 친구 두 명과 함께 자기 집에 있다. 그들은 영화를 볼 예정이지만, 먼저 음식을 주문하기를 원한다. 티나는 피자 가게에 전화해서 페퍼로니 피자와 스파게티를 주문한다. 배달원이 도착할 때, 티나는 주문한 것들을 본다. 그녀는 페퍼로니 피자와 막대빵을 본다. 이 상황에서 티나는 배달원에게 뭐라고 말하겠는가?

Tina: <u>You delivered the wrong food.</u>
음식을 잘못 가져다 주셨어요.

① The pizza looks delicious. 피자가 맛있게 보이네요.
② How much do I owe you? 제가 얼마를 드려야 하죠?
③ I can't wait to see the movie. 빨리 영화 보고 싶어요.
④ How about having some pizza? 피자 좀 드실래요?
⑤ You delivered the wrong food.
음식을 잘못 가져다 주셨어요.

어휘 order 주문하다; 주문품 deliveryman 배달원 arrive 도착하다 breadstick 막대빵

09회 실전모의고사 본문 p.100-101

01 ②	02 ④	03 ①	04 ①	05 ②
06 ③	07 ⑤	08 ⑤	09 ③	10 ①
11 ⑤	12 ②	13 ⑤	14 ③	15 ⑤
16 ⑤	17 ⑤	18 ③	19 ④	20 ④

01 ②

W: Hello. Are you <u>looking for</u> something?
안녕하세요. 무엇을 찾고 계신가요?

M: Yes, today is my friend's <u>birthday</u>. So I want to buy him a birthday <u>cake</u>. 네, 오늘이 제 친구의 생일이에요. 그래서 그에게 생일 케이크를 사주고 싶어요.

W: That's great. How do you like this one with a <u>big heart</u> on it?
잘됐네요. 위에 큰 하트가 있는 이 케이크는 어떠신가요?

M: <u>Sorry, but</u> I don't think he would want that.
죄송하지만 그건 친구가 원하는 것이 아닌 것 같아요.

W: Well, here's a nice <u>strawberry</u> cake. And this one has <u>fruit</u> on top of it. 음, 여기 멋진 딸기 케이크가 있어요. 그리고 이 케이크는 위에 과일이 있고요.

M: They look nice, but they're not big enough.
멋지게 보이지만, 충분히 크지가 않네요.

W: Oh, then <u>how about</u> this one? It has <u>two layers</u> on it. 아, 그럼 이건 어떠세요? 2단으로 이루어져 있거든요.

M: It looks nice. <u>How much</u> is it? 좋네요. 얼마인가요?

W: It's thirty-five dollars. 35달러입니다.

M: Okay, I'll take it. 네, 그걸로 살게요.

어휘 look for ~을 찾다 How do you like ~? ~은 어떤가요?, 마음에 드세요? enough 충분한 layer 층, 단

02 ④

W: I haven't seen you in a while, Jeff.
오랜만이야, 제프.

M: I was busy doing an assignment for school.
난 학교 과제를 하느라 바빴어.

W: Which teacher were you doing that for?
어떤 선생님의 과제를 했니?

M: It was for Ms. Parker. She's my English teacher.
파커 선생님 과제였어. 그분은 내 영어 선생님이셔.

W: She was my teacher last year. She always gave lots of homework. What did you have to do?
그분은 작년에 우리 선생님이셨어. 항상 숙제를 많이 내주셨지. 넌 뭘 해야 했니?

M: I had to write a story, read a book, and write a book report. I was really mad about that.
난 이야기를 쓰고, 책을 읽고, 독후감을 써야 했어. 그것 때문에 정말 짜증이 났어.

W: I understand. She gave you a lot of work. Did you finish? 이해해. 선생님이 네게 많은 숙제를 내주셨네. 끝냈니?

M: Yes, so now I feel so much better. I'm relieved I'm done. 응, 그래서 지금은 기분이 훨씬 괜찮아. 끝내서 안심이야.

어휘 in a while 한동안 assignment 과제, 숙제 book report 독후감 mad 화난(= angry) relieved 안도하는, 안심하는 amused 즐거운

03 ①

M: Do you want to go cycling with me tomorrow?
내일 나랑 같이 자전거 타러 갈래?

W: Okay. Where do you want to go?
좋아. 어디로 가고 싶니?

M: I'd like to go around the lake. 호수 근처로 가고 싶어.

W: The lake? Isn't it far away? 호수? 멀지 않니?

M: It's about five kilometers from here, but it's really nice. 여기에서 약 5킬로미터 정도 거리야, 하지만 정말 멋있어.

W: Okay. What time should we meet?
알았어. 우리는 몇 시에 만나야 할까?

M: How about at nine in the morning? Is that all right?
오전 9시 어떠니? 괜찮니?

W: I'd rather leave one hour earlier. I need to be home by noon.
나는 한 시간 일찍 떠나는 게 좋겠어. 정오까지는 집에 와야 하거든.

M: Okay. That's fine with me. 좋아. 그건 나도 괜찮아.

어휘 go cycling 자전거 타러 가다 lake 호수 would rather ~하고 싶다 earlier 보다 일찍(early-earlier-earliest) noon 정오

04 ①

M: What's the weather forecast for tomorrow?
내일 일기예보는 어떠니?

W: It's going to rain all day long. 하루 종일 비가 올 거야.

M: Are you serious? I'm getting tired of all this rain.
정말이야? 난 이 비가 지겨워지고 있어.

W: So am I, but we're in the middle of the rainy season now. 나도 그래, 하지만 지금은 한창 장마철이잖아.

M: Is it supposed to rain today?
오늘도 비가 오기로 되어 있니?

W: No, it's going to stay cloudy, but it won't rain.
아니, 계속 구름이 끼겠지만 비는 안 올 거야.

M: When are we going to see the sun again?
우리는 언제 다시 해를 볼 수 있을까?

W: I heard it will be sunny on the weekend. So we can enjoy some nice weather then. 주말에는 화창할 거라고 들었어. 그때 좋은 날씨를 즐길 수 있을 거야.

어휘 serious 진지한, 심각한 get tired of ~이 지겨워지다 in the middle of ~의 중앙에, ~가 한창인 rainy season 장마철, 우기 be supposed to ~하기로 되어 있다

05 ②

W: Attention, everyone. We are going to open in five minutes. You can buy tickets by the entrance. Tickets cost ten dollars for adults and seven dollars for children. Please do not bring any food or drinks inside. You may not take pictures of the exhibits, and do not touch them either. Some of them are very old and they can break easily. You can buy posters and postcards of them at the gift shop. We hope you enjoy the exhibits.

주목해 주세요, 여러분. 우리는 5분 후에 개장합니다. 입장권은 입구 옆에서 구매하실 수 있습니다. 티켓은 성인 10달러, 그리고 어린이는 7달러입니다. 박물관 안으로 어떤 음식이나 음료도 반입하지 마십시오. 전시품의 사진은 찍으실 수 없습니다. 그리고 전시품도 만지지 마시기 바랍니다. 일부 전시품들은 매우 오래되었고, 쉽게 깨질 수 있습니다. 여러분은 기념품 상점에서 포스터와 엽서를 구매하실 수 있습니다. 전시회를 즐기시길 바랍니다.

어휘 entrance 입구 bring 가져오다 inside 안쪽에 exhibit 전시(품), 전시회 break 깨지다 postcard 엽서

06 ③

M: What do you need to buy here? 넌 여기서 뭘 사야 하니?

W: I've got to get a notebook for my history class. The notebooks here cost five dollars each.
난 역사 수업에 쓸 공책을 사야 해. 여기는 공책이 5달러씩이야.

M: How about any pens? I think they each cost a dollar here.
펜은 어때? 내 생각에 여기서는 1달러씩인 것 같은데.

W: Yes, I should buy two of them. Oh, no.
응, 난 펜 두 자루를 사야 해. 아, 이런.

M: What's wrong? 무슨 일이니?

W: I don't have any money with me. Can I borrow some money?
나한테 돈이 하나도 없어. 내가 돈 좀 빌릴 수 있을까?

M: Sure. So, you need to buy a notebook and two pens? 물론이지. 그럼 공책 한 권과 펜 두 자루를 사야 하니?

W: That's right. Thanks a lot. I'll pay you back tomorrow. 맞아. 정말 고마워. 내일 갚을게.

해설 공책($5)+펜($1×2=$2) = $7

어휘 notebook 공책 each 각각 borrow 빌리다 pay back 갚다

07 ⑤

W: Why are you going out? You don't have class today. 넌 왜 나가려고 하니? 오늘 수업이 없잖아.

M: Actually, I need to go to school.
사실은, 학교에 가야 해요.

W: Why? It's Sunday. Do you have to study for a test?
왜? 오늘은 일요일이야. 시험 공부를 해야 하니?

M: No. The school festival is this week.
아니요, 학교 축제가 이번 주예요.

W: Oh, are you going to take part in the festival?
아, 네가 축제에 참가하니?

M: No, I'm not. But I'm going to help prepare for it.
아니요. 하지만 축제 준비를 도울 거예요.

W: That sounds interesting. How will you do that?
재미있겠구나. 어떻게 도울 거니?

M: I'm going to make some posters for it. Then, I'll put them up around the school.
저는 축제 포스터를 만들 거예요. 그리고 학교 주변에 붙일 거예요.

어휘 actually 사실은, 실제로 study for a test 시험 공부하다 take part in ~에 참가하다 prepare 준비하다 put up 게시하다, 붙이다

08 ⑤

M: Hi. You look lost. Can I help you?
안녕하세요. 길을 잃으셨나 보네요. 제가 도와드릴까요?

W: Yes, please. I'm trying to find my room.
네, 도와주세요. 제 방을 찾고 있어요.

M: What's your room number? 방 번호가 뭐죠?

W: It's room four two three. 423호예요.

M: Go straight past the elevators. Then, turn left and walk to the end of the hall. 엘리베이터를 지나서 곧장 가세요. 그리고 나서, 왼쪽으로 돌아서 복도 끝까지 걸어 가세요.

W: That's easy. Thanks. Oh, I have one more question.
쉽네요. 감사합니다. 아, 질문이 하나 더 있어요.

M: Sure. What is it? 네. 뭐죠?

W: Where is the restaurant located? 식당은 어디에 있죠?

M: It's on the tenth floor. 10층에 있습니다

어휘 lost 길을 잃은 past ~을 지나 straight 곧장, 똑바로 hall 복도 located 위치한

09 ③

W: Tim, can you give me that box over there?
팀, 저기 있는 상자를 내게 줄 수 있니?

M: Sure. What do you need it for?
응, 상자는 어디에 필요하니?

W: I'm moving tomorrow. So I have to pack all of my things today.

난 내일 이사 가. 그래서 오늘 모든 짐을 챙겨야 해.

M: Tomorrow? Do you have enough time to get ready? You must be really busy.
내일? 준비할 시간이 충분하니? 정말 바쁘겠구나.

W: I am. Do you mind helping me out now?
응. 지금 나를 좀 도와줄 수 있니?

M: Not at all. What do you want me to do?
괜찮아. 내가 무엇을 하면 될까?

해설 여자는 내일 이사 가므로 남자에게 지금 짐 싸는 것을 도와달라고 요청하고 있다. 'Do you mind ~?'로 묻는 질문에 긍정적으로 답변하려면 'No', 'Not at all' 등의 표현을 사용한다.

어휘 over there 저쪽에 move 이사 가다 pack (짐을) 싸다 Do you mind ~? ~해도 될까?

10 ①

W: Mary's sister just called me. Mary had to go to the hospital last night. 메리의 여동생이 방금 나에게 전화했어.
메리가 어젯밤에 병원에 가야 했대.

M: Seriously? What was wrong with her?
정말이야? 메리한테 무슨 일이 생긴 거야?

W: She had a high fever. She's still not well.
고열이 났대. 지금도 여전히 몸이 안 좋다고 하네.

M: We should visit her there now.
우리 지금 메리가 있는 곳에 가보자.

W: Good idea. She's at the hospital across from the police station.
좋은 생각이야. 그 애는 경찰서 맞은편에 있는 병원에 있어.

M: Okay. What should we get for her?
알았어. 우리가 그 애한테 뭘 가져가는 게 좋을까?

W: How about a card and some flowers?
카드와 꽃은 어때?

M: All right. Let's do it. 좋아. 지금 가자.

해설 메리는 어제 병원에 갔다.

어휘 seriously 진지하게, 심각하게 high fever 고열 across from ~의 맞은편에 police station 경찰서

11 ⑤

W: What are you doing on the computer?
넌 컴퓨터로 뭘 하고 있니?

M: I'm writing an email to a restaurant manager. I had a terrible experience there. 식당 지배인에게 이메일을 쓰고 있어. 그곳에서 끔찍한 경험을 했거든.

W: What happened? 무슨 일이 있었니?

M: The service was very bad. My waiter was so rude to me.
서비스가 정말 안 좋았어. 담당 웨이터가 나에게 정말 무례했어.

W: Did you not like the food either? 음식도 별로였니?

M: No, the food was all right, but I couldn't enjoy my meal because of the waiter.
아니, 음식은 괜찮았지만 웨이터 때문에 식사를 즐길 수 없었어.

어휘 write an email 이메일을 쓰다 manager 관리자, 지배인 terrible 끔찍한 experience 경험 happen 일어나다 rude 무례한 all right 괜찮은 meal 식사

12 ②

M: Guess what. My parents <u>gave</u> me a <u>present</u> today.
있잖아. 우리 부모님이 오늘 내게 선물을 주셨어.

W: Cool. What did you get? 멋지다. 뭘 받았니?

M: I got a <u>pet</u>. It's a <u>furry</u> animal.
애완동물을 받았어. 털이 많은 동물이야.

W: Is it a large animal? 큰 동물이니?

M: No, it's actually very <u>small</u>. It has <u>brown</u> fur.
아니, 실제로는 매우 작아. 갈색 털을 가졌어.

W: <u>Where</u> do you <u>keep</u> your pet?
그 애완동물은 어디에서 키우니?

M: I have a <u>cage</u> for it. There's a big <u>wheel</u> in the cage for it to run on. 난 그걸 키울 우리를 가지고 있어. 우리 안에는 애완동물이 타고 달릴 수 있는 큰 바퀴가 있어.

W: I want to see it soon. It must be really <u>cute</u>.
난 그걸 빨리 보고 싶어. 정말 귀여울 것 같아.

해설 작고 털이 있으며, 우리 안에서 바퀴를 타고 노는 동물은 보기 중에서 햄스터가 유일하다.

어휘 pet 애완동물 furry 털이 많은 cage 우리; 새장 wheel 바퀴 cute 귀여운

13 ⑤

W: I <u>wrote</u> <u>about</u> my last <u>trip</u> <u>on</u> my <u>blog</u> today. I wrote that I didn't like the <u>hotel</u> I <u>stayed</u> <u>at</u>. Someone who works at the hotel wrote a <u>message</u> on my blog. He told me that the hotel was great. Then, he said I was a <u>bad</u> <u>guest</u>. I <u>asked</u> him <u>why</u> he thought that. He just called me <u>crazy</u>. I <u>couldn't</u> <u>believe</u> it. It was the <u>worst</u> <u>experience</u> of my life.

나는 오늘 내 블로그에 지난 여행에 관한 글을 썼다. 나는 내가 묵었던 호텔을 좋아하지 않았다고 썼다. 그 호텔에서 일하는 누군가가 내 블로그에 메시지를 남겼다. 그는 내게 그 호텔이 아주 좋다고 말했다. 그리고, 내가 나쁜 손님이었다고 말했다. 나는 그에게 왜 그렇게 생각하는지 물어봤다. 그는 그냥 내가 미쳤다고 말했다. 나는 그 말을 믿을 수 없었다. 그건 내 인생에서 최악의 경험이었다.

어휘 blog 블로그 stay 머무르다, 묵다 write a message 메시지를 쓰다, 댓글을 쓰다 guest 손님, 투숙객 crazy 미친 worst 가장 안 좋은(bad – worse – worst)

14 ③

M: This is a <u>sport</u> that people <u>play</u> <u>indoors</u>. It's a <u>team</u> sport, so there are <u>six</u> <u>people</u> on each team. To play the sport, the players <u>need</u> a <u>ball</u> and a <u>net</u>. They have to <u>hit</u> the ball <u>with</u> their <u>hands</u>, make it <u>go</u> <u>over</u> the net, and try to make it hit the <u>ground</u> <u>on</u> <u>the</u> <u>other</u> team's <u>side</u>. A team can hit the ball

three <u>times</u> before they have to hit it over the net. The first team to score <u>twenty-five</u> <u>points</u> wins the game.

이것은 사람들이 실내에서 하는 스포츠이다. 이것은 단체 경기이고, 각 팀에 6명의 사람이 있다. 이 스포츠를 하려면 선수들은 공과 네트가 필요하다. 선수들은 그들의 손으로 공을 쳐야 하고, 공이 네트를 넘어가게 하고, 공이 상대팀 편의 바닥을 칠 수 있게 해야 한다. 한 팀은 공을 네트 너머로 치기 전에 공을 세 번 칠 수 있다. 25점을 먼저 득점하는 팀이 경기에서 승리한다.

어휘 indoors 실내에서 team sport 단체 경기, 팀 스포츠 go over ~로 건너가다, 넘어가다 net 네트, 그물 score 득점하다 hockey 하키 ping-pong 탁구 volleyball 배구 basketball 농구 baseball 야구

15 ⑤

M: Hey, why are you still <u>at</u> <u>home</u>? I thought you were <u>going</u> <u>out</u>.
얘, 넌 왜 아직도 집에 있니? 난 네가 나가려고 하는 줄 알았어.

W: I was <u>planning</u> <u>to</u>, but I didn't want to <u>see</u> that <u>movie</u>. 나가려고 했지만 그 영화를 보고 싶지 않았어.

M: <u>What</u> movie are you <u>talking</u> <u>about</u>?
무슨 영화를 말하는 거니?

W: Do you know the new action movie?
새로 나온 액션 영화 아니?

M: Are you talking about *The Last Hero*?
'더 라스트 히어로'를 말하는 거니?

M: Yeah. That movie looks really <u>boring</u>, so I just decided to <u>stay</u> home. 응. 영화가 정말 지루해 보여서 그냥 집에 있기로 결정한 거야.

W: No way. I saw it yesterday, and it was a lot of <u>fun</u>. Everyone <u>loved</u> it. 무슨 소리야. 내가 어제 그 영화를 봤는데, 정말 재미있었어. 모두가 그 영화를 좋아했어.

M: Really? Maybe I <u>made</u> a <u>mistake</u>.
정말이야? 내가 아무래도 실수를 한 거 같네.

어휘 go out 나가다, 외출하다 boring 지루한 fun 재미; 재미있는 make a mistake 실수하다

16 ⑤

W: We're going to have fun <u>hiking</u> <u>up</u> the <u>mountain</u> today. 우리는 오늘 등산을 하면서 즐거운 시간을 보낼 거야.

M: I agree. Don't forget to <u>bring</u> a <u>backpack</u> with you.
나도 그렇게 생각해. 배낭을 챙기는 걸 잊지 마.

W: Right. I'm going to bring a <u>water</u> <u>bottle</u>, too.
알았어. 난 물병도 가져갈 거야.

M: Good. And you should also bring a <u>towel</u>.
좋아. 그리고 수건도 챙겨야 해.

M: Why is that? 왜 그래야 하지?

W: You'll <u>sweat</u> a lot. You can use it to <u>dry</u> yourself <u>off</u>.
넌 땀이 많이 날 거야. 몸에 난 땀을 말릴 때 그걸 사용할 수 있어.

M: Good point. I'll bring an <u>extra</u> T-shirt and an <u>umbrella</u>, too.

좋은 지적이야. 여분의 티셔츠와 우산도 가져갈게.

W: The <u>weather</u> <u>forecast</u> doesn't say it will rain.
일기예보에서 비는 오지 않는다고 했어.

M: Okay. Then my umbrella is <u>off</u> the <u>list</u>.
알았어. 그럼 우산은 목록에서 빼야겠다.

어휘 hike 하이킹하다 bring 가져가다 backpack 배낭 sweat 땀을 흘리다 dry off ~을 말리다 off the list 목록에서 지운

17 ⑤

① Mary read <u>the fewest</u> books.
메리가 책을 가장 조금 읽었다.

② Jason read <u>fewer</u> books <u>than</u> Alice.
제이슨은 앨리스보다 책을 덜 읽었다.

③ Alice read more books than Steve.
앨리스는 스티브보다 책을 더 많이 읽었다.

④ Steve read <u>more</u> books <u>than</u> Jason.
스티브가 제이슨보다 책을 더 많이 읽었다.

⑤ Steve read <u>the most</u> books.
스티브가 가장 많은 책을 읽었다.

어휘 more than ~보다 많이 fewest 가장 적은(few-fewer-fewest)

18 ③

① W: Can you buy some <u>groceries</u> at the store?
가게에서 식료품 좀 사올 수 있니?

M: Sure. What do you need me to get?
물론이지. 내가 뭘 사면 될까?

② W: May I <u>borrow</u> this <u>book</u> for a while?
제가 잠깐 이 책을 빌릴 수 있을까요?

M: Sorry, but I'm <u>reading</u> it now.
미안하지만, 지금 제가 읽고 있어요.

③ W: Hello. How may I <u>help</u> you?
안녕하세요. 무엇을 도와드릴까요?

M: Yes, he's <u>helping</u> me. 네, 그가 저를 돕고 있어요.

④ W: Have you <u>heard from</u> Jane lately?
최근에 제인으로부터 소식을 들었니?

M: No, she hasn't <u>called</u> me <u>since</u> last week.
아니, 그 애는 지난주부터 나에게 전화를 하지 않았어.

⑤ W: <u>What time</u> is the game going to <u>start</u>?
경기가 몇 시에 시작하나요?

M: I think it will <u>begin</u> at seven. 7시에 시작할 것 같아요.

어휘 groceries 식료품 for a while 잠시 동안 hear from ~로부터 연락을 받다 lately 최근에 since ~이래로, ~이후로

19 ④

M: I love coming to this <u>park</u>. It's so <u>relaxing</u>.
난 이 공원에 오는 게 너무 좋아. 마음이 정말 편안해.

W: I agree. I love all of the <u>flowers</u> <u>blooming</u>.
나도 마찬가지야. 모든 꽃이 피는 게 좋아.

M: Do you want me to <u>take</u> a <u>picture</u> <u>of</u> you in front of them? 내가 꽃 앞에서 네 사진을 찍어줄까?

W: Sure. That would be great. 응. 그럼 정말 좋겠다.

M: Okay. <u>Stand</u> <u>over</u> <u>there</u>. 알았어. 저기에 가서 서 봐.

W: <u>Right</u> <u>here</u>? 이쪽에?

M: Yes. One, two, three... There you go. You <u>look</u> <u>good</u> in the picture. I'll <u>send</u> a <u>copy</u> to your email.
응. 하나, 둘, 셋. 됐어. 사진이 정말 잘 나오네. 내가 이메일로 한 장 보내줄게.

W: <u>Do you know my email address?</u>
내 이메일 주소를 알고 있니?

① Yes, it's a good picture. 응, 그건 멋진 사진이야.

② No, that's not my email. 아니, 그건 내 이메일이 아니야.

③ Can you send it to my email?
그걸 내 이메일로 보내줄 수 있니?

④ Do you know my email address?
내 이메일 주소를 알고 있니?

⑤ Let me tell you my home address.
너한테 내 집주소를 말해 줄게.

어휘 relaxing 편안한 bloom 꽃이 피다 take a picture 사진을 찍다 in front of ~앞에 copy 한 장, 사본

20 ④

W: Dave and Chris are <u>playing</u> a <u>game</u> of <u>basketball</u> against each other. They are having a good time, but the game is very <u>close</u>. <u>Neither</u> <u>of</u> them wants to <u>lose</u> the game. Dave takes a <u>shot</u>, and Chris tries to <u>block</u> it. Chris <u>accidentally</u> hits Dave and <u>knocks</u> him to the ground. Chris <u>feels</u> <u>bad</u> about that, so he helps Dave up. In this situation, what would Chris most likely say to Dave?

데이브와 크리스는 서로 농구 경기를 하고 있다. 그들은 즐거운 시간을 보내고 있지만 경기는 매우 막상막하다. 그들 중 누구도 경기에 지고 싶어하지 않는다. 데이브가 슛을 던지고, 크리스는 그것을 막으려고 한다. 크리스는 뜻하지 않게 데이브를 치고 그를 바닥에 넘어뜨린다. 크리스는 미안해서 데이브가 일어나는 것을 돕는다. 이런 상황에서 크리스는 데이브에게 뭐라고 말하겠는가?

Chris: I'm really sorry about that. 그건 정말 미안하게 생각해.

① I can't believe I won the game.
내가 경기에서 이겼다니 믿을 수가 없어.

② Let's play a few more minutes. 몇 분만 더 경기를 하자.

③ Why didn't you help me up?
왜 내가 일어나는 걸 돕지 않았니?

④ I'm really sorry about that. 그건 정말 미안하게 생각해.

⑤ That was a great shot. 정말 멋진 슛이었어.

어휘 against each other 서로 대항하여, 맞서서 close (경기가) 막상막하인 neither 둘 다 아닌 lose the game 게임에서 지다 take a shot 슛을 하다 block 막다, 블로킹하다 accidentally 우연히, 뜻하지 않게 knock 넘어뜨리다

01 ③	02 ①	03 ②	04 ⑤	05 ③
06 ⑤	07 ③	08 ①	09 ⑤	10 ③
11 ③	12 ⑤	13 ⑤	14 ③	15 ⑤
16 ④	17 ②	18 ⑤	19 ①	20 ③

01 ③

W: Kevin, what are you doing here?
케빈, 여기서 뭘 하고 있니?

M: I'm walking my dog here in the park. How about you? 여기 공원에서 강아지를 산책시키는 중이야. 너는 뭐하니?

W: I'm here with my brother. It's his birthday.
나는 여기에 남동생이랑 왔어. 오늘이 그 애의 생일이야.

M: You have a little brother? I didn't know that. Where is he?
너한테 남동생이 있었니? 그건 몰랐네. 동생은 어디에 있니?

W: Hmm... I don't see him right now.
음, 지금은 안 보여.

M: Is that him eating the hotdog over there?
저기서 핫도그를 먹고 있는 남자 아이니?

W: No, it isn't. 아니야.

M: Is he the boy holding the baseball bat?
그 애가 야구 방망이를 들고 있는 남자 아이니?

W: No, that's not him either. 아니, 그 애도 아니야.

M: What's he wearing? 동생이 뭘 입고 있니?

W: He's wearing jeans and a T-shirt. He's also got a birthday hat on his head. 청바지와 티셔츠를 입고 있어. 그리고 생일 모자를 머리에 쓰고 있어.

어휘 walk 산책시키다 right now 지금 hold 잡다 baseball bat 야구 방망이 hat 모자

02 ①

M: Hello, everybody. It's time for the global weather forecast. Here's the weather for some major cities around the world. In London, it's going to be rainy all day. It's sunny in Rome but cold and snowy in Moscow. In Mumbai, it's going to be cloudy, and there will be heavy rain in Sydney.

안녕하세요, 여러분. 세계의 일기예보를 알려드릴 시간입니다. 전 세계 주요 도시의 날씨입니다. 런던은 하루 종일 비가 오겠습니다. 로마는 화창하지만, 모스크바는 춥고 눈이 오겠습니다. 뭄바이는 구름이 끼겠고, 시드니에는 폭우가 내리겠습니다.

어휘 global 세계의 major 주요한 around the world 전 세계의

03 ②

W: Pardon me, but I have a question.
실례합니다만, 질문이 있어요.

M: Sure. 말씀하세요.

W: I'm going to City Hall. Which stop should I get off at? 제가 시청에 가고 있는데요. 어느 정류장에서 내려야 하죠?

M: I'm sorry, but this bus doesn't go to City Hall. You need to take the number forty-two bus to get there. 미안하지만, 이 버스는 시청으로 가지 않아요. 거기 가려면 42번 버스를 타셔야 합니다.

W: Isn't this the number forty-two bus?
이 버스가 42번 아닌가요?

M: No, this is the number forty-four bus.
아니요. 이 버스는 44번 버스입니다.

W: Oh, that's terrible. 아, 큰일이군요.

어휘 pardon me 미안합니다, 실례합니다 stop 정류장 get off (교통수단에서) 내리다

04 ⑤

W: This is boring. 지루해.

M: I know, but we can't go outside. It's raining too hard.
나도 알지만, 우리는 밖에 나갈 수 없어. 비가 너무 많이 오고 있어.

W: How about playing a game? 게임을 하는 게 어때?

M: We already played some games.
우리는 이미 게임을 몇 개 했잖아.

W: Then what about watching TV? 그럼 TV를 보는 건 어때?

M: There's nothing good on TV now.
지금 TV에서는 볼 만한 게 안 나와.

W: Look. It's not raining anymore.
이걸 봐. 비가 더 이상 안 와.

M: Seriously? Let me check. You're right. Now we can go outside. 정말? 내가 한번 볼게. 네 말이 맞네. 우리는 이제 밖에 나갈 수 있어.

W: Wait a minute. You won't believe this.
잠깐만 기다려. 너 이 사실을 믿지 못할 거야.

M: Why? What's the matter? 왜? 무슨 일이야?

W: It just started raining again.
방금 비가 다시 오기 시작했어.

어휘 boring 지루한 outside 밖에, 야외에 rain hard 비가 많이 오다 anymore 더 이상 seriously 진지하게, 진심으로 wait a minute 잠깐 기다리다 pleased 기쁜 relaxed 편안한, 긴장이 풀린 nervous 긴장한 disappointed 실망한

05 ③

W: You look worried. 넌 걱정이 있어 보여.

M: I am. My teacher just called my mom.
응, 그래. 우리 선생님께서 방금 우리 엄마한테 전화하셨어.

W: Why did he do that? 왜 전화하셨니?

M: He wants to talk to her about my schoolwork.
선생님께서는 엄마랑 내 학업에 대해 이야기를 나누고 싶어 하셔.

W: Are you getting bad grades? 넌 성적이 안 좋니?

M: Not really, but I didn't write a report last night. It's the third time this month I haven't done my

homework for that class.
그렇지는 않지만, 어젯밤에 보고서를 쓰지 않았어. 그 수업의 숙제를 하지 않은 게 이번 달에만 세 번째거든.

W: Was the report due today? 보고서가 오늘까지였니?

M: Yeah, and I didn't turn it in.
응, 그리고 난 그걸 제출하지 않았어.

W: What did you do last night then?
그럼 넌 어젯밤에 뭐 했니?

M: I went to my friend's house and watched a couple of movies. 친구 집에 가서 영화 두 편을 봤어.

어휘 worried 걱정하는 schoolwork 학업, 학교 공부 grade 성적 due ~하기로 되어 있는 turn in 제출하다, 내다 a couple of 둘의

06 ⑤

W: You must be excited. You're going to France tomorrow, aren't you?
넌 정말 신나겠다. 내일 프랑스에 가지, 그렇지?

M: Yeah, it's going to be lots of fun.
응, 정말 재미있을 거야.

W: Shouldn't you go to bed soon? Your plane leaves early in the morning, doesn't it?
곧 자야 하지 않니? 네가 탈 비행기가 아침 일찍 떠나잖아, 그렇지?

M: No, I'm not taking the six A.M. flight.
아니야, 난 오전 6시 비행기를 타지 않을 거야.

W: Did you change flights? 항공편을 변경했니?

M: Yes, I did. Now, I'm going to be on the two thirty P.M. flight. 응. 난 이제 오후 2시 30분 비행기를 탈 거야.

W: That's much better. 그게 훨씬 낫네.

M: You're right. So I'm going to get to the airport around twelve P.M.
맞아. 그래서 오후 12시쯤에 공항에 도착할 거야.

W: What time will you leave home?
집에서 몇 시에 떠날 거니?

M: I'm going to leave the house at ten thirty A.M.
오전 10시 30분에 집에서 떠날 거야.

W: That's good. You'll have plenty of time.
잘했어. 넌 시간 여유가 많을 거야.

해설 변경 전의 항공편 시각, 남자가 집을 나서는 시각과 헷갈리지 말자.

어휘 excited 흥미진진한, 신나는 plane 비행기 leave 떠나다 airport 공항 plenty of 많은

07 ③

M: Happy birthday, Mom. 생신 축하 드려요, 엄마.

W: Thanks for remembering, dear.
기억해 주어서 고맙구나, 얘야.

M: Since today is your birthday, I'm going to do all of the housework.
오늘이 엄마 생신이니까, 제가 집안일을 모두 할게요.

W: That's very nice of you. 정말 착하구나.

M: First, I'll wash the dishes, and then I'll take out the trash. 첫째로, 저는 설거지를 할 거예요. 그리고 나서 쓰레기를 버릴 거예요.

W: You don't need to take out the trash.
쓰레기는 버릴 필요가 없단다.

M: Why not? 왜요?

W: Garbage day is on Friday, not today.
쓰레기 버리는 날은 금요일이야, 오늘이 아니라.

M: Okay. Well, then I'll clean the living room and do the laundry, too.
알겠어요. 그럼, 거실을 청소하고 빨래도 할게요.

W: Do you mind feeding the dog?
개에게 밥 좀 줄 수 있겠니?

M: Of course not. I can give Rusty his dinner.
물론이죠. 러스티한테 저녁밥을 줄게요.

해설 'Do you mind ~?'에 대한 질문에 긍정으로 답할 때는 'No.', 'Not at all.', 'Of course not.' 등의 표현을 쓴다.

어휘 dear (누군가에게 다정하게 말을 걸 때 사용하는 말) housework 집안일 wash the dishes 설거지하다 take out the trash 쓰레기를 내다버리다 do the laundry 빨래하다 feed 밥을 먹이다

08 ①

M: Hi. Can I help you? 안녕하세요? 제가 도와드릴까요?

W: Good morning. What fruit do you recommend?
안녕하세요. 어떤 과일을 추천하시나요?

M: The oranges are delicious. Each orange costs two dollars. 오렌지가 맛있어요. 오렌지는 개당 2달러입니다.

W: I don't really like oranges. How about the apples?
저는 오렌지를 그렇게 좋아하지는 않아요. 사과는 어떤가요?

M: They're in season now, so they cost one dollar each. But I'll give you seven apples for the price of five. 사과는 지금이 제철이라 개당 1달러예요. 하지만 제가 다섯 개 가격으로 사과 7개를 드릴게요.

W: That sounds good. 좋아요.

M: Would you like to have some? 사과를 좀 사시겠어요?

W: Yes. I'd like fourteen apples, please.
네. 사과 14개 주세요.

해설 상인은 5달러에 사과 7개를 주겠다고 했으므로, 14개를 사면 10달러를 내야 한다.

어휘 recommend 추천하다 delicious 맛있는 each 각각 cost 비용이 들다 in season 제철인

09 ⑤

M: Do you think the city has too much trash on the streets? Then why don't you volunteer? You can help clean up the streets. Make our city beautiful once again. Call five oh nine, six four nine six and tell the person you want to help out. You'll find out when and where to go. You'll work with a team of people for a couple of hours every Saturday. By working together, we can clean up our city quickly.

도시의 거리에 쓰레기가 너무 많다고 생각하시나요? 그럼 자원봉사를 하시는 건 어떠세요? 여러분이 거리를 청소하는 것을 도우실 수 있습니다. 우리 도시를 다시 한 번 깨끗하게 만들어 봅시다. 509-6496으로 전화하셔서, 돕고 싶다고 말씀하세요. 언제, 어디로 가야 하는지를 알게 되실 겁니다. 여러분은 매주 토요일에 두 시간 동안 사람들과 팀을 이루어 일하게 될 겁니다. 우리는 함께 일함으로써 우리 도시를 빠르게 청소할 수 있습니다.

어휘 trash 쓰레기 volunteer 자원봉사하다 clean up 청소하다, 깨끗이 하다 once again 한 번 더 quickly 빠르게

10 ③

W: Stuart, have you finished your homework yet?
스튜어트, 네 숙제를 다 끝냈니?
M: Almost, but I'm going to go to Bruce's house for a while. 거의 했는데, 잠깐 브루스의 집에 갈 거예요.
W: No, you can't do that. 아니, 넌 그러면 안돼.
M: Why not? 왜 안돼요?
W: You haven't done your schoolwork or your chores.
넌 학교 숙제도, 집안일도 안 했잖니.
M: But you and Dad give me too many chores.
그렇지만 엄마랑 아빠가 너무 많은 집안일을 주세요.
W: That's not true. You only have to do one thing each day. 그렇지 않아. 너는 하루에 딱 하나만 하면 돼.
M: Okay. I'll clean the bathroom now.
알겠어요. 지금 화장실을 청소할게요.
W: Good. Hurry up. 좋아. 서두르렴.

어휘 homework 숙제 for a while 잠시 동안 chore 집안일 each day 매일 bathroom 화장실 hurry up 서두르다

11 ③

M: Nowadays, teenagers in many countries are gaining too much weight. Many of them are obese. The main reason is that they eat a lot of fast food. Instead of eating healthy food, they prefer unhealthy food, so they enjoy hamburgers, French fries, and fried chicken. Fast food has few nutrients, but it has lots of calories and fat. This is causing teens to gain a lot of weight. Even if they exercise a lot, they will still become obese.

요즘, 많은 나라의 십 대들의 체중이 너무 많이 증가하고 있습니다. 그들 중 많은 사람들이 비만입니다. 주요 원인은 그들이 패스트푸드를 많이 먹는 것입니다. 건강한 음식을 먹는 대신, 십 대들은 건강에 안 좋은 음식을 좋아해서, 그들은 햄버거, 감자튀김, 그리고 프라이드 치킨을 즐겨 먹습니다. 패스트푸드는 영양분이 별로 없고 칼로리와 지방은 많습니다. 이것 때문에 십 대들의 체중이 많이 늘고 있습니다. 그들이 운동을 많이 하더라도 계속해서 비만 상태를 유지할 것입니다.

어휘 nowadays 요즈음 teenager 십 대 gain weight 몸무게가 늘다 obese 비만의 main 주요한 reason 이유 fast food 패스트

푸드 instead of ~대신에 healthy 건강한, 건강에 좋은 unhealthy 건강하지 않은, 건강에 나쁜 few 거의 없는 calorie 칼로리 fat 지방 cause 야기하다 even if 비록 ~일지라도 exercise 운동하다

12 ⑤

W: I'm thinking about buying a new laptop.
난 새 노트북 컴퓨터를 사려고 생각 중이야.
M: That's good. What are you going to use it for?
좋네. 그걸 어디에 쓰려고 하니?
W: I'll probably just surf the Internet and watch videos.
아마도 그냥 인터넷을 검색하고 동영상을 보는데 쓸 거야.
M: You're not going to play games, are you?
게임은 하지 않을 거지, 그렇지?
W: No, I never play computer games. They aren't interesting to me.
아니, 난 컴퓨터 게임을 하지 않아. 게임은 나한테는 재미 없어.
M: In that case, you don't need an expensive laptop. Just get an average-priced one. 그런 경우라면, 넌 비싼 노트북이 필요 없겠구나. 그냥 적당한 가격의 노트북을 사도록 해.
W: Why is that? 왜 그러니?
M: The expensive ones are for gamers. But since you're going to do basic activities on yours, you don't need to spend a lot of money on it. 비싼 노트북은 게임하는 사람들을 위한 거야. 하지만 너는 네 노트북으로 기본적인 것만 할 거니까, 노트북에 돈을 많이 쓸 필요가 없어.

어휘 laptop 노트북 컴퓨터 probably 아마도 surf the Internet 인터넷을 검색하다 average-priced 평균적인 가격의 since ~이기 때문에 basic 기본적인 activity 활동

13 ⑤

[Telephone rings.] [전화벨이 울린다.]
[Beep] [삐 소리]
M: Hello. My name is Tom Roberts. I'd like to order a birthday cake. I want to get a two-layered chocolate cake. It should have vanilla icing though. It's for my son's birthday, so please write "Happy Birthday, John" on it. You don't need to deliver it. I'll visit your place to pick it up tonight at seven. Thanks a lot.

안녕하세요. 제 이름은 톰 로버츠입니다. 생일 케이크를 주문하고 싶어요. 저는 2단으로 된 초콜릿 케이크를 원해요. 하지만 바닐라 아이싱이 있어야 해요. 그건 제 아들의 생일에 쓸 거라서 케이크 위에 "생일 축하해, 존"이라고 글자를 넣어 주세요. 배달을 하실 필요는 없습니다. 오늘 밤 7시에 가게로 제가 찾으러 갈게요. 감사합니다.

어휘 order 주문하다 two-layered 2단으로 된 icing 아이싱, 당의 deliver 배달하다 pick up ~을 찾다, 가져가다

14 ③

W: Please pay close attention to the rules of the swimming pool. Do not run anywhere near the pool. And you may not <u>have</u> any <u>food</u> or <u>drinks</u> by the pool. <u>Take</u> a <u>shower</u> before you go swimming. When you're in the pool, you may not <u>splash</u> others. And you may not <u>dive</u> <u>into</u> the pool either. Finally, always <u>listen to</u> the <u>lifeguard</u>. Do everything he says. Thank you.

수영장의 규칙에 각별한 주의를 기울여 주시기 바랍니다. 수영장 근처에서는 어디서도 뛰지 마십시오. 그리고 수영장 근처에서는 음식이나 음료를 드실 수 없습니다. 수영하기 전에 샤워를 해주시기 바랍니다. 수영장 안에 있을 때는 다른 사람에게 물이 튀겨서는 안 됩니다. 그리고 수영장에서 다이빙을 해도 안됩니다. 마지막으로 항상 안전요원의 말을 들어 주십시오. 안전요원이 말하는 모든 것을 따라 주십시오. 감사합니다.

어휘 pay attention to ~에 주의를 기울이다 rule 규칙 swimming pool 수영장 anywhere 어디에서도 take a shower 샤워하다 splash 물을 튀기다, 첨벙거리다 dive 다이빙하다 lifeguard 안전요원

15 ⑤

W: Let's <u>get</u> some <u>ice cream</u>. 아이스크림 먹으러 가자.
M: That's a good idea. Where should we go? 좋은 생각이야. 어디로 갈까?
W: Let's go to the ice cream shop <u>by</u> the <u>bank</u>. 은행 옆에 있는 아이스크림 가게로 가자.
M: We <u>can't go</u> there now. 거기는 지금은 갈 수 없어.
W: Why not? 왜 못 가?
M: It's <u>closed</u> <u>for</u> <u>repairs</u>. 그 가게는 수리를 하려고 문을 닫았어.
W: Oh... <u>When</u> is it going to <u>open</u> again? 아, 그 가게는 언제 다시 문을 열까?
M: I think it will <u>reopen</u> next week. 내 생각에는 다음 주에 다시 열 것 같아.
W: So <u>why</u> <u>don't</u> we find <u>another</u> ice cream shop? 그럼 다른 아이스크림 가게를 찾는 게 어때?
M: Good thinking. Do you know where one is? 좋은 생각이야. 가게가 어디에 있는지 아니?
W: Yes, I do. We have to <u>walk</u> <u>five</u> <u>minutes</u> to get there. 응, 알아. 거기 가려면 우리는 5분 정도 걸어야 해.

어휘 by ~옆에 repair 수리(하다) reopen 다시 문을 열다 another 다른

16 ④

① M: Would you like to <u>try on</u> this <u>dress</u>? 이 옷을 입어보시겠어요??
W: Yes, I want to see <u>how it looks</u>. 네, 어떻게 보이는지 보고 싶어요.
② M: <u>What</u> <u>time</u> should we <u>meet</u> tomorrow? 우리는 내일 몇 시에 만나야 하지?
W: How about <u>at</u> <u>three</u> <u>thirty</u>? 3시 30분에 어때?
③ M: Hello. Are you <u>looking for</u> something? 안녕하세요. 무엇을 찾고 계신가요?
W: Yes, I need to <u>buy</u> a new <u>watch</u>.

네, 저는 새 시계를 사야 해요.
④ M: There were two <u>new</u> <u>students</u> at <u>school</u> today. 오늘 학교에 새로운 학생이 두 명이 있었어.
W: I <u>enjoyed</u> the <u>first</u> <u>day</u> of school, too. 나도 학교 첫 날을 즐겁게 보냈어.
⑤ M: Let's <u>watch</u> a <u>movie</u> this evening. 오늘 저녁 영화 보러 가자.
W: That <u>sounds</u> <u>good</u> to me. 좋은 생각이야.

어휘 try on (옷을) 입어보다 look for ~을 찾다

17 ②

M: Good afternoon. What can I do for you? 안녕하세요. 무엇을 도와드릴까요?
W: Hi. I'd like to <u>sign up for</u> the <u>sewing</u> <u>class</u>. 안녕하세요. 바느질 교실에 등록하고 싶어요.
M: No problem. When do you <u>have</u> <u>time</u>? 문제 없습니다. 언제 시간이 되세요?
W: I'm <u>busy</u> on <u>Tuesday</u> and <u>Friday</u> at eleven A.M. I have <u>cooking</u> <u>lessons</u> then. 저는 화요일과 금요일 오전 11시에는 바빠요. 그때 요리 수업이 있거든요.
M: <u>What</u> <u>about</u> on <u>Saturday</u>? 토요일은 어떠세요?
W: Do you have a <u>morning</u> class then? 그때 오전 수업이 있나요?
M: No. We only have an <u>afternoon</u> class on Saturday. 아니요. 저희는 토요일에는 오후 수업만 있습니다.
W: <u>How</u> <u>about</u> on <u>Wednesday</u> <u>evening</u>? 수요일 저녁은 어떤가요?
M: Yes, we have one of those. 네, 수업이 하나 있습니다.
W: Great. I'd like to sign up for it. 좋아요. 그 수업에 등록하고 싶어요.

어휘 sign up for ~에 등록하다, 신청하다 sewing 바느질 cooking 요리

18 ⑤

M: <u>What's</u> <u>wrong</u> with you nowadays? 너 요즘 무슨 문제 있니?
W: I'm <u>having</u> a <u>hard</u> <u>time</u> at work. My boss keeps giving me <u>too</u> <u>many</u> <u>projects</u>. 회사에서 힘든 시간을 보내고 있어. 상사가 나한테 계속 너무 많은 업무를 줘.
M: I <u>understand</u> <u>how</u> you <u>feel</u>. 네 기분이 어떨지 이해돼.
W: You do? 이해해?
M: Sure. My <u>boss</u> always gives me work to do, so I have to <u>stay</u> <u>late</u> at the office almost <u>every</u> <u>night</u>. 물론이지. 내 상사는 항상 나에게 할 일을 주기 때문에 거의 매일 밤 늦게까지 사무실에 있어야 해.
W: <u>How</u> do you <u>handle</u> that? 넌 그 문제를 어떻게 다루고 있니?
M: I try to <u>stay</u> <u>positive</u>, and <u>do</u> my <u>best</u>. In the future, I'm sure that I'll be <u>rewarded</u>. 긍정적이 되려고 노력하고 최선을 다하지. 나는 앞으로 내가 보상 받을 거라고 확신해.
W: That's a good <u>attitude</u>. 좋은 태도구나.

① Easy come, easy go. 쉽게 얻는 것은 쉽게 잃는다.
② Practice makes perfect. 연습이 완벽을 만든다.
③ Too many cooks spoil the broth.
　사공이 많으면 배가 산으로 간다.
④ The early bird catches the worm.
　일찍 일어나는 새가 벌레를 잡는다.
⑤ Look on the bright side of things. 사물의 밝은 면을 보라.

어휘 nowadays 요즘 have a hard time 힘든 시간을 보내다
at work 직장에서, 회사에서 keep –ing 계속 ~하다 stay late 늦
게까지 있다 handle 다루다, 처리하다 positive 긍정적인 in the
future 앞으로, 미래에 be rewarded 보상을 받다 attitude 태도

19 ①

W: Good afternoon, Jim. What are you doing?
　안녕, 짐. 뭘 하고 있니?
M: I'm writing in my diary. 일기를 쓰고 있어.
W: I didn't know you keep a diary.
　난 네가 일기를 쓰는지 몰랐어.
M: I try to write in it every day. I enjoy writing about
　my day, and I also like to write stories.
　난 매일 일기를 쓰려고 노력해. 난 나의 하루에 대해 글을 쓰는 걸
　좋아하고, 이야기를 쓰는 것도 좋아해.
W: What kinds of stories? 어떤 종류의 이야기인데?
M: They are just stories that I make up. How about
　you? What's your hobby?
　그냥 내가 만들어내는 이야기들이야. 너는 어때? 네 취미는 뭐니?
W: I enjoy reading books in my free time.
　나는 여가 시간에 책 읽는 걸 좋아해.
M: So do I. I like to read history books.
　나도 그래. 나는 역사책 읽는 것을 좋아해.
W: Not me. I love reading novels.
　난 아니야. 난 소설을 읽는 것을 좋아해.
① Not me. I love reading novels.
　난 아니야. 난 소설을 읽는 것을 좋아해.
② Yes, I'm reading this book now.
　응, 난 지금 이 책을 읽고 있어.
③ I already finished that book. 난 그 책을 벌써 다 읽었어.
④ I'm going to the library now.
　난 지금 도서관에 가는 길이야.
⑤ No, I haven't read that story.
　아니, 난 그 이야기를 읽지 않았어.

어휘 diary 일기 make up 만들다 hobby 취미 free time 여가
시간 history 역사 novel 소설

20 ③

M: Thank you for coming to Fred's Fried Chicken. May
　I take your order, please? 프레드 프라이드 치킨에 와주셔
　서 감사합니다. 주문을 도와드릴까요?
W: Yes. I'll have an order of fried chicken.
　네. 저는 프라이드 치킨을 주문할게요.
M: How many pieces would you like?
　몇 조각 드릴까요?

W: I'll take three pieces. 3조각 주세요.
M: Do you want regular, crispy, or spicy?
　보통, 바삭함, 아니면 매운맛 중에서 어떤 걸 원하세요?
W: Hmm... I think I'll take spicy. I need some French
　fries, too. 음, 저는 매운맛으로 할게요. 감자튀김도 좀 주세요.
M: Sure. Would you like a large order of fries?
　알겠습니다. 튀김은 큰 걸로 드릴까요?
W: Yes, and what kinds of desserts do you have?
　네, 그리고 후식은 어떤 게 있죠?
M: We have apple pie, shakes, and cheesecake.
　저희는 애플파이, 셰이크, 그리고 치즈케이크가 있습니다.
W: I'll take a chocolate shake, please.
　초콜릿 셰이크 하나 주세요.
① Please give me a chicken burger then.
　그럼 치킨 버거 하나 주세요.
② Okay. I'll have some vanilla ice cream.
　네. 바닐라 아이스크림을 먹을게요.
③ I'll take a chocolate shake, please.
　초콜릿 셰이크 하나 주세요.
④ That's right. I ordered an apple pie.
　맞아요. 저는 애플파이를 주문했어요.
⑤ Yes, I'll take one of those. 네, 그것들 중에 하나로 할게요.

어휘 take order 주문을 받다 piece 조각 regular 보통의 crispy
바삭한 spicy 매운 dessert 디저트, 후식 shake (밀크)셰이크

11회 실전모의고사   본문 p.124-125

01 ②	02 ④	03 ①	04 ③	05 ②
06 ③	07 ④	08 ⑤	09 ④	10 ②
11 ③	12 ④	13 ③	14 ⑤	15 ⑤
16 ③	17 ④	18 ②	19 ⑤	20 ⑤

01 ②

M: Hi. I need to buy a new shirt for work.
　안녕하세요. 회사에서 입을 새 셔츠를 사야 해요.
W: Okay. How about a shirt with polka dots?
　알겠습니다. 물방울 무늬가 있는 셔츠는 어떠세요?
M: No thanks. That's not my style.
　아니요, 괜찮아요. 그건 제 스타일이 아닙니다.
W: This shirt has stripes that go across.
　이 셔츠는 가로 줄무늬가 있어요.
M: I don't like those. But stripes going up and down
　are fine.
　그것도 별로예요. 하지만 위아래로 있는 줄무늬는 좋아요.
W: We have a shirt like that. Here it is.
　저희에게 그런 셔츠가 있습니다. 여기 있어요.
M: Wait a minute. I think this checkered style is better.
　잠시만요. 제 생각에는 이 체크 무늬 스타일이 더 나은 것 같네요.
W: That's a popular shirt. Do you want it?

그건 인기 있는 셔츠예요. 이걸로 하시겠어요?

M: Yes, I'll take it. How much does it cost?
네, 이걸로 살게요. 얼마죠?

어휘 polka dot 물방울 무늬 stripe 줄무늬 across 가로질러
up and down 위아래로 checkered 체크 무늬의

02 ④

W: What do you want to do in the future?
넌 앞으로 뭘 하고 싶니?

M: Well, I really like art. Drawing pictures is fun.
음, 난 미술을 정말 좋아해. 그림을 그리는 게 재미있어.

W: So do you want to be an artist?
그럼 화가가 되고 싶니?

M: No, it's just my hobby. I'd rather be a teacher.
아니, 그건 그냥 내 취미야. 나는 선생님이 되고 싶어.

W: Isn't your father a teacher?
너희 아버지가 선생님 아니야?

M: Yes. He's a science teacher. What do you want to
do? 맞아. 아빠는 과학 선생님이셔. 너는 무엇을 하고 싶니?

W: I'd like to be a pilot. I love flying in airplanes.
나는 비행기 조종사가 되고 싶어. 나는 비행기를 타고 나는 게 좋아.

어휘 in the future 미래에, 앞으로 draw (그림을) 그리다 artist
화가, 예술가 hobby 취미 pilot 비행기 조종사 flying 비행기 여행,
비행기 조종

03 ①

M: Good evening. We had beautiful sunny weather
today. On Wednesday, the sunny weather will
continue in the morning. Then, it's going to become
rainy in the evening. On Thursday, it will be very
foggy in the morning, but it won't rain. On Friday,
there will be cloudy skies all day long. And you can
expect sunny skies again on Saturday.

안녕하세요. 우리는 오늘 아름답고 화창한 날씨를 즐겼습니다. 수요
일에는 화창한 날씨가 오전에 이어질 전망입니다. 그리고 나서 저녁
에는 비가 오겠습니다. 목요일에는, 오전에 안개가 짙게 끼겠으나
비는 오지 않겠습니다. 금요일에는 하루 종일 하늘에 구름이 끼겠습
니다. 그리고 토요일에는 다시 맑은 하늘을 기대할 수 있겠습니다.

어휘 continue 계속되다, 지속되다 rainy 비가 오는 foggy 안개
낀 cloudy 구름 낀 all day long 하루 종일 expect 기대하다

04 ③

M: What do you think we should do next?
우리는 다음에 뭘 해야 하지?

W: We can see the dolphin show.
우리는 돌고래 공연을 볼 수 있어.

M: But that starts in thirty minutes. What should we
do now? 하지만 그건 30분 후에 시작하잖아. 지금 뭘 해야 할까?

W: I'm not sure. 나도 잘 모르겠어.

M: Why don't we go to see the shark tank?
상어 수조를 보러 가는 건 어때?

W: Don't you think sharks are kind of scary?
상어는 좀 무섭지 않니?

M: Sure, but don't worry. They're in a big tank. It's
totally safe. 물론이지, 하지만 걱정 마. 상어는 큰 수조 안에 들
어 있어. 완전히 안전해.

W: You're right. Do you know where it is?
네 말이 맞아. 그게 어디 있는지 아니?

M: Yeah. We just have to walk a bit.
응. 조금만 걸으면 돼.

어휘 dolphin 돌고래 shark 상어 tank (물)탱크, 수조 totally 완
전하게, 전적으로 safe 안전한 a bit 약간

05 ②

M: What are you going to do this weekend?
이번 주말에 뭐 할 거니?

W: I'm going to visit Seoul with my friend.
내 친구랑 서울에 갈 거야.

M: Oh, yeah? Where are you going to go?
아, 그래? 어디로 갈 거니?

W: We're going to visit Namdaemun. She wants to go
to the market there. 우리는 남대문을 찾아갈 거야. 그녀는 거
기 있는 시장을 가고 싶어해.

M: Why don't you go to Dongdaemun, too? That will
be fun. 동대문도 가 보는 게 어때? 재미있을 거야.

W: That's a good idea, but we won't have enough
time. We'll go there later. 좋은 생각이긴 하지만 우리가 시
간이 충분하지 않을 거야. 거기는 나중에 가 볼게.

M: Okay. Well, have fun with your friend.
알았어. 그럼, 네 친구랑 재미있는 시간 보내.

어휘 later 나중에 have fun 재미있는 시간을 보내다

06 ③

[Cellphone rings.] [휴대폰이 울린다.]

W: Hi, Steve. Where are you? 안녕, 스티브. 너 어디니?

M: I'm still on the highway. 난 아직 고속도로에 있어.

W: What's the matter? Why are you still there?
무슨 일이야? 왜 아직 거기 있니?

M: Traffic is terrible. The cars are moving very slowly.
교통 체증이 심각해. 차들이 엄청 느리게 움직이고 있어.

W: But it's already seven, and the concert starts in
thirty minutes.
하지만 벌써 7시야, 그리고 콘서트는 30분 후에 시작해.

M: Don't worry. I think I can be there in fifteen minutes.
걱정하지 마. 15분 안에 그곳에 도착할 수 있을 것 같아.

W: Do you mean by seven fifteen? Okay. I'll be waiting
outside for you.
7시 15분까지 온다는 거니? 알았어. 밖에서 널 기다리고 있을게.

M: All right. I'll get there as fast as I can.
좋아. 최대한 빨리 그곳에 갈게.

해설 현재 시각, 남자가 도착하는 시각 등과 구분해서 들어야 한다.

어휘 on the highway 고속도로상에 traffic 교통(상황) terrible 끔찍한 slowly 느리게 outside 밖에서 as fast as one can 가능한 한 빨리(= as fast as possible)

07 ④

[*Telephone rings.*] [전화벨이 울린다.]
M: Hello. 여보세요.
W: Hello. Is Tim there? 여보세요. 팀 있나요?
M: This is Tim. Who's calling, please?
제가 팀이에요. 전화하는 분은 누구시죠?
W: It's Wendy. Why were you absent from school today? 나 웬디야. 넌 왜 오늘 학교에 결석했니?
M: I felt terrible in the morning. So I stayed in bed all day.
아침에 몸이 안 좋았어. 그래서 하루 종일 침대에 누워 있었어.
W: Do you feel better now? 지금은 좀 괜찮니?
M: Yes, I do. Thanks for asking.
응, 괜찮아. 물어봐 줘서 고마워.
W: Anyway, I'm calling to remind you about our math quiz tomorrow. Be sure to study for it.
아무튼, 난 내일 있을 우리 수학 시험에 대해 너한테 알려주려고 전화한 거야. 꼭 시험 공부를 하도록 해.
M: Oh, that's right. Thanks for letting me know.
아, 맞다. 나한테 알려줘서 고마워.

어휘 be absent from school 학교에 결석하다 terrible 끔찍한, 심한 stay in bed 침대에 누워 있다 anyway 어쨌든, 아무튼 remind 상기시키다 quiz (간단한) 시험, 테스트 be sure to 꼭 ~해라

08 ⑤

W: Good morning, class. Before we begin, I need to give you some instructions. First, do not play with any of the chemicals in the lab. Some of them are dangerous. Next, you need to follow my instructions very carefully. Only do what I tell you. Finally, if you have any questions, please ask me. Now, let's get started.

안녕하세요 여러분. 시작하기 전에, 제가 몇 가지 지시 사항을 알려드리겠습니다. 첫째, 실험실에서는 어떠한 화학약품도 갖고 놀지 마세요. 몇 가지 화학약품은 위험합니다. 다음으로, 제 지시 사항을 매우 신중하게 따라 주셔야 합니다. 제가 말하는 것만 하세요. 마지막으로, 질문이 있으면 제게 물어보세요. 이제 시작하겠습니다.

어휘 begin 시작하다 give instructions 지시하다 chemicals 화학약품 lab 실험실(= laboratory) dangerous 위험한 follow 따르다 carefully 신중하게, 조심스럽게 finally 마지막으로 get started 시작하다

09 ④

M: Take a look at this picture. Who is this?

이 사진을 좀 봐. 이 사람이 누구니?
W: That's Mr. Jackson. He used to be our teacher.
그분은 잭슨 선생님이셔. 우리 선생님이셨잖아.
M: Oh, right. I remember him. 아, 맞아. 그분이 기억나.
W: Do you remember the songs that he used to make us sing in class? 선생님이 수업 시간에 우리에게 부르라고 시켰던 노래들이 기억나니?
M: Yeah, I do. And we got to play some musical instruments, too.
응, 기억나. 그리고 우리는 악기도 몇 개 연주해봤잖아.
W: That was a fun class. 정말 재미있는 수업이었어.

어휘 take a look at ~을 한번 보다 used to (과거에) ~이곤 했다 play a musical instrument 악기를 연주하다

10 ②

M: Ouch. My tooth really hurts. I think I have a cavity.
아야, 이가 너무 아파. 충치가 있는 것 같아.
W: You shouldn't eat so much chocolate. It's bad for your teeth.
넌 초콜릿을 너무 많이 먹으면 안돼. 그건 네 치아에 안 좋아.
M: I know. But it tastes so good.
알아. 하지만 초콜릿은 아주 맛있어.
W: Anyway, you need to see a dentist.
어쨌든, 넌 치과에 가야 해.
M: Do you know a good one? 좋은 의사를 알고 있니?
W: Yes, but he's very busy. Here's the phone number. Why don't you call his clinic and make a reservation? 응, 하지만 그분은 무척 바쁘셔. 여기 전화번호가 있어. 그의 병원에 전화해서 예약을 하는 게 어때?
M: Okay. I think I'll do that. 알겠어. 그렇게 해야겠다.
W: Good luck. I hope your tooth gets better.
행운을 빌게. 네 이가 빨리 나았으면 좋겠어.

어휘 tooth 이, 치아(옝 teeth) cavity 충치 be bad for ~에 해롭다(↔ be good for ~에 이롭다) dentist 치과 의사 clinic 병원, 진료소 make a reservation 예약하다 get better 나아지다, 좋아지다

11 ③

M: Mom, is dinner almost ready?
엄마, 저녁 준비가 거의 다 됐나요?
W: Not yet. I still have to make the salad.
아직 안됐어. 아직 샐러드를 만들어야 돼.
M: Okay. Should I set the table?
알겠어요. 제가 식탁을 차릴까요?
W: Your sister already did it. But there is something you can do for me.
네 여동생이 이미 했단다. 하지만 네가 해줄 수 있는 게 있단다.
M: What's that? 그게 뭔데요?
W: We don't have any milk. Can you go to the store and get some?
우리는 우유가 하나도 없어. 가게에 가서 좀 사올래?
M: Sure. I'll do that right away. 물론이죠. 지금 바로 사올게요.

W: Thanks a lot. 고마워.

어휘 ready 준비된 set the table 식탁을 차리다 right away 지금 바로, 당장

12 ④

M: What did you want to tell me earlier, Sue?
아까 나한테 말하고 싶었던 게 뭐야, 수?

W: I have some possible good news.
어쩌면 좋은 소식이 있을 것 같아.

M: What is it? 뭔데?

W: My mom promised to buy me tickets to the rock concert this Saturday. I just have to get an A on my science test. 우리 엄마가 이번 주 토요일 록 콘서트 티켓을 사주시기로 약속했어. 나는 과학 시험에서 A를 받기만 하면 돼.

M: Science? But that's your worst subject.
과학? 하지만 과학은 네가 제일 못하는 과목이잖아.

W: I know. I'm really worried. What if I don't do well?
알아. 정말 걱정이야. 내가 잘 못하면 어떡하지?

M: You just need to study hard.
넌 그냥 열심히 공부하는 수밖에 없어.

W: I'll do my best. 난 최선을 다할 거야.

어휘 earlier 앞서, 전에 worst 가장 나쁜, 최악의(bad - worse - worst) what if ~이면 어쩌지 do one's best 최선을 다하다 upset 화난, 속상한 confident 자신감 있는 relieved 안도하는

13 ③

M: Excuse me. Could you do something for me?
실례합니다. 제게 뭘 좀 해 주실 수 있나요?

W: Sure. What do you need? 물론이죠. 무엇이 필요하세요?

M: My friend is going to be having dinner with me. When he gets here, can you show him to my table?
제 친구가 저와 함께 저녁식사를 할 건데요. 친구가 여기 도착하면 그를 제 테이블로 안내해 주실 수 있나요?

W: Of course. What's his name?
물론이죠. 친구분 성함이 어떻게 되시죠?

M: His name is Allen Simmons. He's over one hundred eighty centimeters tall, and he has straight brown hair. 그 친구 이름은 앨런 시몬스입니다. 키는 180센티미터가 넘고, 갈색 생머리를 하고 있어요.

W: Do you know what he is wearing?
친구분이 뭘 입고 있는지 아세요?

M: He's wearing a blue suit and a red tie.
파란색 정장에 빨간 넥타이를 하고 있어요.

어휘 get 도착하다 show somebody to a table ~을 테이블로 안내하다 straight 곧은 suit 정장

14 ⑤

① Flying kites is the least popular hobby.
연 날리기는 가장 인기 없는 취미이다.

② More students collect coins than go hiking.
하이킹을 하는 것보다 동전을 모으는 학생이 더 많다.

③ Playing computer games is the most popular hobby. 컴퓨터 게임을 하는 것이 가장 인기 있는 취미이다.

④ Fewer than ten students enjoy hiking the most.
10명보다 더 적은 학생들이 하이킹을 가장 좋아한다.

⑤ More students like flying kites than playing computer games. 컴퓨터 게임을 하는 것보다 연 날리기를 좋아하는 학생들이 더 많다.

어휘 hobby 취미 fly kites 연을 날리다 least 가장 적은(little - less - least) collect 수집하다 go hiking 하이킹을 가다, 도보여행을 가다

15 ⑤

[Telephone rings.] [전화벨이 울린다.]

M: Hello. 여보세요.

W: Hi. I'd like to report a problem with my order.
안녕하세요. 제 주문에 문제가 있다는 것을 알려 드리려고요.

M: What's wrong with the order you made?
주문에 어떤 문제가 있습니까?

W: I ordered some clothes on your website, but you sent me the wrong items. 제가 그쪽의 웹사이트에서 옷을 몇 벌 주문했는데, 잘못된 제품을 보내주셨어요.

M: I'm sorry. What's your order number?
죄송합니다. 주문번호가 어떻게 되시죠?

W: It's four oh five nine five. My name is Soyun Park.
40595입니다. 제 이름은 박소윤이고요.

M: Hold on one moment, please.
잠시만 기다려 주세요.

어휘 report 보고하다 order 주문(품); 주문하다 wrong 잘못된 item 물품, 제품 hold on one moment 잠시 기다리다

16 ③

① M: I just dropped my phone, so there's a crack on the screen.
내가 방금 전화기를 떨어뜨려서 화면에 금이 갔어.

W: You need to have it repaired.
넌 그걸 수리를 받아야 해.

② M: Do you know where the remote control is?
리모컨이 어디 있는지 아니?

W: It should be on the sofa.
소파 위에 있을 거야.

③ M: Would you like a cup of coffee?
커피 한 잔 마실래?

W: Yes, I'm going to make some copies.
응, 내가 몇 장을 복사할 거야.

④ M: When did you visit your parents' home?
언제 부모님 댁에 갔었니?

W: I was just there two days ago.
이틀 전에 갔어.

⑤ M: How many DVDs are you going to rent?
DVD를 몇 장이나 빌릴 거니?

W: I'll just get one or two.

한 개나 두 개 빌릴 거야.

해설 coffee와 copy는 유사한 발음 때문에 어학 시험에서 자주 등
장하는 함정이다.

어휘 drop 떨어뜨리다 crack (갈라져 생긴) 금 screen 화면
repair 수리하다 remote control 리모컨 make copies 복사하다
visit 방문하다 rent 빌리다

17 ④

W: Please listen closely, everyone. The school festival
is going to begin on May tenth. It's going to last for
two days. On the first day of the festival, we will
have class until one P.M. Then, there won't be any
classes for the rest of the day. On the second day,
there will not be any classes. We hope all of you
will come to the festival. There will be many fun
games. The school band is also going to perform.
The concert will be on the second day of the
festival at six P.M.

모두 잘 들어 주세요. 학교 축제가 5월 10일에 열릴 예정입니다. 축
제는 이틀간 계속됩니다. 축제 첫 날에는 오후 1시까지 수업을 하겠
습니다. 그리고 나머지 수업은 모두 하지 않을 것입니다. 둘째 날에
는 아무 수업도 없을 것입니다. 여러분 모두가 축제에 오시면 좋겠
습니다. 재미있는 게임이 많이 있을 것입니다. 또한 학교 밴드가 공
연을 할 것입니다. 콘서트는 축제 둘째 날 오후 6시에 있을 것입니
다.

해설 축제는 5월 10일부터 이틀간 열리며, 첫 날에는 오후 1시까지 수
업이 있다. 그리고 밴드는 오후 6시에 공연을 한다.

어휘 festival 축제 May 5월 last 지속하다, 계속되다 the rest of
~의 나머지 perform 공연하다

18 ②

W: Are you going out now? Why don't you have your
gloves? 너 지금 나가는 거니? 장갑을 끼는 게 어때?
M: What do I need them for? 왜 장갑이 필요하죠?
W: It's going to get really cold today.
오늘은 정말 추울 거야.
M: Is it? I didn't hear the weather forecast.
그래요? 저는 일기예보를 듣지 못했어요.
W: According to the weatherman, it's going to be
minus five degrees later in the day.
기상 캐스터에 따르면, 이따가 오후에 영하 5도가 될 거래.
M: Wow. It is going to be cold. 우와, 추워지는군요.
W: Why don't you go back inside and get your gloves
then? 안에 다시 들어가서 장갑을 갖고 오는 게 어떠니?
M: Yes, I think I should do that. 네, 그래야 할 것 같아요.

① These gloves are made of leather.
이 장갑은 가죽으로 만들어졌어요.
② Yes, I think I should do that. 네, 그래야 할 것 같아요.
③ I'm wearing them right now. 지금 끼고 있어요.
④ No, I don't have my gloves. 아니요, 저는 장갑이 없어요.

⑤ Okay. I'll buy new gloves. 알았어요. 새 장갑을 살게요.

어휘 go out 외출하다 gloves 장갑 weather forecast 일기예보
weatherman 기상 캐스터 degree (온도) 도 inside 안으로

19 ⑤

[Cellphone rings.] [휴대폰이 울린다.]
W: Hi, Tim. It's Wendy. 안녕, 팀. 나 웬디야.
M: What's going on, Wendy? 무슨 일이니, 웬디?
W: I'm bored right now. How about going out and
doing something?
난 지금 심심해. 나가서 뭔가를 하는 게 어때?
M: I'd really love to, but I can't leave the house today.
나도 정말 그러고 싶지만 오늘은 집을 나갈 수 없어.
W: Why not? Are you doing a school assignment?
왜 안돼? 학교 숙제를 하고 있니?
M: No, I'm not. Actually, my parents won't let me go
out this entire weekend. 아니, 그렇지 않아. 사실은 우리 부
모님께서 이번 주말 내내 내가 나가는 것을 허락하지 않으실 거야.
W: They won't? Are they punishing you for something?
허락을 안 하신다고? 무슨 일 때문에 널 벌주고 계신 거니?
M: I came home late last night, so they're mad at me.
내가 어젯밤에 집에 늦게 들어와서 내게 화나셨어.

① Nobody wants to be punished.
아무도 벌 받고 싶어 하지 않아.
② No, we can go out. Where do you want to go?
아니, 우린 나갈 수 있어. 어디를 가고 싶니?
③ That's right. I'm studying for a test right now.
맞아. 난 지금 시험 공부를 하는 중이야.
④ Don't worry. I'm almost finished with my
assignment. 걱정하지 마. 난 숙제를 거의 끝냈어.
⑤ I came home late last night, so they're mad at me.
내가 어젯밤에 집에 늦게 들어와서 내게 화나셨어.

어휘 bored 지루한 leave 떠나다 assignment 과제, 숙제
actually 사실은 let (~하도록) 허락하다, ~하게 하다 entire 전체의
punish 벌을 주다 mad 화난

20 ⑤

W: Joe and Mina are going to meet at the library to
do their homework. Joe goes to the second floor
of the library and waits for Mina. However, Mina
doesn't show up. He waits for thirty minutes, and
then he decides to go home. When he goes to the
first floor, he sees Mina waiting by the front door. In
this situation, what would Joe say to Mina?

조와 미나는 숙제를 하기 위해 도서관에서 만나기로 했다. 조는 도
서관의 2층에 가서 미나를 기다린다. 하지만 미나는 나타나지 않는
다. 조는 30분 동안 기다린 후, 집에 돌아가기로 결심한다. 조가 1층
에 갔을 때, 그는 정문에서 기다리고 있는 미나를 본다. 이런 상황에
서 조는 미나에게 무슨 말을 하겠는가?

Joe: I thought you were coming upstairs.
나는 네가 위층으로 올라온다고 생각했어.

① No, you didn't wait for me. 아니, 너는 날 기다리지 않았어.

② Why was your phone turned off?
왜 네 휴대폰이 꺼져 있었니?

③ I'm glad we decided to meet today.
오늘 우리가 만나기로 해서 기뻐.

④ Did you finish all of the homework? 네 숙제는 다 했니?

⑤ I thought you were coming upstairs.
나는 네가 위층으로 올라온다고 생각했어.

어휘 floor 층; 바닥 wait for ~을 기다리다 show up 나타나다, 등장하다 front door 현관, 정문 turn off (전원을) 끄다

12회 실전모의고사
본문 p.136-137

01 ③	02 ④	03 ①	04 ④	05 ④
06 ①	07 ④	08 ①	09 ⑤	10 ②
11 ⑤	12 ①	13 ⑤	14 ④	15 ⑤
16 ①	17 ①	18 ③	19 ①	20 ①

01 ③

W: What are you looking at, Joe? 뭘 보고 있니, 조?

M: This is a picture from my family reunion.
이건 가족 모임에서 찍은 사진이야.

W: Wow. All of these people are in your family?
우와. 이 사람들이 다 너희 가족이니?

M: That's right. Can you find my cousin Tom?
맞아. 내 사촌인 톰을 찾아볼래?

W: Is he the man wearing glasses and holding a drink?
안경을 쓰고 음료를 들고 있는 남자가 그 사람이니?

M: No, that's my uncle Jim. Tom is wearing shorts.
아니, 그건 내 삼촌인 짐이야. 톰은 반바지를 입고 있어.

W: Does he have long hair? 그는 긴 머리를 하고 있니?

M: No, he has short hair. 아니, 그는 머리가 짧아.

어휘 reunion 모임, 재회 cousin 사촌 glasses 안경 hold 잡다 shorts 반바지

02 ④

M: Today is Monday, May twenty fifth. The weather is finally improving after several days of rain. Today, it will be cloudy most of the day. At night, the clouds will mostly disappear. Expect some fog early in the morning on Tuesday, but there will be sunny skies starting at noon. On Wednesday, however, it is probably going to rain and be very windy.

오늘은 5월 25일 월요일입니다. 며칠 동안 비가 내린 끝에 드디어 날씨가 좋아지고 있습니다. 오늘은, 하루의 대부분이 흐릴 것으로 예상됩니다. 밤에는 구름이 거의 사라질 것입니다. 화요일 이른 아침에는 약간의 안개가 예상되지만, 정오부터 화창한 하늘을 보이기 시작하겠습니다. 하지만 수요일은 강수 확률이 높으며 바람이 세게

불 것입니다.

어휘 finally 마침내, 결국 improve 향상되다, 나아지다 several 몇몇의 mostly 거의, 대개 disappear 사라지다 expect 예상하다, 기대하다 fog 안개 probably 아마도 windy 바람이 부는

03 ①

M: Did you remember to pack our swimsuits?
우리 수영복을 챙기는 건 기억했지?

W: Yes, I did. They are already in the suitcase.
응, 했지. 벌써 여행가방에 들어가 있어.

M: What about some T-shirts and shorts?
티셔츠하고 반바지는?

W: Don't worry. Everything is ready for our trip abroad.
걱정 마. 우리 해외여행은 모든 게 준비됐어.

M: That's great. 잘했어.

W: Do you think we should bring some towels?
우리가 수건을 좀 가져가야 할까?

M: No, the hotel will have those for us. But we should bring some snacks for the ship.
아니, 호텔에 다 준비되어 있을 거야. 하지만 배에서 먹을 간식을 좀 챙겨야 해.

W: Good thinking. 좋은 생각이야.

어휘 pack 짐을 챙기다 swimsuit 수영복 suitcase 여행가방 ready 준비된 trip abroad 해외여행 bring 가져가다 snack 간식

04 ④

M: Pardon me. How much does it cost to take the bus? 실례합니다. 버스 요금이 얼마죠?

W: Adults must pay two thousand won, and students must pay one thousand five hundred won.
어른은 이천 원을 내야 하고, 학생은 천오백 원을 내야 합니다.

M: My son is only eight. How much should he pay?
제 아들은 겨우 8살이거든요. 이 애는 요금을 얼마 내야 하나요?

W He only has to pay one thousand won.
천 원만 내면 됩니다.

M: Great. I need two adult tickets, one student ticket, and one child ticket. 좋아요. 어른 두 명, 학생 한 명, 그리고 어린이 한 명의 표를 주세요.

W: How will you be paying for this? 어떻게 계산하시겠어요?

M: Cash. Here's ten thousand won.
현금이요. 여기 만 원 드릴게요.

해설 어른(₩2,000×2) + 학생(₩1,500) + 어린이(₩1,000) = ₩6,500

어휘 pardon me 실례합니다(= excuse me) cost 비용이 들다 adult 성인 pay 지불하다 cash 현금

05 ④

W: Please listen carefully. The concert is about to begin. Please turn off your cellphones and other electronic devices during the performance. You may not take pictures at all. And you are not allowed to record the show either. Please do not get up to leave the theater during the concert. There will be a short break after about one hour. The concert will begin soon. I hope you enjoy the show.

잘 들어 주세요. 콘서트가 곧 시작합니다. 공연 도중에는 휴대폰과 다른 전자기기들을 모두 꺼주시기 바랍니다. 사진은 절대 찍으시면 안됩니다. 또한 공연을 녹화하는 것도 허용되지 않습니다. 콘서트가 진행되는 도중에는 일어나서 공연장을 나가지 마시기 바랍니다. 약 한 시간 후에 짧은 휴식 시간이 있을 것입니다. 곧 콘서트가 시작합니다. 공연을 즐기시기 바랍니다.

어휘 be about to 막 ~하려고 하다 turn off (전원을) 끄다 electronic device 전자기기 during ~동안에 performance 공연 take pictures 사진을 찍다 allow 허락하다 record 녹화하다 break 휴식

06 ①

W: Are you ready for your trip to Spain?
스페인 여행 준비는 됐니?

M: Almost. I still need to pack a few things.
거의 됐어. 몇 가지만 더 챙기면 돼.

W: You're going to have a great time there.
넌 거기서 즐거운 시간을 보내겠구나.

M: I hope so. It's too bad you can't go with me.
그러길 바라고 있어. 네가 나랑 같이 못 가서 너무 아쉬워.

W: Yeah, but the doctor told me not to travel.
응, 하지만 의사 선생님이 내가 여행을 가면 안된다고 하셔.

M: When does he think you'll get better?
그분은 네가 언제쯤 괜찮아질 거라고 생각하시니?

W: He said I should be better from my illness in two weeks. 2주 후면 병에서 회복할 거라고 말씀하셨어.

M: That's good to hear. 좋은 소식이구나.

어휘 pack 짐을 챙기다 travel 여행하다 get better 호전되다, 회복하다 illness 질병

07 ④

W: Can you put the box on the counter here, please?
상자를 여기 계산대 위에 올려주시겠어요?

M: Sure. I'd like to send it by airmail.
네. 이걸 항공우편으로 보내고 싶습니다.

W: No problem. Did you write the return address on it? 알겠습니다. 발신인 주소를 상자 위에 적으셨어요?

M: Yes, it's in the left-hand corner.
네, 왼쪽 모서리에 있어요.

W: Thank you. That will be twenty-five dollars, please.
감사합니다. 25달러가 되겠습니다.

M: Here's my credit card. 여기 제 신용카드요.

해설 airmail, return address 등이 힌트가 된다.

어휘 counter 계산대, 판매대 by airmail 항공우편으로 return address 발신인 주소 left-hand 좌측의 corner 구석, 모서리

08 ①

W: Thanks for helping me with my math homework.
내 수학 숙제를 도와줘서 정말 고마워.

M: It's my pleasure. I enjoy solving math problems.
내가 좋아서 한 거야. 나는 수학 문제 푸는 걸 좋아해.

W: Do you want to teach math in the future?
넌 나중에 수학을 가르치고 싶니?

M: No. I would like to be a computer programmer.
아니. 나는 컴퓨터 프로그래머가 되고 싶어.

W: That seems like a good job. 좋은 직업 같네.

M: You still want to be an architect, right?
넌 아직도 건축가가 되고 싶지, 그렇지?

W: Yes. I love designing homes and buildings.
응. 나는 집과 건물을 설계하는 걸 좋아해.

M: Good luck. I know you can do it.
행운을 빌게. 네가 할 수 있을 거라고 생각해.

어휘 math 수학 pleasure 기쁨, 즐거움 solve (문제를) 풀다 architect 건축가 design 설계하다

09 ⑤

W: It's noon. Why don't we get some lunch?
12시야. 우리 점심을 먹는 게 어때?

M: All right. Should we go to a restaurant?
좋아. 음식점으로 갈까?

W: Okay. Where would you like to eat?
그래. 넌 어디에서 먹고 싶니?

M: I heard about a new Indian restaurant. I think it's called Delhi Delights. 새로운 인도 식당에 대해서 들었어. 이름이 델리 딜라이트인 것 같아.

W: Oh, I ate there yesterday. 아, 나는 어제 거기에서 먹었는데.

M: Really? How did you like it? 그래? 어땠어?

W: It was great. I promise you will enjoy the food there. 좋았어. 너도 그곳 음식을 즐길 거라고 장담해.

어휘 noon 정오 Indian 인도의 promise 약속하다, 단언하다

10 ②

M: Can I help you with something? 제가 도와드릴까요?

W: What do you recommend today?
오늘은 뭘 추천하시나요?

M: Well, the bananas are fresh. 음, 바나나가 신선해요.

W: I don't really like them.
저는 바나나를 그렇게 좋아하지는 않아요.

M: How about some peaches? They're very sweet.
복숭아는 어떠세요? 매우 달콤해요.

W: How much are they? 얼마죠?

M: They are two for a dollar. 두 개에 1달러입니다.

W: That's a good deal. I'll take ten of them.
가격이 저렴하네요. 10개 주세요.

M: That will be five dollars, please. 그러면 5달러입니다.

어휘 recommend 추천하다 fresh 신선한 peach 복숭아 sweet

달콤한 deal 거래

11 ⑤

M: What are you looking at on your computer?
컴퓨터로 뭘 보고 있니?

W: I'm checking out an online store.
온라인 상점을 살펴보고 있어.

M: What are you going to buy? 뭘 사려고 하는데?

W: I want to get my brother a birthday present. I'm
thinking about getting him some clothes. 남동생에게
생일 선물을 사주고 싶어. 그 애한테 옷을 좀 사주려고 생각 중이야.

M: Clothes? He won't like those.
옷? 그 애는 그걸 좋아하지 않을 것 같아.

W: What should I do then? 그럼 내가 뭘 사줘야 하지?

M: Let's go to the electronics store. I'll find a computer
game he'll like. 전자제품 매장에 가자. 내가 동생이 좋아할 만
한 컴퓨터 게임을 찾아줄게.

W: Okay. Let me get my bag, and then we can leave.
알았어. 내 가방 좀 챙긴 다음에 가자.

M: Sure. 좋아.

어휘 check out 확인하다; 살펴보다 online store 온라인 상점
present 선물 electronics 전자기기 leave 떠나다, 출발하다

12 ①

M: I can't believe it. 정말 믿을 수가 없어.

W: What's up? 무슨 일이니?

M: Do you remember that I was planning to take a trip
this weekend?
이번 주말에 내가 여행 가기로 계획했던 거 기억하니?

W: Sure. You're flying to Los Angeles, right?
물론이지. 너는 로스앤젤레스로 비행기를 타고 가잖아, 그렇지?

M: That was my plan, but I had to cancel my trip
because I need to go to work over the weekend.
그게 내 계획이었지만, 주말에 일해야 하기 때문에 난 여행을 취소
해야 했어.

W: That's disappointing. 그거 실망스러운데.

M: Even worse, the airline won't return my money
because I bought a nonrefundable ticket. I'm so
upset about that.
설상가상으로, 내가 환불이 안 되는 티켓을 구매했기 때문에 항공사
에서 내 돈을 환불해주지 않을 거야. 그것 때문에 너무 화가 나.

W: I'm sorry to hear that. Your ticket was probably
expensive.
그 얘기를 들으니 정말 안됐구나. 티켓이 아마 비쌌을 텐데 말이야.

해설 남자는 실망스러움을 넘어 화가 나 있다.

어휘 plan 계획(하다) take a trip 여행가다 fly 비행기를 타다
cancel 취소하다 even worse 더 안 좋은 것은; 설상가상으로
airline 항공사 return 환불하다, 반환하다 nonrefundable 환불되
지 않는

13 ⑤

M: Hello. Are you looking for something?
안녕하세요. 무엇을 찾고 계시나요?

W: Yes, I'd like to buy some jewelry for my daughter.
네, 제 딸에게 보석을 좀 사주고 싶어요.

M: Here's a nice gold necklace.
여기 예쁜 금목걸이가 있어요.

W: I'm sorry, but gold is too expensive for me.
죄송하지만 금은 저한테는 너무 비싸요.

M: Would you prefer silver then?
그럼 은을 선호하시나요?

W: Yes. Do you have any silver bracelets?
네. 은팔찌가 있나요?

M: Sure. Take a look at these.
물론입니다. 이걸 한번 보세요.

W: This one looks very nice. I'll take it.
이게 정말 예쁘네요. 이걸로 살게요.

M: All right. Let me wrap it up for you.
알겠습니다. 포장해 드릴게요.

해설 남자의 마지막 대사에 포장해 주겠다는 말이 있다.

어휘 jewelry 보석 necklace 목걸이 prefer 선호하다 bracelet
팔찌 take a look at ~을 한번 보다, 살펴보다 wrap up 포장하다

14 ④

그레이트 레이크 놀이공원

	주중	주말 & 공휴일
개장	오전 8:00 – 오후 10:00	오전 8:00 – 오후 11:30
폐장	크리스마스, 새해 첫날, 추수감사절	

① The amusement park is closed four days a year.
놀이공원은 일 년 중 4일 문을 닫는다.

② The amusement park closes at eight on
Wednesdays. 놀이공원은 수요일에는 8시에 문을 닫는다.

③ The amusement park opens at eight on Christmas
Day. 놀이공원은 크리스마스에 8시에 문을 연다.

④ The amusement park closes at different times on
weekdays and weekends.
놀이공원은 주중과 주말에 폐장하는 시간이 다르다.

⑤ The amusement park closes at ten on Sundays.
놀이공원은 일요일에 10시에 문을 닫는다.

어휘 amusement park 놀이공원 weekday 주중 holiday 휴일
Thanksgiving Day 추수감사절

15 ⑤

M: Mom, Eric invited me to his house for dinner. May I
go there? 엄마, 에릭이 자기 집으로 저를 저녁식사에 초대했어
요. 제가 거기 가도 되나요?

W: What time does he want you to go?
그 애는 네가 몇 시에 오기를 원하니?

M: It's four now, and his family eats at six every
evening.
지금이 4시인데, 그의 가족은 매일 저녁 6시에 식사를 해요.

W: You can go if you finish your chores and your

schoolwork.
만약 네가 해야 할 일과 학교 숙제를 다 끝낸다면 가도 좋아.

M: But that might take me a long time.
하지만 그럼 시간이 너무 오래 걸릴 거예요.

W: Then you'd better get started now. Are you going to do your homework first?
그럼 지금 바로 시작하는 게 좋겠구나. 숙제를 먼저 할 거니?

M: No, I think I'll take out the garbage. Then, I'll do my math assignment. 아니요, 쓰레기를 내다버릴게요. 그리고 나서 수학 숙제를 할 거예요.

W: That's good. 좋아.

어휘 invite 초대하다 chore 집안일, 잡일 take (시간이) 걸리다 take out the garbage 쓰레기를 내다버리다 assignment 과제

16 ①

① M: You did really well on the exam.
   넌 시험을 정말 잘 봤구나.
   W: You're welcome. 천만에.

② M: How often does your dog eat?
   네 개는 얼마나 자주 밥을 먹니?
   W: Pepper eats twice a day. 페퍼는 하루에 두 번 밥을 먹어.

③ M: Would you like me to open the window?
   내가 창문을 좀 열까?
   W: Yes, that would be great. 응, 그러면 좋을 것 같아.

④ M: When are you going to visit the gym?
   언제 헬스클럽을 갈 거니?
   W: I'll go there tomorrow morning. 내일 아침에 갈 거야.

⑤ M: How about riding our bicycles for a while?
   우리 자전거를 잠깐 타는 게 어때?
   W: I'd love to, but I'm too tired. 그렇고 싶은데 너무 피곤해.

해설 ①의 질문에 대해서는 'Thanks'와 같은 응답이 이어져야 한다.

어휘 do well on the exam 시험을 잘 보다 twice 두 번 gym 헬스클럽, 체육관 for a while 잠시 동안 tired 피곤한

17 ①

M: How is your history report going?
역사 보고서는 잘 되가니?

W: What history report? 무슨 역사 보고서?

M: Don't you remember? We have to write about a famous person in history.
기억 안 나니? 우린 역사적으로 유명한 사람에 대해서 써야 해.

W: Oh, right. I totally forgot. When is it due?
아, 맞다. 완전히 까먹고 있었어. 그게 언제까지지?

M: We have to give it to Mr. Smith tomorrow morning.
내일 아침에 스미스 선생님께 제출해야 해.

W: I'd better get to work on it.
난 보고서 쓰는 걸 시작해야겠어.

M: It's ten P.M. now. How can you finish on time?
지금은 오후 10시야. 어떻게 시간 내에 끝낼 수 있니?

W: I might not finish in the morning. But I'm sure I can finish it by lunch tomorrow. 아침까지는 못 끝낼 수도 있어.

하지만 내일 점심까지는 반드시 끝낼 수 있어.

① Better late than never.
   늦게라도 하는 것이 아예 안 하는 것보다 낫다.
② Rome wasn't built in a day.
   로마는 하루 아침에 이루어진 것이 아니다.
③ The early bird catches the worm.
   일찍 일어나는 새가 벌레를 잡는다.
④ Too many cooks spoil the broth.
   사공이 많으면 배가 산으로 간다.
⑤ A fool and his money are soon parted.
   어리석은 이는 돈을 오래 지니고 있지 못하는 법이다.

어휘 report 보고서 in history 역사상 totally 완전히 due ~하기로 되어 있는 work on ~을 작업하다 on time 제때에

18 ③

M: Excuse me. Could you do a big favor for me, please? 실례합니다. 제 어려운 부탁을 좀 들어주실 수 있나요?

W: Sure. What do you need? 물론이죠. 뭐가 필요하시죠?

M: Would you please watch my laptop for a moment? I have to go to the bathroom.
잠시 제 노트북을 봐주시겠어요? 제가 화장실에 가야 하거든요.

W: No problem. I'll keep an eye on it.
문제 없어요. 제가 잘 지켜볼게요.

M: Thanks a lot. I don't want to lose something else.
정말 고맙습니다. 저는 다른 것까지 잃어버리고 싶지 않거든요.

W: Why? Did you lose something recently?
왜요? 최근에 뭘 잃어버리셨나요?

M: Yes. I lost my watch. Somebody stole it a couple of days ago.
네. 제 시계를 잃어버렸어요. 누군가가 이틀 전에 그걸 훔쳐갔어요.

W: I'm really sorry to hear that. 정말 안됐네요.
① Sure. I know the time. 물론입니다. 제가 시간을 알고 있어요.
② That sounds good to me. 제게는 좋은 소식이군요.
③ I'm really sorry to hear that. 정말 안됐네요.
④ Okay. We can watch a movie.
   네. 우리는 영화를 볼 수 있어요.
⑤ What do you want me to watch? 제가 뭘 보면 될까요?

어휘 do somebody a favor ~의 부탁을 들어주다 laptop 노트북 컴퓨터 for a moment 잠시 동안 keep an eye on ~을 계속 지켜보다 lose 잃어버리다(lose-lost-lost) recently 최근에 steal 훔치다(steal-stole-stolen)

19 ①

M: I think we can work well together on this group project. 우리는 이번 조별 과제를 함께 잘할 수 있을 것 같아.

W: I agree. It should be fun, too.
나도 그렇게 생각해. 정말 재미있을 거야.

M: What kind of work do you want to do?
넌 어떤 종류의 일을 하고 싶어?

W: I'm good at drawing, so I can make the posters.
나는 그림을 잘 그리니까 포스터를 만들 수 있어.

M: That sounds good. And what should I do?

좋아. 그럼 나는 뭘 하면 될까?

W: You can <u>do</u> the <u>experiment</u>. I'm not that good at
<u>science</u>.
너는 실험을 할 수 있잖아. 난 과학을 그렇게 잘하지 못하거든.

M: Okay, but I can't do it <u>alone</u>. You'll have to <u>assist</u>
me.
알겠어, 하지만 그걸 나 혼자 할 순 없어. 네가 날 도와줘야 해.

W: <u>That sounds fine to me.</u> 그건 나도 좋아.

① That sounds fine to me. 그건 나도 좋아.

② Yes, that's the correct answer. 응, 그게 바로 정답이야.

③ Right. He is a good assistant. 맞아. 그는 훌륭한 조수야.

④ Sure. The experiments are easy. 물론이지. 실험은 쉬워.

⑤ No, I've never made a poster before.
아니, 난 포스터를 만들어 본 적이 없어.

어휘 work well 일을 잘하다 group project 조별 과제 be good
at ~을 잘하다 experiment 실험 alone 혼자서 assist 도와주다
assistant 조수, 조력자

20 ①

M: Take a look outside. It <u>snowed</u> a lot last night.
밖을 좀 봐라. 어젯밤에 눈이 많이 왔구나.

W: That's great, Dad. Since it's Saturday, I can <u>play</u> in
the snow <u>all day</u>. 멋졌어요, 아빠. 오늘이 토요일이니까, 하루
종일 눈 속에서 놀 수 있겠어요.

M: Why don't you <u>take</u> your <u>brother</u> with you?
네 남동생을 데리고 나가는 게 어떠니?

W: Okay. He can come <u>along</u> with me.
알겠어요. 그 애는 저랑 같이 나갈 거예요.

M: Thanks. <u>Where</u> are you going to go?
고맙구나. 어디를 갈 거니?

W: I think we'll go to the <u>park</u> and play with my
friends. 우린 공원에 가서 제 친구들이랑 같이 놀 것 같아요.

M: <u>Okay. Make sure to wear warm clothes.</u>
그래. 따뜻한 옷 입는 걸 명심하렴.

① Okay. Make sure to wear warm clothes.
그래. 따뜻한 옷 입는 걸 명심하렴.

② Do you want to go with your brother?
너는 동생과 같이 가고 싶어?

③ Yes, the park is closed. 그래, 공원은 문을 닫았어.

④ How many friends did you meet?
친구를 몇 명 만났어?

⑤ No, the car isn't parked outside now.
아니, 차는 지금 밖에 주차되어 있지 않아.

어휘 take a look ~을 한번 보다, 살펴보다 since ~이므로 along
with ~와 함께 park 공원; 주차하다

13회 실전모의고사
본문 p.148-149

01 ③	02 ④	03 ③	04 ④	05 ④
06 ④	07 ②	08 ⑤	09 ⑤	10 ②
11 ⑤	12 ⑤	13 ④	14 ③	15 ④
16 ②	17 ②	18 ③	19 ③	20 ④

01 ③

W: I want to buy a <u>necktie</u> for my <u>husband</u> for his
<u>birthday</u>. What do you <u>recommend</u>? 제 남편의 생일 선
물로 넥타이를 사고 싶어요. 어떤 걸 추천하시겠어요?

M: How about this <u>striped tie</u>? It's <u>popular with</u> many
men. 이건 줄무늬 넥타이는 어떠세요? 이건 많은 남성들에게 인기
가 있어요.

W: My husband doesn't like stripes. He <u>prefers solid
colors</u> or ties <u>with designs</u> on them.
제 남편은 줄무늬를 좋아하지 않아요. 그는 단색이나 디자인이 들어
간 넥타이를 선호해요.

M: We don't have any solid colors. But <u>how about</u> this
one with <u>flowers</u> on it? 저희는 단색은 없습니다. 하지만 꽃
이 그려진 이 넥타이는 어떠세요?

W: No, that doesn't look good. But that tie with
<u>triangles</u> on it is nice.
아니요, 별로네요. 하지만 삼각형이 그려진 저 넥타이는 좋은데요.

M: <u>Do you mean</u> this one here?
여기 있는 이걸 말씀하시는 건가요?

W: Yes, I'll take it. 네, 그걸로 살게요.

어휘 necktie 넥타이(= tie) striped 줄무늬가 있는 popular 인
기 있는 prefer 선호하다 solid color 단색 triangle 삼각형

02 ④

W: <u>What's wrong</u> with Tony today?
오늘 토니에게 무슨 일이 있니?

M: Nothing. He seems <u>all right</u> to me.
아무 일 없어. 내가 보기엔 괜찮은 것 같은데.

W: I don't think so. I wanted to borrow his notebook,
but he <u>got</u> really <u>mad</u> at me. He's being <u>selfish</u>.
난 그렇게 생각하지 않아. 그 애의 공책을 빌리고 싶었는데, 나한테
엄청 화를 냈어. 그 애는 이기적이었어.

M: That's strange. Tony is very <u>polite</u> and <u>generous</u> to
everyone.
이상하네. 토니는 모든 사람에게 무척 예의 바르고 친절하잖아.

W: That's what I thought, too. But he was really <u>angry</u>
a few minutes ago.
나도 그렇게 생각했어. 하지만 몇 분 전에는 정말 화를 냈어.

M: Maybe he's got a <u>problem</u> we don't know about.
아마 우리가 모르는 무슨 문제가 있었을 거야.

W: That's possible. I <u>have no idea</u> though.
그럴 수 있어. 그런데 난 잘 모르겠어.

어휘 all right 괜찮은 borrow 빌리다 notebook 공책 mad at ~에게 몹시 화난 selfish 이기적인 polite 예의 바른 generous 관대한, 친절한 maybe 아마도 though 하지만, 그러나 nervous 긴장한 confused 혼란스러운 satisfied 만족스러운

03 ③

W: Did you hear about that big <u>typhoon</u> in the <u>Pacific Ocean</u>? 태평양에서 발생한 큰 태풍에 대해서 들었니?

M: Yeah, it's dropping <u>a lot of rain</u> everywhere.
응, 그게 전 지역에 많은 비를 뿌리고 있잖아.

W: That's right. It's <u>raining heavily</u> in Jakarta and Manilla, too.
맞아. 자카르타와 마닐라에도 비가 엄청 오고 있어.

M: <u>How about</u> in Shanghai? Is it <u>rainy</u> there?
상하이는 어때? 거기에도 비가 오니?

W: No, it's only <u>cloudy</u> there. The typhoon <u>hasn't reached</u> China yet.
아니, 거긴 구름만 끼었어. 태풍이 아직 중국까지는 가지 않았어.

M: So Hong Kong should be all right <u>as well</u>.
그럼 홍콩도 괜찮겠네.

W: That's correct. I just saw the weather report. It's very <u>windy</u> there, but it hasn't started raining.
맞아. 내가 방금 일기예보를 봤어. 홍콩은 바람이 많이 불지만, 비는 오고 있지 않아.

어휘 typhoon 태풍 the Pacific Ocean 태평양 drop 떨어뜨리다 rain heavily 폭우가 내리다 reach 도달하다 correct 정확한 weather report 일기예보

04 ④

W: You <u>drink</u> a lot of <u>coffee</u>, don't you?
넌 커피를 많이 마시지, 그렇지 않니?

M: That's right. I drink <u>several cups</u> each day.
맞아. 매일 몇 잔씩 마셔.

W: Wow, that's a lot of coffee. Why do you drink so much of it?
와, 커피를 많이 마시는구나. 왜 그렇게 많이 마시니?

M: I love the <u>caffeine</u> in it. It helps me <u>stay awake</u> and <u>concentrate on</u> my work. Don't you drink coffee?
난 커피 안에 있는 카페인이 좋아. 카페인은 내가 깨어 있고 일에 집중하는 것을 도와주거든. 너는 커피를 안 마시니?

W: Actually, I've only had it once. I <u>didn't like</u> the <u>taste</u>, so I don't drink it. 사실은, 딱 한 번 마셔 봤어. 나한테는 맛이 없어서, 커피를 마시지 않아.

M: That's interesting. So what do you drink <u>instead</u>?
흥미롭네. 그럼 넌 대신 뭘 마시니?

W: I like <u>iced tea</u>. I <u>prefer</u> cold drinks <u>to</u> hot ones.
나는 아이스티를 좋아해. 난 따뜻한 것보다 차가운 것이 좋아.

어휘 several 몇몇의 each day 매일 caffeine 카페인 stay awake 깨어 있다 concentrate on ~에 집중하다 once 한 번 taste 맛 instead 대신에 iced tea 아이스티 prefer A to B B보다 A를 좋아하다

05 ④

W: You forgot to <u>turn</u> the <u>light off</u> in the living room before you <u>went to bed</u>.
넌 자기 전에 거실의 불을 끄는 것을 잊었더구나.

M: Sorry, Mom. I <u>won't</u> forget the <u>next time</u>.
죄송해요, 엄마. 다음에는 잊지 않을게요.

W: I hope not. We shouldn't <u>waste electricity</u>.
그러길 바란다. 우리는 전기를 낭비하면 안돼.

M: How else can we <u>save</u> electricity?
우리는 또 어떻게 전기를 절약할 수 있죠?

W: We shouldn't <u>leave</u> the computer or TV <u>on</u> when nobody is using them.
아무도 컴퓨터나 TV를 사용하지 않을 때는 그걸 켜두면 안 돼.

M: That's a good idea. 좋은 생각이에요.

W: And we shouldn't leave the <u>refrigerator</u> door open <u>for too long</u>. Open it, get some food, and then close it quickly. 그리고 냉장고 문을 너무 오래 열어 두면 안돼. 냉장고 문을 열고, 음식을 꺼내고, 재빨리 닫아야 한단다.

M: Okay. I'll do that, too. 알겠어요. 그렇게 할게요.

W: Great. Do those things, and you'll be able to <u>save</u> electricity. 좋아. 그렇게 하면 너는 전기를 절약할 수 있을 거야.

해설 여자의 마지막 문장은 동사 do로 시작하는 명령문이다. 여자는 명령문으로 충고의 의도를 나타냈다.

어휘 turn off 끄다 living room 거실 go to bed 잠자리에 들다 waste 낭비하다 save 절약하다 electricity 전기 leave something on ~을 켜둔 채로 두다 refrigerator 냉장고 be able to ~할 수 있다

06 ④

M: Hi, everyone. My <u>name</u> is Ralph, and <u>I am from</u> Canada. Now, my family and I <u>live</u> here <u>in</u> Daegu. We <u>came here</u> two years ago <u>because of</u> my father's job. I'm trying to <u>learn Korean</u>, but it's a difficult <u>language</u>. On the weekend, I often <u>go hiking</u> in the local area, and I sometimes go <u>downtown</u> with my friends. I like <u>taking pictures</u> as well.

안녕하세요, 여러분. 제 이름은 랠프이고, 캐나다에서 왔습니다. 지금 제 가족과 저는 여기 대구에 살고 있습니다. 저희 아버지의 직장 때문에 2년 전에 이곳에 왔어요. 저는 한국어를 배우려고 노력 중이지만, 너무 어려운 언어입니다. 주말에 저는 종종 주변으로 하이킹을 가고, 가끔 친구들과 시내에 갑니다. 저는 사진 찍는 것도 좋아합니다.

어휘 language 언어 on the weekend 주말에 go hiking 하이킹을 가다, 도보여행을 하다 local 지역의, 현지의 area 지역 sometimes 가끔 go downtown 시내에 가다 take pictures 사진을 찍다 as well 또한, ~도

07 ②

W: Steve, are you <u>all right</u> these days?

스티브, 요즘 잘 지내니?

M: Yes, Ms. Martin. I'm <u>fine</u>. Why do you ask?
네, 마틴 선생님. 괜찮아요. 왜 물어 보시죠?

W: You haven't <u>turned in</u> any <u>homework</u> for two weeks. 넌 2주 동안 어떤 숙제도 제출하지 않았더구나.

M: I'm sorry about that. 그 점은 죄송해요.

W: So what's going on? Is there a <u>problem</u>? 그러니까 무슨 일이니? 무슨 문제 있니?

M: The work is <u>too</u> <u>difficult</u> for me. I don't <u>understand</u> it. 그 숙제는 저에게는 너무 어려워요. 이해할 수가 없어요.

W: Then why don't you <u>stay</u> <u>late</u> after school tomorrow? I can <u>show</u> you <u>how</u> to do it. 그럼 내일 방과 후에 좀 남는 거 어떠니? 내가 하는 방법을 알려 줄게.

M: Okay. Thanks a lot. 알겠어요. 정말 감사해요.

어휘 all right 괜찮은 these days 요즘 turn in 제출하다 stay late 늦게까지 머물다 after school 방과 후에

08 ⑤

M: This is a really good <u>painting</u>. Did you make it? 이건 정말 훌륭한 그림이네. 네가 그렸니?

W: No, one of my friends did. But I <u>took</u> the <u>picture</u> she used for the painting. 아니, 내 친구 중 한 명이 그렸어. 하지만 그녀가 그림을 위해 사용한 사진은 내가 찍었어.

M: Can I see it? 내가 그걸 볼 수 있니?

W: Sure. It's right here. I'd like to be a <u>photographer</u> in <u>the future</u>.
물론이지. 바로 여기 있어. 나는 나중에 사진작가가 되고 싶어.

M: The picture and the painting <u>look</u> almost <u>the same</u>. I'm <u>impressed</u>.
사진과 그림이 정말 비슷하게 보이네. 인상적이야.

W: My friend is an <u>excellent</u> <u>artist</u>. Don't you agree? 내 친구는 정말 훌륭한 화가야. 너도 동의하지 않니?

M: Yes, I think so. 응, 나도 그렇게 생각해.

어휘 painting 그림 take a picture 사진을 찍다 right here 바로 여기에 photographer 사진작가 in the future 미래에 look the same 똑같이 보이다 impressed 감명 받은, 인상적인 excellent 훌륭한, 뛰어난 agree 동의하다

09 ⑤

[Cellphone rings.] [휴대폰이 울린다.]

W: Hi, Chris. How are you? 안녕, 크리스. 잘 지내니?

M: I'm good, Mina. What are you doing? 잘 지내, 미나. 뭐 하고 있니?

W: I'm <u>working</u> <u>on</u> my <u>homework</u>. I need to finish <u>writing</u> a <u>paper</u>.
난 숙제를 하고 있어. 보고서 쓰는 것을 끝내야 해.

M: <u>What</u> <u>time</u> do you think you're going to <u>finish</u>? 언제 끝날 것 같니?

W: I need about thirty more minutes. Why? 난 30분 정도 더 필요해. 왜?

M: Wendy and I are going to get some <u>pizza</u> at the <u>restaurant</u>. Would you like to <u>go</u> <u>with</u> us?

웬디와 나는 음식점에 피자를 먹으러 갈 거야. 같이 갈래?

W: Sure. That sounds great. <u>Do</u> you <u>mind</u> waiting a bit? 물론이야. 잘됐다. 조금만 기다려 줄 수 있겠니?

M: <u>Not at all</u>. <u>Call</u> me <u>back</u> when you are ready to go. 당연하지. 갈 준비가 되면 나한테 다시 전화를 해줘.

W: Okay. I'll do that. 알았어. 그렇게 할게.

어휘 work on ~을 작업하다 a bit 약간, 조금 be ready to ~할 준비가 되다

10 ②

M: This is an <u>object</u> that many different <u>items</u> <u>use</u>. This is usually <u>small</u>, and this <u>provides</u> <u>electricity</u>. Without this, many items cannot <u>work</u>. A person <u>puts</u> this <u>into</u> an item such as a <u>remote</u> <u>control</u>, and then the person can use the remote control to change the channels. This often <u>lasts</u> <u>for</u> a <u>long</u> <u>time</u>. But when this <u>runs</u> <u>out</u> of power, people <u>replace</u> this <u>with</u> a new one.

이것은 많은 다른 제품들이 사용하는 물건이다. 이것은 보통 크기가 작고, 전기를 제공한다. 이것이 없다면 많은 제품들은 작동할 수 없다. 어떤 사람이 이것을 리모컨과 같은 제품에 넣으면, 그 사람은 채널을 바꾸기 위해 리모컨을 이용할 수 있다. 이것은 종종 오랜 시간 동안 지속된다. 하지만 전력을 다 소모하면 사람들은 이것을 새 것으로 교체한다.

어휘 object 물건 item 제품, 물품 provide 제공하다 electricity 전기 work 작동하다 remote control 리모컨 channel (방송) 채널 last 지속되다 for a long time 오랫동안 run out of ~을 다 써 버리다, 소모하다 replace A with B A를 B로 교체하다

11 ⑤

M: Good afternoon. <u>What</u> seems to be the <u>problem</u>? 안녕하세요. 무슨 문제가 있으시죠?

W: It's Sandy. She keeps <u>scratching</u> her <u>ears</u>. 샌디가 문제예요. 자꾸 자기 귀를 긁어요.

M: When did this start? 이 문제가 언제 시작됐죠?

W: About two days ago. I looked at her right ear, and it's really red. 약 이틀 전이에요. 제가 샌디의 오른쪽 귀를 봤는데 새빨개져 있었어요.

M: She might <u>have</u> an <u>infection</u>. Can you <u>put</u> her up <u>on</u> the <u>table</u>?
아마 염증이 생긴 것 같네요. 테이블 위로 올려 주시겠어요?

W: Sure. Here she is. Don't worry. She won't <u>bite</u> you. She's <u>wagging</u> her <u>tail</u> now. She's very friendly.
네. 여기 있어요. 걱정 마세요. 물지는 않을 거예요. 지금 꼬리를 흔들고 있잖아요. 샌디는 아주 착해요.

M: Thanks. Hmm… Yes, her ear is very red.
감사합니다. 음, 맞네요. 귀가 아주 빨개요.

W: Is it bad? 심각한가요?

M: Let me <u>give</u> her a <u>shot</u> and some <u>medicine</u>. She'll be fine in a few days. 샌디에게 주사를 놓고 약을 좀 먹일게요. 며칠 후면 괜찮아질 겁니다.

해설 Sandy라는 이름의 동물이 치료를 받고 있는 상황이므로 동물병원이 정답이다.

어휘 keep –ing 계속해서 ~하다 scratch 긁다 infection 감염; 염증 bite 물다 wag one's tail 꼬리를 흔들다 friendly 상냥한, 친절한 give a shot 주사를 놓다 medicine 약

12 ⑤

M: These cookies look great. Do you mind if I have one? 이 쿠키는 정말 맛있어 보인다. 내가 하나 먹어봐도 될까?

W: Not at all. Please go ahead. I just made them.
물론이지. 어서 먹어봐. 내가 방금 만들었어.

M: Thanks. [pause] It's delicious. What did you put in it? 고마워. [잠시 후] 맛있어. 이 안에 무엇을 넣었니?

W: Well, it has sugar, eggs, and flour in it.
음, 설탕, 계란, 그리고 밀가루가 들어갔어.

M: I can see the chocolate chips, too.
초콜릿칩도 보이네.

W: Yes, I added some of those. 응, 몇 개 넣었어.

M: What are these red pieces? Are these cherries?
이 빨간색 조각들은 뭐야? 체리니?

W: No, they aren't. They're cranberries. They give the cookies their unique taste. 아니, 체리가 아니야. 그건 크랜베리야. 그게 쿠키에 독특한 맛을 내주는 거야.

어휘 go ahead (어떤 일을) 계속하다 sugar 설탕 flour 밀가루 add 더하다 piece 조각 unique 독특한 taste 맛

13 ④

W: Hello. Welcome to Dave's Donut Shop.
안녕하세요. 데이브 도넛 가게에 오신 것을 환영합니다.

M: Hi. Which donuts do you recommend?
안녕하세요. 어떤 도넛을 추천하시나요?

W: The chocolate donuts are excellent. They cost one dollar each. 초콜릿 도넛이 아주 맛있어요. 개당 1달러입니다.

M: What about the jelly donuts? I like them a lot.
젤리 도넛은 어떤가요? 제가 그걸 무척 좋아하거든요.

W: We have cherry, blueberry, and raspberry jelly donuts.
저희는 체리, 블루베리, 그리고 라즈베리 젤리 도넛이 있어요.

M: What do they cost? 그건 얼마죠?

W: They are each one dollar and fifty cents. Would you like some?
각각 1달러 50센트입니다. 좀 드셔 보시겠어요?

M: I'll take three raspberry jelly donuts and two chocolate donuts.
라즈베리 젤리 도넛 3개와 초콜릿 도넛 2개 주세요.

W: Hold on just one moment, please.
잠시만 기다려 주세요.

해설 초콜릿 도넛($1×2=$2)+라즈베리 도넛($1.50×3=$4.50)=$6.50

어휘 donut 도넛(= doughnut) recommend 추천하다 excellent 훌륭한, 뛰어난 cost 비용이 들다 raspberry 산딸기, 라즈베리 hold on 기다리다

14 ③

W: Why are you watching TV? 넌 왜 TV를 보고 있니?

M: My favorite program is coming on in a while.
잠시 후에 제가 좋아하는 프로그램이 나올 거예요.

W: But it's eight fifteen, and you have to get ready for your piano lesson.
하지만 지금은 8시 15분이고, 너는 피아노 레슨 준비를 해야지.

M: I know, Mom, but can't I watch this TV program first? 알아요, 엄마, 하지만 TV 프로그램을 먼저 보면 안되나요?

W: When does it start? 그게 언제 시작하니?

M: In ten minutes. 십 분 후예요.

W: Well, how about practicing a bit before the piano teacher gets here? That will only take about five minutes. 음, 피아노 선생님이 여기 오시기 전에 조금 연습하는 게 어떻겠니? 5분 정도밖에 안 걸릴 거야.

M: Okay. I'll do that now. 알겠어요. 지금 할게요.

W: Good. You need to make sure you remember the song you learned during your last lesson.
좋아. 넌 지난 레슨 시간에 배운 곡을 기억할 필요가 있단다.

어휘 favorite 매우 좋아하는 in a while 잠시 후에, 곧 get ready for ~을 준비하다 practice 연습하다 make sure 확실히 하다

15 ④

① M: Where did you buy that dress? 그 옷은 어디서 샀니?
   W: At a store downtown. 시내에 있는 가게에서.
② M: What time is your doctor's appointment?
   병원 진료는 몇 시니?
   W: It's at two thirty. 2시 30분이야.
③ M: Could you pick up that box for me, please?
   나 대신 저 상자를 들어줄 수 있니?
   W: Sure. Where should I put it?
   물론이지. 저걸 어디다 놓아야 하니?
④ M: Why don't we eat out tonight?
   오늘 밤에 외식을 하는 게 어때?
   W: Okay. I'll cook a pizza. 좋아. 내가 피자를 만들게.
⑤ M: What do you think of the new student?
   새로 온 학생에 대해 어떻게 생각하니?
   W: She seems like a nice girl. 좋은 여자아이 같아.

어휘 downtown 시내에 doctor's appointment 병원 진료 예약 pick up ~을 들다, 줍다 eat out 외식하다

16 ②

M: Hi. How can I help you? 안녕하세요. 무엇을 도와 드릴까요?

W: I have this prescription from Dr. Norby. I need to have it filled. 제가 노비 박사님한테서 이 처방전을 받았어요. 처방대로 약을 지어 주세요.

M: All right. That will take a few minutes.
알겠습니다. 몇 분 정도 걸릴 거예요.

W: Okay, I'll wait. 네. 기다릴게요.

M: Do you have health insurance? 의료보험이 있으신가요?

W: Yes. Here's my insurance card.
네. 여기 제 의료보험증이요.

M: Thanks. How will you <u>pay for</u> this?
감사합니다. 계산을 어떻게 하실 건가요?

W: I'll pay with <u>cash</u>. 현금으로 낼게요.

어휘 fill a prescription (처방전대로) 약을 짓다 take (시간이) 걸리다 health insurance 의료보험 pay for ~을 지불하다 cash 현금

17 ②

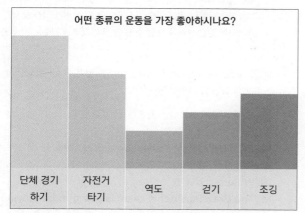

① Playing <u>team</u> <u>sports</u> is the <u>most</u> <u>popular</u> type of <u>exercise</u>. 단체 경기를 하는 것이 가장 인기 있는 운동 종류이다.

② The <u>same</u> <u>number</u> of students like <u>cycling</u> and <u>weightlifting</u>.
같은 수의 학생들이 자전거 타기와 역도를 좋아한다.

③ <u>Walking</u> is not <u>as</u> popular with students <u>as</u> <u>jogging</u>.
학생들에게 걷기는 조깅만큼 인기 있지 않다.

④ Cycling is <u>less</u> popular <u>than</u> playing team sports.
자전거 타기는 단체 경기보다 인기가 없다.

⑤ Weightlifting is <u>one of the least</u> popular activities.
역도는 가장 인기 없는 활동 중 하나이다.

어휘 exercise 운동 team sports 단체 경기, 팀 스포츠 cycling 자전거 타기 weightlifting 역도 activity 활동

18 ③

[*Cellphone rings.*] [휴대폰이 울린다.]

M: Hi, Anna. What are you doing now?
안녕, 애나. 지금 뭐 하고 있니?

W: I'm <u>working on</u> my science <u>project</u>.
과학 프로젝트를 하고 있어.

M: <u>How</u> <u>long</u> are you going to do that?
그걸 하는 데 얼마나 걸릴 것 같니?

W: I'll <u>probably</u> work on it for two more hours.
아마 두 시간은 더 작업해야 할 것 같아.

M: When you're finished, how about <u>seeing</u> a <u>movie</u> with me? 끝나고 나면, 나랑 영화 보러 가는 게 어때?

W: I can't. I need to <u>go to bed</u> early tonight. I'm <u>going</u> <u>hiking</u> with my family early in the morning.
난 안 돼. 오늘 밤은 일찍 자야 해. 내일 아침 일찍 가족과 함께 하이

킹을 가기로 했어.

M: Really? Where are you going to go?
정말? 너희는 어디로 갈 거니?

W: We're <u>going</u> <u>for</u> <u>a</u> <u>walk</u> in the countryside.
우리는 시골길을 걸으러 갈 거야.

어휘 probably 아마도 go hiking 하이킹 가다 for a walk 산책 삼아 countryside 시골

19 ③

W: How are you <u>enjoying</u> the <u>party</u>?
파티는 즐기고 있니?

M: I'm having a great time here. <u>Thanks for</u> the <u>invitation</u>.
난 여기서 아주 즐거운 시간을 보내고 있어. 초대해 줘서 고마워.

W: <u>No problem</u>. And thank you for coming here.
천만에. 여기 와줘서 고마워.

M: I didn't want to <u>miss</u> this party. Everyone from school is here. 난 이 파티를 놓치고 싶지 않았어. 학교의 모든 사람들이 여기 있잖아.

W: Yeah. <u>How do you like</u> the food? 응. 음식은 어떠니?

M: It's great. Did your mother make everything?
맛있어. 너희 어머니께서 전부 만드셨니?

W: <u>Actually</u>, she and I <u>worked</u> <u>together</u> to <u>cook</u> all of the food. 사실은, 엄마랑 내가 모든 음식을 같이 만들었어.

M: You made this? I didn't know you could cook.
네가 이걸 만들었다고? 네가 요리를 할 수 있는지 몰랐어.

W: <u>It's one of my hobbies</u>. 그건 내 취미 중 하나야.

① Here's the menu. 여기에 메뉴가 있어.
② No, I'm not a cook. 아니, 나는 요리사가 아니야.
③ It's one of my hobbies. 그건 내 취미 중 하나야.
④ May I take your order, please? 제가 주문을 받을까요?
⑤ Yes, she works in a restaurant.
응, 엄마는 식당에서 일하셔.

어휘 have a great time 즐거운 시간을 보내다 invitation 초대(장) miss 놓치다 actually 사실은 hobby 취미 cook 요리사; 요리하다 take an order 주문을 받다

20 ④

M: Are you ready for our <u>final</u> <u>exams</u>?
기말 시험 준비는 됐니?

W: Not yet. I <u>haven't</u> started studying <u>yet</u>.
아직 안 했어. 아직 공부를 시작하지도 않았어.

M: But the tests start <u>two</u> <u>days</u> <u>from</u> <u>now</u>. Why haven't you studied for them?
그렇지만 시험은 이틀 후에 시작해. 왜 시험 공부를 하지 않았니?

W: I've been working on my history project.
난 역사 프로젝트를 작업하고 있었어.

M: Oh, I <u>finished</u> it <u>last</u> <u>week</u>. 아, 난 지난주에 그걸 끝냈는데.

W: You did? I'm <u>impressed</u>. Was it hard?
끝냈어? 놀라운데. 그게 어려웠니?

M: <u>Not</u> <u>really</u>. Would you like me to <u>give</u> you <u>a hand</u>

with yours?

그다지 어렵지 않았어. 내가 네 프로젝트를 좀 도와줄까?

W: I would appreciate that a lot. 그러면 정말 고마울 거야.

① Do you expect to do well on the tests?

시험을 잘 볼 것으로 기대하니?

② What exam should I study for first?

난 어떤 시험을 먼저 공부해야 하지?

③ No, I haven't handed it in yet.

아니, 아직 그걸 제출하지 않았어.

④ I would appreciate that a lot. 그러면 정말 고마울 거야.

⑤ I hope I do well on my exams.

난 시험을 잘 보기를 바라고 있어.

어휘 final exams 기말 시험 from now 지금으로부터 work on ~을 작업하다 impressed 감명 받은 give somebody a hand ~을 돕다 do well 잘하다 hand in 제출하다 appreciate 고마워하다

14회 실전모의고사

본문 p.160-161

01 ③	02 ④	03 ⑤	04 ②	05 ③
06 ④	07 ④	08 ②	09 ③	10 ①
11 ③	12 ⑤	13 ②	14 ④	15 ①
16 ④	17 ⑤	18 ③	19 ④	20 ②

01 ③

W: Hi. I need to buy an alarm clock.

안녕하세요. 제가 알람 시계를 사야 하거든요.

M: No problem. We have many of them. Do you like this round one with the bell on top? 알겠습니다. 저희 가게에는 시계가 많아요. 위에 종이 달린 이 둥근 시계는 어떠세요?

W: Not really. It's not my style.

별로네요. 제 스타일이 아니에요.

M: We also have a round one with no bell on it. How about that?

종이 달려 있지 않은 둥근 시계도 있어요. 어떠세요?

W: I'd rather have a rectangular one.

저는 그보다는 직사각형의 시계를 사겠어요.

M: We have a couple of them. This one has hands on it. 저희에게 몇 개 있습니다. 이것은 시계바늘이 있어요.

W: Do you have any digital clocks?

디지털 시계가 있나요?

M: Yes, we have a rectangular one and a circular one.

네, 직사각형의 시계와 둥근 시계가 있습니다.

W: Give me the one shaped like a rectangle, please.

직사각형으로 생긴 시계를 주세요.

어휘 alarm clock 알람 시계 round 둥근, 원형의(= circular) bell 종 rectangular 직사각형의 a couple of 몇 개의, 두 개의 hand (시계) 바늘, (시/분/초) 침 digital clock 디지털 시계

02 ④

M: Here's the weather report for Korea today. In Busan, it's very foggy right now. In Daegu, it's going to rain all day long. There are cloudy skies in Gwangju and Daegu. In Incheon, it's raining a bit now, but there are sunny skies in Seoul. And in Wonju, it's cold and windy right now.

오늘 한국의 날씨를 말씀 드리겠습니다. 부산은 현재 안개가 많이 끼어 있습니다. 대구는 하루 종일 비가 오겠습니다. 광주와 대구의 하늘에는 구름이 끼어 있습니다. 인천은 지금 비가 약간 오지만, 서울에서는 맑은 하늘을 보실 수 있습니다. 그리고 원주는 지금 춥고 바람이 붑니다.

어휘 weather report 일기예보 foggy 안개 낀 all day long 하루 종일 windy 바람이 부는

03 ⑤

M: Check this out. I have some great news.

이것 좀 봐. 좋은 소식이 있어.

W: What is it? 뭐야?

M: The Brazilian soccer team is going to be playing the Korean team next week.

다음 주에 브라질 축구팀이 한국 축구팀과 경기를 할 거야.

W: Really? That's amazing. I'd love to see that game.

정말? 놀라운 소식이네. 난 그 경기를 보고 싶어.

M: According to this article, we can get tickets online.

이 기사에 따르면, 온라인으로 표를 구매할 수 있어.

W: All right. Let's go to the website and book our tickets. [pause]

좋아. 웹사이트에 들어가서 우리 표를 예매하자. [잠시 후]

M: Oh, no. Look at this. This is terrible.

아, 안돼. 이것 좀 봐. 정말 너무하잖아.

W: What's the matter? Is there something wrong?

무슨 일이야? 무슨 문제라도 있어?

M: There aren't any tickets left. They're all sold out.

남은 표가 없어. 다 매진됐어.

어휘 check something out ~을 확인하다 amazing 놀라운 according to ~에 따르면 online 온라인으로, 인터넷에서 book 예약하다 left 남은 sold out 매진된

04 ②

W: Where are you going right now, Dave?

너 지금 어디 가니, 데이브?

M: I've got to go to the library. 난 도서관에 가봐야 해.

W: Are you going to meet John? I know he's studying there now.

존을 만날 거니? 내가 알기로는 존이 지금 거기서 공부하고 있어.

M: Oh, I didn't know that. 아, 그건 몰랐네.

W: Yeah, he needs to study for the science test tomorrow. 응, 존은 내일 있을 과학 시험 공부를 해야 해.

M: I'm not going there to meet him. I need to return

this book.
난 존을 만나러 거기 가는 게 아니야. 이 책을 반납해야 해.

W: Is it late? 기한이 늦었니?

M: No, but it is due today. So I need to return it before the library closes tonight. 아니, 하지만 오늘까지야. 그래서 오늘 밤 도서관이 문 닫기 전에 이걸 반납해야 해.

W: You'd better hurry then. It closes in half an hour. 그럼 서두르는 게 좋겠다. 도서관은 30분 후에 문을 닫을 거야.

어휘 return 반납하다 due 예정인, ~하기로 되어 있는 had better ~하는 것이 좋을 것이다 hurry 서두르다 half an hour 30분

05 ③

W: Excuse me. Where are you going?
실례합니다. 어디 가시죠?

M: I'm here to see Mr. Kent on the ninth floor.
저는 9층에 있는 켄트 씨를 만나러 왔습니다.

W: I'm sorry, but you can't just go up the elevator.
죄송합니다만, 그냥 엘리베이터를 타고 올라가실 수는 없어요.

M: Why not? 왜 안되죠?

W: All visitors to this building have to sign in.
이 건물의 모든 방문자들은 서명을 하셔야 하거든요.

M: Oh, I didn't know that. 아, 그건 몰랐어요.

W: Please sign your name here. And I need to see your ID card, too.
여기에 성함을 적어 주세요. 그리고 신분증도 보여주셔야 합니다.

M: I think I left my wallet in my car. Could you just tell Mr. Kent that I'll be waiting in the lobby?
저는 차에 지갑을 두고 온 것 같군요. 켄트 씨에게 제가 로비에서 기다릴 거라고 말씀해 주시겠어요?

어휘 visitor 방문객 ninth 아홉 번째의 go up the elevator 엘리베이터를 타고 올라가다 sign in 서명하다 ID card 신분증

06 ④

M: Can I help you with something? 제가 도와드릴까요?

W: Yes, I need to take a picture.
네, 제가 사진을 찍어야 하거든요.

M: What is the photo for? 어디에 쓰일 사진이죠?

W: It's for my school ID card. 학생증에 쓰일 사진이에요.

M: That's no problem. We can do that right now.
문제 없습니다. 지금 바로 해드릴 수 있어요.

W: All right. Should I sit down over there?
좋아요. 제가 저쪽에 앉으면 되나요?

M: Yes. Let me set up the equipment. This will just take a moment.
네. 제가 장비를 설치할게요. 잠깐이면 됩니다.

어휘 take a picture 사진 찍다 school ID card 학생증 over there 저기에, 저쪽에 set up 설치하다 equipment 장비

07 ④

W: Are we still going jogging tomorrow morning at nine? 우리 여전히 내일 아침 9시에 조깅하러 가는 거지?

M: Sorry, but I can't go in the morning.
미안한데, 난 아침에는 못 가.

W: Why not? 왜 못 가?

M: My dad wants me to help around the house.
아빠가 내가 집안일을 돕기를 원하셔.

W: Should we go around one or two then?
그럼 1시나 2시쯤에 갈까?

M: It will probably be too hot then. How about sometime in the evening? Six is good for me.
그때는 아마 너무 더울 거야. 저녁때는 어때? 난 6시가 좋아.

W: Five would be better though.
그래도 5시가 더 나을 것 같은데.

M: All right. Let's go jogging then.
알겠어. 그때 조깅하러 가자.

어휘 go jogging 조깅하러 가다 around ~쯤, ~경에 probably 아마도 then 그때

08 ②

M: Are you ready to order? 주문하시겠어요?

W: Yes. I want a chicken sandwich, two orders of fries, and two drinks, please.
네. 치킨 샌드위치, 튀김 2인분, 그리고 음료 두 개를 주세요.

M: Your total comes to seven dollars.
합계 금액은 7달러가 됩니다.

W: Hold on a moment. How much is a slice of apple pie? 잠시만요. 애플파이 한 조각이 얼마죠?

M: It's two dollars. 2달러입니다.

W: I'll also take one of those, please.
애플파이도 한 조각 주세요.

M: Is that all? 다 주문하신 건가요?

W: Yes. Here's ten dollars. 네. 여기 10달러요.

M: And here's your change. 그럼 여기 잔돈 드릴게요.

해설 $10 − ($7+$2) = $1

어휘 order 주문하다; 주문 total 총합; 총액 come to (합계가) ~가 되다 slice 조각 change 잔돈

09 ③

W: You come to school by bus, don't you?
넌 버스를 타고 학교에 오지, 그렇지 않니?

M: That's right. I do that every morning.
맞아. 난 매일 아침 버스를 타.

W: How long does it take? 얼마나 걸리니?

M: It usually takes around half an hour to get to school. 학교에 도착하는 데 보통 30분 정도 걸려.

W: That's a long time. You must be bored on the bus.
오래 걸리는구나. 버스에서 지루하겠다.

M: Not really. 아니 그다지 지루하지 않아.

W: Why not? What do you do? 왜 안 그래? 뭘 하는데?

M: I often play games on my smartphone. And I sometimes surf the Internet.
난 종종 내 스마트폰으로 게임을 해. 그리고 가끔 인터넷 검색을 해.

W: Ah, so you have something to do the entire time.
아, 그럼 넌 버스 타는 시간 내내 뭔가를 하는구나.

어휘 take (시간이) 걸리다 half an hour 30분 bored 지루한 surf the Internet 인터넷 검색을 하다 entire 전체의

10 ①

[*Cellphone rings.*] [휴대폰이 울린다.]
M: Hi, Sue. How's it going? 안녕, 수. 잘 지내니?
W: I'm good, Eric. Are you busy now?
잘 지내, 에릭. 지금 바쁘니?
M: A little. I'm watching my baby sister.
조금. 난 젖먹이 여동생을 돌보고 있어.
W: Do you mind if I come over for a while?
내가 잠깐 들러도 괜찮을까?
M: What for? 무엇 때문에?
W: I want you to look at the paper I wrote for history class.
내가 역사 수업 숙제로 쓴 보고서를 네가 좀 봐줬으면 좋겠어.
M: Why do you want me to look at it?
왜 내가 보길 원하는 거야?
W: You're the best student in class. I know you'll find some mistakes in my paper. 넌 반에서 최고의 우등생이잖아. 네가 내 보고서에서 실수를 찾을 수 있을 거야.
M: Okay. You can come over now. 알았어. 넌 지금 와도 돼.

어휘 do you mind if ~? ~해도 괜찮니? come over (집에) 들르다 for a while 잠시 동안 write 쓰다(write – wrote – written) find 찾다 mistake 실수

11 ③

W: Wow. The house looks great. 우와. 집이 정말 멋져.
M: Thanks. I've been putting up balloons for the past two hours. 고마워. 난 두 시간 동안 풍선을 달았어.
W: Is it your birthday? 네 생일이니?
M: No, it's my brother's birthday. 아니, 내 남동생의 생일이야.
W: Are you having a party for him today?
오늘 남동생을 위해 파티를 열 거니?
M: That's right. It's a surprise party, so I need to finish everything by four. He's coming home then.
맞아. 깜짝 파티가 될 거라서, 4시까지 모든 걸 끝내야 해. 그 애가 그때 오거든.
W: Where's the cake? 케이크는 어디에 있니?
M: Oh, I totally forgot about it. I need to run to the bakery. Can you put up the rest of these balloons for me? 아, 케이크를 완전 잊어버리고 있었어. 제과점에 달려가야겠어. 네가 나 대신 나머지 풍선을 달아줄 수 있겠니?
W: Sure. I'll do that while you're gone.
물론이지. 네가 없는 동안 내가 그걸 할게.

어휘 put up (깃발·돛 등을) 달다 balloon 풍선 surprise party 깜짝 파티 totally 완전히; 전적으로 bakery 제과점 the rest 나머지 while ~하는 동안

12 ⑤

W: Are you looking for something? 뭘 찾고 계신가요?
M: Yes. I need to buy something for my nephew for Christmas. 네. 크리스마스에 조카에게 줄 것을 사야 하거든요.
W: How old is he? 조카가 몇 살이죠?
M: He's six years old. 6살이에요.
W: Does he enjoy games? Here are some games he could play. 그 애가 게임을 좋아하나요? 그가 할 수 있는 게임들이 여기 있어요.
M: I think those aren't good for him. Do you have any robots? 제 생각에 그건 제 조카에게 좋지 않을 것 같아요. 로봇은 있나요?
W: Yes, we have plenty of robots. Please follow me, and I'll show you. 네, 저희는 로봇을 많이 보유하고 있어요. 저를 따라오시면 보여드릴게요.

어휘 nephew (남자) 조카 plenty of 많은

13 ②

① W: Have you met Alice yet? 넌 앨리스를 벌써 만났니?
M: Yes, we talked after class today.
응, 오늘 수업이 끝나고 얘기했어.
② W: When are you going on vacation? 넌 언제 휴가를 떠나니?
M: For three days and two nights. 2박 3일 동안.
③ W: Do you know what time it is? 지금이 몇 시인지 아니?
M: Sorry, but I'm not wearing a watch.
미안하지만 시계를 안 차고 있어.
④ W: How often does John play sports?
존은 얼마나 자주 운동을 하니?
M: Every day after school. 방과 후에 매일.
⑤ W: Could I borrow a pen, please? 펜 좀 빌릴 수 있을까요?
M: Sure, but you need to give it back.
물론이죠, 하지만 다시 돌려줘야 해요.

해설 ②에서는 when 의문문으로 시기를 물었는데, how long(얼마나 오랫동안) 질문에 해당하는 답변을 했다.

어휘 go on vacation 휴가를 떠나다 wear a watch 시계를 차다 borrow 빌리다 give back 돌려주다

14 ④

M: Everyone, please listen carefully. I'm very sorry, but there's a problem with the elevator. It's stuck between the third and fourth floors. A repairman is coming to look at it now. But he won't be here for about twenty minutes. Until he fixes the problem, you need to take the stairs to get to another floor. Please be patient. I apologize for this problem.
여러분, 잘 들어주시기 바랍니다. 정말 죄송합니다만 엘리베이터에 문제가 생겼습니다. 3층과 4층 사이에 멈춰 있습니다. 지금 수리 기사가 엘리베이터를 확인하기 위해 오고 있습니다. 하지만 약 20분 안에는 여기 도착하지 않을 것입니다. 수리 기사가 문제를 해결할 때까지는 계단을 이용하여 다른 층으로 가 주시기 바랍니다. 조금만

참아주시기 바랍니다. 이런 문제가 생기게 되어 죄송합니다.

어휘 stuck 꼼짝 못 하는 between ~사이에 floor 층 repairman 수리공 fix 고치다, 수리하다 take the stairs 계단을 이용하다 patient 참을성 있는 apologize for ~을 사과하다

15 ①

M: Did you enjoy the New Year's holiday, Sally?
새해 첫날 휴일은 잘 보냈니, 샐리?

W: I had a great time. I went to the ocean.
멋진 시간을 보냈어. 난 바다에 갔었어.

M: Did you see the sun rise on the first day of the year? 새해 첫날에 해돋이를 봤니?

W: That's right. It was so beautiful. 그래. 정말 아름다웠어.

M: What did you do after that? 그리고 나서 뭐 했니?

W: My cousin and I went cycling even though it was cold. Then, we went to a ski resort later in the day.
날이 추웠지만 사촌이랑 같이 자전거를 탔어. 그리고 나서 그날 늦게 스키 리조트에 갔어.

M: You can ski? I didn't know that.
너 스키를 탈 수 있구나? 난 그건 몰랐어.

W: It was my first time. I took some lessons.
처음 타는 거였어. 교육을 좀 받았지.

M: It sounds like you had a really busy holiday.
넌 정말 바쁜 휴일을 보낸 것 같구나.

어휘 ocean 바다 cousin 사촌 go cycling 자전거를 타다 even though 비록 ~이지만 first time 처음

16 ④

W: Good afternoon, everyone, and welcome to Super Saver Mart. Right now, we've got a special offer in the meat section. Fresh chicken and pork are on sale for forty percent off, and you can save twenty percent on fresh beef and lamb. This sale is going to last for the next two hours. So go to the back of the store right now and talk to the salespeople in the meat section. They will help you get the best deal.

안녕하세요, 여러분, 슈퍼 세이버 마트에 오신 것을 환영합니다. 저희는 지금 정육 코너에서 특별 할인을 하고 있습니다. 신선한 닭고기와 돼지고기가 40% 할인되어 판매되고 있고, 신선한 쇠고기와 양고기는 20%를 할인 받으실 수 있습니다. 이 할인 판매는 앞으로 두 시간 동안 진행됩니다. 그러니 지금 매장 뒤편으로 가서서 정육 코너의 판매원에게 말씀하세요. 그들이 여러분이 최고로 저렴하게 구매하는 것을 도울 것입니다.

해설 할인 판매는 이틀이 아닌 두 시간 동안 이어진다.

어휘 special offer 특가 제공, 할인 meat 정육; 고기 section 코너, 부문 pork 돼지고기 beef 쇠고기 save 절약하다 last 지속되다 salesperson 판매원(복 salespeople) deal 거래

17 ⑤

W: Why are you smiling so much, Joe?
왜 그렇게 웃고 있니, 조?

M: I just came back from basketball tryouts. Coach Patterson said that I made the team.
난 방금 농구 입단 테스트를 보고 돌아왔어. 패터슨 감독님은 내가 팀에 합류했다고 말씀하셨어.

W: That's great news. Congratulations.
정말 좋은 소식이구나. 축하해.

M: Thanks a lot. 고마워.

W: Wait a minute. You tried out last year but didn't make the team, right? 잠깐만. 넌 작년에도 테스트를 봤는데 팀에 합류하지 못했지, 그렇지?

M: That's right. But I practiced really hard all year long. 맞아. 하지만 난 일 년 내내 정말 열심히 연습했어.

W: Did you improve a lot? 넌 실력이 많이 늘었니?

M: Yeah, I did. I really wanted to make the team. I'm glad that I practiced so much. 응, 많이 늘었어. 난 정말 팀에 합류하고 싶었어. 내가 연습을 많이 해서 기뻐.

① All that glitters is not gold.
반짝이는 것이 모두 금은 아니다.

② There's no place like home. 제 집보다 좋은 곳은 없다.

③ The early bird catches the worm.
일찍 일어나는 새가 벌레를 잡는다.

④ Too many cooks spoil the broth.
사공이 많으면 배가 산으로 간다.

⑤ If at first you don't succeed, try, try again.
만약 처음에 성공하지 못한다면 계속해서 시도하라.

어휘 tryout (운동) 입단 테스트 make the team 팀에 합류하다 practice 연습하다 improve 향상되다 glitter 반짝거리다 spoil 망치다 broth 수프 try 시도하다

18 ③

M: It's already four, Sally. Why are you late for our meeting? 벌써 4시야, 샐리. 왜 우리 회의에 늦었니?

W: I had to stay late after class.
수업이 끝나고 늦게까지 남아 있어야 했어.

M: Did a teacher punish you for some reason?
선생님께서 어떤 이유로 너에게 벌을 주신 거니?

W: Yes, Mr. Harding wasn't happy with me today.
응, 하딩 선생님께서 오늘 나 때문에 기분이 안 좋으셨어.

M: What happened? 무슨 일이 있었니?

W: I forgot to turn in my homework assignment. It's the third time this month I have forgotten. 내가 숙제를 내는 것을 잊어버렸어. 숙제를 잊은 게 이번 달에만 세 번째야.

M: You should write down your homework assignments in a notebook. Then, you won't forget them anymore. 넌 숙제를 공책에 적어 두어야 해. 그러면 더 이상 잊어버리지 않을 거야.

W: You're right. I'm going to buy a notebook this evening. 네 말이 맞아. 오늘 저녁에 공책을 사러 가야겠다.

M: That's smart. 잘 생각했어.

어휘 be late for ~에 늦다 stay late 늦게까지 머무르다 punish

벌을 주다 reason 이유 homework assignment 숙제 write down 적어 두다 not ~ anymore 더 이상 ~아닌

19 ④

W: I'm going to the Hamilton Shopping Mall with Mindy this weekend.
난 이번 주말에 민디랑 같이 해밀턴 쇼핑몰에 갈 거야.

M: I'm sure you'll have a great time there.
넌 거기서 분명히 재미있는 시간을 보낼 거야.

W: Have you been to the mall before?
전에 그 쇼핑몰에 가본 적이 있니?

M: Yes, I have. I went there on the day it opened. My family and I spent a few hours there. 응, 가봤어. 난 개장일에 갔었어. 우리 가족과 난 그곳에서 몇 시간을 보냈어.

W: Mindy and I are planning to eat lunch there. Then, we'll do some shopping. 민디랑 나는 거기서 점심을 먹을 계획이야. 그리고 나서 우리는 쇼핑을 할 거야.

M: What are you thinking of buying? 뭘 사려고 생각 중이니?

W: We're looking for some clothes.
우리는 옷을 좀 찾을 거야.

① This blouse was on sale. 이 블라우스가 할인 중이었어.
② I just bought this new bag. 나는 방금 이 새 가방을 샀어.
③ No, I haven't been there yet.
아니, 난 아직 그곳에 가본 적이 없어.
④ We're looking for some clothes.
우리는 옷을 좀 찾을 거야.
⑤ Yes, that's what we're going to do.
응, 그게 우리가 하려던 거야.

어휘 mall 쇼핑몰 sure 확신하는 do shopping 쇼핑하다 on sale 할인 중인, 판매되는 yet 아직 look for ~을 찾다

20 ②

W: I'm starving. I want something to eat now.
너무 배고파. 지금 뭔가 먹고 싶어.

M: Mom said we're going to have dinner in about two hours.
엄마가 우리는 두 시간 정도 있다가 저녁을 먹을 거라고 하셨어.

W: I can't wait that long. What's in the refrigerator?
그렇게 오래 기다릴 수는 없어. 냉장고 안에 뭐가 있니?

M: I think you're going to be disappointed.
네가 실망할 것 같은데.

W: Why? Don't we have any food?
왜? 음식이 아무것도 없니?

M: No, the refrigerator is almost empty.
없어, 냉장고는 거의 비어 있어.

W: How about going to the convenience store on the corner? 모퉁이에 있는 편의점에 가는 게 어때?

M: Okay. I'm getting hungry, too.
알겠어. 나도 배가 고파진다.

① It's open 24 hours a day. 거긴 하루 종일 문을 열어.
② Okay. I'm getting hungry, too.

알겠어. 나도 배가 고파진다.
③ Yes, that's where the store is. 응, 거기에 가게가 있어.
④ Mom said dinner's almost ready.
엄마가 저녁 준비가 거의 다 됐다고 하셨어.
⑤ Why don't we just make lunch?
그냥 우리가 점심을 만드는 게 어때?

어휘 starving 굶주린, 매우 배고픈 refrigerator 냉장고 disappointed 실망한 almost 거의 empty 비어있는 convenience store 편의점 corner 모퉁이 hungry 배고픈

15회 실전모의고사 본문 p.172-173

01 ④	02 ④	03 ①	04 ③	05 ④
06 ①	07 ⑤	08 ④	09 ⑤	10 ②
11 ③	12 ④	13 ③	14 ④	15 ③
16 ③	17 ①	18 ②	19 ③	20 ⑤

01 ④

W: Good evening. It's six thirty, so it's time to give you an update on the weather. The temperature is falling now, so it's going to be cold the rest of the night. The skies are clear now, but they'll be cloudy in a few hours. It looks like there's a winter storm coming. It's going to rain all day tomorrow, but the rain will turn into snow the day after tomorrow. It looks like we're going to have bad weather for the next few days.

안녕하세요. 6시 30분이므로, 최신 날씨 정보를 알려드릴 시간이 되었네요. 현재 기온이 떨어지고 있어서 밤에는 추워질 것으로 예상됩니다. 현재는 하늘이 맑지만, 몇 시간 후에는 구름이 끼겠습니다. 곧 겨울 폭풍이 다가올 것으로 보입니다. 내일은 하루 종일 비가 오겠습니다만, 모레는 비가 눈으로 바뀔 것입니다. 앞으로 며칠 동안은 날씨가 좋지 않을 것으로 예상됩니다.

어휘 give an update on ~에 대한 최신 정보를 제공하다 temperature 기온 fall 떨어지다 the rest 나머지 clear 맑은, 깨끗한 look like ~할 것 같다 storm 폭풍우 turn into ~로 바뀌다 the day after tomorrow 모레

02 ④

W: Look at everyone in this picture.
이 사진에 있는 사람들 좀 봐요.

M: We had a family reunion last month. There are many babies in that picture. 우리는 지난달에 가족 모임을 가졌어요. 사진에는 아기들이 많이 있어요.

W: That baby with the rattle in her hand is adorable. Is she your daughter?
손에 딸랑이를 쥐고 있는 아기가 사랑스럽네요. 당신 딸인가요?

M: No, she's my niece. She's my sister's daughter.

아니요, 제 조카딸이에요. 제 여동생의 딸이죠.

W: Which one of them is yours then? Is she the one who is sleeping?
그럼 누가 당신 딸인가요? 자고 있는 저 아이인가요?

M: No, that's my cousin's daughter. My daughter has a bottle of milk in her mouth. 아니요, 그 아이는 제 사촌의 딸이에요. 제 딸은 입에 젖병을 물고 있어요.

W: Wow. She looks cute. 와. 귀여워요.

M: Thanks for saying that. 그렇게 말해줘서 고마워요.

어휘 family reunion 가족 모임 rattle 딸랑이(아기 장난감) adorable 사랑스러운 daughter 딸 niece 조카딸 cousin 사촌

03 ①

W: This is something that people around the world can use. They use this to get information about all kinds of things. They also use this to order items and to talk to their friends and family members. Many people use this from their computers, and lots of other people use this with their smartphones. This is very convenient nowadays, so people don't like being without this for a long period of time.

이것은 전 세계의 사람들이 이용할 수 있는 것이다. 사람들은 모든 종류의 정보를 얻기 위해 이것을 이용한다. 사람들은 또한 상품을 주문하고, 친구나 가족과 대화하기 위해 이것을 이용한다. 많은 사람들은 컴퓨터로 이것을 이용하기도 하고, 많은 다른 사람들은 스마트폰으로 이것을 이용한다. 요즘은 이것이 매우 편리해서, 사람들은 오랜 시간 동안 이것이 없는 상태를 좋아하지 않는다.

어휘 information 정보 order 주문하다 item 제품, 물품 convenient 편리한 nowadays 요즈음 without ~이 없이 for a long period 오랫동안

04 ③

[Telephone rings.] [전화벨이 울린다.]

W: Good morning. This is the Prince Hotel. How may I help you?
안녕하세요. 프린스 호텔입니다. 무엇을 도와드릴까요?

M: Hello. My name is Tim Stuart. I have a reservation at your hotel. 여보세요. 제 이름은 팀 스튜어트입니다. 제가 호텔을 예약했거든요.

W: Yes, Mr. Stuart. How can I help you?
네. 스튜어트 씨. 무엇을 도와드릴까요?

M: I'm very sorry, but I have to cancel my reservation.
정말 죄송하지만, 제 예약을 취소해야 합니다.

W: Is there a problem? 무슨 문제라도 있나요?

M: I have to work this weekend, so I can't go on a trip.
이번 주말에 일을 해야 하기 때문에, 여행을 갈 수 없어요.

W: I'm very sorry to hear that, Mr. Stuart. I hope you can stay with us the next time you come to Sydney.
정말 유감이네요, 스튜어트 씨. 다음에 시드니에 오시면 저희 호텔에 투숙해 주셨으면 좋겠습니다.

M: I hope so, too. Thank you. 저도 그러길 바라요. 감사합니다.

어휘 reservation 예약 cancel 취소하다 go on a trip 여행 가다 the next time 다음에

05 ④

M: Wow, today is such a beautiful day.
와, 오늘 정말 날씨 좋다.

W: I agree. I'm glad we decided to come here instead of going to the movies. 동감이야. 영화를 보는 대신 여기 오기로 결정한 게 참 잘한 것 같아.

M: I feel the same way. This is one of the nicest days in summer. It's good to be outdoors. 나도 그렇게 생각해. 오늘은 올 여름 중 가장 좋은 날이야. 야외에 있기에 좋아.

W: So where should we go first?
그럼 우리는 어디를 먼저 갈까?

M: I'd like to stay outdoors for a while, so let's see the zebras.
난 한동안 야외에 계속 있고 싶으니까, 얼룩말을 보러 가자.

W: All right. They're near the giraffes, and I want to see them. They're my favorite animals.
알겠어. 얼룩말은 기린 근처에 있는데, 난 기린이 보고 싶어. 기린은 내가 가장 좋아하는 동물이야.

M: Let's avoid the snake house though. I'm scared of those animals.
하지만 뱀 사육장은 피하자. 난 뱀이 정말 무서워.

W: Sure. I don't want to see them either.
물론이야. 나도 뱀은 보고 싶지 않아.

어휘 agree 동의하다 instead of ~대신에 feel the same way 같은 생각을 하다 nicest 가장 좋은(nice - nicer - nicest) outdoors 야외에 for a while 한동안, 잠시 zebra 얼룩말 giraffe 기린 avoid 피하다 snake 뱀

06 ①

M: Mina, are you going to bring your laptop to school tomorrow? 미나야, 내일 학교에 네 노트북을 갖고 올 거니?

W: I can't. It's too heavy for me to bring.
아니. 내가 들고 오기엔 너무 무거워.

M: But we need to do our group project tomorrow. And all of the files are on your laptop.
하지만 우리는 내일 조별 과제를 해야 해. 그리고 모든 파일이 네 노트북에 담겨 있잖아.

W: What should I do then? 그럼 내가 어떻게 해야 하지?

M: Well, I can ask Gary to bring his.
음, 내가 게리에게 그의 것을 갖고 올 수 있는지 물어볼게.

W: And what about the files? 그럼 파일들은?

M: Save them to a memory stick and bring that with you when you come to school.
USB에 저장해서 학교에 올 때 갖고 와.

어휘 bring 가져오다 too ~ to… …하기에 너무 ~한 group project 조별 과제 save 저장하다 memory stick 휴대용 저장장치

07 ⑤

[*Telephone rings.*] [전화벨이 울린다.]

M: Hello. This is the Fairway Department Store.
여보세요. 페어웨이 백화점입니다.

W: Hi. I'm calling about an item I bought there today.
안녕하세요. 오늘 제가 거기서 산 물건 때문에 전화를 드렸어요.

M: Sure. What did you purchase?
그러시군요. 무엇을 구매하셨죠?

W: I bought a pair of blue jeans. 청바지를 한 벌 샀어요.

M: Is there a problem with them? 청바지에 문제가 있나요?

W: Yes, there is. They're the wrong size. Is it possible to exchange them?
네, 있어요. 사이즈가 안 맞아요. 제가 그걸 교환할 수 있나요?

M: Of course. Simply bring the jeans and the receipt to the store. A salesperson can help you out.
물론입니다. 매장으로 청바지와 영수증을 갖고 오시기만 하면 됩니다. 판매원이 고객님을 도와줄 겁니다.

W: Where should I take them? 제가 어디로 가져가야 하죠?

M: Go to the returns desk on the first floor.
1층에 있는 교환 창구로 가시면 됩니다.

어휘 department store 백화점 item 물품, 제품 purchase 구매하다 a pair of 한 쌍의, 한 벌의 blue jeans 청바지 exchange 교환하다 receipt 영수증 salesperson 판매원

08 ④

W: How are you enjoying your time in Shanghai?
상하이에서 즐거운 시간을 보내고 계신가요?

M: It's a very unique city. I really like it here.
여긴 정말 독특한 도시예요. 이곳이 정말 좋네요.

W: Is your hotel alright? 호텔은 괜찮으세요?

M: Yes, it is. It's located right by the water, so it has a great view.
네, 괜찮아요. 바다 바로 옆에 위치해 있어서 전망이 정말 좋아요.

W: I'm glad to hear that. 그 말씀을 들으니 다행이네요.

M: So what are we going to do next?
그럼 저희는 다음에 뭘 하게 되나요?

W: When everyone gets back to the bus, we're going to have lunch.
사람들이 모두 버스로 돌아오면, 점심 식사를 할 겁니다.

M: And after lunch? 점심 후에는요?

W: We'll visit the best museum in the entire city.
도시 전체에서 가장 훌륭한 박물관을 찾아갈 겁니다.

어휘 unique 독특한 alright 괜찮은(= fine) be located 위치해 있다 view 전망, 경치 get back 돌아오다 museum 박물관 entire 전체의

09 ⑤

M: How was your lunch at the new Italian restaurant?
새로 생긴 이탈리아 식당에서의 점심은 어땠니?

W: It was an interesting experience.
정말 흥미로운 경험이었어.

M: Why do you say that? 왜 그렇게 말하니?

W: Well, the restaurant itself was beautiful. It was

decorated with many beautiful paintings. 음, 식당 자체는 아름다웠어. 식당은 많은 아름다운 그림들로 꾸며져 있었어.

M: How was the food? 음식은 어땠니?

W: The lasagna I had tasted great. But there was only a huge problem. 내가 먹은 라자냐는 무척 맛있었어. 하지만 정말 큰 문제가 딱 하나 있었어.

M: What's that? 그게 뭔데?

W: I ordered spaghetti. But the waiter brought me the wrong dish, and then he wouldn't apologize. He ruined my meal.
난 스파게티를 주문했거든. 하지만 웨이터가 나에게 음식을 잘못 가져다 주었고, 사과를 하지 않았어. 종업원이 내 식사를 망쳤어.

해설 여자는 전반적으로 음식점에 만족했지만, 종업원에게 실망했다.

어휘 decorate 장식하다 huge 거대한, 엄청난 order 주문하다 apologize 사과하다 ruin 망치다 meal 식사 proud 자랑스러운 shocked 충격 받은 satisfied 만족한 confused 혼란스러운 disappointed 실망한

10 ②

W: Are those new sneakers you are wearing, Mark?
네가 신고 있는 게 새 운동화니, 마크?

M: Yes. They just arrived yesterday. 응, 이건 어제 도착했어.

W: Did you order them online?
운동화를 온라인으로 주문했니?

M: That's right. I love online shopping.
맞아. 나는 온라인 쇼핑을 좋아해.

W: How was the price? 가격은 어땠니?

M: The shoes cost one hundred fifty dollars at a shoe store, but they only cost me ninety dollars online.
신발은 매장에서는 150달러였는데, 온라인으로는 90달러밖에 들지 않았어.

W: That's a great deal. Did you have to pay for delivery, or was it free?
정말 괜찮은 가격이구나. 배송비를 내야 했니, 아니면 무료였니?

M: I was charged fifteen dollars for delivery since I requested overnight shipping.
내가 익일 배송을 요청했기 때문에 배송비가 15달러 들었어.

해설 $90(운동화)+$15(배송료) = $105

어휘 sneakers 운동화 order online 온라인으로[인터넷으로] 주문하다 price 가격 cost 비용이 들다(cost-cost-cost) deal 거래 delivery 배송 charge (비용을) 청구하다 request 요청하다 overnight shipping 익일 배송, 특급 배송

11 ③

M: What are you planning to do this afternoon?
오늘 오후에 뭐 할 계획이니?

W: I was thinking of just watching TV and relaxing.
그냥 TV를 보면서 쉬려고 생각하고 있었어.

M: Don't you have any chores to do?
집안일을 해야 할 건 없니?

W: Not today. I cleaned my room and did the laundry

in the morning.
오늘은 없어. 방 청소도 했고, 오전에 빨래도 했어.

M: In that case, how about going to the park?
그렇다면, 공원에 가는 게 어때?

W: What do you want to do there? 공원에서 뭘 하고 싶니?

M: We could go to the lake and relax by the water.
우리는 호수에 가서 물가에서 쉴 수 있어.

W: That sounds good. But I have to finish my homework first. Can we do that in thirty minutes?
그거 좋겠는데. 하지만 난 숙제를 먼저 끝내야 해. 30분 뒤에 갈래?

M: All right. 알겠어.

어휘 plan 계획하다 relax 휴식을 취하다, 느긋하게 쉬다 chore 집안일, 잡일 clean 청소하다 do the laundry 빨래하다 lake 호수 by ~옆에

12 ④

M: May I have your attention, please? Remember that the school festival will be on April twenty fifth. That's the day after midterm exams finish. The festival is going to be lots of fun. There will be a play performed by some students. We'll play sports such as soccer, volleyball, and basketball. There will be a singing and dancing contest. And we'll have a flea market as well. Your friends and family can come to the festival, so please invite them.

잠시 주목해 주시겠습니까? 학교 축제가 4월 25일에 있다는 것을 기억해 주시기 바랍니다. 중간고사가 끝나는 바로 다음 날입니다. 축제는 정말 재미있을 겁니다. 몇몇 학생들이 공연하는 연극도 있을 예정입니다. 우리는 축구, 배구, 그리고 농구와 같은 스포츠도 할 것입니다. 노래자랑과 댄스 경연대회도 있을 예정입니다. 그리고 벼룩시장도 열릴 것입니다. 여러분의 친구와 가족도 축제에 올 수 있으니까, 그들을 초대해 주시기 바랍니다.

어휘 the day after ~의 다음 날 midterm exam 중간고사 play 연극 perform 공연하다 volleyball 배구 contest 경연대회 flea market 벼룩시장 invite 초대하다

13 ③

M: Have you ever been to Bukhan Mountain?
넌 북한산에 가본 적이 있니?

W: No, I haven't. Is it nice? 아니, 안 가봤어. 거기가 좋니?

M: It is, and it's near Seoul, so it's easy to get to.
좋아, 그리고 서울에서 가까워서 찾아가기 쉬워.

W: Are you going to go there soon?
조만간 거기 갈 예정이니?

M: Yes, my friends and I are going hiking there this Saturday.
응, 난 내 친구들이랑 이번 토요일에 그곳으로 하이킹을 갈 거야.

W: Really? That sounds fun. 그래? 재미있겠다.

M: By the way, would you mind lending me your camera? 그나저나, 네 카메라를 나한테 빌려주면 안 될까?

W: Not at all. The leaves must be very colorful there

this time of year.
문제 없어. 이맘때면 산의 나뭇잎들이 정말 알록달록할 거야.

M: Exactly. We'd like to take some nice photographs while we are at the top.
맞아. 우리는 정상에 있을 때 멋진 사진들을 찍고 싶어.

어휘 Have you ever been to ~? ~에 가본 적이 있니? go hiking 하이킹하다, (낮은 산을) 등산하다 lend 빌려주다 leaves 나뭇잎 (⑧ leaf) colorful 다채로운, 형형색색의 while ~하는 동안에 top 정상

14 ④

W: Thank you for attending the first meeting of the school's science club. We have many exciting activities planned for this year. Each semester, we'll go on a field trip. We're going to do some science experiments in the lab as well. We'll go on some nature hikes to learn about the plants and animals in our region, and we're planning to watch some great science documentaries. But first, we need to elect the club president.

학교 과학 동아리의 첫 번째 모임에 참석해 주셔서 감사합니다. 우리는 올해 다양한 흥미진진한 활동들을 계획하고 있습니다. 우리는 매 학기마다 현장 학습을 갑니다. 실험실에서 과학 실험도 몇 번 할 것입니다. 우리는 우리 지역의 동식물들에 대해 배우기 위해 자연 탐사 여행을 갈 것이며, 훌륭한 과학 다큐멘터리들을 시청할 계획입니다. 하지만, 먼저 우리는 동아리 회장을 선출해야 합니다.

어휘 attend 참석하다 meeting 회의 activity 활동 semester 학기 field trip 현장 학습, 수학여행 nature hike 자연 탐사 여행 plant 식물 region 지역 documentary 다큐멘터리 elect 선출하다 president 회장, 사장

15 ③

W: Do you have any pets? 넌 애완동물을 기르니?

M: Sure. I have three dogs. 그럼. 개가 세 마리 있어.

W: Three? You must really like dogs.
세 마리나? 넌 정말 개를 좋아하는구나.

M: That's right. Dogs are lots of fun. They're very friendly, too. 맞아. 개는 정말 재미있어. 무척 다정하기도 해.

W: Don't you like cats? 고양이는 안 좋아하니?

M: I can't stand cats. They often bite and scratch people.
난 고양이를 참을 수 없어. 고양이는 종종 사람을 물고 할퀴잖아.

W: Dogs do that sometimes. 개도 가끔 그래.

M: Not my dogs. My dogs love running, so we go to the park and play a lot. That's fun. Cats can't do that. 우리 개들은 아니야. 우리 개들은 달리기를 좋아하기 때문에, 우리는 공원에 가서 신나게 놀아. 재미있어. 고양이는 그렇게 못 하잖아.

W: You've got a good point. 네 말에 일리가 있어.

M: And my dogs always come to me when I call them.
그리고 우리 개들은 내가 부르면 항상 나에게로 와.

어휘 pet 애완동물 friendly 친절한, 다정한 stand 견디다, 참다 bite 물다 scratch 할퀴다 call 부르다 have (got) a point 일리가 있다

16 ③

① M: How should we go to the museum?
우리는 박물관에 어떻게 가야 하지?

W: We can take the bus or the subway.
버스나 지하철을 탈 수 있어.

② M: Where does your uncle live now?
너의 삼촌은 지금 어디 사시니?

W: He just moved to a city in China.
삼촌은 얼마 전에 중국에 있는 도시로 이사 가셨어.

③ M: Do you think you can make it to the restaurant by five? 넌 식당에 5시까지 올 수 있을 것 같니?

W: I'm making a sandwich now.
난 지금 샌드위치를 만들고 있어.

④ M: What's our test going to be on?
우리 시험 범위는 어떻게 되니?

W: It's on chapters four and five. 4장에서 5장까지 나와.

⑤ M: When is your birthday? 네 생일은 언제니?

W: It's on the last day of November. 11월 마지막 날이야.

어휘 museum 박물관 uncle 삼촌 move 이사 가다 make it to (장소에) 도착하다 chapter 장, 챕터 last 마지막

17 ①

① Documentaries are twice as popular as news programs.
다큐멘터리는 뉴스 프로그램의 두 배만큼 인기가 있다.

② Students prefer variety shows to comedies.
학생들은 코미디보다 버라이어티 쇼를 선호한다.

③ The most popular programs are variety shows.
가장 인기 있는 프로그램은 버라이어티 쇼이다.

④ News programs are the least popular shows with students.
뉴스 프로그램은 학생들에게 가장 인기 없는 프로그램이다.

⑤ Dramas are not as popular as documentaries.
드라마는 다큐멘터리만큼 인기 있지 않다.

어휘 favorite 가장 좋아하는 twice 두 배로 popular 인기 있는 prefer A to B B보다 A를 좋아하다 variety show 버라이어티 쇼, 예능 프로그램 least 가장 적은(little – less – least)

18 ②

W: Look at this. I can't believe it. 이것 좀 봐. 믿을 수가 없어.

M: What's the matter? 무슨 일이야?

W: So many people write on the walls in this apartment building. I hate that. 너무나 많은 사람들이 이 아파트 건물 벽에 낙서를 해. 난 그게 너무 싫어.

M: Why would people do that? 왜 사람들이 그걸 하지?

W: They think it's funny. But it really just makes the building look ugly. 사람들은 그게 재미있다고 생각해. 하지만

낙서는 건물을 보기 흉하게 만들 뿐이야.

M: Do you think we can find out who did it?
누가 그랬는지 우리가 찾을 수 있을까?

W: Probably not. But we can post a message by the elevator asking people not to write on the walls any more.
아마 못 찾을 거야. 하지만 사람들에게 벽에 더 이상 낙서를 하지 말라고 요청하는 메시지를 엘리베이터 옆에 붙일 수는 있어.

M: That should work. Let's write the note now.
그럼 되겠다. 지금 메모를 적자.

① Sure. We can try to erase the writing from the walls.
물론이지. 우리는 벽에 있는 글자를 지우기 위해 노력할 수 있어.

② That should work. Let's write the note now.
그럼 되겠다. 지금 메모를 적자.

③ Okay. I'll stop doing that from now on.
알았어. 이제부터 그걸 그만 할게.

④ What did you just write on the wall?
넌 방금 벽에 무슨 낙서를 했니?

⑤ Yes, I'm going up to the fifth floor.
응, 난 5층으로 올라가고 있어.

어휘 wall 벽 apartment building 아파트 hate 싫어하다 funny 재미있는 ugly 흉한, 못생긴 probably 아마도 post 게시하다 any more 더 이상 erase 지우다 work 효과가 있다 from now on 지금부터

19 ③

[Cellphone rings.] [휴대폰이 울린다.]

W: Hi, Jim. What are you doing right now?
안녕, 짐. 너 지금 뭐 하고 있니?

M: I'm cooking dinner for my parents.
부모님을 위한 저녁식사를 준비하고 있어.

W: That's really nice of you. 정말 착하구나.

M: They are both getting home late tonight, so I decided to do the cooking since they will be tired.
오늘 밤에는 두 분 모두 집에 늦게 오시는데, 피곤하실 테니 내가 요리를 하기로 결심했어.

W: What are you making? 뭘 만들고 있니?

M: I'm making spaghetti with tomato sauce. But I just realized I don't have any green peppers.
토마토 소스를 넣어서 스파게티를 만들고 있어. 하지만 방금 피망이 없다는 걸 깨달았어.

W: Do you want me to stop by the market and buy some? 내가 시장에 들러서 좀 사다 줄까?

M: Would you mind doing that? 그렇게 해줄 수 있겠니?

① I'm at the market right now. 난 지금 시장에 있어.

② No, I didn't buy any of them.
아니, 난 그걸 하나도 사지 않았어.

③ Would you mind doing that? 그렇게 해줄 수 있겠니?

④ Yes, I'm cooking green peppers.
응, 난 지금 피망을 요리하고 있어.

⑤ Okay. What do you want from the market?

알았어. 시장에서 뭐가 필요하니?

해설 ③은 정중하게 요청하는 표현이다.

어휘 cook 요리하다 both 둘 다 get home late 집에 늦게 도착하다 tired 피곤한 realize 깨닫다 green pepper 피망 stop by 잠깐 들르다

20 ⑤

M: Kate has to give a presentation to her class tomorrow. She is good at writing, but she gets very nervous speaking in front of people. Before she makes her presentations, she always starts to sweat, and her hands shake. She also has trouble speaking since she forgets what she's going to say. In this situation, what would Kate's mom most likely say to her to encourage her?

케이트는 내일 수업에서 발표를 해야 한다. 그녀는 글을 잘 쓰지만 사람들 앞에서 말할 때는 무척 긴장을 한다. 그녀는 발표를 하기 전에 항상 땀이 나기 시작하고, 손이 떨린다. 그녀는 또한 말해야 할 것을 잊어버리기 때문에, 발표하는 데 어려움을 겪는다. 이런 상황에서 케이트의 엄마는 그녀를 격려하기 위해 어떤 말을 하겠는가?

Mom: Forget about everyone watching you and do your best.
모든 사람들이 너를 보고 있다는 걸 잊어버리고 최선을 다하렴.

① Your teacher called and said you did a great job.
너희 선생님께서 전화하셔서 네가 정말 잘했다고 말씀하셨어.

② Try rewriting your presentation to make it better.
발표 원고를 다시 써서 내용을 발전시켜 보렴.

③ I'm so proud of you. You didn't get nervous at all.
네가 정말 자랑스럽구나. 넌 하나도 긴장하지 않았어.

④ I think this is the best present you've ever given me. 이건 네가 나에게 준 선물 중에 최고인 것 같아.

⑤ Forget about everyone watching you and do your best.
모든 사람들이 너를 보고 있다는 걸 잊어버리고 최선을 다하렴.

어휘 give a presentation 발표하다 good at ~을 잘하는 nervous 긴장한 in front of ~앞에 sweat 땀을 흘리다 shake 흔들다 have trouble –ing ~하는 데 어려움을 겪다 encourage 격려하다 do a great job 아주 잘하다 rewrite 다시 쓰다 make something better ~을 더 좋게 만들다 proud 자랑스러운 do one's best 최선을 다하다

01 ②	02 ④	03 ④	04 ②	05 ①
06 ⑤	07 ②	08 ④	09 ④	10 ③
11 ④	12 ②	13 ②	14 ④	15 ⑤
16 ⑤	17 ④	18 ⑤	19 ①	20 ③

01 ②

W: What are you looking for in your bag?
가방에서 뭘 찾고 있니?

M: I'm trying to find my student ID. 내 학생증을 찾고 있어.

W: Did you lose it again? 또 학생증을 잃어버렸니?

M: Yes, I don't know where it is. I guess I'll have to go to the Lost and Found Office. Maybe someone turned it in. 응, 그게 어디 있는지 모르겠어. 분실물 보관소에 가 봐야 할 것 같아. 아마 누군가 그걸 갖다 놨을 거야.

W: You ought to get a wallet. Let's go to the store and buy one right now.
너는 지갑을 사야 해. 상점에 가서 지금 당장 하나 사자.

M: A wallet? Do I really need that?
지갑? 나한테 그게 정말 필요할까?

W: Listen. Aren't you sick and tired of losing your ID? If you carry a wallet, you can keep your ID and other cards in the same place.
잘 들어. 너는 신분증을 잃어버리는 게 지겹지도 않니? 지갑을 갖고 다니면 신분증과 다른 카드들을 한 곳에 보관할 수 있다고.

어휘 look for ~을 찾다 lose 잃어버리다 Lost and Found Office 분실물 보관소 turn something in ~을 돌려주다, 반납하다 ought to ~을 해야 한다(= should) wallet 지갑 sick and tired of ~에 진절머리가 나는 keep 보관하다

02 ④

M: I'm so happy that summer is finally here.
마침내 여름이 와서 난 무척 기뻐.

W: So am I. I'm looking forward to hot and sunny weather. 나도 그래. 난 뜨겁고 화창한 날씨를 기대하고 있어.

M: Mark and I are going to the beach this weekend. We're going to go surfing. 마크랑 나는 이번 주말에 해변에 갈 거야. 우리는 서핑을 하러 갈 거야.

W: That sounds like fun, but have you checked the weather report? 재미있겠네, 하지만 일기예보를 확인했니?

M: No, why? Is it going to rain?
아니, 왜? 비가 오기로 되어 있니?

W: I just saw it. We're supposed to get windy weather all weekend. Will that keep you from surfing?
방금 일기예보를 봤어. 주말 내내 바람이 부는 날씨가 될 거라고 했어. 바람이 불면 서핑을 할 수 없지 않을까?

M: Actually, it will help make the waves bigger.
사실, 바람이 파도를 더 크게 만들어 줄 거야.

W: It looks like you're going to have a great time then.

그럼 네가 즐거운 시간을 보낼 수 있을 것 같구나.

해설 마지막의 'have a great time'만 듣고 화창한 날씨를 고르는 실수를 할 수 있으니 조심해야 한다.

어휘 finally 마침내, 결국 look forward to ~을 기대하다 go surfing 파도타기[서핑]를 하러 가다 check 확인하다 be supposed to ~하기로 되어 있다 actually 사실은, 실제로 bigger 더 큰(big – bigger – biggest)

03 ④

M: Why are you smiling so much, Dana?
넌 왜 그렇게 웃고 있니, 데이나?

W: I'm looking forward to this afternoon.
난 오늘 오후를 기대하고 있어.

M: What are you going to do? 뭘 할 건데?

W: I'm going to try out for that singing program on TV.
I want to become a star. 난 TV에 나오는 노래 부르기 프로그램에 도전할 거야. 난 스타가 되고 싶어.

M: Are you talking about the show *Who Wants to Be a Singer*? '가수가 되고 싶은 사람은 누구인가요?'라는 프로그램을 말하는 거니?

W: Right. That's the one I'm going to try out for.
맞아. 그게 내가 도전해 보려고 하는 프로그램이야.

M: The audition for that program was yesterday. My friend Jeff made it to the second round. 그 프로그램의 오디션은 어제였어. 내 친구인 제프가 2라운드에 진출했어.

W: You aren't serious, are you? I can't believe I missed it. 너 장난하는 거지, 그렇지? 내가 그걸 놓쳤다니 믿을 수 없어.

어휘 smile 웃다, 미소를 띠다 try out 시험을 보다; 참가하다 audition 오디션 make it 성공하다, 해내다 serious 진지한, 심각한 miss 놓치다 excited 신이 난 nervous 긴장한 shocked 충격을 받은 concerned 걱정하는

04 ②

W: Good afternoon. 안녕하세요.

M: Hi. How can I help you? 안녕하세요. 무엇을 도와드릴까요?

W: I need to make a reservation for a trip to China.
중국 여행을 예약해야 하거든요.

M: All right. Are you planning on flying there?
알겠습니다. 중국까지 비행기를 타고 가실 계획인가요?

W: Yes. I need to go there in two weeks.
네. 2주 후에 그곳에 가야 해요.

M: Do you already have a visa for China?
중국 비자는 이미 갖고 계신가요?

W: No, I don't. Can you help me with that as well?
아니요, 없어요. 그것도 도와주실 수 있나요?

M: Yes, we can get you a visa. But it will cost fifty dollars to do that. 네, 저희가 비자를 드릴 수 있습니다. 하지만 그렇게 하는 데 50달러의 비용이 들 겁니다.

어휘 make a reservation 예약하다 fly 비행기를 타고 가다 visa 비자(외국인에 대한 출입국 허가의 증명) as well 또한, 역시 cost 비용이 들다

05 ①

M: This is a performance that people give on a stage. This involves a story that the actors tell. Sometimes this is a sad story, and other times it's a comedy. But the actors don't speak their lines. Instead, they sing them. This also includes an orchestra. The orchestra plays music while the performers sing.

이것은 사람들이 무대에서 하는 공연이다. 이것은 배우들이 말하는 이야기를 포함한다. 이것은 가끔은 슬픈 이야기이고, 다른 때는 코미디이다. 하지만 배우들은 그들의 대사를 말로 하지 않는다. 대신, 그들은 대사를 노래로 한다. 이것은 또한 오케스트라를 포함한다. 오케스트라는 배우들이 노래하는 동안 음악을 연주한다.

어휘 performance 공연 stage 무대 involve 포함하다 (= include) actor 배우 comedy 코미디 line 대사 instead 대신에 orchestra 오케스트라 while ~하는 동안에 performer 연기자, 공연자

06 ⑤

[*Telephone rings.*] [전화벨이 울린다.]

W: Hello. 여보세요.

M: Hi, Karen. It's Joe. I didn't go to school today, so could you bring my English textbook home with you? I can drop by your house and pick it up later.
안녕, 캐런. 나 조야. 내가 오늘 학교에 안 가서 그러는데, 네가 집에 올 때 내 영어교과서 좀 가지고 올 수 있겠니? 내가 나중에 너희 집에 들러서 그걸 가져올게.

W: Sorry, Joe, but I'm not at school now. I left twenty minutes ago.
조, 미안하지만, 난 지금 학교에 있지 않아. 20분 전에 출발했어.

M: Oh, no. I called you too late. What should I do about my English homework?
아, 이런. 내가 너무 늦게 전화했구나. 내 영어숙제를 어떻게 하지?

W: I can lend you my book later this evening.
오늘 저녁에 내 책을 빌려 줄게.

M: What time can you do that? 몇 시에 그렇게 해줄 수 있니?

W: Around eight. I will be finished with my homework by then. 8시쯤에. 그때까지는 내가 숙제를 끝낼 거야.

M: That's too late for me. I'd better call someone else to ask for help. 그건 나한테는 너무 늦어. 난 다른 사람에게 전화해서 도움을 구하는 게 좋겠어.

W: Talk to Jenny. She's still at school, and she lives in your neighborhood. Maybe she can bring your book to you. 제니한테 얘기해 봐. 제니는 아직 학교에 있고, 너희 동네에 살잖아. 아마 그 애가 네 책을 가지고 올 수 있을 거야.

M: Thanks for letting me know. I'll do that right now.
알려줘서 고마워. 지금 해볼게.

W: Good luck. 행운을 빌어.

어휘 textbook 교과서 lend 빌려주다 later 나중에 by then 그때까지 neighborhood 인근; 이웃

07 ②

W: [Beep] Hello. You've reached Mary Sanders. I'm really sorry, but I can't take your call at this moment. I'm either in class or doing something else important. If you leave a voice message for me, I'll listen to it and call you back at once. Or you can just send a text message to my cellphone. Thanks for giving me a call. Goodbye.

[삐 소리] 안녕하세요. 당신은 메리 샌더스에게 전화하셨습니다. 정말 죄송하지만 지금은 제가 전화를 받을 수 없습니다. 저는 수업 중이거나, 중요한 다른 용무를 보는 중입니다. 음성 메시지를 남기시면, 제가 그것을 들은 후 즉시 다시 전화를 드리겠습니다. 아니면 제 휴대폰으로 문자 메시지를 보내셔도 됩니다. 전화를 주셔서 감사합니다. 안녕히 계세요.

어휘 You've reached (자동응답기 멘트) ~에 전화하셨습니다 at this moment 현재, 지금 either A or B A와 B 둘 중 하나 leave a voice message 음성 메시지를 남기다 call back 다시 전화하다 at once 즉시 give somebody a call ~에게 전화하다

08 ④

M: Look at all of these pies. 이 파이들 좀 봐.

W: What are you going to buy? 넌 뭘 살 거니?

M: Well, the strawberry pie looks delicious, and it only costs fifteen dollars.
음, 딸기 파이가 맛있어 보이고, 가격도 15달러밖에 안 해.

W: How about the cherry pie for twenty dollars?
20달러 하는 체리 파이는 어때?

M: I love cherry, but my brother doesn't, so I shouldn't buy it. 나는 체리를 좋아하지만 내 남동생이 좋아하지 않아. 그래서 체리 파이는 살 수 없어.

W: Oh, look over there. There's a walnut pie, and it's only twelve dollars.
아, 저기 좀 봐. 호두 파이가 있어, 그리고 12달러밖에 안 해.

M: That's a great deal. I'm definitely going to get that.
가격이 정말 괜찮네. 저건 꼭 살 거야.

W: Are you going to buy more than one pie?
파이를 한 개 이상 살 거니?

M: Why not? The prices here are low. I'll get the strawberry pie, too.
왜 안 사니? 여기는 가격이 저렴해. 딸기 파이도 사야겠어.

해설 앞에서 언급된 딸기 파이를 뒤에서 구매한다고 말하는 것을 놓치지 말자. $15(딸기 파이)+$12(호두 파이) = $27

어휘 strawberry 딸기 delicious 맛있는 over there 저쪽에, 저기에 walnut 호두 definitely 분명히, 확실히 more than ~이상의 price 가격

09 ④

[Cellphone rings.] [휴대폰이 울린다.]

W: Hello, Jake. 안녕, 제이크

M: Hey, Julie. Are you all right? We missed you at Tom's farewell party.
안녕, 줄리. 너 괜찮니? 우린 톰의 송별회에서 널 못 봤어.

W: That's why I'm calling. I'm really sorry that I missed it. I want to apologize to Tom.
그래서 전화한 거야. 못 가서 정말 미안해. 톰에게 사과하고 싶어.

M: He was disappointed you didn't make it. What happened?
톰은 네가 오지 않아서 실망했어. 무슨 일이 있었니?

W: I suddenly got really ill around lunchtime. I felt dizzy, so I lay down on the sofa. Then, I fell asleep.
점심 때쯤에 갑자기 너무 아팠어. 어지러워서 소파에 누웠어. 그때 잠이 들어 버렸어.

M: Did you just get up now? 지금 막 일어난 거야?

W: Yes, but I still don't feel well. I think I'm going to visit the doctor soon.
응, 하지만 여전히 몸이 안 좋아. 병원에 빨리 가볼 생각이야.

M: Yeah, you'd better do that. 응, 그렇게 하는 게 좋겠어.

어휘 miss 그리워하다; 놓치다 farewell party 송별회 that's why 그것이 ~한 이유이다 apologize 사과하다 disappointed 실망한 make it (장소에) 도착하다; (약속을) 지키다 suddenly 갑자기 dizzy 어지러운 lie 눕다(lie-lay-lain) fall asleep 잠들다

10 ③

W: It's very simple to use this machine to buy a train ticket. Let me show you what to do. First, you need to check the time and destination of the train that you want. Second, choose the train that you want to take. After that, choose the seat you want to sit in. You can select an aisle or window seat. Next, press the button to pay either cash or with a credit card and hit the 'Enter' button. It's simple.

기차표를 사기 위해 이 기계를 사용하는 것은 매우 간단합니다. 제가 뭘 해야 하는지 보여드리겠습니다. 첫째, 원하는 시간과 기차의 목적지를 확인하셔야 합니다. 둘째, 타고 싶은 기차를 선택하시기 바랍니다. 그런 다음, 앉고 싶은 좌석을 선택하세요. 통로 자리 또는 창가 자리를 선택하실 수 있습니다. 다음으로, 현금 혹은 신용카드로 돈을 지불하기 위해 버튼을 눌러주시고, '엔터' 버튼을 눌러 주세요. 간단합니다.

해설 지문에 first, second, after that, next 등의 순서에 귀 기울인다. second 이후에 third가 아닌 after that이 등장했다.

어휘 simple 간단한 check 확인하다 destination 목적지 choose 선택하다 seat 좌석 select 선택하다 aisle 통로, 복도 press 누르다 button 버튼 cash 현금 enter 입력하다, 들어가다

11 ④

M: Did you see the news today? 너 오늘 뉴스 봤니?

W: No, I missed it. Did something bad happen?
아니, 못 봤어. 안 좋은 일이 일어났니?

M: Actually, there was some good news.
사실은, 좀 좋은 뉴스가 있었어.

W: Really? Tell me what happened.

정말? 무슨 일인지 말해줘.

M: Do you know the <u>orphanage</u> downtown?
시내에 있는 고아원을 알고 있니?

W: Sure. I <u>volunteer</u> there <u>during</u> vacation.
물론이지. 난 방학 동안 거기서 자원봉사를 해.

M: Well, somebody <u>donated</u> one <u>million</u> dollars to the orphanage today.
음, 누군가 오늘 그 고아원에 백만 달러를 기부했어.

W: That's <u>incredible</u>. Who did that?
믿을 수 없는 일이네. 누가 그랬대?

M: Nobody knows. A <u>lawyer</u> went there <u>with</u> a <u>check</u> and said that his <u>client</u> didn't want anybody to <u>know</u> his <u>name</u>.
아무도 몰라. 변호사가 수표를 갖고 고아원에 가서, 자신의 의뢰인은 아무도 그의 이름을 알기를 원하지 않는다고 말했어.

W: <u>How generous</u>. I love it when people do things like that.
정말 씀씀이가 후하네. 나는 사람들이 그런 일을 하는 게 좋아.

어휘 actually 사실은, 실제로 orphanage 고아원 downtown 시내에 volunteer 자원봉사하다 donate 기부하다 million 백만 incredible 믿을 수 없는, 놀라운 lawyer 변호사 check 수표 client 고객 generous 관대한, 후한

12 ②

W: Hello. Can you tell me <u>where</u> the <u>art exhibit</u> is?
안녕하세요. 미술 전시회가 어디서 하는지 알려주실 수 있나요?

M: You need to <u>go to</u> the <u>second floor</u> for that. Just <u>walk straight</u> ahead and go <u>up</u> the <u>stairs</u>. 그러려면 2층으로 가셔야 합니다. 앞으로 곧장 가서서 계단을 올라 가세요.

W: Thank you. Are visitors <u>allowed</u> to <u>take photographs</u>? 감사합니다. 관람객들이 사진을 찍어도 되나요?

M: I'm <u>sorry</u>, <u>but photography</u> is not allowed. You can <u>buy pictures</u> or <u>postcards</u> of the paintings in the <u>gift shop</u> though.
죄송합니다만, 사진 촬영은 허용되지 않습니다. 하지만 기념품점에서 그림이 나온 사진이나 엽서를 구매하실 수 있습니다.

W: That's <u>good to know</u>. 잘됐네요.

M: Do you have any other questions?
또 다른 궁금하신 점이 있으신가요?

W: Yes, one more. <u>What time</u> does the museum <u>close</u>?
네, 하나 더요. 미술관은 몇 시에 문을 닫죠?

M: Since today is <u>Saturday</u>, we close <u>at six</u>. We close at <u>seven</u> on <u>weekdays</u>.
오늘이 토요일이니까 6시에 닫습니다. 평일에는 7시에 닫습니다.

어휘 art exhibit 미술 전시회 walk straight 곧장 가다 go up the stairs 계단을 오르다 be allowed 허용되다 take photographs 사진 찍다 photography 사진 촬영 postcard 엽서 gift shop 기념품점 weekday 평일

13 ②

M: That's a very nice <u>dress</u> you're <u>wearing</u>.
당신이 입고 있는 옷은 정말 예쁘네요.

W: Thank you for the <u>compliment</u>. 칭찬해 줘서 고마워요.

M: <u>Where</u> did you <u>get</u> it? My <u>wife</u> would love that.
그걸 어디서 사셨어요? 제 아내가 좋아할 것 같네요.

W: I bought it at the <u>clothing store across the street</u> from the cafe on Baker Street.
베이커 가에 있는 카페의 길 건너편에 있는 옷 가게에서 샀어요.

M: Oh, I know where that is. 아, 전 거기가 어딘지 알아요.

W: It was only <u>forty</u> dollars because I got it <u>on sale</u>.
제가 할인을 받았기 때문에 고작 40달러였어요.

M: That's a great <u>price</u>. 아주 괜찮은 가격이네요.

W: I'm <u>going back</u> to the store in a few minutes. I need to <u>do</u> some more <u>shopping</u> there. 저는 몇 분 후에 그 가게에 돌아갈 거예요. 거기서 더 살 것이 있거든요.

M: Do you <u>mind</u> if I go there <u>with you</u>?
제가 함께 가도 괜찮을까요?

W: Not at all. Shall we <u>take</u> a <u>taxi</u>?
물론이죠. 우리, 택시를 탈까요?

어휘 compliment 칭찬 across the street from ~의 길 건너편에 on sale 할인 중인 take a taxi 택시 타다

14 ④

M: Are you still <u>working</u> on your English <u>essay</u>?
넌 아직도 영어 에세이를 쓰고 있어?

W: Yes, I am. I <u>didn't write anything</u> on the weekend, so I need to <u>finish</u> it <u>today</u>.
응. 주말에 아무것도 쓰지 못해서, 오늘 끝내야 해.

M: <u>Good luck</u> with that. 행운을 빌게.

W: Have you finished <u>yours</u>? 네 것은 다 했니?

M: Yes, I did it this morning. 응, 오늘 아침에 했어.

W: What did you do <u>on the weekend</u> then?
그럼 넌 주말에 뭘 했니?

M: I went to a <u>computer store</u>. 컴퓨터 가게에 갔었어.

W: What were you doing there? Did you buy a new <u>laptop or something</u>?
거기서 뭘 했어? 새 노트북 컴퓨터 같은 뭔가를 샀어?

M: No, I didn't do that. I bought a computer <u>game</u> for Mark. 아니, 그러지는 않았어. 마크에게 줄 컴퓨터 게임을 샀어.

W: <u>Why</u> did you do that? 왜 샀는데?

M: Today is his <u>birthday</u>. I'm going to his <u>party</u> after school. 오늘이 그 애의 생일이거든. 난 방과 후에 그의 생일 파티에 갈 거야.

어휘 still 여전히 work on ~을 작업하다 essay 에세이, 과제물 laptop 노트북 컴퓨터

15 ⑤

임대 침실 두 개짜리 집; 집에는 거실, 부엌, 그리고 화장실이 있습니다; 집에는 침대 2개, 소파, 식탁, 그리고 의자 4개가 있습니다.
임대료: 한 달 400달러
전화: 409-3423
애완동물은 허용되지 않습니다.

① There are <u>two bedrooms</u> in the house.

집에는 침실이 두 개 있다.

② The house has <u>furniture</u> in it. 집에는 가구가 있다.

③ The house <u>costs</u> four <u>hundred</u> dollars to <u>rent</u> each month. 집의 임대료는 매달 400달러이다.

④ A person can <u>call</u> a <u>number</u> to ask about the house. 집에 대해 물어보기 위해 어떤 번호로 전화를 걸 수 있다.

⑤ A person <u>with</u> a <u>dog</u> can <u>live</u> in the house.
개 한 마리를 키우는 사람은 집에서 살 수 있다.

해설 'No pets are allowed.'는 주택을 임대할 때 혹은 공공장소에서 자주 볼 수 있는 게시문이다.

어휘 for rent (게시문에서) 임대함, 세놓음 furnished 가구가 비치된 dining table 식탁 per ~마다 pet 애완동물 furniture 가구

16 ⑤

[*Telephone rings.*] [전화벨이 울린다.]

W: Hello. <u>Room service</u>. 여보세요. 룸서비스입니다.

M: Hi. This is John Taylor in room four two three.
안녕하세요. 저는 423호실의 존 테일러라고 합니다.

W: Yes, how can I help you? 네, 무엇을 도와드릴까요?

M: I'd like to <u>order</u> some <u>dinner</u>, please.
저녁식사를 시키고 싶어요.

W: Sure. <u>What</u> do you want to <u>have</u>?
물론이죠. 뭘 드시고 싶으신가요?

M: I'd like the <u>steak</u>, a <u>baked potato</u>, and a cola.
스테이크, 구운 감자, 그리고 콜라를 부탁 드리겠습니다.

W: All right. Your food will <u>be ready</u> in about twenty minutes. How would you like to <u>pay for</u> it? 알겠습니다.
음식은 약 20분 후에 준비될 겁니다. 계산은 어떻게 하시겠습니까?

M: Please <u>charge</u> it <u>to</u> my room.
요금은 제 방으로 달아 주세요.

어휘 order 주문하다 baked 구운 pay for ~에 대한 대금을 지불하다 charge (비용을) 청구하다

17 ④

① M: Do you know <u>how</u> I can <u>get to</u> the flower shop?
꽃 가게에 어떻게 가야 하는지 아세요?

W: <u>Go</u> right <u>down</u> this <u>street</u> and <u>turn left</u> at the <u>intersection</u>. 길을 따라 쭉 가시다가 교차로에서 좌회전하세요.

② M: <u>How many</u> times did you <u>call</u> Doug today?
오늘 더그에게 몇 번이나 전화했니?

W: I only called him <u>once</u>. 딱 한 번 전화했어.

③ M: How would you like to <u>pay for</u> this?
이건 어떻게 계산하시겠습니까?

W: I'm going to use my <u>credit card</u>. 신용카드를 사용할게요.

④ M: Would you <u>prefer</u> pizza <u>or</u> sandwiches for lunch?
점심으로 피자나 샌드위치가 괜찮으세요?

W: Yes, that would be great. 네, 그러면 좋겠네요.

⑤ M: May I please <u>speak with</u> Mr. Simmons?
시몬스 씨와 통화할 수 있을까요?

W: He's <u>on another line</u>. Hold, please.
그분은 지금 다른 전화를 받고 있어요. 잠시만 기다려 주세요.

해설 ④의 질문에 대해서는 둘 중 하나를 선택하거나, 둘 다 선택하거나, 둘 다 선택하지 않는 대답이 이어져야 한다.

어휘 down the street 길을 따라, 길 아래로 turn left 좌회전하다 intersection 교차로 speak with ~와 통화하다, ~와 이야기하다 on another line 다른 전화를 받고 있는

18 ⑤

M: Please <u>listen closely</u>. You're going to <u>take</u> your midterm <u>exam</u> tomorrow, so please <u>do</u> the <u>following</u>. First, do not be <u>late for class</u> because the test will <u>take</u> the <u>entire period</u> to complete. Next, you must use a <u>black pen</u>. You may not use a <u>pencil</u> or blue pen. When you take the test, you must <u>read</u> the <u>questions carefully</u>. Some of them are a bit <u>tricky</u>. You must also <u>answer</u> all of the <u>questions</u>. Even if you don't know an answer, try to <u>guess</u> it anyway. <u>Study hard</u> and good luck tomorrow.

잘 들어 주세요. 내일 여러분은 중간 고사를 보기 때문에, 다음과 같이 해주시기 바랍니다. 첫째, 수업 시간 내내 시험을 보게 되므로 수업에 늦지 마시기 바랍니다. 다음으로, 여러분은 반드시 검정색 펜을 사용해야 합니다. 연필이나 파란색 펜은 사용할 수 없습니다. 시험을 볼 때는 문제를 꼼꼼히 읽기 바랍니다. 몇몇 문제는 약간 까다롭습니다. 그리고 모든 문제에 답하셔야 합니다. 정답을 모르더라도 어떻게든지 정답을 추측해 보십시오. 열심히 공부하시고 내일 좋은 결과가 있길 바랍니다.

어휘 midterm exam 중간 고사 the following 다음, 아래 late for ~에 늦은 take (시간이) 걸리다, 소요하다 entire 전체의 period 수업시간, 교시 complete 완성하다, 완료하다 a bit 약간 tricky 까다로운 guess 추측하다 anyway 어쨌든

19 ①

M: Why don't we <u>order</u> a <u>pizza</u> tonight?
우리 오늘 밤에 피자를 시키는 게 어때?

W: But we had pizza two nights ago.
하지만 우린 이틀 전에 피자를 먹었잖아.

M: I know. But Pizza Express is <u>having</u> a <u>sale</u>. If we buy one pizza, we can get <u>another for free</u>.
알아. 하지만 피자 익스프레스에서 할인을 하고 있어. 피자 한 판을 사면 한 판을 공짜로 받을 수 있어.

W: I <u>don't really</u> like the food there.
난 거기 음식이 썩 마음에 들지는 않아.

M: I thought you loved it. You always eat the pizza when we order it. 난 네가 좋아하는 줄 알았어. 우리가 주문할 때마다 너는 항상 피자를 먹잖아.

W: I <u>just</u> eat it <u>because</u> I know how much you love it.
나는 네가 피자를 얼마나 좋아하는지 알기 때문에 그냥 먹은 거야.

M: I <u>had no idea</u>. In that case, what would you like to <u>have for dinner</u> tonight?
그런 줄 몰랐어. 그럼, 오늘 밤 저녁으로 뭘 먹고 싶니?

W: How about getting Chinese food for a change?

기분 전환 삼아 중국 음식을 먹는 게 어때?

① How about getting Chinese food for a change?
기분 전환 삼아 중국 음식을 먹는 게 어때?

② Okay. That's exactly what I was thinking.
알았어. 그게 바로 내가 생각하고 있었던 거야.

③ I'd love something from Pizza Express.
난 피자 익스프레스에서 뭔가를 먹고 싶어.

④ No, I haven't had anything for dinner.
아니, 난 아직 저녁으로 아무것도 안 먹었어.

⑤ Yes, I already ordered. 응, 내가 이미 주문했어.

어휘 have a sale 할인 판매를 하다 for free 무료로 have no idea 잘 모르다 in that case 그렇다면 for a change 여느 때와 달리, 기분 전환 삼아 exactly 정확하게

20 ③

[Cellphone rings.] [휴대폰이 울린다.]

M: Hello. May I talk to Ms. Gordon, please?
여보세요. 고든 씨와 통화할 수 있을까요?

W: This is Ms. Gordon. Who's calling?
제가 고든입니다. 누구시죠?

M: I'm calling from Speedy Delivery. I have a package I'd like to deliver to you in ten minutes. 스피디 배달에서 전화 드렸습니다. 10분 후에 배달해 드릴 소포가 하나 있습니다.

W: I'm terribly sorry, but I'm not at home right now.
정말 죄송하지만 제가 지금 집에 없어요.

M: Would it be okay if I left the package in your mailbox?
우편함에 소포를 두고 가도 괜찮을까요?

W: I don't think that's a good idea. It contains some valuable papers. 그건 별로 좋은 생각이 아니네요. 소포에는 중요한 서류가 몇 개 있거든요.

M: Then what do you want me to do with the package? 그럼 제가 이 소포를 어떻게 하면 좋을까요?

W: You should leave it with the security guard.
경비원에게 맡겨 주셔야 해요.

① No, I didn't send a package to anyone.
아니요, 저는 누구에게도 소포를 보내지 않았습니다.

② Sorry, but I haven't packed my bags yet.
죄송합니다만 아직 가방을 꾸리지 않았어요.

③ You should leave it with the security guard.
경비원에게 맡겨 주셔야 해요.

④ Yes, I'm going to be home ten minutes from now.
네, 앞으로 10분 후에 집에 갈 겁니다.

⑤ I'm at home now. You can come here and drop it off. 지금 집에 있어요. 여기 오셔서 놓고 가시면 돼요.

어휘 package 소포 deliver 배달하다 right now 지금, 당장 mailbox 우편함 contain 포함하다 valuable 가치 있는, 중요한 pack (짐을) 챙기다, 싸다 security guard 경비원 drop something off ~을 내려놓다, 놓고 가다

---

01 ②	02 ⑤	03 ④	04 ②	05 ④
06 ⑤	07 ④	08 ⑤	09 ②	10 ②
11 ②	12 ②	13 ①	14 ③	15 ④
16 ①	17 ⑤	18 ③	19 ④	20 ⑤

01 ②

W: Mom's birthday is this Saturday. You didn't forget, did you?
엄마의 생신이 이번 주 토요일이야. 너 잊지 않았지. 그렇지?

M: Of course not. I've been saving money to buy her a present. 물론 잊지 않았지. 엄마에게 선물을 사드리려고 돈을 모으고 있었어.

W: That's great. I've saved some money as well.
잘했어. 나도 돈을 조금 모았어.

M: Why don't we combine our money and buy her something from both of us?
우리 돈을 합쳐서 엄마에게 뭔가를 사드리는 게 어때?

W: That's a good idea. What should we buy for her?
좋은 생각이야. 뭘 사드려야 할까?

M: How about some flowers? She loves roses.
꽃이 어때? 엄마는 장미를 좋아하시잖아.

W: Yeah, but I want to get her something she can keep for a long time. We could get her a new scarf.
응, 하지만 나는 엄마가 오랫동안 간직하실 수 있는 것을 사드리고 싶어. 새 스카프를 사드리면 되겠다.

M: She has plenty of those. How about some earrings? 엄마는 스카프를 많이 갖고 계셔. 귀걸이는 어때?

W: Yeah, she said she wants some the other day. Let's buy a pair for her. 그래, 엄마가 지난번에 귀걸이를 갖고 싶다고 하셨지. 귀걸이를 사드리자.

어휘 save 모으다 as well 또한 combine 합치다 keep 보관하다 for a long time 오랫동안 plenty of 많은 earring 귀걸이 the other day 지난번에 a pair of 한 쌍의

02 ⑤

M: People can use this all the time. This is found in all sorts of places. This is in buildings, near people's homes, and even on the streets sometimes. People can use this to get money at any time. They need to have a special card from the bank. But they don't have to go to the bank if they use this. This is very helpful on holidays and weekends.

사람들은 항상 이것을 사용할 수 있습니다. 이것은 모든 종류의 장소에서 찾을 수 있습니다. 이것은 건물 안, 가정집 주변, 그리고 심지어 길에도 있습니다. 사람들은 이것을 이용해 언제든지 돈을 얻을 수 있습니다. 사람들은 이것을 이용하려면 은행에서 받은 특별한 카드가 필요합니다. 하지만 이것을 이용한다면 은행에 갈 필요가 없습

니다. 이것은 휴일이나 주말에 무척 유용합니다.

어휘 all the time 항상 all sorts of 온갖 종류의, 많은 place 장소 on the street 거리에서 at any time 언제든 helpful 도움이 되는, 유용한 holiday 휴일

03 ④

M: I'm really happy that winter is finally ending.
드디어 겨울이 끝나고 있어서 정말 기뻐.

W: I feel the same way. I'm tired of cold weather.
나도 그래. 난 추운 날씨가 지겨워.

M: Yeah, I want warm weather. I want to go outside without wearing a heavy jacket. 응, 난 따뜻한 날씨를 원해. 무거운 재킷을 입지 않고 밖에 나가고 싶어.

W: So have you seen the weather forecast for today?
그래서 오늘 일기예보를 봤니?

M: Not yet. What's the high temperature going to be?
아직 못 봤어. 최고 기온이 몇 도나 된다고 하니?

W: It's going to get up to eleven degrees, but it's going to go down to two degrees above zero tonight.
11도까지 올라갈 거지만, 오늘 밤에는 영상 2도까지 내려갈 거야.

M: That's better than yesterday's weather.
어제 날씨보다는 낫다.

W: I know. It was minus four degrees yesterday. It was freezing. 알아. 어제는 영하 4도였어. 정말 추웠어.

해설 ①은 어제의 기온이고, ⑤는 오늘의 최고 기온이다.

어휘 finally 마침내, 결국 feel the same way 똑같이 생각하다 be tired of ~이 싫증 나다 outside 밖에 temperature 기온, 온도 up to ~까지 degree (기온) 도 above zero 영상의 freezing 몹시 추운

04 ②

M: What are you looking at, Mom? 뭘 보고 계세요, 엄마?

W: This month's electricity bill. It's a lot higher than normal.
이번 달 전기 요금 청구서. 보통 때보다 훨씬 많이 나왔어.

M: I guess we used too much electricity, didn't we?
우리가 너무 많은 전기를 사용했나 보죠, 그렇지 않나요?

W: That's right. We need to start saving electricity. We should turn off the lights in rooms when we leave them. 맞아. 우리는 전기를 절약할 필요가 있어. 방에서 나갈 때는 방의 불을 꺼야 한단다.

M: Will that really work? 그게 정말 효과가 있을까요?

W: Yes, it will. Even though it seems small, it will make a big difference over a month. 응, 그럴 거야. 효과가 작다 하더라도, 한 달이 넘으면 큰 차이를 만들 거야.

M: What else can we do then?
우리가 또 어떤 것을 할 수 있죠?

W: How about using the fan rather than the air conditioner? 에어컨보다는 선풍기를 사용하는 게 어떻겠니?

해설 'How about ~?', 'Why don't ~?'는 제안할 때 자주 쓰이는 표현이다.

어휘 electricity 전기 bill 청구서 normal 보통의, 정상의 guess 추측하다 turn off (전원을) 끄다 leave 떠나다 work 효과가 있다 difference 차이 fan 선풍기 rather than ~라기보다는 air conditioner 에어컨

05 ④

W: Hello. Do you need to check out a book?
안녕하세요. 책을 대출하고 싶으세요?

M: No, but I have a book I need to return. Here you are. 아니요, 제가 반납해야 할 책이 있어요. 여기 있습니다.

W: Thank you very much. 감사합니다.

M: Unfortunately, the book is late, so I guess I need to pay a fine.
유감스럽지만, 책이 연체되어서, 제가 연체료를 내야 할 것 같네요.

W: Let me check. [pause] Yes, it's three days late.
제가 확인해 볼게요. [잠시 후] 네, 3일 연체되었네요.

M: I'm really sorry about that. 정말 죄송합니다.

W: What happened? Did you forget about it?
무슨 일이 있으셨나요? 책에 대해 잊어버리셨나요?

M: No. It's a great book, and I wanted to finish reading it before returning it. 아니요, 좋은 책이어서 반납하기 전에 끝까지 다 읽고 싶었어요.

W: I see. Well, your fine is three dollars.
그렇군요. 음, 연체료는 3달러입니다.

어휘 check out (책을) 대출하다 unfortunately 유감스럽게도, 불행하게도 late 늦은 fine 벌금; 연체료

06 ⑤

[Telephone rings.] [전화벨이 울린다.]

M: Hello. This is the Green Thumb Flower Shop. Can I help you?
안녕하세요. 그린썸 꽃 가게입니다. 제가 도와드릴까요?

W: Hi. This is Melissa Reynolds. I ordered some flowers about thirty minutes ago.
안녕하세요. 멜리사 레이놀즈예요. 약 30분 전에 꽃을 주문했어요.

M: Yes, Ms. Reynolds. Is there something I can do for you? 네, 레이놀즈 씨. 제가 도와드릴 일이 있나요?

W: I need to change my order. 제 주문을 변경해야 하거든요.

M: Sure. How do you want to change it?
네, 어떻게 변경하고 싶으신가요?

W: Well, I ordered two dozen roses and a dozen carnations, right?
음, 제가 장미 24송이와 카네이션 12송이를 주문했어요, 맞죠?

M: That's correct. 맞습니다.

W: I don't want the carnations anymore. I'd like a dozen lilies instead.
이제 카네이션은 원하지 않아요. 대신 백합 12송이를 사고 싶어요.

M: No problem. I'll take care of that right away.
문제 없습니다. 지금 바로 처리하겠습니다.

어휘 order 주문하다 dozen 12개 carnation 카네이션 correct 정확한, 맞는 not ~ anymore 더 이상 ~ 않는 instead 대신에 take care of ~을 처리하다, 돌보다

07 ④

W: Are you <u>hungry</u>? I need some food.
너 배 고프니? 난 뭘 좀 먹어야 해.

M: Okay, let's <u>take a break</u> and get <u>something to eat</u>.
그래, 휴식을 취하고, 뭘 좀 먹자.

W: Thanks. What do you <u>feel like</u> eating?
고마워. 뭘 먹고 싶니?

M: <u>How about</u> going to the <u>snack shop</u>? We can get some <u>instant noodles</u> there.
분식점에 가는 게 어때? 거기서 라면을 먹을 수 있잖아.

W: That sounds fine. And some gimbap and sundae would be nice, too.
그거 괜찮네. 그리고 김밥과 순대도 좋겠다.

M: All right. Do you want a <u>soda</u>? 알았어. 탄산음료 마실래?

W: <u>No thanks</u>. Let's just get some <u>orange juice</u> instead. 아니, 괜찮아. 대신 오렌지 주스를 마시자.

M: Sure. My <u>mouth</u> is <u>watering</u> now. Let's <u>hurry up</u> and go there. 그래. 입에서 군침이 나오네. 어서 가자.

어휘 hungry 배고픈 take a break 휴식을 취하다 feel like ~하고 싶다 snack shop 매점, 분식점 instant noodles 라면 instead 대신에 watering (입이) 침을 흘리는 hurry up 서두르다

08 ⑤

M: Are you all <u>ready for</u> the new <u>semester</u> to begin?
새 학기를 시작할 준비는 다 했니?

W: I think so. I <u>purchased</u> all of my <u>textbooks</u> already.
그런 것 같아. 이미 모든 교과서를 다 구매했어.

M: I <u>did the same</u> thing yesterday.
나도 어제 같은 일을 했어.

W: And I went to the <u>stationery store</u> to buy some <u>notebooks</u>, <u>pens</u>, and <u>pencils</u>.
그리고 나는 문구점에 가서 공책, 펜, 그리고 연필도 몇 개 샀어.

M: I <u>haven't</u> done that <u>yet</u>. I probably have a few pencils <u>at home</u> though. 나는 아직 그건 안 샀어. 하지만 아마도 집에 연필 몇 자루가 있을 거야.

W: But <u>do you have</u> any notebooks? You really need some of them.
하지만 넌 공책은 있니? 공책 몇 권이 정말 필요할 거야.

M: No, I <u>don't</u>. I <u>ought to</u> buy them today.
아니, 없어. 오늘 공책을 사야 해.

W: <u>How about</u> going to the store and getting them now? 지금 가게에 가서 몇 개 사는 게 어때?

M: Okay. But <u>do you mind</u> going along with me?
알았어. 혹시 나랑 같이 가 줄 수 있겠니?

W: <u>Not at all</u>. Let's do that right now.
당연하지. 지금 가자.

어휘 ready for ~가 준비된 semester 학기 purchase 구매하다 stationery store 문구점 notebook 공책; 노트북 컴퓨터 probably 아마도 ought to ~해야 한다 along with ~와 함께

09 ②

M: What are you doing here? I thought you were <u>taking a trip</u>.
여기서 뭐 하고 있니? 네가 여행을 하고 있는 줄 알았는데.

W: I was <u>supposed to fly</u> to Guam today.
난 오늘 비행기를 타고 괌으로 가기로 되어 있었어.

M: Why didn't you go? 왜 가지 않았니?

W: You <u>won't believe</u> what happened. I <u>woke up</u> early and <u>got on</u> the <u>bus</u>. 무슨 일이 있었는지 넌 믿지 못할 거야. 내가 일찍 일어나서 버스를 탔거든.

M: Did you get on the <u>wrong</u> bus? 버스를 잘못 탔니?

W: No. The bus was <u>in an accident</u> on the highway, and I <u>arrived late</u> at the airport, so I <u>missed</u> my <u>flight</u>. 아니. 버스가 고속도로에서 사고가 나서 내가 공항에 늦게 도착했어. 그래서 비행기를 놓쳤어.

M: That's terrible. You must feel <u>awful</u>.
정말 안됐다. 끔찍한 기분이겠다.

W: You can <u>say that again</u>. 정말 그래.

어휘 be supposed to ~하기로 되어 있다 wake up 일어나다 wrong 잘못된 be in an accident 사고가 나다 on the highway 고속도로에서 airport 공항 miss 놓치다 flight 비행 terrible 끔찍한(= awful) you can say that again 네 말에 전적으로 동의해 upset 화난, 속상한 satisfied 만족하는

10 ②

W: Remember that we're going to <u>have</u> our class <u>picnic</u> tomorrow. I <u>checked</u> the <u>weather</u> forecast. Apparently, it's going to <u>rain</u> in the <u>morning</u>. So all of you should <u>bring</u> umbrellas or <u>wear raincoats</u>. But don't worry too much. The rain will <u>stop around ten</u>, and the <u>skies</u> will begin to <u>clear up</u>. We should have <u>sunny</u> weather <u>starting</u> around <u>one</u> P.M. I'm sure we're going to <u>have</u> a <u>great time</u> tomorrow.

내일 우리 반은 소풍을 간다는 것을 기억하시기 바랍니다. 제가 일기예보를 확인했습니다. 보아하니, 아침에 비가 올 것 같습니다. 그래서 여러분 모두는 우산을 가져오거나 우비를 입어야 합니다. 그러나 너무 걱정하지 마세요. 비는 10시쯤 그칠 것이고, 하늘은 맑아질 것입니다. 오후 1시쯤부터는 해가 나기 시작할 겁니다. 우리는 내일 분명히 좋은 시간을 보낼 수 있을 겁니다.

어휘 picnic 소풍 check 확인하다 apparently 보아하니, 분명히 bring 가져오다 umbrella 우산 raincoat 우비, 비옷 clear up 개다, 맑아지다 starting ~부터

11 ②

나이	주민	비거주 주민
성인	12달러	15달러
어린이(12세 이하)	7달러	9달러
노인(60세 이상)	5달러	7달러

W: Good morning. <u>Welcome to</u> the arts center.
안녕하세요. 아트센터에 오신 걸 환영합니다.

M: Hi. I need to buy <u>five tickets</u>, please.

안녕하세요. 티켓 5장을 사고 싶어요.

W: Are you a local <u>resident</u>, or do you <u>live somewhere</u> <u>else</u>? 지역 주민이신가요, 아니면 다른 곳에 사시나요?

M: We <u>live</u> in the <u>city</u>. Here's my <u>ID card</u>.
우리는 이 도시에 살고 있어요. 여기 제 신분증이요.

W: Ah, yes, I can see your <u>address</u> on it. Thank you.
아, 네, 손님 주소가 여기 나와 있네요. 감사합니다.

M: There are <u>two adults</u> and <u>three children</u>.
성인 두 명과 어린이 세 명이에요.

W: All right. Will you be <u>paying with</u> your credit card?
알겠습니다. 신용카드로 결제하시겠어요?

M: Yes. Here you are. 네. 여기 있어요.

해설 성인 2명($12×2)+어린이 3명($7×3) = $45

어휘 adult 성인, 어른 local 지역의 resident 주민 somewhere else 다른 어딘가에 ID card 신분증 address 주소 pay with ~으로 지불하다

12 ②

M: Have you <u>selected</u> a <u>class</u> for the <u>after-school</u> program yet?
넌 방과 후 수업 프로그램을 아직 고르지 못했니?

W: No, I haven't. 응, 아직 못했어.

M: <u>When</u> do we need to do that <u>by</u>?
우리는 그걸 언제까지 해야 하지?

W: I think we need to <u>sign up</u> by tomorrow morning.
내 생각에는, 내일 아침까지 등록해야 할 것 같아.

M: Oh, I didn't know that. 아, 그건 몰랐어.

W: I'm going to Mr. Park's office. He has the <u>registration forms</u>. Would you like to <u>go with me</u>?
난 박 선생님 사무실에 갈 거야. 그분이 신청서 양식을 가지고 있어. 나랑 같이 갈래?

M: I <u>want to</u>, <u>but</u> I'm waiting for Minsu. Can you <u>pick</u> <u>up</u> a form for me? 나도 그러고 싶은데, 난 민수를 기다리는 중이야. 내가 쓸 양식도 가져올래?

W: Sure. I'll <u>give</u> it to you <u>at lunchtime</u>.
물론이지. 점심시간에 줄게.

M: Thanks a lot. 정말 고마워.

어휘 select 선택하다 after-school 방과 후의 sign up 등록하다 registration form 등록 양식 pick up 가져오다 lunchtime 점심시간

13 ①

① M: <u>How</u> did you <u>enjoy</u> the pie? 파이는 맛있게 먹었니?
   W: It was a cherry pie. 그건 체리 파이였어.
② M: Let's <u>see a movie</u> this afternoon.
   오늘 오후에 영화 보러 가자.
   W: Sorry. I <u>don't have</u> enough <u>time</u>.
   미안해. 난 시간이 별로 없어.
③ M: <u>When</u> does soccer practice <u>start</u>?
   축구 연습은 언제 시작하니?
   W: It <u>begins</u> at three thirty. 3시 30분에 시작해.

④ M: You <u>look</u> really <u>good</u> in that dress.
   넌 그 옷이 잘 어울려.
   W: Thank you for saying that. 그렇게 말해줘서 고마워.
⑤ M: <u>Why</u> didn't you <u>come to school</u> yesterday?
   어제 왜 학교에 오지 않았니?
   W: I <u>had</u> a very bad <u>cold</u>. 난 심한 감기에 걸렸어.

어휘 enough 충분한 practice 연습 look good 좋아 보이다
dress 옷, 원피스, 드레스 have a cold 감기에 걸리다

14 ③

M: There are around <u>two hundred countries</u> in the world. Each country has a different number of people in it. <u>China</u> has the <u>world's largest</u> <u>population</u> while <u>India</u> has the <u>second</u> largest. Each country has more than <u>one billion people</u> living in them. <u>The United States</u> has the <u>third</u> most people. <u>Brazil</u> and <u>Indonesia</u> are numbers <u>four</u> and <u>five</u>. Vatican City is a country with <u>one of the smallest</u> populations. Only <u>around five hundred</u> people live there.

세계에는 약 200개의 나라가 있다. 각각의 나라에는 각기 다른 숫자의 사람이 살고 있다. 중국은 세계에서 가장 많은 인구가 있는 반면, 인도는 두 번째로 많은 인구가 있다. 각각의 나라는 10억 명 이상의 사람들이 살고 있다. 미국은 세 번째로 많은 인구를 가지고 있다. 브라질과 인도네시아는 네 번째, 다섯 번째이다. 바티칸 시티는 가장 적은 인구를 가진 나라 중 하나이다. 그곳에는 500명 정도의 사람이 살고 있다.

해설 미국의 인구는 세계에서 세 번째로 많다.

어휘 each 각각의 largest 가장 큰(large – larger – largest)
population 인구 while 반면에 more than ~ 이상의 billion 10억

15 ④

M: Would you like <u>something to eat</u>, ma'am?
무엇을 드시겠습니까, 부인?

W: What are my <u>choices</u>? 뭘 선택할 수 있나요?

M: You can have <u>chicken</u> or <u>seafood</u>.
치킨이나 해산물을 드실 수 있어요.

W: Seafood <u>sounds fine</u> to me. 저는 해산물이 좋은 것 같아요.

M: How about something to <u>drink</u>? 마실 것은요?

W: <u>I'd like</u> a cola, please. 콜라 주세요.

M: Is there <u>anything</u> else you need? 더 필요하신 게 있나요?

W: Yes, I have a question. <u>When</u> are we going to <u>arrive</u> in Hawaii?
네, 질문이 하나 있어요. 우리는 하와이에 언제 도착하나요?

M: We should be <u>landing</u> there <u>in</u> about <u>three hours</u>.
약 3시간 후에 그곳에 착륙할 거예요.

해설 남자의 마지막 말에서 'landing'을 놓치지 말아야 한다.

어휘 choice 선택(권) seafood 해산물 arrive 도착하다 land 착륙하다

16 ①

M: Did you see the new bicycle that Dave got for his birthday? 데이브가 생일에 받은 새 자전거를 봤니?

W: Yeah, it's really nice. 응, 정말 좋더라.

M: I wish I had a bike like that.
나도 그런 자전거가 있으면 좋겠어.

W: But you have a bike. Your parents gave you a new one three months ago. 하지만 넌 자전거를 갖고 있잖아. 너희 부모님께서 3달 전에 새 자전거를 사주셨잖아.

M: I know, but Dave's bike looks nicer than mine.
나도 알지만, 데이브의 자전거가 내 것보다 더 좋아 보여.

W: Who cares about his bike? You've got a great one, and you should be happy you have it.
누가 데이브의 자전거에 신경 쓰겠니? 너도 아주 좋은 것을 갖고 있으니 네가 갖고 있다는 것에 만족해야 해.

M: I don't know. I still think he has a better bike than I do. 난 모르겠어. 아직 그가 내 것보다 좋은 자전거를 갖고 있다는 생각이 들어.

① The grass is always greener on the other side of the fence. 남의 떡이 더 커 보인다.
② A penny saved is a penny earned. 티끌 모아 태산이다.
③ All that glitters is not gold.
반짝이는 모든 것이 금은 아니다.
④ A stitch in time saves nine.
제때의 바늘 한 땀이 아홉 번의 바느질을 던다.
⑤ Seeing is believing. 백문이 불여일견이다.

어휘 bicycle 자전거(= bike) mine 내 것 care about ~에 신경 쓰다, 관심을 갖다 grass 풀 fence 울타리 glitter 반짝이다 save 절약하다, 모으다 stitch (바늘) 한 땀 in time 제때의

17 ⑤

M: Clara, how are you doing? 클라라, 잘 지냈니?

W: Not so well. Do you happen to know Ms. Carpenter's phone number?
별로야. 혹시 카펜터 선생님의 전화번호를 알고 있니?

M: Sorry, but I have no idea. Why do you need it?
미안하지만 모르겠어. 그게 왜 필요해?

W: I need to talk to her about something.
난 그분에게 뭔가를 말씀 드려야 해.

M: What's going on? 무슨 일인데?

W: My grandmother is in the hospital, so my family is going to visit her. Can you tell her why I'm not in class tomorrow?
우리 할머니가 병원에 계셔서, 가족들이 병문안을 하러 갈 거야. 네가 내일 선생님께 왜 내가 수업에 못 왔는지 말해 줄 수 있니?

M: Of course, I'll tell her. And I hope your grandmother gets better.
당연하지, 내가 말씀 드릴게. 너희 할머니가 괜찮아지시길 바랄게.

W: Thanks a lot. 정말 고마워.

어휘 happen to 우연히 ~하다 phone number 전화번호 have no idea 전혀 모르다 get better 회복하다, (병이) 낫다

18 ③

W: I'm thinking of joining a health club. Do you know a good one?
난 헬스클럽에 다닐까 생각 중이야. 괜찮은 곳을 알고 있니?

M: Sure. You should go to John's Health Club. I work out there.
그럼. 넌 존 헬스클럽에 다녀야 해. 나도 거기서 운동해.

W: What do you do? 넌 뭘 하니?

M: I lift weights and swim there. But there are also yoga classes. 난 거기서 역기도 들고 수영도 해. 하지만 거기에는 요가 교실도 있어.

W: That sounds interesting. How much is it?
재미있겠다. 가격은 얼마야?

M: It costs fifty dollars a month. The hours are good, too. It's open from eight in the morning to ten at night every day of the year. 한 달에 50달러야. 시간대도 괜찮아. 일 년 내내 아침 8시에 문을 열고 밤 10시에 닫아.

W: Wow. I should go there. Where is it?
와. 난 거기에 가야겠어. 그게 어디 있니?

M: It's at sixty-eight Maple Street. It's really close to the school. 메이플 가 68번지에 있어. 학교에서 정말 가까워.

어휘 work out 운동하다 lift weights 역기를 들다 close to ~에서 가까운

19 ④

M: Are you going out this evening?
넌 오늘 저녁에 외출할 거니?

W: I am. Karen and I are planning to watch a movie together. 네. 캐런하고 저는 같이 영화를 볼 거예요.

M: Why don't you hang out with Cindy anymore?
왜 넌 더 이상 신디랑 같이 다니지 않니?

W: Karen and I have a great time together. She's more fun than Cindy. 캐런하고 전 함께 즐거운 시간을 보내고 있어요. 캐런이 신디보다 더 재미있어요.

M: But you've been best friends with Cindy for five years. 하지만 넌 5년 동안 신디랑 제일 친한 친구 사이였잖아.

W: That's true, but we don't see each other nowadays.
맞아요, 하지만 우리는 요즘 서로 자주 만나지 않아요.

M: Why don't you try meeting her more often?
그녀를 더 자주 만나보는 게 어떻겠니?

① No, I haven't met Karen before.
아니, 난 전에 캐런을 만난 적이 없어.
② How has Cindy been doing lately?
신디는 요즘 어떻게 지내니?
③ So what are you and Cindy doing tonight?
그래서 너와 신디는 오늘 밤에 뭐 할 거야?
④ Why don't you try meeting her more often?
그녀를 더 자주 만나보는 게 어떻겠니?
⑤ It's good to hear that you're getting along well.
네가 잘 지내고 있다니 다행이야.

어휘 go out 외출하다 hang out (많은) 시간을 보내다 not ~ anymore 더 이상 ~ 않는 fun 재미있는 nowadays 요즘 lately 최근에 get along well 잘 지내다

20 ⑤

M: I can't believe how dirty the park is.
공원이 얼마나 더러운지 믿을 수가 없어.

W: I know. People just throw their trash on the ground.
나도 알아. 사람들이 바닥에 그냥 쓰레기를 버리잖아.

M: Why don't we pick up some of this trash?
우리가 이 쓰레기를 좀 줍는 게 어떨까?

W: We could do that, but there's so much of it.
우리가 그걸 할 수 있지만, 쓰레기가 너무 많아.

M: You're right. But we could still make the park look better. 네 말이 맞아. 하지만 그래도 우리는 공원을 더 보기 좋게 만들 수 있어.

W: We should bring some friends to help us clean up the park.
우리는 공원 치우는 걸 도와줄 친구들을 좀 데려와야 해.

M: Yeah. We could meet here every weekend.
그래. 우리는 매주 주말에 여기서 만날 수 있어.

① The park looks like it's clean to me.
나한테는 공원이 깨끗해 보여.

② What should we do here at the park?
공원에서 우리가 무엇을 할 수 있을까?

③ Why didn't we ask them to meet us here?
우리가 왜 그들에게 여기서 만나자고 하지 않았을까?

④ You're right. I shouldn't have brought them.
네 말이 맞아. 난 그들을 데려오지 말았어야 했어.

⑤ Yeah. We could meet here every weekend.
그래. 우리는 매주 주말에 여기서 만날 수 있어.

어휘 dirty 더러운 throw trash 쓰레기를 버리다 ground 땅, 바닥 pick up 줍다 clean up 치우다, 청소하다 should have p.p. ~했어야 했다

18회 실전모의고사 본문 p.208-209

01 ②	02 ③	03 ④	04 ⑤	05 ③
06 ④	07 ②	08 ⑤	09 ⑤	10 ②
11 ⑤	12 ④	13 ④	14 ③	15 ⑤
16 ①	17 ④	18 ①	19 ②	20 ②

01 ②

W: Hello. May I help you?
안녕하세요. 무엇을 도와드릴까요?

M: Yes, please. I need some shoes for my son.
네. 제 아들에게 줄 신발이 좀 필요해요.

W: Does he need dress shoes like these?

아드님에게 이런 정장 구두가 필요한가요?

M: No, he needs some sneakers.
아니요, 그 애는 운동화가 필요해요.

W: Okay. How about these shoes with small wheels on them? 알겠습니다. 조그만 바퀴가 달린 이런 신발은 어떠세요?

M: I'm not sure. Do you have anything else?
잘 모르겠네요. 다른 것도 있나요?

W: Here are a pair of basketball shoes with three stars on them. 여기 별이 세 개 그려진 농구화가 있어요.

M: Oh, I like the plain ones. Do you have them in a size eight?
아, 저는 무늬가 없는 게 좋아요. 그 신발은 사이즈 8이 있나요?

W: Yes, I do. Let me get it for you.
네, 있습니다. 가져다 드릴게요.

어휘 dress shoes 정장 구두, 신사화 sneakers 운동화 wheel 바퀴 basketball shoes 농구화 plain 무늬가 없는

02 ③

M: It's time for the weather report. Let's look at some major cities in Europe. London has warm and sunny weather today. Berlin has very cold and windy weather though. It's raining in Spain and Italy, so both Rome and Madrid are experiencing rainy weather. In Paris, the skies are cloudy. And it's very foggy in Oslo. That's it for the weather report. I'll be back in thirty minutes with another one.

일기예보 시간입니다. 유럽의 주요 도시들을 살펴보겠습니다. 런던의 오늘 날씨는 따뜻하고 화창합니다. 하지만 베를린의 날씨는 매우 춥고 바람이 붑니다. 스페인과 이탈리아에 비가 오고 있기 때문에, 로마와 마드리드에도 비가 오고 있습니다. 파리의 하늘은 흐립니다. 그리고 오슬로는 안개가 짙게 끼었습니다. 이상 일기예보였습니다. 저는 다른 소식을 가지고 30분 후에 돌아오겠습니다.

어휘 major 주요한 though 하지만, 그렇지만 both 둘 다 experience 겪다, 경험하다 foggy 안개 낀

03 ④

M: Playing sports is one way to become healthier and to have fun. Many people get injured while playing sports these days because they don't know how to take care of themselves. There are several ways to prevent injuries. One of them is to have the proper equipment. People need the correct shoes and protective equipment for certain sports. They should also be sure to warm up properly before playing a sport. Warming up can help them avoid injuries. By doing these two activities, people can reduce their chances of getting hurt.

운동을 하는 것은 더 건강해지고 재미를 즐길 수 있는 하나의 방법입니다. 요즘은 많은 사람들이 운동을 하는 도중 부상을 입기도 하는데, 그들 스스로 어떻게 돌보아야 하는지 모르기 때문입니다.

부상을 예방하는 방법이 몇 가지 있습니다. 그중 하나는 적절한 장비를 보유하는 것입니다. 사람들은 특정 운동을 하기 위해 알맞은 신발과 보호 장비가 필요합니다. 그리고 운동을 하기 전에 제대로 된 준비 운동을 해야 합니다. 준비 운동은 사람들이 부상을 피하는 것을 돕습니다. 이 두 개의 활동을 함으로써, 사람들은 다칠 가능성을 줄일 수 있습니다.

어휘 healthier 더 건강한(healthy-healthier-healthiest) get injured 부상을 당하다 while ~하는 동안 take care of ~을 돌보다 several 몇몇의 prevent 예방하다 injury 부상 proper 적절한 correct 알맞은 protective equipment 보호 장비 certain 특정한 warm up 준비 운동을 하다, 워밍업하다 avoid 피하다 reduce 줄이다 chance 가능성

04 ⑤

W: I'm thinking of cooking spaghetti for dinner tonight.
난 오늘 밤 저녁식사로 스파게티를 만들려고 해요.

M: Why don't we have some leftovers instead?
대신 남은 음식을 먹는 게 어때요?

W: Why do you want to eat leftovers?
왜 남은 음식을 먹고 싶어요?

M: Take a look at the refrigerator. There's a lot of food in there already.
냉장고를 한번 봐요. 이미 많은 음식이 그 안에 있어요.

W: You're right. I didn't realize that.
당신 말이 맞아요. 그걸 깨닫지 못했네요.

M: If we have some leftovers, we can avoid wasting all of the food we have. 우리가 남은 음식을 먹는다면, 우리가 가진 모든 음식을 낭비하는 일을 피할 수 있어요.

W: Wow. I learn a lot from you.
우와. 난 당신에게 많이 배우게 돼요.

어휘 leftover (식사 후에) 남은 음식 instead 대신에 take a look at ~을 한번 보다 refrigerator 냉장고 realize 깨닫다 avoid 피하다 waste 낭비하다

05 ③

W: How tall are you, Kevin? 넌 키가 몇이니, 케빈?

M: I'm one hundred seventy centimeters tall. I'm about average height. 170cm야. 나는 평균 키야.

W: Are you taller than your friend Mark?
넌 네 친구 마크보다 키가 크니?

M: That's right. Both Mark and Steve are around one hundred sixty-six centimeters tall.
맞아. 마크와 스티브는 둘 다 166cm쯤 돼.

W: Are you the tallest boy in your class?
네가 너희 반에서 키가 가장 큰 남자니?

M: No, I'm not. Joe and Peter are both taller than me. Joe's one hundred seventy-five centimeters tall.
아니, 그렇지 않아. 조와 피터는 둘 다 나보다 커. 조는 175cm야.

W: Wow. And what about Peter? 와. 피터는 어때?

M: He's one hundred eighty-two centimeters tall. He's on the basketball team.
피터는 182cm야. 그는 농구팀에 있어.

W: I bet he's really good. 나는 그가 정말 잘할 거라고 확신해.

어휘 average 평균의 height 키, 높이 taller 키가 더 큰(tall-taller-tallest) both 둘 다 bet 확신하다; 내기를 걸다

06 ④

M: Do you have a few moments to help me?
잠깐 날 좀 도와줄 수 있니?

W: What do you need me to do? 뭘 도와줄까?

M: I have to turn in this article for the school newspaper by five P.M., but I'd like you to check it for mistakes. 나는 오후 5시까지 학교 신문에 이 기사를 내야 하는데, 네가 실수가 있는지 확인해 주었으면 좋겠어.

W: I don't have time right now. How about at three?
난 지금 당장은 시간이 없어. 3시는 어때?

M: I've got to meet Sue then. Is three thirty good for you? 그때는 내가 수를 만나야 해. 3시 30분은 괜찮니?

W: No, I've got softball practice. But I can meet you when practice is over. 아니, 난 소프트볼 연습이 있어. 하지만 연습이 끝나면 널 만날 수 있어.

M: When's that? 그게 언제지?

W: Half past four. 4시 30분.

M: Sounds great. I'll see you then. 좋네. 그때 만나자.

어휘 turn in 내다, 제출하다 article 기사 check 확인하다, 점검하다 mistake 실수 practice 연습 over 끝이 난 half 반, 절반 past ~이 지난

07 ②

W: What are you doing right now, Eric?
지금 뭐 하고 있어요, 에릭?

M: I'm just writing in my diary. 그냥 일기를 쓰고 있어요.

W: Do you have some time to help me?
나를 좀 도와줄 시간이 있나요?

M: Sure. What do you need? 물론이죠. 뭐가 필요한데요?

W: Whiskers isn't feeling well. I need to take her to the vet. 위스커스의 몸 상태가 안 좋아요. 수의사에게 데려가야 할 것 같아요.

M: Would you like me to drive you and your cat to the clinic? 자동차로 당신하고 당신 고양이를 병원에 데려다 주었으면 좋겠다는 거죠?

W: That would be great. It's too far away to walk there.
그러면 좋겠어요. 거긴 걸어가기에는 너무 멀거든요.

M: All right. Let me get my car keys.
알았어요. 내 차의 열쇠를 가져올게요.

W: Thanks a lot. I really appreciate your assistance.
정말 고마워요. 도와줘서 정말 감사해요.

어휘 diary 일기 feel well 몸 상태가 좋다 vet 수의사 (= veterinarian) clinic 병원 far away 멀리 떨어져 appreciate 감사하다 assistance 도움

08 ⑤

M: Today, I attended my older brother's wedding. He is

twenty-six years old, and his wife is twenty-four. It was really <u>great to see</u> him and his wife so <u>happy</u>. However, <u>now that</u> he is <u>married</u>, he is <u>moving out</u> of my parents' home. He's going to move to another city, so I'm not going to see him very much <u>anymore</u>. I think I'm starting to <u>feel lonely</u> without him around.

오늘 나는 형의 결혼식에 참석했다. 형은 26살이고, 형수님은 24살이다. 형과 형수님이 행복해하는 것을 보는 것은 매우 즐거웠다. 그러나 형이 결혼했기 때문에, 그는 우리 부모님의 집에서 이사를 갈 것이다. 그는 다른 도시로 이사를 갈 것이고, 그래서 나는 더 이상 형을 자주 볼 수 없을 것이다. 형이 곁에 없어서 외로워지기 시작하는 것 같다.

해설 맨 마지막에 남자의 심정이 나온다.

어휘 attend 참석하다 wedding 결혼식 now that ~이기 때문에 married 결혼한 move 이사 가다 lonely 외로운 without ~없이

09 ⑤

W: What did you do <u>yesterday</u>, Lewis?
어제 뭐 했니, 루이스?

M: I just <u>stayed at home</u> and watched TV most of the day. 난 그냥 집에 있으면서 거의 하루 종일 TV를 봤어.

W: You <u>should have gone</u> to the <u>forest</u> with us. We had a great time. 너도 우리와 함께 숲에 갔어야 했어. 우리는 재미있는 시간을 보냈거든.

M: Yeah? What did you do there?
그래? 넌 거기서 뭐 했어?

W: We <u>went hiking</u> and <u>collected</u> lots of <u>leaves</u> and <u>flowers</u>. 우리는 하이킹을 했고 나뭇잎과 꽃을 많이 수집했어.

M: Collecting leaves and flowers? <u>Why</u> did you do that? 나뭇잎과 꽃을 수집했다고? 그걸 왜 했어?

W: We were trying to <u>identify</u> as <u>many</u> of them <u>as we could</u>. After that, we went to the <u>lake</u> and <u>watched</u> lots of <u>animals</u>. I even saw a <u>deer</u>. 우리는 그것들의 이름을 가능한 한 많이 알아내려고 했어. 그 다음에 우리는 호수에 갔고, 많은 동물들을 보았어. 나는 심지어 사슴도 봤어.

M: Wow. I'll <u>definitely go with</u> you the next time.
우와. 나도 다음에는 너랑 꼭 같이 가야겠다.

어휘 stay 머무르다 should have p.p. ~했어야 했다 forest 숲 go hiking 하이킹을 가다 collect 수집하다 identify (신원을) 확인하다, 알아보다 lake 호수 deer 사슴 definitely 확실히, 분명히

10 ②

[*Telephone rings.*] [전화벨이 울린다.]

W: Hello. Star <u>Airlines</u>. How may I help you?
안녕하세요. 스타 항공사입니다. 무엇을 도와드릴까요?

M: I'd like to <u>fly</u> with my family <u>from</u> Seoul <u>to</u> Osaka tomorrow. 내일 저희 가족과 함께 비행기를 타고 서울에서 오사카로 가고 싶습니다.

W: You're <u>in luck</u>. We have lots of <u>seats available</u>, and we're <u>offering</u> a <u>discount on</u> all <u>flights</u> to Japan.

운이 좋으시네요. 우리는 이용 가능한 좌석이 많이 있고, 일본으로 가는 모든 항공편에 할인을 제공하고 있답니다.

M: That's wonderful. <u>How much</u> are <u>tickets</u>?
그거 좋네요. 티켓은 얼마인가요?

W: Tickets are <u>normally</u> three hundred fifty dollars <u>for adults</u> and two hundred fifty dollars for <u>children</u>. 티켓은 보통 성인은 350달러이고 어린이는 250달러입니다.

M: But <u>what about</u> the discount?
하지만 할인은 어떻게 되나요?

W: Now, they're <u>two hundred fifty</u> dollars for adults and <u>two hundred</u> dollars for children. 지금, 성인은 250달러, 어린이는 200달러입니다.

M: Wonderful. I need two tickets for adults and two tickets for children, please. 좋네요. 성인 2명과 어린이 2명의 티켓을 구매할게요.

해설 성인 2명($250X2)+어린이 2명($200X2)=$900

어휘 airline 항공사 fly 비행기를 타고 가다 seat 좌석 available 이용 가능한 offer 제공하다 discount 할인 flight 비행기 normally 보통

11 ⑤

① M: I'm planning to <u>have dinner with</u> Amy tonight.
나는 오늘 밤에 에이미와 함께 저녁을 먹을 계획이야.

W: <u>Do you mind</u> if I go with you?
내가 너랑 같이 가도 괜찮을까?

② M: <u>When</u> are you planning to <u>visit</u> India?
인도는 언제 방문할 계획이세요?

W: I'll be there in <u>July or August</u>.
7월이나 8월에 그곳에 갈 거예요.

③ M: <u>How</u> did you manage to <u>lose</u> so much <u>weight</u>?
어떻게 몸무게를 그렇게 많이 뺐니?

W: I <u>exercised</u> every day and ate <u>healthy</u> food.
나는 매일 운동하고 몸에 좋은 음식을 먹었어.

④ M: <u>Where</u> is the <u>food court</u> located?
식당가가 어디에 있나요?

W: You need to <u>take</u> the <u>escalator</u> to the <u>second floor</u>.
에스컬레이터를 타고 2층으로 올라가야 해요.

⑤ M: <u>How</u> did you <u>think</u> the <u>homework</u> was?
숙제가 어떻다고 생각했니?

W: I had to <u>solve</u> ten <u>math problems</u>.
나는 수학 10문제를 풀어야 했어.

어휘 Do you mind if ~? ~해도 괜찮을까? manage to (간신히) ~을 해내다 lose weight 체중을 줄이다, 살을 빼다 exercise 운동하다 healthy 몸에 좋은, 건강한 be located 위치하다 escalator 에스컬레이터 solve (문제를) 풀다

12 ④

M: Janet, everyone <u>turned in</u> their <u>homework</u> except you. 재닛, 너를 제외한 모든 사람들이 숙제를 제출했어.

W: I'm sorry, Mr. Walker. I'll <u>give</u> it to you <u>by tomorrow</u> morning. 죄송해요, 워커 선생님. 내일 아침까지 제출할게요.

M: Sorry, but I don't accept late homework.
미안하지만 나는 늦게 내는 숙제를 받지 않는단다.

W: But I have a good excuse this time.
하지만 저는 이번에는 그럴 만한 이유가 있어요.

M: You're not going to tell me that you were sick again, are you?
네가 또 아팠다고 얘기하지는 않을 거지. 그렇지?

W: No, it wasn't that. I did some volunteer work at the hospital all weekend, so I was too busy to do that.
네, 그런 건 아니에요. 제가 주말 내내 병원에서 자원봉사를 했기 때문에 너무 바빴어요.

M: I see. Well, it's nice to see that you care about others.
그렇구나. 음, 네가 다른 사람에게 관심을 갖는 것을 보니 좋구나.

W: So can I please turn my homework in late?
그러면 제가 늦게라도 숙제를 제출할 수 있을까요?

어휘 turn in 제출하다, 내다 except ~을 제외하고 accept 받아들이다 late 늦은 excuse 이유; 변명 sick 아픈 do volunteer work 자원봉사를 하다 hospital 병원 care about ~에 관심을 가지다

13 ④

M: Hello. How can I help you today?
안녕하세요. 오늘 무엇을 도와드릴까요?

W: I'm thinking about traveling to an island.
저는 섬으로 여행을 가는 것에 대해 생각하고 있어요.

M: Why don't you visit Saipan? It's beautiful there.
사이판을 가보는 건 어떠세요? 거긴 아름다운 곳이에요.

W: I was just there five months ago.
저는 5개월 전에 그곳에 갔었어요.

M: Have you been to the Philippines? The islands there are beautiful this time of the year.
필리핀은 가보셨나요? 필리핀의 섬들은 이맘때 아름답답니다.

W: No, I haven't been there. Where do you recommend that I go?
아니요, 거긴 안 가봤어요. 제가 갈 곳을 추천해 주시겠어요?

M: Lots of people enjoy the beaches at Cebu.
많은 사람들이 세부의 해변을 좋아해요.

W: That's interesting. How much are tickets there?
흥미롭네요. 거기 가는 티켓은 얼마인가요?

어휘 travel 여행하다 island 섬 this time of the year 매년 지금쯤 recommend 추천하다

14 ③

M: Good morning, ma'am. What can I do for you?
안녕하세요, 부인. 무엇을 도와드릴까요?

W: I dropped my phone in the sink and it got water all over it. Now, it won't even turn on.
제가 휴대폰을 싱크대에 빠뜨렸는데, 온통 물이 묻었어요. 그리고 지금은 전원이 켜지지도 않아요.

M: Oh, that's not good. Would you like us to fix it?
아, 그건 별로 안 좋네요. 저희가 고쳐 드릴까요?

W: Yes. How long will that take? 네. 얼마나 걸릴까요?

M: This isn't going to be easy to fix, so it's going to take around six hours.
고치는 것이 쉽지는 않아서요, 6시간 정도 걸릴 것 같아요.

W: I have to go back to work. Can you call me at my office number to let me know when the phone is ready? 제가 다시 일하러 돌아가야 하거든요. 전화기가 준비되면 제 사무실 번호로 전화해서 그 사실을 알려주실 수 있나요?

M: Sure. Just write it down for me, and I'll do that.
그럼요. 여기에 전화번호를 적어주시면, 제가 그렇게 해드릴게요.

어휘 drop 떨어뜨리다 sink 싱크대 all over 곳곳에, 온 군데에 turn on (전원이) 켜지다 fix 고치다, 수리하다 take (시간이) 걸리다 write down 적다

15 ⑤

W: John, did you have a good summer vacation?
존, 즐거운 여름 방학을 보냈니?

M: Yes. I did a lot of different things.
응. 나는 여러 가지 일들을 했어.

W: Like what? 예를 들어 어떤 거?

M: I spent some time at my uncle's farm, so I took care of the animals and worked in the fields.
나는 우리 삼촌의 농장에서 시간을 좀 보냈는데, 동물들을 돌보고 들판에서 일했어.

W: That doesn't sound fun. 그건 재미없는 일로 들리는데.

M: Actually, I really enjoyed it. I got to go fishing and cycling in the country, too. 사실은, 난 그 일을 무척 즐겼어. 그리고 시골에서 낚시도 하고, 자전거도 탔어.

W: Wow. I just spent most of my time at the beach.
와. 나는 거의 모든 시간을 해변에서 보냈어.

M: That's why you have a really good suntan.
그게 네가 보기 좋게 탄 이유구나.

어휘 vacation 방학; 휴가 uncle 삼촌 farm 농장 take care of ~을 돌보다 field 들판 go fishing 낚시하러 가다 go cycling 자전거 타러 가다 in the country 시골에서 have a suntan 피부를 태우다

16 ①

M: My friend from America is coming here next week. What should I do with him? 미국에 있는 내 친구가 다음 주에 여기 올 거야. 그 애랑 뭘 해야 할까?

W: Why don't you take him to the Korean Folk Village? He'll love it.
그를 한국민속촌에 데려가는 건 어때? 그가 좋아할 거야.

M: He used to live here, so he went there. He's also been to Insadong and Gyeongbokgung, too.
그는 전에 여기에 살았기 때문에, 거기는 가 봤어. 그는 인사동하고 경복궁에도 가봤어.

W: Why don't you take him to Busan or Gyeongju then? That might be a fun trip. 그럼 그를 부산이나 경주에 데려가는 건 어때? 즐거운 여행이 될 거야.

M: Hmm... He loves history, so Gyeongju would be a good place to go. Thanks for the idea, Sumi.
음.. 그는 역사를 좋아하기 때문에 경주가 여행하기 좋은 곳이 될 거야. 의견 줘서 고마워, 수미.

W: You're welcome. 천만에.

M: Now, I need to start planning everything for when he gets here.
지금부터, 그가 여기 왔을 때 할 모든 것을 계획해야겠어.

어휘 folk 민속의, 전통적인 village 마을 used to ~하곤 했다 trip 여행 history 역사

17 ④

M: We will have a fire drill in a few minutes. First of all, if you hear the fire alarm, everyone needs to line up quickly and quietly at the door. I'll check to make sure the fire isn't right outside the door. Then, we'll all walk quickly out of the room. We can't take the elevator in case of a fire, so we'll take the stairs. Don't push or shove other students. When we get out of the building, go to the middle of playground and listen as I call roll. I need to make sure everyone is there with me.

우리는 몇 분 후에 소방 훈련을 실시합니다. 우선, 여러분이 화재 경보를 듣게 되면, 모든 사람이 신속하고 조용하게 문 앞에 줄을 서야 합니다. 저는 문 밖에 화재가 없는지 확인할 겁니다. 그런 다음, 우리는 모두 교실에서 재빨리 나갈 것입니다. 우리는 화재가 났을 경우에는 엘리베이터를 탈 수 없기 때문에, 계단을 이용하게 될 것입니다. 다른 학생들을 누르거나 밀치지 마세요. 우리가 건물 밖으로 나가면, 운동장 가운데로 가서 제가 출석을 부르는 것을 들으세요. 저는 모든 사람들이 저와 함께 그곳에 있는지 확인해야 합니다.

어휘 fire drill 소방 훈련 first of all 무엇보다도, 우선 fire alarm 화재 경보 line up 줄을 서다 quietly 조용하게 make sure 확인하다, 확실히 하다 in case of ~이 발생할 때에는 take the stairs 계단을 이용하다 shove 밀치다 the middle of ~의 중앙 call roll 출석을 부르다

18 ①

[Cellphone rings.] [휴대폰이 울린다.]

W: Hi, Minsu. What's up? 안녕, 민수야. 무슨 일이야?

M: Hi, Soyun. Do you have some time right now?
안녕, 소윤아. 지금 시간 있니?

W: A bit. I'm just watching a documentary for science class. 조금. 난 과학 수업에서 공부할 다큐멘터리를 보는 중이야.

M: Do you mind taking care of my dog for a couple of days? 네가 이틀 동안 내 개를 돌봐줄 수 있니?

W: Not at all. But why can't you do it?
문제 없어. 그런데 왜 넌 돌볼 수 없니?

M: My aunt in Incheon is very sick, so we're going there to take care of her. I can't bring Snowy with me. 인천에 사는 우리 이모가 너무 아파서, 우리가 이모를 돌보러 가야 해. 난 스노위를 데려갈 수 없어.

W: Okay. Should I go to your house now to pick her up? 알았어. 내가 지금 너네 집에 가서 개를 데려와야 하니?

M: No. We'll drive over there soon and drop her off with you.
아니. 우리가 곧 차를 타고 거기 가서 너에게 개를 줄게.

해설 Snowy는 개의 이름이다.

어휘 documentary 다큐멘터리 take care of ~을 돌보다 aunt 이모, 고모, 숙모 sick 아픈 bring 데려가다 pick up ~을 찾아오다, 데려오다 drop off ~을 내려주다

19 ②

M: Jenny, I heard your science project won first place at the science fair. Congratulations. 제니, 과학 박람회에서 네 과학 프로젝트가 일등상을 탔다는 소식을 들었어. 축하해.

W: Thanks, Jake. I had a lot of fun doing it.
고마워, 제이크. 난 그걸 하면서 아주 재미있었어.

M: What was your project? 네 프로젝트는 뭐였니?

W: I made a robot that can clean the house.
나는 집을 청소할 수 있는 로봇을 만들었어.

M: Wow. That's both creative and useful.
와. 그건 창의적이면서 유용하구나.

W: My dad gave me the idea, but I made the entire robot myself.
우리 아빠가 아이디어를 주셨지만, 전체적인 로봇은 내가 만들었어.

M: Why are you so interested in robots?
넌 로봇에 그렇게 흥미를 가진 이유가 뭐니?

W: I like working with machines a lot.
나는 기계를 가지고 작업하는 게 정말 좋아.

① That's right. I made a robot.
맞아. 내가 로봇을 만들었어.

② I like working with machines a lot.
나는 기계를 가지고 작업하는 게 정말 좋아.

③ I want to go to space in the future.
나는 미래에 우주로 가고 싶어.

④ No, that wasn't an interesting topic.
아니, 그건 흥미로운 주제가 아니었어.

⑤ The robot cleans the house really well.
로봇은 집 청소를 정말 잘해.

어휘 win first place 일등상을 타다, 우승하다 fair 박람회 clean 청소하다 both 둘 다 creative 창의적인 useful 유용한 entire 전체의 be interested in ~에 관심이 있다 space 우주 in the future 미래에 machine 기계 topic 주제

20 ②

M: There's an international food festival at the park today. Shall we go?
오늘 공원에서 국제 음식 축제가 있어. 가 볼래?

W: Why not? It sounds like fun. 안될 거 없지. 재미있겠는데.

M: I went to the festival last year. I got to try all kinds of good food. 나는 작년에 그 축제에 갔었어. 모든 종류의 좋은 음식들을 먹어보았지.

W: What did you eat? 뭘 먹었었니?

M: I had food from Brazil, Thailand, Russia, and Ethiopia.
나는 브라질, 태국, 러시아, 그리고 에티오피아의 음식을 먹었어.

W: Wow. I can't wait to go there. 와, 빨리 가보고 싶어.

M: Which country's food are you interested in trying?
넌 어떤 나라의 음식을 먹어보는 데 관심이 있니?

W: I'd like to have some Spanish food.
난 스페인 음식을 먹어보고 싶어.

① No, I'm not hungry now. 아니, 난 지금 배고프지 않아.

② I'd like to have some Spanish food.
난 스페인 음식을 먹어보고 싶어.

③ I want to try Russian food again.
난 러시아 음식을 다시 먹어보고 싶어.

④ No, I haven't tasted Brazilian food before.
아니, 나는 전에는 브라질 음식을 맛본 적이 없어.

⑤ I've been to that country a couple of times.
나는 그 나라에 두 번 가봤어.

어휘 international 국제적인, 세계적인 festival 축제 try 먹어보다, 맛보다, 시도하다 all kinds of 온갖 종류의 be interested in ~에 관심이 있다 hungry 배고픈 already 이미

19회 실전모의고사
본문 p.220-221

01 ④	02 ④	03 ②	04 ⑤	05 ③
06 ③	07 ②	08 ⑤	09 ③	10 ①
11 ②	12 ①	13 ③	14 ②	15 ④
16 ②	17 ③	18 ①	19 ③	20 ⑤

01 ④

W: Hi. Are you looking for something?
안녕하세요. 무엇을 찾고 계시나요?

M: Yes. I need to buy a notebook for my sister.
네. 제 여동생에게 줄 공책을 사야 해요.

W: Why don't you get this one with the bear on the front? 앞에 곰이 그려진 이 공책을 사는 건 어떠세요?

M: She doesn't really like animals.
여동생이 동물을 썩 좋아하지는 않아요.

W: Okay. Here's a notebook with a rainbow on the front. 알겠어요. 여기 앞에 무지개가 그려진 공책이 있어요.

M: That's nice. But I think she'll prefer the one with the heart.
좋네요. 하지만 여동생은 하트가 들어간 공책을 선호할 거예요.

W: Do you want the notebook with three hearts or one? 하트 세 개가 들어간 공책을 원하세요, 아니면 하나가 들어간 것을 원하세요?

M: The one with three hearts, please.
하트 세 개짜리로 주세요.

W: All right. Here you are. 알겠습니다. 여기 있습니다.

어휘 look for ~을 찾다 notebook 공책; 노트북 컴퓨터 bear 곰 front 앞면, 앞부분 rainbow 무지개 prefer 선호하다

02 ④

M: The school orchestra is putting on a performance tomorrow. 학교 오케스트라가 내일 공연을 가질 거야.

W: Oh, I didn't know that. Are you going to attend it?
아, 그건 몰랐어. 너는 거기에 갈 거야?

M: Actually, I'm going to be in it. I play the trumpet.
사실은, 나도 오케스트라에 참여할 거야. 난 트럼펫을 연주해.

W: Wow. You must be nervous. Have you played in front of many people before?
우와. 긴장되겠다. 전에 많은 사람들 앞에서 연주해 본 적이 있니?

M: I've been in many concerts, so I'm not worried at all. 나는 콘서트를 많이 해봐서 전혀 걱정되지 않아.

W: Do you know all of the music?
넌 모든 노래를 알고 있니?

M: Yes, I do. I have practiced two hours a day for the past month. I'm sure I'll do well. 응, 알고 있어. 지난 한 달 동안 하루에 두 시간씩 연습을 했거든. 난 잘할 거야.

W: Excellent. I'll definitely attend the concert then.
훌륭해. 나도 그때 콘서트를 꼭 보러 갈게.

어휘 orchestra 오케스트라 put on a performance 공연하다 attend 참석하다 trumpet 트럼펫 nervous 긴장한 in front of ~의 앞에 not ~ at all 전혀 ~가 아닌 practice 연습하다 definitely 분명히, 반드시

03 ②

M: Hi. Can I help you? 안녕하세요. 제가 도와드릴까요?

W: Yes, I'm looking for a copy of the new book by Jeff Mercer. 네, 제프 머서가 쓴 신간을 한 권 찾고 있어요.

M: Ah, yes. I believe that we have it.
아, 네. 저희에게 그 책이 있는 것 같아요.

W: That's great. Can you tell me where it is?
좋아요. 어디 있는지 말씀해 주실래요?

M: Let me check the computer for a moment. [pause] It's in aisle number three in the nonfiction section.
제가 컴퓨터로 잠시 확인해 볼게요. [잠시 후] 그건 논픽션 구역 3번 통로에 있네요.

W: Great. And do you know how much it costs?
좋아요. 그리고 그 책 가격이 얼마인지 아세요?

M: It's available for twelve dollars.
그건 12달러에 구매 가능합니다.

W: Thanks. 감사합니다.

어휘 copy 한 부, 복사본 believe 생각하다, 믿다 for a moment 잠시 aisle 통로, 복도 nonfiction 논픽션 available 구매 가능한, 이용 가능한

04 ⑤

[Telephone rings.] [전화벨이 울린다.]

M: Hello. This is Burger World. How can I help you?

안녕하세요. 버거월드입니다. 무엇을 도와드릴까요?

W: Hi. I have a question for you.
안녕하세요. 질문이 하나 있어요.

M: Yes, we're still having a special offer on burgers.
네, 저희는 지금도 버거를 특가에 판매하고 있습니다.

W: Oh, it's not that. I saw an advertisement for your restaurant online. 아, 그런 게 아니에요. 제가 인터넷에서 버거월드의 광고를 봤거든요.

M: Are you interested in working here part time?
여기에서 파트타임으로 일하고 싶으신가요?

W: Yes, I am. What should I do?
네, 맞아요. 제가 어떻게 해야 하죠?

M: Why don't you come here tomorrow at one? You can interview with the manager. 내일 1시에 오시는 게 어때요? 지배인님과 면접을 보실 수 있거든요.

W: Great. Thanks for your assistance.
좋아요. 도와주셔서 감사합니다.

어휘 special offer 특가 판매 advertisement 광고 online 온라인에서; 온라인의 be interested in ~에 관심이 있다 work part time 파트타임으로 일하다 interview 면접하다, 인터뷰하다 manager 관리자, 지배인 assistance 도움

05 ③

W: Next in line, please. 다음 손님 오세요.

M: Good morning. 안녕하세요.

W: How can I be of assistance today?
오늘 무엇을 도와드릴까요?

M: What is the exchange rate for Korean won to American dollars?
원화를 달러화로 바꾸는 환율이 어떻게 되나요?

W: You can get one hundred dollars for one hundred twenty thousand won.
120,000원으로 100달러를 받으실 수 있어요.

M: That's great. 좋네요.

W: How much do you want to exchange?
얼마나 환전하고 싶으세요?

M: I've got two hundred forty thousand won.
저한테 240,000원이 있어요.

해설 십만 단위의 숫자를 읽는 방법은 까다로운 편이다. 이번에 확실히 알아 두자.

어휘 be of assistance 도움이 되다 exchange rate 환율

06 ③

M: How was your weekend, Tina? 주말 잘 보냈니, 티나?

W: It wasn't very good, Mark. 별로였어, 마크.

M: How come? I thought you were going to see a play.
왜? 난 네가 연극을 보러 갔다고 생각했어.

W: I was planning to, but my friend Betty couldn't go.
그러려고 했는데, 내 친구 베티가 갈 수 없었어.

M: That's too bad. What happened to her?
안됐구나. 그녀한테 무슨 일이 있었어?

W: She suddenly got sick while we were at a café before the play.
연극을 보러 가기 전에 카페에 있었는데, 그 애가 갑자기 아픈 거야.

M: Oh, that's terrible. What did you do?
아, 정말 안됐다. 넌 무엇을 했니?

W: I took her back to her home. 베티를 집에 데려다 줬어.

M: That was very kind of you. 정말 친절하구나.

W: I guess. Anyway, she's doing better now, so I'm happy about that. 그런 것 같긴 해. 어쨌든 그 애가 지금은 나아지고 있는데, 그건 기쁜 일이야.

어휘 how come 왜, 어째서 play 연극 happen 일어나다, 발생하다 suddenly 갑자기 get sick 아프다, 병에 걸리다 while ~동안에 anyway 아무튼, 어쨌든

07 ②

W: Excuse me. Are you going to Incheon Airport or Gimpo Airport? 실례합니다. 인천공항과 김포공항 중 어디로 가나요?

M: We're going to Incheon. 저희는 인천으로 갑니다.

W: That's great. I thought I had the wrong bus.
좋네요. 저는 버스를 잘못 탄 줄 알았어요.

M: Are you going to hold your baggage while we go there? 거기까지 가는 동안 짐을 갖고 계시겠어요?

W: Yes, this is just a small bag.
네, 이건 그냥 작은 가방이에요.

M: Okay. It costs ten thousand won for a ticket.
알겠습니다. 표 한 장은 10,000원입니다.

W: Here you are. 여기 있어요.

M: Thank you. Don't forget to fasten your seatbelt.
감사합니다. 좌석 벨트를 착용하는 것을 잊지 마세요.

W: I won't. Thanks. 네, 감사합니다.

해설 승객이 버스에 올라타면서 기사에게 행선지를 묻고 있는 상황이다.

어휘 airport 공항 wrong 잘못된 hold 가지다, 지니다 baggage 짐, 수화물 fasten one's seatbelt 좌석벨트를 착용하다

08 ⑤

M: Many airplane travelers are in a hurry when they get off their flights. So they frequently leave things behind. Which items do they leave behind the most? You might think it's their baggage. But it's not. Only a few people forget that. The items people most commonly leave on airplanes are books. Mobile phones, magazines, and clothes are some other items they frequently forget as well.

많은 항공기 승객들은 비행기에서 내릴 때 서두릅니다. 그래서 그들은 자주 물건을 두고 내립니다. 그들은 어떤 물건을 가장 많이 두고 내릴까요? 수하물일 거라고 생각하실 겁니다. 하지만 아닙니다. 수하물을 두고 내리는 사람은 고작 몇 명뿐입니다. 사람들이 비행기에 가장 많이 놓고 내리는 것은 바로 책입니다. 휴대폰, 잡지, 그리고 옷도 사람들이 자주 잊어버리는 물건들입니다.

어휘 traveler 여행객 in a hurry 서두르는 get off 내리다 flight 항공기, 항공편 frequently 자주 leave something behind ~을 두고 가다 item 물건 baggage 수하물, 짐 commonly 흔하게, 일반적으로 as well 또한

09 ③

[Cellphone rings.] [휴대폰이 울린다.]

W: Joe, are you going home now?
조, 지금 집에 가는 중이니?

M: Yes, Mom. Why? 네, 엄마. 왜요?

W: I need you to do a favor for me, please.
네가 엄마 부탁 좀 들어줬으면 좋겠구나.

M: Sure. Do you want me to set the table or pick up some food from the restaurant?
물론이죠. 식탁을 차리거나, 식당에서 음식을 찾아 올까요?

W: No, you don't have to do either of those two things.
아니, 둘 다 하지 않아도 된단다.

M: All right. 알겠어요.

W: I need you to clean the living room. Your father is bringing some guests home for dinner.
넌 거실 청소를 했으면 좋겠구나. 아빠가 저녁에 집으로 손님들을 모시고 올 거야.

M: Oh, so we need the house to look nice, right?
아, 그럼 집이 깨끗해 보여야겠네요. 맞죠?

W: That's right. 그렇단다.

어휘 do somebody a favor ~의 부탁을 들어주다 set the table 식탁을 차리다 pick up 가져가다 guest 손님, 고객

10 ①

M: Did you join any clubs this semester?
넌 이번 학기에 동아리에 가입했니?

W: Yes. I just signed up for the school's music club.
응. 방금 학교의 음악 동아리에 등록했어.

M: Music? Can you play an instrument?
음악? 넌 악기를 연주할 수 있니?

W: Actually, I can't play any instruments at all.
사실, 난 어떤 악기도 연주를 못해.

M: So what did you join the club for?
그럼 왜 그 동아리에 가입했니?

W: I'd like to learn how to sing.
나는 노래 부르는 방법을 배우고 싶어.

M: Seriously? I didn't know you were interested in singing. 정말? 난 네가 노래에 관심 있는 줄 몰랐어.

W: I'd like to try out for one of those TV programs, so I need to learn a new skill. You know, I can dance, but I can't sing.
나는 TV 프로그램 중 하나에 도전해 보고 싶은데, 그러려면 새로운 기술을 배워야 해. 있잖아, 난 춤은 출 수 있지만 노래는 못하거든.

M: I see. Well, good luck. 그렇구나. 그럼, 행운을 빌게.

어휘 semester 학기 sign up for ~을 등록하다, 신청하다 instrument 악기 what ~ for 무엇 때문에, 왜 join 함께하다, 가입하다 seriously 진심으로 try out 시험해 보다 you know 있잖아

11 ②

① W: Do you prefer baseball or soccer?
넌 야구를 좋아하니, 축구를 좋아하니?

M: Neither. I like basketball more than them.
둘 다 안 좋아해. 나는 그보다는 농구를 더 좋아해.

② W: Is this sweater on sale right now?
지금 이 스웨터가 할인 중인가요?

M: Yes, we sold the last one a while ago.
네, 조금 전에 마지막 제품을 판매했습니다.

③ W: What do you think of my new idea?
내 새로운 아이디어를 어떻게 생각하니?

M: It's pretty good, but you could improve it a bit.
아주 좋지만, 좀 더 발전시킬 수 있을 거야.

④ W: When are you going swimming in the lake?
언제 호수에 수영하러 갈 거니?

M: I'll probably do that next Sunday.
아마 다음 주 일요일에 갈 거야.

⑤ W: How long is this program going to last?
이 프로그램은 얼마나 오래 하니?

M: It's going to finish at seven.
그건 7시에 끝날 거야.

어휘 prefer 선호하다 neither 둘 다 아닌 a while ago 조금 전에 improve 향상시키다, 발전하다 a bit 약간 lake 호수 probably 아마도 last 지속하다, 계속되다

12 ①

W: This is very frustrating. 이건 너무 절망적이야.

M: What's the matter? 무슨 일이야?

W: I have my own blog, but some people are leaving rude comments on it.
내 블로그가 있는데, 어떤 사람들이 무례한 댓글을 남기고 있어.

M: What kind of comments are they making?
그 사람들이 어떤 종류의 댓글을 쓰고 있니?

W: They're writing bad things about my friends and me. 그들은 내 친구와 나에 대해 안 좋은 것을 쓰고 있어.

M: That's not nice at all. 정말 안 좋구나.

W: What can I do about that?
내가 그것에 대해 어떻게 할 수 있을까?

M: You should delete the comments and then ban those people from posting on your blog. 댓글을 삭제하고, 그 사람들이 네 블로그에 글을 올리는 걸 금지시켜야 돼.

W: I don't know how to do that. Would you mind showing me what to do? 난 그걸 어떻게 하는지 몰라. 네가 어떻게 하는 건지 보여줄 수 있겠니?

어휘 frustrating 절망적인, 좌절감을 주는 matter 문제 rude 무례한 leave comments 댓글을 남기다 delete 삭제하다 ban A from B A가 B하는 것을 금지시키다

13 ③

M: Did you finish writing your poem? 시는 다 썼니?

W: Yes, I did. I'm really pleased with it.
　응, 다 썼어. 정말 기분이 좋아.

M: How long is it? 시가 얼마나 길어?

W: It's more than twenty lines. It's pretty long.
　20행 이상이야. 꽤 길어.

M: Wow. How long did it take for you to write it?
　우와. 그걸 쓰는 데 시간이 얼마나 걸렸니?

W: Actually, I was planning to finish it in two days, but it took me more than three weeks.
　실은 이틀 안에 그걸 끝내려고 했었는데, 3주 이상이 걸렸어.

M: What's it about? 무엇에 관한 내용이야?

W: It's a fantasy poem about a knight and a dragon. Would you like to read it?
　기사와 용에 대한 판타지 시야. 읽어 볼래?

M: Sure. It sounds interesting. 물론이지. 재미있겠다.

　해설 이틀은 원래 계획했던 기간이고, 실제로는 3주 이상 걸렸다.

　어휘 poem 시 pleased 기쁜 line (글 등의) 행; 줄 take (시간이) 걸리다 fantasy 판타지, 공상 knight 기사 dragon 용

14 ②

M: Attention, campers. Welcome to Lake Shady. We've got an exciting day planned for you. First, you need to go to your cabins and put your bags there. After that, we'll go on a tour of the camp. Then, we're going to take a break for lunch. When lunch is finished, we're going to go hiking up the mountain, and then we'll swim in the lake for a while. We've got a busy day, so let's get started. Please take your bags to your cabins and be back here in ten minutes.

　캠핑객 여러분은 주목해 주십시오. 셰이디 호수에 오신 것을 환영합니다. 우리는 여러분들을 위해 재미있는 하루를 계획해 놓았습니다. 먼저, 여러분은 여러분의 오두막에 가서 그곳에 가방을 두셔야 합니다. 그 다음에, 우리는 캠핑장을 둘러볼 것입니다. 그리고 나서, 점심 식사를 위해 휴식을 취하겠습니다. 점심 식사가 끝나면, 우리는 산으로 등산을 갈 것이고, 잠시 호수에서 수영을 할 것입니다. 아주 바쁜 날이니 지금 시작하도록 하겠습니다. 가방을 오두막에 갖다 두시고, 10분 후에 이곳으로 다시 모여 주시기 바랍니다.

　어휘 camper 야영객 cabin 오두막, 숙소 take a break 휴식을 취하다 for a while 잠시 동안 busy 바쁜

15 ④

W: The school is giving the students a chance to learn a new foreign language. The students decide to vote to see which language they will study. Twelve students request to study Chinese while ten of them want to learn Latin. Nine students ask to learn Spanish. The same number of them want to learn French. Only four students would like to learn Russian. It's the least popular language.

학교는 학생들에게 새로운 외국어를 배울 기회를 제공한다. 학생들은 어떤 언어를 공부할 것인지 알아보기 위해 투표를 하기로 결정한다. 12명의 학생은 중국어를 배울 것을 요청한 반면, 10명은 라틴어를 배우길 원한다. 9명의 학생은 스페인어를 학습하기를 요청한다. 같은 수의 학생이 프랑스어를 배우고 싶어한다. 고작 4명의 학생만이 러시아어를 배우고 싶어한다. 러시아어가 가장 인기 없는 언어이다.

　어휘 chance 기회 foreign language 외국어 vote 투표하다 request 요청하다 Chinese 중국어 Latin 라틴어 Spanish 스페인어 French 프랑스어 Russian 러시아어 least 가장 적은(little − less − least) popular 인기 있는

16 ②

M: If you want to be a good student, you need to do the following. First, always listen carefully when the teacher is speaking in class. Don't talk to your friends or play with your phone. Instead, focus on what the teacher is saying. Next, be sure to take good notes. Don't write in your textbook though. Get a notebook and take notes in it. Review your notes after class every day, and you'll be able to remember the lesson better. Be sure to do all of your homework as well. Doing homework will help you learn the information you studied in class a lot better.

만약 좋은 학생이 되고 싶다면, 다음 사항들을 따라야 합니다. 첫째, 항상 선생님께서 수업 시간에 하시는 말씀을 잘 들어야 합니다. 친구와 떠들거나 휴대폰을 갖고 놀지 마세요. 대신, 선생님께서 하시는 말씀에 집중하세요. 다음으로, 필기를 잘하세요. 하지만 교과서에는 적지 마세요. 공책을 준비해서 그 안에 필기하세요. 매일 수업이 끝나고 공책의 내용을 복습하면, 수업 내용을 더 잘 기억할 수 있을 겁니다. 또한 모든 숙제도 꼭 하세요. 숙제를 하는 것이 수업시간에 배운 내용을 훨씬 더 잘 익히도록 도와줄 것입니다.

　어휘 the following 다음에 말하는 것 instead 대신에 play with ~을 가지고 놀다 focus on ~에 집중하다 be sure to 확실히 ~하다 take notes 필기하다 review 복습하다 be able to ~할 수 있다 remember 기억하다

17 ③

[Telephone rings.] [전화벨이 울린다.]

W: Hi, Jason. It's Amy. 안녕, 제이슨. 나 에이미야.

M: What's up, Amy? 무슨 일이니, 에이미?

W: Did you forget about our plans to go to the festival today? 오늘 축제에 가기로 한 우리 계획을 잊었니?

M: Not at all. We're still meeting at four, right?
　잊지 않았어. 우린 여전히 4시에 만나는 거잖아, 맞지?

W: Actually, we were supposed to meet at one thirty.
　사실 우리는 1시 30분에 만나기로 되어 있었어.

M: Oh, that's fifteen minutes from now. I don't think I can make it downtown by then. 아, 지금부터 15분 뒤잖아. 내가 그때까지 시내에 갈 수는 없을 것 같아.

W: Then when can you be there?
그럼 몇 시에 거기 올 수 있니?

M: How about at a <u>quarter</u> <u>past</u> <u>two</u>? I can be there then if I <u>leave</u> the <u>house</u> now.
2시 15분 어때? 지금 집에서 출발하면 그때 도착할 수 있을 거야.

W: Okay. <u>Call</u> me when you <u>get</u> <u>there</u>.
알겠어. 도착하면 전화해.

M: I will. Bye. 그럴게. 안녕.

해설 2시 15분은 'two fifteen'과 'quarter past two' 두 가지 방식으로 말할 수 있다.

어휘 be supposed to ~하기로 되어 있다 from now 지금부터 make it (장소에) 도착하다 quarter 15분, 4분의 1 past ~이 지난 leave 떠나다, 출발하다

18 ①

M: You won't <u>believe</u> <u>what</u> <u>happened</u> to me.
나한테 무슨 일이 있었는지 넌 믿을 수 없을 거야.

W: What? Tell me. 뭔데? 말해 줘.

M: Wendy said she was going to <u>come</u> <u>over</u> to <u>work</u> <u>on</u> our group <u>project</u>, but she didn't <u>show</u> <u>up</u>.
웬디가 우리 조별 과제를 하러 온다고 했는데, 나타나지 않았어.

W: Did you <u>try</u> <u>calling</u> her? 그 애에게 전화해봤니?

M: I did, but her <u>phone</u> is <u>turned</u> <u>off</u>.
해봤어, 하지만 전화기가 꺼져 있어.

W: <u>Maybe</u> she just has a lot of <u>work</u> <u>to</u> <u>do</u>.
아마 할 일이 많이 있나 보다.

M: I don't think so. This is the <u>third</u> <u>time</u> she has done that.
난 그렇게 생각하지 않아. 그 애가 그렇게 한 게 이번이 세 번째야.

W: I'm sure she didn't <u>mean</u> <u>to</u>. She always tries to <u>keep</u> her <u>promises</u>. 일부러 그런 건 분명히 아닐 거야. 웬디는 항상 약속을 지키려고 노력하거든.

M: She <u>might</u> <u>try</u> to keep them, but she <u>never</u> does.
지키려고 노력은 할 수 있겠지만, 결코 지키지 않아.

① Actions speak louder than words.
말보다 행동이 중요하다.

② A penny saved is a penny earned. 티끌 모아 태산이다.

③ He who laughs last laughs best.
마지막에 웃는 사람이 최후의 승자다.

④ A watched pot never boils.
지켜보는 주전자는 좀체 잘 안 끓는다.

⑤ Early to bed, early to rise. 일찍 자고 일찍 일어나기.

해설 ①은 말만 하고 실천을 하지 않는 사람에게 말해줄 수 있는 속담이다.

어휘 work on ~에 대한 일을 하다 show up 나타나다, 등장하다 turn off (전원을) 끄다 keep one's promise ~의 약속을 지키다

19 ③

W: I just <u>signed</u> <u>up</u> to take <u>painting</u> lessons.
난 방금 그림 수업을 신청했어.

M: That's interesting. Is the <u>teacher</u> going to <u>visit</u> your <u>house</u>? 재미있겠다. 선생님이 너희 집을 방문하시니?

W: No, I've got to go to her <u>studio</u>.
아니, 내가 선생님의 화실을 찾아가야 해.

M: <u>How</u> <u>often</u> are you going to have lessons?
수업은 얼마나 자주 받게 되니?

W: <u>Twice</u> <u>a</u> <u>week</u>. I'll go there on <u>Thursdays</u> and <u>Saturdays</u>.
일주일에 두 번. 목요일하고 토요일마다 갈 거야.

M: I <u>never</u> <u>knew</u> you liked painting.
네가 그림을 좋아하는지 전혀 몰랐어.

W: I <u>love</u> <u>art</u>, but I've never tried to do any painting.
난 미술을 좋아하지만 그림을 그리려고 해본 적이 없어.

M: <u>What</u> <u>kind</u> <u>of</u> pictures are you going to make?
넌 어떤 종류의 그림을 그릴 거니?

W: I'll probably start with pictures of fruit.
난 아마도 과일 그림으로 시작할 거야.

① No, I haven't seen that picture yet.
아니, 난 아직 그 그림을 보지 못했어.

② Here's a picture I took with my camera.
여기 내 카메라로 찍은 사진이 있어.

③ I'll probably start with pictures of fruit.
난 아마도 과일 그림으로 시작할 거야.

④ I've painted several pictures in the past week.
난 지난주에 그림 몇 장을 그렸어.

⑤ Yes, my mother painted that picture on the wall.
응, 우리 어머니께서 벽에 있는 저 그림을 그리셨어.

어휘 sign up (강좌에) 등록하다 studio 화실, 작업실 twice 두 번 what kind of 어떤 종류의 take a picture 사진 찍다 probably 아마도

20 ⑤

M: This is so frustrating. 이건 정말 절망적이야.

W: Are you <u>talking</u> <u>about</u> your essay? How's it going?
네 과제물에 대해서 말하는 거니? 어떻게 되어가고 있니?

M: Terribly. I haven't written a <u>single</u> <u>word</u> <u>yet</u>.
끔찍하게. 난 아직 한 단어도 쓰지 못했어.

W: Why not? You need to <u>turn</u> it <u>in</u> to Ms. Durham <u>tomorrow</u> <u>morning</u>.
왜? 넌 그걸 내일 아침까지 더럼 선생님께 제출해야 해.

M: But I can't <u>come</u> <u>up</u> <u>with</u> any <u>ideas</u>.
하지만 어떤 생각도 떠오르지 않아.

W: Why don't you <u>try</u> <u>brainstorming</u>? Then, you can write whatever <u>comes</u> <u>to</u> <u>mind</u>. 브레인스토밍을 해보는 게 어때? 그럼 머릿속에 떠오르는 무엇이든 쓸 수 있을 거야.

M: I've <u>never</u> tried that <u>before</u>. Please <u>explain</u> <u>how</u> it works.
난 한 번도 그걸 해본 적이 없어. 어떻게 하는 건지 설명해줘.

W: Write down anything you think of on your paper.
생각나는 아무거나 종이에 적으면 돼.

① I wrote my paper earlier this morning.
난 오늘 아침 일찍 내 과제물을 썼어.

② You should have written two pages by now.
넌 지금까지 두 페이지는 썼어야 해.

③ Yes, I worked there for the past three years.
응, 난 지난 3년 동안 그 곳에서 일했어.

④ Yes, Ms. Durham works very hard every day.
응, 더럼 선생님은 매일 열심히 일하셔.

⑤ Write down anything you think of on your paper.
생각나는 아무거나 종이에 적으면 돼.

어휘 frustrating 절망적인, 좌절감을 주는 essay 과제물, 리포트, 에세이 single 하나의 yet 아직 turn in 제출하다 come up with ~을 떠올리다 brainstorming 브레인스토밍 whatever 무엇이든지 come to mind 머릿속에 떠오르다 explain 설명하다 think of ~을 머리에 떠올리다

20회 실전모의고사
본문 p.232-233

01 ①	02 ④	03 ③	04 ④	05 ④
06 ⑤	07 ⑤	08 ④	09 ④	10 ②
11 ③	12 ④	13 ②	14 ②	15 ④
16 ③	17 ⑤	18 ③	19 ①	20 ④

01 ①

W: Here's the weather report for this week. You're going to need your umbrellas on Monday since it's going to rain all day long. The skies will clear on Tuesday, and we'll have partly cloudy weather. On Wednesday, it's going to be very windy. The temperature is going to get much colder, too. We might get a little snow on Thursday. It's definitely going to snow on Friday. Expect around three to five centimeters of snow then.

이번 주 날씨를 말씀드리겠습니다. 월요일에는 하루 종일 비가 올 것으로 예상되므로 우산을 준비하셔야 합니다. 화요일에 하늘이 개겠으나 부분적으로 구름이 낄 것입니다. 수요일에는 바람이 무척 세게 불겠습니다. 기온도 무척 추워지겠습니다. 목요일에는 눈이 조금 올 수 있습니다. 금요일에는 확실히 눈이 올 것입니다. 그때 약 3 내지 5센터미터 정도의 눈이 올 것으로 예상됩니다.

어휘 umbrella 우산 since ~이기 때문에 clear 깨끗해지다 partly 부분적으로 temperature 온도 definitely 분명히, 확실히 expect 기대하다

02 ④

W: Can I help you, sir? 제가 도와드릴까요, 손님?
M: Yes, I left my laptop bag here in the lobby, and I can't find it now. 네, 제가 여기 로비에 제 노트북 가방을 두었는데, 지금은 찾을 수가 없네요.
W: What does it look like? 그게 어떻게 생겼나요?
M: It's solid black, and it has a shoulder strap.

완전히 검은색이고, 어깨 끈이 달려 있어요.
W: We have several of those. Is there anything on the case? Is there a nametag on it? 그렇게 생긴 게 몇 개 있어요. 케이스 위에 뭐가 있나요? 이름표가 있나요?
M: No, but there is a sticker on it. The sticker shows a picture of a rose. 아니요, 하지만 스티커가 붙어 있습니다. 장미 그림이 있는 스티커입니다.
W: Ah, I believe that we have your bag.
아, 저희가 손님 가방을 갖고 있는 것 같아요.
M: You do? 그래요?
W: Yes, I think this is the bag you're looking for.
네, 이것이 손님께서 찾고 계신 가방 같네요.

해설 기다란 어깨 끈과 장미 그림 스티커가 힌트이다.

어휘 laptop 노트북 컴퓨터 lobby 로비 solid (색이) 단색인 shoulder strap 어깨 끈 several 몇 개의 nametag 이름표 sticker 스티커 look for ~을 찾다

03 ③

W: Why aren't you eating your dinner, Minsu?
넌 왜 저녁을 먹지 않고 있니, 민수야?
M: It hurts every time I bite my food.
음식을 씹을 때마다 아파요.
W: Do you have a sore tooth? 이가 아프니?
M: Yes, I do. I think I have a cavity.
네. 충치가 있는 것 같아요.
W: Well, you need to see a dentist then.
음, 넌 그럼 치과에 가봐야겠구나.
M: But I hate going to the dentist. It always hurts when I go there. 하지만 전 치과에 가는 게 싫어요. 거기 가면 항상 아파요.
W: Don't be afraid of going there. The dentist can help you get better. 치과에 가는 걸 무서워하지 마. 의사 선생님이 네가 낫는 것을 도와주실 거야.
M: I know, but I still don't want to go.
저도 알지만 그래도 여전히 가고 싶지 않아요.
W: If you don't go now, your tooth will hurt even more.
네가 지금 가지 않으면, 이가 훨씬 더 아프게 될 거야.

어휘 hurt 아프다 every time ~할 때마다 bite 씹다, 물다 sore 아픈 cavity 충치 dentist 치과 (의사) be afraid of ~을 두려워하다 curious 궁금한

04 ④

W: Why did you want to come here?
넌 왜 여기 오고 싶었니?
M: I need to buy a few things. 몇 가지 살 게 있어.
W: Well, hurry up. I'm starving and need to get something to eat.
그럼, 서둘러. 난 너무 배고파서 뭘 좀 먹어야 할 것 같아.
M: Hold on just a minute. Let me look around.
잠깐만 기다려. 좀 둘러볼게.
W: What are you looking for? 넌 뭘 찾고 있니?

M: I need an eraser and a stapler.
지우개와 스테이플러가 필요해.

W: Is that it? 그게 다야?

M: No. I should also buy a couple of red pens.
아니. 빨간 펜도 두 자루 사야 해.

W: Okay. Get those items, and then let's go.
알았어. 그것들을 산 다음에 가자.

어휘 hurry up 서두르다 starving 몹시 배가 고픈 look around 둘러보다 eraser 지우개 stapler 스테이플러, 호치키스 a couple of 두어 개의

05 ④

M: Your dog is in good shape. Do you walk her a lot?
네 개는 건강하구나. 산책을 많이 시키니?

W: Yes. We go walking in the park every day.
응. 우리는 매일 공원에 산책하러 가.

M: Did you take her for a walk yesterday?
너는 어제 개를 산책시켰니?

W: No, I didn't. My mom did that instead of me.
아니, 나는 하지 않았어. 우리 엄마가 나 대신 하셨어.

M: Why? Did something happen to you?
왜? 너는 무슨 일이 있었니?

W: I was all right, but I wasn't at home all day long.
아무 일도 없었지만, 난 하루 종일 집에 없었거든.

M: Where were you? 어디 있었니?

W: I was downtown at the museum. I volunteer by giving tours there every weekend. 시내에 있는 박물관에 있었어. 주말마다 거기에서 관람을 시켜주는 자원봉사를 하고 있어.

M: That's fascinating. I should go there and see you.
끝내주는데. 난 거기에 가서 널 봐야겠어.

W: Visit there next Sunday, and I can give you a tour.
다음 주 일요일에 그곳에 오면 내가 관람을 시켜 줄게.

어휘 be in good shape 건강하다 walk 산책하다, 산책시키다 take somebody for a walk ~을 산책시키다 instead of ~대신에 all day long 하루 종일 museum 박물관 volunteer 자원봉사하다 fascinating 흥미로운, 매력적인 give somebody a tour ~에게 관람을 시켜 주다, ~을 안내하다

06 ⑤

W: Why do you look so tired today?
넌 오늘 왜 그렇게 피곤해 보이니?

M: I had trouble getting to sleep.
잠을 잘 수가 없었거든.

W: Were your upstairs neighbors being noisy again?
위층 이웃들이 또 시끄럽게 굴었니?

M: No, they were quiet. I was just thinking about a few things. 아니, 그 사람들은 조용했어. 그냥 몇 가지 일을 생각했어.

W: Like what? 예를 들어 어떤 거?

M: I was worried about our upcoming exams. I really need to do well.
앞으로 있을 우리의 시험에 대해 걱정했어. 난 정말 잘 봐야 해.

W: You need to relax. If you don't, you won't get any

sleep at all. And then you'll do really badly on the tests. 넌 좀 느긋해질 필요가 있어. 만약 그러지 않으면 전혀 잠을 잘 수 없을 거야. 그리고 넌 시험을 정말 못 볼 거야.

어휘 have trouble –ing ~하는 데 어려움을 겪다 upstairs 위층의 neighbor 이웃 noisy 시끄러운 upcoming 다가오는 relax 느긋하게 마음을 먹다, 휴식을 취하다 do badly 잘하지 못하다; 좋은 성적을 거두지 못하다

07 ⑤

W: Sam, are you really going to start a new club?
샘, 넌 정말 새 동아리를 만들 거니?

M: That's right. I'm going to start a history club. Would you like to join it?
맞아. 난 역사 동아리를 시작할 거야. 너도 함께할래?

W: I don't know. What are you going to do?
난 잘 모르겠어. 넌 뭘 할 건데?

M: We're going to watch historical documentaries.
우리는 역사 다큐멘터리를 볼 거야.

W: That sounds boring to me. 그거 내겐 지루한데.

M: That's not it. We'll read history books and talk about important events in the past.
그게 전부는 아니야. 우리는 역사책을 읽고, 과거에 있었던 중요한 사건들에 대해 이야기를 나눌 거야.

W: Have many students signed up yet?
많은 학생들이 등록했니?

M: Yes. Eight boys and four girls are going to join.
응. 남자아이 8명과 여자아이 4명이 참가할 거야.

W: Does that include you? 그게 너까지 포함한 거니?

M: No, it doesn't, and it doesn't include Kevin. I forgot about him.
아니야, 그리고 케빈도 포함된 게 아니야. 내가 그를 깜빡했어.

해설 남자 8명+여자 4명+Sam+Kevin = 14명

어휘 history 역사 join 참여하다, 함께하다 historical 역사적인 event 사건, 행사 in the past 옛날에, 과거에 sign up 등록하다 include 포함하다

08 ④

M: How are your travel plans going?
여행 계획은 어떻게 되어가고 있니?

W: Not bad. I've made the plane reservations to fly to Jeju Island. 나쁘지 않아. 난 제주도로 가는 비행기를 예약했어.

M: How long will you stay there?
거기에서 얼마나 오래 있을 거니?

W: I'm planning to stay there for seven days.
거기서 7일 동안 머무를 계획이야.

M: That's a long time. You'll have a lot of fun.
긴 시간이구나. 재미있을 거야.

W: The only problem is that all of the hotels are booked. I can't find any empty rooms right now.
유일한 문제는 모든 호텔의 예약이 차 있다는 거야. 지금은 빈 방을 찾을 수가 없어.

M: Would you like me to <u>contact</u> my <u>uncle</u>? He has a <u>travel</u> <u>agency</u> on Jeju Island. I'm sure he can <u>help</u> you <u>out</u>. 내가 우리 삼촌한테 연락해 볼까? 삼촌이 제주도에서 여행사를 하시거든. 그분이 너를 도와줄 수 있을 거야.

W: Would you <u>do</u> that <u>for me</u>? That would be great. 날 위해 그렇게 해줄 수 있어? 그러면 정말 좋겠다.

M: Sure. I'll do that <u>right now</u>. 물론이지. 지금 해볼게.

어휘 plan 계획 make reservations 예약하다 plane 비행기 island 섬 stay 머무르다 booked 예약된 empty 빈 contact 연락하다 uncle 삼촌 travel agency 여행사

09 ④

M: Thanks for <u>taking me</u> to the <u>festival</u> today. I had a great time.
오늘 축제에 날 데려와 줘서 고마워. 정말 즐거운 시간을 보냈어.

W: I'm glad you came with me. 네가 나랑 함께 와줘서 기뻐.

M: We <u>saw</u> so many <u>performances</u>. I <u>loved</u> the <u>puppet</u> <u>show</u> by the students.
우린 정말 많은 공연을 봤어. 난 학생들이 하는 인형극이 좋았어.

W: That was nice. I thought the breakdancing <u>performers</u> were good <u>as well</u>. 그건 멋졌어. 내 생각엔 브레이크댄스의 공연자들도 훌륭했어.

M: Were they your <u>favorite</u>? 그게 가장 좋았니?

W: No, but I liked them a lot. The performance I <u>liked</u> <u>the most</u> was the <u>traditional Korean dance</u>. It was very elegant. 그건 아니지만 정말 좋았어. 내가 제일 좋았던 공연은 한국 전통 춤이었어. 정말 우아하더라.

M: Yes, it was pretty nice. It was <u>the first time</u> for me to <u>see</u> that kind of performance.
응, 그건 정말 멋졌어. 난 그런 종류의 공연을 본 게 처음이었어.

W: We should <u>come back</u> here <u>again</u> tomorrow.
우리 내일 여기에 다시 오자.

M: Good idea.
좋은 생각이야.

해설 'The performance I liked the most' 뒤에 여자가 가장 좋아했던 공연이 나온다.

어휘 take (사람을) 데리고 가다 have a great time 즐거운 시간을 갖다 puppet show 인형극 performer 공연자 favorite 매우 좋아하는 traditional 전통의 elegant 우아한 pretty 꽤

10 ②

M: Thank you for coming to the Eastside <u>Library</u> today. This is the <u>first day</u> of a special <u>program</u> we're starting. We're going to <u>teach computer skills</u> to young children. We <u>rely on</u> computers very much <u>these days</u>, so everyone needs to know <u>how to use</u> them. Today, we're going to learn how to do some <u>simple</u> computer <u>programming</u>. All right, everyone, why don't you <u>sit down</u> at a computer? It's time to begin.

오늘 이스트사이드 도서관에 와주셔서 감사합니다. 오늘이 우리가

시작하는 특별 프로그램의 첫 날입니다. 우리는 어린 아이들에게 컴퓨터 기술을 가르칠 것입니다. 요즘 우리는 컴퓨터에 매우 의존하기 때문에, 모두가 컴퓨터 사용법을 알아야 합니다. 오늘 우리는 간단하게 컴퓨터 프로그래밍을 하는 방법에 대해서 배울 것입니다. 좋아요, 여러분, 컴퓨터 앞에 앉아 볼까요? 시작할 시간입니다.

어휘 library 도서관 rely on ~에 의존하다 these days 요즘, 오늘날

11 ③

W: You look <u>tired</u>, Jeff. What's up?
넌 피곤해 보여, 제프. 무슨 일이니?

M: It was my <u>first day</u> of <u>work</u> at my <u>new job</u> today.
오늘이 내 새로운 직장에서의 첫날이었어.

W: Did you <u>get</u> a job? <u>Where</u> are you <u>working</u>?
너 직장 구했어? 어디에서 일하니?

M: I'm working at Chicken Heaven.
난 치킨 헤븐에서 일해.

W: Oh, that's my <u>favorite</u> fast-food <u>restaurant</u>. How was work?
아, 거기는 내가 좋아하는 패스트푸드 음식점이야. 일은 어땠니?

M: It was hard. We got really <u>busy</u> at <u>lunchtime</u>, and I <u>made</u> a few <u>mistakes</u> with customers' <u>orders</u>.
힘들었어. 점심시간에는 정말 바빴고, 내가 손님들의 주문과 관련해 몇 가지 실수를 저질렀어.

W: Did they <u>get upset</u>? 그들이 화났니?

M: <u>A couple of</u> them did. But I <u>apologized</u>, so they were okay.
몇 사람이 화를 냈어. 하지만 내가 사과해서 괜찮았어.

W: That's good to know. 다행이구나.

어휘 get a job 직장을 구하다 hard 어려운, 힘든 make a mistake 실수하다 order 주문; 주문하다 upset 화가 난, 속상한 apologize 사과하다

12 ④

[Cellphone rings.] [휴대폰이 울린다.]

W: Hi, Dad. What's going on? 여보세요, 아빠. 무슨 일이세요?

M: Hi, Kelly. Are you still <u>at school</u>?
안녕, 켈리. 아직 학교에 있니?

W: No, I'm <u>on my way home</u> now.
아니요, 지금 집에 가는 길이에요.

M: That's good. You need to get home <u>as soon as possible</u>. 잘 됐구나. 넌 가능한 한 빨리 집에 가야 한다.

W: Why? Is <u>something wrong</u>?
왜요? 무슨 문제가 있나요?

M: Your mother needs to go to the <u>supermarket</u>. But she can't <u>leave</u> the <u>baby</u> home <u>alone</u>.
너희 엄마가 슈퍼마켓에 가야 해. 하지만 엄마는 집에 아기를 혼자 두고 나갈 수가 없어.

W: Oh, okay. Do you need me to <u>watch</u> her <u>while Mom's gone</u>?
아, 알겠어요. 엄마가 가신 동안 제가 아기를 돌봐야 하나요?

M: Yes. Do you <u>mind</u>? 응. 그렇게 해줄래?

W: Not at all. I'll be home in about five minutes.
네. 저는 약 5분 후면 집에 도착할 거예요.

M: Thanks. I really appreciate your help.
고맙다. 도움을 주어 고맙구나.

어휘 still 여전히, 아직도 on one's way home 집으로 가는 중인 as soon as possible 가능한 한 빨리 leave 남겨두다 alone 혼자 watch 돌보다 while ~하는 동안에 appreciate 감사하다

13 ②

① M: Can I change my order, please?
제 주문을 바꿀 수 있을까요?

W: Sure. What would you like?
물론입니다. 뭘로 하시겠습니까?

② M: What time are you going to meet your sister?
넌 언제 여동생을 만나러 가니?

W: She's fifteen years old. 여동생은 15살이야.

③ M: I got an A on my science test.
나 과학 시험에서 A를 받았어.

W: That's great news. I'm happy for you.
좋은 소식이다. 정말 잘 됐다.

④ M: Have you finished the math problems yet?
수학 문제를 다 끝냈니?

W: I've got two more to do. 아직 두 문제를 더 해야 해.

⑤ M: Did you remember to bring an umbrella?
우산 가져 오는 걸 기억했니?

W: Yes, I've got one here in my bag.
응, 여기 내 가방에 한 개 있어.

14 ②

W: The public library has many DVDs, and students enjoy borrowing lots of them. Most people believe that action movies are the most popular DVDs, but only twenty percent of the students borrow them. Forty percent of the DVDs the students borrow are documentaries. Those are the most popular ones. Animation DVDs are the third most popular after action movies, and science-fiction movies and dramas are popular as well.

공립 도서관에는 DVD가 많이 있고, 학생들이 그것을 많이 빌린다. 많은 사람들은 액션 영화가 가장 인기 있는 DVD라고 생각하지만, 학생들 중 20%만 액션 영화를 빌린다. 학생들이 빌리는 DVD의 40%는 다큐멘터리이다. 그게 가장 인기 있는 것이다. 만화 영화 DVD는 액션 영화 다음으로 세 번째로 인기가 있고, 공상과학 영화와 드라마도 인기가 있다.

해설 앞부분에 있는 액션 영화에 관한 함정을 피해야 한다.

어휘 public 공공의 borrow 빌리다 most 대부분의 animation 만화 영화 science-fiction 공상과학

15 ④

M: Why don't we see a movie tomorrow?

우리 내일 영화 보는 게 어때?

W: Hmm... How about doing something different?
음, 다른 걸 하는 게 어떠니?

M: Why? You like watching movies on Sundays.
왜? 넌 일요일마다 영화 보는 걸 좋아하잖아.

W: That's too boring now. 이제 그건 너무 지루해.

M: Okay. What would you like to do then?
알겠어. 그럼 뭘 하고 싶니?

W: I'd like to see *Nanta*. It's performed in Myeongdong every day. 난 '난타'를 보고 싶어. 명동에서 매일 공연한대.

M: Oh, my friends said it's a great show. Let's book tickets now.
아, 내 친구들이 그게 멋진 공연이라고 말했어. 지금 표를 예매하자.

W: Should we call the theater? 극장에 전화해야 하니?

M: No, we can do that on the website.
아니, 웹사이트에서 예약할 수 있어.

어휘 something different 다른 무엇 boring 지루한 perform 공연하다 book 예매하다 theater 극장

16 ③

W: Hi. Can you give me some assistance, please?
안녕하세요. 저를 좀 도와주실 수 있나요?

M: Sure. What do you need? 물론이죠. 무엇이 필요하세요?

W: I'm looking for a book called *The Ancient Egyptians* by Carl Weathers, but I can't find it. 칼 웨더스가 쓴 '고대 이집트인들'이라는 책을 찾고 있는데, 찾을 수가 없네요.

M: Did you look for it on the computer?
컴퓨터에서 찾아 보셨나요?

W: Yes, I did. It's supposed to be available, but I can't find it on the shelf. 네, 찾아봤어요. 대출 가능하다고 나왔는데, 책꽂이에서 찾을 수가 없네요.

M: That's strange. I remember seeing it an hour ago.
이상하군요. 제가 한 시간 전에 그 책을 봤던 걸 기억하거든요.

W: What do you think happened? 무슨 일이 생긴 것 같나요?

M: Maybe another student is reading it or is going to check it out soon.
아마 다른 학생이 그걸 읽고 있거나, 곧 대출할 예정일 것 같네요.

W: I hope not. I need it for a book report.
그러지 않기를 바라요. 저는 독후감을 위해 그게 필요하거든요.

어휘 assistance 도움, 보조 be supposed to ~하기로 되어 있다 available 이용 가능한 shelf 책꽂이; 선반 strange 이상한 happen 일어나다, 발생하다 maybe 아마도, 어쩌면 check out (책을) 대출하다 book report 독후감

17 ⑤

M: Hi, Sue. What are you doing now?
안녕, 수. 지금 뭐 하고 있니?

W: I'm going to the hospital. 난 병원에 가고 있어.

M: Is your grandfather still there? Are you going to visit him?
너희 할아버지가 아직 거기 계시니? 할아버지 뵈러 가는 거니?

W: Actually, he got out of the hospital two weeks ago.

He's much <u>better</u> now.
사실 할아버지는 2주 전에 퇴원하셨어. 지금은 많이 좋아지셨어.

M: That's good to hear. 다행이구나.

W: Yeah. Anyway, I'm going there to <u>get</u> a <u>flu</u> <u>shot</u>.
응. 어쨌든, 난 독감 예방주사를 맞으러 가는 길이야.

M: Are you <u>sick</u> now? 지금 아프니?

W: No, but <u>winter</u> is <u>coming</u>. I want to be <u>safe</u>.
아니, 하지만 겨울이 다가오고 있잖아. 난 안전한 게 좋아.

M: That's a good idea. I should do the <u>same</u> <u>thing</u>.
좋은 생각이야. 나도 똑같이 해야겠다.

> **어휘** get out of the hospital 병원에서 퇴원하다 flu shot 독감 예방주사 sick 아픈 safe 안전한

18 ③

M: Are you ready to <u>go to</u> the <u>mountain</u>?
산에 갈 준비는 됐니?

W: Yes, I am. 응, 준비됐어.

M: We're going to be really busy <u>cleaning</u> <u>up</u> the <u>area</u>.
우리가 그 지역을 치우려면 정말 바쁠 거야.

W: I know. But it will be <u>worth</u> <u>it</u>. I <u>hate</u> seeing all the <u>litter</u> <u>on</u> the <u>ground</u>. 알아. 하지만 그럴 만한 가치가 있을 거야. 난 바닥에 떨어진 쓰레기를 보는 게 정말 싫어.

M: Do you think we can clean much? <u>How</u> <u>much</u> <u>garbage</u> can we <u>pick</u> <u>up</u> by ourselves?
우리가 많이 치울 수 있을 거라고 생각하니? 우리끼리 얼마나 많은 쓰레기를 주울 수 있을까?

W: We <u>won't</u> <u>be</u> the <u>only</u> <u>ones</u> there today.
오늘 거기에 우리만 있는 게 아니야.

M: Won't we? <u>Who</u> <u>else</u> is going?
우리만 있는 게 아니라고? 누가 또 가니?

W: More than <u>fifty</u> students <u>signed</u> <u>up</u> to help. We should all be able to make the mountain <u>look</u> <u>better</u>. 50명 이상의 학생이 돕기로 신청했어. 우리는 함께 산을 깨끗하게 만들어야 해.

M: That's wonderful. If we all <u>work</u> <u>hard</u>, we'll <u>make</u> a <u>big</u> <u>difference</u>. 멋진걸. 우리 모두가 열심히 하면, 큰 변화를 이룰 수 있을 거야.

① Don't judge a book by its cover.
겉을 보고 속을 판단하지 말라.

② The early bird catches the worm.
일찍 일어나는 새가 벌레를 잡는다.

③ Many hands make light work. 백지장도 맞들면 낫다.

④ Absence makes the heart grow fonder.
떨어져 있으면 그리움이 더해진다.

⑤ The grass is always greener on the other side.
남의 떡이 더 커 보인다.

> **어휘** busy –ing ~하느라 바쁘다 clean up 청소하다, 치우다 area 지역, 구역 worth ~할 가치가 있는 litter 쓰레기 ground 바닥, 땅 by oneself 스스로, 혼자 sign up 신청하다 be able to ~할 수 있다 make a (big) difference (큰) 변화를 가져오다 judge 판단하다 absence 없음, 부재 fond 좋아하는

19 ①

W: Did you <u>have</u> a <u>good</u> <u>day</u> at school?
학교에서 좋은 하루를 보냈니?

M: It was fun, Mom. We got a <u>new</u> <u>student</u> in our <u>class</u>. 재미있었어요, 엄마. 우리 반에 새로운 학생이 왔어요.

W: <u>Where</u> is the student <u>from</u>? 그 학생은 어디에서 왔니?

M: He is from Italy. His family just <u>arrived</u> here <u>last</u> <u>week</u>. 이탈리아에서 왔어요. 가족이 지난주에 여기 도착했대요.

W: Does he <u>speak</u> <u>English</u> <u>well</u>? 그는 영어를 잘하니?

M: No, he only knows <u>a</u> <u>few</u> <u>words</u>.
아니요, 단어 몇 개만 알아요.

W: You ought to <u>help</u> him <u>out</u> then. You should <u>be</u> a <u>good</u> <u>friend</u>. 그럼 네가 그 친구를 도와줘야겠구나. 넌 좋은 친구가 되어야 한다.

M: Don't worry, Mom. I <u>already</u> <u>did</u> a few <u>things</u> for him today.
걱정 마세요, 엄마. 전 이미 오늘 그를 위해 몇 가지 일을 했어요.

W: <u>That's</u> <u>my</u> <u>boy</u>. 잘했다.

① That's my boy. 잘했다.

② Why did you do that? 왜 그 일을 했니?

③ What else did you do? 또 무엇을 했니?

④ When did he move here? 그가 언제 여기로 이사 왔니?

⑤ Teach him how to speak Italian.
그에게 이탈리아어를 가르쳐 주거라.

> **어휘** ought to ~해야 한다 already 이미 Italian 이탈리아어

20 ④

M: Did you remember to <u>clean</u> your <u>room</u> today?
오늘 네 방을 청소하는 걸 기억했니?

W: Sorry. I'll do it <u>tomorrow</u>. 죄송해요. 내일 할게요.

M: You <u>said</u> the <u>same</u> <u>thing</u> yesterday.
넌 어제도 똑같이 말했잖니.

W: I want to clean my room, but I just <u>don't</u> <u>have</u> <u>enough</u> <u>time</u>.
저도 제 방을 치우고 싶지만, 지금은 시간이 충분하지 않아요.

M: But aren't you planning to <u>go</u> <u>out</u> <u>with</u> Lily this evening? 하지만 오늘 저녁에 릴리와 외출하기로 하지 않았니?

W: Yes. We're going to <u>see</u> <u>a</u> <u>movie</u> together.
네. 우리는 같이 영화를 보러 갈 거예요.

M: If you have time to go out, <u>then</u> you have time to clean your room.
네가 외출할 시간이 있다면, 네 방을 치울 시간도 있다는 거야.

W: All right. I'll do that <u>in</u> <u>a</u> <u>few</u> <u>minutes</u>.
알겠어요. 몇 분 후에 할게요.

① Why didn't you help me out at all?
왜 저를 전혀 도와주지 않으셨나요?

② No, we haven't made any plans yet.
아니요, 우리는 아직 어떤 계획도 세우지 않았어요.

③ Thanks. I really appreciate your help.
고맙습니다. 도와주셔서 정말 감사해요.

④ All right. I'll do that in a few minutes.

알겠어요. 몇 분 후에 할게요.

⑤ But I told you my room is already clean.
하지만 제 방은 이미 깨끗하다고 말씀 드렸잖아요.

어휘 remember 기억하다 enough 충분한 plan 계획하다 go out 외출하다 appreciate 감사하다 in a few minutes 몇 분 후에, 곧

01 ③	02 ①	03 ①	04 ①	05 ⑤
06 ④	07 ③	08 ①	09 ④	10 ⑤
11 ③	12 ③	13 ②	14 ②	15 ④
16 ④	17 ②	18 ④	19 ②	20 ⑤

01 ③

W: Welcome to our weather forecast! The snow on the streets will disappear because of a warm wind from the south. Most cities in the country will stay sunny and clear all day tomorrow, but in a few cities like Daejeon and Cheongju, it will rain. So, keep that in mind if you travel to those cities.

일기예보를 말씀 드리겠습니다! 남쪽으로부터 불어오는 따뜻한 바람으로 인해 거리에 쌓인 눈은 녹아 사라질 것입니다. 국내 대부분의 도시들은 내일 하루 종일 화창하고 청명한 날씨가 계속되겠지만, 대전이나 청주와 같은 몇몇 도시는 비가 오겠습니다. 그러니 이 도시를 방문하시는 분들은 그 점을 명심하시기 바랍니다.

어휘 weather forecast 일기예보 disappear 사라지다 stay 머무르다, 유지하다 keep something in mind ~을 명심하다 travel 여행하다, 이동하다

02 ①

W: How was your summer vacation?
여름 방학은 어땠니?

M: Great. This is a picture from my trip to *Horse Hill* on Jeju Island. 좋았어. 이 사진이 이번에 제주도의 말의 언덕을 여행하면서 찍은 사진이야.

W: Wow! You are riding a horse. Weren't you scared?
우와! 넌 말을 타고 있구나. 무섭지 않았니?

M: Not at all. Riding a horse was fantastic.
전혀. 말 타기는 정말 환상적이었어.

W: Who is this man standing next to the horse?
말 옆에 서 있는 남자는 누구니?

M: That's my dad. We had a wonderful time.
우리 아빠야. 우린 정말 좋은 시간을 보냈어.

W: I'm sure you had many happy memories of your trip. 분명히 여행에서 좋은 추억들이 많이 생겼겠구나.

해설 남자는 말을 타고 있고, 남자의 아버지는 옆에 서 있다.

어휘 trip 여행 island 섬 ride a horse 말을 타다 scared 무서워하는 fantastic 환상적인, 멋진 next to ~옆에 sure 확실한 memory 추억, 기억

03 ①

W: Hey, Kevin. What are you doing?
얘, 케빈. 너 뭐 하고 있니?

M: I'm planning a surprise party for my mom's birthday. 우리 엄마 생신을 위해 깜짝 파티를 계획 중이야.

W: You seem so happy. So what are you going to do?
넌 정말 즐거워 보이는구나. 그래서 무엇을 할 계획이니?

M: My family will sing a song together when she opens the door.
엄마가 문을 열고 들어오시면 가족이 함께 노래를 부를 거야.

W: That's a good idea. I'm sure your mom will like that. 그거 좋은 생각이다. 너희 엄마가 분명히 좋아하실 거야.

M: I hope so. I can't wait to see the smile on her face.
나도 그랬으면 좋겠어. 엄마의 웃는 모습을 빨리 보고 싶어.

어휘 plan 계획하다 surprise party 깜짝 파티 I can't wait 빨리 ~하고 싶다, 몹시 바라다 excited 신이 난 relaxed 느긋한 bored 지루한

04 ①

M: You're late! The soccer game started five minutes ago. 너, 늦었구나! 5분 전에 축구 경기가 시작했어.

W: I'm so sorry. I got up late this morning.
정말 미안해. 오늘 아침에 늦게 일어났어.

M: Why? What did you do yesterday? 왜? 어제 뭐 했니?

W: I went on a family trip to Black Water Mountain, so I was really tired.
어제 가족과 함께 블랙워터 산에 갔었어. 그래서 정말 피곤했어.

M: I was worried because you didn't show up.
네가 나타나지 않아서 걱정했어.

W: Sorry, I promise not to be late next time.
미안해, 다음에는 늦지 않는다고 약속할게.

M: That's okay. Let's just watch the soccer game!
괜찮아. 그냥 축구 경기를 보자!

어휘 get up late 늦게 일어나다 tired 피곤한 show up 나타나다, 등장하다 promise 약속하다 next time 다음에

05 ⑤

M: Good morning. How may I help you?
안녕하세요. 무엇을 도와드릴까요?

W: Hi. I bought this picture book yesterday. But there's a problem with it.
안녕하세요. 제가 어제 이 그림책을 샀는데요, 책에 문제가 있어요.

M: What is it? 뭐가 문제죠?

W: I found two pages were missing.
두 페이지가 빠져 있는 걸 발견했어요.

M: Let me check your book. [*Pause*] Oh, we're very sorry. Could you show me your receipt, please?

제가 고객님의 책을 확인해 보겠습니다. [잠시 후] 아, 정말 죄송합니다. 영수증을 좀 보여 주시겠습니까?

W: Yes, <u>here</u> <u>it</u> <u>is</u>. 네, 여기 있어요.

M: Okay, just a minute. I'll get you a new one.
네, 잠시만요. 새로운 책으로 가져다 드리겠습니다.

W: Thank you. 감사합니다.

어휘 buy 사다(buy – bought – bought) problem 문제 missing 없는, 빠진 receipt 영수증 just a minute 잠시만 기다려라

06 ④

W: <u>Look</u> at the baby <u>monkey</u>! It is holding on to its mom so tight!
저 새끼 원숭이 좀 봐! 엄마한테 단단히 매달려 있어!

M: Yeah, that's so <u>cute</u>. I want to <u>give</u> it some <u>snacks</u>.
그래, 정말 귀엽다. 원숭이에게 과자를 좀 주고 싶어.

W: No, you can't. The <u>sign</u> <u>says</u> "Don't <u>feed</u> the <u>monkeys</u>." 그러면 안 돼. 표지판에 "원숭이에게 먹이를 주지 마시오"라고 적혀 있어.

M: Really? <u>Why</u> <u>not</u>? 정말? 왜 안 되지?

W: I think that's because it can <u>make</u> them <u>sick</u>.
내 생각에는 그게 원숭이들을 아프게 만들 수 있기 때문인 것 같아.

M: Oh, is it <u>bad</u> <u>for</u> their <u>health</u>?
아, 그게 원숭이의 건강에 해롭니?

W: Yes. You <u>should</u> <u>not</u> give our snacks to animals.
응. 넌 동물들에게 사람이 먹는 간식을 주면 안 돼.

해설 should는 '~해야 한다'라는 의미로 쓰이는 조동사이다.

어휘 hold on to ~에 매달리다 tight 단단히, 꽉 snack 간식, 과자류 sign 안내문, 표지판 bad for ~에 안 좋은 health 건강

07 ③

M: Sue, do you want to see the <u>musical</u> *The Jungle Story* with me <u>this</u> <u>Saturday</u>?
수, 너 이번 주 토요일에 나랑 '정글의 이야기' 뮤지컬을 같이 볼래?

W: That <u>sounds</u> <u>great</u>! 그거 좋지!

M: Then, I'll <u>buy</u> <u>tickets</u> for the musical.
그럼, 내가 뮤지컬 표를 살게.

W: Thank you, Ted. <u>What</u> <u>time</u> does it <u>start</u>?
고마워, 테드. 뮤지컬이 몇 시에 시작하니?

M: There are shows at <u>one</u>, <u>four</u>, and <u>seven</u> o'clock.
1시, 4시, 그리고 7시에 공연이 있어.

W: I'm going to <u>have</u> <u>lunch</u> with my family at one.
난 1시에 가족들과 점심식사를 할 거야.

M: Then, <u>how</u> <u>about</u> the four o'clock show?
그럼, 4시 공연은 어떻니?

W: <u>Great</u>, I'll call you Saturday morning.
좋아. 내가 토요일 아침에 너한테 전화할게.

해설 남자는 'how about ~?'으로 여자의 의견을 물었고, 여자는 great라며 찬성을 나타냈다.

어휘 musical 뮤지컬 show 공연, 프로그램 have lunch 점심식

사를 하다 how about ~은 어때?

08 ①

W: David, <u>hurry</u> <u>up</u>! It's time to leave.
데이비드, 서둘러! 출발해야 할 시간이야.

M: All right, Mom. I'm <u>putting</u> <u>on</u> my <u>jacket</u> now! <u>When</u> is the <u>train</u> <u>leaving</u>?
알겠어요, 엄마. 지금 재킷을 입고 있어요! 기차가 언제 떠나죠?

W: We need to get there <u>by</u> <u>four</u> P.M. We only have one hour. 우리는 오후 4시까지 거기에 도착해야 해. 한 시간밖에 남지 않았어.

M: Okay, I'm done! Mom, do you have my train <u>ticket</u>?
알겠어요, 저 다 했어요! 엄마, 제 열차 표 갖고 계세요?

W: No, I gave it to you <u>yesterday</u>. Don't you have it?
아니, 내가 어제 너한테 주었잖니. 넌 표를 갖고 있지 않니?

M: Oh, no! It's still <u>on</u> my <u>desk</u>!
아, 안돼! 표가 아직 제 책상 위에 있어요.

W: Go and get it. 가서 가지고 오렴.

M: I'll get it <u>right</u> <u>now</u>, Mom. 바로 가져올게요, 엄마.

어휘 hurry up 서두르다 leave 떠나다 put on (신발, 옷 등을) 입다, 신다 still 여전히 right now 지금

09 ④

W: <u>What</u> are you going to <u>order</u>? 넌 무엇을 주문할 거니?

M: I haven't <u>decided</u> <u>yet</u>. I really want to <u>order</u> some <u>pizza</u> and <u>coke</u>. But I'm afraid it's not <u>good</u> <u>for</u> my <u>health</u>. 아직 결정하지 못했어. 피자와 콜라를 정말로 주문하고 싶어. 하지만 그게 내 건강에 좋지 않아서 걱정이야.

W: Then, <u>how</u> <u>about</u> <u>tomato</u> spaghetti? Tomatoes are really <u>healthy</u>. So, that would be <u>better</u> <u>for</u> you.
그럼, 토마토 스파게티는 어떻니? 토마토는 정말 건강에 좋아. 그래서 너한테 더 좋을 거야.

M: Okay, I will have that. What about you?
그래. 그걸로 할게. 너는?

W: I'm going to <u>have</u> a <u>chicken</u> <u>salad</u>.
나는 치킨 샐러드를 먹을 거야.

M: Sounds great. 좋아.

해설 남자는 토마토 스파게티, 여자는 치킨 샐러드를 주문할 것이다.

어휘 order 주문하다 decide 결정하다 yet 아직, 이미 afraid 걱정하는 good for ~에 좋은 healthy 건강에 좋은, 건강한

10 ⑤

W: Hello, students! May I <u>have</u> your <u>attention</u>, please? We're <u>looking</u> <u>for</u> new <u>members</u> of our <u>volunteer</u> club. In this club, you will <u>help</u> old people and <u>take</u> <u>care</u> <u>of</u> children in the <u>neighborhood</u>. If you're interested, please <u>tell</u> your <u>homeroom</u> <u>teacher</u> by October fifth. You can find more <u>information</u> <u>on</u> the school <u>website</u>. Come and join us!

안녕하세요 학생 여러분! 잠깐 주목해 주시겠어요? 우리는 우리 자

원봉사 동아리의 새로운 회원을 모집하고 있어요. 이 동아리에서는 이웃의 노인들을 돕고, 아이들을 돌보는 일을 하게 됩니다. 관심이 있으면, 10월 5일까지 여러분의 담임 선생님께 말씀해 주세요. 학교 홈페이지에 가시면 더 많은 정보를 알아볼 수 있습니다. 오셔서 우리와 함께해요!

어휘 look for ~을 찾다 volunteer 자원봉사 take care of ~을 돌보다 neighborhood 이웃, 근처 homeroom teacher 담임 교사 join 가입하다, 함께하다

11 ③

M: Hello, Ms. Woods. I'm Inho, a school newspaper reporter. May I interview you, please?
안녕하세요 우즈 씨. 저는 인호라고 하고, 학교 신문의 기자입니다. 제가 인터뷰를 해도 될까요?
W: Sure. Go ahead. 네. 하세요.
M: Thank you. Where are you from?
감사합니다. 어디에서 오셨죠?
W: I'm from Canada. 저는 캐나다에서 왔어요.
M: When did you come to Korea? 언제 한국에 오셨죠?
W: I came here last month with my family. I have three children.
지난달에 가족과 함께 왔어요. 저는 세 명의 아이들이 있답니다.
M: What did you do before coming to Korea?
한국에 오시기 전에는 무슨 일을 하셨나요?
W: I taught English in China for five years.
중국에서 5년 동안 영어를 가르쳤어요.

해설 여자는 지난달에 한국에 왔다.

어휘 newspaper 신문 reporter 기자 interview 인터뷰하다 teach 가르치다(teach – taught – taught)

12 ③

W: Tom, where did you go after school yesterday?
톰, 넌 어제 방과 후에 어디를 갔었니?
M: I went to the Wisdom Bookstore. 위즈덤 서점에 갔었어.
W: My friend told me the books were on sale there. Did you buy any books? 내 친구가 나에게 그 곳에 책들이 세일 중이라고 말해줬어. 책 산 것 있니?
M: No. In fact, I went there to meet my favorite cartoonist, Alex Parker. He signed one of my comic books. 아니. 사실, 나는 내가 제일 좋아하는 만화가 알렉스 파커를 만나러 갔었어. 그가 내 만화책 중 한 권에 사인을 해줬어.
W: Wow! 우와!
M: And I even got a great picture of him.
그리고 심지어 그가 멋지게 나온 사진도 받았다니까.
W: Oh, you're so lucky. 아, 정말 운이 좋았구나.

어휘 after school 방과 후에 on sale 세일 중인 in fact 사실은 favorite 가장 좋아하는 cartoonist 만화가 sign 서명하다 comic book 만화책

13 ②

M: Hey, Julie. Did you know Mike came back?
줄리야. 넌 마이크가 돌아온 걸 알고 있니?
W: No, Todd. I thought he was in Japan.
아니, 토드. 난 그 애가 일본에 있다고 생각했어.
M: He was. But he came back from Japan last Tuesday. 그랬었지. 그런데 지난 화요일에 일본에서 돌아왔어.
W: Really? That's good! Then he can come back to our movie club! 정말? 잘됐다! 그럼 우리 영화 동아리에 다시 들어오겠네!
M: Yes. He told me that he's going to come this Saturday. 응. 그는 이번 주 토요일에 올 거라고 말했어.
W: That's great. 정말 좋구나.
M: Where are we going to meet this Saturday?
우리는 이번 주 토요일에 어디에서 만나는 거니?
W: The club meeting will be in classroom two oh three as usual. 동아리 모임은 보통 때처럼 203호 교실에서 있을 거야.

해설 Mike는 지난 화요일에 일본에서 돌아왔고, 이번 주 토요일에 학교에 올 것이다.

어휘 come back from ~에서 돌아오다 movie 영화 as usual 평상시처럼

14 ②

W: Hi, I want to buy a twelve-color paint set.
안녕하세요. 12색 물감 세트를 사고 싶어요.
M: No problem. Here you are. Anything else?
물론이죠. 여기 있습니다. 또 다른 게 필요하세요?
W: I also need a sketchbook like that one.
저기 있는 것과 같은 스케치북도 필요해요.
M: Here you go. What about a paint brush? Don't you need one?
여기 있습니다. 그림 붓은요? 하나 필요하지 않으세요?
W: You're right. I'll take this one. How much is all that?
맞아요. 이걸 살게요. 모두 얼마죠?
M: All together it's thirty dollars. 모두 30달러입니다.
W: Here you are. 여기 있습니다.
M: Thanks. 감사합니다.

해설 paint, sketchbook, brush 등이 나왔으므로 그림 도구를 파는 문구점에서 벌어지는 대화 상황이다.

어휘 paint 물감 here you are 여기 있습니다 sketchbook 스케치북 paint brush (그림용) 붓 all together 다 함께

15 ④

W: Hojun! Are you still playing that game on your smartphone? You've been playing for more than thirty minutes. 호준아! 넌 아직도 스마트폰으로 게임하고 있니? 30분 넘게 게임을 하고 있구나.
M: I know, Mom. But can I play for ten more minutes, please? 저도 알아요, 엄마. 하지만 10분만 더 하면 안될까요?
W: It's time for dinner. And I need your help.
저녁 먹을 시간이란다. 그리고 네 도움이 필요해.
M: Just a minute, Mom. [Pause] Okay, what do I need

to do? 잠시만요, 엄마. [잠시 후] 됐어요, 제가 뭘 해야 하죠?

W: Please help me to set the table.
식탁 차리는 것을 좀 도와주렴.

M: Okay, Mom. 알겠어요, 엄마.

어휘 smartphone 스마트폰 more than ~이상 set the table 식탁을 차리다

16 ④

W: Hey, Taeyong. What did you do yesterday?
얘, 태영아. 너 어제 뭐 했니?

M: I watched a TV show, *The Great Artist: Vincent van Gogh*.
난 '위대한 예술가: 빈센트 반 고흐'라는 TV 프로그램을 봤어.

W: What was that about? 무엇에 관한 거였니?

M: It was about Vincent van Gogh's life and his works of art.
빈센트 반 고흐의 인생과 그의 예술 작품에 관한 내용이었어.

W: Was it interesting? 재미있었니?

M: Yes! He is my favorite painter.
그럼! 그는 내가 제일 좋아하는 화가야.

W: Oh, I see. It is not easy for me to understand his paintings. Why do you like him? 아, 그렇구나. 나는 그의 그림을 이해하는 게 쉽지 않아. 넌 왜 그를 좋아하니?

M: That's because he used bright colors in his paintings. I like bright colors. 그가 그림에 밝은 색깔들을 사용했기 때문이야. 나는 밝은 색을 좋아하거든.

어휘 TV show TV 프로그램 work of art 예술 작품 bright 밝은 painting 그림

17 ②

① W: Why are you late? 넌 왜 늦었니?
M: I'm sorry. I missed the bus. 미안해. 버스를 놓쳤어.

② W: What are you going to do this Saturday?
넌 이번 주 토요일에 뭘 할 거니?
M: I went to America three years ago.
난 3년 전에 미국에 갔었어.

③ W: Sam, have you ever met Jenny?
샘, 넌 제니를 만나 봤니?
M: No, I haven't. 아니, 만나 본 적 없어.

④ W: Watch out! There is a car coming!
조심해! 차가 오고 있어!
M: Oh, my! Thank you. 아이고! 고마워.

⑤ W: Tony! I lost my bag. What should I do?
토니! 난 가방을 잃어버렸어. 어떻게 해야 하지?
M: Don't worry. Let's find it together.
걱정하지 마. 같이 찾아 보자.

어휘 late 늦은 miss the bus 버스를 놓치다

18 ④

M: Nahyeon, which activity are you going to do at the school festival?

나현아, 넌 학교 축제에서 어떤 활동을 할 거니?

W: I made rockets and soap last year, so I will probably do that again. 난 작년에 로켓과 비누를 만들었는데, 그래서 이번에도 똑같은 것을 할 거야.

M: Really? Why don't you try something new?
정말? 새로운 걸 시도해 보는 게 어때?

W: Like what? 가령 어떤 거?

M: Like face painting! Why don't you do it with me?
페이스 페인팅 같은 것! 나랑 같이 해볼래?

W: Face painting? But I'm not good at painting.
페이스 페인팅? 하지만 난 그림을 잘 못 그려.

M: Don't worry. I can help you.
걱정하지 마. 내가 도와줄 수 있어.

W: Well. Then, I'll do it with you. Thanks.
그럼, 너랑 같이 해볼게. 고마워.

어휘 activity 활동 festival 축제 soap 비누 probably 아마도 like what? (예를 들면) 어떤 것? Why don't you ~? ~하는 게 어때? be good at ~을 잘하다

19 ②

M: Hey, Mina. You look so worried. What's the matter?
야, 미나야. 넌 걱정이 많은 것 같아. 무슨 일이야?

W: I lost my English textbook this morning.
오늘 아침에 내 영어 교과서를 잃어버렸어.

M: Did you check your desk? 네 책상은 확인해 봤니?

W: Yes, I did. But it wasn't there.
응, 해봤어. 그런데 책상에는 없었어.

M: Hmm... Oh, why don't you talk to Ms. Kim, the English teacher?
음, 아, 영어 선생님이신 김 선생님께 말씀을 드려 보는 게 어때?

W: Why is that? 왜 그렇게 해야 해?

M: I heard she found someone's English textbook this morning. 오늘 아침에 선생님께서 누군가의 영어 교과서를 발견하셨다고 들었거든.

W: Oh, thanks! I should talk to her.
아, 고마워! 선생님과 이야기를 해봐야겠다.

① I'm looking forward to meeting you.
난 널 만날 날을 고대하고 있어.

② Oh, thanks! I should talk to her.
아, 고마워! 선생님과 이야기를 해봐야겠다.

③ You can't miss it. 틀림없이 찾을 거야.

④ Let me help you. 내가 도와줄게.

⑤ Here you are. 여기 있어.

어휘 textbook 교과서 check 확인하다 look forward to ~을 고대하다

20 ⑤

M: Susie! Have you seen the movie, *Brave Me*?
수지야! 넌 '브레이브 미'라는 영화를 봤니?

W: Yes. I saw it with my friends. It was wonderful.
응. 내 친구들이랑 봤어. 정말 멋진 영화였어.

M: I've heard many people have seen that movie. I want to see it, too.
난 많은 사람들이 그 영화를 봤다고 들었어. 나도 보고 싶어.

W: You should! It's one of the greatest movies I have ever seen.
꼭 봐야 해! 그건 내가 여태까지 본 최고의 영화들 중 하나야.

M: Really? I am going to ask my brother to go and see it with me. 정말? 우리 형한테 같이 보자고 물어봐야겠다.

W: Don't miss it. You'll love it.
놓치지 마. 넌 그걸 정말 좋아할 거야.

① I don't know where to go shopping.
어디로 쇼핑을 가야 할지 모르겠어.

② How is everything going recently?
요즘 별일 없지?

③ Are you going to watch it again?
다시 그걸 보러 갈 거니?

④ Of course! You can keep it.
물론! 네가 가지고 있어도 돼.

⑤ Don't miss it. You'll love it.
놓치지 마. 넌 그걸 정말 좋아할 거야.

어휘 brave 용감한 wonderful 멋진, 훌륭한 great 훌륭한 (great – greater – greatest) recently 최근에 miss 놓치다

02회 기출 듣기평가

본문 p.256-257

01 ①	02 ④	03 ⑤	04 ⑤	05 ③
06 ①	07 ④	08 ②	09 ②	10 ①
11 ④	12 ⑤	13 ③	14 ③	15 ②
16 ①	17 ②	18 ③	19 ④	20 ⑤

01 ①

W: Good morning! This is the weather forecast for this week. There has been lots of sunshine these days. We will have more sunny days. It will be sunny on Monday, Tuesday, and Wednesday. However, it will rain on Thursday and Friday. On Saturday and Sunday, it will be sunny again. Have a wonderful week. Thank you.

안녕하세요! 이번 주 일기예보입니다. 요즘은 일조량이 많았는데요. 앞으로도 화창한 날씨가 이어질 것입니다. 월요일, 화요일, 그리고 수요일에는 화창하겠습니다. 그러나 목요일과 금요일에는 비가 내리겠습니다. 토요일과 일요일에는 다시 화창하겠습니다. 즐거운 한 주 보내세요. 감사합니다.

어휘 sunshine 햇빛 these days 요즘

02 ④

W: Good morning! May I help you?

안녕하세요! 무엇을 도와드릴까요?

M: I am looking for a T-shirt with a snowman on it.
저는 눈사람이 그려진 티셔츠를 찾고 있어요.

W: How about this one? There is a cute snowman in the middle and one pocket. 이것은 어때요? 가운데에 귀여운 눈사람이 있고, 주머니가 하나 있어요.

M: It looks nice. But I don't need the pocket.
멋져 보여요. 하지만 저는 주머니가 필요 없어요.

W: Okay. Here's the same T-shirt without a pocket. How about this?
알겠어요. 여기 주머니가 없는 같은 티셔츠가 있어요. 이건 어때요?

M: Great. Thanks. I will take it.
멋져요. 고마워요. 그것으로 할게요.

해설 남자는 눈사람이 있고 주머니가 없는 티셔츠를 골랐다.

어휘 snowman 눈사람 cute 귀여운 in the middle 가운데에 pocket 주머니 without ~이 없는

03 ⑤

M: Hi, Sally. Long time no see. What's the matter with your cat? 안녕하세요, 샐리. 정말 오랜만이네요. 당신의 고양이에게 무슨 문제가 있나요?

W: Hello, Dr. Park. He doesn't eat at all.
안녕하세요, 박 선생님. 고양이가 아무것도 먹질 않아요.

M: Oh, I see. When did he stop eating?
아, 그렇군요. 언제부터 안 먹기 시작했나요?

W: Yesterday morning. And he doesn't play much these days. 어제 아침이요. 게다가 요즘에는 통 놀지를 않아요.

M: I'll give him a medical checkup.
제가 고양이를 검사해 볼게요.

W: Please do. I hope it's nothing serious.
그렇게 해주세요. 심각한 게 아니면 좋겠어요.

어휘 long time no see 오랜만이다 at all 전혀 medical checkup 진찰, 검진 serious 심각한 bored 지루한 proud 자랑스러운 peaceful 평화로운

04 ⑤

W: Oh, no! Brian! What happened to your room?
아, 안돼! 브라이언! 네 방에 무슨 일이 있었니?

M: I'm sorry, Mom. I promise to clean it up.
죄송해요, 엄마. 방을 청소하겠다고 약속할게요.

W: Okay. Well, what were you doing?
알겠다. 그런데, 넌 뭘 하고 있었어?

M: I was looking for things to sell at the school flea market. 학교 벼룩시장에서 판매할 물건을 찾고 있었어요.

W: Oh! What did you find? 아! 무엇을 찾았니?

M: I found a baseball cap and some T-shirts. Why don't you come, Mom? 야구 모자 하나랑 티셔츠 몇 개를 찾았어요. 엄마도 오시는 게 어때요?

W: When is it? 그게 언제니?

M: It opens tomorrow at three in the afternoon.
내일 오후 3시에 열려요.

happen (일이) 벌어지다 clean up 청소하다 sell 팔다 flea market 벼룩시장 baseball cap 야구 모자

05 ③

M: I'm so excited! 정말 신 난다!

W: Me, too. We're lucky. The line isn't so long.
나도 그래. 우린 운이 좋아. 줄이 별로 길지 않잖아.

M: Jane, look over there. There's a big parade.
제인, 저쪽을 봐. 거대한 퍼레이드가 있어.

W: Yes, I can see some people walking and waving their hands. 응, 걸어가며 손을 흔드는 사람들이 몇 명 보이네.

M: Oh, look at that man. He's wearing an animal mask and riding a bike.
아, 저 남자를 봐. 그는 동물 가면을 쓰고 자전거를 타고 있어.

W: Wow! There are so many exciting things happening at this amusement park.
우와! 이 놀이공원에는 흥미진진한 일이 많이 있구나.

M: Oh, it's our turn to ride the roller coaster. Let's go.
아, 우리가 롤러코스터를 탈 차례야. 가자.

[해설] amusement park, roller coaster 등을 들었다면 문제를 풀 수 있다.

[어휘] excited 신나는, 흥분한 over there 저쪽에 parade 퍼레이드, 가두 행진 wave one's hands 손을 흔들다 mask 가면 ride a bike 자전거를 타다 amusement park 놀이공원 turn 차례, 순서 ride the roller coaster 롤러코스터를 타다

06 ①

M: Mom, I'm home. 엄마, 저 집에 왔어요.

W: John, you're home already. How was today's baseball game?
존, 벌써 집에 왔구나. 오늘 야구 경기는 어땠니?

M: It was fantastic! We won the game!
환상적이었어요! 우리가 경기에서 이겼어요!

W: Oh, really? Tell me more about it.
아, 정말이니? 좀 더 얘기해 주렴.

M: We were losing in the beginning by two points.
초반에는 우리가 2점 차이로 지고 있었어요.

W: So, everyone was worried, right? Then, how did you win? 그래서 모두가 걱정했겠구나, 그렇지? 그러고 나서 너희가 어떻게 이겼니?

M: Guess what? I hit a home run, and we got three points. 들어 보실래요? 제가 홈런을 쳤고 우리는 3점을 땄어요.

W: That's my boy! You did a great job!
역시 내 아들이야! 정말 잘했어!

[어휘] baseball 야구 fantastic 환상적인 win the game 경기에서 이기다 in the beginning 처음에, 초반에 guess 추측하다 hit a home run 홈런을 치다 do a great job 대단한 일을 하다

07 ④

M: Good morning, Kelly. What class are you in?
안녕, 켈리. 너는 어느 반이야?

W: Hi, Dohoon. I am in Class C. What about you?
안녕, 도훈아. 나는 C반이야. 너는?

M: Wow! We are in the same class this year.
와! 우린 올해 같은 반이야.

W: That's great. Do you know which class Mina is in?
좋아. 미나는 어느 반인지 알아?

M: She is in Class D, right next door to our class.
그 애는 우리 반 바로 옆에 D반이야.

W: I'm sorry she's not in the same class with us.
그 애가 우리랑 같은 반이 되지 않아서 아쉽다.

M: I know, but we can see each other every day.
맞아, 그렇지만 우리는 서로 매일 볼 수 있잖아.

[해설] Kelly와 Dohoon은 Class C이고, Mina는 옆 반인 Class D이다.

[어휘] class 반, 수업, 교실 next door to ~의 옆에

08 ②

W: Tom, did you finish packing your bag to go camping tomorrow?
톰, 넌 내일 캠핑에 가져갈 가방을 다 쌌니?

M: Yes, Mom. I packed snacks, water, clothes, and my sleeping bag.
네, 엄마. 저는 간식, 물, 옷, 그리고 제 침낭을 챙겼어요.

W: Oh, did you get your first aid kit? It is in the bathroom closet.
아, 네 구급상자는 챙겼니? 그건 화장실 서랍장에 있단다.

M: Okay. [Pause] Mom, there is no medicine at all in the box.
알겠어요. [잠시 후] 엄마, 상자 안에 약이 하나도 없어요.

W: Really? Then, you should go and buy some medicine. 정말이니? 그럼, 네가 가서 약을 좀 사오렴.

M: Okay. I will go now. 네. 제가 지금 갈게요.

[어휘] pack (짐을) 싸다 go camping 캠핑을 가다 snack 간식 sleeping bag 침낭 first aid kit 구급상자 closet 서랍장 medicine 약

09 ②

M: Hello, listeners! Welcome to *Health 24*. I am Andy Brown. When I was young, I was very sick for a long time. Do you want to know how I got over it? First, I exercised one hour every day. Second, I drank two liters of water a day. It sounds simple, but it made a huge difference in my life.

청취자 여러분, 안녕하세요! '건강 24시간'에 오신 것을 환영합니다. 저는 앤디 브라운입니다. 저는 어렸을 때 오랫동안 매우 아팠습니다. 제가 어떻게 병을 극복했는지 아십니까? 첫째, 저는 매일 한 시간씩 운동했습니다. 둘째, 저는 하루에 물 2리터를 마셨습니다. 그것은 간단해 보이지만 제 삶에 엄청난 변화를 가져왔습니다.

[어휘] listener 청취자 sick 아픈 for a long time 오랫동안 get over 극복하다 exercise 운동하다 liter 리터 make a huge difference 엄청난 차이를 만들다

10 ①

M: Would you like to <u>taste</u> one of these <u>tomatoes</u>? They're from my grandma's <u>farm</u>.
이 토마토 하나 먹어 볼래? 우리 할머니의 농장에서 온 거야.

W: Thanks. Mmm... They're <u>delicious</u>. Did she <u>grow</u> these <u>herself</u>?
고마워. 음, 맛있다. 할머니께서 직접 이걸 기르신 거니?

M: Yes, she grows lots of things. I want to be a <u>farmer</u> and <u>live</u> in the <u>country</u> like her someday.
응, 할머니께서는 다양한 것들을 재배하셔. 나도 할머니처럼 언젠가는 농부가 되어서 시골에 살고 싶어.

W: Really? Living in the country is not easy. I think it's <u>easier</u> to live in a city as an <u>office</u> <u>worker</u>.
정말이야? 시골에서 사는 건 쉽지 않아. 나는 도시에 살면서 회사원으로 사는 게 더 쉽다고 생각해.

M: It may be difficult, but I still like the country life.
어려울지 모르지만 그래도 난 시골 생활이 좋아.

어휘 taste 맛보다 farm 농장 delicious 맛있는 grow 기르다, 재배하다 farmer 농부 country 시골 office worker 사무직 근로자, 회사원

11 ④

W: Hello, everyone. <u>This is</u> Susan from Book Talk. I am going to <u>talk about</u> *The Purple Orange* <u>written by</u> Monica Smith. It is one of the most <u>famous books</u> in the world. She tells us about <u>friendship</u> and <u>love</u> in this book. This book was written in <u>twelve</u> different <u>languages</u>. It is <u>sold</u> in more than one hundred countries.
안녕하세요, 여러분. 북 토크의 수잔입니다. 저는 모니카 스미스가 쓴 '퍼플 오렌지'에 대해 이야기하려고 합니다. 그것은 세계에서 가장 유명한 책 중 하나죠. 그녀는 이 책에서 우리에게 우정과 사랑에 관해서 이야기합니다. 이 책은 12개의 다른 언어로 쓰였습니다. 그것은 100개 이상의 나라에서 팔립니다.

해설 *The Purple Orange*는 12개의 언어로 쓰여졌다.

어휘 purple 자주색의 friendship 우정 language 언어 be sold 팔리다

12 ⑤

[*Phone rings.*] [전화벨이 울린다.]

M: Flower Guest House. How may I help you?
플라워 게스트 하우스입니다. 무엇을 도와드릴까요?

W: Hi. I am Sujin Park and I have <u>booked</u> a <u>room</u> for <u>tomorrow</u>. 안녕하세요. 저는 박수진이라고 하는데요, 내일 객실 하나를 예약했어요.

M: Hi, Sujin. We are <u>expecting</u> you. Do you need anything?
네, 수진 씨. 기다리고 있었습니다. 필요한 것이 있습니까?

W: Yes. Do you have a <u>hair dryer</u> in the room?
네. 객실에 헤어 드라이어가 있나요?

M: We have a hair dryer in every room. Do you need anything else? 저희는 모든 객실에 헤어 드라이어가 구비되어 있습니다. 더 필요한 것이 있나요?

W: No, thank you. <u>That's all</u>. See you tomorrow.
아니요, 감사합니다. 그게 전부예요. 내일 뵐게요.

어휘 guest house 게스트 하우스, 소규모 호텔 book a room 객실을 예약하다 expect (오기로 한 대상을) 기다리다 hair dryer 헤어 드라이어 that's all 그뿐이다, 그게 전부다

13 ③

M: <u>Thank you for visiting</u> ABC Library. Today, we'll have *Fun Night* on the <u>first floor</u>. Our story lady will read you an interesting story. You can <u>bring snacks</u> or <u>drinks</u>. You can come <u>with</u> your <u>family</u>. *Fun Night* is on <u>every</u> Friday. It <u>starts at</u> <u>six thirty</u> P.M. Come and have fun together at ABC Library!
ABC 도서관을 방문해 주셔서 감사합니다. 오늘 우리는 1층에서 '펀 나이트' 시간을 가지려고 합니다. 저희 이야기꾼 아가씨가 여러분께 재미있는 이야기를 읽어드릴 것입니다. 여러분은 간식이나 음료수를 가져와도 됩니다. 여러분의 가족과 함께 오셔도 됩니다. '펀 나이트'는 매주 금요일에 있습니다. 그것은 오후 6시 30분에 시작합니다. ABC 도서관에 오셔서 함께 즐거운 시간을 보내세요.

해설 행사는 1층에서 열리고, 간식과 음료를 가져올 수 있고, 매주 금요일에 진행되며, 오후 6시 30분에 시작한다.

어휘 fun 재미있는, 즐거운 first floor 일층 bring 가져오다 snack 간식 have fun 재미있게 놀다

14 ③

M: Jisu, you are <u>doing</u> really <u>well</u> in my P.E. class.
지수야, 내 체육 시간에 네가 무척 잘하는구나.

W: Thank you, Mr. Song. I <u>practice soccer</u> on the <u>playground</u> every day.
감사합니다, 송 선생님. 저는 운동장에서 매일 축구를 연습해요.

M: Great. You're beginning to <u>kick</u> like a real <u>soccer player</u>. 훌륭해. 너는 진짜 축구 선수처럼 공을 차기 시작했어.

W: Really? Do you think I'm <u>that good</u>?
정말이에요? 제가 그 정도로 잘한다고 생각하시나요?

M: Yes. <u>Keep practicing</u>, and you'll <u>do well on</u> the <u>test</u> next week.
그래. 계속 연습하면 다음 주에 있을 시험에서 너는 아주 잘할 거야.

W: Okay, I'll do that. 네, 그렇게 할게요.

M: <u>Good luck</u> to you. 행운을 빈다.

어휘 do well 잘하다 P.E. 체육(= physical education) practice 연습하다 soccer 축구 on the playground 운동장에서 kick (발로) 차다 soccer player 축구 선수 do well on the test 시험을 잘 보다

15 ②

W: Where are you going, Taeho? 태호야, 어디에 가니?

M: I'm going to the library to do a history project with my friends.
저는 도서관에 가서 친구들과 역사 숙제를 할 거예요.

W: Okay. Then, would you do me a favor?
그렇구나. 그럼 내 부탁 좀 들어주겠니?

M: Sure, Mom. What is it? 물론이죠, 엄마. 부탁이 뭐예요?

W: I made an apple pie for your grandmother. Please take it to her on your way to the library.
내가 할머니께 드리려고 애플 파이를 만들었어. 네가 도서관 가는 길에 할머니께 그것을 갖다 드리렴.

M: No problem. Apple pies are her favorite. She will love it. 그럼요. 애플 파이는 할머니께서 가장 좋아하시는 거잖아요. 무척 좋아하실 거예요.

W: Thank you. 고맙구나.

해설 여자의 말인 'Please' 뒤에는 부탁하는 내용이 이어진다.

어휘 project 과제, 프로젝트 do somebody a favor ~의 부탁을 들어 주다 on one's way to ~으로 가는 길에 favorite 가장 좋아하는 (것)

16 ①

M: Good afternoon, Katie. Where are you going?
안녕, 케이티. 너는 어디에 가고 있니?

W: Hi, Jason. I'm on my way home.
안녕, 제이슨. 나는 집에 가는 길이야.

M: Then, let's take the bus together.
그러면 우리 같이 버스를 타자.

W: Sorry, but I'd like to walk home today.
미안하지만, 난 오늘은 집까지 걸어가고 싶어.

M: Why? 왜?

W: I am walking home because the weather is so beautiful. Do you want to join me? 날씨가 무척 좋기 때문에 나는 집으로 걸어가는 거야. 너도 나랑 같이 갈래?

M: I'd love to, but I can't. I have a swimming class this afternoon. 그러고 싶지만 안 돼. 나는 오후에 수영 수업이 있어.

W: All right. See you tomorrow. 알겠어. 내일 보자.

어휘 take the bus 버스를 타다 walk home 집까지 걸어서 가다 join 함께하다, 가입하다 swimming 수영

17 ②

① W: When did you get up? 넌 언제 일어났니?
M: At about seven thirty A.M. 오전 7시 30분쯤에.

② W: Did you have a good time at the park?
공원에서 좋은 시간을 보냈니?
M: Sounds great! 그거 좋다!

③ W: Thank you for inviting me. 초대해 주셔서 감사합니다.
M: Make yourself at home. 편하게 계세요.

④ W: Do you know how to make a paper flower?
너는 종이 꽃 만드는 방법을 알고 있니?
M: I have no idea. 전혀 몰라.

⑤ W: How long will you stay there?

너는 그곳에 얼마나 오래 머무를 거야?

M: Maybe about five days. 아마 5일 정도.

해설 ②의 질문에는 Yes, No와 같은 답변이 나와야 한다.

어휘 have a good time 즐거운 시간을 보내다 invite 초대하다 make yourself at home 편하게 있어라 have no idea 전혀 모르다 stay 머물다, 묵다

18 ③

W: Hello, new Hillside Middle School students! I want to explain our lunch system. Our cafeteria is on the first floor of the main building. Lunch starts at twelve thirty, and it's open for one hour. The second graders will use the cafeteria first, followed by the first graders, and then the third graders. After eating, please be sure to clear your table. Thank you.

안녕하세요, 힐사이드 중학교에 새로 온 학생 여러분! 제가 우리의 급식 제도에 대해 설명하고자 합니다. 우리 구내식당은 본관 1층에 있습니다. 점심은 12시 30분에 시작하며 한 시간 동안 이어집니다. 2학년이 먼저 구내식당을 이용하고, 다음에 1학년, 그 다음에 3학년이 이용합니다. 식사 후, 각자의 테이블을 꼭 치우도록 하세요. 감사합니다.

어휘 explain 설명하다 cafeteria 구내식당, 카페테리아 first floor 일층 main building 본관 grader 학생 followed by 뒤이어, 잇달아 be sure to 반드시 ~하다

19 ④

W: What are these posters about?
이 포스터들은 무엇에 관한 거야?

M: They are for our first band performance.
우리 밴드의 첫 공연을 위한 거야.

W: Really? When are you going to have the performance? 정말? 너희는 언제 공연을 할 예정이니?

M: This Friday at five. 이번 주 금요일 5시에.

W: What do you play in the band?
너는 밴드에서 무엇을 연주해?

M: I play the drums. You should come and watch.
나는 드럼을 쳐. 네가 와서 봐야 해.

W: Of course, I will. I really want to see you playing the drums on the stage. 당연하지, 그럴게. 나는 정말로 무대에서 드럼을 연주하는 네 모습을 보고 싶어.

M: Well, I've practiced a lot, but also I'm very nervous now. 음, 난 연습을 많이 했는데, 지금은 긴장되기도 해.

W: Don't worry. You can do it. 걱정 마. 너는 할 수 있어.

① That's a good idea. 그거 좋은 생각이야.

② Please help yourself. 마음껏 먹어.

③ Thank you for your help. 도와줘서 고마워.

④ Don't worry. You can do it. 걱정 마. 너는 할 수 있어.

⑤ You've got the wrong number.
당신은 전화를 잘못 걸었습니다.

해설 여자는 남자의 긴장을 풀어주고 용기를 북돋는 말을 할 것을 예상할 수 있다.

어휘 poster 포스터 performance 공연 stage 무대 practice 연습(하다) nervous 불안한, 긴장하는 You've got the wrong number. 전화를 잘못 거셨습니다.

20 ⑤

M: Cindy! You look happy. What did you do for the holiday? 신디! 너 기분이 좋아 보여. 너는 휴가 때 뭘 했니?

W: I went to Jeonju with my family.
나는 가족과 함께 전주에 갔어.

M: That sounds interesting. How was it?
그거 재미있었겠다. 어땠어?

W: It was wonderful. I think you should go there.
굉장했어. 너도 그곳에 꼭 가 봐.

M: Really? What did you do there?
정말? 너는 거기서 무엇을 했어?

W: I visited the traditional Korean village, and ate delicious food.
나는 전통 한옥 마을에 가 봤고, 맛있는 음식도 먹었어.

M: I'm sure you really enjoyed that. What did you eat there? 굉장히 좋았나 보다. 넌 거기서 뭘 먹었니?

W: I ate bibimbap. 난 비빔밥을 먹었어.

① I wanted to go there again. 나는 그곳에 다시 가고 싶었어.
② Well, I want to buy more. 글쎄, 나는 좀 더 사고 싶어.
③ Yes! That's amazing. 응! 그건 멋져.
④ All right! I will. 알겠어. 그렇게 할게.
⑤ I ate bibimbap. 난 비빔밥을 먹었어.

어휘 holiday 휴가, 휴일 traditional 전통의 village 마을 amazing 놀라운, 멋진

03회 기출 듣기평가
본문 p.268-269

01 ④	02 ②	03 ⑤	04 ①	05 ⑤
06 ③	07 ③	08 ⑤	09 ③	10 ②
11 ②	12 ⑤	13 ①	14 ①	15 ③
16 ④	17 ②	18 ①	19 ④	20 ②

01 ④

W: Tony, why don't we put this picture on the table?
토니, 우리 이 사진을 탁자 위에 놓는 게 어때?

M: Sounds good. How about on the left, next to the clock? 좋아. 시계 옆으로 왼쪽은 어때?

W: Okay. Then let's put the teddy bear between the picture and the clock.
그래. 그럼 사진과 시계 사이에 곰 인형을 놓자.

M: Wait. I don't think that's a good idea. Let's not put

---

the teddy bear on the table. 잠깐만. 그건 좋은 생각이 아닌 것 같아. 곰 인형은 탁자 위에 놓지 말자.

W: Okay. I agree. 알겠어. 나도 찬성이야.

어휘 picture 사진, 그림 on the left 왼쪽에 next to ~옆에 between ~사이에 teddy bear 곰 인형, 테디베어 agree 동의하다

02 ②

M: Rachel, what are you doing? It's already ten thirty.
레이첼, 너 뭐 하고 있니? 벌써 10시 30분이야.

W: I'm checking my bag. I'm almost done.
제 가방을 확인하고 있어요. 거의 다 했어요.

M: You should go to bed. Tomorrow is your first day at your new school.
넌 잠자리에 들어야 한다. 내일이 새로운 학교에서의 첫날이잖니.

W: I know, but I want to make sure I have everything ready. 저도 알지만, 모든 준비가 다 됐는지 확인하고 싶어요.

M: Don't worry. Everything will be fine.
걱정하지 마. 다 괜찮을 거야.

W: Thanks, Dad. But I'm not sure I'll be able to make good friends there.
고마워요, 아빠. 하지만 그곳에서 좋은 친구들을 사귈 수 있을지 잘 모르겠어요.

어휘 check 확인하다, 점검하다 go to bed 잠자리에 들다 make sure 확실히 하다 be able to ~할 수 있다 make friends 친구를 사귀다 nervous 긴장한 alarmed 놀란

03 ⑤

[Telephone rings.] [전화벨이 울린다.]

W: Dr. Benson's Dental Clinic. How may I help you?
벤슨 치과입니다. 무엇을 도와드릴까요?

M: Can I speak to Dr. Benson? This is Tom, Dr. Benson's friend. 벤슨 선생과 통화할 수 있을까요? 저는 벤슨 선생의 친구인 톰입니다.

W: I'm sorry, but she's busy right now.
죄송합니다만 선생님이 지금 바쁘세요.

M: Then, can I leave a message?
그럼, 메모를 남길 수 있을까요?

W: Of course. 물론이죠.

M: Please tell her that I booked a table for dinner at seven P.M. 제가 오후 7시에 저녁식사를 할 음식점을 예약해 두었다고 전해 주세요.

W: Okay, I'll let her know. 네. 그렇게 알려드릴게요.

어휘 dental clinic 치과 speak to ~와 통화하다 right now 지금 당장 leave a message 메모를 남기다 book a table 식당에 자리를 예약하다

04 ①

M: Excuse me. Is it possible to check out books with a student ID card?
실례합니다. 학생증으로 책을 대출하는 것이 가능한가요?

W: No, you need a library card.

아니요. 도서관 카드가 필요합니다.

M: I see. Actually, I don't have one. Can I get a new card here? 그렇군요. 사실, 제가 도서관 카드가 없거든요. 여기서 새 카드를 받을 수 있나요?

W: Sure. Just fill out this form. 물론입니다. 이 양식만 작성해 주시면 됩니다.

M: Okay. How long will it take to make it? 네. 만드는 데 얼마나 걸리죠?

W: About an hour. 약 한 시간 정도요.

M: All right. 알겠습니다.

어휘 check out (책을) 대출하다 student ID card 학생증 fill out ~을 작성하다 form 양식 theater 영화관, 극장

05 ⑤

W: Is something wrong, John? You don't look so good. 무슨 문제 있니, 존? 몸이 좀 안 좋아 보여.

M: I hurt my back while moving a desk into the classroom. 교실 안으로 책상을 옮기다가 허리를 다쳤어.

W: Did you go see the school nurse? 양호 선생님께 가 봤니?

M: No, I didn't think it was serious. 아니, 난 그게 심각하지 않다고 생각했어.

W: But it looks like you're in pain. 하지만 넌 아픈 것처럼 보여.

M: Don't worry. It'll be okay tomorrow. 걱정하지 마. 내일이면 괜찮을 거야.

W: I think you'd better go and see the nurse. 내 생각에는 양호 선생님께 가보는 게 좋을 것 같아.

해설 'you'd better ~'는 '너는 ~하는 편이 좋겠다'라는 충고의 표현이다.

어휘 hurt one's back 등을 다치다 while ~하는 동안에 school nurse 양호 교사 serious 심각한 in pain 아픈 had better ~하는 편이 낫다

06 ③

M: Hello. How can I help you? 안녕하세요. 무엇을 도와드릴까요?

W: Hi. How much are these cookies? 안녕하세요. 이 쿠키들은 얼마죠?

M: The cookies are one dollar each. 그 쿠키는 개당 1달러입니다.

W: And how much is a cup of coffee? 그리고 커피 한 잔에 얼마죠?

M: It's two dollars. 2달러입니다.

W: Okay. I'll take two cookies and a cup of coffee. 알겠어요. 쿠키 두 개와 커피 한 잔 주세요.

M: Please wait a moment. I'll be right back with your order. 잠시만 기다려 주세요. 주문하신 것을 가지고 바로 오겠습니다.

어휘 each 각각 a cup of coffee 커피 한 잔 wait a moment 잠시 기다리다 order 주문(하다)

07 ③

W: Guess what! My friend from the Philippines is going to visit me. 있잖아! 필리핀에 있는 내 친구가 나를 보러 올 거야.

M: Oh, really? You must be excited. 아, 정말? 신나겠구나.

W: Yes. But I don't know where to take him. 응. 하지만 그를 어디로 데려가야 할지 모르겠어.

M: You should take your friend to a traditional Korean restaurant or market. 넌 네 친구를 한국 전통 음식점이나 시장으로 데려가야 해.

W: Good idea. Do you know any good Korean restaurants? 좋은 생각이야. 괜찮은 한국 음식점을 아는 데 있니?

M: Yes. The Seoul restaurant is very well-known. Their menu is on their website. 응. 서울 식당이 정말 유명해. 식당 웹사이트에 메뉴가 있어.

W: Oh, I'll take a look at the website. 아, 웹사이트를 한번 봐야겠다.

어휘 guess what (대화를 시작할 때) 있잖아, 이봐 the Philippines 필리핀 traditional 전통의 well-known 유명한, 잘 알려진 take a look 살펴보다

08 ⑤

W: We have a long weekend. Do you want to go to the swimming pool with me? 우리에게는 긴 주말이 있어. 나랑 같이 수영장 갈래?

M: It's too cold to go swimming. How about going to a baseball game? 수영하기에는 너무 추워. 야구 경기를 보러 가는 건 어때?

W: Well, I don't like baseball that much. How about going to the movies or going shopping? 음, 나는 야구를 그렇게 좋아하지 않아. 영화를 보러 가거나, 쇼핑을 가는 건 어때?

M: Come on, Chicago Bears has a very important game coming up. I'm sure you'll like it. 그러지 말고, 시카고 베어스의 정말로 중요한 경기가 다가오고 있어. 너도 분명히 좋아할 거야.

W: Okay, if you say so, let's go! 알겠어. 네가 그렇게 말한다면, 같이 가자!

어휘 weekend 주말 swimming pool 수영장 go to the movies 영화 보러 가다 go shopping 쇼핑하러 가다 come on 자, 그러지 말고 if you say so 네가 그렇게 말한다면

09 ③

M: Hello, everyone. I'm very happy to receive the award for Player of the Year. I can't express how much I appreciate this honor. I'd especially like to thank my parents for their support during the difficult times. Whenever I wanted to give up, they cheered me on. I really thank them for all their help.

This award is also for them.

안녕하세요, 여러분. 제가 올해의 선수상을 받게 되어 매우 기쁩니다. 이 영광에 대한 감사를 어떻게 표현해야 할지 모르겠습니다. 힘든 시기에 저를 지지해 주신 부모님께 특별히 감사의 말씀을 전하고 싶습니다. 제가 포기하고 싶은 순간마다 부모님께서는 저를 응원해 주셨습니다. 부모님의 모든 도움에 정말로 감사 드립니다. 이 수상은 부모님께 드리는 거나 마찬가지입니다.

[어휘] award 상 Player of the Year 올해의 선수 express 표현하다 appreciate 감사하다 honor 영광 especially 특히 support 지원, 지지 during ~동안에 whenever ~할 때마다 cheer somebody on ~을 응원하다

10 ②

M: Rachel, is this postcard from China?
레이첼, 이게 중국에서 온 엽서니?

W: Yes, I got it from Susan yesterday.
응. 어제 그걸 수잔에게서 받았어.

M: Oh, is she in China? 아, 수잔이 중국에 있니?

W: Yes. She went there with her brother to visit their grandparents.
응. 조부모님을 뵈러 그녀의 오빠랑 중국에 갔어.

M: I see, that's why she couldn't come to the book club this month.
그렇구나, 그래서 이번 달에 독서 동아리에 못 온 거구나.

W: Yeah, but she'll come back next month.
응. 그렇지만 다음 달에는 다시 올 거야.

[해설] Susan은 다음 달에 중국에서 돌아올 것이다.

[어휘] postcard 엽서 visit 방문하다 grandparents 조부모 come back 돌아오다

11 ②

[Telephone rings.] [전화벨이 울린다.]
M: Hello. Grab and Go Vending Machines.
여보세요. 그랩 앤드 고 자판기입니다.

W: Hi. There's a problem with the vending machine in Greenwood Library.
안녕하세요. 그린우드 도서관에 있는 자판기에 문제가 있어요.

M: All right. What's the problem?
알겠습니다. 어떤 문제가 있죠?

W: The vending machine didn't give me my change.
자판기에서 제 잔돈이 나오지 않았어요.

M: Sorry about that. I'll come and check. I'll be there in about five minutes. 그 점은 죄송합니다. 제가 가서 확인해 볼게요. 5분 정도 후에 도착할 겁니다.

W: Okay. Thanks. 네. 감사합니다.

[해설] change를 명사로 쓰면 변화라는 뜻 외에 잔돈이라는 의미도 있다.

[어휘] vending machine 자판기 change 잔돈

12 ⑤

W: Hello, Mr. Smith. I'm so glad to meet a world famous novelist. I'm Kate from ABC Magazine.
안녕하세요 스미스 씨. 세계적으로 유명한 소설가를 만나게 되어 정말 기쁘네요. 저는 ABC 잡지에서 나온 케이트예요.

M: Glad to meet you, Kate. 만나서 반갑습니다, 케이트.

W: I know your latest novel, *Blue Ocean*, is very popular all over the world. How did you get the idea for the novel?
당신의 신작 소설인 '블루 오션'이 전 세계적으로 매우 유명한 것으로 알고 있어요. 그 소설의 아이디어는 어디에서 얻으셨죠?

M: Well, I had an amazing chance to swim with wild dolphins.
음, 저는 야생 돌고래들과 수영할 수 있는 놀라운 기회가 있었어요.

W: Really? Where was that? 정말요? 어디서요?

M: It was in Australia. 호주였습니다.

W: I see. So that's how the story started.
그렇군요. 그래서 이야기가 시작된 거군요.

[어휘] world famous 세계적으로 유명한 novelist 소설가 magazine 잡지 latest 최신의, 최근의 novel 소설 popular 인기 있는 all over the world 전 세계적으로 amazing 놀라운 chance 기회 dolphin 돌고래

13 ①

M: Good morning. How may I help you?
안녕하세요. 무엇을 도와드릴까요?

W: I've had a terrible headache since yesterday.
어제부터 두통이 너무 심하네요.

M: Do you also have a sore throat? 목도 아프신가요?

W: No, but I have a little fever too. Do you have anything I can take?
아니요. 하지만 열이 조금 있어요. 제가 먹을 만한 약이 있나요?

M: This aspirin will ease your pain. But if you don't feel better soon, please go to the doctor.
이 아스피린이 아픈 것을 덜어줄 겁니다. 하지만 금방 나아지지 않으면 병원에 가 보세요.

W: Thank you. How much is it? 감사합니다. 얼마죠?

M: It's two thousand won. 2,000원입니다.

[해설] 약을 먹고도 몸이 좋아지지 않으면 병원을 가보라고 했으므로 남자는 의사가 아니라 약사이다.

[어휘] terrible 심한, 끔찍한 headache 두통 since ~부터, 이후로 sore throat 목 아픔, 인후염 fever 열 ease 완화시키다 pain 고통을 feel better 기분이 나아지다 go to the doctor 병원에 가다

14 ①

[Telephone rings.] [전화벨이 울린다]
M: Hello. 여보세요.

W: Hello. This is Jenny from Alice Online Bookstore. Are you Bradley Smith? 여보세요. 저는 앨리스 인터넷 서점의 제니라고 합니다. 브래들리 스미스 씨 되시나요?

M: Yes, I am. 네, 접니다.

W: I'm calling to let you know that the book you

ordered, *Fantastic Fox*, is currently <u>sold</u> out.
손님께서 주문하신 '판타스틱 폭스'가 현재 매진되었다는 것을 알려 드리려고 전화 드렸습니다.

M: Hmm... <u>What</u> are my <u>options</u> then?
음, 그럼 제가 선택할 수 있는 건 뭐죠?

W: If you want to, you can <u>wait</u> until we get more books. 원하신다면, 책이 더 들어올 때까지 기다리셔도 됩니다.

M: Well, can I just <u>cancel</u> my <u>order</u>?
음, 그냥 주문을 취소해도 되나요?

W: Okay, <u>no problem</u>. I'll do it for you.
네, 물론이죠. 그렇게 해드리겠습니다.

어휘 online bookstore 인터넷 서점, 온라인 서점 let somebody know ~에게 알려주다 currently 현재 sold out 매진된 option 선택권 cancel 취소하다

15 ③

W: Jim, where are you going? 짐, 너 어디 가니?

M: Mom, I'm going to the <u>supermarket</u> to <u>pick</u> up a friend of mine, Minho.
엄마, 제 친구 민호를 마중 나가러 슈퍼마켓에 갈게요.

W: Oh, I thought he knew <u>how to get here</u>.
아, 난 그 애가 여기 오는 길을 알고 있는 걸로 생각했단다.

M: He does, but it's <u>raining</u> really <u>hard outside</u> and he doesn't have an <u>umbrella</u>. 알고 있는데, 지금 밖에 비가 엄청 많이 오고, 민호는 우산이 없어요.

W: So, is he <u>waiting for</u> you <u>in front of</u> the supermarket?
그래서 그 애가 슈퍼마켓 앞에서 널 기다리고 있니?

M: Yes. I'll <u>be right back</u> with him.
네. 민호를 데리고 금방 올게요.

W: All right. 알았다.

어휘 pick up (차에) 태우러 가다, 마중 나가다 rain hard 비가 많이 오다 outside 밖에 umbrella 우산 in front of ~앞에서

16 ④

① W: Long time no see. 오랜만이야.
   M: I've been <u>out of town</u> for a month.
   난 한 달 동안 지방에 있었어.

② W: I think you should <u>get</u> some rest.
   내 생각에 너는 좀 쉬어야 할 것 같아.
   M: I think I should, too. 나도 그래야 한다고 생각해.

③ W: Will you <u>do me a favor</u>? 내 부탁 좀 들어줄 수 있니?
   M: Sure. What is it? 물론이지. 무슨 일이니?

④ W: Are you <u>good</u> at singing? 넌 노래를 잘하니?
   M: Good <u>job</u>! 잘했어!

⑤ W: <u>What time</u> shall we meet? 우리 몇 시에 만날까?
   M: <u>How</u> about at five? 5시 어때?

어휘 long time no see 오랜만이다 out of town 지방에서, 도시에서 벗어나 get some rest 휴식을 취하다 do somebody a favor ~의 부탁을 들어주다 be good at ~을 잘하다

17 ②

[*Cellphone rings.*] [휴대폰이 울린다]

M: Hey, Minju. What are you doing?
야, 민주야. 너 뭐 하고 있니?

W: I'm retyping my <u>essay</u>.
난 내 과제물을 다시 타이핑하고 있어.

M: Why? You told me that you <u>finished</u> it <u>yesterday</u>.
왜? 네가 어제 그걸 끝냈다고 나한테 말했잖아.

W: I did, but I <u>lost</u> my <u>file</u>. My <u>computer</u> got a <u>virus</u>.
끝냈는데, 내 파일을 잃어버렸어. 내 컴퓨터가 바이러스에 걸렸어.

M: What? I told you to <u>update</u> your virus <u>software</u> as often as possible. 뭐? 내가 가능한 한 자주 네 바이러스 예방 소프트웨어를 업데이트하라고 했잖아.

W: Oh, I just updated it. 아, 난 그걸 방금 업데이트했어.

M: Come on. You should be more <u>prepared</u> to prevent <u>something bad</u> from <u>happening</u>. 그건 아니야. 넌 안 좋은 일이 일어나는 것을 막을 준비가 더 되어 있어야 해.

어휘 retype 다시 타이핑하다 essay 과제, 에세이 get a virus 바이러스에 걸리다 update 업데이트하다, 갱신하다 virus software 바이러스 예방 프로그램 prevent something from –ing ~이 ...하는 것을 막다

18 ①

W: Hello. Here's Wednesday night's weather report. We had some <u>snow</u> this <u>Monday</u> and it <u>rained</u> <u>yesterday</u> and <u>today</u>. <u>Tomorrow</u> will be perfect for <u>outdoor activities</u> because it will be <u>sunny</u> all day. However, it's very likely to rain again <u>Friday</u> in the <u>afternoon</u>, which is expected to <u>turn into</u> snow on Friday <u>night</u>. Please be sure to <u>keep</u> yourselves <u>warm</u> because the <u>temperatures</u> are quite <u>low</u> these days. Thank you.

안녕하세요. 수요일 밤의 일기예보입니다. 월요일에는 눈이 조금 왔고, 어제와 오늘은 비가 왔습니다. 내일은 하루 종일 날씨가 화창하기 때문에 야외 활동을 하기에 아주 좋겠습니다. 하지만 금요일 오후에 다시 비가 올 가능성이 매우 높은데, 금요일 밤이 되면 비가 눈으로 바뀔 것으로 예상됩니다. 요즘에 기온이 상당히 낮기 때문에 몸을 항상 따뜻하게 유지하시기 바랍니다. 감사합니다.

어휘 weather report 일기예보 outdoor activity 야외 활동 likely ~할 것 같은, 가능성이 있는 expect 기대하다 turn into ~로 바뀌다 temperature 기온 quite 꽤 low 낮은

19 ④

M: Hey, Sarah. <u>Why the long face</u>?
사라. 왜 그렇게 우울한 얼굴이니?

W: I'm worried that Jaeho might be <u>angry with</u> me.
재호가 나 때문에 화가 났을까 봐 걱정이야.

M: Why? 왜?

W: We <u>had</u> a <u>meeting</u> together this morning, but I didn't go. 오늘 아침에 같이 만나기로 했는데, 내가 가지 않았어.

M: Did something happen? 무슨 일이 생겼니?

W: No. I just completely forgot about it. What should I do? 아니. 그냥 그걸 까맣게 잊고 있었어. 난 어떻게 해야 하지?

M: You should tell him that you're sorry. I'm sure that's the best thing to do. 넌 그에게 미안하다고 말해야 해. 내 생각에는 그게 최선의 방법이야.

W: Thank you for your advice. 충고해 줘서 고마워.

① Please help yourself. 마음껏 먹어.
② I'm sure he can do it. 그는 분명히 할 수 있을 거야.
③ I had a very good time. 정말 좋은 시간을 가졌어.
④ Thank you for your advice. 충고해 줘서 고마워.
⑤ I'm pleased to meet you, too. 나도 널 만나서 기뻐.

어휘 long face 시무룩한 얼굴 worried 걱정하는 angry with ~에게 화가 난 completely 완전히 help yourself 마음껏 드세요 advice 충고, 조언 pleased 기쁜

20 ②

M: Kelly, why are you still here in the computer lab? 켈리, 넌 왜 아직도 여기 컴퓨터실에 있니?

W: Oh, I'm searching the Internet for my science project. 아, 난 과학 프로젝트 때문에 인터넷을 검색하고 있어.

M: You mean the report for Mr. Kim's class? 김 선생님 수업의 보고서를 말하는 거니?

W: Yes, that's right. I need to find an amazing invention and write a report about it. 응, 맞아. 난 놀라운 발명품을 찾아서 그것에 대한 보고서를 써야 해.

M: I see. So, which invention did you choose? 그렇구나. 그럼, 넌 어떤 발명품을 골랐니?

W: Well, I haven't found a good one yet. 음, 아직 좋은 것을 찾지 못했어.

① In fact, I prefer science to history.
사실, 나는 역사보다 과학이 더 좋아.
② Well, I haven't found a good one yet.
음, 아직 좋은 것을 찾지 못했어.
③ Okay. I'm sure I turned off the computer.
그래. 내가 분명히 컴퓨터를 껐어.
④ Right! We should respect inventors' ideas.
맞아! 우리는 발명가들의 생각을 존중해야 해.
⑤ The deadline for the report has already passed.
보고서 마감일은 이미 지났어.

어휘 computer lab 컴퓨터실 search 찾다, 검색하다 mean 의미하다 amazing 놀라운 invention 발명품 choose 고르다 prefer A to B B보다 A를 선호하다 turn off (전원을) 끄다 respect 존중하다 inventor 발명가 deadline 마감일

04회 기출 듣기평가
본문 p.280-281

01 ⑤	02 ③	03 ①	04 ④	05 ①
06 ③	07 ④	08 ①	09 ②	10 ③
11 ④	12 ⑤	13 ③	14 ②	15 ⑤
16 ④	17 ①	18 ②	19 ②	20 ①

01 ⑤

W: Tomorrow is Mom's birthday. Did you get a present for her? 내일이 엄마 생신이야. 넌 엄마 생신 선물을 샀니?

M: Yes, and I made a birthday card for her, too. Look! This is the card. 응, 그리고 엄마에게 드릴 생신 축하 카드도 만들었어. 이것 봐! 이게 그 카드야.

W: Oh, you wrote 'Happy Birthday' on the card.
아, '생신 축하드려요'라고 카드에 썼구나.

M: Yes, I did. What do you think about this ribbon on top? 응. 맨 위에 있는 리본은 어떻게 생각해?

W: It's beautiful. Mom will like it.
예쁘네. 엄마가 좋아하실 거야.

어휘 present 선물 on top 맨 위에

02 ③

W: Hey, John. You're still awake.
얘, 존. 너 아직 안 자고 있구나.

M: Yes, Mom. I can't sleep because of the school trip.
네, 엄마. 수학여행 때문에 잠이 안 와요.

W: Why? Is there something wrong?
왜? 무슨 문제라도 있니?

M: No. I'm just so happy. This is my first visit to Gyeongju.
아니요. 그냥 너무 좋아서요. 이번이 제 첫 번째 경주 여행이에요.

W: I know. You'll learn a lot from this trip.
나도 안다. 넌 이번 여행에서 많은 것을 배울 거야.

M: Yeah. I'm really looking forward to seeing Cheomseongdae the most. I heard it's beautiful.
네. 저는 정말로 첨성대를 보는 게 제일 기대돼요. 아름답다고 들었거든요.

어휘 still 여전히 awake 깨어 있는, 잠들지 않은 school trip 수학여행 look forward to ~을 기대하다, 학수고대하다 bored 지루한 excited 신이 난, 흥분한 relaxed 느긋한

03 ①

M: What are you going to do this weekend, Susan?
이번 주말에 무엇을 할 계획이니, 수잔?

W: I'm going to visit my grandmother on Jeju Island.
난 제주도에 있는 할머니 댁을 방문할 거야.

M: Wow, Jeju Island! I went there last weekend.
우와, 제주도! 난 지난 주말에 거기에 갔었어.

W: Really? What did you do there? 정말? 거기서 뭐 했어?

M: I went horseback riding. It was great!
말 타기를 했어. 정말 재미있었어!

W: Horseback riding? That sounds wonderful!
말 타기? 멋진데!

어휘 weekend 주말 grandmother 할머니 island 섬 horseback riding 말 타기 sound ~처럼 들리다

04 ④

W: Two tickets for *Titanic* at five o'clock, please.
5시 '타이타닉' 티켓 2장 주세요.

M: Sorry, the tickets are all sold out.
죄송합니다만 티켓이 모두 매진되었습니다.

W: When are the next showings? 다음 상영은 몇 시죠?

M: At six thirty or six forty five. The six forty five showing is in 3D.
6시 30분과 6시 45분이요. 6시 45분 상영은 3D입니다.

W: I see. Then we'd like tickets for the 3D movie.
그렇군요. 그럼 우린 3D 영화 티켓으로 할게요.

M: Okay. Please take a look at the computer screen and choose your seats.
네. 컴퓨터 화면을 보시고 좌석을 선택해 주세요.

어휘 sold out 매진된, 다 팔린 showing 상영 would like 원하다 take a look ~을 보다 seat 좌석

05 ①

M: Are you doing anything for your school's festival?
너희 학교 축제 때 뭘 하기로 했니?

W: Well, my friends and I are going to give a dance performance.
음, 내 친구들이랑 나는 같이 댄스 공연을 할 거야.

M: A dance performance? That's cool!
댄스 공연? 멋지네!

W: You know, this is my first time. I feel really nervous.
너도 알다시피, 이번이 나한테는 처음이야. 정말로 긴장돼.

M: Don't worry. I know you'll do great.
걱정하지 마. 난 네가 잘 거란 걸 알아.

W: Thanks a lot. 정말 고마워.

M: I wish you good luck! 행운을 빌게!

해설 'Good luck' 혹은 'I wish you good luck'은 행운을 기원하는 표현이다.

어휘 festival 축제 give a performance 공연하다 nervous 긴장한 do great 잘하다 wish somebody good luck ~에게 행운을 빌다

06 ③

M: Honey, I'm going to make a dinner reservation now.
여보, 내가 지금 저녁 예약을 하려고 해요.

W: Are we going to the Chinese restaurant?
우리는 중국 음식점에 가는 건가요?

M: Yes. There are eight of us, right?
네. 우리는 8명이죠, 그렇죠?

W: Oh, Mr. and Mrs. Brown called and said they can't come. 아, 브라운 씨와 브라운 부인이 전화가 왔는데 못 오신다고 하셨어요.

M: Okay. Hmm... There will be six, then.
알겠어요. 음, 그럼 6명이겠네요.

W: Yes, that's right. 네. 맞아요.

M: Okay. I'll make a reservation right away.
알겠어요. 지금 바로 예약할게요.

어휘 make a reservation 예약하다 Chinese restaurant 중국 음식점 right away 지금 바로

07 ④

W: Daniel, what do you usually do on weekends?
다니엘, 넌 주말에 보통 뭘 하니?

M: I usually play soccer with the school soccer club. How about you?
난 보통은 학교 축구 동아리에서 축구를 해. 너는?

W: I play table tennis. But I would love to play soccer.
나는 탁구를 쳐. 하지만 나도 축구를 하고 싶어.

M: We play soccer every Saturday. Why don't you join the club?
우리는 토요일마다 축구를 해. 너도 동아리에 가입하는 게 어때?

W: Wonderful! How can I join?
좋아! 내가 어떻게 가입할 수 있니?

M: Just go and ask Mr. Kim, our P.E. teacher.
그냥 우리 체육 선생님인 김 선생님께 가서 말씀 드려.

W: Okay! I'll go to see him right away. Thanks.
알겠어! 지금 바로 그분을 만나 봐야겠어. 고마워.

어휘 usually 보통 on weekends 주말에 every Saturday 토요일마다 table tennis 탁구 why don't you ~하는 게 어때? P.E. 체육(= physical education)

08 ①

W: You know what? There will be an after-school tennis class this summer!
너 그거 아니? 이번 여름에 방과 후 테니스 수업이 개설될 거래!

M: Great. I heard there will be a guitar class, too.
좋아. 기타 수업도 개설될 거라고 들었어.

W: I know. Which one do you like more?
나도 알아. 넌 어떤 게 더 좋니?

M: I'd really like to learn how to play the guitar this summer. What about you?
나는 이번 여름에 정말 기타 연주를 배우고 싶어. 너는 어때?

W: Well, at first I wanted the tennis class. But I'll take the guitar class, if you take it.
음, 난 처음에는 테니스 수업을 듣고 싶었어. 하지만 네가 기타 수업을 듣는다면 나도 그 수업을 들을래.

M: Okay. Let's go and sign up for it.
그래. 같이 가서 등록하자.

어휘 after-school 방과 후의 at first 처음에는 sign up for ~에

등록하다

09 ②

W: Good morning, everyone! I have wonderful news. Our girl's volleyball team won the local championship last night. To celebrate the victory, we've cancelled afternoon classes today. Instead, we're planning to have a special party at two o'clock this afternoon. Please come to the gym and enjoy free snacks and drinks. Thank you.

안녕하세요, 여러분! 좋은 소식이 있어요. 우리 여자 배구 팀이 지난 밤에 지역 우승을 차지했어요. 승리를 축하하기 위해 오늘 오후 수업을 취소했습니다. 대신, 오늘 오후 2시에 특별 파티를 열 계획입니다. 체육관으로 오셔서 무료 간식과 음료를 드시기 바랍니다. 감사합니다.

[어휘] volleyball 배구 win 이기다, 우승하다(win-won-won) local 지역의 championship 우승, 결승전 celebrate 축하하다 victory 승리 cancel 취소하다 instead 대신에 gym 체육관

10 ③

M: How was the new shopping mall?
새로 생긴 쇼핑몰은 어땠어?

W: It was huge and very crowded.
엄청 크고 사람이 무척 많았어.

M: What did you buy there? 넌 거기서 뭘 샀니?

W: I bought a hairpin, a belt, and presents for Parents' Day. 머리핀, 벨트, 그리고 어버이날 선물을 샀어.

M: You mean presents for your parents?
너희 부모님께 드릴 선물을 말하는 거야?

W: Yes, I bought a book for my dad and earrings for my mom. 응, 아빠에게 드릴 책과 엄마에게 드릴 귀걸이를 샀어.

M: Oh, you're so sweet. 아, 넌 정말 착하구나.

[어휘] huge 거대한, 엄청난 crowded 붐비는, 혼잡한 buy 사다 (buy-bought-bought) present 선물 Parents' Day 어버이날 earrings 귀걸이 sweet 상냥한, 다정한, 착한

11 ④

[Telephone rings.] [전화벨이 울린다.]

W: Hello. Green Star Library. How may I help you?
여보세요. 그린 스타 도서관입니다. 무엇을 도와드릴까요?

M: Hi. Is it possible to volunteer at your library?
안녕하세요. 도서관에서 자원봉사를 하는 것이 가능한가요?

W: Yes. We always welcome volunteers.
네. 저희는 늘 자원봉사자들을 환영합니다.

M: That's great. 잘됐네요.

W: If you're interested, visit our website. On the website, you'll find information about volunteering.
만약 관심이 있으시면, 저희 웹사이트를 방문해 주세요. 웹사이트에서 자원봉사에 대한 정보를 찾으실 수 있습니다.

M: Oh, I see. Thank you for the information.
아, 알겠습니다. 알려 주셔서 감사합니다.

[어휘] volunteer 자원봉사를 하다; 자원봉사자 interested 관심 있는 information 정보

12 ⑤

M: Hello, everyone. My name is Brian Smith, and I'm the captain of this flight. We're sorry that we departed a little late because of the heavy snow this morning. This flight is for New York. It'll take about twelve hours to get there. We'll land in New York at nine o'clock in the morning. Please enjoy the flight. Thank you.

안녕하세요, 여러분. 저는 브라이언 스미스이고, 이 비행기의 기장입니다. 오늘 아침 폭설로 인해 이륙이 다소 지연되어 죄송합니다. 이 비행기는 뉴욕을 향해 갑니다. 도착까지는 약 12시간 정도가 소요될 예정입니다. 저희는 오전 9시에 뉴욕에 착륙할 것입니다. 즐거운 비행 되시기 바랍니다. 감사합니다.

[해설] 출발 시간은 나와 있지 않으며 9시는 도착 시간이다.

[어휘] captain 기장; 선장 flight 비행기, 항공편 depart 이륙하다, 출발하다 heavy snow 폭설 take 시간이 걸리다 land 착륙하다, 도착하다

13 ③

W: Excuse me. Does this bus go to Victoria Station?
실례합니다. 이 버스는 빅토리아 역으로 가나요?

M: Yes, it does. We're about to leave. If you want to take this bus, you'd better get on now.
네, 갑니다. 이제 곧 출발합니다. 이 버스를 타시려면 지금 탑승하시는 편이 좋습니다.

W: Okay, thanks. [pause] How long will it take to get there? 알겠습니다, 감사합니다. [잠시 후] 거기까지 가는데 얼마나 걸릴까요?

M: About half an hour. 약 30분 정도요.

W: Okay. Can you tell me when we get there please? I'm not from around here. 네. 우리가 그곳에 도착하면 말씀해 주시겠어요? 저는 이 근처에 살지 않거든요.

M: Sure, no problem. Take a seat please.
물론이죠. 문제 없어요. 자리에 앉아 주세요.

[어휘] be about to 막 ~하려고 하다 leave 떠나다, 출발하다 get on 탑승하다 take (시간이) 걸리다 half an hour 30분 from around here 이 근처 출신의 take a seat 자리에 앉다

14 ②

W: Excuse me, sir. Please fasten your seatbelt. We'll take off soon. 실례합니다 손님. 안전벨트를 착용해 주십시오. 우리는 곧 이륙합니다.

M: Sure. But, can I get a blanket? I feel a little cold.
네. 그런데, 담요를 받을 수 있을까요? 약간 추운 것 같네요.

W: Of course. Can I bring you some hot water, too?
물론이죠. 따뜻한 물도 좀 가져다 드릴까요?

M: That's okay. 그건 괜찮아요.

W: Please wait a moment. I'll be right back.
잠시만 기다려 주세요. 금방 다시 오겠습니다.

M: Thank you so much. 정말 감사합니다.

어휘 fasten one's seatbelt 안전벨트를 매다 take off 이륙하다 blanket 담요 a little 약간 be right back 다시 돌아오다

15 ⑤

[Cellphone rings.] [휴대폰이 울린다.]

M: Hi, Nancy. 안녕, 낸시.

W: Hi, Henry. Can you go to the movies with me tomorrow? 안녕, 헨리. 내일 나랑 영화 보러 갈 수 있니?

M: I'd love to, but I can't. 나도 가고 싶지만 갈 수 없어.

W: Why? Do you have other plans? 왜? 다른 계획이 있니?

M: I have to stay home and take care of my younger sister. 집에 있으면서 내 여동생을 돌봐야 해.

W: Really? Aren't your parents home?
정말? 너희 부모님이 집에 안 계시니?

M: No, they're out of town on a trip. 응, 시골로 여행 가셨어.

W: Then, maybe next time. 그럼, 다음에 보자.

어휘 go to the movies 영화 보러 가다 stay home 집에 있다 take care of ~을 돌보다 out of town 도시를 벗어나 on a trip 여행을 떠나

16 ④

① W: How often do you play soccer?
넌 얼마나 자주 축구를 하니?

M: Once a week. 일주일에 한 번 해.

② W: What do you want to wear? 넌 무엇을 입고 싶니?

M: I want to wear blue jeans. 난 청바지를 입고 싶어.

③ W: Can you fix my skateboard?
네가 내 스케이트보드를 고칠 수 있니?

M: Let me see. I'll try. 한번 볼게. 내가 해볼게.

④ W: How do you get to the library? 넌 도서관에 어떻게 가니?

M: I don't feel well. 난 몸이 좋지 않아.

⑤ W: Thank you for your help. 도와줘서 고마워.

M: Sure, anytime! 응, 언제든지!

어휘 how often 얼마나 자주 once 한 번 blue jeans 청바지 fix 고치다 try 시도하다, 해보다 get to ~에 도착하다 feel well 건강이 좋다

17 ①

W: Congratulations on winning the MVP award, Mr. Park. MVP 상을 받은 것을 축하합니다, 박 선수.

M: Thank you. 감사합니다.

W: How did you become such a great player?
어떻게 그렇게 훌륭한 선수가 되셨죠?

M: Actually, I was not really good when I first started playing baseball, but I practiced a lot.
사실, 제가 처음 야구를 시작했을 때는 정말 잘하지는 못했어요. 하지만 연습을 많이 했죠.

W: What did you do? 무엇을 하셨나요?

M: When my team practiced, I was always the first player to arrive and the last player to leave.
저희 팀이 연습을 할 때, 저는 항상 제일 먼저 오고 제일 늦게 가는 선수였습니다.

W: Oh, I see. That's why you became such a good player. 아, 그렇군요. 그래서 이렇게 훌륭한 선수가 되셨군요.

어휘 congratulations 축하해요 MVP 최우수 선수(= most valuable player) practice 연습하다 last 마지막의 leave 떠나다

18 ②

W: Hello. This is the weather report for tonight and tomorrow. The rain that started this morning has stopped for the moment. And it's very likely to be sunny tomorrow morning. In the afternoon, it'll be partly cloudy with no strong winds. Still, the temperatures will be lower than usual all day tomorrow. Thank you.

안녕하세요. 오늘 밤과 내일의 일기예보입니다. 오늘 아침 시작된 비는 지금은 그쳤습니다. 그리고 내일 오전에는 화창할 가능성이 높습니다. 오후에는 약한 바람과 함께 구름이 약간 끼겠습니다. 하지만 내일은 하루 종일 평소보다 기온이 낮겠습니다. 감사합니다.

어휘 for the moment 지금은 be likely to ~할 것 같다 partly 부분적으로 temperature 기온 lower 낮은 than usual 평소보다

19 ②

W: Hey, Mike. How is it going? 얘, 마이크, 어떻게 지내니?

M: Good. Oh, have you heard about James?
잘 지내. 아, 너 제임스에 대해 들었니?

W: No. Did something happen to him?
아니. 제임스한테 무슨 일 있니?

M: He broke his leg yesterday. He's in the hospital now. 어제 다리가 부러졌대. 지금 병원에 입원해 있어.

W: Really? That's terrible. 정말? 끔찍한 일이네.

M: How about going to visit him after school?
학교 끝나고 그를 찾아가 보는 게 어때?

W: Sure, let's go together. 좋아, 같이 가자.

① You did a good job! 넌 정말 잘했어!

② Sure, let's go together. 좋아, 같이 가자.

③ Make yourself at home. 편하게 있어.

④ Wow, you're so lucky. 와, 넌 정말 운이 좋다.

⑤ Cheer up! You can do it. 기운 내! 넌 할 수 있어.

어휘 happen 일어나다, 발생하다 break one's leg 다리가 부러지다 be in the hospital 입원 중이다 terrible 끔찍한

20 ①

M: Helen, this is such a nice dinner.
헬렌, 이건 정말 근사한 저녁식사야.

W: Yes, it is. This restaurant is really great.

응, 맞아. 이 식당은 정말 좋아.

M: How is your food? 네 음식은 어때?

W: It is so delicious. I really love Indian food.
정말 맛있어. 난 인도 음식이 정말 좋아.

M: Oh, do you? Actually, there's another nice Indian restaurant in this mall.
아, 그래? 사실 이 쇼핑몰에는 맛있는 인도 음식점이 또 있어.

W: Really? Let's go there some time.
정말? 다음엔 그곳에 가자.

① Really? Let's go there some time.
정말? 다음엔 그곳에 가자.

② They won't like the restaurant, either.
그들도 역시 그 식당을 좋아하지 않을 거야.

③ Oh, I'm glad to hear that you like this place.
아, 네가 이곳이 마음에 든다고 하니 기분이 좋네.

④ Well, there isn't any Indian restaurant in this mall.
음, 이 쇼핑몰에는 어떤 인도 음식점도 없어.

⑤ Hmm... Many people prefer to eat out on weekends.
음, 많은 사람들이 주말에는 외식하는 걸 선호해.

어휘 delicious 맛있는 Indian food 인도 음식 mall 쇼핑몰 some time 언젠가 either ~도 역시, 또한 place 장소 prefer 선호하다 eat out 외식하다 on weekends 주말에

05회 기출 듣기평가

본문 p.290-291

01 ③	02 ②	03 ①	04 ⑤	05 ④
06 ③	07 ②	08 ④	09 ①	10 ①
11 ④	12 ②	13 ⑤	14 ⑤	15 ③
16 ②	17 ④	18 ③	19 ①	20 ⑤

01 ③

W: Chris, what will you take to the flea market?
크리스, 넌 벼룩시장에 뭘 가져갈 거니?

M: Well Mom, I haven't decided yet.
사실은 엄마, 아직 결정하지 못했어요.

W: How about this soccer ball? 이 축구공은 어떠니?

M: I'm still playing with it. Can I take this jacket?
제가 아직 그걸 가지고 축구를 해요. 이 재킷을 가져갈까요?

W: Sure. I'll wash it for you. 그래. 내가 세탁해 줄게.

M: Thanks. I'm also thinking of selling these books at the market. 고마워요. 이 책들도 시장에서 팔까 생각 중이에요.

W: They're too old. This jacket will be enough.
그건 너무 오래 됐어. 이 재킷이면 충분해.

어휘 flea market 벼룩시장 wash 세탁하다 sell 팔다 enough 충분한

02 ②

M: Where did you go on your winter vacation?

너 겨울 방학에 어디에 갔었니?

W: I visited my uncle's house in Los Angeles.
나는 로스앤젤레스에 있는 삼촌 댁을 방문했어.

M: What was the weather like there? 그곳 날씨는 어땠니?

W: We had sunny days. 날씨는 화창했어.

M: Really? We had a lot of snow here in Korea.
정말? 여기 한국에는 눈이 많이 왔어.

어휘 winter vacation 겨울방학 visit 방문하다 uncle 삼촌 sunny 화창한, 맑은

03 ①

W: How was the water rocket contest today?
오늘 있었던 물로켓 대회는 어땠니?

M: Fantastic, Mom! All the students shot their rockets at the same time.
멋졌어요, 엄마! 모든 학생들이 동시에 로켓을 발사했어요.

W: Sounds great! How did your rocket do?
멋있구나! 네 로켓은 어땠니?

M: It flew about ninety meters!
그건 거의 90미터나 날아갔어요!

W: That's amazing! 놀라운데!

M: Yeah. I won first prize. 네. 제가 1등을 했어요.

W: You did a great job! 정말 잘했구나!

해설 'You did a good[great] job!'은 칭찬할 때 쓰는 표현이다.

어휘 rocket 로켓 contest (경연)대회 shoot 쏘다, 발사하다 (shoot - shot - shot) at the same time 동시에 fly 날아가다 (fly - flew - flown) amazing 놀라운 win 우승하다, 이기다(win - won - won) first prize 1위, 1등 bored 지루한 scared 무서운 relaxed 느긋한

04 ⑤

M: Excuse me, may I ask you something?
실례합니다. 뭐 좀 여쭤봐도 될까요?

W: Sure. What is it? 네. 뭔가요?

M: I borrowed two books last week, but I lost them.
제가 지난주에 책 2권을 빌렸는데, 책을 잃어버렸어요.

W: Oh, that's too bad. Do you have your library card?
아, 정말 유감이네요. 도서관 카드를 갖고 계세요?

M: Here it is. 여기 있습니다.

W: Your name is Andrew Smith, right?
성함이 앤드류 스미스 씨죠?

M: Yes. What should I do? 네. 제가 어떻게 해야 하죠?

W: I'm sorry, but you have to pay for the books you lost.
죄송합니다만, 잃어버리신 책들에 대한 비용을 지불하셔야 합니다.

어휘 borrow 빌리다 library 도서관 pay for ~에 대한 값을 지불하다

05 ④

M: I'm Officer Jones. I heard you saw the thief last

night.

저는 존스 경관입니다. 지난밤에 도둑을 목격하셨다고 들었습니다.

W: Yes. I saw him running out of the house.

네. 도둑이 집에서 뛰쳐나가는 걸 봤어요.

M: What did he look like? 어떻게 생겼습니까?

W: He was very tall. And he was wearing a black shirt.

키가 매우 컸어요. 그리고 그는 검은색 셔츠를 입고 있었어요.

M: Oh, I see. Was he wearing a cap?

아, 알겠습니다. 그가 모자를 쓰고 있었나요?

W: Yes, he was. 네, 쓰고 있었어요.

해설 이름 앞에 officer가 붙으면 경찰관이라는 의미이다.

어휘 officer 경찰관 thief 도둑, 강도(복 thieves) cap 모자

06 ③

M: Welcome to the art gallery. 미술관에 오신 것을 환영합니다.

W: How much is a ticket for a student? 학생 표는 얼마죠?

M: It's six dollars, but we give a one-dollar discount per ticket after six o'clock. 6달러입니다만, 6시 이후에는 표 한 장마다 1달러씩 할인을 해드립니다.

W: That's great! It's six thirty. I need three tickets.

잘됐네요! 지금이 6시 30분이에요. 표 3장 주세요.

M: All right. The total is fifteen dollars.

알겠습니다. 총 15달러입니다.

W: Here you are. 여기 있어요.

어휘 art gallery 미술관 give a discount 할인을 해주다 per ~마다, ~당 total 합계, 총액

07 ②

[Telephone rings.] [전화벨이 울린다.]

W: Hello, ABC Carpet. How may I help you?

안녕하세요, 에이비씨 카펫입니다. 무엇을 도와드릴까요?

M: I'm calling to change my order.

제 주문을 변경하려고 전화 드렸어요.

W: May I have your name, please?

성함을 말씀해 주시겠습니까?

M: This is David Miller. I ordered a blue carpet for my living room yesterday. 저는 데이비드 밀러입니다. 어제 거실에 쓸 파란색 카펫을 주문했습니다.

W: Yes, I found your order. What do you want to change?

네, 제가 주문 내역을 찾았습니다. 무엇을 변경하고 싶으신가요?

M: The delivery date. I want to get it on October seventh.

배송 날짜요. 저는 그걸 10월 7일에 배송 받고 싶습니다.

W: Okay. You want to change your delivery date from October first to October seventh, right? 알겠습니다. 10월 1일에서 10월 7일로 배송 날짜를 변경하고 싶으신 것이 맞죠?

M: That's right. Thanks. 맞습니다. 감사합니다.

해설 남자는 delivery date를 바꾸기 위해 전화했다.

어휘 carpet 카펫, 양탄자 order 주문(하다) living room 거실

delivery date 배송일

08 ④

W: You look tired. What's the matter?

너 피곤해 보이는구나. 무슨 문제 있니?

M: I think I have a cold. 난 감기에 걸린 것 같아.

W: Why don't you go home and get some rest?

집에 가서 좀 쉬는 게 어때?

M: I want to, but I have to study for my math test. It's on Friday.

그러고 싶지만, 수학 시험 공부를 해야 해. 시험이 금요일이야.

W: You have three days before the test. You should go and see a doctor.

시험 전까지 3일이나 있어. 넌 병원에 가서 진찰을 받아야 해.

M: Okay, I'll do that. Thank you for your advice.

알겠어, 그렇게 할게. 조언해 줘서 고마워.

해설 '병원에 가다'라는 표현은 'go to the doctor', 'see a doctor' 등으로 쓰인다.

어휘 tired 피곤한 have a cold 감기에 걸리다 get some rest 휴식을 취하다 math 수학 see a doctor 진료를 받다 advice 조언, 충고

09 ①

M: How may I help you? 무엇을 도와드릴까요?

W: I need to get the medicine my doctor ordered for me. 의사 선생님께서 저 대신 주문하신 약을 받아야 해요.

M: Please wait a moment. 잠시만 기다려 주세요.

W: Okay. [pause] 네. [잠시 후]

M: Here's your medicine. Take one pill three times a day after each meal.

여기 약 나왔습니다. 식사 후에 하루에 세 번 한 알씩 복용하세요.

W: All right. How much is it? 알겠습니다. 얼마죠?

M: It's five dollars. 5달러입니다.

W: Here you are. 여기 있어요.

어휘 medicine 약 wait a moment 잠깐 기다리다 take (약을) 복용하다 pill 알약 meal 식사

10 ①

W: We have more than ten thousand books in our school library. A lot of students borrow various kinds of books there. Among those books, novels are the most popular books. The second most popular books are comic books, and then magazines, followed by dictionaries.

우리 학교 도서관에는 1만 권이 넘는 책이 있습니다. 많은 학생들이 그곳에서 다양한 종류의 책들을 빌립니다. 그 책들 중 소설이 가장 인기 있는 책입니다. 두 번째로 인기 있는 책은 만화책이고, 그 다음은 잡지, 그리고 사전이 그 뒤를 잇습니다.

어휘 various kinds of 다양한 종류의 novel 소설 popular 인기 있는 comic books 만화책 magazine 잡지 followed by 뒤이어,

11 ④

M: Hi, Sumi! Where are you going?
안녕 수미야! 어디 가고 있니?

W: I'm going to the English teachers' office.
난 영어 선생님의 사무실에 가는 중이야.

M: Oh, good. Will you do me a favor?
아, 잘됐다. 내 부탁 좀 들어 줄래?

W: Sure, what is it? 물론이지, 뭔데?

M: Could you give my homework to Mr. Kim? I have to go to my music class now. 김 선생님께 내 숙제 좀 드릴 수 있니? 지금 음악 수업에 들어가야 하거든.

W: Sure, Minsu. 물론이지, 민수야.

M: Thanks a lot. 정말 고마워.

어휘 do somebody a favor ~의 부탁을 들어주다 homework 숙제

12 ②

M: Hello, everyone! Today is Hangul Day. Let me tell you about today's schedule. At ten o'clock, there will be a class about how to write an essay. At two, we will have a writing competition. And at four, we will watch a video about King Sejong. I hope all of you will have a great time! Thank you.

안녕하세요, 여러분! 오늘은 한글날입니다. 제가 오늘 일정을 말씀드리겠습니다. 10시에는 에세이 쓰는 방법에 대한 수업이 있습니다. 2시에는 글쓰기 대회를 갖겠습니다. 그리고 4시에 우리는 세종대왕에 대한 동영상을 시청할 것입니다. 모두 좋은 시간을 보내시기 바랍니다. 감사합니다.

어휘 schedule 일정 how to ~하는 방법 essay 에세이, 보고서 competition 대회, 시합

13 ⑤

W: Did you hear the news? The acting club is looking for actors.
그 소식 들었니? 연극 동아리에서 배우를 구하고 있다.

M: Yes, I heard about it. They are going to perform *Beauty and the Beast* at the school festival. 응, 그 얘기를 들었어. 그들은 학교 축제 때 '미녀와 야수'를 공연할 거래.

W: I really want to be on stage. 난 정말로 무대에 서고 싶어.

M: That would be exciting! 그러면 정말 신나겠는데!

W: Do you know how I can take part in it?
내가 어떻게 참가할 수 있는지 아니?

M: I have no idea. You should ask your English teacher about it. 잘 모르겠어. 넌 영어 선생님께 여쭤봐야 할 거야.

W: Okay, I will. Thanks. 알겠어, 그럴게. 고마워.

어휘 acting 연기 look for ~를 찾다 actor 배우 perform 공연하다 beauty 미인, 미 beast 짐승, 야수 festival 축제 be on stage 무대에 서다, 공연하다 take part in ~에 참가하다

14 ⑤

① *Peter Pan* was read by seven students.
'피터팬'은 7명의 학생들이 읽었다.

② *Snow White* was read by the largest number of students. '백설공주'는 가장 많은 학생들이 읽었다.

③ *Cinderella* was read by more students than *Aladdin*.
'알라딘'보다 '신데렐라'를 더 많은 학생들이 읽었다.

④ *Cinderella* was read by six students.
'신데렐라'는 6명의 학생들이 읽었다.

⑤ *Aladdin* was read by nine students.
'알라딘'은 9명의 학생들이 읽었다.

해설 *Aladdin*은 4명의 학생들이 읽었다.

어휘 read 읽다 the largest number 가장 많은 수

15 ③

W: David, did you get a new cellphone?
데이비드, 넌 새 휴대폰이 생겼니?

M: Yes! It was my birthday present.
응! 이건 내 생일 선물이야.

W: Wow! I really envy you. What can you do with it?
우와! 네가 정말 부러워. 넌 그걸로 무엇을 할 수 있니?

M: I can read books with it. 난 이걸로 책을 읽을 수 있어.

W: That's great! Can you record your voice?
멋지다! 목소리도 녹음할 수 있니?

M: No, I can't. But I can take pictures.
아니, 못 해. 하지만 사진은 찍을 수 있어.

W: What else can you do with it? 또 무엇을 할 수 있니?

M: I can also watch movies. 영화도 볼 수 있어.

어휘 cellphone 휴대폰 envy 부러워하다 record 녹음하다 voice 목소리 take pictures 사진을 찍다 what else 다른 무엇

16 ②

① M: Have you ever heard of Seoul Tower?
서울 타워에 대해서 들어 본 적이 있니?

W: Yes, I have. 응, 들어 봤어.

② M: How long does it take to get to school?
학교에 가는 데 얼마나 걸리니?

W: I go to school by bus. 난 버스를 타고 학교에 가.

③ M: Did you see the TV show, *Quiz King*, last night?
어젯밤에 TV 프로그램인 '퀴즈왕'을 봤니?

W: Yes, it was great! 응, 정말 재미있었어!

④ M: Don't forget to take your umbrella.
네 우산을 챙기는 걸 잊지 마라.

W: I won't, Dad. 잊지 않을게요, 아빠.

⑤ M: What do you like to do in your free time?
넌 여가 시간에 무엇을 하고 싶니?

W: I like to read books. 난 책 읽는 걸 좋아해.

어휘 get to ~에 도착하다 show 프로그램, 쇼 umbrella 우산

17 ④

[*Chime rings.*] [차임벨이 울린다.]

M: Hello, everyone. The school <u>sports</u> <u>day</u> is coming up <u>next</u> <u>Friday</u>! We need <u>thirty</u> <u>volunteers</u> for that day. Everyone is welcomed. If you're <u>interested</u>, please <u>write</u> your <u>name</u> on the <u>list</u> in the school office. You can do it <u>by</u> next <u>Tuesday</u>. Don't <u>miss</u> your <u>chance</u> to become a volunteer!

안녕하세요, 여러분. 학교 체육대회가 다음 주 금요일로 다가왔습니다. 우리는 그날 30명의 자원봉사자가 필요합니다. 누구든지 환영합니다. 관심이 있으시면 학교 사무실에 있는 목록에 이름을 적어 주시기 바랍니다. 다음 주 화요일까지 신청하실 수 있습니다. 자원봉사자가 될 수 있는 기회를 놓치지 마세요.

해설 지원자는 학교 사무실에서 신청할 수 있다.

어휘 sports day 체육대회 volunteer 자원봉사(자) list 목록 miss 놓치다 chance 기회

18 ③

M: <u>How</u> <u>many</u> vacation <u>days</u> do we have <u>left</u>?
우리는 방학이 며칠이나 남았니?

W: Four days. What are you going to do?
4일 남았어. 넌 뭘 할 거니?

M: I'm planning to <u>go</u> <u>hiking</u>.
난 하이킹을 가려고 계획 중이야.

W: Where? 어디로?

M: Halla <u>Mountain</u>. 한라산으로.

W: Really? <u>Who</u> are you going <u>with</u>?
정말? 누구랑 함께 가니?

M: I'm going with my family. 가족과 함께 갈 거야.

① I've been there, too. 난 거기 가봤어.
② That's a great idea! 정말 좋은 생각이다!
③ I'm going with my family. 가족과 함께 갈 거야.
④ Last time, Mike and I went hiking.
  지난번에, 마이크랑 같이 하이킹을 갔었어.
⑤ The mountain is great this time of the year.
  그 산은 매년 이맘때면 정말 멋져.

어휘 left 남은 go hiking 하이킹을 가다. 도보여행을 가다 this time of the year 매년 이맘때

19 ①

M: What are you doing <u>on</u> <u>the</u> <u>computer</u>?
넌 컴퓨터로 뭘 하고 있니?

W: I'm <u>looking</u> <u>through</u> <u>pictures</u> of our family.
우리 가족 사진을 쭉 보고 있어.

M: What will you do with them? 그 사진들로 뭘 할 거니?

W: I'm planning to make a CD for Mom and Dad's <u>wedding</u> <u>anniversary</u>.
엄마와 아빠의 결혼기념일을 위해 CD를 만들 계획이야.

M: That's great! <u>I'm</u> <u>sure</u> they'll like it.
멋지다! 부모님이 분명히 좋아하실 거야.

W: I hope so. What are you going to do for them?
나도 그랬으면 좋겠어. 너는 부모님을 위해서 무엇을 할 거니?

M: <u>I'm</u> <u>going</u> <u>to</u> <u>bake</u> <u>a</u> <u>cake.</u> 나는 케이크를 만들 거야.

① I'm going to bake a cake. 나는 케이크를 만들 거야.
② I'll finish it as soon as I can.
  나는 그걸 최대한 빨리 끝낼 거야.
③ I can't go to the market now.
  나는 지금 시장에 갈 수 없어.
④ I like taking pictures very much.
  나는 사진 찍는 걸 너무 좋아해.
⑤ I don't want to go to the party.
  나는 파티에 가고 싶지 않아.

어휘 look through 살펴보다, 훑어보다 plan 계획하다 wedding anniversary 결혼기념일 bake 굽다 as soon as I can 가능한 한 빨리 take pictures 사진을 찍다

20 ⑤

W: Minji and James like playing badminton. Every Sunday, they <u>play</u> <u>badminton</u> at a <u>park</u> together. Today, they went to the park to play badminton. Minji wanted to <u>win</u> <u>the</u> <u>game</u> this time. <u>However</u>, she <u>lost</u> the game. In this situation, what could James say to Minji to encourage her?

민지와 제임스는 배드민턴 치는 것을 좋아합니다. 매주 일요일, 그들은 공원에서 함께 배드민턴을 칩니다. 오늘, 그들은 배드민턴을 치러 공원에 갔습니다. 민지가 이번에는 경기에서 이기고 싶었습니다. 하지만 민지는 경기에서 졌습니다. 이런 상황에서 제임스가 민지를 격려하기 위해 할 수 있는 말은 무엇일까요?

James: <u>Don't</u> <u>be</u> <u>disappointed.</u> <u>You</u> <u>will</u> <u>do</u> <u>better</u> <u>next</u> <u>time.</u> 실망하지 마. 너는 다음에 더 잘할 거야.

① I like badminton the most. 나는 배드민턴을 가장 좋아해.
② I want to win every game. 나는 모든 경기에서 이기고 싶어.
③ Congratulations! You won the game!
  축하해! 네가 경기에서 이겼어!
④ Hurry up! I need to do my homework.
  서둘러! 난 숙제를 해야 해.
⑤ Don't be disappointed. You will do better next time.
  실망하지 마. 너는 다음에 더 잘할 거야.

어휘 play badminton 배드민턴을 치다 win the game 경기에서 이기다 encourage 격려하다 hurry up 서두르다 disappointed 실망한

강남구청 인터넷 수능방송
강의용 교재 강남구
GANG NAM GU

쎄듀 빠르게 중학 영어 듣기 모의고사 20회 시리즈

전국 16개 시·도 교육청 공동 주관 영어듣기평가 완벽 분석

실전 시험 난이도와 실전 시험보다 높은 난이도 모두 제공

영어권 원어민과 스크립트 공동 개발

개정 교과서 의사소통 기능 반영